OUT FROM THE SHADOWS

Studies in Feminist Philosophy is designed to showcase cutting-edge monographs and collections that display the full range of feminist approaches to philosophy, that push feminist thought in important new directions, and that display the outstanding quality of feminist philosophical thought.

STUDIES IN FEMINIST PHILOSOPHY
Cheshire Calhoun, Series Editor

OUT FROM
THE SHADOWS

*Analytical Feminist Contributions
to Traditional Philosophy*

EDITED BY
SHARON L. CRASNOW
AND ANITA M. SUPERSON

OXFORD
UNIVERSITY PRESS

OXFORD
UNIVERSITY PRESS

Oxford University Press, Inc., publishes works that further
Oxford University's objective of excellence
in research, scholarship, and education.

Oxford   New York

Auckland   Cape Town   Dar es Salaam   Hong Kong   Karachi
Kuala Lumpur   Madrid   Melbourne   Mexico City   Nairobi
New Delhi   Shanghai   Taipei   Toronto

With offices in

Argentina   Austria   Brazil   Chile   Czech Republic   France   Greece
Guatemala   Hungary   Italy   Japan   Poland   Portugal   Singapore
South Korea   Switzerland   Thailand   Turkey   Ukraine   Vietnam

Published by Oxford University Press, Inc.
198 Madison Avenue, New York, New York 10016

www.oup.com

Oxford is a registered trademark of Oxford University Press

Library of Congress Cataloging-in-Publication Data
Out from the shadows : analytical feminist contributions to traditional philosophy.
p. cm.
ISBN 978-0-19-985546-9 (hardcover : alk. paper)—ISBN 978-0-19-985547-6 (pbk. : alk. paper)
1. Analysis (Philosophy)   2. Feminist theory.
B808.5.O88 2012
108.2—dc22
2011011596
ISBN-13: 9780199855469 hardcover; 9780199855476 paperback

1 3 5 7 9 8 6 4 2

Printed in the United States of America
on acid-free paper

For my daughters,
Sascha and Sonia
S.L.C.

For all the daughters of philosophy
who make it matter
A.M.S.

CONTENTS

PREFACE

This collection has its roots in a conference organized by the editors on behalf of the Society for Analytical Feminism, held in Lexington, Kentucky, in April 2008. The goal of the Society, founded in 1993, is to promote analytical feminist work and to provide a forum for exchange of these ideas. Analytical feminists work in the analytical tradition, and apply feminist insights to it, or they use the methods of analytical philosophy to address explicitly feminist issues. In the early days, analytical feminists found themselves defending their methodology from feminist challenges and their feminism from detractors in the analytic tradition. But by 2008, feminist debates about fundamental concepts such as reason, objectivity, and truth had been taking place for some time, and many feminists had moved beyond them and worked squarely within analytical philosophy, unapologetically employing its methodology and many of its concepts, often in revised form. We decided that the time was ripe for a conference that would highlight this transition in feminist work and its impact on traditional philosophy. To this end, we organized the conference whose goal was that of its title: *Analytical Feminist Contributions to Traditional Philosophy*. The speakers were asked to write about how feminist philosophy done in an analytical way advanced the state of the area of philosophy in which they worked. The result was some two dozen or so excellent papers spanning most areas in philosophy, and vivacious discussions of a myriad of issues that these feminists believed needed addressing. Collectively, the discussions represented the current status of analytical feminist work, and one of our goals was to bring some of these ideas together into this collection. Some of the papers from the conference, in revised versions, appear here, but some of the essays in this volume were written independently of the conference and were included because they fit its theme. We believe they offer a comprehensive overview of analytical feminist contributions to traditional philosophy. A secondary goal of this anthology, one we believe to be equally as important as the first, is to reach those who work in mainstream philosophy but not in feminism. Since the essays in this volume are written from an analytical perspective and employ the methods and concepts of analytical philosophy, even while stretching and challenging these at points, they are readily accessible to this audience. The authors in this collection argue that feminism brings to light new issues and new ways of seeing standard issues, or even completely revising traditional takes on certain issues, and they show the ways in which philosophy as a discipline can make progress in light of a feminist perspective. By highlighting many of the ways in which feminism revitalizes traditional philosophy, we hope to engage heretofore uninterested minds.

We would like to thank a number of people who helped this project come to fruition. The Dean of Arts and Sciences and the Office of the Vice President of the University of Kentucky, and the Society for Analytical Feminism, provided financial support for the conference that proved to be the inception of this book. Two anonymous reviewers for Oxford University Press gave detailed and insightful comments on each paper and on the introduction. The editors at Oxford University Press, particularly Peter Ohlin and Cheshire Calhoun, were interested in this project and have supported feminist work in philosophy for some time. Cheshire also found the fabulous photo for the cover which reflects our theme. Anita's mother, Irene, and Sandy Goldberg helped brainstorm about the title, specifically about the phrase "out of the shadows" versus "out from the shadows," and we agreed to settle on the more dramatic reading. Sharon's husband, Stephan Haggard, provided moral support and sound advice on business details related to the project. Our deepest debt is to our contributors for their excellent work, their patience with our comments, their support for this project, and most especially for their courage (particularly on the part of the junior contributors) in taking on what is still viewed in many circles as contentious political material. Because of their work, the relevance of philosophy to real life will be evident to anyone who reads this book.

CONTRIBUTORS

ELIZABETH ANDERSON is John Rawls Collegiate Professor of Philosophy and Women's Studies at the University of Michigan–Ann Arbor. Her research interests include feminist epistemology and philosophy of science, democratic theory, egalitarianism, pragmatism, and theories of rationality and social norms. Her latest book is *The Imperative of Integration* (Princeton University Press, 2010).

LOUISE ANTONY is Professor of Philosophy at the University of Massachusetts–Amherst. In addition to her work in feminist philosophy, she has published numerous articles in the philosophy of mind, epistemology, and the philosophy of religion. She is the co-editor, with Charlotte Witt, of *A Mind of One's Own* (2nd ed., Westview 2002), and with Norbert Hornstein, of *Chomsky and His Critics* (Blackwell, 2003). Most recently, she edited *Philosophers Without Gods: Meditations on Atheism and the Secular Life* (Oxford University Press, 2007).

ANNE BARNHILL is Postdoctoral Fellow in Bioethics and Health Policy at Johns Hopkins University. She is a moral philosopher and bioethicist, and writes about sexual ethics, the ethics of personal relationships, public health ethics, and medical ethics.

SHARYN CLOUGH is Associate Professor at Oregon State University. Her research focuses on epistemology and social values in the context of scientific practice. Her work is informed by feminism, contemporary pragmatism, and analytic philosophy of language, especially the work of Davidson and Quine. Her publications on these topics include "What is Menstruation For? On the Projectibility of Functional Predicates in Menstruation Research" (2002), "Solomon's Empirical/Non-Empirical Distinction and the Proper Place of Values in Science" (2008), as well as her book *Beyond Epistemology: A Pragmatist Approach to Feminist Science Studies* (Rowman and Littlefield, 2003).

ANN E. CUDD is Professor of Philosophy and Associate Dean for Humanities at the University of Kansas. She is the author of *Analyzing Oppression* (Oxford University Press, 2006) and co-author, with Nancy Holmstrom, of *Capitalism, For and Against: A Feminist Debate* (Cambridge University Press, 2011). Her current research is on intervention.

ROBIN S. DILLON is the William Wilson Selfridge Professor of Philosophy and chair of the Department of Philosophy at Lehigh University. She is the president of the Society for Analytical Feminism and was the director of the Women's Studies program at Lehigh for many years. Her research focuses on self-respect and moral character from a feminist perspective.

JULIA DRIVER is Professor of Philosophy at Washington University in St. Louis. She is the author of numerous articles in ethics and moral psychology, as well as *Uneasy Virtue* (Cambridge University Press, 2001), *Ethics: the Fundamentals* (Blackwell, 2007), and *Consequentialism* (forthcoming, Routledge).

MIRANDA FRICKER is Reader in Philosophy at Birkbeck, University of London. She is the author of *Epistemic Injustice: Power and the Ethics of Knowing* (Oxford University Press, 2007); co-editor of *The Cambridge Companion to Feminism in Philosophy* with Jennifer Hornsby (2000); and co-author of *Reading Ethics*, written with Sam Guttenplan, a book of commentaries on selected readings in moral philosophy (Wiley-Blackwell, 2009). Her main areas of interest are in ethics, social epistemology, virtue epistemology, and those areas of feminist philosophy that focus on issues of power, social identity, and epistemic authority.

ANN GARRY is Professor Emerita of Philosophy. She has taught for four decades at California State University, Los Angeles, with visiting appointments including the University of Tokyo, the University of Waterloo, UCLA, and USC. Since the 1970s, she has been active in writing feminist philosophy and in founding the institutions of feminist philosophy in the United States, including the journal *Hypatia*. She co-edited *Women, Knowledge and Reality* (Routledge, 1996) with Marilyn Pearsall and a special issue of *Hypatia* on Transfeminism (2009) with Talia Bettcher. Her articles range from feminist issues in bioethics, pornography, and philosophy of law to intersectionality, analytic feminist epistemology, and philosophical method.

HEIDI E. GRASSWICK is Professor of Philosophy at Middlebury College in Vermont. Her research focuses on feminist epistemology and social epistemology, particularly the relationship between individual and communities as knowers, the role of trust in knowledge, and the ethics of knowing. She edited *Feminist Epistemology and Philosophy of Science: Power in Knowledge* (Springer, 2011) and has published in such journals as *Hypatia, Synthese*, and *Social Epistemology*.

Phyllis Rooney is Associate Professor of Philosophy at Oakland University. Her many publications in feminist epistemology include papers on the following topics: reason and rationality, gender and cognition, feminism and argumentation, values in science, gender metaphors in philosophy, and the connections between feminist epistemology, pragmatism, and naturalized epistemology.

Jennifer Mather Saul is Professor of Philosophy at the University of Sheffield. She began her career writing about substitution puzzle cases in philosophy of language, but her interests have broadened considerably to include lying and misleading, the metaphysics of gender, the psychology of bias, and even the history of the vibrator.

Miriam Solomon received a PhD in philosophy from Harvard University and is Professor of Philosophy at Temple University. Her research interests are in philosophy of science, philosophy of medicine, gender and science, bioethics and epistemology. She is the author of *Social Empiricism* (MIT Press, 2001) and many articles. She is currently writing a book on evidence-based medicine, medical consensus conferences, and narrative medicine, titled *Beyond the Art and Science of Medicine*.

Anita M. Superson is Professor of Philosophy at the University of Kentucky. She specializes in ethics, including metaethics, moral psychology, normative ethics, and applied ethics, and feminism. She is the author of *The Moral Skeptic* (Oxford University Press, 2009), and co-editor with Ann Cudd of *Theorizing Backlash: Philosophical Reflections on the Resistance to Feminism* (Rowman & Littlefield, 2002). She is currently working on bodily autonomy.

Mariam Thalos is Professor of Philosophy at the University of Utah. Her research focuses on foundational questions in the sciences, especially the physical, social, and decision sciences. She has authored numerous articles on causation, explanation and how relations between micro and macro are handled in the context of scientific theorizing, as well as articles in political philosophy, action theory, metaphysics, epistemology, and feminism—some of which has bearing on issues of public policy. She is currently being funded by the NSF to study precaution in decision making, especially in public contexts.

MAURA TUMULTY is Associate Professor of Philosophy at Colgate University and works in the intersection between philosophy of language and philosophy of mind. She is especially interested in the relationship between first-personal and third-personal accounts of mental life.

HELGA VARDEN is Assistant Professor in the Department of Philosophy and Women and Gender Studies at the University of Illinois at Urbana–Champaign. Her main research interests are in legal, political, and feminist philosophy, with an emphasis on the Kantian and the Lockean traditions.

ANDREA WESTLUND is Associate Professor of Philosophy and Women's Studies at the University of Wisconsin–Milwaukee. She works in ethics, moral psychology, and feminist philosophy, and has published in journals including *Hypatia*, *The Monist*, *Philosopher's Imprint*, and *The Philosophical Review*. Her current research focuses on relational autonomy, authority, and self-regarding attitudes.

OUT FROM THE SHADOWS

ANITA M. SUPERSON AND
SHARON L. CRASNOW

▼

INTRODUCTION

PHILOSOPHY IS BY ITS very nature a critical discipline. Philosophers spend much of their time critiquing each other's arguments, all on the way to pursuing wisdom or seeking truth, and even those philosophers who reject truth offer arguments critiquing an entire tradition whose goal is the pursuit of truth. Philosophers define truth in different ways too: some take it to be the best- defended position, while others take it to refer to an objective reality "out there" in the world waiting for human discovery. However truth is defined, and whether or not it is accepted as the goal of philosophy, the fact that there is debate about its very definition and whether and how it might be pursued shows that philosophy is a critical discipline. Due to its critical nature, we can rightfully say that all philosophy is progressive, building on the lessons of the past, offering new ways of thinking about the present and the future. Philosophers working in the analytical tradition rely on a particular methodology, including rigorous argumentation, critical assessment, analysis of terms, and careful attention to detail, as the necessary means to achieve these goals. We might metaphorically describe the progress they seek to make as progress straight up and down, or vertical progress. Over the years, particularly in the past half-century, the debates taking place within the analytical tradition have become much more fine-tuned, rigorous, and detailed, and the hope has been that the progress will reach new heights. Compare this kind of progress to a skyscraper that is flat in its façade. But there is a kind of progress that is informed by political concerns that has been for the most part left out of traditional analytical philosophy. This is social progress, the progress that feminists and other critical philosophers have made or are trying to make toward the goal of "better" knowledge, knowledge that is not only true but relevant for improving our lives. Compare this kind of progress to a skyscraper that has architectural features called "stacked setbacks" that are used to allow in more light at the street level,[1] bringing the streets out from the shadows. The effects of social progress are often even more significant than the effects of vertical progress, since social progress can be tradition-changing at various levels, bringing traditional philosophy out from the shadows. The essays in this collection address social progress. In particular, they examine the ways in which feminists working in analytical philosophy have shaped, are continuing to shape, or need to begin to shape traditional or mainstream philosophy that is nonfeminist in nature. The essays are written from the perspective of feminism because their authors work in this area, but some of the essays also address race and sexual orientation as additional—indeed, interrelated—perspectives from which traditional philosophical issues may be explored (see, for example, the essays by Varden, Fricker, and Garry).

The editors of this volume think of the enterprise of philosophy, and feminist philosophy within it, as an ongoing conversation. We think of this anthology as a new stage in this ongoing conversation. For decades now, feminists have critiqued traditional philosophy—its methods and goals, the issues it deems important, its distinctions and categories, the expanse of conceptual analysis it employs, its representative views about women, and even its downplaying of the contributions of women philosophers throughout the history of philosophy. Some of these critiques have been leveled against the very bedrock of analytical philosophy, particularly against the notions of reason, objectivity, and truth. Other feminists have responded to these earlier feminist critiques of traditional analytical philosophy, rejecting them because they "throw out the baby with the bath water."[2] They have retained these concepts, albeit sometimes refining them, and have maintained much of the methodology used by analytical philosophers while at the same time expanding or, at least, stretching it. Mariam Thalos's essay in this volume, for instance, arguably stretches the boundaries of analytical philosophy itself. The essays in this volume largely presuppose that these earlier, important feminist debates about fundamental concepts have already taken place, and many of the authors endorse both the merits of hanging onto these concepts in some form, and the methodology of analytical philosophy. Thus the essays are written from an analytical perspective, broadly construed.

So why the need for this anthology? First off, we wanted to showcase the contributions that analytical feminism has made, and continues to make, to traditional philosophy. As the essays here demonstrate, analytical feminism continues to offer significant insights to traditional philosophy in a multitude of areas, including social and political philosophy, normative ethics, virtue theory, metaethics, philosophy of language, metaphysics, epistemology, and philosophy of science. Two of the essays, one by Ann Cudd on political philosophy, the other by Phyllis Rooney on epistemology, critically summarize the vast impact of feminist thought on these areas. Other essays represent what might be thought of as a new stage in the conversation that feminism is having with the tradition. They continue this conversation in one of two ways. First, some of them expand on earlier feminist critiques of the tradition, taking them farther or even in a new direction (see, for example, the essays by Westlund, Driver, Tumulty, Antony, Solomon, Thalos, and Garry). These essays answer to Ann Cudd's call for feminism to be self-critical, lest it succumb either to accommodation (adapting one's own perspective to concur with that of the dominant group) or to co-optation (taking on the projects of the dominant group as one's own), thereby becoming "mainstreamed" and immune from critical scrutiny. Second, other essays in this collection aim to bring out from the shadows topics that are only now beginning to be subjected to feminist scrutiny (see, for example, the essays by Dillon, Barnhill, Superson, Saul, Fricker, Grasswick, Anderson, and Clough). Despite the vast philosophical terrain that the eighteen essays in this volume cover, we acknowledge that the collection leaves out certain areas, such as philosophy of mind, and we encourage more feminist analysis to bring out from the shadows these areas too.

A second reason for this anthology is, simply but boldly stated, that feminism, even analytical feminism which employs the methods and such of mainstream philosophy, has not been incorporated into mainstream philosophy. Critiquing the tradition is one thing; having the criticisms incorporated in tradition-changing ways is quite another. Feminist work is beginning to influence philosophy, but it is still too often dismissed as not sufficiently rigorous (male?) or just not good.[3] We suspect that it is being dismissed prematurely, without being read, and given the resources that it provides for social progress, we wonder why.[4] Phyllis Rooney's contribution offers an explicit analysis, but other work in the volume also sheds light on this question. So a second goal that we hope to accomplish with this anthology is to expose feminist ideas to (more) philosophers who work in mainstream philosophy but not in feminism, with an eye to making feminist philosophy part of mainstream philosophy while retaining its critical edge. It is clearly a vital and dynamic subfield—a special one that undergirds other subfields rather than existing alongside them—and should be acknowledged as such.

One of the effects of the dismissal of feminist work is personal, experienced by the very philosophers who incorporate feminist ideas into their work. As things now stand, the journals that are widely believed to be "top tier" in the profession have published very few feminist articles, and there are few feminist philosophers in philosophy departments that are widely believed to be "top tier."[5] The division between mainstream and feminist philosophy has the effect of marginalizing feminist philosophy and feminist philosophers, negatively affecting their careers.

Another effect of the dismissal of feminist work is on the discipline of philosophy itself. As things turned out, we observed that the authors in this collection were collectively and subtly making the strong point that traditional philosophy ignores feminist insights and feminist critiques of traditional philosophy at its own peril. By not endorsing the social progress offered by feminist advancements on traditional philosophy, philosophy remains stagnant, in danger of rehashing the same points, and failing to reflect on its own basic concepts in a constructive, socially critical way. Fundamental presuppositions remain in the shadows. Philosophy sets itself off from other disciplines, including literature, geography, and history, to name just a few, that now regularly incorporate feminist insights. For philosophy to be behind the curve is particularly troublesome, given its fundamental goal of pursuing wisdom or truth that matters: it should be leading the pack.

But furthermore, feminist critique of traditional philosophy rescues it from the ivory tower by speaking to real life issues, showing explicitly how philosophy bears on all our lives, for better or for worse. Most particularly, feminist critique of traditional philosophy speaks to ending the oppression of women, at least. It is this that motivates most if not all of the essays in this volume, and this that makes feminist philosophers see the issues and challenge traditional philosophy in the way they do. Many of the essays in this volume show that much worse than becoming stagnant and boring, traditional philosophy risks leaving out certain groups of persons, thereby becoming an elitist discipline that remains locked behind the walls of the ivory tower. Feminist philosophers recognize that in leaving out some groups, particularly those whose members have been disenfranchised, philosophy is already politicized. They believe that feminism politicizes philosophy in a more reflective way that opens the door to the interests of marginalized groups. By leaving certain groups behind, philosophy risks not exciting their interest in the discipline, and thus not benefiting from the contributions they might make towards philosophy's goals. By not embracing social progress, philosophy risks its own demise.

THE ESSAYS

Given that feminist critique challenges even traditional categories, that it underscores the political nature of seemingly nonpolitical areas of philosophy, and that it sometimes blurs the boundaries between areas of philosophy (see, for instance, Heidi Grasswick's essay that bridges ethics and epistemology), this collection could have been organized in a number of ways. We have chosen to highlight particular points of connection between essays in a way that treats them as falling along a continuum, rather than as grouped into the traditional philosophical categories of value theory, epistemology, and metaphysics. One idea or some key suggestion from an essay is picked up and developed in the next. However, there are themes that recur in several of the essays that suggest alternate groupings. So for example, the importance of context is a crucial idea for the essays by Westlund, Barnhill, Fricker, Saul, Tumulty, Fricker, Anderson, and Clough.[6] A more nuanced clustering might revolve around the role of relationship— we see this theme in Westlund's analysis of autonomy and in Grasswick's analysis of testimonial reliability. Where other such connections exist, we have done our best to point them out.

We begin with a social/political essay, for as Ann Cudd pointedly states, feminist critique of areas of philosophy is by nature political, so "political philosophy has to be seen as the ground zero of feminist influence in philosophy." Feminist contribution to political philosophy, according to Cudd, has been nothing short of significant, changing this area by adding new topics (e.g., oppression[7]), redirecting the focus of other topics (e.g., going from individualistic conceptions of autonomy to a relational view of autonomy), and making more prominent still other topics (e.g., caring labor). Additionally, it has critiqued the public/ private distinction and explained the sex/gender distinction and its bearing on freedom, equality, and justice. One illustration of the impact of feminist analysis on political philosophy can be found in the essay by Helga Varden, who borrows a premise from the history of philosophy— Kant, in particular—that we have an innate right to freedom, to support her argument that there should not be state-imposed restrictions on abortion and homosexual activity. Varden's essay is an example of how feminism uses a traditional concept in a new way, one that functions in an argument for ending the oppression of heretofore disenfranchised group. Andrea Westlund's essay, which crosses the boundary between political philosophy and ethics, is an illustration of how feminism has redefined a well-entrenched notion of autonomy from an individualistic one to a relational one. Expanding on earlier feminist work on this topic, Westlund examines symmetrically shared relational autonomy, and defends the view that the partners in a pair must, to count as autonomous, hold themselves answerable to each other by opening their reasons to assessment by the other. Westlund's account offers a way to assess the autonomy of women who are under the grip of patriarchy or who are in relationships with men whose reasons for action are taken to be more important than the woman's reasons. Likewise, it offers a way to assess the autonomy of those relationships in which men fail to hold themselves answerable to their female partners, as well as ones in which the pair is jointly gripped by its own justificatory perspective. Such facets of autonomy are typically not explored in traditional individualistic accounts of autonomy.

Robin Dillon's essay spans normative ethics and metaethics. Just as Varden turns to the history of ethics, Dillon looks to the history of ethics for its account of virtue ethics, but unlike Varden, she rejects what history has to offer. Dillon argues that if we focus on virtues in connection with flourishing only, as traditional accounts do, we will ignore whether flourishing is at odds with a group's oppression and whether certain traditional virtues will even make the list of virtues. *Critical character theory*, though, examines character traits in terms of whether they contribute to or undermine oppression. This shift in the task of virtue ethics has real bearing on the kind of persons we ought to become, a subject to which our moral theories surely ought to speak. Anne Barnhill's essay serves as an illustration of Dillon's metaethical points about virtue ethics. Barnhill examines sexual modesty as an example of a feminist virtue. Traditional virtue ethics enjoins women to flourish sexually, and under patriarchy this might cash out as recommending sexually provocative dress and demeanor. But, Barnhill argues, when seen through the lens of feminist virtue ethics, the virtue of sexual modesty is called for, since it, rather than sexual display of one's body, is more in line with ending women's oppression.

The next two essays address historically central topics in metaethics, an area of ethics in which there has been very little feminist analysis to date. Anita Superson's essay addresses the issue of defeating the skeptic who wants it to be shown that morally required action is rationally required. She asks us to shift models from the Hobbesian model, which is much like the traditional model of the skeptic in endorsing only reasons of self-interest and in assuming that persons have merely instrumental value, to the Kantian model, which grants persons intrinsic value and allows each to ask, "Why should *I* participate in a system that harms me?" She argues for a combination of these models that has us ask and answer the question, "Why be moral?" from a position that includes anyone, not just the privileged who would find it rational to reject morally required action when it is not in their own interest. This different perspective is likely to force different, more plausible answers to the skeptic. Julia Driver takes up the even more fundamental metaethical issue of moral realism. Driver responds to earlier feminist worries about moral realism, namely, that objective morality might ultimately be determined by members of the dominant group and imposed on members of the subordinate group, and about moral relativism, namely, that relativism about moral truth seems to entrench oppressive norms. Driver defends a sentimentalist constructivist version of moral realism. Her theory is sympathetic to a feminist version of the ethic of care, and yields psychological necessity, according to which we cannot imagine a world *just like* ours in which certain practices under certain conditions are not wrong. It gives feminists a purchase on moral realism that might be used to back up claims about the wrongness of oppression.

Just as Driver wants to hang onto objectivity in ethics, albeit in a nuanced version, Jennifer Saul, in the first of the next two essays in philosophy of language, feels the pull for hanging onto a clear and simple theory of the meaning of terms, but rejects it in favor of a contextualist theory because contextualism best meets feminist political concerns. Terms like "woman" worry Saul, because the common understanding, which picks out those with certain biological traits such as genitalia or chromosomal structure, leaves out people like the intersexed who have XX chromosomes but male genitalia, and transwomen who are born biologically male but who identify as women. Saul's insights call out to traditional philosophers of language to expand their analysis of the meaning of terms by considering politically charged terms, and to test whether their theories survive the scrutiny such terms provide. She suspects that they too will abandon their neat, simple theories in favor of contextualist ones. Maura Tumulty also defends a contextual theory of language. Her essay is about illocution, what one does *in* uttering (e.g., warn). At issue is silencing, a topic that feminists have brought to traditional philosophy of language. Women are harmed by being silenced by pornography because their status as agents is undermined, and because they are unable to ensure that they have sex only when they judge it to be good to do so. Tumulty argues that it is not just that men do not *respond* appropriately to women's refusals of pornographic sex, but that men simply do not *hear* women as refusing. Refusals, she argues, applying a traditional view to this new topic, require uptake—whether women can refuse sex they do not want is a matter of whether they believe their refusals will be listened to, which depends on the context. To protect autonomy, they should be able to refuse. Both Tumulty's and Saul's essays change the terrain of traditional philosophy of language, and the resultant theory of meaning, in ways that matter to women's lives.

While Louise Antony's contribution is also about meaning, it is more generally an essay about analytical feminist methodology. Antony rejects what she calls a "replacement" project—a project calling for feminist philosophy to provide an alternative to deficient masculinist or "malestream" philosophy. She argues that such a replacement project is ill-conceived, and criticizes Jennifer Hornsby's account of meaning at least for the reason that it is engaged in such a project. Antony's essay grapples with a core question of the relationship between feminism and the analytical tradition, and she prescribes that analytical feminists build on that tradition rather than replace it. As we have already noted, philosophy is a critical discipline. Antony's contribution illustrates that analytical feminists may be just as critical of each other as they are of the traditions from which they come.

Phyllis Rooney provides a metaepistemological framework through which to consider the relationship between feminist epistemology and mainstream epistemology. The theme of "failure of uptake," prominent in the essays by Tumulty, Miranda Fricker, and Heidi Grasswick, appears here as well, but Rooney focuses on the failure of mainstream epistemologists to take up the insights made by feminist epistemology. Rooney offers a diagnosis of that failure that includes, among other things, the oversimplification of feminist work. Rooney identifies the association of "feminism" with both "women" and "politics" as leading to a more general misunderstanding of feminist work as a result of such oversimplification. Rooney turns this diagnosis into a prescription for improving mainstream epistemology, arguing that it is through the enhanced understanding of these very associations that feminist epistemology makes its contribution.

Miranda Fricker explores the failure of uptake that features in Tumulty's essay, but in the context of a specific type of epistemic injustice that she calls "testimonial injustice." Testimonial injustice occurs, for instance, when a witness who is a member of a minority group is not even recognized as a credible witness, or when recognized as such, is not properly heard. Fricker's analysis focuses on dysfunction, the failure of testimony, and so advances our understanding by going beyond traditional accounts of testimony that focus strictly on what happens when testimony is successful. Her analysis reveals that testimonial injustice is not only an ethical problem but also a political one, since it can lead to legal injustice. Similarly, Heidi Grasswick highlights one way that epistemology and ethics intersect in giving an account of testimony. Grasswick builds on feminist analyses of moral knowledge, and explores the role of relationships between the participants in testimony, a topic almost completely left untouched by traditional accounts. She offers an analysis that makes clear that there are circumstances under which we have a moral responsibility to resolve seeming contradictions between our beliefs and the testimony of reliable others. While the example she uses focuses on feminist concerns, Grasswick notes that attention to relationships and the moral responsibilities they generate is likely to be relevant when analyzing testimony in other contexts as well.

The emphasis on knowledge in context, that is, knowledge as it affects our lives—especially women's lives—as opposed to knowledge characterized abstractly, is at the same time an emphasis on "knowledge that matters." But the very idea that we are concerned with knowledge that matters challenges the belief that the moral and the epistemological are distinct. When our concerns turn to scientific knowledge, the ideal of value-free, "objective" science comes under scrutiny. The next three essays, by Elizabeth Anderson, Sharyn Clough, and Miriam Solomon, address the question of how to think about values in science in a way that does not require that the objectivity of science means that it is "value-free." Anderson and Clough both argue that empirical evidence can count as evidence for values, illustrating their philosophical arguments with case studies of research. Solomon is more skeptical about the way in which empirical evidence bears on value claims. Specifically, Solomon worries about philosophers she calls "radical feminist empiricists," those who, she believes, insist that all values are empirically grounded as part of the web of belief, or, in a phrase that she coins to emphasize the point, the "web of valief." The feminist nature of these essays enables their authors to identify more explicitly than most established mainstream discussions the values that are at play in science, so they provide a model for furthering both feminist and mainstream research on science and values.

The final two essays in the volume, by Mariam Thalos and Ann Garry, explore key metaphysical concepts for feminism: social identity and the self and the way these are intertwined with freedom and oppression. To construct her account, Thalos draws from existentialism, feminism, and analytical methodology, challenging traditional methodological distinctions as well as traditional concepts. She defends what she calls the "nexus account," which, unlike other traditional conceptions of the self that currently undergird the social sciences, acknowledges the collectivist dimension of human experience. She argues that her analysis provides an understanding of how individuals can choose to identify with and form loyalties to groups, even when these groups are the result of classification by others, which is central to understanding and explaining oppression. Garry is also concerned with the problem of solidarity, and she makes use of the Wittgensteinian notion of family resemblance to give an intersectional account of identity, which she believes answers other feminists' concerns about identities not being appropriately overlapping between groups, or being fragmented in a way that undermines the solidarity that any political movement like feminism needs. Garry's account provides a framework for thinking about the multiple ways that individuals become subject to oppression as a result of their membership in more than one group. These feminist metaphysical accounts of the self and identity join the feminist approaches to political philosophy, ethics, philosophy of language, epistemology, and philosophy of science appearing in this volume in making central the aim of ending women's oppression, arguing for reconstructing our concepts, changing our approaches to issues, and/or building on the tradition in ways important for feminist aims. We hope that the insights contained herein will be incorporated in tradition-changing ways.

Notes

We thank Wiley-Blackwell for granting permission to reprint two essays in this volume. Elizabeth Anderson's essay, "Uses of Value Judgments in Science: A General Argument, with Lessons from a Case Study of Feminist Research on Divorce," appeared in *Hypatia: A Journal of Feminist Philosophy* 19 (1) (Winter 2004): 1–24, and a shorter version of Ann Garry's paper, "Intersectionality, Metaphors, and the Multiplicity of Gender," appears in *Hypatia: A Journal of Feminist Philosophy*, Special Issue on FEAST (Feminist Ethics and Social Theory), (ed. Diana Meyers), 26 (4) (Fall 2011).

1. Both architectural styles are represented by two adjacent, prominent buildings featured in the skyline of downtown Chicago. The idea for this volume came to fruition at a meeting of the Society for Analytical Feminism in Chicago, where the Society has held annual meetings since its inception about two decades ago. The Aeon Center (formerly the Amoco Building and the Standard Oil Building) represents vertical progress, while the

building at Two Prudential Plaza represents social progress. According to the *Encyclopedia Britannica*, many downtown districts of large municipal areas would be in constant shadow were it not for skyscrapers with setbacks, the purpose of which is to allow sunlight to reach streets and lower floors (http://www.britannica.com/EBchecked/topic/536203/setback). Hence the title of this book.

2. This is implied by Louise Antony and Charlotte Witt in the Introduction to their anthology, when they ask: "Wouldn't the abandonment of reason and objectivity be self-defeating for feminists? Wouldn't we be giving up on the possibility of persuading others of the correctness of our views? If we were to dismantle traditional ideals of rational discourse and impartiality, wouldn't we be depriving ourselves of the very norms necessary to ground our own critiques?" See *A Mind of One's Own: Feminist Essays on Reason and Objectivity*, ed. Louise M. Antony and Charlotte E. Witt (Boulder, Colo.: Westview Press, 2002, 2nd ed.), xvi.

3. We debated about the title of this book: should it incorporate the word "feminism" and run the risk that many male philosophers would not buy it as they would not buy a pink Ipod, or should it proudly display the word "feminism" in the title? The title we settled on is, we believe, a happy compromise.

4. For further discussion of these issues, see Anita M. Superson, "Strategies for Making Feminist Philosophy Mainstream Philosophy," *Hypatia: A Journal of Feminist Philosophy* 26(2) (Spring 2011): 410–18.

5. See Sally Haslanger, "Changing the Ideology and Culture of Philosophy: Not by Reason (Alone)," *Hypatia: A Journal of Feminist Philosophy* 23(2) (2008): 210–33. According to Haslanger, between 2002 and 2007, Ethics, Journal of Philosophy, Nous, and Philosophy & Public Affairs published only 2.36% of their papers in feminism, and *Mind, The Philosophical Review*, and *Philosophy & Public Affairs* had not published any articles with feminist or race content during the same five years, though *Nous* published one on race (220). Sharon Crasnow cites data which, while difficult to determine precisely, has the number of women employed as philosophers in 2006 at 21%, and the number of women receiving Ph.D.s in philosophy in 2004 averaging about 27%. See her paper, "What Do the Numbers Mean?" *APA Newsletter on Feminism and Philosophy* 8(2) (Spring 2009).

6. This is not to suggest that context is not relevant in other papers as well. Arguably, sensitivity to context is a hallmark of feminist philosophy, given that a key concept is gender which arguably is dependent on social context.

7. See Ann Cudd's full-fledged analysis of this concept in her book, *Analyzing Oppression* (New York: Oxford University Press, 2006).

ANN E. CUDD
University of Kansas

RESISTANCE IS (NOT) FUTILE:

Analytical Feminism's Relation to Political Philosophy

I. INTRODUCTION: FEMINIST PHILOSOPHY FROM MARGIN TO CENTER

Feminist philosophy emerged as political statement and political philosophy. Looking back at the work of Christine de Pizan, Olympe de Gouges, or Mary Wollstonecraft, we see women philosophers arguing for the moral and political recognition of women as at least dignified contributors to the polis. As their arguments and the activist work of other women began to take hold on the minds of women and men, the arguments became more clearly aimed at political and legal equality. While the twentieth century produced notable works of feminist epistemology, metaphysics, aesthetics, moral theory, philosophy of language, and philosophy of science, political philosophy has to be seen as the ground zero of feminist influence in philosophy.*

Despite significant resistance and protestations to the contrary, feminism has clearly made serious contributions to political philosophy. While feminist philosophy has made important contributions to all the major traditions of philosophy, I will concentrate in this article on the contributions of feminists working in the analytic tradition of feminist philosophy. As I shall argue in this paper, some of the main contributions of analytical feminism to political philosophy include the sex/gender distinction, the critique of the public/private dichotomy, the understanding and explanation of the structural nature of oppression, the conception of autonomy as relational, and the importance of caring labor to both creating and being an autonomous person. Feminism has thus added new topics to political philosophy (gender, care), significantly changed the direction of thought in others (public/private, autonomy), and raised the level of significance of others (oppression). In addition, some of the most important political philosophers of the twentieth century have been women: Carole Pateman, Susan Okin, Seyla Benhabib, Iris Young, Jean Hampton, Nancy Fraser, Marilyn Friedman, and some of the most important male political philosophers today are self-identified feminists: Anthony Appiah, Lawrence Blum, Charles Mills, and Laurence Thomas, to name a few.

Yet, it would be stretching to the truth to say that feminism is a mainstream view in philosophy. In a paper that I presented to the Society for Analytical Feminism in 1998, I cited two prominent philosophers as having stated as much, when I wrote: "In his address as chancellor of Boston University and host of the [1998] World Congress of Philosophy, philosopher John Silber attacked feminist philosophy as 'an assault on reason.' In a review of feminist work in various disciplines, the *Times Literary Supplement* asked Colin McGinn for an overview of the significance of feminism in philosophy. He writes, 'feminism now has a place in many philosophy departments, for good or ill, but it has not made any impact on the core areas of the subject.'"[1]

Further evidence that the profession of philosophy views feminist philosophy as not-yet-ready-for-primetime comes from Sally Haslanger's recent article in *Hypatia*, "Changing the Ideology and Culture of Philosophy: Not by Reason (Alone)," in which she discusses the underrepresentation of women and feminist topics in top philosophy departments and journals. Of the 898 articles in the top seven journals, 111 (12.4%) were written by women and of the 296 articles in the top three journals that commonly publish political philosophy, only seven (2.4%) were feminist (Haslanger, 2008). These facts imply that feminist philosophy has not reached the top level of the philosophy profession, and that philosophy as a profession continues to be somewhat hostile to its radical projects.

It is instructive to compare philosophy in this regard to other humanistic disciplines, such as literature, history, and the humanistic social sciences, where feminist theory is a major theoretical tool that nearly every graduate student learns to at least a passing level of fluency. This is mirrored by the much higher numbers of women professors in these disciplines. There is a common pattern in the penetration of feminism into an academic discipline: first a few women turn attention toward the women of the past as subjects of their fields and to earlier practitioners of their field; then a feminist approach to various women's issues is developed and the traditional topics of the field are explored for their effects on women and women's effects on them; this feminist approach gradually becomes the analysis of the influence of gender more generally on what had always been seen as the central topics and issues of the field, branching eventually to analyses of masculinism as well. Alice Kessler-Harris, an important feminist and women's historian recounted this history of her discipline in a recent article entitled, "Do We Still Need Women's History?" in which she argued for the affirmative. Following this pattern, feminist philosophy seems also to be poised to join the mainstream, since these stages have been attained at least partially in all non-formal fields of philosophy and nearly fully in political philosophy. The only missing link of the evolution of political philosophy is the penetration of the major journals of the field and the related step of equalizing numbers of men and women in the top departments. I believe that we are poised on the edge of that final step and that with just a bit more momentum, it too will be attained.[2]

As an outsider perspective, feminist philosophy, like critical race theory (and for that matter pragmatism and several strands of continental philosophy), offers a critical edge that challenges and, despite its resistance from the mainstream, moves and improves the discipline of philosophy. Philosophy has through its history repeatedly spawned new disciplines as they became applied to specific problems or so empirical that specialists in those areas formed specialized techniques for addressing them. Feminism and critical race theory have revitalized philosophical areas by bringing specialized empirical knowledge *into* philosophical discussion. While the appeal to empirical fact has given some mainstream, influential philosophers an excuse to deny that this is philosophy, it has also breathed new life into a discipline teetering on the edge of total irrelevance. As a marginal area of philosophy, feminism has been fertile ground for new ideas, techniques, and topics for the mother ship.

Mainstreaming is not without its costs, however, in terms of the critique that an outsider analytic can provide to the discipline. Kessler-Harris expresses the ambivalence she feels as part of the generation of women's historians who have made the shift from margin to center in her field. She began as a women's historian, and then readily embraced gender as an analytic category in her work as a labor historian. Yet, she believes that the cost of gendering History has been to leave behind the field of *women's* history, which studies actual women, not only gender as a structural feature of society. Women's history makes two kinds of contributions to history as a discipline. First, by studying actual women of different races, classes, and ethnicities, in their particularity, women's history provided a new set of empirical data for historians to contemplate. Second, by studying women, women's historians stake a claim to agency and power for women in spite of their position as the oppressed gender and as members of other oppressed groups. The notion that agency was not completely eclipsed by oppression, and that oppressed persons commonly resist their oppression in various ways, even while not fully recognizing their own plight, is something women's history and women historians brought to the discipline of history. But in the discipline's mainstreaming of gender as an analytic category, women as such are once again being left out and left behind, and Kessler-Harris worries that in the end, gender itself will become as uncritically standard as any other feature studied in history (such as military power). She writes, "As a scholar, I believe that the cost of mainstreaming women's history may well be to diminish the power of gender as an analytic category." She concludes that "for all the words about mainstreaming, I do not see it either as having happened, or as being desirable just yet" (Kessler-Harris, 2007, B7).

If, as I maintain, feminism is now poised to be mainstreamed in the philosophy collective, its practitioners will need to face a couple of key issues that parallel these worries. First, how can we maintain a critical edge as feminist philosophy enters the mainstream? Once feminist work is fully accepted into the mainstream journals and the top departments, how will feminists maintain their willingness to challenge the status quo of which they have become a part? The dangers that lurk within the internal workings of the discipline are not only stagnation, the endless rehashing of small points that we see so much of in analytic philosophy, but also the more dangerous moral stagnation that comes when one's group is accepted as a part of the dominant group. These are the twin dangers of accommodation and co-optation. Accommodation is adapting one's own perspective to concur with that of the dominant, which can lead to the moral failure of overlooking oppression. Co-optation involves taking on the projects of the dominant group as one's own, which is the moral failing of participating in oppression. It is often difficult to see that one is accommodating or being co-opted. The dominant group's perspective is normative, after all, making it difficult to oppose it. When one is not opposing it, but simply going with the dominant flow of thought, it can be difficult to see that as involving epistemic or moral error. Yet if the feminist perspective is valuable, and if it contradicts or at least lies in tension with the dominant perspective, then accommodating or being co-opted must involve such errors. What are the specific dangers of accommodation and co-optation that feminist philosophy will face?

In this paper, I will argue that feminist philosophers must remain vigilant to these dangers and resistant to complacence with the status quo even as women and feminist analysis are mainstreamed in philosophy. This is for the good of philosophy as well as of progressive political theory. I will try to describe the ways in which analytic feminist political philosophy might tend to accommodate or be co-opted.

Analytical feminists have sometimes been wrongly accused of accommodating or being co-opted in our attempts to cast a critical feminist lens from within mainstream analytic philosophy. It is important, then, to distinguish disagreement with mainstream feminism from accommodation to mainstream political philosophy. This paper is an attempt, in part, to explain how I think we have managed to walk that fine line between being a critical insider and being an excluded outsider, without doing injury to our sensibilities as philosophers or feminists, committed to rigorous and informed pursuit of truth.

II. FEMINIST CONTRIBUTIONS TO POLITICAL PHILOSOPHY

In this section, I focus on the main contributions that I believe feminist analysis have made to political philosophy. As I describe each one, I offer my analysis of how the ambiguities of mainstreaming play out in the attempt by feminist philosophers to make a critique of and yet at the same time to be accepted by the mainstream.

A. The Sex/Gender Distinction

I begin with the sex/gender distinction because, in a sense, feminism begins with the distinction between sex as a biological category and gender, the hierarchical distinction between men and women, masculine and feminine, as socially constructed. On the original construal of this distinction, sex is taken to be a biological category. Males and females are the two sexes, though some have argued that there need to be a few more sex categories to include all the varieties of intersexed persons (Fausto-Sterling, 2000). In humans it is pretty clear that there are biological differences between the sexes beyond production of egg and sperm, but what those differences are remains difficult to discern. Research on these questions is partly empirical, but also partly conceptual. If a difference between males and females is noted, then the feminist should ask how that difference is being understood and what role gender hierarchy plays in the understanding of the difference. For example, it is argued by some that autism is a consequence of the extreme male brain, another consequence of which, namely superior intelligence, accounts for the fact that there are more male geniuses (Baron-Cohen et al., 2005). But autism is claimed to be more an aspect of male genetics because it is carried on the X chromosome, it is a recessive gene, and males have only one, so it is more common in males than females. Yet the feminist notes that the male's X chromosome comes from his mother, so in what sense is that male? There are also women who have autism, just not as many. Why not see women who have two Xs as prone to even greater extremes in this area? It seems a more likely explanation of the tendency of geniuses to be male has to do with gender hierarchy, in other words, that genius is taken to be male and so overlooked, dismissed, or even discouraged in females.

There is a lot of scientific work on human sex difference, but much of it is confused by gender categories. Gender, in contrast with sex, is a social category; gender is said to be "socially constructed." What this phrase means is that how sex difference is significant varies across cultures, and indeed, the social significance of sex difference is believed by most feminists to be a purely contingent, socially determined, matter. This social difference feeds into physical difference in ways that confuse the issue of sex and gender difference. For instance, the fact that women's upper bodies are so much weaker than men's must be in part explained by gender norms of appearance. Men and women are the two genders that are normally found in societies, but many argue that lots of people don't neatly fit into one of them, or they fit into both, and some societies are said to have more than two. One of the main social functions of the category of gender has been to divide labor or social roles. When we look closely at that division of the human species we find quite a wide range of meanings and overlap between the genders across societies.

Margaret Mead noted that in some societies the men fish and the women weave, and in other societies the women fish and the men weave, meaning that how gender difference is expressed can be completely opposite from one society to the next (Mead, 2001, xxxvii). All societies practice some segregation by gender in division of labor. One nearly universal fact has been that in every society men are politically, religiously, and economically dominant and women subordinate. As Mead noted in her discussion of the gendered division of labor, whatever men do is seen as the more valuable activity. Gender is thus not only a social difference, but also a social *hierarchy*, and this makes gender of primary significance to political philosophy.

Feminist political philosophers draw many lessons from the sex/gender distinction. Labor is divided by gender; political power (until very recently) was determined by gender. These facts have led feminists to inquire about freedom, equality, justice, and injustice from the perspective of women, and to argue that the arbitrary social distinction of gender has created a real and non-arbitrary difference in material circumstances between males and females.

However, many feminists now question whether sex is a biological category, and propose instead that sex is also socially constructed.[3] These critiques come from at least three directions. One is the postmodern critique of sex as an objective category, but this view does not claim that there is a one-to-one correspondence of sex to gender, let alone a reduction of gender to sex. The other is the claim from feminist biologist, Anne Fausto-Sterling, that there are five sexes, not just two, based on her analysis of the combinations of hormonal, genetic, and anatomical markers of sex found in nature (Fausto-Sterling, 2000). This also complicates rather than denies the biological nature of sex. Finally, there is the evolutionary biology attempt to derive gender from sex difference. If this reduction were valid, it would show that gender is a superfluous category. I am very doubtful that this reduction can be sustained, but if it could, it would give credence to the biological determinist view that many of our behaviors, particularly those having to do with sexuality and behaviors associated with one or the other sex, are fixed genetically. Although I am convinced that scientists should go where the evidence leads them, I think that feminists have successfully shown that when someone claims that sexual or gendered natures are fixed, one has reason be skeptical (Hrdy, 2002; Bleier, 1985; Fausto-Sterling, 1985; Tavris, 1992). It falls on feminists to raise skeptical opposition to this sort of argument, and this is the sort of role analytical feminists have played in political philosophy.

B. The Critique of the Public/Private Dichotomy

As Carole Pateman (1985) has pointed out, liberal political theory has traditionally recognized a divide between the public world of law and government, and a private realm of civil society, which includes religion, the market, and other non-governmentally determined associations among men. But this fails to recognize a second distinction between the government together with civil society on the one hand, and the domestic private sphere on the other, the distinction which feminists have brought to political philosophy. Feminists point to a second ambiguity concerning the public and private, as well. Traditional liberals carved out the private sphere as the realm of freedom from interference, but this meant freedom for men, conceived as the heads of households, and not women's or children's freedom, as they are the objects of men's free choices. Feminist political philosophers note that privacy must therefore either be done away with or reconceived as the realm of free individual choice in order to serve women as well as men. As Susan Moller Okin writes, "feminists claim that the existing liberal distinction between public and domestic is ideological in the sense that it presents society from a traditional male perspective, that it is based on assumptions about the different natures and natural roles of men and women and that, as presently conceived, it cannot serve as a central concept in a political theory that will, for the first time, include all of us" (Okin, 1998, 125).

While some feminists argue for the overthrowing of privacy and the complete politicization of the personal (MacKinnon, 1989), many still find in privacy an important value for women (Allen, 1988). Privacy is valuable for persons in several ways that feminists can recognize. It is an essential part of intimate relations with others. Intimate relations between persons consist in part in shared stories and values that are not shared with others. Most of us feel that there are things that our intimate partners and friends know about us and our relationships that we would not want to share with others, not only because that might be humiliating or embarrassing, but because it is the very meaning of shared intimacy. Humans find this sharing valuable, and it would not be possible without privacy. Privacy is similarly important for free mental development. If we were not able to keep some thoughts hidden from others, then we would be unwilling to try out new ideas as thought experiments. We need to be able to choose what ideas to share with whom in order to have the confidence that we will not be embarrassed or revealed by every private thought. Finally, privacy is very important to the arguments for reproductive freedom for women. The decision of whether to conceive or bear a child is considered to be private both for the individual who would bear the child and for the couple who would be parents together. Thus privacy is also a positive value for feminists, and this creates a kind of ambiguity for us in mainstreaming feminist political philosophy.

The debate over privacy can lead feminists to accommodate if they begin to see individual liberty as individually and privately achievable, rather than as a social achievement. Viewed as such, valuing privacy may lead to the repudiation of public projects and institutions that support the achievement of liberty for all. But there is a feminist way of valuing privacy that does not imply such possessive individualism. I have noted that privacy is essential for creating and maintaining intimate relationships, both for constituting them and for making reproductive decisions within them. Given the crucial importance of privacy in the abortion debate, it is important for feminists to maintain the value of privacy even while critiquing the way that it historically has been defined and implemented in liberal societies.

C. The Structural Nature of Oppression

Oppression has long been a central topic of feminist philosophy; one might say that feminist philosophy begins with the claim that women are oppressed. Simone Beauvoir (1952) provided one of the deepest analyses of the situation of women as oppressed, showing how interconnected each of the seemingly small and unrelated insults and harms (what Marilyn Frye [1983] compared to the individual wires of the birdcage) come together to form enormous obstacles to women's freedom. The feminist theory of oppression is not a list of grievances, though; it has become a nuanced analysis of the structure of constraint, a theory generally applicable to many different groups in society. Feminists have benefited from Marxist and structuralist theories of oppression that theorize oppression as socially structured, and not just the effect of a tyrannical leader or government. Yet feminists have broadened the application of the term "oppression" to a much wider set of social groups, first women, but also racial groups (Davis, 1981), castes (Narayan, 1998; Nussbaum, 2001), and non-normative sexual groups (Frye, 1983), among others.

On my theory of oppression (Cudd, 2006), which builds on those of Beauvoir and Frye, social groups are constructed by the systematic social constraints they face that either privilege or disadvantage them as a group, vis-à-vis other groups. Oppressed groups are those that face direct and indirect material and psychological forces of oppression, including violence, economic deprivation and discrimination, and cognitive and

affective external and internal forces. Oppression is a network of interlocking forces that create inequality among social groups and suffering of
individuals within them. Women, as a group, are oppressed in contemporary American society by the many types of gender-specific violence they
face, as well as by economic segregation, discrimination, sexual harassment,
and psychological forces that stereotype, traumatize, and humiliate them.
Because they are interlocking forces, the effects of one force make individuals more vulnerable to another, and the harms are exacerbated and mul-
tiplied. So, for example, because women are segregated into lower paid
occupations and part-time work, they have less bargaining power in
domestic negotiations with men over who will do the domestic unpaid
labor, how family income will be distributed, and whose human capital is
to receive a greater investment. These facts make women more vulnerable
to domestic violence, more likely not to leave if they are beaten, and more
likely to return even if they leave. Since women are more likely to be
domestic laborers, they prepare for and prepare their daughters for unpaid
childcare work, including their ability and desire to attach emotionally to
children, which makes it even more likely that they will be vulnerable to
poor bargaining outcomes in domestic situations. By the same token, men
will be less likely to prepare emotionally for domestic work and more
likely to build human capital necessary for public life.

As long as feminist philosophers keep their attention focused clearly on
the social group nature of oppression, it seems to me that the dangers of
accommodation and co-optation are minimized. However, as we make
progress in lessening the oppression of some social groups, it will be important for feminists honestly to assess this progress in order to describe accurately the state of the polis as well as to see what policies or theories work in
bringing about a lessening of oppression. Also, it is important to see what
groups, if any, are left behind or suffer new forms of oppression. In making
these assessments, mainstreamed feminists face the real possibility of seeing
things as the dominant members see them and thereby overlooking or even
actively masking the oppression of others. This, of course, is a longstanding
internal critique of feminists by feminists. The critique has fruitfully introduced the idea of intersectionality, or the notion that we each belong to
intersecting, overlapping, and sometimes opposing social groups that imply
various dimensions of privilege and oppression. While intersectional analysis has deepened our understanding of oppression, it can also lead us away
from the core idea of feminism, that women as women have been the object
of injustice. In being led astray, feminism is vulnerable to co-opting by the
mainstream, and it is essential that feminists resist this trap.

D. Autonomy

Autonomy has long been an important part of moral and political philosophy. But in the mainstream of political philosophy until recent times it has been conceived, with some exceptions (and the nineteenth-century feminist John Stuart Mill comes to mind), individualistically and hyperrationally. That is, autonomy requires both that the agent's mind be independent from her fellows, and that the agent is an integrated self apart from other independent selves, with her own preferences, rationality, and access to the moral law. Liberal political and moral philosophy has made essential use of this notion of autonomy to justify or legitimize governmental authority either on contractarian or contractualist grounds that autonomous agents choose or would choose the authority, or on utilitarian grounds that the authority maximizes the subjective utility of autonomous agents. Feminists have raised serious concerns about both the conception of autonomy and the availability of autonomy to women and other oppressed persons, and hence its usefulness for political theory. I will discuss these two points briefly in order.

Feminists' attention to the lives of women within the private sphere, in which they specialize in and are shaped by caring labor, challenges the ideal of independence in several ways. First, it calls attention to the facts of how persons develop through childhood and dependency on caring others into beings capable of the two moral powers that John Rawls discusses: a sense of justice and a capacity to pursue a conception of the good. These facts reveal our physical, emotional, and epistemic dependency on many others, from those who meet our physical and emotional needs, to the communities that structure our beliefs and values through norms that are always already there for us. There are thus, at the very least, deep social sources and ingredients in our episodic independence. Second, feminist attention to caring labor suggests a moral responsibility both to recognize the nurturance one has received, and to reciprocate or "pay forward" that nurturance for others. Reflecting on the commonness of human disability, Eva Kittay argues for a third moral power as part of the basis for human autonomy: the ability to respond to vulnerability with care (Kittay, 1999, 100).

Feminism has thus given birth to new conceptions of autonomy, called "relational autonomy," which refers to theories of autonomy that share the conviction "that persons are socially embedded and that agents' identities are formed within the context of social relationships and shaped by a complex of intersecting social determinants, such as race, class, gender, and ethnicity" (Mackenzie and Stoljar, 2000, 4). Relational theories of autonomy thus recognize that persons learn and develop their ability to make autonomous decisions and choices within communities, and that the conditions for autonomy are at least partially external to the agent. An oppressive community or relationship can compromise autonomy for some or all of its members.

Feminist attention to the social construction of gender and structural sources of oppression raises the possibility that oppressed persons cannot be autonomous, and leads to a rethinking of liberal political theories premised on the notion of autonomous agents making rational decisions in their own interest. For if their interests are not truly their own, then liberal theories of political legitimacy falter. Feminist attention to oppression and the hierarchy imposed by gender has made clear some of the ways that choice is not autonomous, and so the choices made by oppressed citizens for certain political structures cannot be counted as legitimating those structures. Marilyn Friedman's feminist theory of autonomy is particularly attentive to the ways that social structures can prevent actions from being autonomous. On her account, autonomy requires that actions or choices be one's own in the sense that one self-reflectively considers what one wants, that the choices mirror a reflective endorsement of one's wants and values, that the wants and values are themselves important to one, and that the choices or actions are unimpeded by coercion, deception, or manipulation that can derail those kinds of self-reflection. (Friedman, 2003, 14)

In the introduction to their anthology, *Relational Autonomy*, Catriona Mackenzie and Natalie Stoljar (2000) begin by arguing against what they saw as the prevailing feminist view that autonomy was a hopelessly masculinist notion. Their work, as well as that of Friedman, Diana Meyers, and others, has, I think, demonstrated that they were correct, but also that the mainstream understanding of autonomy was impoverished. Although feminists have at times attempted to accommodate the proceduralism of most pre-feminist thought about autonomy, feminist thought has overall shown that there are some bottom-line requirements for autonomy that oppressive societies deny to some of their people. People must have some degree of self-respect and self-trust to be autonomous. This creates the uncomfortable and now familiar position of having to say of some women (and other oppressed persons) that they do not have the social bases of autonomy, a position that sounds like victim-blaming, but is not. To deny that some women lack the social bases of autonomy, it seems to me, is to accommodate one's perspective so that it fails to notice oppressive social structures because they are too painful or humiliating to face. A mainstream feminism cannot succumb to this, even as feminists become part of the dominant social group. It leads to being co-opted into denying that social structures of oppression exist, or justifying them as the choices of the victims themselves.[4]

Despite pockets of resistance from the mainstream, these contributions of feminism to political philosophy must have their day because political philosophy cannot live without them, and because they form a coherent whole that rationally cannot be divided. Susan Okin writes:

> in the feminist attempt to comprehend gender we find the personal and the political mixed in a way that confounds the separate categories of public and domestic, and points out the necessary incompleteness of theories of politics that persist in confining themselves to the study of what has been defined in a pre-feminist era as legitimately political. (Okin, 1998, 129)

The ideas of gender as constructed and the personal and political as divided along gender lines lead inevitably to the questions about women's role in the domestic sphere. Pointing out that women are unfairly restrained by the domestic sphere implicates questions about justice and personal autonomy, as well as concerns about the role of caring labor and who will be doing the caring if women are free to choose not to do it. The fact that all these ideas are tightly connected means that there are multiple paths leading from feminism to political philosophy, and vice versa. One can start with concerns about caring and women's labor, and that leads to questions about autonomy and oppression, or one can begin with questions about oppression, and that points to women's domestic burden, the public/private dichotomy, and so forth. Similar arguments could be made from other contributions of feminist philosophy that I have not considered here, as well. Thus, feminist political philosophy has intellectually penetrated the mainstream of political philosophy concerns and ideas.

III. MAINSTREAMING FEMINISM IN PHILOSOPHY

One premise of this paper has been that feminism is turning a corner, at least in political philosophy, to becoming a part of the mainstream collective of philosophers. Given the contrary evidence that Sally

Haslanger's piece provides, what evidence would point in the direction of mainstreaming? One thing I would point to is this volume and the careers of the authors. Several of the women who are authors are at top-level philosophy programs, and some of them are full professors. Many of the others are tenured and full professors at so-called Research I institutions, where they are training graduate students in feminism, and others are professors at liberal arts schools or community colleges, where they are whetting the appetites of undergraduates for graduate study in philosophy and teaching them that feminist perspectives are valuable and normative. The fact that Haslanger's article has been widely circulated throughout philosophy departments and has attracted attention among mainstream philosophers who had assumed that the mainstreaming had already occurred is evidence that we are finally getting through. In my home philosophy department, a quiet revolution took place recently when we sought to hire a self-described feminist, who had written a dissertation on a feminist topic, for a position in ethical theory. Since I was hired as a philosopher of economics, and did not self-identify as a feminist philosopher until I received tenure, my department had never hired a self-described feminist.[5] I say this revolution was quiet, though, since there was no discussion of the fact that the job candidate in question was a feminist. Rather, her work was simply seen as stellar work in ethics. It must be noted that she came from one of the top five, some would say the very top, department in rankings of graduate schools in philosophy. This helped my colleagues to see excellent feminist work as excellent work in ethics.

Other areas of evidence in favor of mainstreaming are the many feminist books and book lists published by top academic publishers. (Book publishers seem to be more welcoming to feminist philosophy than journal editors, however.) The *Stanford Encyclopedia of Philosophy* devotes thirty-nine entries (published or planned) to feminist topics in philosophy, not including entries on specific feminist philosophers.[6] Furthermore, many feminist women are in positions of influence at this point, and are beginning to be recognized as the leaders of the profession. For example, Annette Baier and Virginia Held have been recent presidents of the American Philosophical Association, while Eleanor Stump and Claudia Card have presided over the Central Division.

Why would we want feminist political philosophy to be mainstreamed? I think we want this mainly because it would be not only a sign of progress, but **it would be** progress itself. If mainstream political philosophy took in the sex/gender distinction; redrew the public/private distinction so as not to put women and children in the private world of men as their property, but rather preserved a realm of privacy for all that was not a form of ownership; took oppression to be structural and one of the major topics of political philosophy; and understood the relational aspects of autonomy, then this would constitute progress.

IV. THE FUTURE OF FEMINIST PHILOSOPHY: RESISTANCE IS NOT FUTILE

The current state of feminism in political philosophy shows that the resistance of mainstream political philosophy to feminist incursion is futile, but I have also argued that resistance by feminism to accommodating or being co-opted by the mainstream is not futile. By avoiding those twin dangers, feminism has continued to challenge the mainstream and build coherent and complex critiques of mainstream political philosophy. Analytic feminism has walked a fine line between these twin dangers and the internal critique of feminism that it has tried to present. I would argue that because feminism has made room for this internal critique, feminism has been further strengthened. Furthermore, analytic feminism has been able to offer an internal critique of analytic political philosophy in a way that another orientation within feminism could not because it would be doubly rejected.

Unlike the Borg of *Star Trek* fame, the discipline of philosophy has resisted assimilating feminism up to this point, and feminism has likewise resisted accommodation or co-opting, for the most part. Feminism refuses to be assimilated without in turn changing the nature of philosophy. As we move forward, we need to maintain this attitude of resistance, even while we join with the collective to make it stronger. By doing this we change philosophy and make it better. We need to help each other reach positions of authority within philosophy and in the mainstream, applaud each other's successes, and cite each other's work, even while we constructively criticize it. We need to submit our work to and publish in top journals, not accommodating to the status quo by citing only mainstream journals and authors, but rather including women and male fellow travelers on the margins. We need to bring along our students as feminist philosophers. We should honestly assess where progress has been made, and how, and focus on what has yet to be done. Most of all, we need to continue our internal critiques as feminists of feminism, and our internal critiques of philosophy as feminist philosophers. In this way we maintain the vitality of both feminism and philosophy, as well as making philosophy a feminist friendly discipline.

Notes

I gratefully acknowledge helpful comments on this paper from the editors of this volume, Anita Superson and Sharon Crasnow, and two anonymous reviewers for Oxford University Press.

1. Ann E. Cudd, "Analyzing Backlash to Progressive Social Movements," *APA Newsletter on Feminism and Philosophy* 99 (1999). The article cites Scott Allen, "For Philosophers, Criticism and a Call to Service," *The Boston Globe,* August 11, 1998, 1, for the Silber quote, and "Feminism Revisited: A Symposium," *Times Literary Supplement,* March 20, 1998, 13, for the quote by McGinn.
2. For a more pessimistic view, see Margaret Urban Walker, "Diotima's Ghost: The Uncertain Place of Feminist Philosophy in Professional Philosophy," *Hypatia* 20, no. 3 (2005): 153–65.
3. For example, Drucilla Cornell, *The Imaginary Domain* (New York: Routledge, 1997). Postmodern feminists like Judith Butler question whether there is any coherent sense of any gender identity. See Donna Haraway, "'Gender' for a Marxist Dictionary: The Sexual Politics of a Word" in *Simians, Cyborgs, and Women,* New York: Routledge, 1991.
4. See, for example, Christina Hoff Sommers, *Who Stole Feminism?* (New York: Touchstone, 1994).
5. Three other feminist philosophers have come and gone since I was hired, but none of them described themselves as primarily feminist, nor were their dissertation projects explicitly feminist.
6. Edward N. Zalta, editor. *Stanford Encyclopedia of Philosophy*, http://plato.stanford.edu/ accessed 7 July 2011.

References

Allen, Anita. *Uneasy Access: Privacy for Women in a Free Society.* Totowa, N.J.: Rowman and Littlefield, 1988.

Baron-Cohen, Simon, Rebecca C. Knickmeyer, and Matthew K. Belmonte. "Sex Differences in the Brain: Implications for Explaining Autism." *Science* 310, no. 5749 (4 November 2005): 819–23.

Beauvoir, Simone de. *The Second Sex.* Translated by H. M. Parshley. New York: Random House, 1952.

Bleier, Ruth. *Gender and Science: A Critique of Biology and Its Theories on Women.* Elmsford, N.Y.: Pergamon Press, 1984.

Cornell, Drucilla. *The Imaginary Domain.* New York: Routledge, 1997.

Cudd, Ann E. *Analyzing Oppression.* New York: Oxford University Press, 2006.

Cudd, Ann E. "Analyzing Backlash to Progressive Social Movements," APA Newsletter on Feminism and Philosophy 99(1999): 42–46.

Davis, Angela Y. *Women, Race, and Class.* New York: Random House, 1981.

Fausto-Sterling, Anne. *Myths of Gender: Biological Theories about Women and Men.* New York: Basic Books, 1985.

———. *Sexing the Body: Gender Politics and the Construction of Sexuality.* New York: Basic Books, 2000.

Friedman, Marilyn. *Autonomy, Gender, Politics.* New York: Oxford University Press, 2003.

Frye, Marilyn. *The Politics of Reality.* Trumansburg, N.Y.: Crossing Press, 1983.

Haslanger, Sally. "Changing the Ideology and Culture of Philosophy: Not by Reason (Alone)." *Hypatia: A Journal of Feminist Philosophy* 23(April 2008): 210 –23.

Haraway, Donna. "'Gender' for a Marxist Dictionary: The Sexual Politics of a Word" in *Simians, Cyborgs, and Women,* New York: Routledge, 1991.

Hrdy, Sarah Blaffer. "Empathy, Polyandry, and the Myth of the Coy Female." In *The Gender of Science,* edited by Janet A. Kourany, 171–91. Upper Saddle River, N.J.: Prentice-Hall, 2002.

Kessler-Harris, Alice. "Do We Still Need Women's History?" *Chronicle of Higher Education* (7 December 2007): B6–7.

Kittay, Eva Feder. *Love's Labor: Essays on Women, Equality, and Dependency.* New York: Routledge, 1999.

Mackenzie, Catriona, and Natalie Stoljar. "Introduction: Autonomy Refigured." In *Relational Autonomy,* edited by Mackenzie and Stoljar, 3–31. New York: Oxford University Press, 2000.

MacKinnon, Catharine. *Toward a Feminist Theory of the State.* Cambridge, Mass.: Harvard University Press, 1989.

Mead, Margaret. *Sex and Temperament in Three Primitive Societies.* New York: Harper Collins, 2001. First published, 1935.

Narayan, Uma. "Essence of Culture and a Sense of History: A Feminist Critique of Cultural Essentialism." *Hypatia: A Journal of Feminist Philosophy* 13 (1998): 86–106.

Nussbaum, Martha. *Women and Human Development.* New York: Cambridge University Press, 2001.

Okin, Susan Moller. "Gender, the Public, and the Private." In *Feminism and Politics,* edited by Anne Phillips, 116–141. Oxford: Oxford University Press, 1998.

Pateman, Carole. "Feminist Critiques of the Public/Private Dichotomy." In *Public and Private in Social Life,* edited by S. I. Benn and G. F. Gaus, 118–140. London: Croom Helm, 1985.

Sommers, Christina Hoff. *Who Stole Feminism?* New York: Touchstone, 1994.

Tavris, Carol. *The Mismeasure of Woman.* New York: Simon and Schuster, 1992.

Walker, Margaret Urban. "Diotima's Ghost: The Uncertain Place of Feminist Philosophy in Professional Philosophy." *Hypatia: A Journal of Feminist Philosophy* 20, no. 3 (2005): 153–65.

2

HELGA VARDEN
University of Illinois at Urbana–Champaign

A FEMINIST, KANTIAN

CONCEPTION OF THE RIGHT

TO BODILY INTEGRITY:

The Cases of Abortion and Homosexuality

INTRODUCTION

Kant himself did not provide much direct help with regard to giving a philosophical account of the legal permissibility of abortion and homosexuality, and doubtless the feminist movement has been central to illuminating this lacuna in his thought. It seems fair to say that Kant's own writings are at best confusing and at worst of no help. To wit, in the midst of a theory of justice based on a fundamental respect for each person's *innate* right to *freedom*, we are faced with Kant's brief mention of the fetus as a person upon conception, as well as his teleological and notoriously phobic statements about homosexuality.[1] Still, a considered Kantian conception of abortion and homosexuality must be consistent with the overall structure of Kant's theory of justice. I will argue that because of the analytic relation between the person and the body at the heart of Kant's political and legal theory, there is a fundamental commitment to a right to bodily integrity. This commitment entails that a consistent Kantian position defends both a right to abortion and a right to homosexual interaction. Indeed, Kant's political and legal theory affirms a feminist- and queer-friendly conception of abortion and homosexuality that is worth taking seriously.

Pregnant women and persons engaging in homosexual practices compose two groups that have been and still are among those most severely subjected to coercive restrictions regarding their own bodies. From an historical point of view, it is a recent and rare phenomenon that a woman's right to abortion and a person's right to engage in homosexual interactions[2] are recognized. Today, though most Western liberal states do recognize these rights, they are under continuous challenge—sometimes by violent protest—from various political and religious movements. Moreover, though liberal theories of justice typically defend women's rights to abortion and people's rights to homosexual activity, these theories often struggle to capture the fundamental ground for these rights. For example, it appears hard for the liberal to say why and when only the woman and not the embryo/fetus has rights and why the right to certain sexual practices is not on par with rights to other preferences. Contemporary liberal theories of justice, therefore, struggle both to identify what distinguishes questions of abortion and sexual activities from other questions of right and thereby capture the gravity of the wrongdoing involved in coercively restricting homosexual interactions and abortion as such. I will argue that Kant's theory of justice is able to capture the fundamental ground for these rights in his understanding of the bodily integrity of the person. This Kantian position also presents a third alternative to the contemporary stalemate between those privileging the rights of the mother and those privileging the personhood of the embryo/fetus. Just states will neither permit nor outlaw all abortions or sexual interactions, but rather will require all such laws to be reconcilable with the protection of each person's right to freedom.

1. THE POINT OF VIEW OF JUSTICE IS NOT THE POINT OF VIEW OF ETHICS OR RELIGION

It is relatively uncontroversial to say that pregnancies and sexual activities constitute tremendously important aspects of our lives and so naturally constitute major concerns for both ethical[3] and theological theories. In this chapter, however, I am concerned with neither the ethical nor religious value of pregnancies and sexual relations, nor the justifiability of various ethical and theological theories as they have been applied to these issues. Instead, I simply give an account of why, from the point of view of *justice*, it is especially wrong coercively to prevent, including by means of criminalization, abortion as such[4] and homosexual activity. Thus, my account goes against several trends in contemporary thought.

For example, it is often assumed that an analysis of what is right and wrong from the point of view of ethics or theology will yield the same or at least similar results as an analysis from the point of view of justice. Or it is thought that conclusions drawn about what rights we have are dependent on conclusions drawn about what is ethically or religiously required. At least that is the presumption in a large proportion of the papers written on abortion and homosexual activity over the last four decades.[5] I also challenge the view that the rights to abortion and homosexuality are the result of prudential considerations or considerations of tolerance. According to this view, only by granting these rights can we peacefully coexist in a pluralist world given our different ethical and religious ideologies.[6]

Contrary to these dominant views, I will defend the claim that we cannot deny others a right to obtain an abortion as such or to engage in homosexual activity without thereby refusing to interact with them rightfully, namely, in a way reconcilable with their innate right to freedom. Justice is not the enforcement of a subsection of people's ethical or religious duties, nor is it primarily about tolerance of different viewpoints in order to live together peaceably. Rather, justice concerns normative or rightful interaction in the world, that is, normative relations that are in principle enforceable. Even if we try, we cannot force people to be religiously good or to be ethically virtuous. All we can do through legal means is to ensure that when interacting people act in a way respectful of each other's rights. Consequently, justice requires us to look at the issues from the point of view of enforceable rights and duties, which concern rights and duties that are consistent with each person's innate right to freedom. It is therefore entirely possible that what is rightfully enforceable is not coextensive with what is ethically justifiable or religiously defensible.

At the foundation of Kant's conception of justice lies what Kant calls our "Only One Innate Right," namely each person's innate right to freedom (MM 6: 237). And each person's innate right to freedom is defined as her or his right to "independence from being constrained by another's choice...insofar as it [one's freedom] can coexist with the freedom of every other in accordance with a universal law" (ibid.).[7] Importantly, one's right to freedom, for Kant, is something one is born with; it is not something one has before one is born. Hence, even if we concede either that the fetus is a person, as does Judith Jarvis Thomson in her seminal article on abortion, or that metaethical[8] considerations require us to attribute personhood upon conception, as does Kant, we have not thereby established that we can justly criminalize abortion. This is not only a point explicitly emphasized by Thomson but also one acknowledged by Kant when he maintains that the right to freedom is innate even though considerations of metaethics lead him to ascribe personhood upon conception. The important point is that conclusions of ethics are not necessarily also conclusions of justice.

According to the Kantian conception of justice, one's right to freedom is the right to have one's interactions with others restricted only by universal laws (laws of freedom). For example, whether or not Kant himself and others considered some particular sexual ends to be more or less natural (and thus more or less virtuous) than others cannot be a relevant consideration when determining which ends people have a right to set with their own bodies—alone or consensually with others. A law enforcing a particular natural end for all is a contingent restriction and not a law of freedom. Therefore, it is an unjustifiable law according to Kant's own theory. It is for these kinds of reasons that we must ignore Kant's teleological and homophobic statements when applying his theory of justice to the legal status of homosexual practices. In addition, we must make sense of Kant's puzzling claims that personhood is attributed upon conception and yet the right to freedom is innate, namely something we are born with.

The application of Kant's political and legal theory to the question of abortion and homosexuality, I argue below, turns on the fact that persons are embodied beings, which means that the limits of freedom insofar as we are persons must be extended to us insofar as we are embodied. Because we are embodied beings, and because the restrictions on abortion and homosexual activity we are considering are restrictions on what we can do with our own bodies, enforcing unjustifiable restrictions on homosexual activity and abortion denies homosexuals and women a right to freedom. What is more, it is to wrong their persons. And because the state, in establishing itself as a public authority, must provide conditions in which its citizens can interact rightfully, it cannot enforce such laws.

2. EMBODIED FREEDOM

On the Kantian account, it is in virtue of being persons, or beings deemed capable of assuming responsibility for our actions, that notions of rights and duties are possible. And it is in virtue of being embodied that we must determine how we should interact in the empirical world. Justice, then, concerns how we—embodied persons—interact and can be forced to interact normatively in space and time. Moreover, from the point of view of justice, the fact that we are embodied entails that the relation between my person and my body must be considered "analytic," that is, one of necessary unity.[9] Therefore, in conceptualizing a person's legal rights, we must think of a person and her body as one.[10] Since my body and my person are always in the same spatiotemporal location, the empirical boundaries of my person are identical with those of my body. We can illustrate the necessary unity of the body and the person by contrasting it to the relation between a person and her private property. Private property is not necessarily united with my person. I may obtain private property through certain actions, and, indeed, if something is mine, then it is mine even if I am not physically holding it. And if someone takes my property a wrong is done, but not to my person. For example, if I forget my scarf at your house one evening, then the scarf is still mine even though I no longer have it with me. If you steal my scarf, you do not wrong my person since you do not touch my body, but you still wrong me by depriving me of my rightful property. In contrast, were you to forcibly grab the scarf from around my neck as I am leaving your house, not only would you wrong me by depriving me of my property, but also you would wrong my person by touching my body in unauthorized ways. From the point of view of justice, then, my embodiment entails that when you violate my bodily integrity, you wrong my person. Because violations against my body are violations against my person, they are more serious than wrongs involving my property.

Liberal theories of justice, as well as the principles underwriting liberal constitutional democracies, affirm some version of the view that everyone has an innate right to freedom, meaning that everyone has a right to set and pursue ends of his own insofar as he respects the rights of others to do the same, subject to reciprocal laws of freedom. Moreover, according to the liberal position presented above, the fact of our embodiment entails that our innate right to freedom must involve an innate right to our own bodies—as contrasted with acquired rights to material possessions (private property) we appropriate or make part of our means.[11] To be free in this "external" sense—or what Kant calls "external freedom"—involves using oneself (one's embodied person) and one's means (one's rightful possessions) to set and pursue ends of one's own under universal laws of freedom. Thus, when we *interact*, we are free as long as we are setting and pursuing ends of our own subject only to universal laws of freedom that restrict us reciprocally or in the same way. This, for Kant, is rightful freedom.

One way to clarify this liberal conception of freedom is to contrast it, first, with being enslaved and, second, with being deprived of rights. A slave does not have the right to set and pursue ends of his own, since the slave owner literally is seen as "owning" the slave. The slave is seen as a "rightful" possession of the slave owner, namely, as a means with which the slave owner can set and pursue his own ends. The slave is therefore not only deprived of all rights, that is, of any rights to set and pursue ends of his own, but everything the slave does, in principle, is in need of approval from the slave owner. On the Kantian conception of justice, the reason why slave laws are void is that they involve an incoherent notion of rights. Slave laws assume both that some particular persons are mere means for others (things), and so incapable of obligations, and at the same time that they are capable of obligations, and so are not mere means (things). Consequently, such "possessions" and "contracts" can never be rightfully enforced. In contrast to being enslaved, persons who are simply denied rights are not seen as belonging to anyone else, but they too lack the right to set and pursue their own ends. What is common to both cases is the denial of a right to freedom, understood as the right to set and pursue one's own ends independently of the arbitrary choices of another but as subject only to universal laws of freedom that restrict interacting persons reciprocally.

Most commonly, the problem with coercive restrictions outlawing homosexual activity and abortion as such is not that they enslave homosexuals and women.[12] Rather, the typical problem with criminalizing these activities is that it denies women and homosexuals the right to their own bodies. And since our bodies and persons must be seen as necessarily united, such restrictions are irreconcilable with respect for one another's person, which is the foundation of any liberal notion of rights and duties. Such restrictions involve, in other words, a refusal to interact with women and homosexuals rightfully or as persons. Consequently, a state that enforces such laws fails to set itself up as civil society, since the civil condition just is one in which all persons can interact rightfully.[13] Such a state fails to provide conditions under which all its citizens can interact as persons or on terms consistent with each other's innate right to freedom.[14] Instead, such a state forces its subjects to interact as they would in a brutal version of the state of nature, where the many or the powerful have no intention of interacting in ways consistent with respect for everyone's right to freedom.[15] In fact, some set it as their end to deprive others of this basic right. But if anything is wrong, this is wrong, since it violates the very foundation of a liberal notion of rights and duties. Hence, under such conditions, women and homosexuals must protect themselves from the violence perpetrated against them by others—including the state—to the best of their ability.

2.1 Abortion: Rightful Restrictions

Before applying the above conception of rightful embodied freedom to the current controversial, proposed legislation to criminalize abortion, let me first illustrate how the above Kantian conception of justice can explain why all liberal constitutional democracies firmly reject certain proposals to deny the right to abortion. As we will see, the reason why these particular proposals are rejected is primarily that they so clearly involve depriving women of their bodily integrity, though one type of proposal involves enslavement.

Consider first the enslavement case. Liberal constitutional democracies typically reject laws that subject a woman's decision regarding abortion to some other private person's choice. For example, liberal constitutional democracies do not permit laws according to which the other parent or the parents of the woman are seen as having the right to veto the woman's choice to have an abortion.[16] According to the theory presented above, the reason why such restrictions are rejected is that they involve the enslavement of women. They are fundamentally inconsistent with a woman's freedom subject to universal laws, since the woman's freedom in this case is subjected to another private person's arbitrary choice (the other parent or the woman's own parents). A liberal constitutional democracy considers such laws to be fundamentally inconsistent with each citizen's rights—they are necessarily "unconstitutional"—since any liberal notion of right is inconsistent with depriving legally responsible persons of the right to make such decisions regarding themselves. To use Kantian language, such a law is fundamentally inconsistent with each citizen's innate right to freedom, which is why no just state will uphold it.

Second, no modern liberal constitutional democracies hold that women and their embryos/fetuses have equal legal status. Importantly, they all hold that the fetus acquires full legal rights only once it is born. Up until the point of birth, the life and health of the mother has priority, and therefore, if carrying the fetus to term presents a health risk to the mother, there is a right to abort. Like Kant, they all agree that the right to freedom is "innate," something a person is born with. It is not something that persons have prior to birth. Why is this so? In accordance with the conception of rightful interaction presented above, the reason is simply that a liberal constitutional democracy requires its laws to be consistent with each citizen's right to freedom. Since we are embodied beings and since women give birth to babies, the only way to protect a woman's embodied freedom—to protect her constitutional rights as a citizen—is by giving her priority over the fetus. That is to say, in an important sense, the mother and the fetus are an analytic unity: they are necessarily united up until birth. But, since the fetus is inside the mother's body, it is united with and dependent on the mother—not the other way around. Therefore, only the mother is an independent, embodied person. The fetus is not an independently existing embodied person until it is born. To treat the fetus otherwise, that is, as an independently existing person prior to birth, is necessarily to deprive the mother of her bodily integrity and therefore of her embodied personhood. It is necessarily to treat the mother merely as a means for the fetus.[17]

Finally, all liberal modern constitutional democracies argue that no woman can be rightfully coerced to carry forward a pregnancy that is the result of force (rape). Again, no liberal legal system can permit any of its citizens to violate another citizen's bodily integrity and thereby force that other person to pursue a particular end (carry forward a pregnancy). To permit this would be to deprive some of its citizens—women—a right to freedom at all, or to permit the replacement of right with might.

These above examples constitute the easy cases for liberal theories, including the Kantian theory, and they do not, in my view, constitute the heart of the current controversies surrounding abortion. Indeed, both liberal positions and reasonable ethical/religious positions arguing against the right of abortion have some way of accommodating the above claims made concerning enslavement, unequal status of mother and fetus until birth, and pregnancies as a result of rape. These kinds of cases do not represent the core of the present controversy, since at least the reasonable participants in current discussions agree that they are exceptions to the general rule.[18] Rather, the hard question concerns what the general rule should be: should women have a right to abortion under "normal" circumstances or not? Much of the debate focuses not only on the assumption granted in the arguments above namely, that the fetus is a person, but also on the question of whether the embryo is a person. The reason seems to be that both camps in the debate agree that if we accept that an embryo/fetus is a person—for metaethical or theological reasons—then we must also accept the general rule that abortion in all stages of embryonic/fetal development should be coercively prevented and criminalized (again with the exceptions being cases of enslavement, protecting the life or health of the mother, and rape). Consequently, much effort on the part of those in favor of abortion focuses on challenging this assumption with regard to earlier stages of embryonic/fetal development, whereas anti-abortion defenders focus on justifying it. Thus the current debate is mired down in trying, to this point unsuccessfully, to give some sort of conclusive metaethical or theological arguments for why, why not, or at what stage we should consider the embryo/fetus a person.[19]

The most important challenge to the assumption that solving the metaethical or theological problem will solve the problem of whether or not abortion should be prohibited comes from Thomson, for she grants that the fetus is a person in all stages of development. She then argues famously—through the example of the violinist who gets kidnapped and hooked up to another person overnight—that it does not follow that abortion can be coercively prevented or criminalized. As is evident by now, I share Thomson's view. Nevertheless, I believe that Thomson's argument succeeds only in justifying the exceptions to the general rule outlined above, namely, the cases of prohibiting one person to have an arbitrary veto power over the pregnant woman, of the pregnant woman's priority over the fetus, and of the right to abort in cases of rape. That is, Thomson establishes why no liberal theory and constitutional democracy will permit these kinds of coercive legislation, and her reasoning seems to be quite similar to the Kantian reasoning presented above. What we are looking for, however, is the possibility of a stronger argument, one that justifies abortion also in the "normal" cases and not only in these exceptional cases.[20] That argument, I suggest, must tackle the harder question of whether or not it matters from the point of view of justice that the woman has permitted embryonic/fetal development to reach a certain stage. The stronger justification of a right to abortion will show that even if we grant personhood upon conception for metaethical or theological reasons, this does not entail that as a matter of justice, normal cases of abortion can be coercively prevented or criminalized. Moreover, if we can show why women must choose whether or not to abort before a certain stage of embryonic/fetal development, then we might have an argument convincing to both camps. The hope is that this argument can provide a way out of the current deadlock between pro-choice and anti-abortion activists and advocates, by driving home the point that their disagreement is about metaethical or theological positions on personhood and not about considerations of justice. Once this important distinction is brought to light, it will be clear that the argument can satisfy most pro-choice advocates. And although it will challenge the conclusion upheld by the anti-abortionists, it proceeds from the anti-abortionists' own metaethical or theological foundation, namely that an embryo/fetus is a person upon conception.[21]

This third approach to abortion I am suggesting requires accepting the view that an analysis from the point of view of justice or right is not the same or coextensive with an analysis from the points of view of ethics or theology. As such, this is not a terribly upsetting assumption for most. After all, no major religions argue that one can be forced to become religious. One is only a religious person if one has accepted it freely, taken the religion "to heart." Moreover, everyone accepts that much of what might be considered ethically praiseworthy or blameworthy should not be made a matter of law. For example, no one thinks that it should be a matter of justice that one is generous, kind, friendly, or considerate. Rather, what will strike many as controversial, and hence what is important to show, is that the issue of abortion should be seen similarly. Abortion is one of those issues where from the point of view of justice ethical and theological arguments are not, and therefore should not be, considered directly relevant. Consequently, when we individually—as citizens, as politicians, as legislators and as judges—think about whether or not abortion should be criminalized, ethical or theological arguments should not be what settles the issue. Rather, what is important from the point of view of justice is how to make our interactions in the world just or rightful. What we ought to be thinking about when considering abortion rights is how we ensure what Kant calls "rightful interaction."

Rightful interaction concerns external freedom. External freedom requires, as we saw above, the human ability consciously to set and pursue ends of one's own in the world, which Kant also calls "choice." *External freedom*, simply put, is to subject one's choices in the empirical world (of space and time) only to universal laws of freedom. Finally, justice or right is a relation between persons' exercise of external freedom, namely, the relation enabling *interaction* under laws of freedom that restrict reciprocally. Moreover, it is because external freedom is exercised in space and time that it can be coerced, since to coerce is to hinder the exercise of external freedom—hinder the setting and pursuing of ends in the world (in space and time). Coercion is rightful, in turn, only if it enables interacting persons to exercise their external freedom under universal laws of freedom that restrict reciprocally. In fact, it is precisely because rightful interaction tracks only what is coercible that ethics and religiosity are fundamentally beyond the proper grasp of just laws. Being religious, just as being virtuous, fundamentally requires a first-personal involvement and motivation that coercion cannot in principle reach and hence we cannot legislate it.[22] It follows that having laws that prescribe virtuous or religiously inspired actions is nonsensical.[23] In addition, laws demanding religiosity or virtue are fundamentally inconsistent with setting and pursuing ends of one's own, which is to say that they are inconsistent with an individual's innate right to freedom. The innate right to freedom therefore includes the right to set and pursue immoral ends, such as undertaking stingy or unfriendly actions.

How, then, does the above conception of rightful interaction entail that abortion as such cannot be rightfully and coercively prevented or criminalized? It helps to remember that justice, and consequently legal argumentation, is limited to the kind of beings who are capable of external freedom, even if this ability is not fully developed and even if temporarily incapacitated.[24] In light of this consideration, it is important that at very early stages of pregnancy the embryonic cells merely divide and multiply. At this stage, there is yet no spatiotemporal being with a capacity for choice developed to protect.[25] At this stage there is no human capacity for or ability to act on one's own initiative, that is, engage in what I will call "spontaneous unified action" even in a minimal sense. Therefore, we simply cannot attribute legal rights upon conception even if we, for metaethical or theological reasons, want to attribute person-hood. Consequently, legal personhood is limited to beings with a spatio-temporal or empirically detectable capacity for spontaneously unified action, whereas moral/religious personhood may not be so limited.

To clarify this point, let me draw an analogy to the legal discussion surrounding legal death. Even though there is significant disagreement exactly when it occurs, most states consider a person legally dead when he or she is "brain dead," meaning that there is no longer any brain activity. So, from the point of view of justice, the crucial consideration is whether or not the person is presumed (by medical experts) permanently to have lost all spatiotemporal capacity (let alone ability) spontaneously to unify action. When this happens, legal guardians have the right to end treatment. The main reason why legal guardians are not required to end treatment at this point, I believe, is to ensure that the legal system is com-patible with the brain dead person's deep ethical or religious views.[26] Analogously, at early stages of pregnancy, when the unit of cells (the embryo) merely divides, there is no spatiotemporal human capacity or minimal ability to spontaneously unify any kind of action.[27] It follows that up until this point it has not acquired any legal rights, and the decision whether or not to abort lies with the mother. In other words, we may grant that from a metaethical or religious point of view, the person already exists, say, as a being only in time or an immaterial being, but justice and the law must be restricted to regulating interaction in space and time, between beings capable of external freedom, which starts with *evidence* of a capacity spontaneously to unify action. Cells dividing at early stages of embryonic development simply cannot be ascribed such a capacity. Legal rights as such can be conferred only at the point at which the fetus has developed into a unified spatiotemporal being with minimal yet human capacities for external action. This point, therefore, is the normatively important moment from the point of view of justice and the law. Since justice and the law are limited to regulating external freedom, or interaction in space and time, justice and the law must be silent until the human capacity for minimal external action exists.

From the point of conception to the point at which the embryo/fetus is able spontaneously to unify action in this minimal sense, the fetus can have no rights and the law cannot coercively restrict abortion. Up until this point, ethical and religious considerations are what must regulate people's thoughts and actions about the matter. To legislate otherwise is to deprive women of their innate right to freedom in a most radical sense. Having coercive restrictions that require women to carry forward pregnancies before the fetus can acquire legal rights is to treat women as being subject to the law in a different way or for different reasons from anyone else. Hence, women are denied equal protection under the law.[28] In addition, requiring women to carry forth pregnancies before the fetus acquires legal rights deprives women of their rights to their own bodies (and thus their own persons) by forcing them to set and pursue particular bodily ends not of their own choosing.

Moreover, as in the case of legal death, there seems to be a reasonable disagreement about exactly when the point of embryonic/fetal[29] development occurs that confers legal rights. Indeed, there is significant, informed disagreement concerning what constitutes sufficient embryonic/fetal development even within and among states that protect women's right to abortion. For example, some advocate the time of viability, others the moment of "quickening," still others minimal consciousness or certain neurological processes, and so on. The effect of this disagreement is that states that protect women's right to abortion have different laws determining the time after which abortion is no longer legally permissible. Some states permit women to abort only up until the eighth week, others later. Still, what is common to all these reasonable suggestions is that they focus on evidence of the development of human cells into what may be deemed a unified, minimally acting human being. Therefore, each suggestion is a reasonable empirical candidate in light of the common normative principle being applied. Furthermore, the disagreement seems not only to be reasonable, but also inevitable, since the question of when the fetus can exercise minimal unified, external action requires a normative judgment, namely, when we should ascribe movements in space and time to a fetus/embryo's spontaneous ability to unify external action. The judgment is normative in that we are ascribing actions to the fetus by saying that it seems reasonable to hold that the movements are actions initiated by the fetus rather than merely determined by cells dividing. Because we are looking for a normative principle to determine the issue, there will be more than one reasonable empirical interpretation of how the principle applies. And though some empirical suggestions are more reasonable than others, it will not be possible to determine one single empirical answer to the question.

My suggestion, then, has been twofold. First, all of the aforementioned contemporary proposals for which time is the normatively significant moment from the point of view of justice and the law can be seen as applications of the same normative principle. The principle would state something like, "the moment of embryonic/fetal development at which some legal rights are acquired is the moment that evidences a minimally acting human being." And because there is a problem of reasonable indeterminacy in trying to choose between the many reasonable, yet competing, applications of the normative principle, we find a significant diversity of legal practice in liberal constitutional states that recognize women's right to abortion. Second, because this diversity arises as a result of a *reasonable* disagreement regarding the correct application of a normative principle, only the state—and not individuals—can have the right to enforce any specific restrictions on abortion. That is to say, since many of the choices are equally reasonable, for any particular private party to make the determination is merely for that party arbitrarily to impose her choice on others.[30] This would result in one person being seen as having the right to subject another person's body and person to her arbitrary choices, which is inconsistent with due respect for that person's right to freedom. Since there is reasonable disagreement as to what constitutes the appropriate evidence of sufficient embryonic/fetal development, there can be rightful enforcement of one restriction over another only if the restriction is determined, applied, and enforced by a *public* authority. Only a public authority can be seen as representing everyone and yet no one in particular, and thus only it can issue a restriction that can be deemed impartial in principle. Therefore, only a state can impose abortion restrictions on women, namely, that they can terminate their pregnancies only before a particular stage of gestation. The reason is that due to the indeterminacy in applying the normative principle, only the state can rightfully determine the time at which the embryo/fetus acquires some legal rights. Moreover, once the baby is born and hence is no longer physically dependent on the mother's body, it has full legal rights, including the right that both parents take care of it.[31] The baby has not consented to being born, but is the result of the parents' actions and hence it is reasonable to claim that they are responsible for the baby. The parents must act on behalf of the child and teach the child, insofar as possible, what is needed for the child to become capable of choice, external freedom and rightful interaction.[32]

The position presented here gives a strong defense for abortion, but only before the embryo/fetus has reached a certain legally significant point—a point in time at which it acquires some legal rights due to having developed a capability or ability to act externally (minimally understood). And this point in time must be determined by the state.[33] Therefore, up until the point at which the fetus acquires legal rights, the choice whether or not to keep the embryo/fetus lies with the pregnant woman, and if she chooses to let the fetus develop beyond this point, she must also accept that the fetus has acquired legal rights to her. Finally, it is worth pointing out that the state cannot enforce such abortion laws if it does not also make sure that those in need, whether adolescent or adults, actually have access to the resources required for abortions. It is reasonable to argue, first, that adolescents must be guaranteed information and financial help in order to make sure that they are not subjected to their parents' lack of ability or unwillingness to pay for abortions, since this would be to allow the parents to enslave their children in the sense I have described. Second, poor persons' rights to abortion must also be guaranteed by a state that enforces abortion laws. Such guarantees are necessary to ensure that poor persons have opportunities to have abortions independent of being sub-jected to other private person's arbitrary choices to provide them with the required means (as perhaps through charitable donations). After all, women cannot make a choice to abort without the required means. Hence, if a state imposes and enforces a deadline on abortions, as on this account it should, it must also institutionally guarantee access to the means, say, through welfare measures, that make either choice possible. If the state were to uphold a monopoly on coercion and a legal system in which women have neither the appropriate knowledge nor the requisite actual access to services to exercise their freedom, it would fail to provide them with civil society. Instead, it would force some of its citizens to be subject to the arbitrary choices of others, namely, their private choices to provide education or charity. The state must set up its monopoly on coercion such that it is reconcilable with each person's innate right to freedom, which requires systemic institutional guarantees against being trapped in such private dependency relations. If it does not provide such institutional guarantees, it cannot justly enforce abortion laws.

2.2 Homosexual Activities: Rightful Restrictions

Somewhat surprisingly, perhaps, attempts to justify coercive restrictions on homosexual interactions, including criminalization, encounter similar kinds of problems faced by those attempting coercively to restrict abortion as such. Nevertheless, it should no longer be surprising. Because we are embodied beings, a person's innate right to freedom gives each person a right to bodily integrity. Restrictions on homosexual activity, like restrictions on abortion as such, fail to respect an individual's right to bodily integrity. The main difference between the two cases is that the argument against coercively restricting homosexual activity is simpler and more straightforward, since homosexual interactions involve consensual actions between two legally responsible embodied persons. In short, coercively preventing, including criminalizing, homosexual interaction involves denying homosexual persons sole control over their own bodies and thus also their persons. Instead, it permits homophobic persons the right to determine how other persons should use their own bodies, which is to deny interaction in a way consistent with an individual's innate right to freedom. Therefore, legal restrictions on homosexual activity aim at the annihilation of rights as such. Moreover, a state that enforces such restrictions fails to institute civil society. A "de facto" state thereby fails to set itself up as a *public* authority, for it fails to represent each of its citizens and yet no one in particular, since it posits and enforces laws that fail to treat each citizen as having an innate right to freedom. Thus, the state forces homosexual persons to stay in the pre-state condition, or the so-called "state of nature" and, indeed, in a particularly barbaric or brutal version thereof, namely, one in which there is no respect for their persons as such. Hence, homosexuals are not obliged to obey such laws, but must defend themselves, even against the state, as best they can.

As far as I can see, it is impossible to justify any particular restrictions on homosexual activity as contrasted with heterosexual activity, since any attempt to do so would result in asymmetrical restrictions by the law. For example, were homosexuality outlawed, only heterosexuals would be allowed to use their bodies in consensual sexual activity as they choose. This is not to say that there should not be any coercive restrictions regulating sexual interactions, including homosexual interactions, but that their determination will not concern whether or not the activity is homosexual or heterosexual. In addition, I believe that only the state, not private individuals, can rightfully determine, apply, and enforce these restrictions. The reason the state is essential to ensuring rightful interaction with regard to sexual relations is that here also there appear to be problems of indeterminacy, albeit of a different sort. Where indeterminacy with respect to abortion arises in the application of the normative principle governing the time at which abortion is rightful, indeterminacy with respect to the rightfulness of sexual activities seems to arise with regard to disagreements about whether or not there is consent to engage in the activity. This is why rightful sexual activity, including homosexual activity, also requires the state. That is to say, mutual consent seems to be the normative principle we all must accept as governing the rightfulness of any particular sexual interaction, as well as in all other private interactions. Yet situations arise in which there is reasonable disagreement in the application of the principle, that is, about whether or not consent has been given. For example, there are questions of required maturity, the use of alcohol and drugs, relations of power, and so on. So, unless the state, which represents both interacting parties and yet none of them (or anyone else) in particular, determines restrictions on consent and applies these restrictions when controversies arise, we appear to have another situation in which one person's choice runs roughshod over another's. The upshot of this last point is twofold: private individuals cannot be seen as having the right to determine, apply, and enforce restrictions concerning whether or not there is consent, and states that outlaw homosexual activity fail to provide rightful solutions to such disputes among its homosexual citizens.[34] Instead, this "de facto" state forces mere might to reign between them.

Finally, as with restrictions on abortion, this argument against restrictions on homosexual activity is irrelevant to, and therefore reconcilable with, various ethical and theological views. Because the demands of justice are not coextensive with the demands of ethics or religion, homosexual activities can still be considered vicious and/or wrong from an ethical or religious point of view. It is also not an argument about tolerance. The reason why homosexual activity cannot be coercively restricted is not that we must tolerate our differences in order to achieve a minimum of stability and peace. In fact, it is also not an argument of the kind, "if heterosexuals have the right, then in all fairness homosexuals must have it too." Instead, the position maintains that from the point of view of *justice*, what we are after is a conception of coercion and authority that is reconcilable with each person's innate right to freedom, and according to such a conception everyone must have a right to engage in any consensual interaction, including sexual interaction. Consequently, from this point of view, ethical and religious discussions and disagreements are beside the point—as are considerations of tolerance and equal laws as such. From the point of view of justice, the problem with such restrictions on homosexual activity is that fundamentally they are irreconcilable with respect for other persons. They involve the authorization of wrongs against homosexuals' persons since they deny them a right to their own bodily integrity, which just is to deny interaction on the basis of reciprocal rights and duties at all. Therefore, no just state can criminalize homosexual interactions.

3. CONCLUDING REMARKS

The most important issue for theories of justice concerns delineating legitimate from illegitimate types of coercion—whether by individuals or by states. It follows from the above arguments that no one (state or private individual) can have the right coercively to prevent abortion or homosexual interaction as such, since such restrictions are irreconcilable with each person's innate right to freedom. Moreover, there are two reasons why these kinds of laws are constitutive of a graver injustice than many other unjust laws. First, having coercive authority with regard to how another person uses her own body is to have the right to that other person's person—and no one can have such a right. Coercive restrictions making abortion and homosexuality impossible are therefore antithetical to interaction based on reciprocal rights and duties among free persons. Second, anti-abortion and anti-homosexuality *laws*, that is, when such restrictions are posited, applied, and enforced by the state, are particularly unjust because by issuing such laws the state fails to establish itself as a public authority, namely, as an authority that represents all and yet no one in particular, and so posits, applies, and enforces laws that enable its citizens to interact in ways irreconcilable with each citizen's innate right to freedom. By positing such laws, the state thereby denies women and homosexuals entrance into civil society. Instead, it forces them to fend for themselves in a brutal version of the state of nature.

One way to illustrate the point about the severity of the wrongdoing involved in these kinds of coercive restrictions is to see how they are structurally similar to, and yet different from, restrictions that deny some groups or particular persons the right to own private property. To have material means subject to one's own choice only (private property) is a precondition for external freedom, since it is impossible to set and pursue ends of one's own without means distinct from oneself. Without private property, therefore, there is no external freedom and no one can be seen as having the right to deny another person the right to appropriate private property. Moreover, when the state is denying some of its subjects the right to own private property, the state denies them the possibility of interacting with others in a way reciprocally respectful of their freedom, and, hence, these people are not obliged to obey the state's private property laws. In enforcing these laws, the state forces some people to stay in a brutal version of the state of nature with regard to material possessions, and so they must defend their means as best they can against others—including the "de facto" state.[35] In the same way that those denied a right to private property are forced to stay in a violent and brutal version of the state of nature, women and homosexuals are forced into the same condition by states that enforce laws that criminalize all abortion and homosexual acts. Both groups find themselves in situations where they must defend their rights on their own.[36,37] The difference between denying people private property rights and denying them a right to their own bodies is that by denying people a right to their own bodies, you deny them the right to exist as persons at all. This is why the enforcement of such coercive restrictions is amongst the gravest types of wrongdoing.

Notes

I would like to thank Shelley Weinberg for many and involved discussions of all aspects of this chapter. I would also like to thank Arthur Ripstein and the editors of this volume, Sharon Crasnow and Anita Superson, for their encouragement and most useful comments on earlier drafts. Special thanks too to Lucy Allais for her invaluable help on the final version of the chapter. Finally, thanks to the audiences at the 25th International Social Philosophy Conference ("Gender,

Inequality, and Social Justice") at the University of Portland in Oregon, July 17–19, 2008, and at the Society for Analytical Feminism Conference ("Analytic Feminist Contributions to Traditional Philosophy") at the University of Kentucky, April 4–6, 2008.

1. For example, Kant says about homosexual interaction in the "Doctrine of Right" in the *Metaphysics of Morals* that it involves an *"unnatural* use" of one another's "sexual organs and capacities" (MM 6: 277). Moreover, he argues that because "such transgressions of laws…do wrong to humanity in our own person, there are no limitations or exceptions whatsoever that can save them from being repudiated completely" (ibid.). About the fetus being a person, Kant says: "For the offspring is a *person*, and it is impossible to form a concept of the production of a being endowed with freedom through a physical operation. So from a *practical point of view* it is a quite correct and even necessary idea to regard the act of procreation as one by which we have brought a person into the world without his consent and on our own initiative, for which deed the parents incur an obligation to make the child content with his condition so far as they can" (MM 6: 280). I have used Mary Gregor's translation and edition of Immanuel Kant's *The Metaphysics of Morals* (Cambridge University Press, 1996). I abbreviate *The Metaphysics of Morals* as "MM" in the remainder of this text.

2. Although the argument presented here can be reformulated as an argument against sodomy laws, it cannot be transformed into an argument against discrimination and oppression against queer people in general. The reason is that the argument is grounded on the importance of our embodiment, whereas other queer rights, such as the right to marry, do not have such a foundation. This is not to say, however, that there are not other Kant-inspired arguments that will do the job. See my "A Kantian Conception of Rightful Sexual Relations" for one example of such an argument.

3. For reasons that will become clear, an "ethical theory" is taken to focus on issues of morality strictly from the first-personal point of view.

4. By "abortion as such" I mean to signal that my main argument targets any argument against abortion—at any stage or for any reason whatsoever. As will become clear shortly, I do not argue that all limits on abortion are impermissible. In fact, I will defend some limits.

5. For some exemplary articles, see note 20 below.

6. This is not to say that distinguishing between analyzing an issue from the point of view of justice and from the point of view of ethics or theology is novel. In her famous article "A Defense of Abortion," Judith Jarvis Thomson argues along similar lines. See pp. 60–61. Similarly, the stronger readings of John Rawls's later philosophy, as found, for example, in *Justice as Fairness: A Restatement* and in *Political Liberalism*, proceed on a similar assumption. Note, however, that it is tempting to read Thompson and Rawls as defending "tolerance" arguments, meaning arguments according to which the great differences in overall moral or religious conceptions entail that justice must stay neutral amongst them. Such an interpretation is advanced by

Robert P. George in "Public Reason and Political Conflict: Abortion and Homosexuality." I believe that this interpretation of both Rawls and Thompson is mistaken and fails to capture the strength of their positions. In contrast, with respect to Rawls, I believe that the better interpretation is the one provided by Arthur Ripstein in "Private Order and Public Justice: Kant and Rawls," and I believe the stronger reading of Thomson follows similar interpretive lines. Consequently, I am not defending a "neutrality tolerance" argument of the kind criticized by George. My view is that it is *wrong* from the point of view of justice to deny persons a right to obtain an abortion or to engage in homosexual activity independently of conclusions drawn from the points of view of tolerance, ethics, and religion.

7. The same idea informs the Universal Principle of Right, which states: "[a]ny action is *right* if it can coexist with everyone's freedom in accordance with a universal law, or if on its maxim the freedom of choice of each can coexist with everyone's freedom in accordance with a universal law" (MM 6: 230–31).

8. Although these are also metaphysical considerations, I want to follow Kant's distinction between the metaphysics of ethics (virtue) and the metaphysics of justice (right) as composing the metaphysics of morals. In *The Metaphysics of Morals* we find this distinction also in his understanding of the difference between "internal" and "external" freedom, where "internal" freedom is the domain of ethics (virtue) understood as first-personal aspects of morality, and "external" freedom is the domain of justice (right) or enforceable aspects of morality. I am here using "metaethical" to refer to the former.

9. The position defended here is silent on whether the same must be granted from the point of view of virtue.

10. We see this in Kant's discussion of the relation involved in empirical possession: "All propositions about right are *a priori* propositions, since they are laws of reason... An *a priori* proposition about right with regard to *empirical possession* is *analytic*, for it says nothing more than what follows from empirical possession in accordance with the principle of contradiction, namely, that if I am holding a thing (and so physically connected with it), someone who affects it without my consent (e.g., snatches an apple from my hand) affects and diminishes what is internally mine (my freedom), so that his maxim is in direct contradiction with the axiom of right. So the proposition about empirical possession in conformity with rights does not go beyond the right of a person with regard to himself" (MM 6: 249–50). Since justice is a normative perspective tracking external interaction in space and time from the third-personal point of view, it is impossible from the point of view of justice to distinguish between a person and her body. The distinction between the person and the body is, however, available from the internal first-personal perspective, which is tied to the normative perspective of virtue and is tracked only in time.

11. I do not engage Kant's argument concerning how we acquire rightful possessions beyond our bodies, since it is irrelevant to the present discussion. I discuss this issue at length in "Kant's Non-Voluntarist Conception of Political Obligations." I deal with issues of economic justice more generally in "Kant and Dependency Relations."

12. As we shall see, however, there are some proposed restrictions on the right to abortion that can be classified as enslavement of women.

13. I expand upon this point below, but it may be useful to note that this does not entail that the state thereby fails to establish rightful relations across the board, since it may, for example, have succeeded in establishing rightful private property relations.

14. Let me reiterate that this argument is a legal-political argument, in which each person's right to freedom refers to her basic political right.

15. I use "brutal" here in the same sense that Kant uses the word "barbaric," namely, to describe actions that are fundamentally in conflict with or uninformed by reason. In *Anthropology from a Pragmatic Point of View*, Kant defines barbarism as a society in which there is "Power without freedom and law" (7: 331). Since criminalizing abortion and homosexuality is inconsistent with a respect for a person's person, it is inconsistent with basic requirements of freedom (reason). Moreover, it matters not to the brutality of the restriction whether it is enforced by a de facto state or an individual, since in enforcing a law that contradicts the fundamental ground for justice (the innate right to freedom) the state ceases to yield political obligations on this issue.

16. Although liberal democracies cannot allow consent restrictions on adults, they can require parental consent for pregnant children. Nevertheless, in a just state there will be cases in which the parents' consent or lack thereof can be overridden by the state. I deal with some of these issues in my "Kant and Dependency Relations," though more extensively in "The Priority of Rightful Care to Virtuous Care" (unpublished).

17. A Kantian liberal conception would foreclose an argument that the woman agrees to be enslaved to the fetus in becoming pregnant through consensual sex, that is, that concerns of the fetus can justifiably override her own. Like slave laws, slave contracts are void according to Kantian conception because they involve an incoherent notion of rights. Therefore, they cannot be rightfully enforced.

18. As is often pointed out in the literature, it is notable that the Catholic Church actually denies women a right to abortion even when the life of the mother is at stake.

19. See for example H. Tristram Engelhardt, Jr., "The Ontology of Abortion"; L. W. Sumner, "The Ontology of Abortion," and Michael Tooley, "Abortion and Infanticide." Moreover, whether the fetus is or is not granted the status of a person, arguments are typically provided for or against the conclusion that it is always wrong to kill it. For example, Michael Tooley argues, "One reason the question of the morality of infanticide is worth examining is

that it seems very difficult to formulate a completely satisfactory liberal position on abortion without coming to grips with the infanticide issue. The problem the liberal encounters is essentially that of specifying a cutoff point which is not arbitrary: at what stage in the development of a human being does it cease to be morally permissible to destroy it?" (p. 37–38). Tooley argues that in order to justify the criminalization of abortion as such, we must establish the moral impermissibility of it. Therefore, the two analyses (from justice and from morality) are seen as yielding the same results, which means that the analysis of justice is dependent upon the ethical analysis of abortion. See also Don Marquis, "Why Abortion is Immoral"; Norman C. Gillespie's "Abortion and Human Rights"; and Robert P. George in "Public Reason and Political Conflict" for arguments that proceed on the same assumption. For a brief overview of both kinds of arguments (for and against), see Don Marquis, "Why Abortion is Immoral" esp. pp. 183–89. Marquis grants that a fetus is not a person, but a potential person. This difference, however, is seen as irrelevant to the issue of abortion, since what makes killing immoral is that one deprives another being of a valuable future. Hence, whether one kills a potential or an actual person, the immorality of the action is the same (pp. 189–92). Michael Tooley, in "Abortion and Infanticide," famously argues that if it's correct that fetuses are not persons because they lack self-consciousness in some minimal sense, then one must not only defend the right to abortion until birth, but also the right to infanticide.

20. The argument I am providing is a type of dependency argument of the kind Thomson mentions on p. 58. If successful, it shows that a pregnant woman living under conditions in which abortion is legally secured (including economically) and choosing not to abort before the deadline as legally defined has, as Thomson says, a "special kind of responsibility for it," since in this case she has chosen to let a human being (as legally defined) become dependent upon her. My argument leaves it open whether or not pregnancies constitute the only case in which we can have a right to let another human being become dependent upon our bodies in this way.

21. Naturally, the argument will not be acceptable to those who think that there should be a right to abortion through any stage of the pregnancy or to those who deny that there is a distinction between ethics and justice. As will become clearer below, I do not, however, believe that those positions are able to produce the most coherent, convincing interpretations of the legal traditions of liberal, constitutional democracies.

22. This is why Kant argues that issues of virtue concern "internal" and not external freedom. Internal freedom is to act on universalizable maxims from a moral motivation, whereas external freedom is to set and pursue ends of one's own in the world subject to universal laws of freedom. For example, Kant argues, "In contrast to laws of nature, the...laws of freedom are called *moral* laws. As directed merely to external actions and their conformity to law they are called *juridical* laws; but if they also require that they (the laws)

themselves be the determining grounds of actions, they are *ethical* laws, and then one says that conformity with juridical laws is the *legality* of an action and conformity with ethical laws is its *morality.*" (MM 6: 220, cf. 225)

23. In Kant's terminology, the scope of justice is limited to external freedom; it cannot reach internal freedom—or first-personal freedom (MM 6: 213f, 21–20).

24. The unconscious or comatose patient, for example, is only temporarily unable, but not permanently. In contrast, the minimally acting embryo, I will argue, has started to develop this ability.

25. Kant would say that there is neither "outer" and "inner sense" nor "outer" and "inner use of choice." Consequently, it is also absurd to say that at this stage there exists a capacity for choice even in its minimal sense.

26. The two exceptions to the rule are New Jersey and New York, where in addition to brain death, the heart and the lungs must also have stopped functioning before death is pronounced. For our purposes, this difference seems irrelevant, since the important point is that even though death cannot be pronounced until also the heart and lungs have stopped functioning, the legal guardians have the right to stop treatment at the point of brain death.

27. In Kantian language, it is yet to exhibit (even minimal) capacity for spontaneous, unified external action, which is the capacity enabling "outer sense" and "outer use of choice."

28. This would be a philosophical argument for why the 14th amendment to the US Constitution cannot permit restricting abortion in early stages of pregnancies.

29. The distinction between embryo and fetus is usually drawn at eight weeks— a time that corresponds with many, but not all, state legislation on this issue. Consequently, for the argument pursued here, we cannot appeal to this distinction as particularly significant or determining for the issue at hand.

30. Unreasonable applications of the principle are precluded by considerations of justice as already argued. For a more extensive treatment of the issue why the state or the public authority is the only way to solve reasonable disagreements concerning the application of principles of justice, see my "Kant's Non-Voluntarist Conception of Political Obligations."

31. The decision whether or not to abort cannot be made dependent on the father's or the second parent's choice, since, as we saw above, this would involve enslaving women, namely, by making their freedom subject to the arbitrary choices of others. This is also why fathers or the second parent do not have parental duties until the child is born. Fathers or the second parent may have duties to the *pregnant women* before the child is born, since the father or the second parent is partially responsible for the pregnancy, but neither the father nor the second parent has rights or duties to the *fetus or child* until it is born.

32. Once the child is born, the nature of the dependency changes since it is not physically united with the mother. Still, the mother continues to act on

behalf of the child, since the infant is not yet capable of exercising choice or external freedom responsibly—or what Kant calls "deeds" or "rightful interaction." The scope and justification of children's rights is naturally beyond the scope of this chapter. For a thorough account of these issues, including related redistributive issues, see my "Kant and Dependency Relations" and "The Priority of Rightful Care to Virtuous Care."

33. For example, the position appears to support the general principle that if there is good evidence that the fetus has such serious impairments that (a) if born, it will commit the mother (and the second parent, if there is one) to the dependency relation for the rest of her life, and (b) this evidence is available only after the general deadline, then there might be an extension of the time by which the decision must be made.

34. So, to sum up, there are two wrongs involved when a state outlaws homosexual activity. On the one hand, it denies homosexuals the right to bodily integrity, which is to force them to stay in the brutal version of the state of nature. On the other hand, such a state also forces homosexuals to stay in the "normal" or normative state of nature with regard to their sexual interactions, since they are denied the possibility of a rightful authority settling issues of reasonable disagreements regarding consent.

35. The case that naturally comes to mind here is Nazi Germany's denial of private property rights to Jews. I discuss these particular issues in "Kant's Murderer at the Door."

36. Indeed, if the state at some point decides to eradicate such illegitimate laws, it seems reasonable to argue that those against whom they have been enforced should be compensated. For example, women and homosexuals should be given reparation insofar as they have been subjected to oppression regarding their own bodies just as persons who at some point lose their right to private property must have a right to restoration after their private property rights have been reestablished.

37. This does not, however, entail that those who live in a state with anti-homosexuality or anti-abortion laws cannot have *any* political obligations. For example, assuming that the state has rightful private property and contract laws, homosexuals and pregnant women are politically obligated to obey these laws. They are not, however, obligated to obey the anti-homosexuality or anti-abortion laws. An interesting implication of this is that the issue of political obligations is not exclusively disjunctive. Persons may have political obligations to obey a state's laws governing many relations, such as private property and contract laws, but nevertheless cannot be politically obligated to obey laws governing all relations, in this case sexual relations and abortion.

References

H. Tristram Engelhardt, Jr., "The Ontology of Abortion," *Ethics*, Vol. 84, No. 3 (April 1974), pp. 217–34.

Robert P. George, "Public Reason and Political Conflict: Abortion and Homosexuality," *The Yale Law Journal*, Vol. 106, No. 8 ("Symposium: Group Conflict and the Constitution: Race, Sexuality, and Religion"), (June 1997), pp. 2475–504.

Norman C. Gillespie, "Abortion and Human Rights," *Ethics*, Vol. 87, No. 3 (April, 1977), pp. 237–43.

Immanuel Kant, *The Metaphysics of Morals*, ed. and transl. Mary Gregor (Cambridge: Cambridge University Press, 1996).

———, *Anthropology from a Pragmatic Point of View*, transl. Mary Gregory (the Hague: Martinus Nijhoff, 1974).

Don Marquis, "Why Abortion is Immoral," *Journal of Philosophy*, Vol. 86, No. 4 (April 1989), pp. 183–202.

John Rawls. *Political Liberalism* (New York: Columbia University Press, 1996).

———. *Justice as Fairness: A Restatement* (Cambridge, Mass.: Harvard University Press, 2001).

Arthur Ripstein, "Private Order and Public Justice: Kant and Rawls," *Virginia Law Review*, Vol. 92 (2006), 1391–438.

L. W. Sumner, "The Ontology of Abortion," *Ethics*, Vol. 84, No. 3 (1974), pp. 217–34.

Judith Jarvis Thomson, "A Defense of Abortion," *Philosophy and Public Affairs*, Vol. 1, No.1 (Autumn 1971), pp. 47–66.

Michael Tooley, "Abortion and Infanticide," *Philosophy and Public Affairs*, Vol. 2, No. 1 (Autumn 1972), pp. 37–65.

Helga Varden. "Kant's Murderer at the Door…One More Time: Kant's Legal Philosophy and Lies to Murderers and Nazis," *Journal of Social Philosophy*, Vol. 41, No. 4 (Winter 2010), pp. 403–21.

———. "Kant's Non-Voluntarist Conception of Political Obligations: Why Justice is Impossible in the State of Nature," *Kantian Review*, Vol. 13-2 (2008), pp.1–45.

———. "Kant and Dependency Relations: Kant on the State's Right to Redistribute Resources to Protect the Rights of Dependents," *Dialogue* XLV (2006), pp. 257–84.

———. "A Kantian Conception of Rightful Sexual Relations: Sex, (Gay) Marriage and Prostitution," *Social Philosophy Today*, Vol. 22 (2007), pp. 199–218.

———. "A Kantian Critique of the Care Tradition: A Kantian Response to Virginia Held's and Eva Kittay's Conception of Family Law and Systemic Injustice" (unpublished).

ANDREA C. WESTLUND
University of Wisconsin–Milwaukee

AUTONOMY IN RELATION

ANNETTE BAIER ONCE WROTE that "A person, perhaps, is best seen as one who was long enough dependent upon other persons to acquire the essential arts of personhood. Persons essentially are *second* persons, who grow up with other persons" (Baier 1985, 84). This idea has been embraced by feminist critics of traditional theories of autonomy, who follow Baier in reminding us that many distinctively human capacities, including the capacity for responsible action, could not come to be but for the long, slow, process of maturation during which human young remain dependent on their elders. Certain ideals that have been associated with traditional theories—such as those of radical independence and self-sufficiency—come to look fanciful and even pernicious when viewed with this fact in mind. If the concept of autonomy is inextricably bound up with such ideals, one wants to say, then so much the worse for autonomy.*

Along with a growing number of feminist philosophers, however, I take the real moral of Baier's story to be that autonomy must itself be understood to be a relational capacity. Feminists have argued forcefully that autonomy is not only *compatible* with human embeddedness in social and personal relationships, but in some important respects *depends* on these relationships. As I will explain below, different theorists have developed this general thesis in different ways. But the resulting accounts of personal autonomy have, in general, been much friendlier to the realities of (many) women's lives—which have historically been more pervasively structured than men's by the demands of caring relationships—while at the same time bringing to light respects in which women's agency may be damaged by a social context of sexist oppression.

In both of these respects, feminist work on relationality has added depth and subtlety to our understanding of the nature and conditions of individual agency. What I find surprising, however, is that feminist theorists of relational autonomy have thus far had relatively little to say about the concept of *shared* agency. When one sees the phrases "relational autonomy" and "shared agency" side-by-side on the page, or hears them uttered in close proximity to one another, it is hard not to suspect that they must be somehow related. Yet Baier herself is the only philosopher routinely cited within both literatures. Drawing on her notion of second-personhood, Baier challenges the presumption (which she takes to pervade the literature on shared agency) that individual action is somehow less mysterious or more fundamental than joint action. We act together long before we act on our own, she argues, and, developmentally speaking, it is individual action that is the more difficult feat, achieved at first only with the assistance and support of others (Baier 1997). Although Baier does not explicitly frame this point as one about relational autonomy, her argument suggests that one respect in which autonomy is relational is that the capacity for autonomy is developmentally dependent on the not-yet-autonomous agent's inclusion in activities that are shared with caregivers and other significant others. That is, individually autonomous agency is relational at least in the sense that it (necessarily) grows out of a form of shared agency, through which immature humans acquire the competencies that are eventually exercised in self-governed action from others on whom they depend for guidance and support.

While my own approach to shared agency may be more individualistic than Baier herself would endorse, I am sympathetic to the idea that there are deep connections between the social conditions of individual autonomy and the capacity to act together with others. Indeed, I think these connections go beyond the developmental one that Baier emphasizes. My aim in this essay is to flesh out one such further connection. I will argue that there is a centrally important form of shared agency, which, in virtue of its dialogical structure, does not just contribute to the development of autonomy competencies, but actually constitutes us as autonomous in relation to one another. This form of shared agency, unlike the interactions Baier describes between caregivers and children, is symmetrically shared, and it depends on the presence of mutually referring attitudes that are also integral to the individual autonomy of the participants.

In the first part of this essay, I argue that autonomy is constitutively relational in the sense that it depends upon a dialogical disposition to hold oneself answerable to external, critical perspectives.[1] In the second part, I argue that this disposition is intimately tied to a capacity for symmetrically shared or "joint" deliberation. When we engage in symmetrically shared decision-making and planning, a disposition for mutual answerability constitutes us at once as individually autonomous and as a deliberative pair. Under such conditions, we do not just *function* autonomously; we also *present* ourselves to one another as autonomous agents and treat the possibility of such mutual self-presentation (and recognition) as a constraint on our deliberative relationship.

In the third section of the essay, I revisit the significance of this argument from a feminist point of view. The question of how agency can be symmetrically shared is closely related to the question of how autonomy can be maintained within personal or, more broadly, social relationships. The latter question is a culturally gendered one, since maintaining autonomy within relationships has been seen as more of a problem for women than for men. Women have, historically, been allotted a disproportionate share of caregiving labor (both paid and unpaid), and as a result may be expected to put others' interests ahead of their own or even to define their own interests in terms of serving others. Women may also be socialized to defer and behave submissively rather than to assert themselves, particularly in their relationships with men. The conceptions of relational autonomy and joint deliberation I develop here do not exclude the possibility that autonomous choices might be influenced by problematic social norms. But both autonomy and joint deliberation require a form of answerability that equips us to challenge those norms. Indeed, under moderately favorable conditions, we should expect such answerability to destabilize acceptance of norms that are at odds with the agent's own self-presentation as autonomous.

1.

Whatever connections may hold between the concepts of relational autonomy and shared agency, the two literatures at issue are organized around importantly different questions. Whereas the literature on shared agency takes up questions about what it is for us to act together, the concept of relational autonomy is designed to highlight the social dimensions of *individual* agency—in other words, it takes up questions about how relations with others are implicated in one's ability to act, not as a part of a collective, but as a singular agent. Relational accounts of autonomy have provided a variety of different answers to this latter question, which can be divided into two broad, overlapping categories. In the first category we find accounts according to which autonomy is a *causally* relational property and, in the second, accounts according to which it is a *constitutively* relational property.

An account of autonomy is causally relational if it holds that some social or relational factor(s) make a necessary causal contribution to the development or sustenance of the capacity for autonomy. Theorists who have explicitly argued for or endorsed this sort of view include (among others) Jennifer Nedelsky, Diana Meyers, Marilyn Friedman, Carolyn McLeod, and John Christman. I confess I don't know of any philosophers (feminist or otherwise) who explicitly deny it. It would, after all, be difficult to argue against the claim that the capacities needed for autonomy require socialization and care from others in order to develop.[2] What complex human capacities do not? At a certain level of abstraction, then, the thesis of causal relationality should not be terribly controversial. Nonetheless, feminist theorists have done valuable work in making this kind of relationality explicit and devoting serious attention to fleshing it out. Feminists have tended, for example, to highlight a wider range of capacities (or, as Meyers calls them, "autonomy competencies") than their non-feminist counterparts, and are also much more likely to focus on ways in which these competencies can be undercut by oppressive circumstances (see, for example, Meyers 1987, 2004 and McLeod 2002). Causally relational accounts of autonomy have, for this reason, tended to have relatively clear social and political implications, and have also yielded rich insights into practical problems such as those encountered in biomedical ethics (see, for example, McLeod 2002).

Constitutively relational accounts of autonomy seem, on their face, to pose a deeper challenge to mainstream accounts. An account of autonomy is constitutively relational if it holds that some social or relational factor(s) play an ineliminable role in the definition of autonomy itself. Views that fall unambiguously into this category are less common, but have attracted more critical attention. Marina Oshana, for example, offers an "externalist" conception of autonomy according to which autonomy is a matter not just of what goes on in an agent's head but also of "what goes on in the world around her" (Oshana 1998, 81). To be autonomous, on her view, an agent must (among other things) enjoy a significant range of viable options and retain authority over her social circumstances. Paul Benson, too, defends a constitutively relational account of autonomy, but he thinks that the special authority exercised by autonomous agents depends not on the agent's control over social circumstances but on her "ownership" of her motives or desires. Whereas most recent accounts of autonomy treat ownership as a matter of what authorizes particular motives or desires to represent the agent's own point of view, Benson thinks we should ask instead what authorizes *agents* to speak and answer for those attitudes. Autonomy is constitutively relational, on his view, because agential ownership cannot be achieved independently of persons' "socially structured authority to stand by what they do" (Benson 2005, 108).

I agree with Oshana and Benson that autonomy is constitutively relational, but there are aspects of each of their particular views with which I disagree. While I share some of the intuitions that lead Oshana to reject standard internalist accounts, I believe her externalist view is more strongly substantive than necessary.[3] And while I think Benson is right to shift the focus from identification to answerability, I hesitate to follow him all the way in reframing the problem of autonomy as a question of what authorizes *agents* with respect to their wills.[4] For this move seems to presuppose an answer to the very question over which theorists of autonomy have traditionally been puzzled: how do we demarcate, among all the attitudes that make up an agent's psychic economy, a "will" that counts as *hers* in the first place? In virtue of what may we attribute, to the agent, the very will for which she may (or may not) be socially authorized to answer? Deployed slightly differently, I believe the concept of answerability can help us to answer this prior question, by giving us a handle on two core problems about autonomy.

The core problems to which I refer are what Michael Bratman (2007b) calls the problems of agential authority and subjective normative authority. According to a broad and widely shared conception, personal autonomy is a matter of *self-governance* of choice and action. Self-governance of choice and action seems to require motivation by attitudes bearing both of the just-mentioned forms of authority. For an action to count as autonomous, that is, it must be motivated by attitudes that (a) have the authority to speak for or represent the agent, and (b) express or articulate what the agent sees as having justificatory force. When these two requirements are satisfied, action is guided by what I'll call *the agent's own practical perspective*—that is, by a (practically) justificatory perspective that represents or speaks for the agent herself.

Not all attitudes by which a person is moved to action, much less all that occur within her psychic economy, have a claim to this sort of authority, despite belonging to her in some literal sense. As Harry Frankfurt famously noticed, for example, a person might experience some of her "first-order" desires as alien forces to be ignored, resisted, or expunged, and this seems to matter to our intuitions about the choices and actions to which they give rise. Actions motivated by desires from which one is alienated should not, it seems, be counted as bearing the relevant sorts of authority. Proponents of hierarchical views of autonomy go on to argue that agential authority depends on the presence of higher-order endorsing attitudes of some form, perhaps combined with other structural or historical constraints.

Hierarchical approaches to autonomy have been theoretically fruitful in part because they shed light on genuinely interesting dimensions of human agency, but also in part because it can be so illuminating to reflect on their limitations. Ever since Gary Watson first raised a worry about the status of higher order volitions, asking what could give another mere desire (regardless of its order) authority to speak for the agent, the literature has seen a proliferation of attempts to refine, supplement, or replace the hierarchical approach in a way that will prevent a vicious regress from arising (Watson 1975; Frankfurt 1988; Bratman 2007b). From another direction, various philosophers (myself included) have worried about the apparent inability of hierarchical accounts to deal adequately with cases in which agents act on the basis of internalized, oppressive social norms (Stoljar 2000; Westlund 2003; Benson 2005). In at least some of these cases, it is intuitively implausible that the oppressed agent should count as autonomous.

I cannot here provide an exhaustive review of such critiques or attempts to respond to them.[5] Instead, I will try to say more positively how I think the concept of answerability can move us beyond a persistent kind of impasse about agential authority. On pain of having to appeal to an ultimately mysterious, unexplained notion of agent causation, it seems that we must locate agential authority in some attitude or complex of attitudes within the agent. But we need a principled reason for thinking that some particular attitude or complex of attitudes should count as representing the agent's perspective, and this sort of reason is hard to come by. For almost any attitude or complex of attitudes one might propose, it is conceivable that the agent might find herself alienated from *it* in something like the way Frankfurt saw that we could be alienated from our first-order desires. Even an agent who does not seem to experience an attitude as an alien force may strike us as being merely *in its grips*, if her acceptance of that attitude itself has a genesis that intuitively undercuts agential authority. Acceptance that is based in nothing other than deference or depression-based resignation, for example, arguably falls into this category (Westlund 2003, 2009a).

What we need is a principled way of distinguishing between cases in which an agent is merely in the grips of a practical perspective and cases in which that agent counts as self-governing in virtue of that perspective's guidance of her action. This is where I think it helps to appeal to the concept of answerability. One thing that is so distinctive about cases of deep deference or depression-based resignation is the way in which these psychological conditions insulate agents from any real engagement in critical dialogue—either imaginatively or with other people—about the commitments that guide their practical reasoning. When we exclaim "But that's the depression talking, not you!" or "But that's his reason, not yours!" we are flagging a significant failure of responsiveness to ordinary, interpersonal justificatory demands. Resistance to such demands may sometimes demonstrate mere lack of confidence about one's grasp of practical reasons, or perhaps offense at presumptions exhibited by one's interlocutor. But *imperviousness* to such demands—however well-placed or constructively articulated those demands may be—is another story. Such intransigence in the face of external, critical challenge is an excellent candidate for what it is to be gripped by a practical perspective rather than self-governing in virtue of its guidance. In short, I argue that autonomy requires a disposition to hold oneself answerable to external, critical perspectives on one's motives and desires, because such a disposition marks the relevant distinction between being gripped by and governing the practical reasoning that guides one's actions.[6]

In embracing this view, I go some distance with Oshana in rejecting what she calls "internalist" accounts of autonomy: to count as autonomous, it is certainly not sufficient that the agent choose and act on the basis of lower-order desires she has endorsed from elsewhere within her own hierarchy of desires. Unlike Oshana, however, I do not think that autonomous functioning depends conceptually on the agent's actual social standing. An agent's *freedom* may, of course, be compromised by her social standing, and constraints on freedom may in some cases lead to the erosion of the reflective (and other) capacities required for autonomy.[7] But even severe constraints on freedom are not in principle incompatible with autonomy, since they do not necessarily undermine those capacities. Even oppressed agents may retain the disposition to answer for the commitments that guide their choices and actions, and it is important to recognize that this is so.

In sum, I take autonomy to be constitutively relational not because it requires the agent to stand in particular kinds of relations to others, but because the kind of reflectiveness it requires of the agent is itself dialogical in form: the autonomous agent has a disposition to hold herself answerable, for elements of her motivational hierarchy, in the face of critical challenges posed by others. It is potentially misleading to think of this account as an externalist one, at least in Oshana's sense of the term: while the disposition to hold oneself answerable to others is a disposition to be engaged by points of view external to one's own, this very disposition is a feature of the agent's psychology, and thus internal to the agent. In focusing on the role of this aspect of the agent's psychology, however, the account does bring to light an important form of relationality. Speaking figuratively, the agent who is merely gripped by her practical commitments is trapped in a deliberative echo chamber, effectively cut off from the shared space of practical reasoning that is occupied by self-governing agents.

2.

So how does this dialogical conception of autonomy shed light on the phenomenon of shared agency? As Baier points out, most prominent views of shared agency are individualistic in the sense that they seek to explain shared agency in terms of the interlocking intentional attitudes of two or more individual agents. Unlike Baier, I am basically sympathetic to this approach—at least as applied to paradigm cases of shared agency between mature adults. Being individualistic in this sense does not commit a theorist of shared agency to an anti-social or non-relational conception of autonomy. It is at the very least compatible with such views of shared agency that the autonomy of individual participants in a shared action might have social conditions—including, but not necessarily limited to, the social and personal dependencies required for human young to develop autonomy competencies. Nor does it commit us to any implausible thesis about the ontogenetic priority of individual agency. Even if shared action depends on interlocking intentional attitudes of individual agents, it is possible that children begin to participate in such structures before they have the capacity to carry out much by way of intentional action on their own.

Developmentally speaking, the capacities for full-blown individual and full-blown shared agency seem to arise simultaneously out of what I would call *assisted* agency. I hesitate to treat the interactions of very young children with their caregivers as full-blown instances of shared agency, because the sharing in these cases is asymmetrical in a special and developmentally necessary way. It is not just that such interactions involve leading and being led. Many activities shared between mature agents, such as the oft-mentioned example of ballroom dancing, involve that, perhaps even to a greater extent: after all, very young children do not yet know *how* to be led. Doing something with a toddler is often more about dealing creatively and constructively with the toddler's resistance to one's guidance. My point here is that members of a parent-child pair not only play different roles in the activity in question, but also participate in fundamentally different ways, with agency initially coming much more from one side than the other. The child is learning not merely, say, to color Easter eggs with his mother, but (in this and all other shared endeavors) to *do* things in an organized, purposeful way. This requires, among other things, developing a basic grasp of the temporality of action and learning how to form and execute plans over time, whether by oneself or with another.

Paradigm examples of shared agency between mature agents are strikingly different from this sort of parent-child interaction, even in cases of teaching and learning and leading and following. While parties to a shared action may contribute different things (I sing while you strum, you lead while I follow), in paradigm cases they each contribute *agentially*. Even Margaret Gilbert's account of shared agency, which, as Baier notes, is less individualistic than most, counts an action as genuinely shared only if both parties have "put into" it intentionally (Gilbert 1989, 410). This kind of symmetry is still quite thin: it is compatible with considerable asymmetries of other sorts, including asymmetries in power and influence over shared activities. But even this thin agential symmetry is not fully present in interactions between very young children and their adult caregivers, and it only begins to appear over time as some assisted actions become individual actions and others become, in a fuller sense, shared.

So, I do not take shared agency, in its fullest sense, to be ontogenetically prior to individual agency, even though assisted agency obviously is. Nor do I think we have grounds for treating shared agency as *conceptually* prior to individual agency, in the sense that we could only understand individual agency in terms that already include reference to its shared forms. This line of argument might appear to lead to the unexciting conclusion that relational autonomy and shared agency are not deeply linked, after all—except in the sense that both have socio-relational roots in our interactions with caregivers, teachers, friends, and so on. Actually, however, I think that the dialogical account of autonomy that I've sketched reveals another, different kind of link between the two concepts—or, at least, between relational autonomy and a special form of shared agency in which it is expressed.

This link emerges when we focus on the processes of joint deliberation through which a shared intention may be formed. Of course, not all shared intentions are formed deliberatively: some are the product of mutually self-interested bargaining, others of voting, others, perhaps, of mere contagious whim. And as long as neither party's intentional agency is bypassed entirely, some may be the product of coercion, domination, or other forms of duress. Even among shared intentions that *are* based on deliberation, we should not assume that both parties are necessarily symmetrically involved. In some cases, for example, we might agree that I'll do the deliberating and you'll defer to my decision.[8] In all of these cases, we are (in one way or another) individually guided by reasons, and we are guided by reasons in a more-or-less coordinated, though not always cooperative, way. Still, these means of coming to share an intention do not require that we regard the reasons by which we are guided, in coordinating our intentions and actions, as *themselves* shared. The link I want to draw between relational autonomy and shared agency emerges in cases that manifest this further form of sharing. Such cases are ones in which we aim to deliberate our way to agreement in a way that is more deeply *ours*: we aim to be guided by reasons that are attributable, jointly, to *us*, as the product of a symmetrically shared deliberation.

Such deliberation, which I call *joint* deliberation, is a dialogical process in which we attempt jointly to establish a set of practical reasons that will serve as a basis for shared intention, action, and further deliberation.[9] Otherwise put, it is a process aimed at establishing a shared practical perspective—a perspective from which certain considerations but not others will count as reasons-for-*us*. Insofar as we are engaged in such deliberation, I argue, we are subject to special normative constraints that require us to hold ourselves answerable to one another. In what follows, I briefly elaborate this picture, and then argue that agents who meet the relevant normative constraints will also count as individually autonomous with respect to their shared practical perspective. I argue, in sum, that joint deliberation is a special type of shared, cooperative activity that not only preserves but also requires the autonomy of its participants.

I believe the aim of symmetrical sharing is most easily recognized and analyzed in relationships of close friendship and reciprocal love.[10] These relationships provide a natural home for joint deliberation both because their participants share a complex structure of robust mutual concern (which I'll sketch out below), and because each party sees him or herself as, at least to some extent, sharing a life with the other. As friends and lovers we face the challenge of figuring out how to live together, which is in part a matter of coming up with a unified practical stance on many matters of joint concern. To put it in terms borrowed from Bratman, we will want to devise shared policies regarding what we will treat as reasons to act (Bratman 2007a). But we will want to do so in a way that preserves and supports a conception of the relationship we share as one of robust mutual concern. How do we accomplish this?

Joint deliberation, as I understand it, is a dialogical process that culminates in the joint acceptance of certain considerations as shared reasons—reasons which, when taken together, make up a shared practical perspective. To accept something as a reason, as I use the phrase, is to commit oneself to treating it as having justificatory force within one's deliberation and planning. *Joint* acceptance of something as a reason involves a *joint* commitment to treating it as having such force. Loosely following Margaret Gilbert's model of joint commitment, I take us to jointly commit ourselves to treating R as a reason when we exchange interlocking expressions of conditional acceptance: each of us must express, to the other, something equivalent to "I hereby accept R as a reason-for-us, if you likewise accept R as a reason-for-us." My readiness to accept R as a reason, in other words, is conditional on your expressing a precisely parallel readiness—a readiness that is conditional on mine in just the same way that mine is conditional on yours.

But if this is where joint deliberation ends, where does it begin? I believe that in cases where no overriding (for example, moral) norms prescribe a unique course of action, our individual preferences, desires, and other components of our individual practical perspectives provide an appropriate starting point.[11] But they are only a starting point. We cannot always construct a coherent joint perspective simply by aggregating our individual preferences, since those preferences will not always be compatible with one another. Nor can we solve the problem simply by each taking the preferences of the other as decisive. Where our preferences conflict this stratagem will lead just as surely to impasse, only now in the form of a familiar sort of competitive deference.[12] Evidently, we must sometimes compromise. But to say this is simply to restate the problem in other terms, since compromise may take many forms. Only under certain conditions will a proposed compromise cohere with our conception of our relationship as one of robust mutual concern.

I borrow the term "robust concern" from Alan Soble (1997). Soble argues that x does not have an attitude of robust concern for y unless "x desires for y that which is good for y, x desires this for y's own sake, and x pursues y's good for y's benefit and not for x's" (Soble 1997, 68). There is room to quibble about certain features of this definition. Arguably, for example, robust concern is compatible with x pursuing y's good both for y's benefit *and* for x's own.[13] One might even question whether the attitude of concern must always manifest itself in a desire to benefit the other (see Velleman 1999). But Soble's core idea is, I believe, deeply right: for another person to be the object of my robust concern, I must treat that person as a final end.[14] And this means that, insofar as we do desire and pursue the good of those we care about, we must do so for their own sake. Cases of close friendship and reciprocal love are paradigmatic examples of relationships that include robust concern, thus understood, and in which such concern is generally both mutual and mutually desired. In these relationships, each of us cares about the other for his or her own sake and also values and cares about being the object of such concern from the other.[15]

When this structure of mutual concern is in place, it will constrain individuals' willingness to accept certain considerations as shared reasons. Suppose, for example, that Jane and Joe are trying to decide where to spend their vacation. Jane proposes that they visit her family, despite the fact that this rules out spending time with Joe's family or, alternatively, taking any significant vacation time by themselves this summer. She hopes (for various reasons) that Joe will agree, but she does not want him to agree grudgingly, or only because he despairs of reasonable discussion of alternatives, or because he wants, strategically, to position himself to win the next battle. Nor does she feel comfortable with the prospect that he might simply defer, even if it would make him happy to do so. Jane (by stipulation) cares about Joe's good for Joe's own sake, and if he appears to be motivated entirely by the affective rewards he derives from pleasing her, she may legitimately worry about whether he is taking his own good sufficiently into account, or is reflecting adequately on what his good actually involves.[16]

Indeed, the question of what Joe's (or Jane's) good actually involves, and what will count as adequate reflection on this matter, is itself central to the project of joint deliberation, and how the parties go about answering this question bears directly on the conditions for autonomy within such relationships. Further reflection on the notion of robust concern reveals, I think, that relationships of friendship or love are threatened not only by failures to care properly for the other's good (that is, to care for it for the other's own sake), but also by failures to grant appropriate authority to each party's understanding or interpretation of his or her own good. Put briefly, the kind of regard for persons on which robust concern depends must itself include regard for persons as self-interpreting beings.

Consider, for example, the husband of the diarist in Charlotte Perkins Gilman's well-known story "The Yellow Wallpaper." Arguably, this husband cares about his wife's good for her own sake, but he certainly does not allow her self-understanding to weigh with him in deliberation or move him to action. While he schedules "a prescription for each hour of the day" (Gilman 1997, 2), focused on tonics and rest and air, the diarist herself longs for work and companionship, excitement, and change. She frankly disagrees with her husband, who is also a physician, that such activities would keep her from getting well. In fact, she strongly suspects they would do her some good. But, as she puts it, "If a physician of high standing, and one's own husband, assures friends and relatives that there is really nothing the matter with one but temporary nervous depression—a slight hysterical tendency—what is one to do?" (Gilman 1997, 1). However hard she tries to muster gratitude for her husband's "care," his paternalistic dismissal of her point of view ultimately pits him, from her increasingly unapologetic (if otherwise confused) point of view, as foe rather than friend.[17]

My point is not that a concerned friend or lover must always take the other's perspective on her own good as decisive as it stands. If I think a loved one is self-destructively confused, for example, I will certainly want to engage her on the question of where her good lies, and I will not be comfortable formulating joint plans on the basis of preferences that I take to be harmful to her. What Gilman's diarist calls a "real earnest reasonable talk" (Gilman 1997, 7) would be in order. But having one's interpretation of one's own good *discounted* is as much a violation of robust care as the sort of merely instrumental concern (or simple lack of concern) on which Soble and others have focused. Relationships of close friendship and reciprocal love are flawed insofar as either party claims unilateral interpretive authority over the other's good.

But they are also flawed, I would argue, insofar as either party completely refuses the other authority to question or challenge her self-interpretations. Dean Cocking and Jeanette Kennett (1998) have argued convincingly that it is characteristic of close friendships that each party is receptive to interpretation by the other.[18] Such interpretation can affect us in more or less deep ways: for one thing, our close friends often notice things about us that we have not noticed about ourselves, and their observations may change the way in which we view ourselves. In some cases, a friend's interpretation of my character traits might improve my self-understanding, including, I would argue, my sense of what would contribute to my good. But the effects of "friendly interpretation," if

I may call it that, can also be more subtle. Cocking and Kennett argue that friends' interpretations of one another's character traits can make a difference to how (and presumably whether) those traits continue to be realized. In one of their examples, "Judy teasingly points out to John how he always likes to be right" (Cocking and Kennett 1998, 505), an observation that becomes a running joke in their relationship and leads John to take himself less seriously and adopt a more "self-consciously ironic tone" (Cocking and Kennett 1998, 505). If character traits are subject to modification, in this way, through responsiveness to the interpretations offered by a friend, it seems likely that my sense of what is important and interesting and worthwhile in life will be similarly interpretation-sensitive. And if my good is at least partly shaped by my character traits, interests, and values, then there will also be a sense in which my good is a moving target in such contexts. Relationships of friendship and love are, I would argue, relationships in which we engage in mutual and collaborative interpretation. As such, they are relationships in which we *share* interpretive authority over ourselves and our respective goods.

This renders the process of joint deliberation deeply dialogical: it is as much a process of jointly articulating and assessing our individual reasons for "signing on" to a would-be shared practical perspective as it is a process of generating that shared perspective. Or, more precisely, it is a process of generating a shared perspective *by way of* articulating and assessing our individual reasons for accepting it. Only when we are mutually satisfied that we each have good reasons for signing on—reasons that cohere with a conception of our relationship as one of robust mutual concern—will we complete an exchange of conditional commitments. And cohering with that conception, as we've just seen, requires that whatever reasons we share emerge from a collaborative process in which we share interpretive authority over our own goods. In the context of such a relationship, the reasons we offer one another must pass what I call (borrowing a term from Baier) an "expressibility test": that is, the reasons that move individual deliberators to express conditional commitment to a shared practical perspective must survive expression within a dialogue that is partly aimed at the joint articulation and joint acknowledgement of each party's good.[19]

We might, of course, deliberate poorly, and allow considerations to survive that should not. But there is a significant difference between deliberating within the constraints set by mutual concern and failing to live up to them, and not deliberating within those constraints at all. Joint deliberation aims at (though it might sometimes fall short of) establishing a symmetrically shared practical perspective. The activity of joint deliberation is defined by this constitutive aim, but regulation by this aim does not guarantee success. What it does provide is an open-ended venue for revisiting the self-interpretations that underlie our willingness to be jointly committed to a certain justificatory perspective. Sharing interpretive authority with another requires an attitude of humility about one's conception of each party's interests, such that one remains prepared to consider relevant challenges to one's interpretations and to revise those interpretations as appropriate.

Relevant challenges to one's interpretive framework will include (at the very least) good-faith challenges posed by one's deliberative partner, and joint deliberators must hold themselves answerable to such challenges in an ongoing way. The physician-husband in Gilman's story clearly fails to do this, as he affectionately belittles and gently disciplines his wife's "excited fancies" (Gilman 1997, 4). His failure begets a similar failure on her part: it is difficult for her to "answer" to challenges that do not seem to be addressed *to* her as a mature moral agent at all. This failure of mutual recognition has important implications for autonomy. It does not, perhaps, decisively show that either party fails to function autonomously. But if they do function autonomously, it would appear to be in spite of their relationship to one another and not because of it. The husband clearly treats his wife as non-autonomous, and over time she, too, begins to take what P. F. Strawson (1974) called an "objective" attitude toward him: instead of a person with whom she can reason, he becomes a force with which she must reckon.

If the spouses in "The Yellow Wallpaper" had instead treated each other's perspectives as relevantly authoritative, and held themselves answerable to one another in the articulation of a shared perspective, would they thereby have been constituted as autonomous, in relation to one another? Ultimately, I think the answer to this question is yes: in holding themselves dialogically answerable to one another, they would have taken responsibility for their action-guiding commitments (including shared ones) in just the way specified in the first part of this essay. But this answer depends on a point that has not yet been made clear: in addition to requiring openness to the perspective of one's co-deliberator, I would argue, joint deliberation also requires receptivity to challenges emanating from sources external to the deliberating dyad. Genuine humility about one's own interpretive framework involves receptiveness to relevant critical challenge in general—not just to critical challenge from some privileged source.

Why should this be so? The idea, in short, is this: if one does not acknowledge the possibility of local error—that is, of error shared by a deliberating duo—it is not clear that one ought to be counted as engaged in *justificatory* dialogue at all, as opposed to something like a project of joint rationalization (in the pejorative sense). As Gilbert notes, individuals who have "fused" intensively in a relationship such as marriage may, over time, come to hold fewer and fewer diverging views, preferences, and values (Gilbert 1996, 223). Shared echo chambers may be very comfortable—but they may also be very misleading. For this reason, meaningfully accepting the interpretive authority one is granted in a deliberative relationship means accepting responsibility for one's interpretations in the face of more widely, intersubjectively shareable norms. In order to avoid deliberative *folie à deux*, in which we are each captive to the same delusions about what we have reason to do, each party must hold herself answerable not only to the other but also to critical perspectives external to the deliberative relationship itself.

If I am right that joint deliberation involves this complex structure of mutual answerability (answerability to one another *and* to external critical perspectives), we arrive at the conclusion that a participant in joint deliberation will be constituted at one and the same time as part of a deliberative pair *and* as individually autonomous. In the process of attempting to develop a shared practical perspective with her deliberative partner, she will exercise the very disposition that renders her an autonomous agent—namely, the disposition to hold herself answerable to perspectives external to her own. She will not be in the grip of practical reasons stemming from her own (or even a shared) practical perspective, but will be, by the very nature of the enterprise, open to reassessing them in light of the reasons offered by another. Nor, despite the fact that she answers to the perspective of a particular other whose perspective she treats as normative, is she at risk of simply *deferring* to that perspective (and hence losing her autonomy), because the kind of answerability in question includes sensitivity to the possibility of local error and responsiveness to external perspectives on the deliberative relationship itself. Being jointly gripped is no more conducive to the project of joint practical deliberation than is being individually gripped to the project of individual practical deliberation.

3 .

Feminist critiques of oppressive gender norms suggest a common source of local error, along with a kind of diagnosis of our susceptibility to being gripped (or jointly gripped) by such error. In circumstances in which women's opportunities and expectations are sharply curtailed by customs and institutional practices that systematically disadvantage them, women may adapt their preferences to those circumstances, in ways that are actually harmful to them, without being aware that they are doing so (Superson 2009). These adaptive preferences may be sincerely held by women and regarded (equally sincerely) as genuine by their partners in deliberation. In such a scenario, the mere fact that the two parties hold themselves answerable to one another is unlikely to lead to any change in their mutual self-interpretations, and may permit their acceptance of wildly unfair reasoning-governing policies. Suppose that, like the "Deferential Wife" described by Thomas Hill, Jr. (Hill 1991), Jane actually derives much of her happiness from serving her husband, and does not take herself to have any important interests above or beyond serving his. Instead of expressing a preference to visit her own family for vacation, for example, she will express a preference to do whatever he prefers. Suppose further that Joe also prefers that he take the lead in such matters, and agrees with Jane about the propriety of her role in the family. Even if Joe is concerned about Jane's good for Jane's own sake, and does not want simply to impose his own interpretation of Jane's good on her, the fact that their preferences have been formed in response to the same system of norms leaves little room for critical discourse between them— unless, of course, Jane and Joe also hold themselves (and one another) answerable to *external* critical perspectives on their preferred gender roles in the course of their deliberations.

Now, even where deliberators do hold themselves answerable to external critical perspectives on their mutual self-interpretations, there is no guarantee that the shared practical perspective they construct will be free of distortion by any adaptive preferences or deformed desires. The range of critical perspectives that are likely to be encountered, or even to be imaginatively accessible, from within a community that widely shares certain problematic gender norms might not be sufficient to destabilize the perceived acceptability of arrangements which, in more ideal circumstances, would not be deemed acceptable. In my view, however, this empirical possibility does not undermine either the jointness of their deliberation or their individual autonomy. Deliberators who hold themselves mutually answerable to external critical perspectives are not in the grips of the action-guiding commitments they bring to bear on their joint decision-making (even if those commitments are legitimately criticizable), for their attitudes toward those commitments at least render them engageable in critical discourse that may lead to revision and change.

Fortunately, I believe, it is rather rare that no such discourse is available. Michele Moody-Adams points out that a growing number of social scientists have begun to question a "holistic" view of cultures, on which cultures are fully coherent structures containing no vantage points for selective criticism of traditional norms or practices (Moody-Adams 1998, 266). Instead, cultures are and always have been complex enough to contain conflicting strands and multiple sources of internal challenge. Of course, attempts to suppress such sources, or to exclude certain segments of the population (such as women) from exposure to them, may well have the effect of eroding the capacity for autonomy in affected individuals over time, as might explicit teaching or training that members of certain groups are not—and cannot be—answerable for themselves. Still, the conception of shared deliberation I've articulated here suggests that a local source of resistance to oppressive norms may be found within the (sometimes imperfect) relations of friendship and love that are ubiquitous in our lives. Individuals who engage in symmetrically shared deliberation both treat one another and present themselves to one another as autonomous, and they do so as a result of their aim to share reasons, as constrained by their robust concern for one another.

I do not mean to sound Pollyannish about this possibility: all too often the relevant forms of answerability are lacking, even within relationships that purport to be founded on (or to include) robust mutual concern—and sometimes this lack is a clear result of unfavorable social and institutional conditions, which trivialize the importance of the interests of some and exaggerate the importance of the interests of others, or miscast members of particular groups as having too little (or, conversely, too much) authority over the interpretation of those interests. To address these problems, we need feminist and other forms of political critique and action, including critical perspectives on the cultural norms that shape our personal relationships.

Nonetheless, it is an important and interesting fact about human agency that a link between individual autonomy and joint deliberation exists within relations of robust mutual care. A person may well function autonomously within other forms of shared agency: even when coerced or blackmailed into a shared activity, I might hold myself answerable to external critical perspectives for my decision to go along with the other's demands. But joint (or symmetrically shared) deliberation is special insofar as its very aim seems to include the autonomy of its participants.

In joint deliberation, answerability to external critical perspectives is mutually expected and required for the relevant form of sharing to get off the ground. This is what I meant, at the outset, when I suggested that in joint deliberation we not only *function* as autonomous agents but also *present* ourselves to one another as such.

Relational autonomy, on this view, has a special connection to shared deliberative agency—at the very least, within relations of robust mutual care. This form of shared agency expresses full mutual respect and support for the dialogical capacities that are always involved in autonomous agency, and, as such, it provides a particularly hospitable environment for autonomous agents. Although my primary concern has been with constitutive relationality, I suspect that involvement in such relationships may be among the important causal contributors to sustained personal autonomy over the course of a life, and that, at earlier stages, involvement in proto-deliberations with caring others is an important causal condition of the capacity for full-blown autonomy. The connections between autonomy and shared agency are bound to be rich and multi-layered, and attention to these connections will undoubtedly reward us with further insight into what Baier calls "the essential arts of personhood."

Notes

I would like to thank Anita Superson and Sharon Crasnow for their helpful comments on earlier drafts. I also benefitted from discussion of this paper with audiences at Marquette University, the University of Washington, and the University of Wisconsin–Madison. I am grateful to the Institute for Research in the Humanities at the University of Wisconsin–Madison, for its support during the writing of this paper.

1. My argument in the first section recapitulates a view of autonomy that I have defended in more detail elsewhere (Westlund 2003, 2009a).
2. It is slightly less obvious that social relations must play an ongoing role in *sustaining* autonomy in mature human persons, and there is certainly much interesting and potentially valuable work to be done in elaborating how or why this should be so.
3. I argue this point in Westlund 2009a.
4. As Benson puts it, his view is that "the authorization that constitutes autonomy is an authorization of *agents* with respect to their wills, not, in the first instance, authorization of their motives or courses of action" (Benson 2005, 107). Even if social authorization is an important question, I think we still need an answer to the question of what authorizes certain motives or other attitudes to represent the agent in the first place. Although I do not

have space fully to make the case here, I think that a view that ties agential authority to answerability can avoid the sorts of problems to which Benson points (Benson 2005) without departing from the general framework set by the traditional problem of agential authority.

5. I have, however, discussed a number of them elsewhere (Westlund 2003, 2009a).

6. My argument here draws on and recapitulates the fuller account given in Westlund (2003) and (2009a).

7. I do think that connections between freedom and autonomy need further elucidation. In their work on pornography, Jennifer Hornsby and Rae Langton (1998) argue that pornography might compromise women's freedom of speech (literally silencing them) by undermining the uptake conditions for certain illocutionary acts—including, for example, acts of refusal and protest. Though I do not have the space to do it here, I would like to explore the effects of these and other cases of illocutionary disablement (or unfreedom) on autonomy. If there are, for example, cases in which members of oppressed minorities cannot succeed in answering or accounting for themselves, because certain felicity conditions are absent or uptake is lacking, it seems quite likely that their disposition for answerability—and with it, their autonomy—will be put at risk. It is here that I think the social authorization of agents may come, indirectly but importantly, to bear on the problem of agential authority itself.

8. This kind of case is of particular interest to feminists, and I'll return to it below.

9. Here and below I draw on Westlund 2009b, which gives a fuller account of joint deliberation and its normative dimensions.

10. I suggest elsewhere (Westlund 2009b) that it might also be present in some other relationships, but that will not be my concern here.

11. See Westlund 2009b. Other components might include personal projects or commitments that we treat as sources of practical reasons. For simplicity's sake, I will speak in terms of preferences in what follows.

12. My favorite example of such mutual deference comes from a Garrison Keillor monologue in which he describes the citizens of Lake Wobegon as frequently vacationing on the "outer edges of Hell"—places where no one wants to be, but everyone thinks someone else might. For philosophical discussion of related problems and paradoxes, see David Estlund (1990) and F. C. T. Moore (1985a, 1985b).

13. Certainly, it is compatible with x actually benefitting (for example, deriving happiness) when he acts on a motive to benefit y, but I doubt that Soble meant to deny that.

14. On the notion of persons as ends, and what it is to treat them as such, see J. David Velleman (1999).

15. For influential discussions of the alienation that may arise in personal relationships that lack robust concern, in the sense at issue, see Michael Stocker (1976) and Peter Railton (1984).

16. Here I cast Joe in the role of one who derives happiness from pleasing others to avoid reinforcing a feminine stereotype that is associated with such motivational tendencies. This is not to say, of course, that we should not acknowledge and be critical of feminine gender norms that demand precisely such attitudes from women, especially with respect to their husbands and families. I return to this point in section 3 below.

17. For another fictional work that explores the phenomenon of self-disintegration in the face of the denial of epistemic authority, see Simone de Beauvoir, "The Woman Destroyed" (Beauvoir 1969). Lorraine Code treats a related theme in her paper "Persons and Others" (Code 1993), and issues of epistemic authority also arise prominently in feminist discussions of anger (see, for example, Frye 1983). From another direction, the literature on deliberative democracy includes several very interesting and empirically grounded discussions of asymmetries in epistemic authority, especially as they arise from status hierarchies and affect uptake conditions for the contributions of lower status participants. See James Bohman (1996; 1997), Jack Knight and James Johnson (1997), and Lynne Sanders (1997).

18. They also argue that each party is receptive to being "directed" by the other, meaning that each party is open to allowing her choices and activities to be shaped by and oriented toward the interests of the other. I think that they are right about this, but their claims about mutual interpretation are more directly relevant to my point in this paragraph.

19. See Westlund 2009b.

References

Baier, Annette. 1985. *Postures of the Mind: Essays on Mind and Morals*. Minneapolis: University of Minnesota Press.

———. 1986. Trust and Anti-Trust. *Ethics* 96: 201–30.

———. 1997. Doing Things With Others: The Mental Commons. In *Commonality and Particularity in Ethics*, edited by Lilli Alanen et al. London: MacMillan Press.

Beauvoir, Simone de. 1969. The Woman Destroyed. In *The Woman Destroyed*. Tr. Patrick O'Brien. London: William Collins Sons.

Benson, Paul. 2005. Taking Ownership: Authority and Voice in Autonomous Agency. In *Autonomy and the Challenges to Liberalism: New Essays*, edited by J. Christman and J. Anderson. Cambridge: Cambridge University Press.

Bohman, James. 1996. *Public Deliberation: Pluralism, Complexity, and Democracy*. Cambridge, Mass.: MIT Press.

———. 1997. Deliberative Democracy and Effective Social Freedom: Capabilities, Resources, and Opportunities. In *Deliberative Democracy*, edited by J. Bohman and W. Rehg. Cambridge, Mass.: MIT Press.

Bratman, Michael. 2007a. Shared Valuing and Frameworks for Practical Reasoning. In *Structures of Agency*. Oxford: Oxford University Press.

————. 2007b. *Structures of Agency*. Oxford: Oxford University Press.

Cocking, D. and J. Kennett. 1998. Friendship and the Self. *Ethics* 108:502–27.

Code, Lorraine. 1993. Persons and Others. In *A Reader in Feminist Ethics*, edited by Debra Shogan. Toronto: Canadian Scholars Press.

Estlund, David. 1990. Mutual Benevolence and the Theory of Happiness. *Journal of Philosophy* 87 (4):187–204.

Frankfurt, Harry. 1988. *The Importance of What We Care About*. Cambridge: Cambridge University Press.

————. 1999. *Necessity, Volition, and Love*. Cambridge: Cambridge University Press.

Frye, Marilyn. 1983. A Note on Anger. *The Politics of Reality: Essays in Feminist Theory*. Freedom, Calif.: Crossing Press.

Gilbert, Margaret. 1989. *On Social Facts*. Princeton, N.J.: Princeton University Press.

————. 1996. *Living Together*. Lanham, Md.: Rowman & Littlefield.

Gilman, Charlotte Perkins. 1997. *"The Yellow Wallpaper" and Other Stories*. Mineola, N.Y.: Dover Publications.

Hill, Thomas E., Jr. 1991. Servility and Self-Respect. In *Autonomy and Self-Respect*. Cambridge: Cambridge University Press.

Hornsby, Jennifer and Rae Langton. 1998. Free Speech and Illocution. *Legal Theory* 4:21–37.

Knight, Jack, and James Johnson. 1997. What Sort of Political Equality Does Deliberative Democracy Require? In *Deliberative Democracy*, edited by J. Bohman and W. Rehg. Cambridge, Mass.: MIT Press.

MacKenzie, Catriona, and Natalie Stoljar. 2000. Introduction: Autonomy Refigured. In *Relational Autonomy: Feminist Perspectives on Autonomy, Agency, and the Social Self*, edited by C. MacKenzie and N. Stoljar. New York: Oxford University Press.

Meyers, Diana Tietjens. 1987. Personal Autonomy and the Paradox of Feminine Socialization. *Journal of Philosophy* 84 (11): 619–28.

————. 2004. *Being Yourself: Essays on Identity, Action, and Social Life*. Lanham, Md.: Rowman & Littlefield.

McLeod, Carolyn. 2002. *Self-Trust and Reproductive Autonomy*. Cambridge, Mass.: MIT Press.

Moody-Adams, Michele M. 1997. *Fieldwork in Familiar Places: Morality, Culture, & Philosophy*. Cambridge, Mass.: Harvard University Press.

Moore, Francis Charles Timothy. 1985a. The Martyr's Dilemma. *Analysis* 45:29–33.

————. 1985b. A Problem about Higher Order Desires. *Acta Philosophica Fennica* 38:149–55.

Oshana, Marina. 1998. Personal Autonomy and Society. *Journal of Social Philosophy* 29 (1):81–102.

Railton, Peter. 1984. Alienation, Consequentialism, and the Demands of Morality. *Philosophy & Public Affairs*. 13 (2):134–71.

Sanders, Lynn M. 1997. Against Deliberation. *Political Theory* 25 (3):347–76.

Soble, Alan. 1997. Union, Autonomy, and Concern. In *Love Analyzed*, edited by Roger E. Lamb. Boulder, Colo.: Westview Press.

Stocker, Michael. 1976. The Schizophrenia of Modern Ethical Theories. *Journal of Philosophy* 73 (14):453–66.

Stoljar, Natalie. 2000. Autonomy and the Feminist Intuition. In *Relational Autonomy*, edited by C. MacKenzie and N. Stoljar. New York: Oxford University Press.

Strawson, P.F. 1974. Freedom and Resentment. In *Freedom and Resentment and Other Essays*. London: Methuen.

Superson, Anita. 2009. Feminist Moral Psychology. *Stanford Encyclopedia of Philosophy*, edited by Edward N Zalta. http://plato.stanford.edu/archives/spr2009/entries/feminism-moralpsych/.

Velleman, J. David. 1999. Love as a Moral Emotion. *Ethics* 109:338–74.

Watson, Gary. 1975. Free Agency. *Journal of Philosophy* 72 (8):205–20.

Westlund, Andrea. 2003. Selflessness and Responsibility for Self: Is Deference Compatible With Autonomy? *Philosophical Review* 112 (4):37–77.

———. 2009a. Rethinking Relational Autonomy. *Hypatia* 24 (4):26–49.

———. 2009b. Deciding Together. *Philosophers' Imprint*. 9 (10). www.philosophersimprint.org/009010/.

4

ROBIN S. DILLON
Lehigh University

CRITICAL CHARACTER THEORY:

Toward a Feminist Perspective on "Vice" (and "Virtue")

I. INTRODUCTION/MANIFESTO

One central focus for moral philosophy has always been virtue theory: theorizing about human character to understand what it is to be a morally good person and how being morally good relates to acting rightly and living well. However, traditional virtue theory neglects two significant matters. The first is the sociopolitical dimensions of character: how character is shaped by, supports, and resists domination and subordination. By contrast, feminist ethics is chiefly concerned to theorize the moral nature and meaning of relations of unequal power, and feminist ethicists have recently begun to theorize virtue in relation to oppression, identifying traits of character that enable people to survive and resist subordination in morally justifiable ways and envisioning morally desirable modes of being toward which emancipatory struggles might aim.[1] But like traditional virtue theory, feminist ethics also neglects a second thing of importance for understanding character and moral life, namely, what has traditionally been called "vice" or bad character. Yet rich accounts of vice are as important as accounts of virtue: we need to understand not only what kinds of persons to be but also what kinds not to be, not only what traits foster resistance to oppression and emancipation but also what traits support domination and thwart emancipation, and what costs to character struggles for liberation and struggles to maintain domination might exact.

This chapter calls for a substantive reorientation in moral theory in general and feminist ethics in particular, arguing for two significant changes.[2] The first is a move to what I call "critical character theory,"[3] which seeks to understand moral character as affected by domination and subordination and by the struggles both to maintain and to resist and overthrow them. I want to argue that feminist ethics needs critical character theory and that feminists engaged in the work of theorizing about moral life in societies that are structured by domination and oppression should put work on critical character theory higher on the agenda. I also want to argue that virtue theory as it has traditionally been done is inadequate to the task of understanding human character to the extent that it neglects to think about character critically, and so I would argue that critical character theory ought to replace virtue theory in non-feminist moral philosophy as well. The second change I propose is that more serious and sustained attention be given, in moral theory in general and feminist ethics in particular, to theorizing vice (or, rather, what has traditionally been called "vice"[4]).

By critical character theory, I mean something that might be seen as a version of what is nowadays called virtue theory. By virtue theory, I mean something different than what is nowadays called virtue ethics. To start with the last concept, virtue ethics is the project of basing ethics on virtue, of developing, that is, an ethics in which the notion of virtue is central, in which the basic judgments are judgments about character, and so in which conceptions of rightness of action, goodness of ends, the good life, the moral point of view, and so on, are derived from and justified in terms of a conception of good character.[5] In virtue ethics, the central focus is on the traits of individuals rather than on, for example, actions or social institutions and practices. Aristotelian ethics is the most obvious example of a virtue ethics; other contemporary examples include Rosalind Hursthouse's neo-Aristotelian virtue ethics, Christine Swanton's Nietzschean and pluralistic virtue ethics, Michael Slote's "agent-based" approach, inspired by Hutcheson, Hume, Martineau, and some versions of the feminist ethics of care.[6] A virtue theory, by contrast, offers an account of what vice and virtue are, as well as accounts of particular virtues and vices. Every moral theory or approach to moral theorizing can have as a part of it a theory of virtue. Thus, although Kant, for example, is hardly a virtue ethicist (at least as he is standardly read), he has a well-developed theory of virtue, and Julia Driver has recently elaborated a consequentialist virtue theory.[7]

However, although some theorists would argue that there is such a thing as a feminist virtue ethics,[8] I think there cannot, or should not, be a feminist virtue ethics. But I do think that theorizing character critically from a feminist perspective can and should be part of feminist ethics. Let me say first why I think there cannot be a feminist virtue ethics. Virtue ethics, as I said, is centrally focused on traits of individuals. But for feminist ethics, the focus is not just, or even first, on traits of individuals. Where the concern of feminist ethics is with individuals, it is with individuals as members of groups of people living among social institutions that organize life along lines of hierarchies of power, at least some of which are morally illegitimate. Character is important to feminist ethics, or so I will argue; but so are actions, ends, and social institutions and practices. Feminist ethics tends to be pluralistic, stressing the complexity of interconnections among what are traditionally regarded as the core organizing concepts of ethical theory, rather than identifying one, say character or action, as the basic focus or the central concept in terms of which to make sense of everything else. If, however, there is a concept that is the focus and central organizing concept for feminist ethics, it is *power*. As Margaret Walker has said, "feminist ethics is inevitably and fundamentally about morality and power and the moral meaning of relations of unequal power"[9]; indeed, as Susan Sherwin has noted, feminist ethics asks about power, about domination and subordination, even before it asks about good and evil.[10] So I conclude that making virtue or character the central organizing concept for a feminist ethics is either not possible or not wise. But taking power as a central organizing concept gives feminist ethics a distinctive take on what is now called virtue theory, or as I think we should say, critical character theory.

What, then, do I mean by "critical character theory"? Critical theory in general seeks human emancipation; it aims, as Horkheimer puts it, "to liberate human beings from the circumstances that enslave them."[11] It is thus every bit as practical as it is theoretical; indeed, the theory is in service to the practical aims. Feminist theory is, of course, a critical theory. Now, critical theory tends to focus at the social level of human life, seeking emancipatory change through the elimination of the social, political, and material causes of human suffering and enslavement. Critical character theory, however, springs from the recognition that enslavement is not only social and material but also operates on and through character: what Blake called "the mind forg'd manacles" and Sandra Bartky called "psychological oppression" are dimensions of the distortions of character that both result from and result in domination and subordination.[12] More specifically, critical character theory holds that (a) domination and oppression inflict moral damage on the characters of those who live within them, preventing them from living fully good human lives, and (b) certain structures of character dispose or enable individuals to acquiesce in, resist or struggle against, or live, unwittingly or intentionally, in ways that maintain and strengthen systems of domination and oppression. Thus, critical character theory seeks liberation of and through character. As a response to pressing social justice concerns, critical character theory has two important tasks. The first is to understand character in the circumstances of domination and oppression with an eye toward dismantling unjust hierarchies of power both for and through the liberation of character. The second task is to examine mainstream moral philosophy and character theory to understand how dominant accounts of "character" operate ideologically in the service of power.[13] This shift in focus and aims significantly alters what is now called virtue theory.

Why not call the altered approach "critical virtue theory"? As the terms "virtue theory" and "virtue ethics" indicate, philosophical theorizing about character has traditionally taken the form of theorizing about what we have traditionally called "virtue."[14] Some groundbreaking work in feminist ethics has involved theorizing virtue. There are, however, serious problems with the exclusive focus on virtue, not the least of which is the real but unacknowledged difficulty of identifying a character trait as genuinely good without asking, "Does this trait contribute to or undermine the continuation of systems of domination and subordination?" or "Does the possession of this trait enable the individual to survive under or to resist or struggle against domination and oppression but only at the cost of disabling the individual from living a good human life?"[15] These are questions that traditional virtue theory does not ask. Moreover, virtuous character is not the only form of character, and there is reason to believe, as I discuss below, that character distorted by vice is more common within systems of domination and oppression than is generally acknowledged. And to the extent that vice is both one of the forms of damage that domination and oppression inflict on individuals and one of the mechanisms through which they are sustained, attention to vice as well as virtue is of central importance to theorizing character critically. Given the dearth of attention to vice, I want to shift the focus and approach theorizing character critically by giving special emphasis to vice.

One might analyze character critically from a non-feminist perspective; I want in this chapter to work toward a distinctively feminist critical character theory. In her critique of Aristotle's decidedly noncritical virtue ethics, Susan Moller Okin once asked, "how does virtue ethics look from a feminist point of view, i.e., from a perspective that expects women and men to be treated equally as human and as equally worthy of due concern and respect?"[16] I would answer thus: feminist critical character theorizing puts the wrongness of the oppression of women front and center and examines, on the one hand, actual practices of character development and, on the other, appraisals of character and theoretical treatments of virtue and vice, in the light of women's oppression. Further, it seeks to develop accounts of character and character traits that take women's experiences seriously but not uncritically, that carry in them right valuing of women, and that provide insight, guidance, and cautions for liberatory struggle that seeks to make the world one in which women and men are treated equally as human and equally worthy of concern and respect.[17]

Ethics in general and feminist ethics in particular need to engage in critical character theorizing in which vice is a central concern for five reasons: (1) in order to fully understand and engage with the nature and mechanisms of domination and oppression; (2) in order to theorize the kinds of persons people need to be in order to survive and resist domination and oppression in morally justifiable and non-self-corrupting ways, and to envision morally desirable modes of being that promote emancipation; (3) in order to understand morally undesirable modes of being that support domination and oppressio n and thwart emancipation; (4) in order to conceive the kinds of good lives toward which struggles for liberation might aim and the kinds of bad lives which misguided struggles might produce; and (5) in order to understand the costs to lives and character which both struggles for liberation and struggles to maintain domination might exact.

II. WHY IT IS IMPORTANT TO THEORIZE VICE AND TO DO SO FROM A CRITICAL FEMINIST PERSPECTIVE

One might analyze character critically by focusing on virtuous character, which has held the center of attention at least since Plato. But I want to argue that feminist critical character theory ought to proceed by giving priority to the analysis of what has traditionally been called "vice." Making the case for doing so requires raising and answering five questions:

1. Why is it important to theorize vice at all?
2. Why is it important to theorize vice critically from a feminist perspective?

3. Assuming the importance of doing so, how might we go about theorizing vice (and virtue) from a critical feminist perspective?
4. What are the criteria that from a feminist perspective would enable us to identify and understand vice, or to understand and evaluate some dimensions of character as constituting vices?
5. How should we understand character, and should we continue to talk about character (or "character") in terms of "vice" and "virtue"?

I want in the rest of this chapter to address questions 1, 2, 3, and 5, saving the fourth for another occasion. Let me start, then, with the first question: why theorize vice at all? This is an important question to ask, for it would appear that contemporary moral philosophers on the whole *do not* think it is worth doing so. For even with the contemporary resurgence of interest in virtue ethics, relatively little work has been done on vice in general or on particular vices.[18] In this lack of attention we may hear echoes of Hume: "Why rake into those corners of nature which spread a nuisance all around? Why dig up the pestilence from the pit in which it is buried?"[19]

One of the things that taking a feminist perspective involves is looking for what Cheshire Calhoun calls "patterned sets of silences" concerning topics, concepts, cases, and the like that seem to have been neglected or marginal in a discipline, and asking: why these silences?[20] So, I ask: why the relative lack of attention to vice in contemporary moral philosophy generally and in feminist ethics?

I can think of three answers:

1. Vice, it might be thought, is just the contradictory or contrary of virtue. So, if you understand what virtue is in general or understand a particular virtue, then you need only negate or invert the account, or move the indicator from "just right" to "too much" or "too little," to know what vice or a particular vice is. There is thus nothing to be gained from looking at vice directly.

2. Cheshire Calhoun has argued that patterns of silence are a byproduct of the participants in discussions in moral philosophy settling upon features of moral life they regard as theory-worthy and fit subjects for further philosophical dialogue, and she underscores the value of bringing to light and examining the assumptions that underlie these implicit judgments about what is worth discussing philosophically.[21]

Lisa Tessman has argued that there is a set of unexamined assumptions permeating virtue ethics, among them that most people are basically good, that vice is unusual, and that when vice is a problem it is a problem in others but not in oneself (the theorist or reader.)[22] These assumptions connect, she notes, with the dominant approach in moral philosophy to theorize the ideal rather than the nonideal, an approach that connects in turn with the sociopolitical position of the folks who dominate professional philosophy, by numbers, ideology, and culture. The dominant view in moral philosophy generally, then, is that it is uninteresting and unimportant to theorize vice.

Now, we all know that this world is far from ideal and we know that lots and lots of people are far from wholly virtuous. Indeed, as Lisa Tessman puts it, "in oppressively structured societies, a large proportion of the population will display" what she calls "ordinary vices of domination," which include callousness, greed, self-centeredness, dishonesty, cowardice, and indifference to the preventable and unjust suffering of others.[23] Yet, given the pervasiveness of such vices and the suspicion, which Anita Superson nicely articulates,[24] that these vices not only enable members of dominant groups to maintain their own positions of dominance but also may contribute to the general maintenance and continuation of oppressive and dominating social institutions and practices, we can reasonably wonder why feminist ethicists have been relatively silent about vice in general and vices of domination in particular.

3. A third reason for the general silence in feminist ethics about vices of domination is suggested by an objection Louise Antony raises against Anita Superson's claim that vices such as "arrogance, self-centeredness, and denial of responsibility regarding one's privilege issue in a staunch resistance to recognizing, understanding, and eradicating women's oppression" and "cause the agent to engage in various forms of sexist immoral behavior that in turn function to maintain privilege," behavior for which, she argues, the agent is responsible and blameworthy.[25] Louise Antony believes that "it is a mistake to think that individual agency ought to be the main explanatory factor in conceptualizing social and political phenomena," and she argues that Superson places "far too much emphasis on individual intentions, actions and responsibility in her proffered explanations of social injustice and in her proposed strategies for dismantling it."[26] A better strategy, Louise Antony maintains, would be to focus on the social and material bases for oppressive structures. This strategy is better

for two reasons. First, since the real source of oppression and domination is social structures and not defects in the characters of some individuals, focusing on understanding and changing their social and material bases is a more effective way of understanding and dismantling domination and oppression; and second, telling people that their characters are vicious and challenging them to undertake personal reform is a strategy likely to backfire, inasmuch as "people deeply resent personal accusations." We might add to Louise Antony's second reason an objection derived from the idea of constitutive bad luck, which Lisa Tessman and Claudia Card have illuminatingly discussed: it might be not only ineffective but also unfair to blame people for characters that they are not fully responsible, in the backward-looking sense, for having.[27]

So, why the silence about vice? Because, one might think, analyzing vice, in general or in connection with theorizing oppression and domination, is unnecessary, uninteresting and unimportant, and/or both seriously misguided and morally perilous.

Now, it would clearly be a mistake to think that if one paid attention only to vice, one would have paid attention to everything that matters with respect to understanding and eradicating oppression and domination. It would indeed be misguided to think that all of the ills of domination and oppression can be reduced to and blamed upon vices in individuals. An ethics of vice, or of vice and virtue, or of character, would not by itself be sufficient for understanding domination and oppression thoroughly; we do need to theorize and engage in liberatory struggle at the structural and material levels. But I disagree that it is useless or worse to theorize vice or even to focus one's theorizing on vice. I want to resist the suggestion that none of the ills of domination and oppression can be understood in terms of or traced to vices, and I want to resist the suggestion that liberatory struggle does not also need to involve active engagement with vices of individuals. I also want to resist backing away from engaging with vice out of worries about blame, for two reasons. First, I think blame can be appropriate.[28] Second, I think worries about the fairness of blaming individuals for vice and social ills are among the things that indicate that the dominant understanding of vice, virtue, and character needs to be revised in light of the recognition by feminist theorists, among others, that character is not simply a matter of what is inside the individual, for which the individual is wholly and solely responsible, but is also a matter of interpersonal, social, cultural, and political contexts,[29] a point to which I will return.

I think that we need to theorize and engage vice, and to do so from a feminist perspective. So, I need respond to these three reasons for not doing so. To do that, let me ask another question, one prompted by Sally Haslanger's suggestion, in another context, that we begin thinking about gender and race by asking what we want those categories for—what is the point in having these concepts? What cognitive or practical function do they enable us to accomplish?[30] Let me ask, what could we (moral philosophers and feminist ethicists) want the concept of vice for? Of what cognitive or practical use is such a category? One might think that the main function that the category of vice serves is to enable and perhaps encourage us to hold individuals responsible in a blaming way for engaging in domination and subordination or for supporting or not working to eradicate structures of domination and oppression; and one might think that this blaming would not be a worthwhile activity. I would argue that wanting to assess people's characters in order to know whom to blame for wrongdoings or social ills is not among the principal reasons for attending to vice. There are, rather, at least five other important cognitive and practical tasks for which the category of vice is not only useful but required.

The first three tasks are familiar ones. First, I take a central moral task facing every moral agent to be the task of trying to become a morally good person leading a life that is and that she can rightly regard as morally worthy. I take the kind of person that a person is to matter a great deal, and not just because of the ways in which the kind of person one is affects others, but because it is intrinsically important. I take being a person with a good character to be an intrinsically good thing and being a person whose character contains significant vices to be an intrinsically bad thing. I also take the exercise of one's agency in taking responsibility in the forward-looking sense for the kind of person one is and could be, through activities of development of self, reflective evaluation and regulation of self, and improvement of self, to be intrinsically valuable. And I believe that even though social and interpersonal forces are powerful shapers, and often distorters, of character, there is still a moral demand and significant room for exercising one's agency in taking responsibility for one's character.

Second, I take another central moral task facing a great many moral agents to be that of raising and educating children and young people and thus of helping to develop their characters, and the allied task of contributing to the continuing character development of those who are no longer children whom we love or care for or over whom we exercise various legitimate forms of control. The task of helping to develop the characters of others is made all the more difficult when, under non-ideal conditions, we face, on the one hand, forces that operate in ways that can distort character, and on the other, the need to navigate among three potentially conflicting goals: (1) helping to shape people who are fit to live in and contribute to society as it currently is; (2) helping to shape people who are able to survive or to resist the social forces that work to diminish or corrupt selves and lives; and (3) helping to shape people who are able to struggle actively against forces of domination and oppression and perhaps able to live both toward and in a less oppressive society. The task of contributing to the development of others' characters thus involves mediating, and determining for what end and how to mediate, both these goals and the powers of social institutions and practices and interpersonal interactions that shape and distort character.

Third, a great many of us face repeatedly the task of having to make decisions about other people, decisions that very often require character assessment—voting, choosing friends, hiring, deciding whether to dump this guy or forgive him, writing recommendations, determining with what others to engage in a wide range of projects, including those of social transformation, figuring out with whom solidarity is possible, worthwhile, and not integrity-threatening, and so on. Here, the point of character assessment is not to blame, but to understand in order to determine what to do, with or for whom, and how.

In order to engage well in these three tasks of taking responsibility for character development in oneself and in others and of making character-based decisions, we need to understand a whole lot about material and social possibilities and limitations, dangers and opportunities; but we also need a clear sense not only of the kinds of persons that it is good to be but also of the kinds of persons that it is bad to be, not only of virtues but also of vices that distort character and thwart attempts to live appropriately and to engage effectively in projects one regards as worthy of and perhaps calling for one's engagement.

An essay in *Time* published in the midst of the 2008 presidential campaign focused on Bill Clinton's role in Hillary Clinton's campaign for the Democratic nomination and asked "how much of the blame for her predicament [her string of primary losses before winning Ohio and Texas] belongs to him?" "A Hillary friend and supporter" is quoted as saying, "I think he just did her so much damage... They'll never see it that way, because they can't. And he has no self-knowledge. This has magnified all his worst traits."[31] To be sure, self-knowledge and theoretical knowledge of bad traits are two different things, but at least sometimes being able to know oneself and to see certain bad traits in one's character involves or is made possible by understanding the various guises of these particular traits, why they are bad, and what other traits make it difficult for us to know ourselves.

We need nuanced understandings of vice and vices because many of them are not always easy to recognize or comprehend. For example, while it may be easy to know that arrogance (one of the traits said to be responsible for Bill Clinton's inflicting "damage" on Hillary Clinton's campaign, despite efforts to help it), is called a vice (although, I have found, that is not always easy, as there is plenty of praise around nowadays for arrogance), it can be very difficult to know precisely what it is to be arrogant and to know whether one is or is heading toward becoming arrogant. It can also be difficult to know why one should care about whether one is arrogant or not. Under conditions of domination and subordination, it can be even more difficult to tell whether a trait is one that should be encouraged or discouraged, cultivated or resisted, and for what end, or to determine whether the possession of certain vices might be offset or tempered by possession of certain virtues. And it can be difficult to know whether character repair is possible, and if so, how it might be accomplished. On some journeys, it can be as important to know where and how not to go as to know where and how to go, and it can be especially important along the way to have some means of telling if one is headed in the right, or at least not a wrong, direction, and whether course correction is even possible, and if so, how.

We do not, however, have enough to go on in carrying out these three cognitive and practical tasks if we just have an account of virtue and then negate or invert it. In my own work on the (putative) vice of arrogance,[32] I found that the few theorists who have written about it take the virtuous opposite of arrogance to be humility; but much of the work on humility makes it clear that it cannot be seen as a virtue unless one first sees the badness of arrogance and then sees humility as the proper corrective for it.[33] Sometimes we cannot know what is good or why it is good until we know what is bad and why it is bad. Moreover, sometimes we do not get a good understanding of what the virtuous opposite of some vice is until we have examined that vice thoroughly. In my case, it was only by working out from both a Kantian and a feminist perspective what arrogance is and why and when it is a vice (and why and when it is not) that I came to believe that arrogance is not a matter of "too much"—of thinking too highly of one's worth—but is a matter of thinking wrongly about the worth of oneself and everything else, that humility, a low or moderate opinion of one's worth, is not the virtue opposed to arrogance (self-respect, which is thinking rightly about one's worth, is), and that humility is at best an ancillary and context-dependent virtue, not a virtue for all humans, and at worst not a virtue at all.

The fourth and fifth cognitive and practical tasks for which understanding vice is necessary address as well my second question: why should we theorize vice critically from a feminist perspective? The fourth task is one I take to be important for moral philosophers generally but which is too often neglected: to understand how people's characters come to be distorted by vice and whether and how such distortions can be corrected. Such understanding, I believe, requires understanding the actual moral conditions within which people have to live their lives and engage in various projects, including the projects of character development and improvement. This understanding requires a critical perspective, for the conditions in which people live are thoroughly interpersonal, social, cultural, and political and are shot through with hierarchies of power whose structure and functioning shapes life contexts and hence lives in profound ways. One important dimension of this understanding concerns the nature and extent of the damage wrought upon persons through their living in unjust societies, including the deep damage to character that is both intrinsically bad and bad because of how life possibilities for self and others are affected. Vice is a form of character damage.

The lack of explicit, prioritized attention in most theorizing about character to the effects of systemic forces of unjust power hierarchies on the constitutions of selves and characters is problematic for two reasons. First, it makes us, both theorists and "ordinary folks" engaged in the first three tasks, liable to understand virtue and vice in general and specific virtues and vices in ways that reflect and reinforce domination values, and in particular, ways that normalize and buttress vice in members of dominant groups (a point to which I'll return). It makes us liable also to neglect or distort what would count as flourishing and what would count as damage for both those who are subordinated and those who occupy positions of dominance in various power hierarchies. Such mis-understanding may subvert not only our sincere efforts to assess character properly and guide its development and improvement, which may result in continuing damage to character, but also our efforts to end oppression, resulting in the continuation of injustice. Second, I would argue that we are, in some cases, unable to understand that there is something wrong about the conditions of moral life until we understand that something is wrong with many lives as they are lived under those conditions and that what is wrong is, in part, that the lives express vices of character—just as we sometimes do not understand that there is something wrong with a machine until we understand that there is something wrong with what it produces, tracing back from specific effect to specific cause. A good understanding of the nature, operation, and effects of domination and subordination, I would argue, requires a good understanding of vice and vices.

In this context, I am particularly interested in understanding more fully the distortions of character wrought upon members of dominant groups. Most feminist theorizing, understandably, focuses on the oppressed. When dominant groups are considered, it is typically by way of discussing privilege; indeed, it has become commonplace to discuss oppression in terms of two groups, the oppressed (or subordinated) and the privileged.[34] While the concept of privilege is enormously useful in understanding some dimensions of domination, it has this odd effect. We are used to thinking of privilege and privileges as good things—who would not want to have privilege, to be privileged? It is not hard to begin to think that there is nothing intrinsically bad about being a member of a privileged group, that it would be great if everyone had privileges, and that all we have to do is to figure out a way to separate privilege from the harm that those without privilege suffer, to keep the privilege and extend it to those now without it—just give everyone one of those backpacks full of "special provisions, assurances, tools,...codebooks,...and blank checks" that facilitate a smooth and thriving progress through life.[35] I know that subtle analyses of privilege make it clear that this dream is incoherent,[36] but I have found it a hard dream to overcome in my students. What is more sobering is coming to understand that much privilege comes at a great price for the self, that being a member of a dominant group is damaging to one's character and in ways of which one is usually unaware and is prevented in various ways from becoming aware.

In her discussion of ordinary vices of domination, Lisa Tessman notes that it might seem to some people (although it does not seem so to her) counterintuitive to claim that oppression is harmful to its perpetrators as well as to its victim.[37] I would argue that oppression damages everyone, though in different ways and to different degrees. It would not be good to try to quantify damage to determine who is damaged more or more seriously. But I hold the view that inasmuch as injustice and wrongdoing require and foster such vices in dominants as arrogance, self-centeredness, callousness, indifference, and social irresponsibility,[38] the characters of those who perpetrate or are complicit in oppression, however unwittingly, are deeply damaged, and that damage to character is not compensated for by the privileges that members of dominant groups unknowingly enjoy. It is important to theorize vice critically in order to understand the kinds of damage and the insidious nature of the damaging to which individuals as members of dominant groups are liable, and the ways in which such damage may be expressed in efforts (some perhaps unconscious) of dominants to maintain their own positions of dominance, in the continued support by dominants of the maintenance and continuation of oppressive and dominating social institutions and practices, and in the resistance by dominants to feminist emancipatory critique and activity. This task of understanding the nature and effect of character damage in dominants is made all the more difficult when vices are normalized in members of dominant groups, and I would argue that only a critical perspective has the resources to investigate whether and to what extent traits that are regarded as morally innocuous or even virtuous are better understood as normalized vices. It is also important to theorize vice critically in order to understand the limitations, possibilities, resources, and means for efforts to recognize, address, and attempt to repair damage to character in dominants as well as subordinates.

My insistence that oppression damages dominants as well as subordinates is not meant to call for compassion for members of dominant groups or to let dominants off various hooks of responsibility (although the questions of whether compassion would be justified and what hooks any of us are on remain open). But I do want to focus on damage to dominants not only because there are important theoretical and practical reasons for doing so, but also because I am someone who, when we sort though the various axes of oppression and domination, ends up among the dominants along all the axes but one, and someone whose most loved ones are dominants by every measure. So, to return to the first three cognitive and practical tasks, it is also important to me personally, as someone with the important moral task of taking responsibility for character, to have some way of understanding both how domination and oppression distort character and the possible resources, in and outside of me, for character repair.

The fifth cognitive and practical task for which theorizing vice is important is the critical activity of theorizing and engaging in the eradication of oppression and domination. But—what needs to be changed, restructured, repaired, dismantled, thwarted, and how can these things be done? Certainly, ending domination and oppression requires altering the social and material conditions of life, and repairing the conditions under which moral life has to be lived may be what it takes to repair and prevent character damage. But it may not be, or it may not be sufficient, and repairing social conditions may take longer than many of us have to wait for character repair. What is more, it may be that repairing or transforming character is a necessary condition for or an effective way of repairing or transforming social conditions. A better understanding of vice and vices may help us to determine the connections between character correction and social correction, and to determine how it is possible and how it might be best to repair character. And I think the repair of character itself has to be on the agenda for change, as an intrinsically valuable project.

Moreover, if I am right that having a character distorted by vice (or at least, certain vices) is part of what enables members of dominant groups to maintain their positions of dominance and to participate in the perpetuation of oppressive social structures, and that the possession of certain vices makes it very unlikely that members of dominant groups will accurately understand the fact of or the injustice of the positions of dominance they hold and makes it very likely that they will resist rather than support social transformation, then it is essential to address vice in members of dominant groups in efforts to dismantle unjust hierarchies of power.

We can engage in these five tasks well only if moral philosophers in general and feminist ethicists in particular engage explicitly in examining vice from the perspective of a feminist critical character theory. I do not mean to say that critical character theorizing is the most important critical work to be done or that theorizing vice is the only dimension of critical character theory. There are so many ways in which we are damaged by domination and oppression characterologically, psychologically, materially, and with regard to life prospects, and so many targets, aspects, modes, and resources of repair and change. I do, however, mean to claim a space for doing what I have argued is important work of theorizing vice from a critical feminist perspective.

III. HOW WE MIGHT THEORIZE VICE (AND VIRTUE) FROM A CRITICAL FEMINIST PERSPECTIVE

Having explained why it is important to theorize vice from a critical feminist perspective and as an important part of feminist ethics, let me now turn to the third question: how might we go about theorizing vice (and virtue) from a critical feminist perspective? Let me approach this by identifying eight dimensions of feminist critical character theory, saying how an analysis of vice (and virtue) would be part of each dimension.

First, feminist critical character theory has an explicitly political orientation and aim. It puts front and center, as Susan Okin says, the notion that women and men are equally human and equally due concern and respect, and it aims explicitly to end domination and oppression.[39] Thus, one of its chief concerns would be to understand the ways in which, in circumstances of oppression, both actual practices of character development and appraisal and non-feminist theories of vice and of virtue ignore or deny the humanity and worth of women, reinforce the oppression of women, damage the characters of women and men in different ways, and hide all this from non-feminist observers. Think, for example, of the damage done to women by the view that the failure of a woman to devote herself wholeheartedly to the well-being of others manifests the worst of the many feminine vices, the vice of selfishness, the correction for which is the greatest of the feminine virtues, selfless love— a trait that feminist analysis reveals in this context to be self-destructive self-abnegation.[40]

Another chief concern would be to develop accounts of vice and virtue in general and of specific vices and virtues that carry in them right valuing of women and that build understandings of sociopolitical realities and emancipatory goals into the evaluation of traits as vices or virtues. Feminist critical character theory would thus seek to determine, for example, whether certain traits that are traditionally called "virtues" are in fact virtues for members of oppressed and subordinated groups, and whether traits that are traditionally regarded as vices in humans might be reclaimed through revision or revaluation as potentially liberatory virtues for women and other subordinated people. I argue, for example, both that arrogance is what I call a "deadly vice," indeed the deadliest of vices, insofar as it is fundamentally a failure to respect self and others, and that a certain form of arrogance, while a vice in members of dominant groups, can be a virtue in members of subordinated groups insofar as it can express self-respect and enable subordinates to struggle against oppression.[41] Although I cannot say much more here about what criteria we might use to define vice and virtue(the fourth of the five questions), it is plausible to think that chief among them would be those that link the badness of vice to the tendency to reinforce oppression and the goodness of virtue to the tendency to subvert it. I anticipate that a fair amount of revision in canonical lists of vices and virtues would result from examining traits systematically from a feminist perspective. I also anticipate that as a result of feminist analysis, we will come to understand vice/vices and virtue/virtues as much more complex than is standardly thought.

One dimension of that complexity is the focus of a second feature. Feminist critical character theory emphasizes power; hence, it would theorize character by taking unequal relations of power to be central to character: to its development, its structure and functioning, its social moral meaning and value, and the differential possibilities for different groups of humans for becoming and being good or bad. Thus, among the things this approach would seek to understand are the following: how unjust power hierarchies shape character differentially, that is, how character, vice, and virtue are gendered, racialized, classed, and so on; the roles played in maintaining unjust power hierarchies by the possession and exercise of vices such as arrogance, self-centeredness, callousness, indifference, and social irresponsibility; the damage to character resulting from the encouragement or toleration in certain groups of certain vices (for example, by relabeling the aforementioned as confidence, self-esteem, strong-mindedness, focus, and conservatism); and the damage resulting from the lack of opportunities of certain groups to develop or exercise certain virtues deemed especially distinctive of a good or fully human life.

The third feature of feminist critical character theory also concerns power, for it would seek to understand not only how power shapes character differentially but also how it shapes analyses and evaluations of character and how such analyses and evaluations function to reinforce domination and oppression. So this approach would ask, among other things, about the ways in which distributions and exercises of power affect what particular vices and virtues are understood to involve and entail; about whether and how they get recognized and in whom, and in particular, whether the possession and exercise of certain vices is recognized in members of certain groups or is regarded as making individuals and their lives less morally good. Hence it would ask what traits get identified as virtues or vices in women but not men and vice versa and on what grounds and in what domains of human life. Critical character theory, that is, holds that the identification of particular traits as virtues and vices has political as well as moral dimensions and functions: certain traits are differentially identified as virtues or vices, and given differential social moral attention and inattention, depending on what groups of people are being evaluated. For example, different traits are now identified as virtues or vices for women and for men;[42] some traits are given different content or valence for women and men or are regarded as more or less appropriate, possible, or typical for each, in ways that reflect and reinforce power hierarchies;[43] and the political function of labeling some trait as vice or virtue X can be different, depending on where the subjects stand in some power hierarchy. One thing that made me realize I needed to analyze arrogance from a feminist perspective was noticing that women are called arrogant far less frequently than men and that women who are called arrogant tend to be ones who defy feminine stereotypes by exercising power in masculine ways in arenas traditionally regarded as masculine, whereas men exhibiting the same qualities in exercising power in those same ways and same arenas are not called arrogant. This suggests that the epithet "arrogant" is used in ways that function both to undercut women's legitimate claims to power and to normalize the arrogance that social domination necessarily involves. I call this the "politics of character assessment," and it is part of what makes it hard to understand what it is, really, to be a good and worthy person and the extent to which one is, really, good and worthy, and to understand what it is, really, to be a person whose character is made unworthy by being distorted by various vices and the extent to which one's character is distorted and unworthy. Theorizing vices critically would put us in a better position to assess character assessments and the uses to which they are put, to ask whose interests the assessments serve and at whose expense.

Fourth, feminist critical character theory would, as Alison Jaggar says of feminist ethics generally, take women's experiences seriously but not uncritically, as every bit as worthy of respect as men's experiences and yet as likely to reflect in manifold ways the circumstances of domination and subordination within which women live and develop characters and moral conceptions of themselves as women and as good or bad.[44] Let me mention three of the many things I think taking women's experiences seriously for theorizing vice would involve. The first is attention to diversity among people who are differentially shaped by gender, race, class, ethnicity, sexual orientation, and social and historical context. This means taking seriously the possibility that character and character assessment may be deeply context dependent, that, for example, some vices may be specific to social positions. It also means recognizing that different kinds of people can have different developmental journeys to moral maturity and so not assuming, as so much mainstream theory does, that all humans are subject to the same deficiencies of character for which the same virtues are universally corrective. Consider, for example, the view that arrogant, overconfident self-assertion and desire for superiority is a vice, perhaps the central vice, to which all humans are inherently liable (it's what used to be called the sin of pride, the worst of the deadly sins), and that humility (as self-constraint, recognition of limitation, acknowledgment of lowness) is the corrective virtue and an excellent trait that all humans should cultivate in order to value themselves properly. This view is, I would argue, one that is deeply damaging to selves that tend to underdevelopment and self-abnegation as a result of subordination.

A second thing that taking women's experiences seriously would involve is taking seriously the complexity of the intrapsychic self that is shaped by multiple and sometimes fractious sources of social identity, recognizing, as Claudia Card does, that fragmentation of the self can be characteristic of selves formed under conditions of domination and oppression and that the resulting warring inclinations, needs, motivations, and so on, can distort character and make development or exercise of certain vices more likely or certain virtues less likely.[45] But we should also take seriously the possibility that there might be distinctive virtues that develop through or are called for in circumstances of psychic disunity, as well as certain traits that might in other circumstances reasonably be viewed as virtues (or vices) but that in these circumstances are better understood as vices (or virtues) because of their role in disabling (or enabling) individuals in the project of living well despite or through their psychic disunity.

A third thing that taking women's experiences seriously might involve is giving special emphasis to appropriate self-valuing as infusing some, if not all, virtues and inappropriate self-valuing as involved in or related to some, if not all, vices. Given the long tradition of, on the one hand, both requiring women's self-sacrifice and morally ignoring the ways in which it is absolutely essential to the sustenance of human life and moral community, and, on the other, regarding women's positive self-valuing (but not men's) as exhibiting the vice of selfishness, we would do well to center the moral importance of self-respect and proper self-love, not only as specific virtues but also as bases of anything that would count as a virtue. This suggests that it is not sufficient for re-identifying as a virtue something traditionally regarded as a vice that it is useful to subordinates for opposing and dismantling oppressive social conditions; it is also necessary, I would argue, that the trait express or support self-respect, and in particular, to borrow from Rawls, that it support the self-respect of those who have been least able to respect themselves.

The fifth dimension of feminist critical character theory is related to its emphasis on women's experiences: it would, as I stressed earlier, give special emphasis to issues of character development. With the notable exception of Aristotle, whose virtue ethics is, Okin argues, in many other ways a prime example of what a feminist theory of virtue would *not* look like,[46] most non-feminist philosophical theories of virtue ignore issues of character development. In particular, none of them, to my knowledge, addresses the character-focused tasks that are part of rearing children insofar as they take place within systems of domination and subordination. When virtue theorists address development, it is typically only through saying, "We have to learn to be good," but then focusing almost exclusively on adult character. Moreover, analyses of vice typically assume that adult individuals are wholly and solely responsible both for acquiring and for correcting vices in their characters. A feminist critical theory, however, would insist on carefully examining how people develop virtues and vices from early childhood on, examining the interpersonal, social, cultural, political, and educational contexts within which the characters of differently situated people develop differently, and examining the social conditions that make characters more or less resistant or amendable to change. This would connect with the feminist attention to the interrelatedness of humans and to conditions of dependency, vulnerability, immaturity, incapacity, and disability that affect all humans at various times in their lives and some humans for all of their lives. Feminist critical character theory would also ask how relations, practices, institutions, and responses at each of these levels to dependency, disability, and immaturity would have to be reconfigured so that no group of humans is excluded from the possibility of becoming and staying good, and no group is systematically subjected to conditions that distort character with vice and then make that vice hard to detect or dislodge.

Sixth, feminist critical character theory would problematize the central concepts of traditional virtue theory. One such concept is "human"; another is "happiness" or "flourishing." Most theories of character assume that character analysis applies to humans as such, not to particular groups of humans, that character psychology is universally human, and that vices and virtues are tied to human badness and goodness, human flourishing, and human happiness. Most virtue theories are, moreover, implicitly built on particular conceptions of human nature and human psychology. But feminist theorizing has shown us that conceptions of "human nature" are often really about only certain kinds of humans, namely, the dominant ones,[47] and that psychological theories of the structure and functioning of "normal" humans are often depictions of how dominants do or want to see themselves.[48] Thus, feminist critical theory asks of conceptions of vice and virtue, "what kind of human does this take as its model, and whose interests are reflected in and protected by the identification of this as a *human* vice or virtue?"

Similarly, most mainstream virtue theories also implicitly assume a particular conception of human happiness or flourishing, assume that happiness and flourishing so conceived are the same for all humans, and assume that virtues are traits that contribute to human happiness or are partially constitutive of human flourishing and that vices make flourishing impossible and may make happiness (or at least "true happiness") impossible as well. Lisa Tessman has called these assumptions into question by identifying ways in which oppression disrupts the presumed linkage between virtue and flourishing, arguing that resistance and liberatory struggle might well call for traits that are rightly called virtues but that are inimical to the flourishing of their bearer.[49] Similarly, if we assume that vices of domination are widespread, we might well think that it is not at all obvious that most or very many members of dominant groups, whose privilege depends on the subordination of other people, are not or cannot be happy or that their lives are not or cannot be regarded, by themselves or others, as flourishing, at least given familiar accounts of happiness and flourishing.[50] Thus, critical character theory might question the assumption that the happiness or flourishing of every human is intrinsically valuable, or might call for reconceptualizing flourishing or happiness, or might decenter or remove these concepts altogether as criteria for virtue and vice.

IV. RECONCEPTUALIZING "CHARACTER," "VICE," AND "VIRTUE"

"Human," "flourishing," and "happiness" are not the only concepts that feminist critical character theory would problematize. The most central concepts, those of character, vice, and virtue, would themselves be reconceptualized by feminist critical theorizing. This reconceptualizing would involve at least three things.

First, once we take unjust arrangements of power to be the central organizing concept for feminist theorizing, then since power is inevitably about social context, social relations among persons, and social institutions and practices, it follows that a feminist critical theory of character and hence of vice cannot be methodologically individualist about character or character traits. That is, character would not, from a critical perspective, be thought of as something that is "inside" individuals, a function or result solely of individual life choices, as traditional virtue ethics assumes. Character would, rather, be thought of as not only shaped by but also partially constituted by the complex interconnections and interactions among personal, interpersonal, cultural, social, and political structures, practices, ideologies, relations, and activities. Thus, vice and particular vices would not be seen simply as matters of facts about individuals' psychologies, such as an individual's motivations, values, and cognitive, affective, and desiderative dispositions, nor would vicious character traits continue to be viewed as states for which individuals are, as some virtue ethics seems to assume, primarily responsible for developing and solely responsible for maintaining or changing. Rather, character dispositions would be understood to be inculcated, nurtured, directed, shaped, and given significance and moral valence as vice or virtue in certain ways in certain kinds of people by social interactions and social institutions and traditions that situate people differentially in power hierarchies; and we would understand vices in and among individuals as, among other things, dispositions that support, direct, shape, and give significance and value to social interactions and institutions. So, to understand whether and how an individual is arrogant or compassionate or profligate or responsible and whether it is good or bad to be like this, a critical character theorist would not look only or even primarily "inside" the individual; she would also examine the sociopolitical context in which character develops and in which certain complexes of psychological elements are identified as character traits or not and are given meaning and moral valence in ways that can reflect and reinforce or subvert power hierarchies.

At the same time, however, critical character theory would not deny that human individuals (at least most of us much of the time, but not all of us all of the time) are, or are capable of becoming if circumstances are kind, fully agents, with powers and responsibilities that are morally relevant to the transformation of the characters of individuals and of societies. That is, critical theory recognizes that the characters of individuals are actively and continually shaped not only by interpersonal, cultural, social, and political dimensions of human living but also by and through the exercise of individual and collective agency in actively and continually shaping the personal, interpersonal, cultural, social, and political. To think of character from a critical feminist perspective would thus involve holding together in creative tension a perspective that views the individual through the social and a perspective that views the social through the individual.

The complex of perspectives also indicates a second dimension for reconceptualization. Character—as the original Greek meaning of the word, "engraved mark," invites—has traditionally been thought of as a fixed collection of relatively simple, isolable, and static traits that are expressed straightforwardly in action. A critical theory would think of character instead as fluid, dynamic, and contextualized, both bodily and socially, as better understood as processive rather than substantive, as capable of stability without being static,[51] the various expressions of which involve complex interactions among a host of psychological and interpersonal components, developmental aspects, and environmental features and cues. It may be useful to think of character and character "traits" the way geneticists now think of genes: as complex processes that play a major role in making us what we are and that underlie what goes on with us as living, embodied, and minded creatures and that underlie much of what can go wrong with us biochemically, cellularly, physiologically, and psychologically, but whose expression is by and large related in complicated ways to the interplay among a host of physical, developmental, and environmental factors. Our genetic make-up is real and matters enormously, but our genes and genetic processes turn out to be real and to matter in very complexly dynamic ways; the same may fruitfully be said of character.

The third thing I think a feminist critical reconceptualizing of character would involve is figuring out how to talk better about these things. The terms we have inherited—"character," "virtue," "vice"—are deeply problematic terms. Just as the term "character" invites us, etymologically, to think of character as fixed, so the term "vice" and particular vice terms are typically understood to invite blaming individuals for having vices. It is not unreasonable to hear that invitation, for the term "vice" is related etymologically to terms for fault, failing, blameworthiness, crime, offense, violation, injury, and uselessness.[52] But a revised understanding of character would call traditional activities of blaming into question, both as regards justification and as regards usefulness (recall Louise Antony's objection to centering vice in trying to understand oppression: telling people that their characters are vicious and challenging them to undertake personal reform is a strategy likely to backfire, inasmuch as "people deeply resent personal accusations"). Nuanced examinations from a feminist critical perspective of particular "vices" could give us the means for talking about certain kinds of distortions of character without being focused on blaming and yet without dismissing the possibility that blaming may be both morally appropriate and useful, for fully acknowledging not only the ways in which sociopolitical conditions shape and partially constitute character but also the ways in which individual agents, working "alone" and collectively, at the personal, intrapersonal, interpersonal, and social levels, have powers to take forward-looking responsibility for the kinds of persons that persons could become.

I conclude that it is very important for moral philosophers to theorize about moral life in societies that are structured by domination and subordination by doing three things: engaging theoretically and practically with "character" and with "vice" from a feminist critical perspective; reconceptualizing the understanding of "character" and the philosophical examination of "character" in sociopolitical contexts; and seeing "character," and especially "character" distorted by "vice," as both a site and source of oppression, as a center of resistance both to oppression and to change, and as both subject and object of liberatory struggle.

Notes

1. Among these are Lisa Tessman, *Burdened Virtues: Virtue Ethics for Liberatory Struggles* (New York: Oxford University Press, 2005); Lisa Tessman, "Critical Virtue Ethics: Understanding Oppression as Morally Damaging," in Peggy DesAutels and Joanne Waugh (eds.), *Feminists Doing Ethics* (Lanham, Md.: Rowman & Littlefield, 2001); Lisa Tessman, "Dangerous Loyalties and Liberatory Politics," *Hypatia* 13:4 (1998): 18–39; Lisa Tessman, "On (Not) Living the Good Life: Reflections on Oppression, Virtue, and Flourishing," *Canadian Journal of Philosophy* Supplementary Volume 28 (2002) on Feminist Moral Philosophy; Claudia Card, *The Unnatural Lottery: Character and Moral Luck* (Philadelphia: Temple University Press, 1996); Margaret McLaren, "Feminist Ethics: Care as a Virtue," in DesAutels and Waugh (eds.), *Feminists Doing Ethics*; Barbara S. Andrew, "Angels, Rubbish Collectors, and Pursuers of Erotic Joy: The Image of Ethical Women," in DesAutels and Waugh (eds.), *Feminists Doing Ethics*; Nancy Potter, "Is Refusing to Forgive a Vice?" in DesAutels and Waugh (eds.), *Feminists Doing Ethics*; Nancy Nyquist Potter, *How Can I Be Trusted? A Virtue Theory of Trustworthiness* (Lanham, Md.: Rowman & Littlefield, 2002); James Lindemann Nelson, "The Social Situation of Sincerity: Austen's *Emma* and Lovibond's *Ethical Formation*" in Peggy DesAutels and Margaret Urban Walker (eds.), *Moral Psychology: Feminist Ethics and Social Theory*, (Lanham, Md.: Rowman & Littlefield, 2004); Rebecca Wisnant, "Woman Centered: A Feminist Ethic of Responsibility," in DesAutels and Walker (eds.), *Moral Psychology*; Susan Moller Okin, "Feminism, Moral Development, and the Virtues," in Roger Crisp (ed.),

How Should One Live? (Oxford: Clarendon Press, 1996); Nancy Snow, "Virtue and the Oppression of Women," *Canadian Journal of Philosophy* Supplementary Volume 28 (2002) on Feminist Moral Philosophy; Margaret Urban Walker, "Moral Luck and the Virtues of Impure Agency," *Metaphilosophy* (January–April 1991): 14–27; Damien Cox, Marguerite la Caze, and Michael P. Levin, *Integrity and the Fragile Self* (Aldershot, U.K.: Ashgate, 2003); Joanne Woolfrey, "Feminist Awareness as Virtue: A Path of Moderation," *American Philosophical Association Newsletters: Newsletter on Feminism and Philosophy* 1–2 (2002): 64–67; Anita Superson, "Privilege, Immorality, and Responsibility for Attending to the 'Facts about Humanity,'" *Journal of Social Philosophy* 35 (2004): 34–55; Robin S. Dillon, "'What's a Woman Worth? What's Life Worth? Without Self-Respect!' On the Value of Evaluative Self-Respect," in DesAutels and Walker (eds.), *Moral Psychology*; Robin S. Dillon, "Kant on Arrogance and Self-Respect," in Cheshire Calhoun (ed.), *Setting the Moral Compass: Essays by Women Philosophers* (New York: Oxford University Press, 2004).

2. The impetus for calling for these changes is the realization in my own work on arrogance that both traditional and feminist approaches to analyzing character traits and vices of character were inadequate to ground what I want to be able to say about arrogance. I found that I needed to develop a different theoretical framework for analyzing character; this paper is a gesture toward such a framework.

3. This call was suggested to me by a recent move at the intersection of social psychology and personality psychology toward the development of what Suzanne Ouellette calls "a critical personality psychology." Within this approach, as Suzanne Ouellette says, "personality is understood to be an expression of (1) a multifaceted organization that includes individual, interpersonal, social, cultural, and political contexts; (2) individual and social change; and (3) the moral dimensions of human psychology." Suzanne C. Ouellette, "Notes for a Critical Personality Psychology: Making Room Under the Critical Psychology Umbrella," *Social and Personality Psychology Compass* 2:1 (2008): 1–20, 10.1111/j.1751-904.207.00039.x. See also Tessman, "Critical Virtue Ethics."

4. I will, at the end of the paper, urge that we discard the terms "virtue" and "vice," so I am uncomfortable using the terms without scare quotes. However, scare-quoting the terms throughout the rest of the paper will seem odd and be distracting, so I will use the terms without scare quotes although I really mean for them to be there.

5. I take the distinction between virtue ethics and virtue theory from Julia Driver, "The Virtues and Human Nature," in Crisp (ed.), *How Should One Live*, p. 111, n.1; and Christine Swanton, *Virtue Ethics: A Pluralist View* (Oxford: Oxford University Press, 2003), pp. 4–5.

6. Rosalind Hursthouse, *On Virtue Ethics* (Oxford: Oxford University Press, 1999); Michael Slote, *Morals from Motives* (Oxford: Oxford University Press, 2001); Swanton, *Virtue Ethics*.

7. Immanuel Kant, *The Metaphysics of Morals, Part II: Metaphysical First Principles of the Doctrine of Virtue* (*Die Metaphysik der Sitten. Metaphysische Anfangsgründe der Tugendlehre*, Akademie vol. 6, 1797); translated as "The Metaphysics of Morals," in *Practical Philosophy*, ed. and trans. Mary J. Gregor (Cambridge: Cambridge University Press, 1996); Julia Driver, *Uneasy Virtue* (New York: Cambridge University Press, 2001).

8. Michael Slote, personal communication. See Michael Slote, "Autonomy and Empathy," *Social Philosophy and Policy* 21:1 (2004): 293–309. See also Tessman, *Burdened Virtues* and "Critical Virtue Ethics."

9. Margaret Walker, "Seeing Power in Morality: A Proposal for Feminist Naturalism in Ethics," in DesAutels and Waugh (eds.), *Feminists Doing Ethics*, p. 4.

10. See, e.g., Susan Sherwin, *No Longer Patient: Feminist Ethics and Health Care* (Philadelphia: Temple University Press, 1992), pp. 54–55.

11. Max Horkheimer, *Critical Theory* (New York: Seabury Press, 1982), p. 244. Quoted in James Bohman, "Critical Theory," *Stanford Encyclopedia of Philosophy*, ed. Edward Zalta (http://plato.stanford.edu/entries/critical-theory/).

12. William Blake, "London," in *Songs of Experience* (1794); Sandra Lee Bartky, "Psychological Oppression," in Bartky, *Femininity and Domination: Studies in the Phenomenology of Oppression* (New York: Routledge, 1990).

13. See Ian Parker, "Critical Psychology: What It Is and What It Is Not," *Social and Personality Psychology Compass* 1:1 (2007): 1–15, DOI 10.1111 /j.1751-9004.2007.00008.x; here p. 2.

14. See the entries for "Virtue Ethics" and "Moral Character" in *The Stanford Encyclopedia of Philosophy*, where talk of character immediately shifts to talk of virtue. Marcia Homiak, "Moral Character," *Stanford Encyclopedia of Philosophy* (Fall 2008 Edition), Edward N. Zalta (ed.), http://plato.stanford.edu/archives/fall2008/entries/moral-character/; Rosalind Hursthouse, "Virtue Ethics," *Stanford Encyclopedia of Philosophy* (Fall 2008 Edition), Edward N. Zalta (ed.), http://plato.stanford.edu/archives/fall2008/entries/ ethics-virtue/.

15. Lisa Tessman asks the second question and develops the concept of "burdened virtues" to apply to traits "that could be recommended as virtues within the context of liberatory political movements," in that they are "practically necessitated for surviving oppression or morally necessitated for opposing it," but that impose a moral cost on their bearers, in that they may make it difficult or impossible for the bearer to flourish; *Burdened Virtues*, p. 4.

16. Okin, "Feminism, Moral Development, and the Virtues," p. 211.

17. I take inspiration about the goals of critical character theory from Alison Jaggar, "Feminist Ethics," in Lawrence C. Becker and Charlotte B. Becker (eds.), *Encyclopedia of Ethics*, 2nd ed. (New York: Routledge, 2001), p. 533.

18. One indication of this lack of attention: a quick search in the *Philosopher's Index* turned up nearly 3000 hits for the descriptor "virtue" but only about 88 for the descriptor "vice," of which only about 30 items were either

focused on vice or on particular vices, or asked of a quality, "is this a virtue or a vice?" It is interesting that in psychology, the focus in personality research was overwhelmingly on defects, malfunctioning, neuroses— "abnormal psych" and the psychological dimensions of "unhappiness"— until about ten years ago when there was a conscious effort to redirect attention to normal, good functioning, and happiness, to do "positive psychology." (See, e.g., Christopher Peterson, *A Primer in Positive Psychology* [New York: Oxford University Press, 2006]). Psychologists focused on what goes wrong in personality and only recently came to see that it was just as important to pay careful attention to what is good; moral philosophers have focused on what is good in character and have just barely begun to attend explicitly to what is bad.

19. David Hume, *Enquiry Into the Principles of Morals* (Indianapolis: Hackett, 1983 [1751]), Section IX "Conclusion," Part II. Annette Baier pointed me to this passage many years ago.

20. Cheshire Calhoun, comments prepared for symposium on *Setting the Moral Compass*, Central Division APA, April 19, 2008.

21. Cheshire Calhoun, *Moral Compass* comments.

22. Tessman, *Burdened Virtues*, p. 55

23. Tessman, *Burdened Virtues,* pp. 55, 77.

24. Anita Superson, "Privilege, Immorality, and Responsibility for Attending to the 'Facts about Humanity,'" *Journal of Social Philosophy* 35 (2004): 34–55.

25. Superson, "Privilege, Immorality," p. 38.

26. Louise Antony, "Comments on Superson," *Symposia on Gender, Race, and Philosophy* 2 (January 2006): pp. 1, 2; available at https://wikis.mit.edu/confluence/display/SGRP/January+2006+Symposium+II+(Superson).

27. Tessman, *Burdened Virtues*; Card, *Unnatural Lottery*.

28. Anita Superson argues for this, as does Margaret Walker, "Resentment and Assurance," in Calhoun (ed.), *Setting the Moral Compass*, pp. 145–60.

29. Ouellette, "Critical Personality Psychology."

30. Sally Haslanger, "Gender & Race: (What) Are They? (What) Do We Want Them to Be?" *Nous* 34 (2000): 31–55.

31. Karen Tumulty, "The Bitter Half," *Time*, March 10, 2008, p. 36.

32. Dillon, "Kant on Arrogance and Self-Respect," and *Arrogance: The Deadliest Sin?* in progress.

33. See, for example, among the older theorists, Augustine, *The City of God; Against the Pagans* (418 C.E.), trans. Philip Levine, Loeb Classical Library (London: William Heineman and Cambridge, Mass.: Harvard University Press, 1966), Book 14; Bernard of Clairvaux, *The Twelve Degrees of Humility and Pride* (1124 C.E.), trans. B. R. V. Mills (New York: Macmillan, 1929); Thomas Aquinas, *Summa Theologica,* trans. Fathers of the English Dominican Province (London: Burns Oates & Washborne, 1921), II, 2, Q. 161; and, among contemporary theorists, Robert C. Roberts and W. Jay Wood, "Humility and Epistemic Goods," in Michael DePaul (ed.), *Intellectual Virtue: Perspectives from Ethics and Epistemology* (Oxford: Clarendon Press, 2003).

34. To what extent has this shift from talking about "oppressors" or "members of the dominating group" to talking about "the privileged" been motivated by the consideration that Louise Antony raised: to call someone an oppressor or dominator is likely to be politically counterproductive, inasmuch as "people deeply resent personal accusations"?

35. The "backpack" metaphor is Peggy MacIntosh's; see, e.g., "White Privilege and Male Privilege," in Lisa Heldke and Peg O'Connor (ed.), *Oppression, Privilege, and Resistance* (New York: McGraw-Hill, 2004).

36. MacIntosh, for example, argues that while it is reasonable, even morally required, to extend certain privileges to everyone, there are other privileges that dominants can enjoy only because they are upheld by corresponding oppressions, and still others that no one ought to have. Thanks to Anita Superson for reminding me of this.

37. Tessman, *Burdened Virtues*.

38. These are among the "ordinary vices of domination" that Tessman nicely discusses.

39. Okin, "Feminism, Moral Development, and the Virtues," p. 211.

40. One of the earliest analyses is Lawrence Blum, Marcia Homiak, Judy Housman, and Naomi Scheman, "Altruism and Women's Oppression," *Philosophical Forum* 5 (Fall–Winter 1973): 222–47.

41. See Dillon, *Arrogance: The Deadliest Sin?* and "Kant on Arrogance and Self-Respect." Similarly, Nancy Potter has argued that being defiant and being unforgiving, typically regarded as a vices, could be seen as virtuous in oppressed people ("Defiance," paper presented at Pacific APA session on "Feminist Virtue Theory," March 26, 2006, and "Is Refusing to Forgive a Vice?") Lynne McFall makes a similar argument for the revaluation of bitterness in "What's Wrong with Bitterness?" in Claudia Card (ed.), *Feminist Ethics* (Lawrence: University Press of Kansas, 1991).

42. For example, think of the way in which giving attention and any priority to oneself is regarded as the hideous vice of selfishness in women but as normal and even necessary (for success, etc.) in men. To take another example, in the film *Out of Africa* (Universal, 1985), Meryl Streep's character, Karen Blixen, notes, on the occasion of her husband being called to war, that "men go off to be tested, for courage; if we are tested, it is for patience and doing without, or how well we can endure loneliness."

43. Consider: courage, pride, charity, modesty, humility, assertiveness, ambition, being self-sacrificing, obedience, self-control, knowing one's place, serenity, discretion, cheerfulness, perseverance, chastity, curiosity, nurturance; and meekness, vanity, impulsiveness, spitefulness, gullibility, rashness, boastfulness, complacency, ill-temperedness, bulliness, overprotectiveness, vengefulness, weakness of will, spitefulness...to name just a few.

44. Jaggar, "Feminist Ethics," p. 533.

45. Card, *Unnatural Lottery*.

46. Lisa Tessman, however, argues for a feminist Aristotelian virtues ethics in *Burdened Virtues*.

47. See, for example, Simone de Beauvoir, *The Second Sex*, and Elizabeth Kamark Minnich, *Transforming Knowledge* (Philadelphia: Temple University Press, 2005). As Minnich says, "The root problem...is, simply, that while the majority of humankind was excluded from education and the making of what has been called knowledge, *the dominant few not only defined themselves as the inclusive kind of human but also as the norm and the ideal.* A few privileged men defined themselves as constituting mankind/humankind and simultaneously saw themselves as akin to what mankind/humankind ought to be in fundamental ways that distinguished them from all others. Thus, at the same time they removed women and nonprivileged men within their culture and other cultures from "mankind," they justified that exclusion on the grounds that the excluded were by nature and culture "lesser" people...Their notion of who was properly human was *both* exclusive *and* hierarchical..." (p. 88).

48. For example, a systematic survey of forty years of gender difference research in four journals published by the American Psychological Association by Hegerty and Buechel found that "the psychological literature tends to contrast women's and girl's psychologies against an implicit male norm more often than the reverse" and conclude that men are "the prototype for modern psychology's picture of the typical person." This finding is "all the more striking as between 1965 and 2004 the journals studied ceased to be male-dominated. Roughly equal numbers of the study authors and roughly equal numbers of the participants in the studies now published in these journals are male and female" (P. Hegarty and C. Buechel, "Androcentric Reporting of Gender Differences in APA Articles, 1965–2004," *Review of General Psychology* 10 [2006]: 377–89). Quotations from a University of Surrey online press release of December 12, 2006, available at http://portal.surrey.ac.uk/portal/page?_pageid=799, 1258756&_dad=portal&_schema= PORTAL

49. Tessman, *Burdened Virtues.*

50. Marilyn Friedman, "Feminist Virtue Ethics, Happiness, and Moral Luck," *Hypatia* 24 (2009): 29–40.

51. I owe the ideas about process and stability to Mark Bickhard.

52. Charlton T. Lewis and Charles Short, *A Latin Dictionary*, available at http://www.perseus.tufts.edu/cgi-bin/resolveform?lang=la.

Bibliography

Andrew, Barbara S. 2001. "Angels, Rubbish Collectors, and Pursuers of Erotic Joy: The Image of Ethical Women." In Peggy DesAutels and Joanne Waugh (eds.), *Feminists Doing Ethics*. Lanham, Md.: Rowman & Littlefield, pp. 119–34.

Antony, Louise. 2006. "Comments on Superson." *Symposia on Gender, Race, and Philosophy* 2. Available online at https://wikis.mit.edu/confluence/display/SGRP/January+2006+Symposium+II+(Superson).

Aquinas, Thomas. 1274/1921. *Summa Theologica.* Literally translated by Fathers of the English Dominican Province. London: Burns Oates & Washborne.

Augustine. 418/1996. *The City of God; Against the Pagans.* Translated by Philip Levine. Loeb Classical Library. London: William Heineman and Cambridge, Mass.: Harvard University Press.

Bartky, Sandra Lee. 1990. "Psychological Oppression." In Bartky, *Femininity and Domination: Studies in the Phenomenology of Oppression.* New York: Routledge.

Beauvoir, Simone de. 1949/2009. *The Second Sex.* Translated by Constance Borde and Sheila Malovany-Chevallie. New York: Knopf.

Bernard of Clairvaux. 1124/1929. *The Twelve Degrees of Humility and Pride.* Translated by B. R. V. Mills. New York: Macmillan.

Blake, William. 1794/1984. "London." In Blake, *Songs of Experience.* Mineola, N.Y.: Dover.

Blum, Lawrence, Marcia Homiak, Judy Housman and Naomi Scheman. 1973. "Altruism and Women's Oppression." *Philosophical Forum* 5: 222–47.

Bohman, James. 2008. "Critical Theory." In Edward Zalta (ed.), *Stanford Encyclopedia of Philosophy*, http://plato.stanford.edu/entries/critical-theory/

Card, Claudia. 1996. *The Unnatural Lottery: Character and Moral Luck.* Philadelphia: Temple University Press.

Cox, Damien, Marguerite la Caze, and Michael P. Levin. 2003. *Integrity and the Fragile Self.* Aldershot, U.K.: Ashgate.

Dillon, Robin S. 2004a. "Kant on Arrogance and Self-Respect." In Cheshire Calhoun (ed.), *Setting the Moral Compass: Essays by Women Philosophers.* New York: Oxford University Press, pp. 191–216.

———. 2004b. " 'What's a Woman Worth? What's Life Worth? Without Self-Respect!' On the Value of Evaluative Self-Respect." In Peggy DesAutels and Margaret Urban Walker (eds.), *Moral Psychology: Feminist Ethics and Social Theory.* Lanham, Md.: Rowman & Littlefield, pp. 47–68.

Driver, Julia. 1996. "The Virtues and Human Nature." In Roger Crisp (ed.), *How Should One Live? Essays on the Virtues.* New York: Oxford University Press, pp. 111–30.

———. 2001. *Uneasy Virtue.* New York: Cambridge University Press.

Friedman, Marilyn. 2009. "Feminist Virtue Ethics, Happiness, and Moral Luck," *Hypatia* 24: 29–40.

Haslanger, Sally. 2000. "Gender & Race: (What) Are They? (What) Do We Want Them to Be?" *Nous* 34: 31–55.

Hegarty, P., and C. Buechel. 2006. "Androcentric Reporting of Gender Differences in APA Articles, 1965–2004." *Review of General Psychology* 10: 377–89.

Homiak, Marcia. 2008. "Moral Character." In Edward N. Zalta (ed.), *Stanford Encyclopedia of Philosophy* (Fall 2008 Edition), http://plato.stanford.edu/archives/fall2008/entries/moral-character/.

Horkheimer, Max. 1982. *Critical Theory.* New York: Seabury Press.

Hume, David 1751/1983. *Enquiry Into the Principles of Morals*. Indianapolis: Hackett.

Hursthouse, Rosalind. 2008. "Virtue Ethics." In Edward N. Zalta (ed.), *Stanford Encyclopedia of Philosophy* (Fall 2008 Edition), http://plato.stanford.edu/archives/fall2008/entries/ethics-virtue/.

———. 1999. *On Virtue Ethics*. Oxford: Oxford University Press.

Jaggar, Alison. 2001. "Feminist Ethics." In Lawrence C. Becker and Charlotte B. Becker (eds.), *Encyclopedia of Ethics*. 2nd ed. New York: Routledge.

Kant, Immanuel. 1797/1996. *The Metaphysics of Morals, Part II: Metaphysical First Principles of the Doctrine of Virtue* (*Die Metaphysik der Sitten: Metaphysische Anfangsgründe der Tugendlehre*). Vol. 6 in *Kant's gesammelte Schriften* (Berlin: Georg Reimer, 1907). Translated as "The Metaphysics of Morals," in Mary J. Gregor (ed. and trans.), *Immanuel Kant Practical Philosophy*. Cambridge: Cambridge University Press.

Lewis, Charlton T. and Charles Short. 1879. *A Latin Dictionary*. Available online at http://www.perseus.tufts.edu/cgi-bin/resolveform?lang=la.

MacIntosh, Peggy. 2004. "White Privilege and Male Privilege." In Lisa Heldke and Peg O'Connor (eds.), *Oppression, Privilege, and Resistance*. New York: McGraw-Hill, pp. 317–27.

McFall, Lynne. 1991. "What's Wrong with Bitterness?" In Claudia Card (ed.), *Feminist Ethics*. Lawrence: University Press of Kansas, pp. 146–60.

McLaren, Margaret. 2001. "Feminist Ethics: Care as a Virtue." In Peggy DesAutels and Joanne Waugh (eds.), *Feminists Doing Ethics*. Lanham, Md.: Rowman & Littlefield, pp. 101–18.

Minnich, Elizabeth Kamark. 2005. *Transforming Knowledge*. Philadelphia: Temple University Press.

Nelson, James Lindemann. 2004. "The Social Situation of Sincerity: Austen's *Emma* and Lovibond's *Ethical Formation*." In Peggy DesAutels and Margaret Urban Walker (eds.), *Moral Psychology: Feminist Ethics and Social Theory*. Lanham, Md.: Rowman & Littlefield, pp. 83–98.

Okin, Susan Moller. 1996. "Feminism, Moral Development, and the Virtues." In Roger Crisp (ed.), *How Should One Live?* Oxford: Clarendon Press, pp. 211–30.

Ouellette, Suzanne C. 2008. "Notes for a Critical Personality Psychology: Making Room Under the Critical Psychology Umbrella." *Social and Personality Psychology Compass* 2(1): 1–20, 10.1111/j.1751-904.207.00039.x.

Parker, Ian. 2007. "Critical Psychology: What It Is and What It Is Not." *Social and Personality Psychology Compass* 1 (1): 1–15, DOI 10.1111/j.1751-9004.2007.00008.x.

Peterson, Christopher. 2001. *A Primer in Positive Psychology*. New York: Oxford University Press.

Potter, Nancy. 2001. "Is Refusing to Forgive a Vice?" In Peggy DesAutels and Joanne Waugh (eds.), *Feminists Doing Ethics*. Lanham, Md.: Rowman & Littlefield, pp. 135–52.

Potter, Nancy Nyquist. 2002. *How Can I Be Trusted? A Virtue Theory of Trustworthiness*. Lanham, Md.: Rowman & Littlefield.

Roberts, Robert C., and W. Jay Wood, 2003. "Humility and Epistemic Goods." In Michael DePaul (ed.), *Intellectual Virtue: Perspectives from Ethics and Epistemology*. Oxford: Clarendon Press, pp. 257–79.

Sherwin, Susan. 1992. *No Longer Patient: Feminist Ethics and Health Care*. Philadelphia: Temple University Press.

Slote, Michael. 2001. *Morals from Motives*. Oxford: Oxford University Press.

———. 2004. "Autonomy and Empathy." *Social Philosophy and Policy* 21: 293–309.

Snow, Nancy. 2002. "Virtue and the Oppression of Women." *Canadian Journal of Philosophy* (Supplementary Volume 28: Feminist Moral Philosophy): 33–63.

Superson, Anita. 2004. "Privilege, Immorality, and Responsibility for Attending to the 'Facts about Humanity.'" *Journal of Social Philosophy* 35: 34–55.

Swanton, Christine. 2003. *Virtue Ethics: A Pluralist View*. Oxford: Oxford University Press.

Tessman, Lisa. 1998. "Dangerous Loyalties and Liberatory Politics." *Hypatia* 13(4): 18–39.

———. 2001. "Critical Virtue Ethics: Understanding Oppression as Morally Damaging." In Peggy DesAutels and Joanne Waugh (eds.), *Feminists Doing Ethics*. Lanham, Md.: Rowman & Littlefield, pp. 79–100.

———. 2002. "On (Not) Living the Good Life: Reflections on Oppression, Virtue, and Flourishing." *Canadian Journal of Philosophy* (Supplementary Volume 28: Feminist Moral Philosophy): 3–32.

———. 2005. *Burdened Virtues: Virtue Ethics for Liberatory Struggles*. New York: Oxford University Press.

Tumulty, Karen. 2008. "The Bitter Half," *Time*, March 10, 2008.

Walker, Margaret Urban. 1991. "Moral Luck and the Virtues of Impure Agency." *Metaphilosophy* (January–April): 14–27.

Walker, Margaret. 2001. "Seeing Power in Morality: A Proposal for Feminist Naturalism in Ethics." In Peggy DesAutels and Joanne Waugh (eds.), *Feminists Doing Ethics*. Lanham, Md.: Rowman & Littlefield, pp. 3–14.

———. 2004. "Resentment and Assurance," in Cheshire Calhoun (ed)., *Setting the Moral Compass: Essays by Women Philosophers*. New York: Oxford University Press, pp. 145–60.

Wisnant, Rebecca. 2004. "Woman Centered: A Feminist Ethic of Responsibility." In Peggy DesAutels and Margaret Urban Walker (eds.), *Moral Psychology: Feminist Ethics and Social Theory*. Lanham, Md.: Rowman & Littlefield, pp. 201–18.

Woolfrey, Joanne. 2002. "Feminist Awareness as Virtue: A Path of Moderation." *American Philosophical Association Newsletters: Newsletter on Feminism and Philosophy* 1–2: 64–67.

5

ANNE BARNHILL
Johns Hopkins University

MODESTY AS A FEMINIST

SEXUAL VIRTUE

INTRODUCTION

One of the most interesting philosophical accounts of sexual ethics—and one of the most frustratingly anti-feminist—is given by the moral philosopher and renowned conservative thinker, Roger Scruton.

In his book, *Sexual Desire*, Scruton identifies ethical ideals for sexual desire, sexual activity, and our erotic lives. According to Scruton, the paradigm case of sexual desire is desire for a person, and not desire just for a person's body or desire just for sexual contact. Scruton writes: "Sexual arousal has, then, an epistemic intentionality: it is a response to another individual, based in revelation and discovery, and involving a reciprocal and cooperative heightening of the common experience of embodiment. It is not directed beyond that individual, to the world at large, and it is not transferable to another, who "might do just as well."[1] And: "Only people can experience arousal and only people or imagined people can be the object of sexual arousal."[2]

According to Scruton, sexual desire is "inherently 'nuptial'"; sexual desire for a person prompts sexual activity with her, and this sexual activity leads naturally to knowledge of her, to intimacy with her, and ultimately to erotic love.[3]

According to Scruton, the flourishing sexual life is centered around erotic love for one person. But erotic love is possible only if we cultivate our sexual lives in certain ways: we must cultivate chastity, and we must avoid too much sexual fantasy and pornography. Scruton argues, in this way, for traditional, conservative sexual mores.

Scruton also argues for traditional *masculine* and *feminine* virtues. In "Modern Manhood," Scruton bemoans the demise of traditional marriage, in which men have the traditional masculine role of occupying the public sphere and women have the traditional feminine role of occupying only the private sphere. Scruton describes how this kind of marriage brought rewards accepted and appreciated by both men and women: "The two sexes respected each other's territory and recognized that each must renounce something for their mutual benefit."[4]

Scruton argues that traditional marriage was supported by traditional masculine and feminine virtues. The masculine virtues suit men to their masculine role of protector and provider: men should be courageous but not belligerent, protective but not possessive, even-tempered but not aggressive, and loyal. Feminine virtues complement the masculine virtues: women should match men's protectiveness and loyalty with the traditional feminine virtues of modesty and chastity. Scruton laments the denigration, by feminists, of these traditional masculine and feminine virtues: "And the feminist ideology has encouraged her to think that only one thing matters—which is to discover and fulfill her true gender identity, while discarding the false gender identity that the 'patriarchal culture' has foisted upon her. Just as boys become men without becoming manly, therefore, so do girls become women without becoming feminine. Modesty and chastity are dismissed as politically incorrect...."[5]

Along with arguing for traditional masculine and feminine virtues, Scruton argues that it's morally necessary to maintain masculine and feminine *appearance*. According to Scruton, gender categories and the physical manifestations of gender difference—the different appearance of men and women, the different hair, skin, demeanor, and especially the different clothes—are what humanize sexual activity.[6] So it's morally important for men and women to construct and maintain masculine and feminine appearances, especially in their style of dress.[7] (Scruton's argument for this claim is complex, and I explain it in more detail in this footnote.[8])

I disagree with most of Scruton's conclusions about gender, and think they can be refuted. But I present these conclusions here not so that I can refute them, but to give you a sense of Scruton's work on sexual ethics—work that I take as a model in many respects. Scruton exhorts us to think deeply about sex and romance: about what the ethically ideal sexual life is, about how our social context (especially feminism) has affected our sexual and romantic lives, and about how our sexual mores and sexual behavior in turn affect the social context. Scruton thinks about the body, and how our presentation of our bodies shapes our attitudes toward sex and our sexual partners and helps us or hinders us in recognizing our sexual partners as fully human. Scruton gives us a virtue ethics of sex: he describes what sexual flourishing is like—it's centered around erotic love (and traditional marriage)—and then he describes the character traits that allow and promote that kind of sexual flourishing.

In all of these ways, Scruton's work goes beyond most work on sexual ethics by analytic moral philosophers. Analytic sexual ethics is focused almost exclusively on the question of moral permissibility: under what conditions is it morally permissible to have sex? A standard answer given by analytic moral philosophers is: sex is morally permissible if and only if the participants give free and informed consent and it doesn't harm anyone. Most work on sexual ethics is an effort to refine this standard answer by determining exactly what counts as free and informed consent to sex. Is the consent of a drunk person sufficient? How informed must the consent be? At what age can people give free consent?

These questions about the conditions under which sex is morally permissible are important, but there's more to be said about sex. Also important are the questions asked and answered by Scruton's virtue ethics of sex: what is an ethically ideal sexual experience? What is it to flourish sexually? What are the character traits that allow an individual to flourish sexually? What are the character traits that support the social roles that allow individuals to flourish sexually? Sexual ethics should address these questions, and so should include a virtue ethics of sex—a virtue ethics that avoids Scruton's valorization of traditional, gendered virtues, gender roles, and gendered appearances. In other words, we should give a *feminist* virtue ethics of sex.

Scruton's project proceeds by describing sexual flourishing (which for Scruton is romantic, marital, and erotic flourishing), the social roles that allow sexual flourishing, and the character traits that support both those social roles and sexual flourishing. A feminist virtue ethics of sex that mirrors Scruton's project would identify then describe individual sexual flourishing, the social roles that allow sexual flourishing, and the character traits that support both those social roles and sexual flourishing. However, the character traits that allow individual flourishing might not be the character traits and social roles that support feminism. As Lisa Tessman has pointed out, one of the harms of oppression is that in some instances we must choose between counteracting sexism and flourishing as individuals.[9] For example, speaking out against sexism in the workplace can, realistically, chill a woman's relationships with her colleagues.

I think that sexual flourishing is a case in point. The sexual attitudes and behaviors that allow us to flourish sexually are often sexual attitudes and behaviors that perpetuate sexism rather than counteracting it; for example, sexually provocative dress and demeanor perpetuates sexism—or so I'll contend in this paper—but also arguably allows women to flourish sexually, given the expectation that women will display their bodies and their sexuality in provocative ways.

Thus there are two distinct kinds of feminist sexual virtues: those character traits that allow individual sexual flourishing given the realities of sexism, and those character traits related to sex that help to counteract sexism. We might optimistically try to identify character traits that are feminist virtues in both senses or we might, more realistically, identify character traits that are feminist virtues in one sense or the other.

Here I focus on identifying a character trait that is a feminist sexual virtue in the second sense: a character trait related to sex that helps to counteract sexism. This is the character trait—the virtue—of sexual modesty. Sexual modesty, I'll argue, helps to counteract rather than perpetuate the sexual dehumanization of women. But I don't think that sexual modesty is necessarily a virtue in the first sense; being modest doesn't necessarily allow individual sexual flourishing, rather than putting a damper on women's sex lives.

In identifying sexual modesty as a virtue for women, I find a point of agreement with Scruton (though Scruton and I might disagree about what exactly is the virtuous form of sexual modesty). But I put myself at odds with some feminist writers who, as I'll explain below, argue that women's sexually provocative display of their bodies and their sexuality is a feminist act.

SEXUAL MODESTY

Virtues are character traits. Character traits, as I understand them here, are dispositions to thought, feeling, and action. In the founding text of virtue ethics, the *Nicomachean Ethics*, Aristotle describes virtues by describing the vices that virtues are the mean between, and by identifying paradigms and pitfalls—paradigm behaviors that the possessor of the virtue performs, paradigm behaviors that the vicious man performs, pitfalls that the possessor of the virtue avoids, and pitfalls that the possessor of the virtue must be careful to avoid.

For example, Aristotle describes *liberality* (sometimes translated as "generosity"), the virtue concerning the proper use of money, as the mean between the vices of prodigality and meanness.[10] The liberal man avoids the extremes of prodigality and meanness/stinginess. A paradigm action of a mean/stingy man is lending money at a high interest rate, whereas a paradigm action of a prodigal man is giving away all his money and then taking money from other people. The liberal man avoids the pitfall of giving too much, so that he doesn't have enough left for himself. The liberal man also avoids the common pitfall of asking for too much from other people (in other words, being a mooch). The most likely pitfall is not giving away enough; this pitfall is more likely than asking too much from other people. So what's most characteristic of the liberal man is that he gives away enough, and in so doing avoids the most likely pitfall of not giving away enough.[11]

I will follow suit and describe the virtue of sexual modesty by identifying the vices that it's a mean between, and by identifying paradigms and pitfalls. The virtue of *sexual modesty* is a character trait relating to the sexual display of the body and expression of sexual thoughts and feelings. The sexually modest person displays her body in sexually provocative ways only when it's appropriate. The sexually modest person avoids the extremes of immodesty and prudery.

This description of sexual modesty is empty unless I also specify what exactly counts as immodesty and prudery, and *when* it's appropriate to display your body in sexually provocative ways. So when is it? My short answer, developed more fully in what follows, is *not that often*. Insofar as we're concerned with the feminist impact of women's bodily display—that is, insofar as we're judging it appropriate if it counteracts sexism and inappropriate if it contributes to/perpetuates sexism—it's not often appropriate for women to display their bodies in sexually provocative ways.

This is a controversial conclusion. We might've thought that sexual modesty is precisely what feminist women should avoid. Sexual modesty is, after all, a traditional feminine virtue: women should be chaste, and this chastity should be enabled and expressed by women dressing modestly and revealing their bodies only in prescribed ways, even if this requires women to wear uncomfortable and impractical clothing and prevents them from expressing themselves sexually.

In light of this history, we might conclude that sexual modesty is a pitfall that feminist women must take care to avoid—and that the feminist virtue is immodesty, not modesty. I think there *is* a pitfall here for women: women are in danger of not asserting their sexuality, given the historical background of controlling women's sexual activity and sexual expression. But the more likely pitfall for women—in particular, younger women—is that they display their bodies in ways that contribute to their own and other women's sexual objectification. Aristotle thought that a virtue is the mean between two extremes, but that the virtue errs away from the more common extreme. Following him, and thinking that sexual immodesty is the more common extreme for women, I conclude that the virtue of sexual modesty requires that women err on the side of not displaying their bodies in ways found to be sexually provocative.

Some feminist writers reach the opposite conclusion and advocate immodesty. For women to display their bodies and their sexuality in provocative ways, they argue, is consistent with gender equality and even is a component of the gender equality that women seek. I'll make my case for modesty by refuting this case for sexual immodesty. I'll first describe the aspect of gender inequality that forms the backdrop of this discussion: women are sexually objectified, and in particular, women more than men are cast as objects of sexual arousal rather than as subjects who feel sexually aroused. I'll then describe the case for sexual immodesty—the case that immodesty transforms, or at least avoids, the sexual objectification of women. I'll then refute the case for sexual immodesty by critiquing the initial account of sexual objectification: my criticism is that it's an incomplete account of the gender inequalities created by women's sexual display. With a more complete understanding of how women's sexual display perpetuates gender inequality, we'll see how immodesty perpetuates rather than mitigates it.

OUR SEXUALLY OBJECTIFYING SEXUAL CULTURE

American popular culture is sexist and it reinforces the sexism of American society; I'll take this as uncontroversially true. Here I focus on one much-discussed dimension of sexism: the sexual objectification of women. I focus in particular on one kind of sexual objectification of women that pervades American popular culture: women are presented as objects of sexual arousal whereas men are presented as subjects who feel sexually aroused.

American popular culture—as manifested in film and television, in advertising, in popular music, and on the internet—is saturated with sexually arousing depictions and images, and expressions of sexual arousal. Mainstream advertising tries ceaselessly to arouse us, especially if we're men: cars, shaving products, electronics, and much more are sold to men by associating these products with sexually arousing women. Mainstream films and television shows are cast with sexually attractive actresses who show off their bodies in sexually arousing ways—and to a lesser extent, cast with sexually attractive actors. Even news anchors are often sexualized, if they're women: for example, Katie Couric regularly shows some leg. And then there's internet porn and its endless articulation of the possibilities of sexual arousal. The argument that the primary medium of American popular culture is sexual arousal has been made by many groups (Christian conservatives, for example), and it is compelling even to those who do not share their conservative politics: so much of popular culture, no matter what its medium (film, television, music, internet, etc.) or its content (advertising, news, etc.) is designed to be sexually arousing.[12]

Our arousal-obsessed popular culture is focused disproportionately on what arouses heterosexual men, as opposed to heterosexual women or gay women or gay men. There's just less emphasis on what arouses women—fewer depictions or descriptions of it, less discussion of it—than on what arouses men. There's just less in our popular culture that's designed to sexually arouse women than to sexually arouse men.[13]

Our arousal-obsessed popular culture is focused on what's arousing to straight men and, in particular, is focused on presenting women's bodies in ways that are arousing to straight men. There are vastly more sexually provocative depictions of women's bodies than men's bodies in the popular media, and women more than men are encouraged to display their bodies in sexually provocative ways and are rewarded for that display. There's a high premium on being sexually arousing to men, if you're a woman—a higher premium than is placed on being sexually arousing to women if you're a man. Consequently women do display their bodies in sexually provocative ways more than men.

The greater emphasis on what arouses men than on what arouses women amounts to this: there's less emphasis on women as *subjects* who get aroused than on men as subjects who get aroused. There's more emphasis on women as *objects* of sexual arousal than on men as objects of sexual arousal. Women more than men are cast as objects of sexual arousal, and men more than women are cast as subjects who feel sexually aroused. For short, women are cast as sexual objects and men are cast as sexual subjects.

One sense in which women are cast as sexual objects is innocuous: women are the intentional objects of men's sexual arousal; women are what men find sexually arousing. But there are other, problematic senses in which women are cast as sexual objects. Women are cast as the arousing visual items, rather than the subjects who feel arousal. Women are cast as those who shape their appearance and behavior to fit others' sexual desires, rather than those whose subjective experience of arousal and desire sets the expectations that others try to meet. Women are treated more like sexual objects and less like sexual subjects than men, in both of these senses.

THE CASE FOR IMMODESTY

I turn now to the case for sexual immodesty made in some recent feminist writing.

A paradigm example is found in *Manifesta*, a book by feminists Jennifer Baumgardner and Amy Richards that lays out the landscape of contemporary American feminism. Baumgardner and Richards celebrate women's display of their bodies and their sexuality, and they see themselves as breaking with feminists of the past who found women's sexual self-display to be sexually objectifying. Baumgardner and Richards think that women's sexual self-display is not objectifying—or at least, it is not objectifying in a problematic way, and it is empowering as well as objectifying. They write: "Whether or not you believe, as Camille Paglia and others do, that showing herself in sexual ways makes a woman feel powerful and men powerless, there are positive examples of women's 'subjectification.' These women aren't objects, because they hold the power. The obvious 'subjectifier' is Madonna, but there is also hip-hop diva Missy Elliott, soccer pinup Brandi Chastain, and TV star Rosanne. All have parlayed their sexual selves into power in feminist ways. These women aren't exploited. They are whole women—both confident and conscious."[14]

Tamara Straus, a journalist who interviewed Baumgardner and Richards, writes, in a favorable description of their book *Manifesta*: "Third Wavers, say Baumgardner and Richards, want to continue the fight for equal rights, but not to the detriment of their sexuality. They want to be both subject and object, when it comes to their sexual roles, their political power and their place in American culture."[15]

In another excerpt from her interview of Richards and Baumgardner, Straus asks, "Why is sex or sexual self-esteem so important for this generation rather than issues of economic and social equality? Why has so-called lipstick or girlie feminism emerged?" Richards responded:

> What people don't understand is that talking about sex and sexual self-esteem is talking about equality. When I meet with high school students

and they want to discuss sex, I realize we are talking about equality. It's just a different path to the same goal. In our book, we put emphasis on the "Do-Mes," the lipstick feminists, because that's been our culture. I think we've seen women in our generation—*Bust* magazine is a great example of this—who say, adamantly, "I'm going to be female, and being female is just as valuable as being male." I don't think these women are saying, "I'm going to be female, going to be objectified, going to wear sexy clothes and so on and be part of the backlash against feminism." I think they're saying, "I'm going to do all these things because I want to embrace my femininity."[16]

In the same interview, Baumgardner said: "In our chapter on girlie culture, 'Barbie vs. the Menstrual Kit,' we argue that young women's primary expression these days is a joy and ownership of sexuality and that's a form of power, a type of energy."[17] These feminist writers give several arguments in favor of women flaunting it (that is, displaying their bodies and expressing their sexual thoughts and desires in sexually provocative ways). They argue that flaunting it doesn't exacerbate women's inequality but in fact promotes women's equality, because flaunting it gives women power. They also seem to be arguing that having a "lipstick" feminine sexuality is a way for women to assert the equality of men and women because it asserts the equality of femininity and masculinity.

They also argue—and this is the argument of interest here—that it's not sexually objectifying in a problematic way for women to flaunt it. This is because women who flaunt it can be sexual subjects even while they're seen as sexual objects: they are sexual subjects because they "own" their sexuality, they have their own sexual style (which presumably reflects their own sexual feelings and sexual desires), and they choose how to express themselves sexually.

THE CASE AGAINST IMMODESTY

There is a countervailing stream of feminist writing which argues that we're just fooling ourselves if they think that women's sexual self-display really empowers women or promotes gender inequality. Women's sexual self-display is just sexual objectification with an awful new twist: women are now complicit in their own sexual objectification to an unprecedented extent.

For instance, the writer Rochelle Gurstein expresses skepticism about women's sexual self-expression in her essay, "On the Triumph of the Pornographic Imagination." Gurstein considers the merits of "alt porn"—alternative porn made by young women, some of whom consider themselves feminists. Gurstein quotes the writer, Katie Roiphe, who is positive about alt porn:

> "Younger women today are growing more comfortable with their sexuality," she said, "and it makes perfect sense that they'd want to create a hip corner of the pornographic universe where they can express themselves."[18]

Gurstein, unlike Roiphe, is not persuaded that women's sexual display amounts to a valuable form of self-expression. Gurstein writes:

> "Naughty" S&M lingerie displays in the windows of upscale department stores; "cardio striptease" classes at health clubs; revealing fashions on the street—I wondered if Katie Roiphe had any of these hackneyed, stereotypical images of dominatrixes and porn stars and hookers in mind when she spoke with enthusiasm of how younger, more liberated women were "expressing themselves" in pornography. From what I could see, the erotic imagination of women had never been more flat.[19]

As Gurstein points out, it's not obvious that young women who flaunt their sexuality are expressing their own sexual feelings and desires, rather than mimicking the sexual display that pervades American culture.

Another worry is that women's motivation for expressing sexual desire and sexual arousal is that it makes them more sexually appealing to men. Most straight men are aroused by women's sexual arousal—a sexually aroused woman is a turn-on, and physical signs of arousal (parted lips, come-hither look, arched back) are common in sexually provocative images. So women might express arousal and desire because it makes them more sexually desirable to men—not because they really feel arousal or desire, and not because expressing arousal or desire in that way is satisfying or important to them. In this case, women's expression of arousal and desire is a way of conforming themselves to men's sexual desires—that is, the desire that women desire them and are aroused.

So we should worry that women's sexual self-expression isn't authentic—that the sexual feelings and sexual desire they express aren't their own (as Gurstein worries), and that their expression of sexual arousal and sexual desires isn't a satisfying form of self-expression but is an effort to conform to men's sexual desires. But let's put aside these worries here and assume that at least some cases of flaunting it are cases of authentic sexual self-expression. I want to argue that even these cases of authentic sexual self-expression are problematic.

Another immodesty critic is the columnist Maureen Dowd. In her book, *Are Men Necessary?* Dowd expresses dismay at the amount and kind of flaunting in our current sexual culture:

> Before it curdled into a collection of stereotypes, feminism had fleetingly held out a promise that there would be some precincts of womanly life that were not all about men. But it never quite materialized.
>
> It took only a few decades to create a brazen new world where the highest ideal is to acknowledge your inner slut. I am woman, see me strip. Instead of peaceful havens of girl things and boy things, we have a society where women of all ages are striving to become self-actualized sex kittens. Hollywood actresses now work out by taking pole-dancing classes.[20]
>
> A lot of women now want to be *Maxim* babes as much as men want *Maxim* babes. So women have traveled an arc from fighting objectification to seeking it.
>
> "I have been surprised," *Maxim*'s editor, Ed Needham, confessed, "to find that a lot of women would want to be somehow validated as a *Maxim* girl type, that they'd like to be thought of as hot and would like their boyfriends to take pictures of them or make comments about them that mirror the *Maxim* representation of a woman, the Pamela Anderson sort of brand. That, to me, is kind of extraordinary."[21]

Like Gurstein and Dowd, I'm skeptical of the merits of flaunting it. I think that the sexual self-expression of women that pervades American pop culture ultimately exacerbates gender inequality, even when this sexual self-display is freely chosen and makes the woman feel powerful, and makes her rich, like Madonna or Missy Elliot.

But there is something compelling about the idea that when a woman flaunts it, she is choosing how to express herself, and she is expressing that she has her own sexual feelings and desires, or at least her own sense of sexual style, her own sexual aesthetic.

How exactly is a woman being sexually *objectified* when she chooses to express her sexual feelings and sexual desires? Rather than sexual objectification, this does seem like an assertion that she has sexual subjectivity. Think of Madonna, or more recently, the hip-hop star Beyonce, flaunting it: they strut, they're confident they have their own unique style. They are expressing—asserting, even—that they are sexual subjects and unique sexual subjects.

Women who authentically express their sexual feelings and desires aren't casting themselves as sexual objects in the ways described above—they aren't casting themselves as objects of sexual arousal rather than subjects who feel sexually aroused, and they aren't conforming themselves to the sexual desires of men rather than asserting their own sexual desire. But there is a way in which this authentic sexual self-expression can be dehumanizing.

Even if women present themselves as sexual subjects (who have sexual desires and thoughts, get sexually aroused, and decide for themselves how to express themselves sexually), they still might be treated as nothing more than *sexual* subjects. Madonna and Beyonce are expressing that they're sexual subjects, but not expressing that they're intellectual subjects or spiritual subjects or professional subjects. Their expression of sexual subjectivity is merely the expression of *sexual* subjectivity, and not the expression of a complicated, multi-faceted subjectivity.[22] Even though they're presenting themselves as sexual *subjects* (in multiple ways) and not just sexual *objects*, they still are presenting themselves as merely sexual subjects, not complete, multi-faceted subjects.[23] In presenting themselves as merely sexual subjects, they are presenting themselves as less-than-full persons; we might say that they're *sexually depersonalizing* themselves, even if they're not strictly speaking sexually objectifying themselves.[24]

In presenting themselves as merely sexual subjects, women play into and reinforce the widely shared tendency to overvalue women's sexuality and focus on it rather than other aspects of them. We're disposed to notice and care about women's sexual properties, and disposed not to care nearly so much about women's other features; a woman's sexual attractiveness is quite often under consideration, and a woman's sexual attractiveness is quite often her most salient feature to us. Even when other aspects of a woman should be of primary or exclusive concern, we often focus on women's sexual attractiveness. Consider, for example, how much attention is given to the sexual attractiveness (or unattractiveness) of women news anchors, women athletes, and women politicians.

I'm claiming that when a woman presents herself as a merely sexual subject rather than a multi-faceted subject, she plays into this tendency to focus on her sexuality rather than other aspects of her. But this claim seems to ignore the fact that sexuality is a multi-faceted part of our personalities, incorporating bodily desires and bodily responses but also emotion, intellect, humor, and spirituality. An expression of this kind of multi-faceted sexuality is of necessity an expression of a multi-faceted subjectivity; so women can express their sexuality in a way that expresses many aspects of their personalities.

However—and regrettably—the expression of a multi-faceted sexuality isn't always interpreted as such. A woman who's trying to communicate something about the emotional and intellectual dimensions of her sexuality might succeed only in drawing sexual attention to her body and her bodily desires—especially when she's expressing her sexuality in sexually provocative ways. An authentic expression of multi-faceted sexuality often succeeds only in drawing attention to one dimension of her sexuality (her bodily desires and her body) that occludes all other aspects of her sexuality.

To make a long story short: I allow that women can display their bodies, and express themselves sexually, in ways that reveal their own sexual subjectivity rather than just positioning themselves as mere objects of sexual arousal. However, even if women succeed in being seen as sexual subjects rather than sexual objects, they still might be playing into and reinforcing the tendency to see women as primarily sexual subjects and to overvalue women's sexuality. Because we're more likely to sexually dehumanize women by overvaluing their sexuality rather than undervaluing it, the greater danger and the more likely pitfall—and hence the danger and pitfall that the virtuous feminist takes care to avoid—is that women contribute to their sexual dehumanization by displaying their bodies and their sexuality. So the virtuous feminist errs on the side of modesty rather than immodesty.

There is a necessary qualification of this conclusion. Our tendency to see women as primarily sexual subjects is not a tendency to see *all* women equally as primarily sexual subjects. The sexuality of some women is overvalued as a part of themselves, but the sexuality of other women is undervalued. The sexuality of some women is too salient to us, but the sexuality of some women is almost invisible to us. For instance, we tend to overvalue the sexuality of younger women but to undervalue the sexuality of older women, perhaps because we just don't see older women as sexual anymore.[25] The undervaluation of women's sexuality, like the overvaluation of it, is a form of sexual dehumanization—a way of treating someone as a less-than-full person.

There are cases in which flaunting it can work against a tendency to undervalue or even ignore a woman's sexuality. For example, when older women assert that they're still sexually desirous and sexually active, this works against the tendency to see older women as no longer sexual. The lesson here is that the appropriate kind of sexual self-display for a woman depends upon the social forces she's contending with—whether others are apt to overvalue her sexuality or to undervalue it. So what counts as sexual modesty—as the golden mean between too little sexual expression and too much sexual self-display—is different for different women.[26]

A FEMINIST *VIRTUE ETHICS* OF SEX?

In this paper, I've identified sexual modesty as a character trait that encourages feminist change of our sexually objectifying and thereby sexist sexual culture. This project is the beginning of what I'm calling a *feminist virtue ethics of sex*—identifying the character traits that encourage feminist change. It's obvious that my project is feminist, and that it's concerned with sex, but it is, I must admit, somewhat controversial that my project is virtue ethics.

A first worry is that my project deviates fundamentally from Aristotelian virtue ethics. According to Aristotelian virtue ethics, virtue is essentially connected to individual flourishing. In Aristotle's (translated) words, flourishing is the "prize and end of virtue" and is "an activity of the soul in accordance with perfect virtue."[27] Flourishing consists of being virtuous.[28]

The connection between virtue and individual flourishing that's central to Aristotelian virtue ethics drops out of my virtue ethics project and is replaced with a connection between virtue and social change. I identify a character trait that has a beneficial effect—it encourages feminist change (though, of course, one virtue alone won't cause wholesale social change). But modesty isn't a virtue in the Aristotelian sense that links virtues to the individual's flourishing. My feminist virtue ethics project departs from Aristotelian virtue ethics in a fundamental respect.

But this departure from Aristotelian virtue ethics is an important revision of it. As Lisa Tessman points out, the character traits that allow individual flourishing might not be the character traits that encourage social change. The golden means that allow individual flourishing might not be the means that encourage social change—social change might require more courage, more anger, or more generosity than individual flourishing requires. Given this, we should clearly distinguish the theoretical project of describing individual flourishing, and the character traits that allow it, from the theoretical project of describing social ideals (i.e., gender equality) and the character traits that promote them. These two projects *are* interrelated: for instance, one aspect of individual flourishing is having equal rather than domi-nating personal relationships, and one aspect of the social ideal of gender equality is that women flourish as individuals as much as men. But however interrelated, these projects are distinct and conflating them will breed confusion.

I've argued here that sexual modesty is a feminist sexual virtue in the sense that it is a character trait that promotes feminist change. In favoring modesty as a virtue, I make a point of contact with Scruton—though it's a single point of contact, as Scruton and I have very different reasons for favoring modesty. Though I argue that modesty is a virtue in one sense, I don't claim that sexual modesty allows individual women to flourish sex-ually in our society. Receiving less sexual attention might take a toll on individual women's sex lives (e.g., they'll have fewer or no sexual part-ners). Forgoing authentic sexual self-expression might have psychological and emotional costs for women. Doing what promotes feminist change won't always be in the best interests of individual women. This is something that, as Tessman writes, we should grieve and should be mad about, but not something that we should deny.[29]

There's a second reason to worry that despite a superficial simi-larity to virtue ethics, my project of figuring out which character traits promote feminist change is not properly classified as virtue ethics. Some moral philosophers claim that for an ethical theory to be a virtue ethics, it must give us a theory of right action that's an alternative to deontology and consequentialism, and in particular it must claim that virtue/character in some sense has priority over the right and the good.[30] The thought is that deontologists prioritize the right over the good and consequentialists prioritize the good over the right, so if virtue ethics is to be a genuine alternative to both deontology and con-sequentialism, it must prioritize virtue or character over the right and the good.

Let's call this demand the priority demand: for an ethical theory to be a virtue ethics, it must assign virtue/character priority over the right and the good. There are different kinds of priority that virtue/character is claimed to have over the right and the good. According to Gary Watson, the defining feature of a virtue ethics is that character has *explanatory* priority over action. He writes: "An ethics of virtue is . . . the claim that the basic moral facts are facts about the quality of character." And: "On an ethics of virtue, how it is best or right or proper to conduct oneself is explained in terms of how it is best for a human being to be. I will call this the claim of explanatory priority."[31]

According to Watson, the explanatory priority of virtue requires that being virtuous is intrinsically valuable. Only when virtue is intrinsically valuable is virtue explanatorily prior to the good and the right. What is *not* a virtue ethics according to Watson, because it doesn't make the priority claim, is the theory that virtues are character traits that are valuable because they tend to promote flourishing. According to Watson's accounting, this is a consequentialist theory, because what's taken as basic—what's explanatorily prior—is the good state of affairs (flourishing) and not virtue. The virtues are valuable *because* they promote flourishing; what explains the value of the virtues is the value of the state of affairs (flourishing) they promote.

Watson would, similarly, classify my feminist virtue ethics of sex as a consequentialist view rather than a virtue ethics: what explains the value of the virtues is the state of affairs (a less sexist society) they promote, not the intrinsic value of virtue.

Along with failing Watson's version of the priority demand (i.e., a theory is a virtue ethics only if it claims the explanatory priority of virtue), my feminist virtue ethics of sex also fails other versions of the priority demand. Roger Crisp and Michael Slote describe a different way in which virtue can have priority over the right and the good: the rationality of right action and of goodness-promoting action is based in the rationality of virtue. In other words: virtue-based moral reasons are the most basic moral reasons.[32] My virtue ethics project is silent on this priority issue; I don't claim that virtue-based moral reasons are the most basic moral reasons.

Another way in which virtue has priority over the right is this: we cannot even specify principles of right action; all we can say is that the right actions are those that would be performed by the virtuous person. Stephen Gardiner identifies another, fourth kind of priority in his discussion of Seneca's virtue ethics.[33] According to Gardiner, the key priority issue is not whether we can specify moral principles (rather than just saying, right actions are those that would be performed by the virtuous person). Rather, the key priority issue is whether the principles are accessible to everyone or only to the virtuous person. Seneca's view, according to Gardiner, is that only the virtuous person can fully understand the evaluative concepts that feature in these principles—only the virtuous person can fully understand what's virtuous.

My virtue ethics project is again silent on the last two priority issues. I don't claim that it's impossible to specify principles of right action; nor do I claim that only the virtuous person can understand what's virtuous.

So if any of these versions of the priority demand are true (that is, if a virtue ethics must claim that virtue has priority in one of these senses), then my project fails to be a virtue ethics.

But I reject the priority demand. Why must an ethical theory claim priority for virtue in order to be properly classified as "virtue ethics"? Why must we accept this definition of virtue ethics?[34] Insistence on the priority view is based in a particular and overly restrictive way of classifying ethical theories—that we classify them according to which moral facts they claim are prior. Determining which moral facts are the basic moral facts is an important theoretical project, so it's useful to distinguish ethical theories according to the relative priority they assign to facts about the right, facts about the good, and facts about virtue. But there are other important theoretical projects, and so other differences between ethical theories that are usefully marked, and so other ways to classify ethical theories.

What I consider importantly different about my virtue ethics project as compared to deontological and consequentialist analyses is not that virtue has priority over the right and the good, but that the concepts and terms used to describe moral reality are virtue concepts and terms. This feature of a virtue ethical analysis makes it especially well-suited for feminist analysis of personal conduct. This is because moral judgments that employ virtue concepts and terms are often more compelling—and more motivational and therefore more likely to change behavior—than moral judgments employing the concepts and terms characteristic of consequentialist or deontological theory.

Allow me to illustrate this point with examples. Responding to someone's mistreatment of an animal with the judgment "That's cruel" or "That's brutal" is more compelling than responding with "That causes more suffering than good and it doesn't maximize utility to cause more suffering than good" or "That causes excessive harm" or "That violates the animal's rights."

To give another example, responding to someone who doesn't speak out against a sexist joke with "That's cowardly" is more compelling than responding with "Your silence will contribute to gender inequality" or "By being silent, you're failing to acknowledge the equal worth of all people."

These virtue judgments are more compelling and motivational for the simple reason that they employ moral concepts that we use most frequently in our everyday lives and hence are most familiar with, as opposed to the unfamiliar or less familiar concepts, terms, and principles of deontological and consequentialist theory.[35]

These virtue judgments are also more compelling and motivational for another reason: many people are more motivated to change behavior that reflects badly on their character than behavior that is morally wrong but doesn't otherwise reflect badly on their character. People don't want to be cowardly or brutal, and to be seen as cowards or brutes; some people take note of the judgments that they're being cowardly or brutal, even after they've become inured to the charge that their behavior contributes to sexism or violates animal rights.

For both of these reasons, virtue judgments are more motivational than the judgments characteristic of deontological and consequentialist theory involving harm, equality, utility, rights, and so forth.[36] In this way, virtue has what we might call *motivational priority* over the right and the good: we're typically more motivated by virtue judgments.[37]

Thus even if we accept the priority demand—that an ethical theory is a virtue ethics only if it asserts that virtue/character have priority over the right and the good—we can classify my project here as a kind of virtue ethics. And we can see one reason why feminist theorists would want to give a virtue ethics of this kind: not because we think virtue has explanatory priority or rational priority and we're concerned to give a theory about the explanatorily or rationally basic moral facts, but because virtue concepts are motivationally prior and we're concerned to give a moral theory that will actually help motivate people to change.

Notes

1. Scruton, *Sexual Desire*, 30.
2. Scruton, *Sexual Desire*, 36.
3. I don't think this is a claim about the typical case of sexual activity, or the paradigm case of sexual activity. I think that Scruton is giving us an ethical ideal for sexual activity: in ideal cases, sexual activity leads to erotic love.
4. Scruton also writes: "Marriage was once permanent and safe; it offered the woman social status and protection, long after she ceased to be sexually attractive. And it provided a sphere in which she was dominant. The sacrifice permanent marriage demanded of men made tolerable to women the male monopoly over the public realm, in which men competed for money and social rewards." (Scruton, "Modern Manhood.") The flawed logic of this passage is worth noting: even if traditional marriage did afford women social status and protection, why is the social status and protection that comes with traditional marriage better for women than the social status and protection that comes from having your own career?
5. Scruton, "Modern Manhood."

6. Scruton acknowledges that the outward, visible manifestation of gender is to some extent a social construction, while still insisting that gender is not *just* a social construction and is more than skin deep: "The artifact of gender is not merely one of display. Men and women develop separate characters, separate virtues, separate vices and separate social roles. The modern consciousness is less disposed to admit those facts than was Aristotle, say, or Hume. Nevertheless, it cannot be denied that, whatever men and women ought to do, they have persistently conspired to create an effective 'division of moral labour,' with the virtues and aptitudes attributed to the one sex being complemented, but by no means always imitated, by the other." Scruton, *Sexual Desire*, 267.

7. Scruton, *Sexual Desire*, 268–69, 272–73.

8. If the target of sexual desire is a mere body, then sexual activity is a mere animal act. To transform sexual activity into a human act (rather than a mere animal act), the target of sexual desire must be a person (rather than a mere body). When we gender bodies—when we notice and accentuate the physical differences between male and female bodies, and we attach meaning and personal attributes to these physical differences—we transform them from the bodies of two kinds of animal (male and female) into the bodies of two distinct kinds of person (masculine and feminine persons). Scruton writes: "The basic differences between the sexes—hair, skin, voice, form and movement—are redeemed from their arbitrariness by being represented as integral to a moral condition"—that is, the moral condition of being an instance of the moral kind "man" or an instance of the moral kind "woman." For example, women's bodies are softer than men's, and we take this softness to represent something about women's characters—that they are passive. When we experience a soft body, we experience it as the body of a person who's passive, rather than experiencing it just as a body. By reading meaning into the physical differences between male bodies and female bodies, we can read meaning off those bodies—and thereby avoid experiencing our sexual partners' bodies as mere bodies. Scruton writes: "Given the existence of gender, we can no longer assume that the sexual act between humans is the same act as that performed by animals. Every feature of the sexual act, down to its very physiology, istransformed by our conception of gender. When making love I am consciously being a man, and this enterprise involves my whole nature, and strives to realise itself in the motions of the act itself…It is 'man uniting with woman' rather than 'penis entering vagina' which focuses their attention." Scruton also writes: "The argument that I have given suggests at least that something integral to the experience of sex is missing without it. Without gender, sex ceases to play a part in human embodiment, and the sexual act, far from being liberated from its 'mere animality', is in fact detached from its most natural moral interpretation." Scruton, *Sexual Desire*, 277, 268.

9. Tessman, *Burdened Virtues*.

10. "Liberality, then, being a mean with regard to giving and taking of wealth, the liberal man will both give and spend the right amounts and on the right objects, alike in small things and in great, and that with pleasure; he will also take the right amounts and from the right sources" Aristotle, *Nicomachean Ethics*, 39.

11. Aristotle writes: "Hence it is more the mark of the liberal man to give to the right people than to take from the right sources and not to take from the wrong…It is easier, also, not to take than to give; for men are apter to give away their own too little than to take what is another's." Aristotle, *Nicomachean Ethics*, 38.

12. It's not just our popular culture as elaborated in the media that's overly focused on sexual arousal. Our dominant sexual identities—heterosexual, homosexual, bisexual, and also pedophile, fetishist, etc.—categorize people according to who or what they sexually desire and find arousing. We consider a man to be homosexual if he primarily desires and is aroused by men, even if he never has sex with men. We could have different sexual categories that define people not by what arouses them, but by some other feature of their sexual lives. For example, in Macedonia, the group of men who are classified as "gay" is not men who are sexually attracted to other men, or men who have sex with other men, but men who are penetrated by other men (though "gay" is not an adequate translation, because there's just a very different concept in play). Sasho Lambevski, "Suck my nation: Masculinity, ethnicity, and the politics of (homo)sex," 414.

13. This is an empirical claim that I don't have hard evidence for, but I think it is uncontroversially true; I'll just assert it.

14. Baumgardner and Richards, *Manifesta*, 103.

15. Straus, "Manifesto for Third Wave Feminism," 1.

16. Straus, "Manifesto for Third Wave Feminism," 1.

17. Straus, "Manifesto for Third Wave Feminism," 1.

18. Gurstein, "On the Triumph of the Pornographic Imagination."

19. Gurstein, "On the Triumph of the Pornographic Imagination."

20. Dowd, *Are Men Necessary*, 175.

21. Dowd, *Are Men Necessary*, 183.

22. But don't we often present only one aspect of our subjectvity? Yes. Often this is unproblematic; for example, my tennis partner experiences only the tennis-player aspect of my subjectivity, and there's nothing wrong with that. What's problematic is when the emphasized aspect occludes other aspects of our subjectivity—even when these other aspects should become salient. This is what too often happens with women's sexuality—people remain focused on their sexuality when other aspects of their subjectivity should become salient (e.g., we remain focused on the sexual appeal of women athletes and women journalists when their performance of their jobs should be salient).

23. In another paper in progress ("Sexual Objectification and Sexual Subjectification"), I discuss this phenomenon in more detail and term it

sexual subjectification. Sexual subjectification, as I define it, is *seeing or treating someone as a primarily sexual subject.*

24. "Sexual objectification" is sometimes used to refer to any sexual treatment that's demeaning or sexist or, more generally, that fails to treat someone as a full and equal person. However, we might use "sexual depersonalization" to refer to sexual treatment that fails to treat someone as a full and equal person, and reserve the term "sexual objectification" for treating someone, more precisely, in a way that objects are typically treated. One might protest that treating someone as less than a full and equal person is treating her in a way that objects are typically treated, but to understand objectification so broadly blunts the concept in a way that probably won't improve theoretical work on objectification.

25. We also tend to overvalue the sexuality of women who conform to mainstream standards of sexual attractiveness more than women who don't so conform—but this is complicated, because women with certain non-mainstream sexualities *are* intensely sexually subjectified. An example is the sexual subjectification of lesbians by some people: their sexuality is of primary concern and eclipses all else. Some people don't see the whole person but just the lesbianism.

26. Also, what counts as sexual modesty varies for different societies.

27. Aristotle, *Nicomachean Ethics*, 10, 13.

28. Julia Annas writes: "How do the virtues contribute to my flourishing? Classical theories of virtue ethics claim that virtue is, more weakly, necessary, or, more strongly, sufficient for flourishing. How is this to be understood? Classical virtue theories reject the idea that flourishing can be specified right at the start, in a way that is both substantive and makes no reference to the virtues... Rather, virtue ethics tells us that a life lived in accordance with the virtues is the best specification of what flourishing is." Annas, "Virtue Ethics," 521.

29. I've identified a kind of virtue—doing what promotes feminist change—and acknowledged that being virtuous in this way might impede a woman's own flourishing. But do women have a moral obligation to be virtuous in this way, even though it impedes their flourishing? I think so, but I won't justify that position here because that would require addressing a number of issues: do we have a moral obligation to address social injustice that we didn't cause? When a behavior contributes only marginally or negligibly to injustice, are we required to refrain from that behavior? What costs are we required to bear in order to address injustice?

30. Watson, "On the Primacy of Character"; Crisp and Slote, *Virtue Ethics.*

31. Watson, "On the Primacy of Character," 232.

32. It's not obvious from what Crisp and Slote write that their "rational priority" of virtue is different from Watson's "explanatory priority" of virtue. Crisp and Slote write: "How, then, is a virtue ethicist to carve out his or her own niche? It must be by providing an account of ultimate moral reasons which not only is neither utilitarian nor Kantian, but makes essential

reference to the rationality of virtue itself. Thus, for example, the real reason why I should not lie to you is not that it is against the moral law, nor that it is likely not to maximize well-being, but because it is dishonest. The notions of virtue, then, are more basic than the notions at the heart of utilitarian and Kantian theory. They may even replace some of these notions, including perhaps 'obligation' itself. The virtue ethicist at least does not need such language. Certainly, it is characteristic of modern virtue ethics that it puts primary emphasis on aretaic or virtue-centered concepts rather than deontic or obligation-centered concepts." Crisp and Slote, *Virtue Ethics*, 3.

33. Stephen Gardiner, "Seneca's Virtuous Moral Rules."

34. Admittedly, this is merely a terminological issue—a tussle over who gets to apply the term "virtue ethics" to her theory. But it's an important terminological issue. At stake, potentially, is the relegation into obscurity of theories of virtue that aren't crowned "virtue ethics."

35. Admittedly, it is possible to translate *some* deontological judgments, such as "the maxim you're acting on is one that you cannot will be universally accepted" into familiar moral exhortations, such as "What if everyone did that?" and "Why are you so special that you get to treat others like that?"

36. As Rosalind Hursthouse points out, Elizabeth Anscombe makes a related point in her famous essay, "Modern Moral Philosophy": moral rules employing virtue and vice terms (e.g., "Do what is charitable") succeed, as a matter of fact, in giving us a great deal of specific action guidance. Hursthouse, "Virtue Ethics."

37. This is not to say there's no place for theories of the right or the good. There are moral truths about what's right and what's good that are best expressed in terms of rights, equality, utility, harm, and so on.

References

Annas, Julia. 2006. Virtue ethics. In *The Oxford companion to ethical theory*, ed. David Copp. New York: Oxford University Press.

Anscombe, G. E. M. 1958. Modern moral philosophy. *Philosophy* 33:1–19.

Aristotle. 2005. *Nicomachean ethics*. Trans. W. D. Ross. Stilwell, Kans.: Digireads. com Publishing.

Baumgardner, Jennifer, and Amy Richards. 2000. *Manifesta*. New York: Farrar, Straus, and Giroux.

Crisp, Roger, and Michael Slote, eds. 1997. *Virtue ethics*. Oxford: Oxford University Press.

Dowd, Maureen. 2005. *Are men necessary? When sexes collide*. New York: G. P. Putnam's Sons.

Gardiner, Stephen. 2005. Seneca's virtuous moral rules. In *Virtue ethics, old and new*, ed. Stephen Gardiner. Ithaca, N.Y.: Cornell University Press.

Gurstein, Rochelle. 2005. On the triumph of the pornographic imagination. *The New Republic Online*. http://www.tnr.com/article/books-and-arts/the-triumph-the-pornographic-imagination (accessed September 1, 2009).

Hursthouse, Rosalind. 2009. Virtue ethics. In *The Stanford Encyclopedia of Philosophy* (Spring 2009 Edition), ed. Edward N. Zalta. http://plato.stanford.edu/archives/spr2009/entries/ethics-virtue/ (accessed September 1, 2009).

Lambevski, Sasho. 1999. Suck my nation: Masculinity, ethnicity, and the politics of (homo)sex. *Sexualities* 2(4):397–419.

Scruton, Roger. 1999. Modern manhood. *City Journal* 9(4). http://www.city-journal.org/html/9_4_a3.html (accessed July 16, 2011).

———. 1986. *Sexual desire.* New York: The Free Press.

Straus, Tamara. 2000. A manifesto for Third Wave feminism. *AlterNet.* http://www.alternet.org/story/9986/ (accessed S 1, 2009).

Tessman, Lisa. 2005. *Burdened virtues: Virtue ethics for liberatory struggles.* New York: Oxford University Press.

Watson, Gary. 2003. On the primacy of character. In *Virtue ethics*, ed. Stephen Darwall. Malden, Mass.: Blackwell Publishing.

6

ANITA M. SUPERSON
University of Kentucky

STANDARDS OF RATIONALITY

AND THE CHALLENGE OF THE MORAL

SKEPTIC

I. THE ISSUE

Several years ago a publisher invited me to write a short book on how men benefit from feminism. I agreed to do this, but only after I finished my long book on moral skepticism. I realized quickly that these issues bore great similarity to each other, if they were not exactly the same: "How do men benefit from feminism?" seems much the same as the age-old question, "Why be moral?" Each question is asked from the perspective of self-interest, or "What's in it for me?" The skeptic who asks, "Why be moral?" wants it to be shown that each person can expect to benefit more from being in a world with morality than in one without, from having a moral character or disposition, and from acting morally on any occasion. The person who asks, "How do men benefit from feminism?" wants it to be shown that for each man, he can expect to benefit from a world absent women's oppression instead of a world with patriarchy firmly in place, from being disposed to feminism, and from acting in feminist ways, that is, ways consistent with ending women's oppression. And upon further reflection, I began to think that the question of how men benefit from feminism was fundamentally misguided, and in a way different from the way some people think the traditional construal of the skeptic about acting morally is misguided. The latter is misguided because we can never justify acting morally on every occasion—even if we could show that it was to each person's advantage to be in a moral world and to be morally disposed—to a skeptic steeped in a self-interest model of rational choice and action, because of the many cases of conflict between morally required and self-interested action. And even if we could show this, doing so would, as David Gauthier claims, make morality otiose because all talk of moral reasons could be replaced with talk of self-interested reasons.[1]

The question about men's benefiting from feminism, though, raises the worry that it takes a position of privilege, namely, men's social privilege, as the one to defeat. Why should we have to defeat *this* position, having to appeal to a person who does not have to concede unless it is in his self-interest? After all, the challenge of the skeptic about acting morally is uninteresting or unimportant if it is asked from a position of privilege, since there is no problem for morality if it turns out that privileged people who exploit others have no interest in giving up their position of privilege. Furthermore, this position takes an instrumental view of persons, which automatically puts women in a disadvantaged position in patriarchal societies. It will be difficult to answer the question about men's benefiting from feminism in a way that is acceptable to feminists, who are likely to insist that all persons have intrinsic value in virtue of being persons. The question of men's benefiting from feminism got me thinking more about the traditional approach to defeating skepticism about acting morally, and what feminists might have to say about it. The issue I want to take up is whether the traditional view of the skeptic is doomed from the very start for feminist purposes: is it amenable or antithetical to feminist concerns? If it is problematic from a feminist perspective, then philosophers need to construct it in a way that avoids these problems yet at the same time gives us the most complete skeptical stance such that a defeat of it will leave no further skeptical question remaining. I examine two models—Hobbesian and Kantian—that we might use to defeat the skeptic, and ask of each two questions: (1) is it problematic for feminism? and (2) is it problematic for a successful defeat of skepticism?

II. WHY DEFEAT THE SKEPTIC?

Before assessing the traditional skeptic from a feminist perspective, I should say a bit about the significance of the issue of moral skepticism. Why should philosophers be concerned with the issue of why one should be moral, and should feminist philosophers have any special interest in it? The issue is certainly one of the most intractable in moral philosophy and has attracted the attention of many philosophers since at least Plato. Philosophers have at least two reasons for defeating the skeptic about moral action (hereafter, "the skeptic" for short).[2] First is the theoretical reason that demonstrating the rationality of acting in morally required ways[3] would strengthen morality by backing it with reason. Justifying our widely held beliefs, including our beliefs about the rational required-ness of acting morally, is the very enterprise of philosophy. But moral beliefs are special for the reason that we have a practical reason to justify them, which is that we hope to make headway in having people actually act morally.[4] For we have a real worry that people who are skeptics about acting morally will treat others badly if we do not show that moral rea-sons override other reasons for action, but not that people who are skep-tics about the existence of the external world, for instance, will step in front of trains, cars, and raging bulls. This is not to say, of course, that if we justify acting morally, people will act morally, necessarily or other-wise. But for people who try to follow the dictates of reason, we can pin our hopes on them aligning their behavior with morality.

Feminists should have a particular stake in defeating the skeptic about acting morally since women have been and still are subject to a particularly flagrant form of immorality, on top of other immoralities that take anyone as their victim. These are the harms resulting from sex-ist acts caused by individual agents, as well as the harms caused by insti-tutionalized sexism or oppression. Feminists should want it to be shown that those who act in blatantly sexist ways (e.g., rapists and sexual harassers), those who are indifferent to women's oppression or insuffi-ciently motivated to try to eradicate it, and perhaps even those who do not harbor bad attitudes about women but who nonetheless benefit from a system that oppresses women, act irrationally when they act in these ways and against morality. Surprisingly, though, feminists have not weighed in, in any extensive way, on the issue of why one should be moral. I attempt to remedy this in my book, *The Moral Skeptic*,[5] where I aim to re-construe the traditional picture of the skeptic's position in ways that serve to ground a complete defeat of skepticism according to which no immoral acts, including sexist ones or ones that contribute to wom-en's oppression, turn out to be rationally permissible. To this end, I argue for changing the skeptic's position to be one according to which the skeptic endorses reasons relating to privilege rather than only reasons of self-interest, since privilege includes self-interest but goes beyond it in covering many other immoral acts that are at least as much in opposition to morality as self-interest. My account of privilege, very briefly, is this.

I endorse the Kantian view that each person, in virtue of her capacity for rationality, which is marked by having desires, interests, goals, plans, and the like, has intrinsic value. I borrow from Stephen Darwall and Christine Korsgaard, who say that we have equal standing to make claims on each other or put forward reasons relating to our ends.[6] These reasons are recognizable to other rational persons, and are sufficient for making one a being we ought to respect. A person who privileges himself fails to respect another's rationality, either by not recognizing it, by disregarding the other's worth, by acknowledging it and seeking to set it back, by failing to focus on it, or by not caring about it. He privileges himself, or privileges his reasons, over others and their reasons.[7] Re-construing the skeptic's position as the view that rationality requires acting in ways that privilege oneself and one's reasons captures all kinds of immoralities that involve disrespect for a person's intrinsic value or dignity; a successful defeat of the skeptic will show them to be irrational, thereby leaving no immoral acts rationally permissible. The topic of this chapter, though, is whether there is something wrong with the traditional model of the skeptic in the sense that it has built into it a kind of privilege that is problematic either for feminist aims or for a successful defeat of skepticism.

The general idea that I want to tweak is this. There are two approaches—both contractarian—that we might take to posing and answering the skeptical question: Hobbesian and Kantian. According to the Hobbesian, self-interest-based contractarian approach, which is most in line with the traditional picture of the skeptic, we must demonstrate to the skeptic who accepts only reasons of self-interest that morality benefits those who follow it. This approach takes an instrumental view of persons. Gauthier, who defends a Hobbesian contractarian theory, notoriously says that only those who are able to contribute to others' well-being are included in the bargaining scheme from which morality is derived.[8] In terms of the question of how men benefit from feminism, the Hobbesian view would require that in order to demonstrate that rationality requires acting in nonsexist or even feminist ways, we have to show that it is in men's interest to act thusly even when it means surrendering some, most, or all of their economic, social, and political power.

Alternatively, we could also ask the skeptical question, "Why be moral?" from a position other than one of expected self-benefit. Such is the case with a Kantian approach, present in the Categorical Imperative, which allows us to ask the skeptical question from the perspective of anyone because it grants all persons intrinsic value instead of regarding them as self-interested maximizers who have only instrumental value.

This approach allows *women* to ask why they should participate in a sexist system when it is harmful to them, which is interesting since Kant was not known for endorsing feminist views.[9] Women would go along with a sexist scheme only when coerced or lied to, which Kant identifies as the two ways that an immoral maxim might pass the Categorical Imperative. Otherwise women would not consent, and maxims reflecting sexist behavior would be immoral and irrational. The Kantian approach, it seems, puts the burden squarely and rightly on those who do not respect the equal personhood of their fellows. I want to develop these intuitions, and argue ultimately that each approach has elements that are either amenable to or antithetical to feminist concerns. The Kantian approach moves us in the right direction for asking the right skeptical question, but the Hobbesian approach in the end gives us a more empowering view of rational agency that involves an agent's *asserting* her interests, not merely *protecting* them. Finally, I suggest an alternative approach that aims to use the best of both models for purposes of successfully defeating the skeptic in a way that promotes feminist aims.

III. THE TRADITIONAL SKEPTIC

The skeptic's position is meant to capture or express the kind of actions that are rationally required and against which morally required acts are to be defended. Serving as a philosophical tool designed to represent a challenge for justification, the traditional skeptic about moral action denies that there is reason to act morally, and endorses only reasons of self-interest.[10] More precisely, the skeptic endorses the expected utility theory of practical reason, or, EU, according to which rationality dictates that the agent act in ways that *maximize* her expected utility, which is commonly identified with promoting one's own interest, benefit, or advantage, or satisfying one's desires or preferences.[11] The skeptic is taken to hold EU because it is allegedly the best-defended theory of rational choice and action available, though, of course, it has been criticized on many grounds,[12] and because self-interested action is assumed by many philosophers to be the farthest removed from, or the most in opposition to, morality. So as not to beg the question in favor of morality by assuming either that anyone has moral desires, or that it is rational to have moral desires, which the skeptic denies, the skeptic is taken to believe that it is rational to have desires that, when satisfied, would promote one's self-interest.[13] So even though EU (at least in its formal version[14]) does not

144 | OUT FROM THE SHADOWS

rationally assess desires themselves, and according to EU, rationality requires acting in ways that maximize the satisfaction of whatever desires the agent has,[15] for purposes of defeating skepticism, philosophers impose the assumption that a rational person can have any desires but moral ones, defined as those that involve taking an intrinsic interest in the interests of others.[16] The skeptic is set up this way for strategic reasons: a successful defeat of the skeptic will show both that acting morally is rationally required even in the worst-case scenario against morality when morality competes with self-interest, and that no matter what desires a person has, excepting moral ones, acting morally is rationally required.[17] The moral philosopher's task is to demonstrate that acting in morally required ways is, in the face of EU, rationally required. But the skeptic is not wedded to EU: if some other theory of practical reason were shown to be better than EU, the skeptic will accept it. If not, though, a failure to defeat the skeptic means that rationality requires self-interested action, even when it conflicts with morally required action.

Defeating this kind of skeptic is, of course, no easy task. Indeed, whichever way we set up the skeptic constrains the kind of answer we can give to him. Since on the traditional view the skeptic accepts only self-interested reasons, we have to justify acting morally, or at least being morally disposed, by appealing in some way to self-interest. The option of showing that there is a better theory of practical reason than EU would foreclose setting up the skeptic to endorse EU—the skeptic is taken to endorse it mainly because it is the best-defended theory of its kind, and, as a matter of fact, it flies in the face of morally required action unless such action promotes one's self-interest. The skeptic's position privileges or favors EU as the theory of practical reason to defeat. By this I mean that it privileges one's own reasons of self-interest over others' reasons of self-interest and over moral reasons when the former conflicts with the latter two reasons. Hobbes famously, but unsuccessfully, tries to show that *every* morally required action is rationally required because in the agent's self-interest. Gauthier makes a dispositional move, aiming to show that *adopting a moral disposition,* which he calls "constrained maximization," is rationally required because having it best promotes one's self-interest in comparison to "straightforward maximization," which requires that one act in ways that, for each action, best promotes one's interest. Having the disposition of constrained maximization means that one can expect to benefit from a *system* of morality in place, even though at the same time one expects to have to make moral sacrifices from time to time. The overall expected benefit of morality is, for each person, greater than the benefit she could expect from not being morally disposed and acting in her self-interest on every occasion, as a straightforward maximizer does. Still, Gauthier's dispositional move faces problems, including demonstrating that the rationality of the moral disposition carries over to the rationality of the actions expressing this disposition.[18]

But there are decided advantages to setting up the skeptic to demand a self-interested grounding of moral action. If we abandon the project of defeating skepticism in a way grounded in reasons of self-interest, we risk not reaching someone who endorses only these reasons, and leave it be that rationality requires acting self-interestedly in cases of conflict with morality. And if we do defeat this skeptic, we will have shown, significantly, that even in a case as far removed from morality as self-interested action, acting in morally required ways is rationally required. This is a positive result for feminist concerns, since a successful defeat of this skeptic would mean that self-interested sexist behavior will turn out to be irrational. If we expand the skeptic's position in the way I suggested to one of endorsing reasons relating to privilege, a successful defeat of this skeptic will show that even more kinds of sexist behavior are irrational.

In addition, the best strategic move is to give one's opponent the strongest position possible. Even though self-interested action might not be as much in opposition to morality as some other immoral actions, it is grounded in a well-defended theory of rational choice; and the position makes no moral assumptions—indeed, it assumes the absence of moral desires.[19] The strategy is philosophically laudable for several reasons. First, it avoids setting up a straw-person argument that is unfairly easy to knock down, as would be the case were we to take some action less far-removed from morality than self-interested action as rationally required. Second, the strategy avoids begging the question against the opponent by in some way assuming that acting in morally required ways is rationally required. Third, it lends strength to the moral philosopher's argument, should the opponent be defeated. Arguing from a weak, underdog position bolsters the position from which the moral philosopher begins, should her argument against skepticism succeed. Compare defeating the skeptic about acting morally to "Descartes'" attempt to defeat the epistemological skeptic by digging himself into a deeper and deeper skeptical abyss to the point that he doubts everything he once believed to be true. Although most philosophers agree that Descartes does not succeed in defeating his skeptic, his attempt was ingenious because had it succeeded it would have left his skeptic with no further challenge. The same can be said of a robust skeptical position in ethics.

So there are good reasons, both for feminist concerns and for a successful defeat of skepticism, for taking the traditional view of the skeptic (or some stronger version of it) as the position for moral philosophers to defeat; privileging oneself and one's reasons as evidenced in the formal version of EU that the skeptic is assumed to endorse, is not a worrisome sense of privilege.

IV. THE HOBBESIAN MODEL

However, philosophers have expanded the skeptical position along self-interest-based contractarian lines, making the additional assumptions that persons have only instrumental value and that hypothetical persons may be embedded in a social context that accords them power over their fellows. Such assumptions introduce a problematic sense of privilege.

We find this view in Hobbes and Gauthier, both of whom develop their contractarian morality in the context of defeating the skeptic. They take on the skeptic on his own terms, attempting to defeat him by appealing to reasons of self-interest, which is arguably the strength of their position despite the widely acknowledged failure to defeat the skeptic. The Hobbesian model they employ assumes the truth of EU, and they aim to show that we can derive morality from a hypothetical agreement among persons who, at least for Gauthier, have whatever desires or preferences they may but moral ones. These features the Hobbesian model has in common with the traditional picture of the skeptic. I next want to examine the reasoning of the hypothetical bargainers in the Hobbesian model, and show how the model expands in problematic ways beyond the traditional view of the skeptic.

Both Hobbes and Gauthier start from the position of hypothetical bargainers who set out to define the terms of morality through an agreement they make with others. Hobbes famously begins with the State of Nature, or, state without morality and laws, where each person acts rationally in satisfying whatever desires he happens to have, the only constraint on desires being that the strongest desire of each person is their desire for self-preservation, a desire that none of us ever loses. Hobbes idealizes the State of Nature by assuming that everyone is relatively equal in strength: whatever one lacks in physical strength, one makes up with mental acumen, and vice versa. Everyone also has the right to everything, meaning that anyone is at liberty to treat another person according to the former's desires. Self-interest drives the bargain

STANDARDS OF RATIONALITY | **147**

and is the reason for keeping one's contract. It is, Hobbes argues, in *each person's* interest to move from a State of Nature to a state with morality because of each person's desire for self-preservation and the promise of achieving the goods that can only be achieved from cooperation. The contract "comes about" from each person's "laying down" certain rights he has in the State of Nature for the sake of an expectation of benefit that morality brings. It is also, Hobbes argues, in each person's self-interest always to keep the contract he makes, lest he be caught for reneging and "placed back" in the State of Nature in which others no longer cooperate with him. Each hypothetical bargainer, like the skeptic, finds that rationality requires agreeing to act, and actually acting, in morally required ways if and only if she or he expects to benefit, whether it be from the particular interaction, as is the case for Hobbes, or from the practice of morality, as is the case for Gauthier. In agreeing to the hypothetical bargain, each puts forward claims that aim to maximize the satisfaction of her interests or preferences. She asks herself how much she can expect to get given what others expect to get and what they will concede. Each is constrained by her desire not to drive away the others so each can achieve the state of affairs in which they can have self-preservation, the goods of cooperation, and the maximization of the satisfaction of their interests. If they cannot expect to benefit in these ways from the agreement, perhaps because the others have little or nothing to offer or because they are renegers, then rationality requires not making or keeping the agreement.

The idea that self-benefit is the only reason for entering and keeping the hypothetical contract introduces the notion that persons have only instrumental value: interacting with another is rational if and only if one can expect to benefit from such interactions, and there is no other feature of persons that would make it rational to interact with them. The expected utility theory itself does not presume that persons have only instrumental value; the formal version says only that rationality requires acting in ways that maximize one's utility. But when we build EU into the position of the hypothetical bargainers, who, like the skeptic, demand that we demonstrate the rationality of acting in morally required ways when only self-interested reasons are acceptable, and who are considering whether interaction with others is rationally required, it is a quick step to the view that persons have only instrumental value. Jean Hampton explains this feature of the Hobbesian model as follows: "... if you ask me why I should treat you morally, and I respond by saying that it is in my interest to do so, I am telling you that my regard for you is something that is merely instrumentally valuable to me; I do not give you that regard because there is something about you yourself that merits it, regardless of the usefulness of that regard to me."[20] Hampton quotes a passage from Hobbes in which he unabashedly states that the value or worth of a man is his price. Hampton concludes, rightfully, I believe, that Hobbesian morality "fails in a serious way to capture the nature of morality, which is that people are owed respect in virtue of being persons."[21] Morality, that is, should make room for the intrinsic value of persons instead of seeing persons simply as beings from which we stand to benefit or not. I will have more to say on this point in the next section.

Since self-interest-based contractarian models couple EU with the conception of persons as having only instrumental value, they run the risk that those who have *greater* instrumental value than others because they have more goods, strengths, talents, and the like have more bargaining power, and hence their interests and reasons relating to them will be privileged over the interests and reasons of others. But this is problematic, as many have pointed out, because only those who have enough to offer so as not to drive away other potential bargainers or cooperators, that is, who offer others an expectation of benefit from interactions with them, will be included in the self-interest-based contractarian scheme. Hobbes may have tried to stave off this possibility by assuming that the contractors are equal in strength, desire for power, and pursuit of their own desires. But it is not entirely obvious that such features affect a person's social position. More likely, factors such as stereotyping are the most salient ones determining whether a person is a member of a dominant or a dominated group, so that even the assumptions that Hobbes makes to ensure equality of persons will not achieve their goal.[22] In addition, feminists such as Alison Jaggar object to this model on the grounds that it conceives of individuals as ontologically prior to society, with their needs and interests, capacities and desires being given independently of their social context and not created or altered by that context. Jaggar objects particularly to Rawlsian contractarianism that invokes the veil of ignorance, because it does not deem as philosophically important "accidental" features of persons stemming from class, gender, race, and so on.[23] Although Rawls invokes the veil of ignorance precisely to avoid the bias that such features can bring to the contract, some feminists and race theorists have argued that we are already in a social context with a long history of sexism and racism, and that abstracting from these features fails to repair existing injustices that are part of the basic structure of society, with the result that these injustices will perpetuated by the contract.[24] The conception of humans on the contractarian, liberal model is abstracted away from features that persons have that individuate them and/or can be the source of their oppression. Finally, Gauthier believes that the Hobbesian assumption of equality is too idealistic and will never be actualized, so he takes his hypothethical bargainers to have features that real persons have.

One problem Gauthier runs into, though, is that he explicitly excludes those we cannot expect to benefit from—"animals, the unborn, the congenitally handicapped and defective."[25] Obviously, women do not fit into the same category because there is nothing defective about their reasoning or physical capacities, but some feminists have complained that women's lesser social power might exclude them from some interactions with men. To be sure, though Gauthier assumes that the bargainers come to the bargaining table knowing their particular interests and having a certain social position, he introduces two constraints—the proviso and minimax relative concession—that are designed to ensure impartiality in the bargaining scheme. No one can claim just anything, nor be forced to make unfair concessions to others.

Still, even with these constraints in place, no one need enter or keep agreements unless she or he expects to benefit from doing so, and those occupying positions of power are among the most likely to be in this position when they are in the company of those with less to offer. The better positioned are not rational, by EU, to interact with those who do not have enough to offer to provide the former a sufficiently high expectation of benefit from the interaction. Women's having less economic, social, and political power than men in patriarchal societies makes it likely that they have less to offer men, so they may be excluded from at least some bargaining schemes with men. This is not to say that men do not stand to benefit from many of their interactions with women: women have been the primary caretakers of men's children, have done the menial homemaking tasks for men, and have done the lion's share of underrated and underpaid labor that lies behind men's successful work. Some economists have argued that men even gain from women's having more rights, the satisfaction of which increases women's bargaining power. Men stand to gain by improving the human capital of their future grandchildren, and they do this by improving their own daughters' bargaining position by their being well-educated and being treated well by their husbands.[26] Despite these benefits, however, men stand to gain even more from interactions with their equals because their equals have more to offer.[27] And men certainly benefit from having a sexist system in place—whether they are oppressors who intend to harm women or whether they are merely advantaged vis-à-vis women's being in a subordinate social position[28]—and it is this system that lowers women's instrumental value. The list of such benefits is long, including being paid significantly more than women for the same work; having the opportunity to make it into the top professions, succeed in them, and enjoy the perks they bring; not being judged solely on the basis of their appearance and having these judgments count against them in the workplace; not being divided into classes on the basis of their sexual practices; not being stereotyped in degrading and harmful ways; not having to deal with catcalls; not having to live in fear of rape or violence from a partner and the subsequent loss of freedom; being taken seriously; being taken for their word; being assumed to be intellectual, strong, and decisive, and having doors opened on this basis; having a real choice about whether to raise their children or stay in the paid workforce; and having their right to bodily autonomy respected. Men would have to weigh these benefits against the benefits they could expect were they in a society where women were not an oppressed group, and in the case of *following* morality, they would have to weigh the benefits of following a moral system without oppression against enjoying such benefits. The former benefits might include the opportunity to live in a just world, and to have relationships with women who have authentic desires, are psychologically stable, do not fulfill sexist and harmful stereotypes, and who are able to have autonomy and express it in ways that allow everyone to be better off. Showing that rationality requires disposing oneself to act in ways contributing to ending women's oppression, and showing that rationality requires acting these ways on every occasion in the face of the expectation of great benefits men gain from being in the dominant group, would be difficult indeed. In terms of the issue of men's benefiting from feminism, showing that *whenever* a man acted in a non-sexist way he would promote his self-interest would be pretty hard.

A further worry is that if persons have only instrumental value, the Hobbesian model runs the risk of slighting women for the reason that when women and men mimic the gendered roles a patriarchal society sets out for them, women will not see themselves as having enough instrumental value due to deformed desires, false consciousness, or lack of self-worth, while men will see themselves as having too much instrumental value, thereby setting up women for exploitation.[29]

The Hobbesian model, then, particularly when it allows a person's social position to be a factor in determining the rationality of agreement and compliance, allows men legitimately to ask why they should participate in feminist schemes when such schemes will require them to sacrifice their position of power. The model enables a person, due to their social position, to privilege themselves and their reasons over others and their reasons. Because of its grounding in self-interest, and its instrumental view of persons, it allows the privileged to ask, "Why should *I* participate in a system that requires self-sacrifice?" The Hobbesian model builds in a kind of privilege that is problematic for feminism because it either does not allow women into its scheme, or it allows them in, but they lose out on it because their social position weakens their bargaining position. In the next section, I introduce an alternative, Kantian model, which shifts the perspective from which the skeptical issue can be asked and answered. The shift takes place because the model accords persons intrinsic value, which puts everyone in the "moral game." This holds promise for feminist concerns, for only when we accord everyone an equal standing can the nonprivileged ask the skeptical question, "Why should *I* participate in a system that harms me?" Thus there is a prima facie reason to favor the Kantian over the Hobbesian model.

V. THE KANTIAN MODEL

We find in Kant's Categorical Imperative another contractarian approach to morality and a possible way to answer the skeptic about acting morally, as it asks not only what any rational agent would agree to *have* as a duty, but what any rational agent would agree to *follow*. To see how the Kantian model incorporates the perspective of the nonprivileged, we need to examine the three main versions of the Categorical Imperative and their interconnections. The Universal Law Formulation requires that one ask oneself whether one can will—both imagine and want—a maxim to be a universal law. The agent is primary in the sense that he asks from his own perspective whether he can will the universalization of the maxim at issue. But his perspective is not one of self-interest: the agent does not agree to and follow a maxim for the reason that doing so promises to maximize the satisfaction of his desires or preferences. Rather, the agent asks whether some non-self-interested sense of rationality would require him to agree to and follow the maxim. Kant's case of the imperfect duty to aid those in need when one is able but does not want to serves as a clear illustration. The agent considers whether he can will—both imagine and want—a maxim that when universalized will turn the tables and put him on the short end of the stick where no one aids him when he is in need. Kant believes that we can imagine this situation but would not want it. Kantian rationality invokes consistency rather than EU: if in willing a maxim to be a universal law the agent runs into a contradiction in her desires, rationality requires rejecting the maxim as one we ought to follow. The agent who tries to universalize the maxim at issue runs into a conflict between her desire to be helped when in need of aid and her desire not to help others when she is able to—she can't consistently will these two states of affairs, one of which is brought about by universalizing the maxim. The Kantian model, unlike the Hobbesian model, does not reflect the traditional view of the skeptic who adopts EU, but appeals to a basic principle of logic that enjoins us not to have inconsistencies in our desires and beliefs. It does not seem problematic to me to build into the skeptic's position a requirement about consistency. To defeat the skeptic on the Kantian model, consistency would make moral norms into rational norms.

The kind of reasoning the Kantian agent employs in the Universal Law Formulation takes him some way toward seeing matters from the perspective of the nonprivileged. The Universal Law Formulation requires that the agent imagine himself not being in a position of privilege, as when the tables are turned and he is in the subordinate position in need of aid. Here his interests are vulnerable, in jeopardy of being sacrificed for the promotion of others' desires. The Hobbesian agent never has to think this way, but has to consider only whether making and acting on an agreement provides him an expectation of maximizing his utility. He is constrained only by whether the extent to which he puts forward his interests might drive away other potential bargainers. The Kantian agent, in contrast, takes his own perspective, but has to imagine what he would will when his circumstances have changed in such a way that when others aim to satisfy their desires, he might end up in a position that he would not want, a desire that conflicts with the desire he would fulfill were only he to act on the maxim. The Kantian agent considers his hypothetical self: what could *it* will were the tables turned and his situation different from the one in which he initially considers the maxim?

Indeed, the Kantian model, when seen in light of all three versions of the Categorical Imperative, goes even a step further by requiring the agent to take the perspective of *others*. This is seen in the Principle of Autonomy, but to understand how it requires the agent to take this perspective, we first need to speak to the Principle of Humanity. The Kantian model ascribes to persons intrinsic value, which they have in virtue of having the capacity for rationality or being self-determining agents,[30] which is evidenced by their having interests, desires, plans, and goals.[31] Christine Korsgaard states that your humanity is your power of rational choice, the condition of all value and what gives your needs and desires the justifying force of reasons.[32] In virtue of having the capacity for rationality, persons are deserving of respect.[33] This means that we must treat them as ends in themselves, and never merely as means to our own ends. When we treat a person as a mere means to our ends, we fail to respect some aspect of the person's rationality, say, by putting our own desires or interests first, ignoring another's capacity to make her own decisions about something or discounting her plans. The Principle of Humanity requires that the agent acknowledge the humanity of others. Significantly, it puts everyone who has at least the capacity for rationality in the moral game in the sense that *their* interests matter to what it is rational for anyone to do; significantly for our purposes, it grants women equality to men in respect to their intrinsic value. In doing so, the Principle of Humanity serves as a basis from which the privileged have to consider maxims from the perspective of the nonprivileged, as seen in the Principle of Autonomy. The intrinsic value of persons constrains an agent's pursuit of the satisfaction of his desires. As Kant remarks, "This principle of humanity and of every rational nature generally as an end in itself is the supreme limiting condition of every man's freedom of action . . . it applies to all rational beings generally."[34]

The Principle of Autonomy, which requires that moral maxims be self-legislated, makes the agent actually take the perspective of the non-privileged; the agent has to make another's reasons his own. This principle underlies the first two versions of the Categorical Imperative as follows.[35] When an agent tries to universalize a maxim that involves making an exception for himself, he treats another person merely as a means to his own ends. No one else would consent to such a maxim unless coerced or deceived. Similarly, when others try to universalize a maxim that makes them an exception to the rule, allowing them, for example, to act self-interestedly, they treat the agent merely as a means to their own ends. The agent would not consent to such a maxim unless coerced or deceived. When considering whether a maxim will pass the Principle of Autonomy, the privileged person can see that just as he could not autonomously legislate maxims that would give him the short end of the stick, no other being like him could autonomously legislate the same. None would agree to maxims that failed to grant them the same worth as others, or that failed appropriately to respect it. Put another way, the

Principle of Autonomy requires that the agent put forward reasons for his desires and have others bound by them as he is bound by their reasons; he must make others' reasons his own. Kant's notion of the kingdom of ends is that situation in which persons see each other as co-legislators of morality, as beings whose reasons count equally for all.[36]

Despite its promise for feminist aims, not all feminist philosophers like the Kantian model. Annette Baier objects to it on the grounds that it opens the door to the privileged deciding for the nonprivileged the matters to which they would consent. This is so, Baier believes, because the Kantian account allows an agent to run maxims through the Categorical Imperative by himself without consulting others who would provide a check on this abuse. Baier puts it thusly:

> A view like Kant's makes a halfhearted gesture toward recognizing the relevance of the question, "What do *we* will to will?" Kant's own preferred question is, "What can *I* will that we all will?" But unless my metawilling is responsive to and corrected by what my fellows will to will, we will merely risk proliferating, at the metalevel, the discord and troublesome self-will that drove us in the first place to take a step away from the simple, "What do *I* want?" ... As long as the difference between autonomy and heteronomy, between obeying "self alone" and obeying "others" ... is left unmediated by any recognition that "I" of necessity includes my reflective passions and a concern for others' agreement with me, autonomy will be in danger of deteriorating into pretend-sovereignty over compliant subjects. ... Simply to assume that what I can will others to do to me, they also can and do will me to do to them, without verifying that assumption case by case, is to arrogate to oneself the right to decide for others ... all Kantian persons ... are licensed by Kant's tests to treat all others as virtual women or virtual servants, as ones whose happiness is to be aimed at by other moral agents who are confident they know where that happiness lies. Moral decision making, for Kant, is responsible patriarchal decision making, made without any actual consultation even with the other would-be patriarchs.[37]

If Baier is correct, then the Kantian model fares no better than the Hobbesian model because privileged persons can push through maxims that when acted on promote only their own interests. The Kantian model would then be problematic for feminism, despite the promise it holds due to its according all persons intrinsic value.

I think the Kantian model requires that the agent ask not what *any* rational being would consent to, absent the particularities of the other person and her circumstances. Consider the Universal Law Formulation again, which has the agent consider whether he as a socially embedded person with certain desires and interests could will a particular maxim to be a universal law. He should not abstract away from his desires and interests, but in fact must be aware of them to see if a conflict arises when he attempts to universalize the maxim. He will have to ask, for any other agent, whatever desires and interests she has, when she finds herself in similar circumstances, whether she could will the maxim to be a universal law. Barbara Herman notes that the Categorical Imperative procedure assesses actions through their maxims, which express the agent's conception of what he is doing and why, making them particularized in that they reflect the agent's interests and desires.[38] To put oneself in another's shoes is to consider the maxim from another's perspective in all of its particularities. If this is correct, then the Kantian model does not allow the promotion of one's interests, and is one up on the Hobbesian model because it accords persons intrinsic value. It closes the door on the possibility in the Hobbesian model that bargainers can bring benefits of their social position to the bargaining scheme and get ahead of others unfairly. Significantly, for purposes of assessing the position of the traditional skeptic, it turns the tables on the traditional skeptical position because it allows the nonprivileged to ask, "Why should *I* participate in a system that harms me?" instead of allowing the privileged to ask, "Why should *I* participate in a system that I cannot expect to benefit from?" The Kantian model rightly puts the burden on the privileged to show what gives *them* the right not to respect women's equal personhood and not see them as potential co-legislators of morality. Granting everyone intrinsic worth denies anyone the right to favor their own perspective and their own reasons in determining whether it is rational to agree to and follow morality.

An objector might claim that the Kantian model could not serve as a satisfactory way of defeating the skeptic for the reason that assigning to persons intrinsic value imports moral premises into the argument against the skeptic, thereby begging the question in favor of morality. So while the model fares better for feminist reasons, it is problematic for defeating skepticism. I now want to add to Hampton's point that assigning persons only instrumental value does not capture the nature of morality, which is that persons are owed respect in virtue of being persons. To diffuse the objection, note that the idea underlying Kantian intrinsic worth is the very premise upon which the Hobbesian model is built. Both Hobbes and Kant believe that our having interests is central to our being subjects of morality, though each assigns radically different value to persons in connection with our being interest-bearers. Kant believes that persons are distinguished from things and animals on account of having interests and the like that are indicative of the capacity for rationality. In addition, Kant distinguishes among desires: some are ones that nonhuman animals have, while others are ones that involve reason or reflection and whose satisfaction promotes our well-being. He states that

> the human being is a being with needs, insofar as he belongs to the sensible world, and to this extent his reason certainly has a commission from the side of his sensibility which it cannot refuse, to attend to its interest and to form practical maxims with a view to happiness in this life and, where possible, in a future life as well. But he is nevertheless not so completely an animal as to be indifferent to all that reason says on its own and to use reason merely as a tool for the satisfaction of his needs as a sensible being. For that he has reason does not at all raise him in worth above mere animality if reason is to serve him only for the sake of what instinct accomplishes for animals... he needs reason in order to take into consideration at all times his well-being and woe... Someone who submits to a surgical operation feels it no doubt as an ill, but through reason he and everyone else pronounce it good.[39]

Kant seems to be suggesting that it is particularly reflective desires, ones had only by rational beings, that are indicative of rationality and so essential for putting them in the moral game as beings who are owed certain treatment.[40]

For Hobbes, being an interest-bearer—and he does not specify the kind of interests—allows one to enter rational bargaining schemes from which moral agreement arises, though it warrants one's having only instrumental value. Rational agents are ones who exercise their capacity for rationality by acting in ways that maximize the satisfaction of their interests. Just being an interest-bearer puts one in the moral game for Hobbes, as it does for Kant. For Hobbes it means that these beings are positioned to consider whether a system of morality or the occasion of acting morally will bring them greater expected benefit than the benefit they could otherwise expect.

I am suggesting that being an interest-bearer does not import morality at the start for either philosopher, but that for each it provides the grounds for the very *possibility of morality*. Along these lines, Judith Thomson explains that having what she calls "inherently individual interests," such as interests in life and bodily integrity, is essential for understanding and following morality because they allow a person to understand what it is to make a moral sacrifice, which involves doing something that she ought when it is not necessarily in her interest.[41] For if you do not have interests (for Thomson, inherently individual interests), you do not know what it is like to have to sacrifice their satisfaction or to have someone else's actions stand in the way of your satisfying your own interests. This reasoning aids the Hobbesian model by explaining why having interests puts one in the moral game. But, since the Kantian model is not about maximizing and sacrificing the satisfaction of one's interests, we can explain the importance of having interests by the fact that they are necessary for self-determination. For it is the agent's reflective desires that are tied to her self-determination, since they are ones that she believes that, when satisfied, will promote her well-being.

VI. PROTECTING VERSUS ASSERTING INTERESTS: A NEW MODEL

So far, I have argued that the Hobbesian model invokes a kind of privilege that is problematic for feminist concerns, but that the Kantian model attempts to resolve this problem by assigning all persons intrinsic value. I raised the objection that the Kantian solution begs the question against the skeptic by introducing a moral assumption, but then tried to diffuse it by showing that both models make being an interest-bearer essential for the very possibility of morality. So we have two models before us, each with strengths and weaknesses regarding our two concerns of skepticism and feminism. How do we decide between these models? We notice that each model describes a certain kind of agent as ideally rational. I want to suggest that what might help us choose between these models is the one that supports the best view of rational agency. For we want to defeat skepticism by showing that rationality requires acting morally for agents who are rational in the fullest sense, as I will explain.

Elizabeth Anderson distinguishes different articulations of rational choice theory, and critiques the formal theory of EU, which disregards the contents of the agent's preferences and her reasons for having the preferences she has.[42] Anderson favors the rhetorical theory of rational choice, which provides a narrative about how people behave. It describes the rational agent as follows:

He (this is popularly coded a masculine ideal) is *self-transparent*: he knows what he wants, and suffers from no unconscious drives that thwart his conscious desires. He is *opportunistic*: he takes the initiative in pursuing his goals, and actively seeks and promptly takes advantage of every opportunity to advance his goals. He is resourceful and enterprising: neither passive nor procrastinating. He is *self-reliant*, and expects others to likewise look after themselves. He is *coolly calculating*: he is good at probability theory and engages in no wishful thinking, self-deception, or superstition in calculating means to his ends. Most importantly, the rhetoric of economic rationality portrays the rational agent as *autonomous* and *self-confident*.[43]

By autonomous, Anderson means two things. First, the agent regards himself as authorized to order his own preferences as he sees fit, understanding himself as having preferences of his own, having no compunctions about pursuing his preferences and feeling no obligation to defer to convention, tradition, morality, or others' opinions about how to act— the choice about how to act is up to him.[44] Second, the agent regards himself as a self-originating source of claims and expects others to acknowledge his authority in this regard. Regarding the agent's self-confidence, Anderson notes that the rhetoric of rational choice has it that the agent is self-confident in his self-knowledge about what he wants and how he acts, never questioning his own self-image or having any ambivalence or shame about his preferences, and feeling entitled to see himself as a self-originating source of claims.[45]

The agent of rhetorical rational choice theory bears similarity to Carol Gilligan's description of Jake, an eleven-year-old boy who confidently answers Gilligan's question about conflicts between responsibility to oneself and to others, by claiming that "[y]ou go about one-fourth to the others and three-fourths to yourself."[46] Jake explains that he arrives at his answer "[b]ecause the most important thing in your decision should be yourself." Underlying Jake's confidence, and the confidence of many males, in Gilligan's view (which puts them high on Lawrence Kohlberg's scale of moral reasoning), is the fact that he sees his interests as counting, and counting more than those of others.[47] The Hobbesian agent thinks the same way, but goes even further, since he is a *maximizer* about his interests, seeking to satisfy as many of them as possible without driving away other potential bargainers or risking being put back in the state of nature.

The Kantian agent, we might say, also possesses self-confidence, but its grounding is different. His self-confidence stems from the fact that he sees his own worth, recognizes others' worth, and is confident that they recognize his worth. So he is not like eleven-year-old Amy, Jake's counterpart in Gilligan's interview (and here I am relying on Hampton's analysis), who vaguely explains that *maybe* she can put herself first in conflicts about responsibility, but only if not doing so would mean losing out on something she "really, really wants." Amy is not confident that her interests even count, has trouble asserting their priority, and "borders on outright servility," making her highly exploitable.[48] Although he is hardly subservient, the Kantian agent is not autonomous in the way the Hobbesian agent is. The Kantian agent considers his preferences one at a time, as they appear in the maxim at issue, and tests them against a preference he has about the situation that arises when he attempts to universalize the maxim. Rather than seeing his choice of action as being up to him, he defers to morality, or to the fact that others have interests and intrinsic value—*these* factors determine how he is to act or refrain from acting. Rather than having preferences of his own that are distinct from preferences others have about how he should act, he must consider, and is constrained by, whether others would agree to his acting on certain reasons that reflect his preferences. He is autonomous in the sense that he self-legislates maxims that he would consent to were he not coerced or deceived. His goal is to *protect* himself (and any other rational being) from being taken advantage of or from having his humanity disrespected. The Kantian agent takes a defensive stance, and forces others to recognize him as an interest-bearer who will defend his interests against invasion. He is prepared to stand up for himself as an interest-bearer, making sure that no one is trampling on his interests. He aims to have his interests secured. The Kantian model, I suggest, makes paramount *protection* of one's interests.[49]

The Hobbesian model, in contrast, emphasizes *asserting* interests. To be sure, there is one main element of protecting interests in the Hobbesian model, which arises in connection with the desire for self-preservation, which Hobbes takes to be each person's strongest desire, one that is never rational to concede. According to the Hobbesian scheme, one protects one's interest in self-preservation by agreeing to move from the State of Nature with like-minded fellows and by acting morally on every occasion. But beyond this, each person is rational to *assert* his interests, to get as much as possible that would promote his own good from his interactions with his fellows, conceding the satisfaction of his own interests only if he can expect to benefit from doing so. Since the Hobbesian model conceives of rationality in terms of maximizing the satisfaction of one's interests, it makes *asserting* interests paramount. Asserting one's interests involves putting them forward and maximizing their satisfaction. The Hobbesian agent is prepared to stand up for *his interests themselves*, not just *himself as an interest-bearer*, and to insist upon their satisfaction without undue interference from others or even bringing about the conditions under which they can be satisfied. The Hobbesian agent takes an offensive stance regarding his interests, aiming to promote their satisfaction.

It seems that those who ask how men benefit from a feminist system think of men as taking the position of the Hobbesian agent, which allows them to assert their interests because they are thinking in maximizing terms. But when women ask why they should participate in a system that contributes to their oppression, they align themselves with the Kantian agent because they are thinking in terms of their worth as persons being disrespected and want first and foremost to defend themselves against this. But why should men be allowed to assert their interests, and women only to protect their interests? I am not suggesting that women frame the skeptical question in terms of self-interest, asking, "What's in it for me?" which implies that they see morality as instrumental, even if they grant that all persons have intrinsic value. This would put the privileged and the nonprivileged on a par, but not in the way we want.

It seems to me that women have not been allowed to assert their interests as freely as men have, but that they could benefit from doing so. I agree with Hampton that while Amy is too servile, and Jake too self-interested, there is a "constrained" happy medium: Amy would benefit from becoming more Jake-like but in a way that does not deny anyone's self-worth. Ann Cudd voices a similar view: she believes that rational choice theory can be a tool for progressive feminist social theory, and one interpretation of it has it that it prescribes an ideal to which rational persons should strive.[50] She argues that women, who have done the lion's share of caring work in society, should withhold care from men or others who refuse to reciprocate, as it is in their interest not to be exploited. I now need to say a bit more about what is involved in asserting interests, how women have been prevented from doing so, and why it is good for women and men alike to do so.

Asserting interests involves being able to *define* them for oneself rather than have them defined for one by others. Some patriarchal practices stand in the way of women's being self-definers about their interests. According to Marilyn Frye's feminist analysis, the practice of a man's being expected to open a door for a woman, no matter how burdened he is and how unburdened she is, discounts what women really need and lets men define for women what their needs are.[51] Men are also in the driver's seat in defining women's interests when it comes to sex, as is evident in current rape laws in the United States, which turn the issue of *mens rea*, or guilty mind of the perpetrator, into an issue of the victim's consent, which is determined by her resistance rather than what she says.

Patriarchy's deforming women's desires is another way women are prevented from being self-defining about their desires. Jon Elster describes how a person acquires deformed desires by the process of adapting her preferences according to her opportunities and without her control or awareness. Elster calls this the "sour grapes" phenomenon, according to which the fox's conviction that he is prevented from eating grapes that are out of his reach causes him to believe that grapes are sour and so to prefer not to eat them.[52] Feminists are divided as to whether deformed desires involve reflection by the agent, some believing that they overcome the agent, completely brainwashing or duping her, but others believing that they exist alongside other desires, both of which are subject to reflection by the agent.[53] The Hobbesian model does not exclude any desires or interests; if it allows the agent to have deformed desires that factor into the content of morality, this is a strike against it from a feminist perspective, since deriving morality from these desires is likely not to rectify women's oppression. Anderson notes that the formal version of EU not only fails to distinguish autonomous from heteronomous preferences, but represents people as acting on their own preferences when they in fact may be under the sway of oppressive social norms or under the control of others.[54] The Kantian model *might* fare better on this score because for it, reflective desires, which are related to the agent's well-being, are the ones the Kantian agent uses to determine the content of morality.[55] Deformed desires do not promote the agent's well-being, but benefit the system or the dominant members in society, as when a woman's desire to settle for a part-time job in order to have time to raise children disadvantages her economically and psychologically in terms of her own self-fulfillment, while men gain at least economically by concentrating their efforts fully on their careers. Kant's emphasis on morality being autonomous rather than heteronomous makes me suspect that he would exclude deformed desires from the Categorical Imperative procedure, but of course more needs to be said to show this really is the case.

Asserting interests also involves being free to *express* one's interests. By this I mean in part that the agent should be free from external impediments that would prevent her acting on her interests, including unfair judgments from others, threat of violence, restrictive laws, and the like. Women have been denied freedom of sexual expression under patriarchy, as they have been constrained by the fact that safe, effective, and affordable birth control is not widely available, by restrictive abortion laws, by the threat of being labeled promiscuous or frigid, and by the fact that the law can take their dress or whereabouts as a sign of consent to sex despite their desires. The agent has to be able to express her interests in order for her interests to define her; merely *having* interests is not sufficient. The Hobbesian model, of course, cannot guarantee that such external impediments are eradicated (this would come under ideal theory), but the Hobbesian agent as an interest-asserter would express the interests she had—and this is the second thing I mean by being free to express one's interests—because she feels she has the *right* or is entitled to express or put forward her interests.

Why is asserting one's interests a good thing? My original question asks which model is best for purposes of defeating the skeptic and for feminist aims. For purposes of defeating skepticism, we want to employ a model that best captures what we take to be the ideal rational agent. Antony Duff suggests that one critique of "one traditional philosophical account of practical rationality," which Duff does not explicitly name but I take to be EU, is that it allows it to be the case that even a psychopath will turn out to act rationally, and this is because EU, at least in its formal version, requires only bare minimum standards for rational action—just act in ways that best promote your own interest by maximizing the satisfaction of your preferences and you count as rational.[56] Duff does not defend a theory of practical reason, because the topic of his paper is to examine philosophically the notion of psychopathy. But we can glean from his analysis of psychopathy what a better theory of practical reason than EU would include.

According to Duff's analysis, the psychopath often does act in his own interest, knows what he is doing and does what he wants, and has pro- and con-attitudes toward actions and states of affairs, all of which meet traditional standards of rationality. What is lacking in the psychopath—and in theories of practical reason that count agents as rational if they simply meet these standards—are deep emotions, values, and interests, and their logical connection to reasons for action in his own case and in that of others. Duff says that the psychopath lacks emotions such as love that are critical to moral understanding and being a part of the moral world. Hervey Cleckley, a psychiatrist who cites empirical evidence in agreement with Duff's claim, notes that the psychopath shows only half-hearted emotions and is even unresponsive to things like special consideration and kindness.[57] Shaun Nichols cites data showing that psychopaths have an abnormally low responsiveness to pictures of faces of people in distress.[58] This emotional impairment impedes the psychopath's understanding of morality. Nichols describes the psychopath as using moral terms in an "inverted commas" sense, that is, using moral terms conventionally and offering conventional reasons for moral wrongs, but not really understanding what moral terms mean. Duff describes the psychopath as having only limited comprehension of morality, being able only to parrot simple moral rules, while not being able to apply moral rules to tough cases or to understand complexities of moral behavior (e.g., why insulting a friend is bad). The psychopath can deliberate instrumentally and often acts self-interestedly; his behavior is unpredictable because he lacks a true understanding of morality. According to this description, the psychopath misses out on most of morality.

This point is explained further by Duff's analysis that the psychopath fails to see how moral concerns, values, or interests, which have an emotive component, generate reasons for action for others or even for himself. The psychopath can see *that* others have values, such as caring about their families and friends, but he fails to understand what it means for them to *have* deep, complex values and emotions, and how these values yield reasons for actions, because he fails to understand the emotional significance these values have for them. He fails to see this in his own case because he is emotionally impaired. His emotional responses run no deeper than immediate feeling. I assume, then, that for Duff, a plausible theory of practical reason would not judge an agent's rational status simply by whether she maximizes the satisfaction of her preferences; rather, it will judge whether the agent has the appropriate emotional attachment to her preferences, and understands that this is what links her preferences and those of others to reasons.

The point I want to take from Duff's critique is that we need a robust model of the ideal rational agent incorporated into a theory of practical reason. This, I would add, is important for the project of defeating skepticism. We want to show that for a robustly rational agent, rationality requires acting morally. This kind of agent is in control of her person, so to speak; she does not just have interests and act to maximize them, but connects reasons to her interests because she is emotionally connected to her interests, and so sees the significance of having interests and how they would generate reasons for action for herself and others like her. She also sees whether her interests are connected to moral reasons, and so contemplates in the right way whether to have moral reasons. She cares about her own preferences and sees that others care about their own preferences. She makes a real choice about whether her reason dictates following morality or self-interest and the like. If we can show that for this kind of agent, rationality requires acting morally, we will have shown something much stronger and more compelling than were we to show that an agent who is minimally rational by meeting the standards of EU is rationally required to act morally.

Duff's implied view of the ideal rational agent is a rich and plausible one. Neither the Hobbesian model nor the Kantian model explicitly endorses it. What seems crucial for ideal rational agency is that the agent be *self-determining*. Satisfying one's interests plays a significant role in self-determination, especially when it is the case that one cares appropriately about one's interests. Asserting one's interests entails defining one's own interests and being able to express them and seeing oneself as having the right to express them because one cares about them and their satisfaction. The rational agent's interests matter to her and she understands that they do, unlike the psychopath. Coupled with the maximizing element, asserting allows the agent to test out her interests to see if their satisfaction is what she really wants—acting on as many of her interests as she can gives her the opportunity to keep ones she wants because they will (partly) define her as the person she is. In addition, this cultivates an environment that is rich with the possibility of developing new interests, also important for self-determination. The maximizing model aids the agent in developing and growing—in determining herself—in this way. Full rational agency requires not just being an interest-bearer, but being able to determine oneself, at least in part, through one's interests—their expression and development and even rejection. One does this only when one cares appropriately about one's interest, unlike the psychopath Duff describes. In addition to a model of ideal rational agency that we ought to strive for, we need to ensure the removal of external impediments to persons' self-determination, including those constraining women.

This is not to say that the Kantian model does not aid the agent in self-determination. Universalization helps the agent become aware that she has desires or interests, and ones that she cares about appropriately, that conflict or not with the desire she has for the maxim to apply only to herself. The agent determines herself through her desires by not acting on or even ridding herself of desires that conflict with ones she is made aware of when trying to universalize a maxim. The Kantian model is important for self-determination in still other ways. One sign of ideal rational agency is that an agent cares enough about her interests to protect them from being set back in ways to which she would not autonomously consent. To avoid being Amy-like, women under patriarchy should strive for this kind of rational ideal. Furthermore, it is a sign of rationality to be consistent about seeing that others want to protect against their interests being set back just as much as you want to protect your own interests—everyone cares about their own interests. This is not to be confused with being deferential, which means putting others' interests ahead of your own at all costs.

We need the best of both the Hobbesian and the Kantian models, tempered with the insights from Duff. We need a model of the ideal rational agent that accords the nonprivileged, not just the privileged, full rational standing and self-determination. I suggest putting together the models in such a way that any of us should be able to ask, "Given that I have intrinsic value, *and* that I am able to protect and assert my interests because I care appropriately about them, what kind of action is rationally required?" We need a fuller model of practical reason, and a robust model of ideal rational agency, both of which should inform the position of the skeptic. I am not sure what this theory of practical reason would look like, but it would define rationally required action as more than interest-satisfaction, even combined with consistency. The intriguing question is whether the kind of agents who determine themselves at least partially through their interests act rationally when they act in morally required ways. This question cannot be answered in an abstract, mechanical way by ticking off whether and how many of an agent's preferences are satisfied. Rather, it calls for a deeper understanding of rational agency that reflects real choices of agents to act in certain ways and to be certain kinds of persons.

Notes

I thank audiences at the Society for Analytical Feminism conference, "Analytical Feminist Contributions to Traditional Philosophy," Lexington, Kentucky (2008), the Central Division, American Philosophical Association (2007 and 2010), and the Philosophy Departments at Marquette University and Trent University. I also am indebted to David Copp, Sharon Crasnow, Ann Cudd, Nancy Snow, and Helga Varden for very useful comments on drafts of this paper.

1. David Gauthier, *Morals by Agreement* (New York: Oxford University Press, 1986).

2. There are different ways of construing the skeptic about morality, including as a nihilist (a skeptic about moral truths), a moral subjectivist (a skeptic about objective truth, or truth that is independent of a person's feelings), and a moral relativist (a skeptic about universal truth that holds for all persons at all times). See Russ Shafer-Landau, *Whatever Happened to Good and Evil?* (New York: Oxford University Press, 2004), 8. I am concerned with the practical skeptic, who doubts the existence of moral reasons, whatever the content or source of morality. Even here I have labeled different kinds of skeptics. The action skeptic is a skeptic about whether every morally required act is rationally required. This skeptic is my concern in this chapter. But a disposition skeptic is a skeptic about the rational requiredness of adopting a moral disposition, a motive skeptic believes that going through the motions in acting in morally required ways is rationally permissible, and the amoralist is not moved by moral reasons though he recognizes their existence.

3. The action skeptic need not take a stand on acts that are merely morally permissible, that is, neither obligatory nor wrong. Rationality might be indifferent between morality and self-interest when it comes to morally permissible acts. The skeptic's concern is that the moral philosopher demonstrate that rationality requires acting in morally required ways.

4. One kind of internalist position is that a person's having a reason (to act morally) *necessarily* motivates her to act. For purposes of this paper, I will not take a stand on the internalism/externalism debate. I take up this issue in chapter 6 of my book, *The Moral Skeptic* (New York: Oxford University Press, 2009).

5. New York: Oxford University Press, 2009.

6. Stephen Darwall, *The Second-Person Standpoint: Morality, Respect, and Accountability* (Cambridge, Mass.: Harvard University Press, 2006); Christine M. Korsgaard, "Kant's Formula of Humanity," in *Creating the Kingdom of Ends*, ed. Christine M. Korsgaard (New York: Cambridge University Press, 1996), 106–32, at 114, 117, and 119.

7. See my discussion in *Moral Skeptic*, at 98–105.

8. Gauthier, *Morals by Agreement*, 17.

9. On this point, see, for example, Nancy Tuana, *Woman and the History of Philosophy* (New York: Paragon House, 1992). Tuana cites passages demonstrating that Kant believes that all humans have the capacity for rationality, which accords them dignity. Humanity is realized only when choice is fully rational. Tuana cites conflicting passages where Kant says that women are less rational than men, suggesting that their moral capacity is not the same as men's. Women, for Kant, have a "beautiful understanding," so they are excluded from "deep meditation and a long-sustained reflection," the latter of which is essential for figuring out one's duties by way of the Categorical Imperative. It turns out that while men use reason to figure out their duties, women do not act on principle, but on inclination. This, Tuana notes, is

inconsistent with Kant's view that the Categorical Imperative is derived from the universal concept of a rational being. Kant believes that women should develop the beautiful virtues rather than follow reason, for the sake of refining men. This again flies in the face of Kant's injunction that no rational being is to be used merely as a means to the ends of another. See Tuana's discussion of these points at 60–65.

10. I argue in *The Moral Skeptic* for expanding the traditional skeptic's position to include not only the action skeptic, but the disposition skeptic, the motive skeptic, and the amoralist.

11. See, for example, Gauthier, *Morals by Agreement*, 6. Gauthier speaks loosely on this point at first, but then tightens his view in line with the expected utility theory of rational choice and action, and talks in terms of maximizing the satisfaction of one's (considered) preferences for states of affairs, which is measured in terms of utility (22–23). For ease, I will not distinguish between desires, interests, preferences, and the like, though in the literature these refer to different things. Gauthier speaks in terms of interests or preferences, and Hobbes speaks in terms of desires or interests.

12. Gauthier says that it is almost universally accepted and used in the social sciences. (*Morals by Agreement*, 8) Recent feminist critiques of EU have been offered by Elizabeth Anderson, *Values in Ethics and Economics* (Cambridge, Mass.: Harvard University Press, 1995); Jean Hampton, *The Authority of Reason* (New York: Cambridge University Press, 1998) and "Feminist Contractarianism," in *A Mind of One's Own: Feminist Essays on Reason and Objectivity*, ed. Louise M. Antony and Charlotte E. Witt (Boulder, Colo.: Westview Press, 2nd ed., 2002), pp. 337–68; and myself, *Moral Skeptic*.

13. See, for example, Gauthier, *Morals by Agreement*, 8.

14. See Elizabeth Anderson, "Should Feminists Reject Rational Choice Theory?" in *A Mind of One's Own*, 369–97, at 379, for this point.

15. Some philosophers have imposed weak requirements that a person's preferences be coherent, consistent, and transitive. See Gauthier, *Morals by Agreement*, for example.

16. Gauthier explicitly makes this assumption. See *Morals by Agreement*, 87, 100–104.

17. I argue in *The Moral Skeptic* that there are other immoral acts that are at least as much in opposition to morality as self-interested acts.

18. I discuss this issue extensively in *The Moral Skeptic*, chapter 2.

19. In *The Moral Skeptic*, I argue that in order to defeat my modified version of the skeptic, we should appeal to reasons of consistency rather than reasons of self-interest. My modified version of the skeptic's position is that rationality requires that one privilege oneself vis-à-vis morality: it is rational to privilege oneself in the sense of advantaging oneself, including doing so in ways that disrespect others' humanity. To defeat the skeptic, then, we need to show that rationality requires not privileging oneself by disrespecting others' humanity, but instead acting in morally required ways—taking the

worth of others to give one a reason not to privilege oneself, which involves an inconsistency in treating the humanity of self and others.

20. Hampton, "Feminist Contractarianism," 345.

21. Hampton argues in favor of modifying Hobbesian contractarianism by assigning intrinsic value to the bargainers to the hypothetical contract, and she favors a feminist version of contractarianism as a device by which to measure whether the distribution of benefits and burdens—distributive justice—in so-called private relationships, those to which contractarian schemes have not historically been applied.

22. Ann Cudd argues that this is the cause of oppression. See Ann E. Cudd, *Analyzing Oppression* (New York: Oxford University Press, 2006), esp. 68–77.

23. Alison Jaggar, *Feminist Politics and Human Nature* (Totowa, N.J.: Rowman and Allanheld, 1983), 28–33.

24. See also Charles W. Mills, "Racial Justice," paper presented to the Department of Philosophy, University of Kentucky, November 2009.

25. Gauthier, *Morals by Agreement*, 268. He does not exclude the aged, for the reason that they already "paid for their benefits by earlier productive activity" (18, fn. 30).

26. For this argument, see Mark Thoma, "Women's Rights: What's In It for Men?" *Economist's View*, (posted May 26, 2008), 1–5. At http://economistsview.typepad.com/economistsview/2008/05/womens-rights-w.html. I thank Sharon Crasnow for this reference.

27. Here we might recall Sandra Bartky's argument that even though women give men emotional support, believing that men really value it, it turns out that men would rather get approval from their equals—other men—than from women. See Bartky, "Feeding Egos and Tending Wounds," in *Femininity and Domination: Studies in the Phenomenology of Oppression*, ed. Sandra Lee Bartky (New York: Routledge, 1990), 99–119.

28. Ann Cudd nicely makes this distinction in *Analyzing Oppression*.

29. Hampton believes that Carol Gilligan's well-known cases of Amy and Jake "betray perspectives that seem to fit them perfectly for the kind of gendered roles that prevail in our society." Amy loses herself to others, not seeing her own interests as counting, while Jake sees his own interests as counting far too much, overriding or even ignoring others' interests. Hampton argues that neither voice should inform our moral theorizing if morality is going to attack the oppressive relationships that now hold in our society. See "Feminist Contractarianism," 343.

30. See James W. Ellington, p. x, Introduction, Immanuel Kant, *Grounding for the Metaphysics of Morals*, translated by James W. Ellington (Indianapolis, Ind.: Hackett Publishing Company, 1981 [1785]).

31. Kant says that humanity is the capacity to set ends through reason. See Kant, *Grounding*, p. 42, AKA 437.

32. Christine Korsgaard, "The Right to Lie: Kant on Dealing with Evil," *Philosophy & Public Affairs* 15 (1986): 328–40, at 338.

33. Exactly which entities have intrinsic value? Kant says "humanity." But what does this mean? Thomas Hill has weighed in on this issue in two papers. He examines what Kant might mean by the second formulation of the Categorical Imperative: "Act in such a way that you always treat *humanity*, whether in your own person or in the person of any other, never simply as a means but always at the same time as an end." (Thomas E. Hill, Jr., "Humanity as an End in Itself," *Ethics* 91 (October 1980): 84–99, at 84 (emphasis mine). In the most general sense, Kant means to include anything that is a human being, which would mean that merely having human genes puts a being into the moral game, being owed respect by others. This, I would add, would include fetuses and any other humans at the margins of life. Thus when Kant says that having the *capacity* for rationality gives an entity dignity, he understands "capacity" in the weakest sense, as that humans are the kind of beings capable of exercising rationality, though we do not know whether *this* human will ever develop this capacity. Hill goes on to say that Kant's frequent use of "humanity" strongly suggests that he thought of humanity as a characteristic, or a set of characteristics, of persons. It is the power to set ends, and other powers associated with rationality (e.g., the capacity to act on maxims, the capacity to follow rational principles of prudence, the power to foresee consequences and adopt goals, and the like), which distinguish us from nonhuman animals (85–86). Kant even includes the most foolish and depraved persons as having humanity. This reading implies that one has to have the capacity in the sense of having the ability, or mental power, for rationality, right here and now, whether it is exercised in the right (moral) way or not; the entity has the right equipment, as it were, to be rational. This would exclude fetuses and others at the margins.

   In a second paper, Hill says that "[i]f some people are not now willing and able to deliberate morally, though they have the potential capacity to do so, their interests and voice can to some extent be represented by proxy…" He supposes that at least all but the severely brain-damaged infants might have their interests represented and protected because they have humanity. Their humanity is latent, but can be ready and developed. But Hill believes that it would be "too complex and difficult" to figure out whether fetuses, the comatose, the permanently retarded, and the like, had humanity, and he even worries about adults who are so blindly devoted to authorities for answers to moral questions that they can't engage in reasonable deliberation about moral issues (Thomas E. Hill, Jr., "Must Respect Be Earned?," in *Respect, Pluralism, and Justice: Kantian Perspectives*, ed. Thomas E. Hill, Jr. [New York: Oxford University Press, 2000], 87–118, at 102, fn. 18 and 19).

   Kant himself says this about whether fetuses are persons: "For the offspring is a *person*, and it is impossible to form a concept of the production of a being endowed with freedom through a physical operation. So from a *practical point of view* it is a quite correct and even necessary idea to regard the act of procreation as one by which we have brought a person into the world without his consent and on our own initiative, for which deed the parents incur an obligation to make the child content with his condition so far as they can.—They cannot destroy their child as if he were something they had *made* (since a being endowed with freedom cannot be a product of this kind) or as if he were their property…" (Immanuel Kant, *The Metaphysics of Morals* 6:280, in *Immanuel Kant: Practical Philosophy*, trans. and ed. Mary J. Gregor (New York: Cambridge University Press, 1996 [1797]), 429–30. (I thank Helga Varden for this source, and Ann Cudd for bringing this issue to my attention.) So Kant believes that the fetus is a person, and that abortion is wrong. But this is at odds with Hill's view of Kant's most frequent use of "humanity" as a capacity that an entity now has, or at least, in the case of children, will have because it can be ready and developed. I agree with Hill that it is too difficult to defend Kant's view on those at the margins of life. Even if we could, we would have to speculate how to weigh the fetus's humanity against that of the mother, in the case of abortion. My main concern is to show that having humanity or intrinsic value puts *women* into the moral game.

34. Immanuel Kant, *Grounding*, p. 37, AKA 431.
35. See Christine Korsgaard, "Kant on the Right to Lie," for this view.
36. This interpretation is one that Korsgaard offers. See, for example, "The Right to Lie," 332 and 338.
37. Annette Baier, "Hume: The Reflective Women's Epistemologist?" in *A Mind of One's Own*, 38–53, at 44–46.
38. Barbara Herman, "Mutual Aid and Respect for Persons," in *The Practice of Moral Judgment*, ed. Barbara Herman (Cambridge, Mass.: Harvard University Press, 1993), 45–72, at 51.
39. Kant, *Critique of Practical Reason*, in *The Cambridge Edition of the Works of Immanuel Kant: Practical Philosophy*, trans. and ed. Mary J. Gregor (New York: Cambridge University Press, 1999 [1788]), 133–271, at AKA 5:61–62, pp. 189–90.
40. Kant admits that even the would-be murderer's desire to kill another person should be respected on grounds of the Formula of Humanity, since even this desire is indicative of the would-be murderer's rationality. See Korsgaard, "Right to Lie." Korsgaard notes that the Formula of Humanity entails that it is a rational being's prerogative to share in determining the destiny of things, and that any attempt to control another's actions and reactions except by appeal to reason treats the other as a mere means (336). This would hold for the would-be murderer who wants to kill your friend you have hidden in your attic, when the would-be murderer asks you where your friend is. Lying to the would-be murderer does not respect his humanity, even though his desires are bad ones. In a footnote, Korsgaard suggests that kicking the would-be murderer off the porch would be "cleaner" than lying to him, because it treats him more like a human being than lying does (339, fn. 12).

41. Judith Jarvis Thomson, "Trespass and First Property," in *The Realm of Rights* (Cambridge, Mass.: Harvard University Press, 1990), 205–26, at 215.
42. Elizabeth Anderson, "Should Feminists Reject Rational Choice Theory?" in *A Mind of One's Own*, 369–97, at 373–74.
43. Anderson, "Should Feminists Reject," 375.
44. Anderson, "Should Feminists Reject," 375.
45. Anderson, "Should Feminists Reject," 378.
46. Hampton, "Feminist Contractarianism," 338–39.
47. Hampton, "Feminist Contractarianism," 340.
48. Hampton, "Feminist Contractarianism," 340.
49. I am considering the Kantian view as put forward in the Categorical Imperative procedure. Kant may have other things to say elsewhere about maximizing the satisfaction of one's interests.
50. Ann E. Cudd, "Rational Choice Theory and the Lessons of Feminism," in *A Mind of One's Own*, 398–417, at 412–13.
51. Marilyn Frye, "Oppression," in *The Politics of Reality: Essays in Feminist Theory* (Freedom, Calif.: Crossing Press, 1983), 1–16, at 6.
52. Martha C. Nussbaum, "American Women," in *Sex and Social Justice*, ed. Martha C. Nussbaum (New York: Oxford University Press, 1999), 130–53, at 149.
53. See, for example, Uma Narayan, "Minds of Their Own: Choices, Autonomy, Cultural Practices, and Other Women," in *A Mind of One's Own*, 418–32. Narayan describes the "dupes of patriarchy," who completely subscribe to patriarchal norms and practices of their culture and impose them on themselves, and the "bargainers with patriarchy," who have both deformed and nondeformed desires, and who choose between them what is best for themselves in a context of further external constraints on their liberty. Narayan herself believes that women are the latter. For a fuller discussion of deformed desires, see my entry on "Feminist Moral Psychology," *The Stanford Encyclopedia of Philosophy*, ed. Edward Zalta (Stanford, Calif.: Stanford University Press, 2008; available online at http://plato.stanford.edu/contents.html).
54. Anderson, "Should Feminists Reject," 392.
55. I am skeptical that informed desire tests that invoke a notion of well-being or objective good will exclude deformed desires as irrational. See my "Deformed Desires and Informed Desire Tests," *Hypatia: A Journal of Feminist Philosophy*, Special Issue on Analytical Feminism, 20 (4) (Fall 2005): 109–26.
56. Antony Duff, "Psychopathy and Moral Understanding," *American Philosophical Quarterly* 14 (3) (1977): 189–200.
57. Hervey Cleckley, *The Mask of Sanity: An Attempt to Clarify Some Issues about the So-Called Psychopathic Personality*, 5th ed. (St. Louis: Mosby, 1976), esp. 337–64.
58. Shaun Nichols, "How Psychopaths Threaten Moral Rationalism," *Monist* 85 (2) (2002): 285–303, at 299–301.

Bibliography

Anderson, Elizabeth. 1995. *Values in Ethics and Economics.* Cambridge, Mass.: Harvard University Press.

———. 2002. "Should Feminists Reject Rational Choice Theory?" In *A Mind of One's Own: Feminist Essays on Reason and Objectivity,* 2nd. ed., ed. Louise M. Antony and Charlotte E. Witt, pp. 369–97. Boulder, Colo.: Westview Press.

Baier, Annette. 2002. "Hume: The Reflective Women's Epistemologist?" In *A Mind of One's Own: Feminist Essays on Reason and Objectivity,* 2nd ed., ed. Louise M. Antony and Charlotte E. Witt, pp. 38–53. Boulder, Colo.: Westview Press.

Bartky, Sandra. 1990. "Feeding Egos and Tending Wounds: Deference and Disaffection in Women's Emotional Labor." In *Femininity and Domination: Studies in the Phenomenology of Oppression,* ed. Sandra Lee Bartky, pp. 99–119. New York: Routledge.

Cleckley, Hervey. 1976. *The Mask of Sanity: An Attempt to Clarify Some Issues about the So-called Psychopathic Personality.* 5th ed. St. Louis: Mosby.

Cudd, Ann E. 2002. "Rational Choice Theory and the Lessons of Feminism." In *A Mind of One's Own: Feminist Essays on Reason and Objectivity,* 2nd ed., ed. Louise M. Antony and Charlotte E. Witt, pp. 398–417. Boulder, Colo.: Westview Press.

———. 2006. *Analyzing Oppression.* New York: Oxford University Press.

Darwall, Stephen. 2006. *The Second-person Standpoint: Morality, Respect, and Accountability.* Cambridge, Mass.: Harvard University Press.

Duff, Antony. 1977. "Psychopathy and Moral Understanding." *American Philosophical Quarterly* 14 (3): 189–200.

Frye, Marilyn. 1983. "Oppression." In *The Politics of Reality: Essays in Feminist Theory.* Freedom, Calif.: Crossing Press.

Gauthier, David. 1986. *Morals by Agreement.* New York: Oxford University Press.

Hampton, Jean. 1998. *The Authority of Reason.* New York: Cambridge University Press.

———. 2002. "Feminist Contractarianism." In *A Mind of One's Own: Feminist Essays on Reason and Objectivity,* 2nd ed., ed. Louise M. Antony and Charlotte E. Witt, pp. 337–68. Boulder, Colo.: Westview Press.

Herman, Barbara. 1993. "Mutual Aid and Respect for Persons." In *The Practice of Moral Judgment,* ed. Barbara Herman, pp. 45–72. Cambridge, Mass.: Harvard University Press.

Hill, Thomas E., Jr. 1980. "Humanity as an End in Itself." *Ethics* 91: 84–99.

———. 2000. "Must Respect Be Earned?" In *Respect, Pluralism, and Justice: Kantian Perspectives,* ed Thomas E. Hill, Jr., pp. 87–118. New York: Oxford University Press.

Jaggar, Alison. 1983. *Feminist Politics and Human Nature.* Totowa, N.J.: Rowman and Allanheld.

Kant, Immauel. 1981. *Groundwork for the Metaphysics of Morals.* Trans. James W. Ellington. Indianapolis, Ind.: Hackett. Originally published, 1785.

———. 1996. *The Metaphysics of Morals.* In *Immanuel Kant: Practical Philosophy.* Trans. and ed. Mary J. Gregor. New York: Cambridge University Press. Originally published, 1797.

———. 1999. *Critique of Practical Reason.* In *The Cambridge Edition of the Works of Immanuel Kant: Practical Philosophy.* Trans. and ed. Mary J. Gregor. New York: Cambridge University Press. Originally published, 1788.

Korsgaard, Christine M. 1986. "The Right to Lie: Kant on Dealing with Evil." *Philosophy & Public Affairs* 15: 328–40.

———. 1996. "Kant's Formula of Humanity." In *Creating the Kingdom of Ends,* ed. Christine M. Korsgaard, pp. 106–32. New York: Cambridge University Press.

Mills, Charles. "Racial Justice." Unpublished paper presented to the Department of Philosophy, University of Kentucky, November 2009.

Narayan, Uma. 2002. "Minds of Their Own: Choices, Autonomy, Cultural Practices, and Other Women." In *A Mind of One's Own: Feminist Essays on Reason and Objectivity,* 2nd ed., ed. Louise M. Antony and Charlotte E. Witt, pp. 418–32. Boulder, Colo.: Westview Press.

Nichols, Shaun. 2002. "How Psychopaths Threaten Rationalism." *Monist* 85 (2): 285–303.

Nussbaum, Martha C. 1999. "American Women." In *Sex and Social Justice,* ed. Martha C. Nussbaum, pp. 130–53. New York: Oxford University Press.

Shafer-Landau, Russ. 2004. *Whatever Happened to Good and Evil?* New York: Oxford University Press.

Superson, Anita M. 2005. "Deformed Desires and Informed Desire Tests." *Hypatia: A Journal of Feminist Philosophy,* Special Issue on Analytical Feminism 20 (4): 109–26.

———. 2008. "Feminist Moral Psychology." *The Stanford Encyclopedia of Philosophy,* ed. Edward Zalta. Stanford, Calif.: Stanford University Press. http://plato.stanford.edu/contents.html.

———. 2009. *The Moral Skeptic.* New York: Oxford University Press.

Thoma, Mark. 2008. "Women's Rights: What's In It for Men?" *Economist's View.* http://economistsview.typepad.com/economistsview/2008/05/womens-rights-w.html.

Thomson, Judith Jarvis. 1990. "Trespass and First Property." In *The Realm of Rights.* Cambridge, Mass.: Harvard University Press.

Tuana, Nancy. 1992. *Woman and the History of Philosophy.* New York: Paragon House.

7

JULIA DRIVER
Washington University in St. Louis

CONSTRUCTIVISM AND FEMINISM

> "But this is our culture" is a response so often given by male elites
> around the world to justify the continued infringement of women's
> rights.
>
> —SUSAN MOLLER OKIN[1]

SUSAN MOLLER OKIN RAISED the issue of how cultural relativism did
not go hand-in-hand with progress on women's issues. She was focusing
on the issue of group rights being granted in liberal cultures to certain
non-liberal groups, that is, groups that discriminate against women as
part of the cultural norms for that group. Women are often harmed by
deference to cultural norms that are taken to be legitimate simply because
they are cultural norms. In Okin's view, one that I concur with, many
feminists have failed to confront such issues because of "...a hypercon-
cern to avoid cultural imperialism that leads, at worst, to a paralyzing
degree of cultural relativism."[2] The worry she expressed is familiar to
many critics of the version of moral relativism that is based on observation of cultural differences. The view that some moral claims are true, but
their truth dependent on cultural beliefs, would seem to entrench *oppressive* norms, the very norms that feminists have fought to expose as
shams.[3] Yet, some feminists are suspicious of moral realism, the view that
moral properties are objective in the sense that they exist "out there" in
the world, independent of us. Robust forms of moral realism hold that
moral claims have truth conditions that are "stance-independent" and
objective in this sense. This conflicts with the view that one of the tasks
of feminism is "transformative," that is, that new "realities" are created in
the midst of social change.

   In addition to, or maybe in light of, worries about relativism, there
has also been some feminist criticism of care approaches to ethics as
lacking in the means to engage in constructive and legitimate social

criticism, which requires taking an impersonal perspective on some problem or issue. In its early years, the care ethics approach did not grapple adequately with issues of perspective, and how moral perspective might be one that needs to be corrected *away* from both our own personal sentiments and relationships, and away from purely cultural norms. The care approach, relying as it did on the idea that moral behavior involves sympathetic response to others, includes, in some way, caring for them. It was also seen as being based in the sentimentalist approach to morality championed by writers such as Adam Smith and David Hume.[4] In general, sentimentalism holds that morality is based on affect. This, as far as it goes, is compatible with rationalism, since a rationalist could maintain that reason is both the basis for morality itself, and, further, guides the emotions properly, and that care, appropriately guided, is fundamental to moral *judgment*, though not the source of normativity itself. Thus, it is possible for the rationalist to reconcile to an emotional element in our practice of morals, just as the sentimentalist has always reconciled to the use of reason in modulating and guiding judgment.[5] Sentimentalism when it is contrasted with rationalism holds that the source of normativity is provided by affect.

Sentimentalism is anti-realist because it is committed to the view that norms are not stance-independent. But the anti-realism is not necessarily one that leads to "anything goes" in morality. There are standards. One way to establish the standards as holding independently of individual stances is to develop a constructivist version of sentimentalism. Constructivism is the view that normative standards are constructed via a particular process or procedure, and/or relative to a perspective, rather than discovered. Further, some moral claims are true (or appropriate) relative to the constructed norms. In this way, one can hold the view that there are some true moral claims, and yet the norms of morality depend on (in some sense, to be discussed later) our responses to them. The most plausible version, and the one I explore in this paper, does not claim that this procedure constructs norms at the individual level. At the very most, the proper level is that of the species. However, a plausible argument can be made that we can be even more general and hold that the proper method of construction takes place at the level of social beings. This will not completely eradicate worries about relativism. However, it will eradicate the worries about relativism that are of concern to feminists focused on the systematic mistreatment of women by other social beings.

David Hume is probably the most well-known sentimentalist.[6] His view of virtue can be developed along substantive constructivist lines.

According to Hume, whether a trait is a virtue or a vice is determined by whether the trait is approved of or disapproved of from "the general point of view."[7] The virtuous person is responding to reasons with a certain content—for example, the usefulness of a given trait, or its agreeableness—all underwritten by sympathy. Thus, when a person judges another to be courageous or generous, she does so because either she finds the trait in question immediately agreeable, or she detects something useful about the trait. Virtues are traits we ought to possess, that is, they have normative force, due to their being approved of from the general point of view.

> The notion of morals, implies some sentiment common to all mankind, which recommends the same object to general approbation, and makes every man, or most men, agree in the same opinion or decision concerning it. It also implies some sentiment, so universal and comprehensive as to extend to all mankind, and render the actions and conduct, even of the persons the most remote, an object of applause or censure, according as they agree or disagree with that rule of right which is established.[8]

In more detail, the right perspective for determining whether an act is a virtue or a vice is that of the general point of view, that is, the perspective from which the *observer* would approve or disapprove of the act or corresponding trait when stripped of biases and prejudices, and when thinking of how the act or trait in question would affect those around the agent. In some cases, a trait is a virtue just because it results in actions we always tend to find pleasing, such as generous acts. In some cases, such as justice, the story is more complicated. Justice is an example of what Hume called an "artificial" virtue since its goodness, and hence its pleasing quality, depends on the usefulness of the system of justice as a whole. Justice is a virtue, but not because we find the individual acts of justice pleasing or useful. In fact, we may feel bad when a poverty-stricken thief is sent to jail. But, realizing that society needs a system of justice in order to flourish, we find the overall system useful.

In the *Treatise*, Hume provides a vivid example of how the corrective of the general point of view works:

> The good qualities of an enemy are hurtful to us; but may still command our esteem and respect. 'Tis only when a character is consider'd in general, without reference to our particular interest, that it causes such a feeling or sentiment, as denominates it morally good or evil.[9]

Hume often employs the analogy with aesthetic judgments that also require perspectival correction.[10] That we think it is appropriate to correct for biases and prejudices in our sympathy is clear when we consider how important many people feel impartiality is to ethics. Sympathy, uncorrected, would lead people to favor the near and dear in an illegitimate manner. It is not morally good to steal even if one really wants a new television and one feels sorry that one's children are forced to miss their favorite shows. Further, if sympathy is not corrected, then Hume believes that a host of practical problems would follow. We strive for consistency in moral judgments, but without correcting for our own idiosyncratic interests and how they affect our feelings, we would not be able to achieve this. Bob, for example, ought to admire the political courage of his rival for public office, even though it makes *him* feel bad whenever that rival succeeds, just because the success of his rival makes his own success less likely.

Thus, the responses of the observer, under the circumstances that are considered corrective to the sentiment of sympathy, provide the standard of evaluation.[11] We are correct in regarding Benedict Arnold's disloyalty as bad since the impartial observer disapproves of it. It's clear this approach is intended to provide a standard for the correct application of moral terms. Someone who approves of Arnold would be mistaken.

One can employ this framework in providing an account of the appropriateness or inappropriateness of moral commitments. Further, sentimentalism *can* be developed in such a way as to hold that there are some moral *truths*, and the truth value of moral claims is not culturally determined. In Hume's view all normal human beings possess sympathy. It is part of human nature and not a cultural artifact. He is open to the possibility that how intensely individuals feel may be influenced by cultural standards. But this is irrelevant to the overall account since the variability is corrected for by the general point of view. Thus, on this view, it is not simply individual norms that are criticizable, but cultural norms are as well. Judgments appealing to those norms are true or false, but the truth or falsity is due to the correspondence with norms that are reflectively endorsed. They are not, therefore, stance-independent norms.

In this paper I try to bring together these two threads—that there is a correct standard for moral evaluation and that norms are constructed—in order to explore an option that seems quite friendly to feminist concerns, and yet does not commit one to a kind of robust moral realism that some find suspect. But the rejection of realism does not imply a rejection of standards that have some degree of objective basis. A sentimentalist approach can provide this, while also keeping with the spirit of a feminist approach to ethics based on a care perspective. I use "care perspective" here rather loosely. Many feminists reject the early care approach as being too noncritical, as rejecting considerations of justice and fairness, for example—and I agree with this take on the early care approach. But the kernel of the care approach that is worth preserving is the idea that, at its basis, morality is more a matter of how we feel both about certain reasons for action and about certain sorts of actions themselves. This does not at all rule out a role for reason or critical reflection. Indeed, critical reflection is crucial to refining our views on how we *ought* to feel, regardless of how we do feel. I do not think the view is feminist in particular—just that it allows a good deal of what feminists want to do with moral criticism without the need to jettison other, anti-realist, commitments to which some feminists subscribe. Further, this approach allows for the development of a more refined normative theory that has often been associated with feminism—the ethics of care. The caring that forms the foundation of the system, however, is not uncritical caring. The correction of bias and prejudice allows for the critique of oppressive norms. The general approach might be termed "constructivism," though it is a sort of constructivism that takes as its starting point third person moral evaluation rather than the standpoint of the agent deliberating about what she should do—thus, the standpoint is evaluative rather than deliberative; it involves a judger who considers a trait or an action from the third- person perspective. This variety of constructivism is quite different from Kantian brands of constructivism. Kantian forms of constructivism, such as those developed by John Rawls and Christine Korsgaard, take the practical standpoint, or the first-person standpoint, to be the starting point for the construction of norms.[12]

SOME DISTINCTIONS

"Sentimentalism" refers to a family of theories regarding the nature of morality and moral judgment. The general idea is that morality in some way depends upon sentiments, or desires, that is, what we care about. The dependency in question can be semantic, epistemological, or metaphysical. If it is semantic, then the idea is that moral claims either express emotions, in which case they have no truth value, or express claims with truth value, but the truth value is determined in some way by a connection to an emotional response, usually one that has been corrected through an idealized procedure. Expressivism, the view that moral claims do not have truth value, falls into the first category. According to expressivism, we are expressing a feeling, either positive or negative, when we make a normative judgment, and that expression cannot be "true" or "false" any more than the utterance "Yay!" can be. "Yay!" makes no assertion, no claim about the world. The standards for evaluating these sorts of expression revolve around notions such as "apt" or "inapt," "appropriate" or "inappropriate." These standards are usually tied to pragmatic considerations, not evidential ones.

However, one can be a sentimentalist about the semantics of moral claims and also believe that those claims have truth value, and even that some are true. There are many ways to spell out the latter approach. One could be a subjectivist, and tie truth conditions to the beliefs of the speaker. This approach is afflicted with serious problems. For example, it makes no sense of genuine moral disagreement because when people disagree about moral issues, on this view all this amounts to is that they express different reactions to the issue in question. But this does not reflect how we intuitively think about disagreement. Many of us believe that when two people argue over the moral permissibility of abortion, something more is at stake than just a disagreement over how they *feel* about abortion. However, the idealizing procedure mentioned above could be such as to set common standards of evaluation for the moral claims, so that a speaker can be mistaken in making a claim if the claim falls short of those standards, whatever they happen to be. Constance may truly and deeply believe that female circumcision is obligatory, and that may well be the normal view in her culture, but she is mistaken relative to the constructed norms. The practice would not be approved of from an unbiased, impartial viewpoint that sets the standard for the norms.

As an epistemological claim, sentimentalism holds that we come to understand morality—acquire moral *beliefs*—via the sentiments. Without the right kind of emotions, we would not be able to acquire *moral* beliefs. This view, that our moral judgments depend on having feelings of the right sort, can be attributed to philosophers such as Francis Hutcheson. Hutcheson holds that the perception of moral failing in particular, as opposed to some other kind of failing on the part of nature, requires a moral sense that conveys distinctive sentiments regarding moral goods and evils.

> This will perhaps be equally evident from our ideas of evil, done to us designedly by a rational agent. Our sense of natural good and evil would

> make us receive, with equal serenity and composure, an assault, a buffet, an affront from a neighbour, a cheat from a partner, or trustee, as we would an equal damage from the fall of a beam, a tile, or a tempest; and we should have the same affections and sentiments on both occasions.[13]

The house one lives in may be defective, and cause one discomfort, but Hutcheson's point is that moral defects are perceived differently by us. Evidence for this is gleaned from our reactive attitudes. We do not resent a house for its defects, though we do resent a moral agent when that agent intentionally causes us harm.

This view is compatible with the view that moral norms are derived from reason, since it is simply a view about what we need in order to recognize or understand those norms. For example, it is possible to hold that if we did not care for each other we would not recognize our obligations to each other, though those obligations would still exist since they would be derived from reason.

If viewed as a metaphysical claim, sentimentalism purports that moral properties, or moral facts, are dependent on emotional responses of the right sort. This view is independent of the other two theses; however, those sentimentalists who hold that some moral claims are true will often appeal to some version of the metaphysical claim to account for their truth. These approaches typically view the properties in question as response-dependent in some way, on analogy with secondary qualities. It is possible to interpret Hume this way, when he explicitly draws the analogy between perception of virtue and secondary qualities: "Vice and virtue, therefore, may be compar'd to sounds, colours, heat and cold, which, according to modern philosophy, are not qualities in objects, but perceptions in the mind: And this discovery in morals, like that other in physics, is to be regarded as a considerable advancement of the speculative sciences...."[14] In this passage, Hume is simply drawing an analogy between virtue and vice judgments and color judgments. Hume himself did not have the view that response-dependent properties resided in objects. Depending on how one interprets claims he made about our inability to perceive moral facts, is seems clear that he did not think there were such properties that we were able to pick up on in making moral judgments. Indeed, one could hold that the above passage supports the view that there are no dispositions of things in the world that do cause various responses in us. However, some writers such as David Wiggins have seen in Hume's overall account of morality a way to modify the view toward what Wiggins dubbed a "sensible subjectivism." It does not follow that virtue and vice are not real, just that they depend on our perceptions. They are not "stance-independent." This position blurs the distinction between realism and anti-realism, since the "virtue" property of some mental qualities is an actual property of those mental qualities, yet it is not a property that can be understood independently of the responses of the observer. On this type of view, moral goodness is not stance-independent, so it makes appeal to a subject or judger, yet it also holds that a particular judger can get things right or wrong when he or she makes a judgment of virtue.[15]

One deep problem for the semantic approach, which is committed to truth values for moral claims, and the metaphysical approach, which is committed to the existence of moral properties, is the *contingency problem*. The fact that we have the emotional responses that we do is dependent on features of human nature that are contingent. Features of human nature are evolved. We have the feelings that we have due to selective pressures. Thus, if the truth of moral claims depends upon what our emotional responses happen to be, even ones that are suitably idealized, we need to recognize that these could have been very different, and thus there seems to be the possibility that moral truths will vary given variances in the emotional responses of the creatures that make moral claims. This is a problem because it runs against moral phenomenology. We have a very strong sense of the necessity of moral claims—that is, if it is true that suttee (i.e., the immolation of a widow on her husband's funeral pyre) is wrong, then it must be true, and it *must* be true independent of our feelings about suttee itself.

This same worry can be brought out for the metaphysical issue as well. We seem to have a strong sense that if there is a property of "wrongness" supervening on the physical aspects of the practice of suttee, then that property is really "out there," and is neither a simple projection of a negative emotional response to that action, nor dependent on whether or not we exist and experience those negative emotions.

The sentimentalist denies one or both of these views. That is, the sentimentalist may hold that truth values are not necessary, so that the claim that

(1) Torturing babies just for fun is wrong

is not true in all possible worlds; and/or, the sentimentalist holds that if this claim is true at all, it is true in virtue of correspondence with *response-dependent* properties.[16]

However, we need to distinguish another way that moral norms seem "necessary." There is a practical sense, which I call the *binding thesis*: morality binds unconditionally. If it is wrong to engage in suttee (under conditions C), one must not engage in suttee (under conditions C), no matter what. These are independent theses, but both speak to the moral phenomenology that resists contingency. The connection is that in one case, the semantic case, the truth of the moral claim is not contingent on our responses (or some other non-objective feature), and in the second case, the practical requirement set by the true claim is not contingent on some aspect of our nature such as our desires. The sentimentalist has something to say about both sorts of necessity, but in this paper I will be focusing on the semantic thesis. I will argue that the semantic thesis is false: the necessity is actually psychological in nature.

The contingency worry that the semantic thesis tries to avoid is related to a worry about relativism. While many feminists have embraced relativism, others have not, precisely because of the moral phenomenology: it *seems* very clear to most of us that if abusing someone is morally bad, it must be morally bad, regardless of how someone, or some group of persons or sentient beings, happens to feel about it. The worry would be allayed by realism about morality, or the view that there are *robust* moral properties, ones that are *not contingent* on emotional responses in the way sentimentalism seems to hold.

However, a non-realist view could hold that the properties in question are response-dependent, but in a way that does not commit them to being dependent on the *individual's* response. Consider a property that is a paradigm of a response-dependent property, that of being irritating. Screeching noises are irritating. A response-dependent property is a property such that the extension of the property term is determined by our responses, and not merely by features external to those responses.[17] Given this understanding, then the property, let's say, of moral goodness, is a disposition to elicit a response of approval in the observer.[18] We then have the issue of specifying the nature of the "observer." Problems of subjectivism can be avoided by idealizing the observer. Adam Smith, for example, ruled the observer impartial.[19] Roderick Firth added that the observer was fully informed.[20] These additions are important to preserving the recognition of moral error. Individuals make lots of mistakes, including moral mistakes, and a simple subjective form of response-dependence cannot account for this. According to simple subjectivism, when Sarah says "abortion is wrong" and Isabel says "abortion is permissible," they are both right since they are just reporting something about themselves, not about abortion itself. But insulating agents from moral error leads to highly counterintuitive views about the nature of moral disagreement.

To avoid the problems with subjectivism, and to preserve what I take to be the virtues of Hume's theory, ones that I believe many feminists would endorse, I propose that we integrate response-dependence with a constructivist view of moral norms. These are distinct ways of understanding how norms can be mind-dependent and yet confer a degree of objectivity to our moral claims. To hold *simply* that moral goodness is a property that causes a feeling of approval in the spectator is not constructivist. What makes the account constructivist is that one endorses the feeling caused, and the endorsement under certain specified conditions generates legitimacy for the norms in question. To clarify, first consider a non-moral case:

(P) The peony is gorgeous.

The peony is gorgeous (crudely) because the normal response to the peony is one of appreciation. We could consider "gorgeous" to be a response-dependent property. But we have not yet generated a norm. On the view I am recommending, to generate a norm we need to *endorse* the appreciation. While I am not sure this can be done for aesthetic properties, I claim it can be for moral ones. Murder is wrong because of the response it generates in the observer, appropriately construed, who further endorses the response relative to other norms.

It is important to clarify the sort of response-dependence I am specifying here. Richard Holton discusses various kinds of response-dependence. For example, some concepts are response-dependent because they are *judgment-dependent*. So, we might hold that something is red when it is judged to be red: X is red if and only if it is judged to be red. In the case of color judgments, the judgers will be normal observers, those who use the concept of "red" in describing the world around them. However, the idealizations appealed to in ethics have another source, so that it may be the case that the concept in question does not fit with *statistically* normal usage of the term. Often, for example, the responses must be those of an *ideal*, rather than normal, observer in order to rule out distorting influences such as biases and prejudices of various sorts. But another difference between judgment-dependence and the sort of response-dependence I have in mind is that the response-dependence I am talking about does not necessarily involve judgment. Holton uses the example of "stimulant": a stimulant is a substance that causes an increased heartbeat—that is the response typical of stimulants. But this response is not a *judgment* that a particular substance is a stimulant. The same point can be made in the moral case. Moral goodness may cause a response that is not a *judgment*; the approval could manifest in other ways. Perhaps it is just a feeling of approval with respect to an action. This would be compatible with an expressivist view that moral language simply expresses attitudes. However, though the response-dependence may not be judgment-dependent, it will provide the building blocks for judgments. The response, *combined* with a procedure of reflective endorsement regarding the response, can lead to the recognition of moral reasons to engage in some behaviors and avoid others. That is what the constructivist project holds is actually the case with our moral judgments.

MIND-INDEPENDENCE

If one adopts the view that moral claims are true in virtue of responses of the appropriate sort of observer, properly endorsed, then one can be a sentimentalist and hold that some moral claims are true, and are true mind-independently in the sense that we care about here—independently of individual *and* cultural beliefs. This is because the contingency problem can be understood at many different levels. The sentimentalist is committed to some degree of contingency, but it certainly need not be at the level of the individual observer or the community, or even the species.

Sentimentalist approaches always deploy a corrective mechanism on the emotional response. This is precisely to avoid the problems associated with a fine-grained relativism. Without a mechanism to correct for idiosyncratic responses, each person's response would be self-validating and moral truth would vary from person to person. Hume himself justified the correction as necessary for people to communicate with each other meaningfully about virtue. His worries in this regard seem overblown. The real worry has to do with fidelity to the phenomenology of moral facts. We disagree about moral issues, and that disagreement does not boil down simply to incompatible responses. The corrective mechanism appeals to an idealization of some sort, sometimes having to do with the capacities of the responder. As noted earlier, the idealizations can occur along differing parameters, but will tend to include factors such as impartiality and adequate levels of information possessed by the observer. Of course, on these models within the sentimentalist tradition the observer is a sympathizer. The observer *cares*. In the idealizations, the caring is modulated by the other cognitive features of the observer, that is, how much she knows, her impartiality, how well she reasons, and so forth. One thing that often seems to be missed is that caring is perfectly compatible with impartiality. One can care about both of one's children, and be impartial between them. One can care about other human beings, and be impartial between them as well.

But getting full-fledged norms is a two-stage process. Consider a case adapted from one of Hume's examples:

> Valerius is the commander of a squadron of soldiers holding a castle. As he looks over the battlements he sees enemy troops approaching, led by his counterpart, Valeria. Valerius hates Valeria. He observes her bravery in battle and it causes him great unhappiness. Valeria's bravery does not cause Valerius to have a pleasant reaction.

But this does not mean that Valeria lacks virtue. Instead, it is clear she has the virtue of bravery when Valerius's perceptions are stripped of biases and prejudices and her actions are perceived from the idealized perspective. Then it *is* pleasing. The second step is to endorse the corrected finding. Why have the second step? Isn't it redundant? No, because it helps separate out norms. Consider (P) again. When a person's distorted vision is corrected, and the peony viewed in normal lighting conditions, and so on, it is gorgeous. But we cannot *universally* endorse this. We understand the truth of (P) as genuinely relative in a way that moral norms are not. The claim that "Valeria has the moral virtue of bravery" appeals to a different sort of norm, a norm that applies to all persons judging Valeria and others, as well as judging themselves.

Again, the type of model is constructivism since it understands the correctness of moral claims to rest on whether or not those claims, such as "generosity is a virtue" or "murder is wrong," pass an endorsement test.[21] It is not the more familiar Kantian constructivism that holds that moral goodness is the result of a procedure of rational "self-legislation," in which rational agents construct for themselves (and, by extension, for others), moral laws that demand obedience on pain of irrationality. Rather, moral goodness is a disposition to be viewed a certain way by caring, rational agents and thus is understood relative to those responses. The sentimentalist approach further side-steps a problem identified by Russ Shafer-Landau in discussing the constraints of impartiality and full information generally placed on the observer: "...agents satisfying these constraints may be perfectly callous, or entirely indifferent to human welfare...."[22] As mentioned earlier, impartiality does not entail callousness. Sentimentalism adds to the view that the endorsement test be conducted from a sympathetic point of view to generate endorsement of *moral* norms.[23] The agent is sympathetic at the first level, where perception is corrected to rule out distortions, and again, at the second level, where he views the findings of his perception to provide norms that are universally applicable.

On Hume's view, the background theory is that there are some things that we, as human beings, are psychologically committed to believing. These beliefs are referred to by Hume commentators as "natural beliefs."[24] Examples are claims such as "there is an external world," "the external world resembles, at least roughly, one's perception of it under the appropriate perceptual conditions," and so forth. We can, I argue, include normative claims of the form "*it must be the case that* willful killing of an innocent person is (*pro tanto*) wrong" in this category. Natural beliefs are those that cannot be abandoned by human beings, however much we reason about them.[25] They withstand rational reflection, but not in a way that makes them ultimately justified. Instead, they withstand reflection in that they cannot simply be dispensed with in either practical or theoretical reasoning. Writers such as Norman Kemp Smith took this to mean that Hume held reason to be utterly subordinated to "feeling and instinct." The object of reason is belief, but human nature is such that some beliefs—which, presumably, serve our interests in some way—are only pragmatically justified rather than justified by evidence (reason employed to discover truths about the world). Indeed, they cannot be justified by reason. I strongly believe that "body" exists, but cannot prove it with evidence. Such a belief is arational, but not irrational. It is not irrational to hold such a belief because there is reason to hold such a belief, even though the belief may not be true or backed by adequate evidence. Thus, the endorsement test is pragmatic on the Humean account.

My view is not that *particular* moral beliefs themselves have this character. Indeed, I believe that individual moral beliefs can be true and we can have adequate evidence for their truth. For example, the evidence for my belief that killing an innocent person is *pro tanto* wrong is that such an act has great disutility. Disutility that is not overridden by some other consideration is not approved of by the impartial observer. But this does not yet *fully* get at the source of moral authority, the feeling that the norms represented in such judgments are fully binding. In addition to being part of an account of the force of moral norms and their genuineness, sympathy can *explain* how it is that we are motivated, and how it that we do *feel*, as part of normal human nature, bound by the norms in question. But that is only part of the story. It is the commitment to *necessity* that cannot be eradicated through rational reflection. We do not so much endorse the necessity as fail to entertain not endorsing it, as a practical matter. That is, it is not a *practical* possibility for us that we take seriously claims that seem outrageously immoral, such as "torturing kittens for fun is permissible." It may be we entertain it in abstruse philosophical discussions, but, like the claim that "the external world is totally different from our perceptions of it," we cannot as a practical matter, take it seriously. The phenomenon of imaginative resistance, I have discussed elsewhere, provides some evidence for this.[26] Imaginative resistance refers to the phenomenon that, when reading works of fiction, we seem to refuse to go along with morally outrageous "truths" presented in the fiction, and this seems odd given that we go along with all kinds of descriptively outrageous "truths" in the fiction, such as talking mice, ghosts, wizards, and so forth. But for this to be plausible in my argument in this paper, we need to be very clear about what we feel the necessity *about*. Consider again the claim that

(S) Suttee under conditions C is wrong.

The claim is not that one cannot imagine a world in which suttee might be morally indifferent or even good. Rather, the claim is that one cannot imagine a world *exactly like ours in all respects* except that suttee under conditions C is not wrong. This explains the psychological necessity. It is true that in any world exactly like our world in all descriptive respects, that world will be exactly like ours in all normative respects as well. Of course, this does not mean that "suttee is wrong" is a necessary truth in some other respect. It is not—if conditions in other worlds are different, it may not be.

The nature of the commitment is also important. The claim here, as in Hume's discussion of natural belief, is not that one cannot bring oneself to consider an alternative hypothesis. Perhaps there is no external world. Perhaps it is question-begging to insist that if all descriptive elements are the same, the normative one must be as well. It may be that one could get oneself into a frame of mind where one questioned such beliefs. Indeed, it seems certain that people regularly do this. But the commitment is not theoretical; it is practical. One does not leave by the window because one cannot prove the door is really there.

The sentimentalist picture as outlined here does give one an account of mind-independent truths in morality without realism. It does so in a way that attaches significance to features of our normative lives that feminists in the past have found to be neglected. The necessity in question is not truth in all possible worlds where one allows for differing descriptive circumstances, but involves the rejection of there being a possible world exactly like ours descriptively but with different norms.

However, it should also be pointed out that to avoid relativism we do not need *necessity*, nor do we need the truth of moral claims in all possible worlds. All we need is *universal* truth in the actual world.

UNIVERSALITY

A universal moral claim is one that holds for all agents. Relativism challenges *universality*, not necessity. One can deny the necessity of moral claims, where that is understood as their truth failing to be contingent on appropriate responses, and yet commit to the universality of moral claims, where universality is understood in the following way:

> (UMC) If x is a general moral claim and x is true, then x is true for all agents.

The requirement for agency here is that the being in question be rational and engage in goal-directed behavior.

There has been a suspicion of universal moral truth, which is usually also described as "timeless" in the feminist literature. For example, Alison Jaggar writes:

> Most of the dominant voices in Western ethics have sought to transcend the changing world of the senses and the contingencies of historical situations by pursuing timeless and universal moral truths through practices of moral reason that also have been conceptualized as timeless and universal. Feminist ethics, by contrast, is inhospitable to such idealized portrayals of moral philosophy.[27]

It is not entirely clear in such passages whether the claim is simply that male bias has distorted what are perceived to be the universal truths of morality, or whether there is also the claim that this process itself cannot work even if a neutral stance is taken by those seeking universal and timeless truths. Further passages indicate that Jaggar is highly skeptical of there being a timeless universal moral truth independent of "... a culturally specific set of texts and practices produced by individuals inhabiting particular social locations and laden with historically particular preoccupations and preconceptions."[28]

We should distinguish different ways in which a moral claim can be "universal" and/or "timeless." Scope issues have to be clearly spelled out. A claim can be a universal truth with a limited scope. Presumably Jaggar means to include in the scope truths applicable within all human cultures. This would be the view that true moral claims provide reasons for everyone either to approve or disapprove, or to engage in or fail to engage in, a certain behavior or attitude. The constructivist of the sort spelled out above can hold to such truths. These are set by the norms for human beings; or, even more generally, social beings. Are they "timeless"? If this means "timeless with respect to the course of human history," and if we are also talking about basic truths such as "causing unnecessary pain is wrong," then, "yes." The worry Jaggar has need not lead us to embrace relativism at all. The reactions of privileged men do not determine the content of actual morality any more than the reactions of any particular subgroup—or any group at all.

Hume believed that universality was achieved by appeal to a universal human nature. All "normal" persons possess the capacity for sympathy. Thus, all persons are able to make moral judgments and feel the weight of moral norms. Of course, this is different from the consideration that these norms have universal force or application, as specified in (UMC). But they are connected. For Hume, sympathy accounts for the force we feel attached to moral norms. If one takes a cognitivist route, then that force can also be explained by the perception of the true moral claims being true for everyone, not just some people, such as those who happen to react differently. This provides a response to relativism and a response to Jaggar as well. Cultural norms can be distorting. This is because they may be due to historical factors in a given culture that enshrined unjust norms. In the case of suttee, for example, the practice is approved of as a way of recognizing the purported ownership of women by men. This does not withstand impartial, sympathetic scrutiny. When it comes to cultural practices like suttee, they would fail to be pleasing from the general point of view, or claims of their goodness would fail endorsement.

The model that I have been proposing in this paper, which is derived from Hume, is one that I believe to be amenable to the two strands of feminist thought outlined above. It is that when the observer finds a trait or an action pleasing, and reflects on why it is pleasing, the observer focuses on features that, given our sympathetic natures, are ones that we take to be directing our actions in unique ways. These features relate to our actions with respect to each other, and they are ones that caring agents must endorse, in order to be caring agents. We may fall short of the highest level of universality—we may not be able to get endorsement from the non-caring—but then these agents may not then count as moral agents at all. That argument, however, calls for an entirely different paper.

Notes

I thank Anita Superson for her helpful comments on an earlier draft, and the participants of the Society for Analytical Feminism meetings in Lexington, Kentucky, April, 2008, where an earlier version of this paper was read.
1. Susan Moller Okin, "Feminism and Multiculturalism: Some Tensions," *Ethics* (1998): 661–84.
2. Ibid., 665.
3. Of course, many writers have pointed out that arguing from cultural differences to ethical relativism is fallacious. See, for example, James Rachels's well-known discussion in chapter 2 of *The Elements of Moral Philosophy* (New York: McGraw-Hill, 1993). The worry I am mainly concerned with here, however, is that legitimating cultural norms for whatever reason has serious problematic implications for our ability to criticize or praise legitimately, and thus to engage in social reform.
4. Adam Smith did not in fact ground morality in self-interest, as some writers have commonly supposed.
5. Indeed, Michael Slote has ended his new book, *The Ethics of Care and Empathy* (New York; Routledge, 2007), p. 121 with the statement: "Care-ethical sentimentalism may not think that practical reason grounds morality, but it has, or can have, its own distinctive conception of practical reason, and it allows great scope and use for other kinds of reason and reasoning within morality, and in human life generally."
6. References to David Hume's work cite David Fate Norton's and Mary J. Norton's critical edition of *A Treatise of Human Nature*, vol. 1 [THN] (Oxford: Clarendon Press, 2007) and Thomas Beauchamp's critical edition of *An Enquiry Concerning the Principles of Morals* [EPM] (Oxford: Clarendon Press, 1998).
7. There is a very large literature on what Hume meant by the "general point of view." Some have argued that it is an ideal observer standard, other that such

a standard would be inaccessible and so not the one actually offered by Hume. I discuss this in more detail in "Pleasure as the Standard of Virtue in Hume's Moral Philosophy," *Pacific Philosophical Quarterly* 85 (June 2004), 173–94. In this essay, I will not be going into the details of the distinction and assume that Hume had in mind a kind of ideal observer standard, though the details of the idealization may vary.

8. EPM 9.1.5.
9. THN 3.1.2.4.
10. Ibid. In THN 3.1.2.4, Hume notes that we may need to correct for our prejudices when we judge whether or not an enemy's voice sounds "agreeable."
11. Note that the standard itself does not require that agents actually employ the general point of view to correct their sentiments. However, to the extent that the moral judgment the agent makes is warranted, it is corrected as required to rule out biases and prejudices.
12. See John Rawls, "Kantian Constructivism in Moral Theory," *Journal of Philosophy* 77 (September 1980): 515–72 and Christine Korsgaard, *Sources of Normativity* (New York: Cambridge University Press, 1996).
13. Francis Hutcheson, *An Inquiry Concerning the Original of Our Ideas of Virtue or Moral Good, Treatise II*, in *British Moralists: 1650–1800*, ed. D. D. Raphael (Oxford: Oxford University Press, 1969), p. 265.
14. THN 3.1.1.27.
15. David Wiggins, "A Sensible Subjectivism," in *Needs, Values, Truth: Essays in the Philosophy of Value* (New York: Oxford University Press, 1998), pp. 185–214.
16. This is a tricky issue. Some sentimentalists retain the semantic thesis via rigid designation. See, for example, Michael Slote's "Moral Sentimentalism," *Ethical Theory and Moral Practice* 7 (March 2004): 3–14. If one opts for this sort of strategy, then "suttee (under conditions C) is wrong" is true in all possible worlds because the reference of the key terms is rigidly fixed in our world, where suttee is wrong.
17. Richard Holton discusses this characterization of response-dependence, and uses "irritating" as an example, in "Intentions, Response-Dependence, and Immunity from Error," in *Response-Dependent Concepts*, ed. Peter Menzies (ANU Working Papers in Philosophy 1, 1991), 1–26. Holton, however, holds that although some *concepts* are response-dependent, properties are not.
18. This can also be specified in an explicitly normative way, as a disposition to elicit a "proper" or "warranted" response. If one were not using the account itself to describe the source of warrant, then one would be free to pursue this characterization.
19. Adam Smith, *A Theory of the Moral Sentiments*, ed. Knud Haakonssen (New York: Cambridge University Press, 2002).
20. Roderick Firth, "Ethical Absolutism and the Ideal Observer," *Philosophy & Phenomenological Research* 12 (1952): 317–45.

21. See Sharon Street's "Constructivism About Reasons," in *Oxford Studies in Metaethics* 3, ed. Russ Shafer-Landau (Oxford: Oxford University Press, 2008), p. 2, where she provides the following, very general, account of constructivism: "Constructivist views in ethics understand the correctness or incorrectness of some (specified) set of normative judgments as a question of whether those judgments withstand some (specified) procedure of scrutiny from the standpoint of some (specified) set of further normative judgments."
22. Russ Shafer-Landau, *Moral Realism: A Defense* (New York: Oxford University Press, 2005), p. 41.
23. Note that this leaves to the side the issue of constructivism regarding other norms.
24. Norman Kemp Smith first discussed Hume on natural belief. See his "The Naturalism of Hume (I)," *Mind* 54 (1905): 149–73, at 161.
25. See, for example, THN 1.4.2.1 where Hume discusses the example of our belief in body as something "…which we must take for granted in all our reasonings."
26. "Imaginative Resistance and Psychological Necessity," in *Objectivism, Subjectivism, and Relativism in Ethics*, ed. Ellen Frankel Paul et al. (New York: Cambridge University Press, 2008), pp. 301–13.
27. Alison Jaggar, "Ethics Naturalized: Feminism's Contribution to Moral Epistemology," *Metaphilosophy* 31 (2000): 452–68, at 458.
28. Ibid.

Bibliography

Driver, Julia. "Pleasure as the Standard of Virtue in Hume's Moral Philosophy." *Pacific Philosophical Quarterly* 85 (June 2004): 173–94.
———. "Imaginative Resistance and Psychological Necessity." In *Objectivism, Subjectivism, and Relativism in Ethics*, edited by Ellen Frankel Paul et al., pp. 301–13. New York: Cambridge University Press, 2008.
Firth, Roderick. "Ethical Absolutism and the Ideal Observer." *Philosophy and Phenomenological Research* 12 (1952): 317–45.
Holton, Richard. "Intentions, Response-Dependence, and Immunity from Error." In *Response-Dependent Concepts*, edited by Peter Menzies, pp. 1–26. ANU Working Papers in Philosophy 1, 1991.
Hume, David. *A Treatise of Human Nature.* Edited by David Fate Norton and Mary Norton. Oxford: Clarendon Press, 2007.
———. *An Enquiry Concerning the Principles of Morals.* Edited by Thomas Beauchamp. Oxford: Clarendon Press, 1998.
Hutcheson, Francis. *An Inquiry Concerning the Original of Our Ideas of Virtue or Moral Good, Treatise II.* In *British Moralists: 1650–1800*, edited by D. D. Raphael. Oxford: Oxford University Press, 1969.
Jaggar, Alison. "Ethics Naturalized: Feminism's Contribution to Moral Epistemology." *Metaphilosophy* 31 (2000): 452–68.

Korsgaard, Christine. *Sources of Normativity*. New York: Cambridge University Press, 1996.

Okin, Susan Moller. "Feminism and Multiculturalism: Some Tensions." *Ethics* 108 (1998): 661–84.

Rachels, James. *The Elements of Moral Philosophy*. New York: McGraw Hill, 1993.

Rawls, John. "Kantian Constructivism in Moral Theory." *Journal of Philosophy* 77 (September 1980): 515–72.

Shafer-Landau, Russ. *Moral Realism: A Defense*. New York: Oxford University Press, 2005.

Slote, Michael. *The Ethics of Care and Empathy*. New York: Routledge, 2007.

———. "Moral Sentimentalism," *Ethical Theory and Moral Practice* 7 (March 2004): 3–14.

Smith, Adam. *A Theory of the Moral Sentiments*. Edited by Knud Haakonssen. New York: Cambridge University Press, 1992.

Smith, Norman Kemp. "The Naturalism of Hume (I)." *Mind* 54 (1905): 149–73.

Street, Sharon. "Constructivism About Reasons." In *Oxford Studies in Metaethics* 3, edited by Russ Shafer-Landau, pp. 207–46. Oxford: Oxford University Press, 2008.

Wiggins, David. "A Sensible Subjectivism." In *Needs, Values, Truth: Essays in the Philosophy of Value*, pp. 185–214. New York: Oxford University Press, 1998.

8

JENNIFER MATHER SAUL
University of Sheffield

POLITICALLY SIGNIFICANT TERMS

AND PHILOSOPHY OF LANGUAGE:

Methodological Issues

PHILOSOPHERS OF LANGUAGE HAVE tended to focus on examples that are not politically significant in any way. We spend a lot of time analyzing natural kind terms: We think hard about "water" and "pain" and "arthritis." Some of us even obsess over issues about co-referential names raised by comic book plots.[1] But we don't think much about the far more politically significant kind terms (natural or social—it's a matter for dispute) like "race," "sex," "gender," "woman," "man," "gay," and "straight."

My work in feminism has recently led me to turn my attention as a philosopher of language to the more politically significant terms. What I expected to find was some new puzzles, perhaps similar in form to the old ones, but likely amenable to the same solutions. I thought my knowledge of the older, drier debates would help me to make some useful interventions in these newer, more significant (in the real-world sense) debates. I did indeed find puzzles—and puzzles of the sort that any traditional philosopher of language should find well worth considering. But I also found something that I hadn't expected (though perhaps I should have): that these newer puzzles bring with them challenging new methodological issues. And that, once raised, these methodological issues are not confined to politically significant puzzles. Some of them, at least, are issues that every traditional philosopher of language would do well to consider.

My strategy in this essay will be to examine a case study. That case study is the evolution of my own thinking about sex/gender terms like "woman" and "man." My reason for examining this is that the methodological issues that will in the end be my focus are ones that concern what sorts of factors should be relevant in theorizing about philosophy of language. This case study is as good a way as any to illustrate the sorts of factors that arise in thinking about politically significant terms. Although I'll be examining various views about how to treat terms like "woman," my goal isn't so much to pass judgment on these views as to bring out the methodological concerns.

1. A PUZZLE ABOUT "WOMAN"

1.1 Background

According to most ordinary speakers and dictionaries, "woman" is a sex term—a term that picks out those who have certain biological traits. Traditionally, feminist academics used "woman" as a gender term—a term that picks out those who have certain social traits or who occupy a particular social role. Both of these views face severe difficulties. These difficulties will be familiar to most who work in feminist philosophy, but for the benefit of others, what follows is a very brief overview. It suffers the faults common to brief overviews, such as important omissions and oversimplifications. But my goal is simply to provide enough information to make the debate comprehensible to outsiders. For a more complete overview and lots of useful references, see Mikkola 2008.

1.1.1 "WOMAN" AS A GENDER TERM

In feminist academia, it used to be assumed that "woman" was a gender term, a term meant to pick out a category of people who share something social—a role, a place in a hierarchical society, and so on. "Woman" was often carefully distinguished from "female human," which was meant to pick out a category of people who share something biological—chromosomes, genitalia, and so on. More generally, the social category of gender was meant to be sharply distinguished from the biological category of sex. One key reason for this was to draw attention to the thought that biology is not destiny: the sex we're born with needn't determine the sort of life we live.

In recent decades, there has been a lot of pressure on the idea that "woman" picks out anything at all. This pressure has come in part from the recognition that there are huge and important differences between women from different classes, races, nationalities, religions, and so on. Once we reflect on the wide variety of social roles lived out by women (consider a Somali refugee mother of five, the Queen of England, and a childless Californian lesbian artist, for a few examples), it becomes clear that there is no one "women's social role." (See, e.g., Spelman 1988.) This variety has led many to believe that there is simply not enough in common between these people for the word "woman" to pick out a kind at all.[2]

This led to a kind of crisis in feminist theorizing: how could feminism have a distinctive political aim or a subject matter, if we can't even pick out and discuss those who are meant to be its subject, women? There has been a variety of responses to this crisis. Some have argued that feminism can and should do without the concept *woman*, some argued that we can go on using the concept *woman* and the term "woman" even if we cannot explain them, some have suggested analyses as a family resemblance concept, and some have suggested analyses that at least seem to be rather revisionary.

My initial, naïve (I now see) reaction to this "crisis" and to the responses to it was that they didn't take seriously enough the option of using "woman" as a sex term—that this was far more viable than it appeared.

1.1.2 "WOMAN" AS A SEX TERM

If one asks an ordinary speaker what it is to be a woman, she/he will almost certainly answer in terms of biological traits, most likely genitalia or chromosomes. The same is true of dictionaries. Given that feminists need to communicate successfully both with each other and with those who are not (yet) feminists, feminists should want to avoid large-scale misunderstandings wherever possible. And many views of "woman" as a gender term—even those designed in response to the problem noted above—bring with them the potential for such misunderstanding. For example, one view with such potential for misunderstanding is Sally Haslanger's, on which to be a woman is (very roughly) to be subordinated on the basis of one's perceived sexual characteristics (Haslanger 2000). On Haslanger's view, then, feminists should happily endorse "we must eliminate all women"—since feminists should not want anyone to be subordinated in this way. This slogan could all too easily be misunderstood (and the wrong people might show up for one's protests). Of course, there are ways to deal with and even prevent such misunderstandings. In the end, one may decide that this extra work is worth doing. My point here is simply that this is a cost of the view.

Using "woman" as a sex term accords better with ordinary usage. And this provides important communicative advantages for feminists. Moreover, using "women" as a sex term leaves feminists far more flexibility in thinking about social roles than is generally realized. Feminists can still talk very effectively about the fact that sex should not determine the sort of life one should lead, and can still make (at least many of) the sorts of claims and arguments that feminists want to make. For example, one can still maintain that women *tend* to be subordinated on the basis of their perceived female sex characteristics, even if this is not true by definition.

But problems lurk.

1.1.2.1 Intersexed People: The "folk" view of human biological sex is that (a) there are two mutually exclusive and jointly exhaustive categories of human, male and female; (b) people fall neatly and easily into these categories. This view is false—there are people with XX chromosomes but male genitalia, people with XY chromosomes and female genitalia, people with various mixtures of male and female genitalia, and various permutations of chromosomes, genitalia, and secondary sex characteristics. (See, for example, Fausto-Sterling 2000.) As a result of the folk view (in combination with other attitudes), these people, who I will call "intersexed," often suffer a great deal: they may be subjected to painful and harmful surgeries at an early age; they may be ostracized or otherwise mistreated for not being "normal"; and they may be forced to live out roles that simply do not feel right to them.

If "woman" is a sex term, then we need to know which of the biological markers associated with sex determine who is a woman. Moreover, this decision is not one to take lightly, given the huge repercussions that sex categorization have. It is hard to see any good, clear answer to this. What this shows is simply that using "woman" as a sex term is not a quick or easy solution: it carries with it its own problems. But it does not show that "woman" should be used as a gender term—we already know that problems lurk there as well.

So, one problem for understanding "woman" as a sex term is that intersexed people show that it is far from clear whom the sex term "woman" refers to. Consideration of intersexed people, and the way that they are often medically forced into one of our two sex categories, also helps to motivate the thought that a strict division between sex (biological) and gender (social) is not as tenable as it may have seemed. Sex is arguably, at least in part and in some cases, socially determined. But these are not the only problems for the view that "woman" should be understood as a sex term.

1.1.2.2 Trans Women: If we use "woman" as a sex term which refers only to those possessing certain biological features such as vaginas, ovaries, XX-chromosomes, and the like—no matter how many or few of these we require—some people who identify themselves as women will not count as women. These people are those who possess what are standardly taken to be the biological features of womanhood, but who identify themselves as women. It is generally very important to trans women that they be considered women, and most if not all trans women face enormous obstacles due to this self-identification, obstacles that include discrimination, ostracization, and violence. I will call these people "trans women." (There is considerable dispute over the proper meanings of "transgender" and "transsexual," and I'd like to avoid this.) Some trans women have none of the biological markers associated with female sex, some have many of them (due to surgery and hormonal treatments), but none have all of them. The proportion of trans women excluded from the sex category woman will depend on exactly how "woman" is defined, but some are bound to be excluded from any biologically based category. (For more on these issues see Bettcher 2009.) Those whose gender identity matches the gender they were assigned at birth are known as "cis women".

Some feminists will be happy with this result, as will some other speakers more generally. Many others, like me, feel that it is important to count trans women as women. One who agrees with the latter group will most likely not want to use "woman" as a sex term. Importantly, however, it is not only this latter group that should reject the view that "woman" is a sex term, after considering the case of trans women. Another view— perhaps a widespread one—is that it really isn't clear whether trans women are women, and that perhaps they sometimes count as women and sometimes don't. This view also fits most comfortably with a denial that "woman" is simply a sex term.

1.3 "Woman" as a Contextually Shifting, Similarity-Based Term

As we have already noted, ordinary speakers and dictionaries both take "woman" to be a sex term. But sex is far from a straightforward matter. And many speakers will sometimes use "woman" as though it is not a sex term after all—this is what they do when they refer to trans women who have not undergone reassignment surgeries as "women," a usage that seems perfectly acceptable to many of us. But using "woman" as a gender term brings with it its own problems. And this collection of ordinary usage data is a part of what motivates the view I develop here.

My own usage and understanding of the term "woman" is complex. I suspect this is true of many speakers, but I'll take my case as a starting point. First, I feel quite strongly that we should recognise the preferred categorisations of trans women (and trans men). I think (1) is true:

> (1) Trans women are women, even if they have not had "reassignment" surgery or hormonal treatments.

This is clearly a case in which I am using "women" as something other than a sex term. Similarly for (2):

> (2) Some of those who were identified at birth as boys are women, and always were.

Yet I also do use "woman" as a sex term. I have no problems with forensic scientists uttering sentence (3).

> (3) This is the DNA of a woman.

And this is not because I think DNA is a very good, though fallible, guide to who is likely to live out a woman's gender role. I would also assent to (4), with "woman" used as a sex term.

> (4) It is important for scientists testing drugs to study both men and women.

I strongly suspect that many other speakers are like me in their acceptance of all of these sorts of sentences. We (many of us, anyway) use "woman" in more than one way. This at first seems to complicate things even more. But the last few decades in philosophy of language have seen the development of context-sensitive accounts of a wide range of terms and constructions. The natural thought for one familiar with both the data regarding "woman" and the literature on context-sensitivity is to try a context-sensitive analysis of "woman." And, for some time, I felt drawn to this approach. In the next section, I'll outline the account I developed.

1.3.1 A CONTEXT-SENSITIVE DEFINITION OF "WOMAN"
Here is the definition I developed.

> *X is a woman* is true in a context C iff X is human and relevantly similar (according to the standards at work in C) to most of those[3] possessing all of the biological markers[4] of female sex.[5]

This would be accompanied by a parallel definition of "man":

> *X is a man* is true in a context C iff X is human and relevantly similar (according to the standards at work in C) to most of those possessing all of the biological markers[6] of male sex.

The thought behind these definitions is to incorporate the commonsense view that the biological sex traits are somehow of central importance to womanhood and manhood, but without using these as necessary or sufficient conditions. The definitions are sufficiently flexible that according to them "man" and "woman" can each sometimes pick out a biological kind and sometimes a social kind—and different biological and social kinds in different contexts. I think the virtues of these definitions are not immediately apparent. They emerge best through a close look at cases and through considering some apparent problems for the definitions.

1.3.2 SOME CASES
1.3.2.1 Intersex cases: As we have already noted, some people are born with physical features associated with both biological maleness and biological femaleness: they may, for example, have XY chromosomes but female genitalia, or both ovaries and male genitalia, or any of a wide range of other combinations. Consider, for example, Amanda, who has XX chromosomes, testicles, and a vagina, and sincerely says, "I am a woman." Is Amanda a woman or a man, according to our analyses? The answer will depend on the context in which the question is asked.

First imagine a context in which our concern is with how people self-identify. In this context, we are all committed to the view that how people think of themselves is in general the most important factor in whether they should be considered a man or a woman, and we are focused on this view. Call this context C1.

> *X is a woman* is true in C1 iff X is human and relevantly similar (in sincerely self-identifying as a woman) to most of those possessing all of the biological markers of female sex.

In this context, "Amanda is a woman" will be true. It will be true because Amanda is relevantly similar, in this context, to most of those who have all the biological markers of female sex. She is relevantly similar because in this context what matters is similarity of self-identification, and most people with these physical features self-identify as women—as does Amanda.

Now imagine a context in which we are medical professionals screening for testicular cancer. The NHS has decided that all and only men of Amanda's age should be screened for testicular cancer. Our focus is exclusively on testicular cancer. In this context, Beau says "We should test Amanda, because Amanda is a man." In this context, Beau's utterance is true, because Amanda meets the "man" definition: what matters in this conversation is not self-identification but the presence of testicles. Call this context C2.

> *X is a man* is true in C2 iff X is human and relevantly similar (in possessing testicles) to most of those possessing all of the biological markers of male sex.

Most (indeed all) of those with all the biological markers of male sex have testicles, as does Amanda. So in this context Amanda is relevantly similar to these people, and therefore counts as a man.

Note that these two conversations might well take place at the same time. This means that at exactly the same moment utterances of "Amanda is a man" and "Amanda is a woman" could be true. This is surprising, perhaps, but I think it is also well-motivated.

Could a single utterance, "Amanda is both a man and a woman," ever be true? It seems to me that it could. Suppose that we are medical professionals screening for both testicular cancer and vaginal diseases. The NHS has ruled that all and only men of Amanda's age should be screened for testicular cancer, and that all and only women of Amanda's age should be screened for vaginal diseases. Beau's job is to indicate which people fall into which categories so that we can carry out proper screening procedures. In this context, it would be true for Beau to say "Amanda is both a woman and a man": in this context, what matters to being a woman is possession of a vagina and what matters to being a man is possession of testes.[7]

1.3.2.2 Trans Women: Consider the case of a trans woman, Charla. When self-identification is what matters in a context, "Charla is a woman" is true. When what matters is something biological—as in the cancer-screening examples—"Charla is a woman" may well not be true. But this does not yet begin to deal with all the complexities of the politics of these cases (or of some intersex cases).

In many, perhaps even most, contexts that I find myself in, I take sincere self-identification as a woman to be sufficient for womanhood. We've already seen one such context, C1:

> *X is a woman* is true in C1 iff X is human and relevantly similar (in sincerely self-identifying as a woman) to most of those possessing all of the biological markers of female sex.

So, if my conversational partners are in agreement with me on this, my utterance of "Trans women are women" is true.

But not everyone holds this view. Some people hold a view on which trans women never count as women, in any context. One reason for holding this view is the belief that chromosomes determine womanhood. Another is the belief that experiencing the life of a girl/woman from birth is essential to womanhood. Both of these views are used to exclude trans women from places where they want to be and things that they want to do—the first, for example, frequently excludes them from the right to use women's restrooms and from being legally recognized as women; the second most commonly excludes them from certain feminist organizations and activities.[8] Such views are also used in attempted justifications for violence and abuse against trans women (though one who holds these views need not support violence, abuse, or even exclusion). Let's call a context where the participants hold the chromosome view C3:

> *X is a woman* is true in C3 iff X is human and relevantly similar (in having XX chromosomes) to most of those possessing all of the biological markers of female sex.

As I've noted, I think the chromosome view is the wrong one to take in most contexts. Imagine, for example, that we're discussing the issue of who should be allowed to use women's toilets. I would argue that trans women are women and should therefore be allowed to use women's toilets. But many others, some of them perhaps lawmakers, would insist that trans women are not women and that therefore they should not be allowed to use women's toilets. I would like to say that these lawmakers are wrong when they say "Trans women are not women" to one another.

But according to the contextualist view, their utterances of this sentence are perfectly true. I can insist all I want that "Trans women are women" is true—and it is, when I say it to my like-minded friends, but this does not mean that *their* utterance of "Trans women are not women" is false. Nor can I argue that their law banning trans women from women's restrooms is at odds with the meaning of "women." There are simply different standards at work in the lawmakers' context. This seems both paradoxical and politically paralyzing. A case can be made in response to both of these worries.

To dissolve the air of paradox, consider an analogy. I am discussing a four-year-old girl and I say, "Lydia is tall." In fact, Lydia is tall for a four-year-old girl, and this is the standard that's relevant to my context, so my utterance is true. But now imagine that Dave is discussing who could wear the very long women's coat he has found, and somebody says "Lydia is tall." In this context, what matters is being tall for an adult woman, so "Lydia is tall" is false. In my context, "Lydia is tall" is true, but in another context it is false. No paradox here. And, similarly, there should be no air of paradox in the trans woman example.

One reason that the trans woman example seems more paradoxical is surely that "woman," unlike "tall," is not generally thought to be a term whose reference can shift with context. But another is, I think, that the lawmakers' standards seem simply *wrong* to me (as mine undoubtedly do to them). This is not at all the case in the Lydia example: in that example, the two standards seem perfectly right for two different contexts. Recognizing this and reflecting on it also offers the way out of political paralysis. On my view of "woman," I cannot argue that the lawmakers are making a mistake about how the word "woman" works. But what I can do is argue that they are morally and politically wrong to apply the standards that they do. On my view, then, disagreements over who counts as a woman are simply not to be settled by appeal to the facts of language. They are to be settled by appeal to moral and political principles.[9] There may well be a single *right* answer about what standards should be applied for determining who satisfies the definition of "woman" in a particular context; but it will be right because it is morally and politically right. So I can coherently, and maybe even correctly, insist that the lawmakers are wrong and I am right. But we must recognize this claim for what it is: a moral and political, rather than merely linguistic, claim.

1.3.2.3 Errors: Some interesting features of this view emerge as we consider the consequences of certain mistaken beliefs—in particular, the sort of mistaken beliefs that have played an unfortunate role in the history of feminist discussions of gender.

Suppose that it's 1973, and an all white, middle-class, heterosexual Northeastern American consciousness-raising group is discussing the plight of women. Betty utters sentence (5):

(5) Most women are raised to be physically weak.

Sentence (5) is, we would think pre-theoretically, false: many, many women, all over the world, do huge amounts of heavy labor. And they are raised to do this sort of heavy labor. (5) is just the kind of false generalization that comes from ignorance about all the many kinds of lives that women lead. Unfortunately, all of the women in Betty's conversation have the mistaken belief that (5) is true. What does my view say about (5)? Well, it will depend on what standards of similarity are at work in Betty's context.

If Betty and her friends are trying to talk about all of those with all the biological markers of femaleness, then those will be what are relevant to determining who is in the extension of "woman": all of those humans possessing all the biological features of female sex will count as women. Call a context like this one C4. Plugging this into my definition of "woman," we get:

X is a woman is true in C4 iff X is human and relevantly similar (in having all the biological markers of womanhood) to most of those possessing all of the biological markers of female sex.

Since it's clearly not true that most of these people are raised to be physically weak, (5) is false. Just the result we want.

But now suppose that Betty and her friends take her claim to be about those of the gender woman (having just discussed the sex/gender distinction). Betty and her friends take women to be a group united by their role as physically weak, dependent helpmates for men. For this reason, Betty is very confident that (5) is true. What does my view say now? Well, according to the standards at work in this context, C5:

X is a woman is true in C5 iff X is human and relevantly similar (in playing the role of a physically weak, dependent helpmate for men) to most of those possessing all of the biological markers of female sex.

But it's simply not the case that most of those possessing the biological markers of womanhood play the role of a physically weak, dependent helpmate for men. Many, perhaps most, of those with these biological markers are physically strong. Nobody, then, can be relevantly similar to most of those with the biological markers of womanhood by virtue of playing the role of physically weak, dependent helpmate. So *nobody* satisfies the criteria for womanhood in Betty's context: given the facts of the world, these standards are just too deeply mistaken to pick out anybody. Betty's utterance, then, is simply confused: there are no women, according to the standards she is using, so her utterance lacks a truth value.

At first, it may seem strange that these contexts lead to such different results. But I think there is some plausibility to the thought that in C5, Betty's understanding of "woman" is just too deeply flawed to pick out anyone.

1.3.3 SOME INITIAL EVALUATIVE THOUGHTS

The contextualist view sketched above is far from perfect or complete. Like other contextualist views, it faces particular challenges from mixed contexts (where speaker and audience have different standards in mind); from the fact that ordinary speakers would reject the thought that the terms at issue ("woman" and "man") have meanings that vary with contexts; and from examples involving belief reports (to name just a few problems). It also runs the risk of counting what we would like to consider non-literal uses of "woman" as literally true—for example, "Margaret Thatcher's not a woman."[10]

Further, there are lots of complications about how to understand "self-identification" and about whether it could even begin to do the work it's meant to do. Here are a few worries one might have, briefly stated, which are especially pressing if we take self-identification as a woman to be merely a matter of being disposed to assent to "I am a woman" or its translation.[11]

1. Many trans women take themselves to have been women even before they realized that they were. A self-identification view of womanhood has difficulty accommodating this.

2. Trans women take their claims of womanhood to be substantive, rather than merely claims about what sentences they're disposed to accept. They think that when they begin to self-identify as women this is made true by their womanhood, rather than the other way around.

3. We could imagine a case in which a person is maliciously deceived into believing that he is a woman, when he is not. (A hoax is perpetrated on a man previously totally comfortable identifying a man: all sorts of documents and clues are left around his house that convince him that he has had false beliefs about himself all his life. Or perhaps an unscrupulous therapist wrongly convinces a credulous male patient that the reason for his unhappiness is that he is really a woman.) Such a person would come to accept the sentence "I am a woman," but we would want to be able to say that he is wrong to do so.

It may be that there is an understanding of self-identification that doesn't suffer from these problems, though it's not obvious to me what that would be. But it's also important to remember that the self-identification understanding of "woman" is just one of those permitted by the contextualist view. A problem for the self-identification view is, then, a problem for this particular understanding rather than for the contextualist view itself, which *of course* permits flawed understandings of womanhood to be at work in contexts where people are using these flawed understandings.[12]

The contextualist view, then, does suffer from problems. But the problems that I want to focus on here are not the ones noted above.

2. METHODOLOGICAL ISSUES

Now, with the above case study in mind, I'd like to turn to the methodological issues that are my real focus. (As I work through these, we'll also see some very good reasons to reject the contextualist view developed above.)

2.1 Do Real-World Consequences Distort or Reveal?

I was more than a little bit surprised to find myself putting forward a contextualist view, as in general I tend to dislike contextualist views. I usually like to endorse a nice, neat, simple semantic view and explain away the intuitions that seem to conflict with it (e.g., Saul 2007). In the case of "woman," what I would have expected myself to do was simply to argue for a view of "woman" as a sex term. I could, for example, insist that "woman" and "men" only truly apply to those who have all the biological markers of femaleness and maleness. Intersexed people are not women and men, nor are trans women. But, my standard theoretical self would say, we can still accommodate the intuition that "Amanda is a woman even though she has testicles" is true; it communicates that *Amanda considers herself a woman*, or that *Amanda has some of the biological markers of womanhood.* Similarly for "Trans women are women": while false, it communicates a very important truth: *that trans women deserve to be treated as women.*

However, I find this move wholly unappealing. Here are two possible explanations of the differences in my views:

1. When I focus only on examples which in a real-world sense *don't matter,* it's easy to accept a view that violates and explains away contextualist intuitions. But this is a mistake, and contemplating examples that matter forces me to take these intuitions more seriously. One might even be so cynical as to suggest that in ordinary cases what I care most about is my anti-contextualist views, which allows them to have a pernicious influence over me. In cases that matter, that influence is trumped.

2. When I focus on examples that in a real-world sense don't matter, my intuitions are more pure and uncorrupted, and my theorizing more likely to be guided only by standardly accepted theoretical considerations. But when I turn to politically charged cases, my politics begin to corrupt my intuitions and to have a pernicious effect on my theorizing.

I think it's far from obvious which of these is right. And I think this sort of issue is a very important one for any philosopher of language to consider. Views in philosophy of language are supported in part by reflections on particular cases. If cases with real-world significance yield different sorts of results from cases without such significance, philosophers who focus on only one or the other are taking a bit of a gamble unless they can offer a compelling argument that the sort of cases on which they focus are the right sort of cases to focus on.

2.2 Making Sense of a Compelling Objection to Contextualism

A further methodological issue arises from the facts that

1. An argument can be made that the contextualist view fails to do justice to the womanhood claims of trans women;

2. I think that, if this argument is right, it constitutes a legitimate objection to it; but

3. it is far from obvious how the traditional philosopher of language can countenance the legitimacy of this objection.

All of this needs spelling out.

2.2.1 THE OBJECTION

Despite my attempts in section 1 to defend the contextualist view, I found myself recurringly plagued by the concern that this view really did not do justice to trans women's claims of womanhood. But it took me a while to articulate this concern properly. My first attempt was this:

> According to the contextualist view, trans women's self-ascriptions of womanhood are true. But so too are their opponents' denials of their womanhood. The view therefore fails to do justice to trans women's claims of womanhood. It grants them, but only in a fairly meaningless way—since it also grants the truth of their denials.

But this does not actually get at the problem, as we can see from the response below.

> The contextualist view does not grant the truth of the denials of trans women's claims. After all, the denials take place in different contexts. An utterance of (6) is true in, for example, a context in which self-identification is what matters to womanhood.
>
> (6) Trans women are women.
>
> An utterance of (7) will not be true in such a context.
>
> (7) Trans women are not women.
>
> For an utterance of (7) to be true, it must be made in a context in which *something else* (perhaps chromosomes) is what matters to womanhood. So a true utterance of (7) is not a denial of a true utterance of (6) The contextualist does not grant the truth of denials of trans women's claims.

Nonetheless, I think it may be right to say that there is something trivializing about the way that the contextualist grants the truth of trans women's claims. The reason the trans woman's claims are true, on the contextualist view, is simply that there is a huge range of acceptable ways to use the term "woman" and the trans woman's way of using "woman" isn't ruled out. The trans woman's use of "woman" is perfectly acceptable—just as acceptable as her opponent's. In effect, I am saying, "Yes, your claim to be a woman is true—because 'woman' can mean so many things." And this, I can't help but think, would be deeply unsatisfying to the trans woman who wants to be recognized as a woman simply because *she is a woman* rather than because "woman" is such a flexible term. What the trans woman needs to do justice to her claim is surely not just the acknowledgement that her claim is true but also the acknowledgement that her opponent's claim is false. And the contextualist view does not offer that.

2.2.2 THE METHODOLOGICAL WORRY: POLITICAL OBJECTIONS TO VIEWS IN PHILOSOPHY OF LANGUAGE

The objection raised in the last section turns on the thought that *we should seek an analysis of "woman" that does justice to trans woman's claims.* This desideratum is a very different one from others that we have considered, and very different from those we normally consider in philosophy of language. In reflecting on my pro-contextualist intuitions about "woman," I wondered how the term's political significance might be shaping my intuitions. Here there is no room for such wondering. The objection is simply one of political unacceptability. The thought is that it is politically unacceptable to give an analysis of "woman" that doesn't do justice to trans women's claims. And the question is whether a thought like that has any place in philosophy of language.

2.2.2.1 Haslanger on Kinds of Analysis: Sally Haslanger (2000, 2006), writing about concepts, distinguishes three sorts of projects that one might engage in.

1. A *conceptual* inquiry proceeds by examining our intuitions about various cases, both actual and hypothetical, and also by examining the definitions that we formulate when asked to reflect upon our concepts. Such an inquiry is very likely to proceed by way of reflective equilibrium. It is concerned with arriving at what Haslanger calls our *manifest* concept.
2. A *descriptive* inquiry is not so much concerned with what we *take* our concepts to be when asked about them or with our intuitions about hypothetical cases. Instead, a descriptive inquiry into F-hood might start by examining the things in the world to which we apply the predicate *F.* It would then ask what kind (natural or other), if any, we seem to be tracking with our use of

  F. The concept that we arrive at through this method is our *operative* concept.

3. An *ameliorative* inquiry is very different from either of the above. It attempts to discover what concept we *should* be using. This concept—the *target* concept—will be the one that best serves our legitimate purposes. (In her 2000 article, she calls this an *analytic* inquiry.)

It is, I think, pretty straightforward to arrive at parallel distinctions for the meanings of words rather than concepts. The manifest meaning will be the one arrived at by testing definitions against cases; the operative meaning will be the one arrived at by looking at actual usage; and the target meaning will be the meaning that best serves our legitimate purposes.

It then looks initially very straightforward to find a place for the objection that the contextualist account fails to do justice to trans women's claims. This objection obviously has a home in the ameliorative project: it can be understood as insisting that the contextualist theory is not the best one for serving our legitimate purposes. Done!

But I think this is too fast. The problem is that there is a very easy response to the objection, thus understood: this is a change of topic. Once we distinguish the various possible projects, it becomes clear that the objection is relevant only to the ameliorative project. But it's far from clear that this is the project that I was engaged in: after all, I was looking at definitions and considering cases, refining my definitions in light of cases considered—and that sounds like I was seeking the manifest meaning. And I was looking at actual usage and trying to find a meaning that would accord with that usage—which sounds like I was seeking the operative meaning. But I wasn't asking what meaning would best suit my purposes. It would be perfectly possible, then, to insist that the objection is simply relevant to a *different* project.

What, then, would be required for the political objection to be a legitimate objection to the project I've been engaged in? Here are some possible answers:

1. Despite appearances, the project I've been engaged in *is* the ameliorative project. As I noted in my brief discussion of other views on "woman," I think it's important for feminists to communicate effectively both with each other and with other speakers. This gave me pause about very revisionary analyses. But it also gives me good reason to engage in

conceptual and descriptive inquiries *as a part of* my ameliorative inquiry, and that's what I've been doing.

2. Haslanger suggests that our ultimate goal should always be to bring the descriptive, conceptual, and ameliorative projects together: to arrive at an analysis that is manifest, operative, and our target. If that's right, then there is good reason to move back and forth between the projects and to consider an analysis's unsuitability for one role to be at least a potential objection to using it for another.

3. One might further argue that it is in fact not so easy in practice to separate out Haslanger's different projects, at least in some cases. It may help to turn to a more familiar example of a politically significant term in a time of transition and disputed meaning: "marriage." Suppose that you are asked whether or not same-sex partnerships can count as marriages (linguistically speaking, not legally). You might at first try to distinguish two questions: whether they *do* count as marriages and whether they *should* count as marriages. Suppose we opt for the first question. This question looks like it calls for purely descriptive and conceptual inquiries. But since we are dealing with a term in a state of conflict and transition, decisions will surely have to be made about which data to place the most weight on: some people clearly do take "marriage" to be applicable to same sex partnerships, while others clearly do not.

If such decisions are to be made, it seems very natural to let them be guided by ameliorative—and therefore political—considerations. Certainly, I do find myself attending to these considerations in my own reflections. It matters a great deal to me to find out how trans women want to use and to define "woman." I consider their views more important than, for example, those of right-wing Christians. And I would be very lacking in self-knowledge indeed if I did not acknowledge that political considerations inform this preference.[13] For at least certain kinds of terms, then, at certain stages in their development, it may not be possible fully to separate out the kinds of analyses. A descriptive project may not be able to avoid ameliorative aspects.

4. Continuing a bit further with the "marriage" example, one might argue that with a politically significant term like this, one has a moral and political responsibility to consider the political consequences of one's views. At least arguably, one would be doing something morally wrong

to respond to the query above by reflecting solely on, for example, current usage without thinking about the political consequences of the view one is putting forward. If this is right, then political considerations should always be taken seriously when one is dealing with a politically significant term.

2.2.2.2 Explaining Away Political Worries in Philosophy of Language: As I described the political objection, it was one that concerned *doing justice to trans women's experiences.* But a closely related objection would be that the contextualist view is *offensive* to trans women—either because it trivializes their claims to womanhood or because it grants the truth of their opponents' claims. And objections grounded in offensiveness (as political concerns about language often are) pose special difficulties for certain standard strategies in philosophy of language.

As I noted earlier, one common strategy in philosophy of language is to find a way of explaining away intuitions that seem to conflict with one's view. So, for example, one might insist:

> I know it seems wrong to you to say that Lois really does know Superman is Clark Kent. But that's because you're making a mistake regarding what's strictly speaking said and what's otherwise communicated. Here, let me explain my theory in more detail...

This strategy is sometimes convincing and sometimes not, but it is widely used.

But now imagine the same strategy applied to concerns of offensiveness rather than clashes with intuitions.

> I know it seems offensive to you as a trans woman to say that your opponents' denials of your womanhood are true. But that's because you're making mistakes regarding the way that context works in determining what claims of womanhood say. My theory doesn't really grant the truth of denials of your claims to womanhood, so it's not really offensive. Here, let me explain my theory in more detail...

It is hard to shake the thought that there would be something deeply offensive about saying something like the above. But surely sometimes it *is* acceptable to explain away offensiveness. A Spanish friend of a friend, for example, happened to have a name that, in British English, is a deeply offensive racial slur. Explaining that a British interlocutor who takes offense at a mention of the name is mistaken to be offended in this case seems wholly appropriate—and *not* offensive in itself. Working out how to deal with claims of offensiveness and responses to such claims seems to me to be a substantial and worthwhile project for philosophers of language—and one that becomes very salient once we begin to think about politically significant terms.

3. CONCLUDING THOUGHTS

Considering politically significant terms like "woman" raises novel methodological challenges for an analytic philosopher of language. Some of these are minor and technical, like how best to formulate a contextualist analysis of such a term. But in trying to decide whether such an analysis is the right analysis (and I now suspect it isn't), I uncovered far more interesting issues concerning the relevance of political issues for philosophy of language. And these, upon reflection, at least potentially have implications for work not concerning politically significant terms. This seems to me to give good reason for traditional philosophers of language to pay attention to—and indeed to join in—discussions in areas like feminist philosophy of language.

Notes

I am grateful to many people for helpful discussions of the material in this paper, including: Heather Arnold, Elizabeth Barnes, Laura Beeby, Ross Cameron, Samara Casewell, Lorraine Code, Josep Corbi, Sharon Crasnow, Esa Díaz-León, Ray Drainville, Alex Fleetwood, Michelle Garvey, Michael Glanzberg, Sally Haslanger, Avram Hiller, Jules Holroyd, Chris Hookway, Michael Hymers, Rosanna Keefe, Kathleen Lennon, Dan López de Sa, Mari Mikkola, Christine Overall, Lina Papadaki, Angie Pepper, Cristina Roadevin, Komarine Romdenh-Romluc, Stella Sandford, Frank Saul, Julie Saul, Alison Stone, Anita Superson, and Alessandra Tanesini. I'm also grateful to audiences at Cambridge University, Cork University, Leeds University, the *Sex and Gender* conference in Lancaster, the *SWIP* conference on *Feminism in the Analytic Tradition* in Stirling, the *NOMOS* Meeting in Barcelona, and the Pacific APA in Vancouver.
1. In the most extreme manifestation, whole books (e.g., Saul 2007) can be written on such topics.
2. The neglect of these issues by many earlier feminists has led to charges of classism and racism.
3. "Most of those" is not relativized to the context.
4. I'm taking these to be ovaries, vagina, and XX chromosomes.

5. I should emphasize that when I write of "biological markers associated with female sex" I am referring to those traits *commonly taken to be biological* which are *commonly associated with female sex*. Which traits are actually biological, which traits are in fact associated with female sex, and what the terms "biological" and "sex" mean are matters of significant controversy. I thank Alex Fleetwood for discussion of these complex issues.
6. I'm taking these to be penis, testes, and XY chromosomes.
7. I don't mean to suggest that the policies described in this section would actually be good ones for the NHS to adopt—surely it would be better if they require simply that people with testicles be tested for testicular cancer and that people with vaginas be tested for vaginal diseases. My goal was simply to offer a somewhat artificial set of examples to show the flexibility of the view. (Thanks to the editors for pressing me on this.)
8. A well-known example of feminists excluding trans women is the Michigan Womyn's Music Festival, which initially excluded all trans women because they did not have "entire life experiences as female" (Sreedhar and Hand 2006: 163). They insisted that participants must be "womyn born womyn." The festival then considered a rule excluding those with penises, which was criticized as classist since only some trans women can afford the necessary surgery (Sreedhar and Hand 2006: 164–65). The current status of the "womyn born womyn" rule is unclear (Wikipedia). For more examples, and a fuller discussion, see Scott-Dixon 2006.
9. They may also sometimes be settled by appeal to practical considerations, as in the NHS screening examples.
10. I heard this frequently in 1997, when Tony Blair came to power along with a large quantity of new female members of Parliament. It was often suggested that all of these women would make British politics kinder and gentler. Puzzled, I would ask how people who lived through Thatcher could be convinced of this. The reply was always the same: "Margaret Thatcher's not a woman."
11. We needn't do this, but it's certainly the most obvious understanding.
12. My discussion of problems for self-identification is very much indebted to Bettcher 2009b and to discussions with Joseph Corbi.
13. This sort of choice can even be read as an expression of *solidarity* with one group rather than another.

References

Bettcher, Talia. 2009a. "Feminist Perspectives on Trans Issues," *The Stanford Encyclopedia of Philosophy* (Winter 2009 Edition), Edward N. Zalta (ed.), http://plato.stanford.edu/archives/win2009/entries/feminism-trans/.
———. 2009b. "Trans Identities and First Person Authority." In Laurie Shrage (ed.), *You've Changed: Sex Reassignment and Personal Identity*. New York: Oxford University Press.
Fausto-Sterling, Anne. 2000. *Sexing the Body*. New York: Basic Books.

Haslanger, Sally. 2000. "Gender, Race: (What) Are They? (What) Do We Want Them To Be?" *Noûs* 34, no. 1, 31–55.

———. 2006. "What Good Are Our Intuitions: Philosophical Analysis and Social Kinds," *Proceedings of the Aristotelian Society*, supplementary volume 80, no. 1, 89–118.

Mikkola, Mari. 2008. "Feminist Perspectives on Sex and Gender," *The Stanford Encyclopedia of Philosophy* (Fall 2008 Edition), Edward N. Zalta (ed.), http://plato.stanford.edu/archives/fall2008/entries/feminism-gender/.

Saul, Jennifer. 2007. *Substitution, Simple Sentences, and Intuitions*. New York: Oxford University Press.

Scott-Dixon, Krista. 2006. "Section III: Inclusion and Exclusion." In Krista Scott-Dixon (ed.), *Trans/forming Feminisms: Transfeminist Voices Speak Out*. Toronto: Sumach Press.

Spelman, Elizabeth V. 1988. *Inessential Woman: Problems of Exclusion in Feminist Thought*. Boston: Beacon Books.

Sreedhar, Suzanne, and Michael Hand. 2006. "The Ethics of Exclusion: Gender and Politics at the Michigan Womyn's Music Festival." In Krista Scott-Dixon (ed.), *Trans/forming Feminisms: Transfeminist Voices Speak Out*. Toronto: Sumach Press.

Wikipedia. "Michigan Womyn's Festival." http://en.wikipedia.org/wiki/Michigan_Womyn's_Music_Festival, consulted 30 March 2010.

MAURA TUMULTY
Colgate University

ILLOCUTION AND EXPECTATIONS

OF BEING HEARD

INTRODUCTION

An interest in women's silence—in the many ways that silence has been
enforced, and in the many ways women have found of speaking in the
face of such force—is common to a wide variety of feminist work.
Feminist philosophy of language, especially its analytic variant, has been
interested in silence of two kinds.[1] Some silence is topic specific, and
results when a language lacks words for certain phenomena—or when
the words it does make available have connotations a woman using those
words might disavow. In such a situation, not only are women unable to
speak in the way they wish about a topic of concern to them, no one is
able to state explicitly what it is those women wished to say but could
not. After all, if there were a way to state their intentions to say that such-
and-such, then the women could simply say that such-and-such.
Examples of this kind of silence are easily given only in retrospect, when
we note the work now done by the phrases "sexual harassment" and
"marital rape," and consider the difficulty of expressing, and perhaps
even of thinking, certain thoughts without them. To show that this kind
of silence is a coherent possibility—that our intuitive treatment of these
examples is not misleading—we must investigate the relationships between thought and talk, speaker-meaning and semantic-meaning, and
what is strictly meant and what is implied.

Another kind of silence is marked not by a literal lack of words in
connection with certain topics, but with the relation between certain
speakers and certain audiences. Here, the claim is that words that would
be available for various uses are not available to women, or not to all
women, for those uses. Suppose a woman wants to use some words for a

certain purpose—say, to report that she is being sexually harassed—but she is frightened of the consequences of doing so, and remains silent. Now suppose instead that a woman intends to use some words for a certain purpose, and utters those words, but is not heard as speaking with that purpose. She may, for example, intend to say, "About face!" as an order, but her male subordinates fail to hear it as an order (perhaps because they fail to see her as a relevant authority). On some accounts of force, as distinct from sense, a speaker is not able to put forward words with a certain force—of declaring, or warning, or ordering—unless her audience hears her as so doing. If something impedes an audience's ability to hear a female speaker properly, then she is silenced in that she cannot speak with the kind of force she intends. Arguing that this kind of silence is a coherent possibility requires work on the distinction between sense and force, and on the relationships among speaker intention, audience reception, and what is said. Feminist concern about the serious consequences of such silence has encouraged work in philosophy of language to probe the reasons for failures of communication and to sharpen our general accounts of communicative success, wherever it is achieved. It has produced subtle accounts of the task of communicating that have enriched both Gricean and Austinian approaches to language.[2]

This essay addresses Jennifer Hornsby's and Rae Langton's argument that there is a clear, literal sense in which pornography or a pornographic culture, broadly speaking, could silence women.[3] They look at the "rape myths" pedaled by pornography, which represent women not only as coyly saying "no" to offers of sex they in fact intend to accept, but as enjoying forceful sexual domination by men—as enjoying, in the end, encounters that are violent and which they do not, at their beginning, enjoy. If these myths are widely believed, it may come to be the case that any time a woman says "no" in (what we are normally inclined to call) an attempt to refuse sex, she in fact is unable to refuse (at least not in saying "no").[4] Horsnby and Langton make their case in part by accepting J. L. Austin's distinction between locutions, illocutions, and perlocutions.[5] A locution is a meaningful utterance, such as "There is a large wasp on your arm." An illocution is what one does in uttering a locution—such as *warn*, by saying "There is a large wasp on your arm," to one's friend. And perlocution is what one does by uttering a locution—such as frightening one's friend in this case. Hornsby and Langton rely on Austin's claim that for the making of an utterance to be an illocutionary act (e.g., refusing), *uptake* must be secured. An illocutionary act's being the act it is depends in part on its being perceived by its audience as an act of just that kind.

In the absence of uptake, it fails to be the illocution the speaker intended, and will likely fail to be any illocution at all.

If all these claims are true, then something of grave consequence occurs when a man attempts to force sex and a woman attempts to refuse.[6] If he thinks "no" means "yes" (in the limit, because it has come to mean that in this context), he will not understand "no" as having a negative meaning, nor understand it in this case to have been uttered with refusing force. But if proper uptake, that is, his understanding, is impossible, successful refusal is apparently impossible. The woman cannot perform the illocutionary act of refusing sex. She has been silenced. And this is a harm distinct from the sexual violence that may follow.

Three serious criticisms have been made of their argument:[7]

1. It appears to make rape conceptually impossible. If Hornsby and Langton are correct, a man who proceeds to force sex after a woman has uttered "No" is not doing so while thinking that the woman has refused.[8]

2. If responsibility for the woman's inability to refuse sex in saying "No" lies with the porn industry, or with the collusion between that industry and our collective social imagination, then it seems as if the responsibility for the man's inability to perceive an utterance of "No" as a refusal of sex must also be put down to those forces. That is, if the woman is subject to an expressive disadvantage, the man must be subject to an interpretive disadvantage.[9] And yet we often want to say that any individual man who claims he thought a woman meant to accept sex in saying "No" is either (a) insincere; or (b) sincere and truthful only because he so systematically disvalues women that he just did not care enough about this woman's autonomy to make sure that she was welcoming the sex before proceeding.

3. Hornsby and Langton, like Austin himself, are simply mistaken in thinking that any effect of a locution—including a hearer's grasp of the meaning and (illocutionary) force of an utterance— is ever essential to illocution. Illocution has many necessary preconditions, but audience uptake is not among them—neither in general, nor for refusal in particular.[10]

The first two objections do not directly attack the validity of Hornsby's and Langton's argument, but urge us to reject it because its conclusion has undesirable consequences. Even if we concede that these consequences are entailed by their conclusion, we could argue that the consequences are not as painful as the objectors suppose. I will first present a version of such an argument and conclude that it deepens our thinking about the moral wrong of forced sex in ways with which Hornsby and Langton might not disagree. In the rest of the chapter, I address the third objection and concede that it is a successful attack on Hornsby's and Langton's argument for silencing. If we accept that *actual* uptake is not necessary for refusal, then we cannot accept their argument. But I argue that speakers' expectations about uptake play a role in their refusals, and that acknowledging this preserves the claim that women are silenced. Using a distinction Austin makes between the act of performing a particular illocution and the act of attempting to perform a particular illocution, we can hold on to a key insight from Hornsby's and Langton's work: that forced sex in some cultural contexts entails at least two distinct kinds of harm.[11]

INTERPRETIVE DISADVANTAGE AND TWO KINDS OF RESENTMENT

Whenever there are wide, deep, and serious patterns of injustice, there will be cases where individuals are clearly suffering harm at the hands of other individuals, and yet those inflicting the harm appear not to understand their actions in a way that would warrant our assigning them full moral culpability. Part of the injustice of a particular system of thinking about men and women might precisely be that it enables a man to force sex on a woman without seeing his action for what it in fact is. The way to cope with this is not necessarily to abandon the claim that women are silenced in sexual encounters, but to increase the conceptual resources we have for assessing the moral status of the agents who cause harm. Perhaps certain men, in certain contexts, are subject to an interpretive disadvantage when it comes to their efforts to understand whether or not women want sex. And perhaps for some of these men (certainly not for all) we wish to say that the disadvantage was such that, however grave the harm inflicted on their victims, they ought not be blamed as individuals for the entirety of that harm.

This possibility can be developed by means of Miranda Fricker's distinction between those moral judgments that issue in a resentment of blame and those that issue in a resentment of disappointment.[12] We blame someone for an action when he would have realized that it was wrong, had he used the most basic of moral resources available to him in his context. Presumably a man who uses the threat of a loaded gun to force sex on a woman is blameworthy in just this robust sense, however much pornography has permeated his culture. But we resent someone in the manner specific to moral disappointment when he could have used contextually available moral resources to recognize his action as wrong, though he would have had to use them in more creative and self-reflective ways. A man who really believes "no" means "yes" should still have been able to stop and secure a more convincing consent before proceeding, had he thought at all about such facts as that he would not like another person to take action towards him were his own consenting so ambiguous, or that in any of his business dealings, such ambiguous consent from a potential partner would make him uneasy.[13]

There are also cases in between these two extremes that seem to call for a kind of resentment that blends both blame and disappointment. Fricker allows that it is often a matter of degree which type of resentment is appropriate, and that there may even be some moral luck involved in shifts between the two. The fewer resources a culture has for thinking about sexual autonomy, for example, the harder a man would have to work to overcome his interpretive disadvantages, and so the less blameworthy he is individually for certain kinds of sexual aggression.[14] This does not eliminate blame for forced sex, but alters its character and distribution in some contexts.[15] This is appropriate, because blame and responsibility admit of greater nuance in a social context in which both victims and victimizers are subject to certain kinds of distortions.

Suppose we accept this way of thinking about moral condemnation. And suppose, with those theorists making the second objection, we accept that social forces can put women at the truly serious expressive disadvantage tantamount to silencing only by putting men at a correlative interpretive disadvantage. In some cases it may appear that this interpretative disadvantage means a man will not meet *mens rea* standards for at least some legal definitions of rape. Presumably we ought not to construe women as genuinely subject to this expressive disadvantage if this means we are entirely declining to blame men for their failures to hear "no" as a refusal of sex, or deciding not to prosecute any such men for rape (or other sexual crimes). That is, if those were the consequences of Hornsby's and Langton's view then, regardless of its other merits, we would be right to reject it. But the consequences are not that stark if we refine our tools for explaining what has gone wrong and where to lay what kind of blame. We can remain open to arguments for the claim that women do suffer from this kind of expressive disadvantage, and accept them (or not) on their merits.

MORE-OR-LESS SUCCESSFUL ILLOCUTIONS

The silencing theory is compelling in large part because of its claims about how women are harmed. It is clear that women suffer harm whenever they are not effectively able to prevent sex from being forced on them. But the silencing view enables us to notice another kind of harm—the harm of being unable to say, in the full sense of "say," that one does not want sex when one does not. That is, it suggests that in some cultural contexts, women can be harmed in the face of a threat of unwanted sex in two distinct ways: by having their autonomy violated when they are unable to ensure that they have sex only when they judge it good to do so; and by having their status as agents capable of forming and communicating judgments on this crucial matter undermined. But to make their case that women are in fact harmed in the second way, Hornsby and Langton must do more than show that men intent on forcing sex do not *respond* appropriately to women's refusals. They need to show that men in that context do not *hear* women as refusing, and that therefore women *are not*—cannot be—refusing in anything but a very thin sense. Alexander Bird argues, however, that Hornsby and Langton—like Austin himself—are wrong to think refusal is prevented by failure of actual uptake.

Austin held that to perform any illocutionary act—to say anything in the full sense he has in mind—requires uptake, where that means that what one does in saying is grasped as such by one's intended audience.[16] The question is whether men ever do in fact fail to grasp what women are (trying) to do in saying "No," and whether, if so, we should conclude that therefore those women do not refuse. If we do draw this conclusion, then we must think of these women either as performing some other determinate act—perhaps the act of *trying* to refuse—or acknowledge that they are not illocuting at all.[17] In the latter case, the noises coming out of their mouths are recognizable as belonging to a language—as something other than mere noise—but the women are not doing anything with their words.[18]

Let us assume for the sake of argument that there are some contexts in which at least some men will not grasp that a woman is refusing in saying "no." Can a woman, in such a context, successfully refuse sex from such a man? (Remember that even if she can, he may still force sex on her—successful refusal does not ensure that what one refuses does not happen.) There is certainly *a* notion of "successful refusal" on which she cannot. Success, on this stringent notion of it, requires that both speaker and audience are perfectly clear about which speech act is being performed. The audience fully grasps the content of the speech act, fully appreciates its force, and is disposed to respond appropriately to it. (A response can be appropriate without being the response most desired by the speaker, but it must be a conversationally sensible response and not, for example, a random changing of the subject.) There is no real interpretive struggle on the part of the hearer, and the understanding he achieves effectively matches the understanding the speaker has of what she said. Now, if that is what successful illocution requires, it seems that many of our attempted illocutions fail to be successful: the force and content of illocution often fail to be clearly perceptible to all participants in a communicative context.[19]

But presumably the notion of successful illocution at issue between Hornsby and Langton, and Bird, is not this one. All three would agree that in this stringent sense of success, a woman who ends up having sex forced on her was probably unable to perform successfully the illocutionary act of refusal. Someone who really grasps a refusal *as* a refusal, even if he ultimately decides not to respect it, is committed to seriously deliberating about its claim on him. That is, to hear something as a refusal is to hear it as placing a (perhaps defeasible) claim on one to *stop* or *remove* what was refused. The hearer who hears properly is aware of the perlocutionary object of a refusal: that its audience stop. Of course, the hearer can decide not to, and in some cases this may even be the morally correct thing to do, as in the case when a suspect may refuse the police entry to his home, and yet they may be warranted (literally) to enter. But in such cases, one is still weighing, and so recognizing, the refusal as such. However, a man who seriously deliberates about whether or not he ought to attempt to force sex on someone who has refused it is hardly a typical rapist. That is, any context in which a man does deliberate in this way either will not end with his forcing sex, or is very far removed from the standard scripts for forced sex that are at play in discussions of the silencing view.

So we need a slightly thinner notion of illocutionary success, of managing to refuse in saying "No," if there is to be daylight between Bird's position and that of Hornsby and Langton. And the question is whether the fact that a man will not understand what we pre-theoretically class as the woman's refusal could ever entail that nothing she does can in fact be a refusal, even in this thinner sense. What could such a thinner sense be? Here is one proposal: something counts as a refusal in this thin sense if it is not obviously wrong to take a speaker to have intentionally produced some locution, and for it to be more proper to classify what she does in producing it as refusing rather than, for instance, promising or criticizing or any other specific candidate illocutionary act. Thinly successful refusals are illocutions that are plausibly interpreted as refusals, without being clearly perceptible as refusals (and so clearly perceived as refusals) in the way that thickly successful refusals are.

I will argue that even in this thinner sense, there are contexts in which a woman having sex forced on her cannot refuse—cannot perform the illocutionary act of refusal. These failures are not directly due to the absence of uptake, but to speakers' beliefs about that absence. To make this case, I will use recent work on the epistemology of testimony to question one of the assumptions Bird makes in his criticisms of Hornsby and Langton.

Bird has very general reasons for objecting to Hornsby's and Langton's claims, and all of them are directed at Austin's claims as well as theirs. His first reason concerns our ability to use the tools Austin provides us—in particular, the distinction between illocutionary acts (such as arguings) and perlocutionary acts (such as convincings). Bird thinks that if utterance-effects are allowed to determine illocutions as well as perlocutions, we lose any grip on the nature of the distinction between those two sorts of acts.[20] Since something like the illocutionary/perlocutionary distinction is essential, it seems better in theorizing to be quite strict and insist that *no* effect can determine whether an illocution is or is not performed—not even the effect, of an utterance, of a hearer understanding the meaning and force of that very utterance.

But quite apart from this methodological point, Bird argues that it is simply false that actual uptake is required for illocution. He uses the example of a diary whose entries are never read after being written—not even by the diary keeper.[21] He asks, rhetorically, whether we really suppose that the absence of an audience, and so of any actual uptake, really prevents the diary-keeper from "being able to deplore the state of the nation, praise a colleague, or predict the outcome of an election" (13). And presumably we think she can do those things.[22]

Bird argues that it is clearly wrong to suppose that *actual* uptake is what is essential to an illocution being what it is. Uptake does matter, he allows, but counterfactually: "[a]lthough no-one reads the secret diary, it is true that if some normal person had read it they would have realized that the writer intended to deplore the state of the nation" (13). But what explains this counterfactual—the fact that uptake would have occurred given a properly positioned hearer—is simply that the illocution was exactly the illocution that it was *without the uptake*. And while Bird notes that we are far from having a complete, detailed story about what makes it the illocution that it is, he remarks that:

> we know the sort of factors which are relevant: primarily the words actually written, and their meanings; context, including institutional setting if relevant, is obviously important too, as indeed may be certain other background information including facts about human nature. These things, which include appropriate felicity conditions, fix the illocution performed. They do not *include* actual effects of the locution though they do determine what effects would typically occur...failure of the effect to occur would be *evidence* that the conditions for illocution had not been fulfilled...not...a sufficient condition for failure.[23]

What is most striking about this (by his own admission, highly general) story about the necessary conditions for determinate illocutionary acts is that speaker intentions do not get a look in at all. Bird's reference to intentions in the counterfactual case of a reader perusing the diary is only an apparent exception. The reader would realize that the diary keeper intended to deplore, because she would read the keeper's sentence *as* a deploring. That Bird does not mention speaker/writer intention in the long passage quoted suggests that it would be a mistake to take him to mean, in the previous remark, that the diarist's intention to deplore was essential to, for example, "Things are going to hell in a hand-basket" being a deploring. In fact, Bird explicitly endorses the claim that there are some illocutionary acts—grumbling and gossiping are his examples—where the speaker neither has an intention to perform them nor knows that she is.[24] Even if we grant that there are some illocutionary acts for which no speaker intentions at all are necessary, is it true they never are?

Two truths about language and convention might initially incline us to say so. First, linguistic meaning is in large part conventional, but such social conventions do not need propping up at each moment by individuals intending to mean as the conventions do. And second, it is a phenomenological fact that once we have been successfully initiated into the conventions of language use, much of our speech feels completely spontaneous and is not preceded by the formation of explicit intentions (to mean such-and-such, or to accomplish this or that in or by saying such-and-such). We can, however, recognize both points without having to concede that no illocution ever depends on speaker-intention.

Rather than argue this point on general grounds, I will argue that at least one illocutionary act, namely, telling, does so depend, and then make the case for an analogous treatment of refusing. I will draw on two recent accounts of testimony: Elizabeth Fricker's and Richard Moran's.[25] Both discuss the illocutionary act of *telling* within a specifically epistemological framework, but they both depend on and propose various positions in philosophy of language. At a very high level of generality, both Fricker and Moran understand a telling to be an act in which a speaker vouches for the truth of p or offers her assurance that p. When I tell, I commit myself to the truth of my utterance p: I speak because I (justifiably take myself to) know, and because I take my hearer *not* to know.

Certainly there can be infelicitous tellings. We all know at least one person who is always trying to tell us, at great length, of things we already know, and for which we may in fact have been the teller's original source. But for a telling to be a telling, felicitous or not, the speaker has to do something, namely, commit herself to the truth of p. And she does so in order to inform her audience. She offers her assurance that p to another so that he might also know that p. She need not, of course, have consciously thought to herself, before asserting that p, "I shall tell Smith that p." But informing Smith is her reason for uttering p and for vouching for its truth (in so saying).

Telling, on these accounts, is an illocutionary act to which speaker intention is essential. Speaker intention is also essential to its perlocutionary object—the hearer's forming a belief in what he was told. And since on this account that requires the hearer to trust the speaker—in Moran's terms, to believe her, and not only to believe what she says—that requires the hearer to believe that the speaker is trustworthy about the subject of her speech and that she is (intentionally) vouching for its truth. So for fully successful illocutionary telling, the hearer, even if he does not come to believe what he is told, needs clearly to understand that he is being invited so to believe, and being assured that doing so is proper. Sometimes these intentions—to vouch for p, and to inform some person or persons that p—are fully explicit. But they need not be. When they are not, a speaker must nevertheless meet an important condition, which I will dub the Not-Not Condition. She must *not* believe that it is *not* possible for her intended action to succeed.[26]

This looks like a general point about action. One can surely do something intentionally without having antecedently formed an explicit intention to do that thing, and one can surely do something without antecedently and explicitly believing that all the necessary conditions for one's successfully doing that thing in fact obtain. But it is not clear that one can do something intentionally if one believes that an absolutely necessary condition for success in so doing will *not* obtain.[27] In any case, the Not-Not Condition applies to telling, at least on Fricker's and Moran's accounts of it. A speaker cannot successfully tell (in either the thick or thin senses of success) unless she meets the Not-Not Condition. In order to tell my husband that my daughter is upstairs in her room, I need not have answered all the skeptic's doubts about object-persistence in the absence of current perception. But I cannot vouch for her being upstairs if I am aware of a reason to doubt it. And in order to tell you that the provost is out for your blood, I need not run through a conclusive proof to the effect that you are in fact ignorant of this, but I cannot proceed if I know you already know (at least not without doing something quite other than telling: namely, rubbing it in).

This point complicates Bird's claims about actual uptake, because it appears that for at least one kind of illocutionary act, telling, a speaker's beliefs about the possibility of uptake matter to her ability to perform that act. It is nevertheless true, as Bird notes, that in many cases, an illocutionary act can be the illocutionary act it is without actual uptake being secured. For example, consider inviting. If the colleague with whom I have been occasionally chatting this morning through our too-thin shared office wall has slipped out for coffee, that does not prevent my utterance of, "I'm starving; may I treat you to lunch?" being an invitation. But this does not tell against the Not-Not Condition's applying to inviting, because I meet it in this case. I do not know that actual uptake will not happen. What if I did? In the case of inviting, I would surely wait until I thought uptake would succeed. And likewise for telling, though perhaps not for grumbling or even complaining. I might grumble about the provost without any need for my next-door audience, and perhaps even without any intention to grumble at all. What about refusing? Specifically, what about refusing sex? Is that illocution's relation to speaker intention more like inviting and telling, or more like grumbling?

Refusal is more like telling than like grumbling or deploring. While some illocutions might not need any intended audiences or are able to make do with the illocutor herself as a kind of default audience, refusals and tellings are directed at intended audiences. Both illocutions are partially defined by the fact that their uptake is supposed to effect a reaction from a person other than the speaker.[28] The aim of telling is to transmit knowledge, and the aim of refusal is to effect a change in audience behavior. One can certainly fail to achieve one's aims. But having a fully determinate aim is sometimes required to perform a determinate action, and sometimes having such an aim requires one not to believe it cannot be achieved. Both prongs of this requirement apply to refusing.

Refusals aim to bring it about that one's audience cease and desist, in virtue of their recognition of one's refusal. One cannot be refusing if one lacks an intended audience and if one lacks this aim towards that audience.[29] One can succeed in refusing—in performing the illocution defined by that aim—even if one does not achieve that aim, that is, even if one's audience does not respond to one's refusal as one hopes. And perhaps one can succeed in refusing even if one's audience fails to hear one's refusal as a refusal—they faint as one is speaking, or they assume one's refusal is insincere, or they assume that in this context "no" means "yes." If so, then actual uptake is not, by itself, necessary to refusal. But if one believes uptake will not be secured, one will believe one cannot achieve the aim of getting the audience to cease in virtue of recognizing one's refusal. And so one cannot intentionally perform an action defined by that aim: one cannot refuse.[30] Of course one can still want the relevant action to cease, and plan to bring that about by other means, but that is a separate issue.

Suppose a woman says "no," intending it to be a refusal of sex. But this first refusal is not respected, nor is the next—and in a way that plants a serious (and terrifying) doubt in her mind as to whether the man is willing or able to hear her as refusing. That is, the kind of disregard with which the man is treating the woman in this context leads her to suppose not that he is proceeding in the face of what he hears as a refusal, but rather that he fails to hear her as refusing. At this point, the would-be refuser ceases to meet the Not-Not Condition: she does believe that conditions are hostile to uptake. She comes to believe she cannot achieve the aim of refusing. And so she ceases to be able to refuse.[31]

Holding that violations of the Not-Not Condition prevent refusals, while failure of uptake by itself does not, preserves the core of Hornsby's and Langton's conclusion: that some women's refusals of sex are silenced. Allowing that some intended refusals of sex *are* refusals (even if they are not heard as such) is compatible with their conclusion. That is because Hornsby and Langton are not arguing that women in a patriarchal culture are never able to refuse sex (by saying "no," or in any other way). They hold only that *some* women—those whose attempted refusals fail to secure uptake—are sometimes unable to refuse.

However, allowing that "a failure of uptake—or even uptake opposite to the one intended—is not sufficient to prevent an act of refusal" does undercut Hornsby's and Langton's own argument for the conclusion that women are silenced.[32] As Bird notes, because they believe that uptake is necessary for illocution generally, they do not argue that it is needed specifically in the contexts of attempts to refuse sex. So if one accepts that actual uptake is not necessary for refusal, then one appears to have to give up Hornsby's and Langton's conclusion: that women in some contexts not only have sex forced on them, but are silenced, unable to refuse that sex.

I have argued that one can preserve the conclusion not by arguing that actual uptake is necessary for refusals of sex in particular, but by arguing that refusing requires a speaker to meet the Not-Not Condition and that some contexts in which sexual violence is threatened may be such that women fail to meet that condition. In some contexts, the failure might be complete—that is, the woman realizes, at one and the same time, that she needs to refuse sex and that no refusal will be properly heard. Such women are immediately silenced. In other contexts, the woman might initially meet the Not-Not Condition, at least if that condition applies to her beliefs about a stretch of communication, rather than simply to her beliefs about her first utterance. That is, she might be tacitly assuming that her first "No!" serves only to get the man's attention, so that her second "No!" could be heard as a refusal. But it is possible that at some point she will cease to meet the condition, perhaps because she forms a belief like, "A man who has not heard my words as refusals by now *never will*."[33] Women in these contexts are silenced, but not immediately.

That not all such silencing is immediate does not rob the phenomenon of importance. Of course, if one wants to claim that such silencing is frequent, one will eventually have to answer some non-philosophical questions. How many women find themselves in communicative contexts where they believe they will not be heard as refusing sex is an empirical question. But the bare possibility of such cases is of philosophical interest. It highlights the deepest part of the dispute between Bird, and Hornsby and Langton: a disagreement over the role that *particular* contexts play in determining who can perform illocutionary acts of which kinds. Bird assumes that provided that the very general background conditions for successful illocution are met—the conditions for *anyone* to perform an illocution of a certain kind—a particular speaker can perform whatever illocutionary acts she wishes.[34] Hornsby and Langton hold instead that one cannot say what will not be heard. Even if the general background conditions for successful illocution have been met, the particular illocutions a particular person can perform depend on what illocutions her particular audience is capable of understanding her as making.

As a general claim about illocution, this is too strong. There are some illocutions, like grumbling, that one can perform whenever one wishes—or sometimes, even, without truly so wishing—provided the very general background conditions that fix such illocutions are met. But not all illocutions are like this, and they are governed by the Not-Not Condition. This gets back, for key illocutions like refusing, some of the dependence on particular contexts that makes Hornsby's and Langton's account so valuable. On my account, speakers need (not to have) certain beliefs about their audiences and their audiences' reactions to them. Those beliefs are formed in the uncomfortable space where speaker and audience size each other up. The forces, cultural and otherwise, that affect those beliefs are numerous and vary widely from context to context.[35] We can grant Bird's argument that actual uptake is not necessary for refusal without losing the theoretical license to attend closely to context, and to the forces that operate differently on male and female speakers, that Hornsby's and Langton's account wanted to secure.[36]

There is a cost to this account, but it is acceptable.[37] With Hornsby's and Langton's account, the silencing effect of the failure of uptake is direct—it happens regardless of whether a given speaker is thinking about it. On my account, the effect is mediated by the speaker's beliefs about the likelihood of such failure. This raises two concerns.[38] It might seem that women now share some of the blame for their loss of expressive power, or at least, that this blame cannot be put as squarely as it ought to be on the men who fail to hear them, and on the culture that encourages this. But that women's beliefs play a causal role in the harm they suffer is not enough to make women responsible, in a morally weighted way, for any part of that harm. When women decline to pursue an activity they would otherwise enjoy—taking solitary star-lit walks, to choose a well-worn example—because they believe they may fall victim to gender-specific crimes, we can see that the diminishment of their options is a harm for which they are not to blame, even though their belief is causally necessary to their decision not to pursue the option. A woman unable to refuse because she believes uptake cannot be secured is similarly not to blame for the fact that she is not refusing, though on my account this is an action she *cannot* now perform, not (like the star-lit walk) an action she chooses not to perform. In both cases, however, it is true that a blithely optimistic woman, who foresees no problems for her walk or her speech, is not prevented from embarking on the activity. But this simply seems appropriate: it is a fact about the operations of injustice that some of its harms fall on those who are most alert. A particular woman who goes for a dangerous walk *may* safely return home, after all.

But this raises the second concern. In order to use the loaded term *silenced* to describe a woman whose failure to meet the Not-Not Condition renders her unable to refuse, it seems her belief that uptake will not be forthcoming should be justified. It is not clear that a woman suffering from a delusion that *no one* can hear her, or in the grip of a prejudice that men from a certain ethnic group all believe "no" from a woman means "yes," should count as silenced, and yet my account appears to let her count. This points up a need to distinguish two facets to the notion of silencing: the fact that some women cannot perform certain illocutions and the judgment that this fact represents a wrong. On my account, a paranoid or prejudiced woman will be unable to refuse. But we need not judge that *this* is a wrong. (Of course, were sex to be forced on such a woman, *that* would still be a wrong.) In order to blame someone or something other than the female speaker for her silencing, in order to think that something in society rather than her mind ought to change, we do need to take her beliefs about uptake to be justified.[39]

A woman who cannot refuse because she ceases to satisfy the Not-Not Condition is silenced by the factors responsible for her justifiable belief that she cannot secure uptake. And a woman whose naïveté allows her to meet the Not-Not Condition in a situation where uptake in fact will not be forthcoming is able to perform the act of refusal—but only because her beliefs are not what they ought to be.[40] The kind of speaking we have reason to value is missing in both cases. Refusals, especially refusals of anything that, if forced, threatens one's autonomy, should be heard properly. And women should be able to engage in refusals without having to labor under false beliefs.

REASONS FOR ATTEMPTING TO REFUSE

A woman may surely keep saying "no" even after it is clear to her that she cannot change the outcome of what happens. She might have many motives for doing so. Perhaps she is coping with the situation by already thinking about pressing charges against her attacker and wants to be able to describe herself, later, to the police as "saying 'No' the whole time."[41] But a consequence of accepting the Not-Not Condition is that she cannot, in saying "no" past the point where she believes her attacker to be unable to respect a refusal, be refusing. She is not uttering nonsense. But what illocutionary act is she performing? She may simply be evincing distress; that is, she may be chanting "No," and it has its usual locutionary meaning, but she is not performing any determinate illocutionary act in saying it. But it is also possible that she is performing the act of *attempting to refuse*. It might be that we have reason to admit a special status for this act, and perhaps also *attempting to tell* in some related contexts.[42]

Miranda Fricker's notion of epistemic injustice can be used to make this case. Speaking somewhat loosely, someone is subject to epistemic injustice when a social-identity-related prejudice causes her audience to perceive her as not trustworthy. Using language from the account of telling discussed above, we could say that in some cases, a speaker is viewed as so worthless that she has nothing of value to *stake* in vouching for the truth of a claim. She is taken to be so far from being an agent worthy of respect that there is no sense in taking her assurance for anything, and even something ridiculous in the idea of her offering assurance. Such a speaker would be what Fricker calls pre-emptively silenced.[43] She certainly is never asked to tell anything, at least not on certain topics; at nightmarish levels of injustice, the non-asking might be global. And she never volunteers anything, at least not to individuals outside her social group. Drawing on the account developed above, we can see how she might attempt to tell—perhaps in a kind of desperate hope that this time things will be different, that she will be believed. If the hope is strong enough then, even if it is not borne out, she will in fact have told (even if she is not heard)—because she will have met the Not-Not Condition, however fleetingly. But she might attempt to tell in full knowledge that she will not be heard, and so in a kind of awareness that she cannot tell. But her attempting to tell, at least on topics of grave importance to her, would be a way of expressing, if only to herself, her self-respect—the fact that she takes herself as able to assure, and vouch for truth.

Some attempted sexual refusals could be similarly treated. A woman might continue to say "no" while knowing that she will not be heard as refusing, in saying "no," and this could be a distinctive illocutionary act: attempting to refuse. One might make it because one wants to know of oneself that one has made it. In this limited sense, one's illocution has oneself as audience. That only this limited assertion of autonomy is possible here is part of the tragedy.

CONCLUSION

Both because accurate statements of facts matter in the pursuit of truth and because finer-grained representations of facts can make it easier to rectify injustice, it is important to be able to distinguish all the different harms potentially involved when women are subject to forced sex. The forced sexual action is itself a harm. The way in which women are not taken to be trustworthy testifiers, even on topics central to their own well-being and their own sexuality, is another. This second harm may involve women having their status of credible refusers of sex undermined. A credible refuser of X is someone whose refusal of X places a prima facie obligation on a listener to stop pressing X on the refuser. A typical adult is a credible refuser of candy; a typical child is not a credible refuser of bad-tasting medicine. It is unjust to view someone as a noncredible refuser when she in fact is, and women are thus wronged if they are not viewed as credible refusers of sex. Miranda Fricker uses this point to present her own argument for the claim that some of women's sexual refusals are silenced. The non-credible refuser is improperly viewed as lacking the status needed to secure respect for her refusals. In the limit, her credibility may be so low that others even have trouble hearing her refusals as such.[44]

The harm Hornsby and Langton identify reaches all the way to what women are able to say, and not only to how their sayings may be dismissed. In any given case where a woman suffers the harm of forced sex, it is of course an empirical question whether her refusal was understood but not respected; whether the refusal she succeeded in making was not heard as such because she was viewed as lacking relevant epistemic status; or whether she was unable to perform the illocutionary act of refusal. And it is a separate empirical question why, in any of these cases, her attacker in fact forced sex on her. It may turn out that in the majority of cases refusals are made and even heard, but disrespected and discounted. Perhaps only under very specific kinds of injustice is the belief that uptake will not be secured justified, rendering illocutionary acts of refusal impossible. But if that harm, that loss of appropriate expressive power, can happen, it is important that we should be able to take account of it. Distinguishing the harm of not-being-able-to-make-a-refusal from the harm of not-being-able-to-be-heard-as-refusing is a fine distinction but an important one.

Making fine distinctions is useful when faced with very tangled forms of injustice, and the injustices feminism is interested in addressing are often tangled in a particular way. It can be hard to get everyone to see key harms *as* harms; hard for even victims to find words to articulate exactly *how* they have been harmed; hard to notice, sometimes, that women are being *deprived* of something rather than declining to seize it. I have argued that women could be deprived of the opportunity to refuse by arguing that speaker beliefs about audience response matter to refusals. This keeps Hornsby's and Langton's conclusion that women's refusals of sex are silenced available to render free-speech defenses of pornography and hate-speech less obviously compelling. And because speakers' and audiences' beliefs about one another are shaped by social identities and power relations, focusing on how such beliefs affect what can be said ensures that appropriate attention is paid to social life—even in speech-act theories that limit the power of actual audience response to determine what gets said.

Notes

Marianne Janack provided helpful comments on a very early version of this chapter. A later version was presented at a group session of the Society for Analytical Feminism held at the Central Division Meeting of the American Philosophical Association (Chicago, Ill., 2009). I was helped a great deal by insightful criticism from my commentator on that occasion, Anne Barnhill, and by discussion with her and members of the audience. Anita Superson's reflective suggestions much improved the final essay.

1. Both types of silence are discussed by Jennifer Hornsby, "Disempowered Speech," *Philosophical Topics* 23, no. 2 (1995): 127–47 and Jennifer Saul, "Feminist Philosophy of Language," in *The Stanford Encyclopedia of Philosophy* (Fall 2008 Edition), ed. Edward N. Zalta, http://plato.stanford.edu/archives/fall2008/entries/feminism-language/. Saul discusses feminist criticisms of traditional philosophy of language as too individualistic, as well as the quite recent move by some feminist philosophers to use traditional philosophy of language to explore issues of importance to feminists.

2. As Saul notes, this project is quite new ("Feminist Philosophy of Language"). A significant portion of the work drawing on Austin will be discussed in this essay. Ishani Maitra has explored, within a Gricean framework, the effect speakers' perceived social roles play in how their speech is interpreted ("Silence and Responsibility," *Philosophical Perspectives* 18 [2004]: 189–206). For J. L. Austin's own approach, see *How To Do Things With Words*, 2nd ed.,

ed. J. O. Urmson and M. Sbisà (Cambridge, Mass.: Harvard University Press, 1962). For Paul Grice's, see *Studies in the Way of Words* (Cambridge, Mass.: Harvard University Press, 1989).

3. In several papers, including Jennifer Hornsby and Rae Langton, "Free Speech and Illocution," *Legal Theory* 4 (1998): 21–37, and Rae Langton, "Speech Acts and Unspeakable Acts," *Philosophy & Public Affairs* 22, no. 4 (1993): 293–330. Hornsby's "Disempowered Speech" discusses such silencing with respect to judges' presumption of victims' insincerity during rape trials (citing two English cases). Broader, and perhaps less literal, notions of silencing-by-pornography are argued for in Catharine MacKinnon's *Feminism Unmodified* (Cambridge, Mass.: Harvard University Press, 1987) and *Only Words* (Cambridge, Mass.: Harvard University Press, 1993).

4. I am glossing over several complexities. For example, it is surely possible that "no" might come to be unavailable for refusal-making for reasons other than a specific rape myth whose source was pornography. (Only if pornography causally contributes to this silencing, however, is the fact of the silencing able to play a role in free speech arguments against pornography. For analysis of the difficulties involved in assessing any causal link between pornography and harm to women, and a proposal that we look to epidemiology for dealing with them, see A. W. Eaton's "A Sensible Antiporn Feminism," *Ethics* 117, no. 4 [2007]: 674–715.) And we might want to distinguish between a relatively weak claim that pornography diminishes women's expressive resources—it takes away one method, uttering "no," that was once available for refusing sex—and a much stronger claim. The stronger claim would be that pornography eliminates women's linguistic capacity to refuse—that pornography (or some other causal factor) has effected a change such that no words a woman utters in the course of an unwanted sexual encounter will count as refusal. This latter claim may, in its strongest form, shade into a claim that, for example, Catherine MacKinnon appears at times to want to make: that a pornographic culture has constructed 'woman' in such a way that it is a conceptual impossibility for a woman to refuse sex to a man who wants it. That is, "woman" is defined in terms of sexual availability to men. To refuse to have sex is at the very least not something women are encouraged to feel comfortable about (see "Sex and Violence," in *Feminism Unmodified*, 94). To refuse offered sex is not feminine; in fact, femininity is the desire for male sexual dominance (see "Desire and Power" in *Feminism Unmodified*, 50). Of course, Mackinnon does not deny that individual women can escape these patterns of domination on particular occasions. Her point is that doing so is difficult, and that until our society as a whole changes, those escapes will count as escapes from full femininity as well as from forced sex. While I find this compelling, I share Miranda Fricker's concern that MacKinnon's work "essentializes the multifarious nature of women's historical subordination to men as foundationally a matter of sexual subordination" (*Epistemic Injustice: Power and the Ethics of Knowing* [Oxford: Oxford University Press, 2007], 138).

Fricker's own acknowledgment of a version of MacKinnon's claim about silencing is discussed below.

5. See Austin, *How To Do Things With Words.*

6. The debates I am interested in all focus on cases in which a woman does *not* want sex (at least not at this time) with a particular man and in which she *knows* this about herself. None of the views discussed in this paper, my own included, are therefore addressing the complicated question of when and how a sexist culture could alter a woman's sense of what is good for her to such an extent that she desires, or thinks of herself as desiring, sex in conditions that are likely to do her harm or are incompatible with her autonomy. That is, none of us is taking up the case of a woman who fails even to attempt to refuse in a case where it might appear she *should*.

7. Because I am focusing on the question of the illocutionary force of "no" in attempting to refuse sex, I am not addressing objections to the view that pornography itself has illocutionary force (as argued in Langton's "Speech Acts and Unspeakable Acts," and criticized in Jennifer Saul, "Pornography, Speech Acts, and Context," *Proceedings of the Aristotelian Society* 106 [2006]: 229–48.)

8. This objection originates with Daniel Jacobson (in his "Freedom of Speech Acts? A Response to Langton," *Philosophy & Public Affairs* 24, no. 1 [1995]: 64–79) and is pressed by Alexander Bird (in his "Illocutionary Silencing," *Pacific Philosophical Quarterly* 83 [2002]: 1–15) and Nellie Wieland (in her "Linguistic Authority and Convention in a Speech Act Analysis of Pornography," *Australasian Journal of Philosophy* 85, no. 3 [2007]: 435–56). There are complicated questions about the relation between non-refusal and non-consent and about the distinction between what is required for a legal verdict of rape and what is required for a moral judgment that a man committed a gross violation of a woman's autonomy in forcing sex on her. But even without resolving these questions, some version of this objection does seem serious. Forced-sex-in-the-face-of-clear-refusal is a particularly heinous act, one it seems some men do commit, and it is problematic if we lose the capacity to represent them as doing what they are apparently doing.

9. Wieland, "Linguistic Authority and Convention." I have taken the phrase "collective social imagination," and the idea of its use in such a context, from Miranda Fricker's *Epistemic Injustice.*

10. Bird, "Illocutionary Silencing." Jacobson had expressed a worry that any view of illocution that required the securing of uptake would "hold the performance of an illocutionary act hostage to the perversity of one's audience" ("Freedom of Speech Acts," 74).

11. Ishani Maitra argues that a Gricean account can fund a notion of communicative disablement amounting to silencing, and that this notion avoids some of the criticisms leveled at Hornsby's and Langton's ("Silencing Speech"). I consider only the question of how much of Hornsby's and Langton's work can be preserved within an Austinian framework and do

not attempt to adjudicate the question of whether Austin or Grice has the better line on communication in general.

12. See §4.2, "History, Blame, and Moral Disappointment" in Miranda Fricker, *Epistemic Injustice*.

13. It has been argued that men may sometimes strategically avoid this kind of reflection, relying instead on culturally sanctioned understandings of women as ineffective communicators about their sexual desires. See Susan Ehrlich, *Representing Rape: Language and Sexual Consent* (New York: Routledge, 2001) and Rachael O'Byrne, Susan Hansen, and Mark Rapley, "'If a Girl Doesn't Say "No" ...': Young Men, Rape, and Claims of Insufficient Knowledge." *Journal of Community and Applied Social Psychology* 18 (2008): 168–93. A case in which a man avoids reflection in this way would be one of the complicated cases, discussed in the next paragraph, which call for a mixture of kinds of blame in our responses to them.

14. Fricker introduces her illuminating contrast by means of an example that is less morally weighted. However, she uses the contrast to argue generally against moral relativism, so I do not think she would object to my using it for a wrong as dramatic as this.

15. The relevant objections held that Hornsby's and Langton's view would make men either not responsible at all, or only to an inappropriately diminished degree, for forcing sex. I have argued that we can use Fricker's account of blame to deny this. Of course, sorting out *exactly* what kind and degree of responsibility a given man has for forcing sex in a particular cultural context is bound to be difficult. Feminist moral psychology has been interested in considering how false beliefs about the persons one harms do and, importantly, do *not* diminish or alter the nature of one's responsibility for those harms. No one wants to inappropriately let victimizers off the hook. There are reflective tasks we should blame victimizers for failing to pursue. But the difficulty of such tasks can be increased or decreased, depending on the kinds of conceptual tools available for aiding such reflection—tools that may be first sharpened by feminist analysis. For an approach to responsibility that, like Fricker, seeks to hold people responsible for wrongs they do while recognizing how hard it is to be moral, and how corrupt cultural understanding can contribute to this difficulty, see Michelle Moody-Adams, "Culture, Responsibility, and Affected Ignorance," *Ethics* 104, no. 2 (1994): 291–309. The attitude of Moody-Adams's "forgiving moralist" may not line up exactly with that of someone feeling Fricker's resentment of disappointment. The greater rigor Moody-Adams appears to favor stems, I think, from her being more optimistic than Fricker about empirical constraints on the human capacity for reflection. Moody-Adams holds, for example, that "one has the capacity to question existing social practices merely by virtue of learning to form the negation of any statement" (296 n.14). For a survey of different approaches to this issue in feminist ethics generally, see Anita Superson, "Responsibility of Oppressors for Oppression," §3.1 in her "Feminist Moral Psychology," in *The Stanford*

Encyclopedia of Philosophy (Spring 2009 edition), ed. Edward N. Zalta, http://plato.stanford.edu/archives/spr2009/entries/feminism-moralpsych/. For specific discussion of responsibility for silencing, see Maitra, "Silence and Responsibility," and Ishani Maitra and Mary Kate McGowan, "On Silencing, Rape, and Responsibility," forthcoming in the *Australasian Journal of Philosophy* (2010).

16. Austin, *How To Do Things With Words*, 116–17.

17. Austin construes the distinction between the act of φ-ing, and the act of attempting to φ, to be basic to the theory of action, and so not as specially directed to linguistic actions (*How to Do Things With Words*, 105–6).

18. See Hornsby and Langton, "Free Speech and Illocution," on the distinction between "produc[ing] intelligible sounds and marks" and doing things with words (37).

19. Presumably, unless there were enough illocutions that succeed in this thick sense, we would not go in for illocuting at all, at least not for illocutions where success really makes a difference (e.g., to knowledge transmission, in testifying). Presumably there is no mechanical way to specify what would count as "enough" here. See Elizabeth Fricker, "Second-hand Knowledge," *Philosophy and Phenomenological Research* 73, no. 3 (2006): 602, especially n. 23.

20. Bird does not say it would be impossible to make this out, only that "Austin's distinction between φ-ing *in* saying that *p* and φ-ing *by* saying that *p* is not enough" ("Illocutionary Silencing," 12). This criticism refers to Austin's suggestion that ordinary language marks the distinction between perlocutionary and illocutionary acts, because in many cases we find it more natural to say, of an illocutionary act, that someone performed it *in* saying what she did, and of a perlocutionary act, that she performed it *by* saying what she did. Thus, we might say that *in* saying "I do," I married my spouse; and that *by* saying "I do," I made my grandmother happy. Austin appears to be trying to capture the difference between a constitutive connection between two actions, such that it turns out we only *apparently* have two actions; and a means/end connection between what remain in fact two actions. That is, to continue the example, my saying "I do" and my marrying are, in the right conditions, one action. But my speaking is the means by which I accomplish something else, the cheering of my grandmother. For explicit claims that illocution may be tied to one utterance effect—uptake—without vitiating the usefulness of appeals to other effects in our account of perlocution, see Jennifer Hornsby, "Feminism in Philosophy of Language: Communicative Speech Acts," in *The Cambridge Companion to Feminism in Philosophy*, ed. Miranda Fricker and Jennifer Hornsby (Cambridge: Cambridge University Press, 2000), 92–93; and Hornsby and Langton, "Free Speech and Illocution," 24.

21. Bird takes it that focusing only on face-to-face communications prejudices an inquiry into the nature of illocution, since illocution is to be found not only in those contexts but wherever there is language use ("Illocutionary

Silencing," 8). And he faults Hornsby and Langton for focusing only on the communicative function of language in their discussions of the reciprocity that is (in their view) required for illocution. I do not need to contest either of these moves in order to pursue my criticism of Bird. But an alternative line of attack could begin by contesting Bird's apparent assumption that, for theoretical purposes in philosophy of language, no one context of language use is privileged over any other—what matters is only that one look at a broad selection of contexts.

22. We might think so because we take the diarist to be, at the moment of writing, a kind of audience for herself—in which case we might think we can accept the example without abandoning the Austinian view.

23. Bird, "Illocutionary Silencing," 13; emphases original.

24. Bird, "Illocutionary Silencing," 9.

25. Elizabeth Fricker, "Second-hand Knowledge," and Richard Moran, "Getting Told and Being Believed," *Philosopher's Imprint* 5, no. 5 (2005): 1–29. Fricker notes that she has altered her earlier view on testimony in response to Moran's work.

26. The condition is formulated negatively to respect the point that the illocutions of ordinary competent speakers may not be preceded by explicit intentions so to speak, nor by occurrent beliefs about the advisability of so speaking. The negative formulation also leaves open the possibility that, for example, very young children manage (if we think they do) to perform illocutionary acts like telling before they have the capacity to formulate the relevant explicit intentions and beliefs. They, too, could satisfy the Not-Not Condition.

27. Similarly, one cannot intend that something be the case if one believes it is impossible for it to be the case. Intending that p is not simply wishing that p. So even accounts of illocution that eschew any role for *audience-directed* speaker intentions will need to respect the Not-Not Condition. Consider, for example, Mitchell S. Green's analysis of illocutionary speaker meaning: "S illocutionarily speaker-means that P ϕ'ly where ϕ is an illocutionary force, iff (1) S performs an action A intending that (2) in performing A, it be manifest that S is committed to P under force ϕ, and that it be manifest that S intends that (2)" (*Self-Expression* [Oxford: Clarendon Press, 2007], 212–13; I have substituted parentheses around for full stops after the first two occurrences of 1 and 2). I certainly can intend that something be manifest without believing that each of the preconditions for manifestibility in this context obtains. But I cannot intend that something be manifest if I believe that one or more of the conditions for manifestibility does not obtain.

28. Both Fricker and Moran present a teller as offering her assurance to an intended audience. Fricker is most explicit about this, in part because she wants to allow that hearers not in the speaker's intended audience could still acquire the relevant knowledge from her telling. But on both accounts, assurance has to be offered—and offerings require intended recipients (see

Fricker, "Second-hand Knowledge," 596–97, and Moran, "Getting Told and Being Believed," 11, 15–16). As a consequence, an individual speaker cannot assure, and hence tell, if she believes there is *no* audience.

29. Bird claims that a refusal could be unintentional, as when a speaker with a poor grasp of idiomatic French utters "Merci" intending to accept some offered food ("Illocutionary Silencing," 4). I agree with Bird that such a speaker will be interpreted as refusing, and that "Merci" in that context has a locutionary meaning like, "No, thank you." But the account above commits me to denying that the speaker has performed the illocutionary act of refusing. In any case, I am inclined to agree with Strawson that non-intentional illocutionary acts make sense primarily in institutional contexts, or in structured games, *and* that even then, such acts have a very non-standard character (see his "Intention and Convention in Speech Acts," *The Philosophical Review* 73, no. 4 [1964]: 457).

30. In thinking about this, I have been helped by P. F. Strawson's discussion of the different roles played by the *aim* of securing uptake and the *achievement* of uptake. Strawson is closer to Austin than Bird on the role of uptake in illocution, outside of explicitly institutional contexts (see "Intention and Convention in Speech Acts," 458). (So I think Hornsby and Langton could be even more forceful than they are in claiming Strawson as a partial ally; see "Free Speech and Illocution," 26, 29 n. 22.) A clarification: when theorists want to resist Austin's linking of illocution to uptake, they describe an illocution as aiming at the securing of an uptake that may not be achieved. In the text above, I have used 'aim' to describe not uptake but the desired effects of uptake (such as cessation).

31. What she can do instead will be discussed in the next section.

32. Bird, "Illocutionary Silencing," 11.

33. I am grateful to Anne Barnhill for convincing me that the Not-Not Condition should not be framed as a condition on single utterances. This applies not only to refusals but to many other illocutions as well. For example, in a crowded store one often says "Excuse me" fairly mildly, to attract the attention of the person blocking your way, and then more loudly. Similar examples could be constructed using "Wait for me!" or "Watch out!" The exact size of the relevant portion of communication—how much longer than a single utterance, how much shorter than a whole conversational exchange—would depend on the specific illocution (pleading, warning) being performed, and specific facts about one's audience (partially deaf, distracted).

34. Institutional facts do need to be included in the background conditions. I cannot pronounce sentence on anyone, because I am not a judge. But the conditions for being a judge and being in the right setting to pronounce sentence can be spelled out without any reference to any particular person.

35. This fact could be part of the explanation for why fully communicative sexual encounters, of the kind advocated by Lois Pineau, are so difficult.

Pineau argues that our discussions, legal and otherwise, about rape should focus not on whether a woman can prove she signaled non-consent but on whether a man can prove he secured consent. A man must secure consent, and must be able to show that it would have been reasonable for the woman to consent to sex on the terms he was offering it. Pineau argues that the reasonableness of granting consent will be clearest in cases where a sexual encounter is set up to involve clear communication, on the part of both participants, of their desires, for the end of mutual pleasure. (Desires deformed by violent threats are obviously ruled out.) But if intentions to communicate can be hampered by false or incomplete beliefs about what one's audience is capable of understanding, it may be hard to say everything one might wish in such a context—even a context free of obvious violence. See Pineau, "Date Rape: A Feminist Analysis," in *Date Rape: Feminism, Philosophy, and the Law*, ed. Leslie Francis (University Park: Pennsylvania State University Press, 1996).

36. See the beginning of Hornsby and Langton, "Free Speech and Illocution," where they express an interest in exploring, in connection with Hornsby's account of reciprocity between speakers and hearers, and MacKinnon's work, "the conditions that constrain women's speech" (27). See also Hornsby's statement that on an account of language like hers that recognizes the paramount importance of communication, "[a] certain transparency between those who share a language is acknowledged. But the possibility is admitted that relations of power and authority, which differentiate speakers, will affect which speech acts they are capable of performing" ("Feminism in Philosophy of Language," 97).

37. Finding these costs unacceptable might lead one wholeheartedly to embrace Bird's account. After all, if he is correct about illocution, then women's abilities to refuse are *never* impaired as a direct or indirect result of facts about their audiences. So if Bird is right, then something feminists have reason to want to be true *is* true: women can illocutionarily refuse sex no matter how perverse their audience. I would like that to be true, but because I do not think Bird is correct about illocution in general, I cannot accept that it is true. That is, I have to admit that women are vulnerable to a harm that on Bird's account does not even exist. The remainder of this section argues that this is not sufficient reason to reject the criticisms of Bird's account of illocution that I have presented above. (It is, of course, reason to attempt to change society so that no woman ever actually suffers the harm that remains a conceptual possibility on my view.)

38. I am grateful to Anne Barnhill, David Enoch, and other participants at the Society for Analytic Feminism group session where I presented the earlier version of this paper for raising these concerns.

39. She needs to have justifiable beliefs that she will not be able to secure uptake from this particular man. That will not always require her to have justifiable beliefs about all the factors actually responsible for his inability to hear her properly.

40. This is why it would be perverse to suppose that the remedy for women whose refusals are silenced would be for more of those women to be blind to the fact that their sexual refusals are not heard as such. The remedy is to change social facts so that any fear of uptake-failure is no longer justified.

41. The vexed history of why and when a "clearly articulated 'No,'" as opposed to physical resistance, was taken as constitutive of non-consent to intercourse for legal purposes is discussed in Susan Estrich's "Rape," in *Applications of Feminist Legal Theory to Women's Lives: Sex, Violence, Work and Reproduction*, ed. D. Kelly Weisberg (Philadelphia: Temple University Press, 1996), 431–54.

42. It is a consequence of the general way I framed the Not-Not Condition that these are the options any time someone fails to meet that condition with respect to some action, even if it is not a linguistic action. That is, if I really am intentionally φ-ing, then I must have met the Not-Not Condition (even if I started from a position of disbelief). If I do not now meet the Not-Not Conditions relevant to φ-ing, then I cannot be φ-ing. I am therefore performing some action other than φ-ing or attempting to φ, or I am attempting to φ. Many of the cases we might pre-theoretically label as someone's "praying for a cure," "begging for mercy," or "pushing the car up the hill" actually fall in this last category. If the agent fails the Not-Not Condition, then she is really only attempting the relevant action, perhaps to express how important the desired (but believed to be out of reach) end of that action is to her.

43. Miranda Fricker, *Epistemic Injustice*, 130–31.

44. Fricker draws to a limited extent on MacKinnon's work to argue that in some contexts, women's credibility is so diminished that men simply do not register that their testimony (to the fact that they do not want sex) *is* testimony. She distinguishes this "epistemic model" from Hornsby's and Langton's "communicative" model, and concludes that "[e]ither conception of silencing presents a coherent social possibility, but I tend to think that the epistemic model describes the more empirically likely possibility, simply because it requires less erosion of women's human status before the silencing effect kicks in" (*Epistemic Injustice*, 141–42). Accepting the Not-Not Condition on refusal means that a woman who realized her refusals were not heard as such, because of epistemic injustice, would be unable to continue making them—thus indicating a grey area between the "epistemic" and "communicative" models.

References

Austin, John L. *How To Do Things With Words*, 2nd ed. Edited by James O. Urmson and Marina Sbisà. Cambridge, Mass.: Harvard University Press, 1962.

Bird, Alexander. "Illocutionary Silencing." *Pacific Philosophical Quarterly* 83 (2002): 1–15.

Eaton, Anne W. "A Sensible Antiporn Feminism." *Ethics* 117, no. 4 (2007): 674–715.

Ehrlich, Susan. *Representing Rape: Language and Sexual Consent.* New York: Routledge, 2001.

Estrich, Susan. "Rape." In *Applications of Feminist Legal Theory to Women's Lives: Sex, Violence, Work and Reproduction,* ed. D. Kelly Weisberg, 431–54. Philadelphia: Temple University Press, 1996.

Fricker, Elizabeth. "Second-hand Knowledge." *Philosophy and Phenomenological Research* 73, no. 3 (2006): 592–618.

Fricker, Miranda. *Epistemic Injustice: Power and the Ethics of Knowing.* Oxford: Oxford University Press, 2007.

Green, Mitchell S. *Self-Expression.* Oxford: Clarendon Press, 2007.

Grice, Paul. *Studies in the Way of Words.* Cambridge, Mass.: Harvard University Press, 1989.

Hornsby, Jennifer. "Disempowered Speech." *Philosophical Topics* 23, no. 2 (1995): 127–47.

———. "Feminism in Philosophy of Language: Communicative Speech Acts." In *The Cambridge Companion to Feminism in Philosophy,* ed. Miranda Fricker and Jennifer Hornsby, 87–106. Cambridge: Cambridge University Press, 2000.

———, and Rae Langton. "Free Speech and Illocution." *Legal Theory* 4 (1998): 21–37.

Jacobson, Daniel. "Freedom of Speech Acts? A Response to Langton." *Philosophy & Public Affairs* 24, no. 1 (1995): 64–79.

Langton, Rae. "Speech Acts and Unspeakable Acts." *Philosophy & Public Affairs* 22, no. 4 (1993): 293–330.

MacKinnon, Catherine. *Feminism Unmodified: Discourses on Life and Law.* Cambridge, Mass.: Harvard University Press, 1987.

———. "Desire and Power." In *Feminism Unmodified: Discourses on Life and Law,* 46–62. Cambridge, Mass.: Harvard University Press, 1987.

———. "Sex and Violence." In *Feminism Unmodified: Discourses on Life and Law,* 85–92. Cambridge, Mass.: Harvard University Press, 1987.

———. *Only Words.* Cambridge, Mass.: Harvard University Press, 1993.

Maitra, Ishani. "Silence and Responsibility." *Philosophical Perspectives* 18 (2004): 189–206.

———. "Silencing Speech." *Canadian Journal of Philosophy* 39 (2009): 309–38.

——— and Mary Kate McGowan. "On Silencing, Rape, and Responsibility." *Australasian Journal of Philosophy* 88 (2010): 167–72.

Moody-Adams, Michelle. "Culture, Responsibility, and Affected Ignorance." *Ethics* 104, no. 2 (1994): 291–309.

Moran, Richard. "Getting Told and Being Believed." *Philosopher's Imprint* 5, no. 5 (2005): 1–29.

O'Byrne, Rachael, Susan, Hansen, and Mark Rapley. "'If a Girl Doesn't Say "No"…': Young Men, Rape and Claims of Insufficient Knowledge." *Journal of Community and Applied Social Psychology* 18 (2008): 168–93.

Pineau, Lois. "Date Rape: A Feminist Analysis." In *Date Rape: Feminism, Philosophy, and the Law*, ed. Leslie Francis. University Park: Pennsylvania State University Press, 1996.

Saul, Jennifer. "Pornography, Speech Acts, and Context." *Proceedings of the Aristotelian Society* 106 (2006): 229–48.

———. "Feminist Philosophy of Language." In *The Stanford Encyclopedia of Philosophy* (Fall 2008 Edition), ed. Edward N. Zalta, http://plato.stanford .edu/archives/fall2008/entries/feminism-language.

Strawson, Peter F. "Intention and Convention in Speech Acts." *The Philosophical Review* 73, no. 4 (1964): 439–60.

Superson, Anita. "Responsibility of Oppressors for Oppression." Section 3.1 of "Feminist Moral Psychology." In *The Stanford Encyclopedia of Philosophy* (Spring 2009 edition), ed. Edward N. Zalta. http://plato.stanford.edu/ archives/spr2009/entries/feminism-moralpsych.

Wieland, Nellie. "Linguistic Authority and Convention in a Speech Act Analysis of Pornography." *Australasian Journal of Philosophy* 85, no. 3 (2007): 435–56.

10

LOUISE ANTONY
University of Massachusetts–Amherst

IS THERE A "FEMINIST"

PHILOSOPHY OF LANGUAGE?

THIS IS A POLEMICAL paper, thinly disguised as a methodological paper. The broad question I am concerned with is how to understand the phrase "feminist philosophy." I do not intend to argue *for* one specific way of construing it; rather, I want to make a case *against* one specific way of construing it. My case is philosophically sound, I believe, but my hope is that my political plea will be effective as well—that it will move some feminist philosophers to think a bit differently about what they are doing.

While there is enormous variety among the projects in which feminist philosophers are currently engaged, we can discern two overarching kinds of project. Each of these project types originated in a particular kind of feminist engagement with mainstream philosophy in the 1960s and 1970s. The first type of project I'll call "critical": this is the project of exposing, analyzing, and theorizing masculinist bias within mainstream philosophy, including both canonical and contemporary work. The landmark anthology, *Discovering Reality*, edited by Sandra Harding and Merrill Hintikka in 1983, could be regarded as containing the founding documents of this stream of feminist work. The other type of project I'll call "practical:" this is the project of training existing philosophical methods onto issues that were (and, sadly, remain) pressing for women: abortion, affirmative action, sexuality. Early examples of this sort of work would be Judith Jarvis Thomson's "A Defense of Abortion," (1971) and Ann Ferguson's "On Conceiving Motherhood and Sexuality: A Feminist Materialist Approach" (1984). In calling such work "practical," I mean to be evoking an analogy with "practical ethics," sometimes called "applied ethics." The idea is to apply philosophy to areas of concern to women.

There need be no incompatibility between projects of one type and projects of the other, but their mutual coherence depends to some extent on the outcome of the critical project. Some feminist philosophers engaged in the critical project quickly came to the conclusion that philosophy was too deeply imbued with masculinist bias for feminists to work comfortably within existing frameworks. New philosophical frameworks and new foundations were needed, these critics said—we needed a new kind of philosophy, a *feminist* philosophy. Thence was born a new type of feminist project, a type I'll call the *replacement* project. The agenda: replace "malestream" ethics, philosophy of science, epistemology, etc., with *feminist* ethics, *feminist* philosophy of science, *feminist* epistemology, and so forth. It is the replacement project I want to argue against.

The replacement project is ostensibly *constructive*, but in fact, I think the results of the project to date have been mainly negative. That is not to say that nothing positive has been produced under the headings of "feminist ethics" or "feminist epistemology"—quite the contrary. There has been wonderful work appearing under rubrics like this. My contention is that, whatever it is *called*, the best work in feminist philosophy is work that would easily count as "feminist" in the practicalist sense. The best feminist philosophy, in my opinion, is work that has developed simply from the application of a feminist mind to a philosophical problem, with free appeal to whatever concepts and background theories seemed to that feminist thinker to be the right ones to use.[1]

But what, then, is the difference between the replacement approach and the practicalist approach? Only this—that the replacement approach depends on a prior *de-legitimation* of some alternative to the view being defended. That is, in order for someone to advertise her theory as a *feminist* theory, she must first show that the view hers opposes is a *masculinist* theory—the *kind* of theory that necessitates the replacement. She must insist that the view she disagrees with is not only incorrect, but pernicious, and that toleration of that view helps—in however small a way—to sustain patriarchy.[2] The practicalist, on the other hand, does not need to impugn the politics of her opponents. Although she may argue against other views in the course of defending her own, she does not need to take the extra step of *discrediting* the opposition. A feminist, working, for example, within the consequentialist framework, may believe that Kantian and virtue theoretic frameworks are fundamentally flawed; she may even argue that that is so. But she doesn't need to establish that either of these frameworks is disconsonant with feminism. She needn't show that there cannot be a "feminist Kantian" or a "feminist virtue theorist."

It may appear that what I am really calling for is the ending of the critical project. I don't think so. It is possible, I believe, to point to the operation of male bias in the development of a certain line of thought without discarding as "masculinist" everything in the lineage. This point is tacitly acknowledged by feminist philosophers in the cases of certain figures. Many feminists feel that there is value to be found in Freud's account of subconscious psycho-dynamics, despite the sexism displayed in his refusals to credit female patients' reports of sexual abuse, and the likely role these played in the development of his theory of repression.[3] Bias, after all, can operate in a variety of ways, and the response we make to the discovery of bias ought to be keyed to the kind of harm the bias has produced. When the bias consists in there being too narrow a set of perspectives informing the kinds of questions asked or the phenomena surveyed, the obvious response is to pose the unasked questions and expose the unnoticed phenomena (all the while working to democratize the relevant fields). Or, consider the statements of overt sexism found in the work of several Enlightenment thinkers. I believe (although many feminist theorists certainly disagree with me about this) that the best response here is to use the thinkers' own principles against them: demonstrate that banal empirical fact combines with their own criteria of moral personhood to entail the inclusion of women in the moral community. In a society with avowed commitment to Enlightenment principles, this can be (and has been) a highly effective way to extend civil rights to women and to men in other marginalized groups.

What I am cautioning against, really, is the *selective* pursuit of the critical project. Since virtually everything in the philosophical canon was produced by men, one needs a justification for training the lens of gender on some views but not on others. This is especially true if the outcome of the intellectual genealogy is supposed to tell us something about the aptness of a view for feminist appropriation. It would be patently circular to hold one's own view immune from gender-critical scrutiny on the grounds that it is antecedently known to be feminist. Yet this is what is likely to happen if one frames one's own philosophizing in terms of the replacement strategy. In search of a feminist theory of X, what better place to start looking than the theory of X one favors to begin with? Another form of objectionable selectivity occurs when a feminist philosopher presumes that opposition to her view must stem from some masculinist bias hidden in her opponents' theories, which she then sets out to expose. Once again, it must be remembered that there is no philosophical tradition that has *not* been dominated by men, and, likely, no philosophical disagreement without men on every side. Why think that gender is more operative in one's opponents' thinking than it is among the men with whom one happens to agree?

Let me repeat: virtually everything in the philosophical canon was produced by men. If, as many of us believe, *all* views are shaped equally by the social positions of their authors, it is surpassingly likely that any philosophical position *that is subjected to scrutiny* will come out of the examination looking male.[4] This process of selective scrutiny is akin to the process I have argued is operative in the construction of dissident perspectives as "biased" in American political discourse and in the academy: since *all* views are shaped by the perspectives of their authors, *any* charge of "partiality" against *any* view will be sustained. But if the charge of bias is only leveled selectively, the bias present in the uncriticized views is never exposed. The illusion that these views are "impartial" is thereby sustained. The danger becomes acute if we take it as our goal merely to *explain why* our opponents hold the views they hold instead of *arguing* against the views. There are general reasons against attempting such explanations.

In the first place, we ought all to be modest about what we know about other people's reasons and motivations. Explanations why someone believes something are not a priori, and few of us really know enough about the psychologies and circumstances of the people we argue with to be confident that we understand where their beliefs come from. Even if a certain cognitive dynamic has been shown to be at work in some cases, it hardly follows that it's at work in *every* one. Secondly, explanations of this sort, even if correct, rarely have probative value. As Roger White points out, there are lots of utterly contingent factors that play crucial roles in the development of anyone's beliefs about anything. For any of these factors, it may be true to say, "You only believe that because..." Schooling provides a good example. It may be only because one went to school that one values or knows certain things. The content of one's opinions, too, can be shaped by contingent factors. It is not merely self-selection that accounts for the alignments between the philosophical orientations of students and those of their teachers.[5] Yet it would be bizarre to criticize someone's views on the grounds that he or she "only believes that because" he or she has been educated.

What would we lose if we were to abandon the replacement project? Well, if replacement theorists are right, then not all philosophical frameworks are suitable for use in the practical project. Feminists who tried to draw insight from one of these blighted frameworks would be, at best, wasting their efforts, and at worst, facilitating patriarchal oppression. These risks may seem too great to take. But there is no safe strategy here: the constraint goes in both directions. If a practicalist manages to throw light on a theoretical issue of pressing importance to feminists, then whatever philosophical framework it was that structured her work would be politically vindicated by the practical achievements flowing from it. It would then be the critics condemning the framework who would be impeding feminist progress, by deflecting feminist philosophical attention away from a promising line of research.

In what follows, I propose to defend my methodological recommendations by means of a case study. I'll look at Jennifer Hornsby's essay, "Feminism in Philosophy of Language: Communicative Speech Acts" (2000). Hornsby there tries to promote, *as feminist*, a particular version of speech-act theory. "An idea of communicative speech acts," she says, "belongs in the philosophy of language." Hornsby complains, however, that this notion has been missing from "malestream accounts of linguistic meaning." She attributes this lacuna to masculinist thinking: the "absence of such an idea from malestream accounts of linguistic meaning might be explained by ways of thinking which are arguably characteristically masculine" (p. 87). Hornsby hints that this fact alone gives feminists a reason to reject, or at least to ignore, the picture of linguistic meaning found in conventional philosophy of language. But more urgently, Hornsby argues that her view offers *political* advantages over the conventional view. The latter view, because it is shaped by the allegedly masculine habit of thought Hornsby dubs "decompositional- ism," inevitably separates meaning from communication. In doing so, she argues, the view deprives us of theoretical tools useful for crafting an appropriate response to the problem of hate speech.

I want to distinguish two lines of argument in Hornsby's essay. One line aims at discrediting opponents of Hornsby's view by revealing both their criticisms and their positive views to be rooted in masculine "ways of thinking." Call this line of argument *etiological*. The second line—what I'll call the *practical* line—tries to show that adoption of Hornsby's posi- tion facilitates important political work. Neither line, I'll argue, is suc- cessful. But what I hope to make clear in the course of my discussion is that these two ways of arguing are importantly different. The arguments in the etiological line exemplify the kind of invidious "ground clearing" that I've claimed the replacement strategy always brings in tow. In my discussion of these arguments, I'll dispute some of the specific claims Hornsby makes about what various views entail and what they don't, but my overall aim will be to expose the sterility of this strategy. No light is shined, I'll argue—neither on any philosophical issue nor on any matter of importance to feminists.

Hornsby's second line of argument is different. Here Hornsby is trying to draw out the consequences of a particular set of philosophical commitments for issues of importance to feminists. I believe—and I'll argue—that here, too, Hornsby gets the philosophy wrong. But the differences between her and me on this issue are of exactly the sort that we should expect to arise between feminist philosophers with different philosophical backgrounds and different philosophical sympathies. Hornsby's work here fits nicely within the practicalist paradigm, confirming my general claim that feminist philosophy can flourish without the replacement strategy. I hope, too, that my discussion, critical as it will be, will yet serve to demonstrate the value, for both feminism and philosophy, of the practicalist approach. Whether you side in the end with me or with Hornsby—indeed, even if you think we're both wrong—I hope you will agree that my engagement with her work has been productive.

THE ETIOLOGICAL LINE

I claimed earlier that in order for a feminist philosopher to position her view as a "replacement" view, it is necessary for her to show, minimally, that it is different from masculinist views. But what, exactly, is a masculinist view? How does a philosophical view get gendered? Hornsby makes two different suggestions about this. One is that a view is gendered masculine if it has been mostly articulated and defended by men. The other is that philosophy is gendered male when it reflects or embodies a distinctively male mode of thought, a "masculine way of thinking." I'll focus, for now, on the first suggestion.

Hornsby makes this suggestion in a footnote, following her first use of the term "malestream." She writes:

> "Malestream"...remains a useful term for the preponderantly male mainstream. It might seem tendentious to identify a body of philosophical work by allusion to its maleness. But the claim need only be that the contributors are *de facto*, nearly all men.[6]

In this sense, it would be very difficult to find any body of philosophical work that is *not* "malestream." That is why I was initially perplexed by

Hornsby's contention that the notion of a "communicative speech act" has been missing from "malestream" philosophy of language. No one could plausibly claim mainstream philosophy has ignored speech acts. The study of verbal performatives has been a *central* part of analytic philosophy of language ever since the notion of a "speech act" was introduced by J. L. Austin in the middle of the last century. The posthumous publication, in 1962, of *How To Do Things With Words*, Austin's acclaimed 1955 William James lectures, was followed by a monograph on speech acts written by his student, John Searle, in 1969.[7] Between then and now, there have appeared at least seven other monographs and hundreds, if not thousands, of articles and chapters devoted to the theory of verbal performatives. A section on speech acts is de rigeur for any teaching anthology or introductory textbook on the philosophy of language. The roster of major analytic philosophers who have devoted sustained attention to this topic is lengthy and impressive.[8] Mitchell Green, himself the author of many essays on speech-acts, points out that the impact of Austin's idea has not been limited to philosophy. It has also been influential, Green says,

> in linguistics, psychology, legal theory, artificial intelligence, literary theory and many other scholarly disciplines. Recognition of the importance of speech acts has illuminated the ability of language to do other things than describe reality. In the process the boundaries among the philosophy of language, the philosophy of action, the philosophy of mind and even ethics have become less sharp. In addition, an appreciation of speech acts has helped lay bare an implicit normative structure within linguistic practice, including even that part of this practice concerned with describing reality.[9]

Clearly, the notion of a speech act has not been "absent" from *mainstream* philosophy of language. But "mainstream" philosophy of language just *is* "malestream" philosophy of language, if we adhere to the non-tendentious sense Hornsby claims to be using. Speech-act theory itself, according to this definition, could hardly be more "malestream." The progenitor of speech-act theory, Ludwig Wittgenstein, as well as the philosopher who explicitly introduced the term and who developed the standard speech-act taxonomy, J. L. Austin, were both men. So have been the philosophers most strongly associated with speech-act theory since that time. (An interesting exception is feminist philosopher Marilyn Frye, whose early work was on speech-act theory.[10])

What, then, does Hornsby mean? What is the lacuna she is complaining about? Going back to her text with this question in mind, I noticed that she does not exactly say that malestream *philosophy of language* has ignored *speech-acts*. Her precise claim, rather, is that the notion of a *communicative* speech-act has been absent from malestream *accounts of linguistic meaning*. These careful qualifications, I surmised, were meant to signal the specific features that Hornsby takes to differentiate *her* view of language from those of "malestream" philosophers of language, including many proponents of speech-act theory. Given that supposition, I arrived at the following interpretation.

Hornsby mainly wants to challenge the idea that linguistic meaning can be separated, even analytically, from linguistic communication. According to her, the presumption that it is possible to *characterize* meaning without reference to acts of communication leads to a view of meaning as being *actually* independent of communication. If one conceives of meaning as that which can be fully specified by an abstract semantic theory, then, she thinks, it follows that *knowledge* of such a theory would constitute knowledge of meaning. Meaning itself then would become radically individualistic—it would turn into the content of "an isolable psychological state belonging to each of the individual speakers of the language." This move would have two problematic consequences. First of all, it would make the connection between meaning and *saying* merely contingent, leaving open the possibility that a person could possess knowledge of a language, "but lack what it takes to communicate." It would, secondly, disconnect *saying* from *communication*, by making it possible for someone to say something without anyone else's hearing or understanding what was said (p. 96). Hornsby finds these consequences not merely incorrect, but utterly absurd. She believes that there is, as a matter of necessity, "[n]o linguistic meaning without saying, and no saying without communication" (p. 96). The only way for a theorist to properly certify these connections, Hornsby contends, is to resist the analytical separation in the first place: we must embrace as fundamental and primitive the notion of a *communicative speech-act*, the act of *saying something to someone*.

I will agree that Hornsby's hostility toward compositional semantic theories marks a significant difference between her and many other philosophers of language. Most philosophers, including most speech-act theorists, have accepted the *analytical* separation of meaning (or "content") from what Frege called "force," and, they have considered the theory of verbal performatives to be part of an account of force rather than of meaning. So let me grant Hornsby that with her notion of a "communicative" speech-act, she has indeed put herself at odds with "malestream accounts of linguistic meaning." But notice the following curiosity. One man within the malestream tradition with whom Hornsby seems eager to maintain an association is J. L. Austin. Yet Austin never seemed to have questioned the separability of the theory of content from the theory of force, and did seem to have regarded the latter as a supplement to, rather than a replacement for, the theory of linguistic meaning. Why doesn't Hornsby indict Austin along with his malestream colleagues?

I think it's clear why Hornsby maintains her allegiance to Austin: she thinks Austin had a beautiful idea, an idea she wants to preserve and develop. Furthermore, she believes that the malestream has gotten Austin wrong, and she wants to set things right. Looking at Austin through a feminist's eyes, she sees something in Austin that others have missed. And so she defends her view *as an interpretation* of Austin, rather than as a "repair" of his malestream view. And she does—if I may say so—a very good job. I had always taken the distinction between "illocution" and "perlocution" to be simply that the latter does, while the former does not, refer essentially to effects on the hearer. Hornsby shows, however, that the text makes it far from clear that this is what Austin had in mind, citing passages that support her view that Austin considered one kind of hearer effect—understanding, or "uptake"—to be necessary even for the performance of an illocutionary act.[11] I'll read and teach Austin differently from now on.

However, let's consider what Hornsby has accomplished here. She has *redeemed* a canonical philosopher—a member of the malestream. But in that case, what is the point of calling a philosopher or a philosophical view "malestream?" If one of them can be redeemed, why not others? Here we must turn to the second meaning of "malestream" that Hornsby deploys, to indicate a different and more invidious way in which philosophical work can be gendered male. This alternative meaning comes out as Hornsby is trying to explain why her conception of "illocution" (and, presumably, her interpretation of Austin) has not been widely adopted. She admits that she cannot respond to "every objection that might be made" to her view, but she does think that "many of [the objections] spring from a common fount" (p. 92). This "common fount" is "[d]ecompositionalist thinking," a mode of thought that "pervades analytic philosophy whenever necessary and sufficient conditions are sought" (p. 93).

Decompositionalist thinking, according to Hornsby, is a habit of mind that strives always to subject phenomena to "conceptual arithmetic"—to find within a phenomenon some set of separable components. A philosopher trapped in this frame of thought will want to treat *saying something to someone* as containing a basic speaker-related ingredient from which any reference to communication, or to hearers, can be separated off.

Decompositionalism, this compulsion to analyze and divide, "might be regarded as a *masculine way of thinking*. For we are sometimes told that men—men in our culture, that is—'prefer what is separable,' and that women 'assign importance to relational characteristics'" (p. 93, emphasis mine). So Hornsby here claims that there is a new way in which a philosophical idea can be gendered: it can spring from a *distinctively* male way of thinking. Further support for her diagnosis is found, Hornsby says, in the fact that "decompositionalist thinking underwrites a kind of individualism that has independently been castigated as male" (p. 94).

I appreciate Hornsby's caution here in formulating her charges. She says only that decompositionalism "might be" regarded as distinctively masculine, not that it is, and that individualism has been "castigated" as male, not that it has been demonstrated to be so. That just barely makes room within the company of respectable feminists for someone like me, who holds individualist views.[12] But Hornsby soon ceases to be even-handed. In the next line, she commits herself: individualism is a terrible thing. The decompositionalist thinking behind it leads (in epistemology) to solipsism, and (in the philosophy of language) to reactionary politics. Lest the reader think that I am caricaturing Hornsby's position, here is the relevant passage, quoted in its entirety:

> When "seeing *x*" is treated as decomposable, subjects of experience are cut off from visible objects. But when communicative linguistic concepts are treated as decomposable, human beings are cut off from one another. The treatment of language then exhibits the kind of individualism which has been taken to be characteristic of liberal political theory—in which accounts of social arrangements are based in properties of individuals atomistically conceived. Such theory, which lacks a conception of politics which gender can easily mix with, does not suit feminists. (p. 94)

This, surely, is hyperbole. Hornsby appears to be suggesting that one cannot hold the philosophical view that communication is relational without turning into Ayn Rand. Does she intend to give offense? Permit me a little speculation of my own. I see in Hornsby's discussion a philosophical method that comes directly out of a particular tributary to what is by any definition malestream philosophy, one with the later Wittgenstein at its source. This is the strategy of refutation by diagnosis. In its original deployment, this method was underwritten by the idea that philosophical problems are chimerical, and that they only arise when someone is in the grip of a philosophical obsession. Given this diagnosis of the obsession should make the problem go away. Argument against the idée fixe is not only unnecessary, it is counterproductive.

This is a strategy that, in fact, is often used by male chauvinists outside of philosophical contexts, as well as by anti-feminists within academia, to deflect feminist critique, and we rightly complain about it when they do. You know what I'm talking about—you make an argument, for, say, the proposition that pornography harms women. Your male interlocutor, ignoring everything you've just *said*, announces that the reason you dislike pornography, obviously, is that you are sexually inhibited. Where do you go from there? Do you deny that sexual inhibition lies behind your critique? (If so, is that because you're not sexually inhibited, or because your sexual inhibitions just didn't come into it?) Do you point out that whatever your personal motivations may be, you've made an argument that stands on its own, and deserves an answer? Whatever you do, your interlocutor has successfully forced a change in subject.

I feel exactly the same way when I read Hornsby's discussion of individualism. *I* hold the views that Hornsby thinks are so pernicious; how am I now to defend them? Must I display my own feminist credentials, to show that one can be a feminist and still like Fodor? I'd rather just argue about individualism. I'd rather see Hornsby's responses to the arguments I've presented on behalf of individualism. I'd rather address the philosophical objections to individualism that Hornsby has made. I'd rather not have someone else tell me *why* I believe something.

This brings me to a second aspect of the Wittgensteinian legacy that I think is bad, one that is also evident in Hornsby's writing. Wittgenstein saw himself, and his philosophical method, as standing in opposition to the philosophical mainstream. What happened, though, was that his own view of philosophy caught on. Wittgenstein became *part of* the mainstream. Once this happened, the term "philosopher" as it was used by Wittgenstein and his followers underwent a forced change in denotation. In order for Wittgensteinian claims about the invidiousness of the "philosopher's" ideas to make sense, the term could no longer be used to refer just to any of the group of individuals who held paid positions in an academic philosophy department or who published work in philosophy journals. These criteria would have captured the Wittgensteinians themselves. "Philosopher" had to signify, instead, a kind of *normative* construction—it had to denote only those philosophers with the *wrong* views—the ones who persisted in taking seriously, or in asking anew, the questions Wittgenstein had disparaged. Wittgenstein had alleged that the views of philosophers derived from their inattention to the workings of ordinary language and from their distance from the activities of ordinary people. Assuming the truth of this allegation, and armed with the new, normative notion of the Philosopher, Wittgenstein's followers began to construct *themselves* as representatives of non-philosophers, as "Ordinary Persons." And as the Philosopher became increasingly "othered," the community of Ordinary Persons became simply "We." Unlike a Philosopher, whose observations and intuitions are corrupted by his philosophical theories, We have direct access to the workings of language and the significance of behavior. We can tell immediately what the purpose or function of a thing is. We can simply see, for example, that the purpose of language is communication. Anyone who would deny this must be a Philosopher, working away in his ivory tower, disconnected from the world of real human beings.

Hornsby sounds these themes repeatedly. Here is the trope of the cloistered, out-of-touch Philosopher, deployed in connection with the idea that language *might* have, as *one* of its functions, the expression of thought:

> When it comes to language, alone in one's study one may think of one's language as something one could know in isolation from others. The sentences of one's language can appear to equip one simply to "express beliefs;" directing remarks to another person appears to be a separate matter, requiring "other minds"....By what right does a philosopher in his study assume that a person could possess the skill that a semantic theory records but possess no communicative abilities? (pp. 96–97)

Or again: "Philosophers who think in isolation about language make an assumption about the self-sufficiency of the individual language user." And also: "The philosopher who thinks about language in abstraction from use forgets about its function: he forgets what sentences are *for*" (both quotes, p. 97). I marvel at the presumption of such claims, and at the arrogance that disregards the many *arguments* that have been made by philosophers in defense of theoretical positions that Hornsby has dismissed as mere "assumptions."

One might think here—and I did for a moment—that Hornsby is excoriating the Philosopher for his *a priorism*—that she's urging philosophers to get out of the academy and into the field with the cognitive scientists, to look at actual data about language acquisition and speech processing, instead of relying on personal intuitions. I would have been quite sympathetic to such a criticism, although it is far less apt now than it was a few decades ago. But that is hardly what Hornsby means. Hornsby fails even to consider the idea that there might be broad *empirical* support for some form of individualism, as I—for one—have argued there is.[13] Indeed, Hornsby fails to consider *any* other idea. She seems never to consider the possibility that her views about language might not be shared by sensible people everywhere. Identifying herself in opposition to the "philosopher in his study," she takes the next step and imagines she is speaking in the *vox populi*. "Here one takes Wittgenstein's side," says Hornsby in a footnote.[14] If "one" doesn't, I suppose that "one" must then be a Philosopher.

Here is some psychological speculation that strikes me as plausible: confidence in the universality—among normal people—of one's conceptions of things begets confidence in the correctness of one's own judgments. Believing oneself to be a good exemplar of humanity in general, one either fails to notice that some people have different conceptions, or else stigmatizes the dissenters as corrupt or defective (as, being, for example, Philosophers alone in their studies). This is pretty much the process that "has independently been castigated as male," by Iris Young and other postmodernist feminists. Young, following Adorno (male), called this the "logic of identity." She saw it at work in the construction of the Enlightenment subject as simultaneously "universal" and normatively male.[15] I am suggesting that Hornsby has effected a similar sleight of hand: she has produced a normative construction ostensibly representative of the ordinary person (all the while ignoring her own highly partial and thoroughly philosophical situation) and then has dismissed all apparent counterexamples as products of philosophical corruption. She does something similar, although opposite in valence, in her construction of "malestream" philosophizing. The term is initially introduced as a non-tendentious abbreviation for "produced by men," but then is deployed to stigmatize *selected* malestream views as displaying a "masculine way of thinking." How can a distinctively male way of thinking be at work in some, but not all, "malestream" thought? (Cf.: how can reason be a distinctively human capacity if it is found in some, but not all, human beings?) If decompositionalism is not always at work when men philosophize, what makes it a particularly *masculine* way of thinking?

There is one final irony. The idea of "decompositionalism," along with the speculation that it drives misguided philosophizing, is *itself* a "malestream" idea. One can see the roots of this line of critique in the work of Austin,[16] as well as in that of Austin's near-contemporary, J. M. Hinton.[17] But it is perfectly explicit in Jonathan Dancy's article, "Arguments from Illusion."[18] Dancy first identifies, through consideration of the original "argument from illusion" in epistemology, the following argumentative pattern: a certain phenomenon, X, is observed to resemble some other phenomenon, Y, in some salient way. From this it is inferred that there is a common element between X and Y—call it Z. X is then taken to decompose into Z plus "something-else." Thus, because illusions can be introspectively indistinguishable from veridical perceptions, it is concluded by many that veridical perception must be composed of an internal state of "mere seeming"—the element common to perceptions and illusions—plus something-else. Similar forms of argument, Dancy says, lie behind many other philosophical analyses or oppositions: acting/trying, knowledge/justified belief, and others. Dancy thinks that the failure of philosophers to successfully identify the "something-else," the addition of which would turn seeming-to-see into *really* seeing (and so forth), is good reason to give up on the idea that phenomena like perceiving and knowing have internal "cores."

Dancy's article was one important piece in the emergence of a philosophical trend now known as "disjunctivism"—a version of direct realism in epistemology that denies the existence of any inner mental "core" state present in veridical and non-veridical sense experiences alike, so as to reject the existence (or fundamentality) of any overarching kind subsuming experiences of both kinds. Almost everyone who has or does defend disjunctivism is male: in addition to Austin and Hinton, there is John McDowell, Paul Snowden, Timothy Williamson, John Campbell, William Child, Bill Brewer, and Michael Martin (apologies to those I've forgotten).[19] One might possibly count Elizabeth Anscombe among the ancestors of contemporary disjunctivism, but by and large it's a malestream movement.

If decompositionalism is a distinctively masculine mode of thought, how is it that it was *men* who identified and criticized it? Have all of these men managed to evade a form of thinking that is distinctive of their gender? My guess is that Austin, Dancy, and the others are *not* regarded by Hornsby as men whose thinking counts as *distinctively* male.

Hornsby embraces the philosophical bloodline that goes back through Austin to Wittgenstein, and she identifies with the intellectual community in which disjunctivism thrives. How then could the way of thinking displayed within that group be masculinist? Is the thought this: that since Hornsby finds it congenial, it cannot be. Such reasoning would be tightly circular.

But enough. I really have no interest in pressing countercharges against Hornsby. My point is only that it would be easy enough to do so if I wanted to. The etiological exercise in which Hornsby is engaged is too poorly constrained for any results to be meaningful. The level of generality at which allegedly masculine "ways of thinking" are characterized, the richness of the texts in play, and the lability of analogical interpretation all together guarantee that almost any philosophical work can be given a masculinist reading. And this is my point: once one indulges the suspicion that one's opponents are corrupted by masculine bias, masculine bias will be there for the discovering.

Perhaps the most lamentable result of Hornsby's focus on etiology is that she never confronts any possible non-etiological explanations—arguments, in other words—for putting a semantic theory in one's overall account of human language. But philosophers who advocate systematic treatments of linguistic meaning have in fact offered explicit defenses of their positions; Hornsby is unfair in ignoring them. But setting aside this (perhaps mild) injustice, Hornsby's failure to survey these arguments leaves the reader with the quite mistaken impression that all the philosophers in the "malestream" who appeal to semantic theories have the same philosophical commitments, and the same philosophical outlook on language and communication. That is decidedly not the case. Even some philosophers who share both Hornsby's social view of language, and her antipathy toward psychologism, have argued for the utility of semantic theories.

Let's address the question head-on: what *is* this creature of darkness, the "semantic theory?" Within analytic philosophy of language, the term refers to any systematic characterization of the relation between linguistic expressions and extra-linguistic reality. There is a wide consensus that such theories ought to be *compositional* in form, and that they ought to associate *truth-conditions* with each declarative sentence in the language. But while there's general agreement about what a semantic theory should look like, there's no consensus about what, exactly, a semantic theory is a theory *of*. Hornsby, however, seems to be saying that anyone who sees any need for such a theory as part of her overall account of language will be bound to interpret the theory as describing psychological reality. I am unclear just what kind of necessity Hornsby thinks is at work here—psychological?—but it surely isn't logical. The demonstration is that many philosophers who argue for truth-conditional, compositional semantic theories specifically abjure this interpretation.

Donald Davidson, for example, held that an overall theory of natural language needed a compositional, truth-conditional theory of meaning at its heart, and he argued that a Tarskian truth-theory[20] could serve this purpose. Contrary to Hornsby's suggestion, though, Davidson's *ontology* of meaning was neither decompositionalist, nor individualist. Quite the contrary. He was actually an instrumentalist about meaning-theories; they were, on his view, tools for the theorist, rather than descriptions of an objective phenomenon. Davidson believed, with Quine, that a meaning-theory (or "translation manual," as Quine[21] thought of it) could only be justified *holistically*. That is to say, there could be no sentence-by-sentence or term-by-term verification of the lines of a meaning-theory; the only way a meaning-theory could be justified empirically was through the predictions about speaker behavior entailed by the theory as a whole. Because there will always be many different meaning-theories that correspond equally well in this way with the total body of empirical data, there could be no basis for viewing the particular articulations of linguistic expression and semantic content imposed by any one semantic theory as answering to some kind of objective linguistic structure. Reference, which is for many semantic realists the ontological foundation of all semantic value, was for Davidson, a necessarily *social* relation. It did not exist as a static relation between word and thing; rather, it existed only insofar as two or more linguistic beings were engaged cooperatively in "triangulating" on an object.[22]

Davidson, then, was an instrumentalist about meaning-theories. He did not think that they described any really existing linguistic structure, but were, rather, a kind of bookkeeping tool convenient for the theorist. Individualism, of the sort Hornsby deplores, clearly does not follow from this view. But individualism about meaning doesn't follow even on a realistic interpretation of semantic theories. It is a perfectly consistent position to hold that semantic theories aim to describe objective linguistic reality, while denying that that objective reality is located within the heads of individual speakers. Michael Devitt, for example, believes that languages exist objectively, that they have objective semantic structure, and that semantic theories aim to describe that structure. He is adamant, however, in his insistence that a *language* is not the same thing as an individual speaker's *linguistic competence*, that a theory of one is not a theory of the other. Indeed, he has written an entire book arguing *against* the Chomskian view that linguistic theories (including semantic theories) should be construed as descriptions of individually internalized grammars—*I-languages*, as Chomsky calls them.[23] On Devitt's view, facts about human natural languages supervene on facts about the use of language within a community. Facts about meaning, in particular, depend on semantic conventions, which are, of course, a particular kind of social practice.

Finally, even if one thinks that semantic theories *do* aim to characterize some feature of individual speakers, one is not committed to individualism about meaning. Michael Dummett, for example, believes that a meaning-theory is a theory of speaker knowledge, a theory of what someone knows in knowing a language. But although Dummett allows this degree of individualism about *knowledge* of meaning, his *ontology* of meaning is social, for all that. Dummett, like Devitt, does not identify the *object* of semantic knowledge with the knowledge itself. Dummett's position also illustrates that one can think that a semantic theory describes some feature of an individual speaker without reifying that feature as an "isolable" psychological structure. Dummett would vigorously deny that his position commits him to any *psychological* thesis at all. In particular, he would deny that it commits him to the view that the semantic theory is *mentally represented* by the speaker.[24] If Hornsby were to argue that Dummett's position—epistemic realism without psychological realism—is unstable, I would have to agree.[25] But the view is out there, nonetheless.

To review: it's important to distinguish the question whether an overall account of human language use must contain within it a semantic theory from the question how that semantic theory is to be interpreted. Hornsby seems to assume that anyone who sees a role for semantic theories at all must be committed to one particular interpretation of them, namely, the interpretation on which semantic theories aim to describe the contents of "isolable" psychological states of individual speakers. This is simply not the case: there is no necessary connection between semantic theories and ontological individualism.

Why do all these philosophers, so various in their interpretations of semantic theories, believe that semantic theories are necessary? Recall the area of consensus I identified above. All these theorists agree that semantic *theories* must be compositional, even if the reality these theories describe is not composite (as might be the case if semantic theories are systematizations of dispositions to behave), and even if they describe no reality at all. The reason that realists and non-realists agree on this constraint is they must all confront the problem of how to specify truth-conditions for an infinite number of possible utterances, using only a finite set of resources. For the anti-realist, this problem is a technical problem for the theorist—how can she contrive a usable tool for inter-preting the speech of another person, given that there are an infinite number of things that that person might say? A compositional theory—a theory that presents the language *as if* the meanings of complex expres-sions were functions of the meanings of their parts—fills the bill.

Realists will claim to have direct evidence (of whatever sort they deem relevant) that linguistic reality actually *is* compositional. Linguistic intuition concurs with observation: human languages display logical form and contain mechanisms for recursion and recombination. The epistemic realist will argue that unless meaning is compositional, minds could not comprehend the unlimited number of distinct meanings that it is possible to express in a human language. The psychological realist will cite empirical reasons for treating language compositionally; she'll say that the best theories of language acquisition, comprehension, and production posit internalized compositional structures.

What about the overall separation of meaning from communica-tion? Once again, the *analytical* separation of the one from the other can be a feature of a *theory* of human language without committing the the-orist to the idea that linguistic meaning could *subsist* without there being communicative interactions among speakers of the language. And once again, there is ample justification for the theorist's making such a separa-tion. Without a compositional semantics in the background, an account of linguistic communication would have to treat every single utterance as a sui generis performance. There would be, in consequence, a host of reg-ularities the theory could not take note of: (1) regularities among differ-ent speech-acts involving (what a truth-conditional semanticist would call) the same contents (I can *assert* that the door is open, *ask if* the door is open, and *command that* the door be made open); (2) regularities among similar speech-acts with different contents (I can assert that the door is open and I can assert that the door is closed) and (3) regularities involving (what a compositionalist would call) recurring semantic ele-ments within the contents (all of the speech-act types listed above were about doors). Again, one needn't be a semantic realist, much less a psychological realist, to regret such results as these. They would be fatal, for example, to the project of Davidson's interpreter. The absence of a free-standing compositional semantic component to the translation manual would entail a separate entry for every piece of linguistic behavior, depriving the theorist of any surveyable means of translating or predicting speakers' utterances. For the psychological realist, the question would be pressing how hearers actually manage to understand speakers—if speech-acts are sui generis, then how could anyone ever understand a novel utterance, that is, a speech-act not type-identical to any other the hearer has already encountered? (Notice that I don't say that it's *impossible* for speech-acts to lack separable contents; I would just like to know how Hornsby proposes to address these issues if they do.)

An interesting philosopher to consider at this point is Paul Grice, who Hornsby takes as her chief example of malestream thinking run amok. Grice, I would argue, was a semantic realist. He believed that languages had objective semantic structures, and that those structures could be adequately described by semantic theories. In this, he set himself against philosophers like Wittgenstein and Strawson, who held that ordinary language was too richly nuanced and too context-sensitive for its semantic properties to be captured by a free-standing formal theory. At the same time, though, Grice would have agreed with those particular philosophers that meaning *itself* was an artifact of human *communicative* behavior. Whereas Grice thought that, on any particular occasion, the meaning of a speaker's uttered sentence could be separated from its use, he hardly thought that meaning was an individualistic matter. For Grice, it was *coordinated communicative* intentions that were, ultimately, *constitutive* of linguistic meaning.

Grice drew a distinction between what he called "natural meaning" and "non-natural meaning."[26] The former is the kind of "meaning" or signification carried by natural signs, the way smoke "means" fire. The latter is a distinctive kind of meaning that is carried by symbols and other artifacts, such as words or traffic signs. In the first case, the "meaning" is simply the legible manifestation of a natural regularity; a lawful co-occurrence that allows us to take one phenomenon as indicating the presence or immanent occurrence of another. In the case of "non-natural" meaning, however, the signification relation has to be established through *convention*. Conventions, crucially, are *not* simply regularities to be noticed and exploited. They necessarily involve *intentions*. In order for a convention to be set up or to persist, there has to be a network of intentions and recognition of intentions coordinating everyone involved. Many conventions arise to solve coordination problems, but this they do only if everyone following the convention is confident that everyone else knows the convention and follows it *because* it is the convention.

Intentions can be made explicit, as happens when conventional practices are encoded in law, as perhaps happened with traffic rules, or with the codification of the rules of various sports. But they needn't be explicit. People in some parts of England[27] wait for buses by "queuing"— lining up single-file, but this is not prescribed by civil law, as is keeping on the zebra when you cross the street. The intentional structure underlying an informal convention may be wholly implicit, but it is there nonetheless. This implicit knowledge is evidenced in the way a whole range of behavioral dispositions are structured. You cannot, as I said, get arrested for failing to queue in the United Kingdom, but you can (and will) experience some serious social sanctioning if you try to enter the bus ahead of someone else who's been waiting longer. You will, that is, if people construe your failure to follow the convention as a failure of *courtesy* or *concern*. Everything changes if people come to understand that you *didn't know what the convention was* and that you *didn't intend any disrespect*. Someone might figure out (as happened, luckily in my case, when I inadvertently jumped the queue) that you are from the United States. Once it's realized that you've grown up in the wilderness, the sanctions may well be withdrawn (and some explicit instruction may be provided.)

Grice's account of the institution of linguistic meaning draws from this background understanding of conventions in general. On Grice's account, linguistic meaning is a particular kind of convention, structured essentially by *communicative* and *reciprocal* intentions. For "snow" to denote snow, it must be that speakers intend to refer to snow in uttering the word "snow," but also that their hearers recognize that they have this intention in uttering the word. These two intentions, however, represent just a small part of the intentional structure that Grice posited, which Hornsby disparages for its complexity: "I think this ought to seem ludicrous. Real people regularly get things across with their utterances; but real people do not regularly possess, still less act upon, intentions of this sort" (p. 95). (Notice, by the way, Hornsby's intemperate rhetoric. It is not enough for her to say that she disagrees; she enjoins the reader to agree that it is "ludicrous." *I* do not find it ludicrous. What is wrong with me?) Hornsby's complaint, however, depends on a very blunt and uncharitable understanding of what's involved in the attribution of intentionality. It *would* seem implausible to me if someone were to suggest that, in every act of saying something, one consciously and explicitly—or even unconsciously and explicitly—represented to oneself thoughts even as complex as these. But Grice didn't need to commit himself (and didn't, as far as I know) to the kind of crude intellectualism that would demand such explicit rehearsal or representation of these contents in order for an ascription of intention to be true. Someone who is a pure dispositionalist about intention—someone who denies that intentions ever involve explicit representation—could easily take Gricean intentions on board. Possession of a Gricean communicative intention would, according to such a theorist, be constituted simply by a speaker's possessing a certain subtly sensitive behavioral disposition.[28]

I believe it is clear that convention is going to have to play *some* role in any account of human language. We human beings differ from the bees and (some) birds in that the semantics of our verbal communication systems are not built into us. But whether or not *that's* true, it's clear that conventions play an important role in human social life. Any adequate account of convention in general is going to have to explain the difference between conventions and de facto behavioral regularities— this task, I contend, is going to have to appeal to intentions, and these intentions are not going to be simple to characterize. The difference between people's simply having a natural tendency to line up one-by-one (as perhaps, sheep do) and their following a convention of queuing is going to have to appeal to *counterfactual* differences—what would happen, what people would do, under this circumstance or that. My point is that all Grice needs is whatever *anyone* needs to ground these counterfactual differences. If the grounding can only be done with intentions of Gricean complexity, then we'll have to make sense of them apart from any work Grice wants them to do. If, on the other hand, the grounding can be done without appeal to intentions, then a Gricean can simply co-opt whatever the general story turns out to be.[29]

There is another point at which Hornsby presumes an overly intellectualized reading of Grice's appeal to intentions. She says that it's obvious that Gricean intuitions could not be required for being able to say things to others. "Developmental psychologists find it doubtful whether three year old children possess the concept of belief; but they do not find it doubtful that three year olds can, for instance, tell them things" (p. 95). Setting aside quibbles about Hornsby's reading of the empirical literature,[30] the problem here is that Hornsby badly overestimates the amount of theoretical sophistication a person needs to have in order to possess a Gricean intention. It is in fact irrelevant to the adequacy of Grice's account whether young children do or do not have a concept of belief, or whether they possess the meta-belief that other people possess beliefs. Children of an age to fail the false-belief test nonetheless do evince intentions with the kind of contents Grice's account requires. A toddler who comes to me holding out a shoe very well might do so with the intention of getting me to put it back on her, and to get me to do it *by* getting me to see that she wants me to do that, and to do that *by* showing me the dislocated shoe. But in order to have such an intention, she needn't deploy all of the concepts I just did in characterizing her intention. She might simply think, "I'm going to show Mommy my shoe so she'll put it back on." The concept of belief needn't enter into it. She doesn't have to have a theory of the *mechanism* that underlies showing— "showing" might be a primitive concept for her and perfectly adequate for her purposes.[31]

There is, finally, an important feature of Grice's view that Hornsby's criticism seems to ignore: Grice does *not* hold that meaning is newly constituted or reconstituted with every act of linguistic communication. Communicative intentions *establish* conventional connections between sentence-types and meanings. But once a semantic convention has arisen, the facts about the content of that convention can float free of the particular communicative intentions of any individual speaker on any individual occasion. Indeed, there can be, in various ways, a sizeable gap between the conventional meanings possessed by a group of words, and the message one aims to communicate by means of those words. This gap is not only philosophically defensible, but also, as I'll show, politically invaluable. I'll explain the philosophical considerations here, and return to the political applications in the next section.

Grice coined the term *implicature* to denote a message that a speaker intends to convey but which is not part of, nor is strictly entailed by, the meaning of the sentence the speaker chooses to utter in order to convey that message.[32] Consider a team of burglars robbing a bank. The lookout, noticing a marked car pulling up outside, whispers urgently to his partners, "the police are coming." By uttering *this* sentence in *this* context, the lookout surely intends to communicate to the rest of the gang that they need to get out, fast. But on Grice's analysis, this is not what the lookout *said*. If the gang gets the message that they have to leave right away, it's because they were able to infer from what the lookout *literally* said, together with certain assumptions about the norms of conversation, that that's what the lookout was trying to convey to them. One might want to say that the lookout performed the illocutionary act of *warning* his comrades, but if so, he did it by *telling them that the police were coming.*

What communicative speech act does Hornsby think has been performed in such a case? Was it the act of warning the gang to get out quick? Or was it the act of informing them that the police were coming? Both at once? The difficulty of treating the communicative act as simple is well-illustrated in this case. Somehow or other, the lookout managed to warn the gang to get out. What Hornsby is going to have to explain, somehow or other, is how a speaker could convey that message *by* uttering a sentence of the linguistic type "the police are coming." An utterance of a sentence of the same linguistic type could easily serve to convey a quite different message in a different context. One might, for example, use that sentence to reassure the victim of a crime that help is on the way. If we cannot separate the literal meaning of a sentence from the message it can be used to convey on a given occasion, or if we insist on making the message conveyed determinative of the meaning, there is nothing that can be said about the apparent commonality between the two speech-acts, other than that words of the same type were uttered on both occasions. And this is assuming that Hornsby will allow us to abstract out at least the phatic properties of each speech-act; if she does not, then the two speech-acts would have to have counted as being as different from each as each is from an utterance of "Merry Christmas."

Grice, on the other hand, has a plausible and elegant explanation of the same set of phenomena. On his account, the literal meaning of the sentence-type "the police are coming" is the same on both occasions of its utterance, as is the respective hearers' understanding of that literal meaning. What differs is the presumptions the speaker/hearer pairs have about the significance of the arrival of the police. In the first case, the robbers all fear capture by the police; in the second case, speaker and hearer share confidence that the police will be helpful. (And we can think of yet different cases where yet different attitudes toward the police, with correspondingly different messages, are implicated by the utterance of the same sentence.) But what is crucial to Grice's account of the operation of implicature is that speakers and hearers be *psychologically connected*. It's not enough for implicature to work that speaker and hearer *happen* each to have a particular piece of semantic knowledge, and *happen* to share attitudes. Speaker and hearer must have *mutual* knowledge of each other's states of mind. They have to *understand* each other in order to communicate with each other at all, on Grice's view, but particularly when the message is only implicated.

On Grice's account, it is the speaker's particular knowledge of the literal meaning of uttered sentences, *together with* the speaker's belief that her hearer has and will deploy the same knowledge, that explains a lot about how the communication of subtle messages occurs. For example: someone once introduced me to a new acquaintance of theirs by saying, "This is Alice—she and I met at her church when I was speaking there." This doesn't look like a warning, but I took it as one. I understood by my friend's inclusion of the otherwise gratuitous information that Alice is a churchgoer that she wanted me to realize that I would give offense if I happened to launch into one of my rants against organized religion. She couldn't bring up the matter explicitly—to do so would be to introduce the very topic she wanted us to avoid—so she didn't *say* "Don't ridicule religion around Alice." Instead, she said something that she had reason to believe would induce me to draw the proper conclusion. It is noteworthy that conversational implicatures are extremely difficult for autistic people to "take up." It is not knowledge of the meanings of words in the language that they are missing; it's *social understanding.*[33]

THE PRACTICALIST LINE

I have argued that commitment to the *analytical* separation of meaning from communication does not entail the *ontological* separability of meaning from either its social or its communicative context. In particular, I argued, Grice's theory is not individualistic about meaning in either of these ways. In that case, there is no necessary link between commitment to semantic theories and commitment to any form of semantic individualism. I've also surveyed a variety of arguments for the inclusion of a semantic theory in an overall account of language, to show that there is no need to cite "decompositionalist thinking" to explain commitment to this view. But notice that, once the connection between commitment to semantic theories and commitment to individualism is broken, there is no longer any good basis for worrying about decompositionalism. So what if this habit of thought is involved? And so what if it is a *masculine* mode of thought? As Hornsby herself says:

> One cannot make a case for communicative speech acts merely by showing that they emerge when habits of thought that may strike one as male are rejected. Of course not. If men are indeed acculturated to think in one way and women in another, then that is not yet to say that either style of thinking has a monopoly on the truth in any area. (p. 94)

The badness of decompositionalism was supposed to run through the badness of the individualism it was supposed to either motivate or express. With that connection severed, decompositionalism looks now to be "malestream" only in Hornsby's "non-tendentious" sense.

Recall, however, that there are *two* kinds of abstraction to which Hornsby is opposed: abstraction of linguistic meaning from the communicative function of language (the *what's said* from the *saying something*) and abstraction of communicative intention from communicative effect (the *saying something* from the *saying something to someone*). While Hornsby thinks both are bad, it is really only the *second* abstraction that turns out to play a role in Hornsby's discussion of hate speech. It is mainly the thought that communication involves two *discrete* intentional episodes involving two individuals that (in her view) opens the door for the arguments against the regulation of hate speech that she wants to criticize.

This idea is absolutely central to the work of Paul Grice, which is perhaps why Hornsby takes him, rather than Davidson or Dummett—prominent proponents of semantic theories—as her chief stalking horse. I think that the preceding discussion has shown that the charges of masculinist corruption against semantic theories must be dropped. But Hornsby still has a constructive line to pursue. She has a chance of demonstrating the *political utility* of her preferred view of speech acts if she can show that Grice's separation of speaker intention from hearer effects leaves us unable to theorize adequately a linguistic phenomenon of central concern to feminists, namely, hate speech.

In what follows, I intend to do two things. First, I want to show that, despite Hornsby's claims, there is nothing in a Gricean view of communication that makes it difficult to do the political work Hornsby (rightly) wants done. Second, I want to go further, and show that there are forms of sexist oppression that cannot be adequately characterized *without* the two abstractions that Hornsby descries. Ironically, it will emerge that it is Grice, rather than Hornsby, who offers feminists the tools we need to characterize the role of language in the perpetuation of sexism.

Hornsby begins the constructive part of her essay by saying that she will attempt to illustrate "the difference it makes for feminists to recognize that language is social *au fond*." But she doesn't exactly do this in the way one might have expected, by showing us why the notion of a communicative speech-act is *necessary* for an understanding of hate speech or of the harm it does women. Rather, she proposes to show us how the notion can be used to criticize two "libertarian" arguments against the regulation of hate speech. Hornsby defines a "libertarian"—for her purposes—as any of those "who claim that any regulation of hate speech is bound to be contrary to a defensible principle of free speech." These demonstrations will support her overall view (defended elsewhere, she tells us) that "when speech is treated as illocution, an egalitarian position about *free speech* is lent a distinctive content and argumentative foundation" (all quotes p. 98).

The arguments she discusses, are, I presume, ones that have actually been made by someone in some context, perhaps by a lawyer in court or in a scholarly article; they are unattributed. In any case, the first argument looks like this:

> (1) The "effects of speech on a hearer are brought about through a certain kind of 'mental intermediation.'"
> Therefore,
> (2) "the construction put on the words is the responsibility of [the hearer]"
> Therefore,
> (3) "When a word is construed as conveying visceral hatred, this construction is . . . more the fault of the hearer than the speaker. (p. 98)

I am not sure exactly how the final conclusion—that hate speech should never be regulated—is supposed to be obtained, whether it goes through a premise about the necessary innocence of the speaker, or by showing that there is no such thing as "hate speech" to be regulated. But that doesn't matter, because I want to focus on this fragment that Hornsby gives us.

The first thing that struck me about this argument is how very bad it is as an argument—how *many* things there are that are wrong with it The move from (1) to (2) is patently invalid. There are plenty of ways for (1) to be true while (2) is false. It's perfectly consistent for one to hold that verbal communication involves the hearer's recovering an interpretation of the speaker's words, without holding that the hearer is therefore *responsible* for the words' having that interpretation. It could be (as is likely) the semantic conventions of the language that are responsible for the words' meaning what they do. Now perhaps Hornsby's libertarian—or Hornsby herself—will say that if there is *any* mental act that the hearer must perform in order for the speaker's speech to be effective, then that mental act is a necessary condition of the effect's occurring, and thus can (or should?) be counted as a *cause* of the ultimate effect on the hearer. But if (2) means only that the hearer bears some *causal* responsibility for the effect of the speaker's speech, then the move from (2) to (3) is invalid. Causal responsibility never, on its own, entails any kind of moral responsibility, nor does it relieve other causally involved agents of their moral responsibility.

The point is that with so much going wrong in this argument, there is no justification for pinning the blame on premise (1). And that's a good thing, because, depending on what exactly is meant by "mental interme-diation," it's overwhelmingly likely that (1) is true. Hornsby claims that it's a selling point of her view that "hearer reactions to speech are attuned directly and simultaneously to the significance of words and to speakers' performances" (p. 98). I don't really know what Hornsby has in mind here, but if she means that language processing does not involve infer-ence or computation, then she disagrees with every linguist[34] I've ever encountered. Speech processing involves *at least* auditory (or visual or tactile) processing—the speech signal has to be *perceived* before it can be understood, and perception is not mere transduction. Once the signal has been perceived to be speech, linguistic processing commences, and once again, information processing, rather than mere transduction, is involved. This is all typically unconscious, but it is mental—or "psychological" if "mental" connotes consciousness to you, since the processing involved is certainly unconscious.

But here's the real point: *it's an empirical question* whether or not there is "mental intermediation" involved in communication. This is not something a philosopher can determine by reflecting on the con-cept of "language," or by surveying her beliefs about the nature of communication. (This is why I find Hornsby's scolding philosophers for staying alone in their ivory tower studies so ironic.) By identi-fying her own view—the "direct attunement" view—as a *feminist* view, Hornsby yokes feminism to her own personal bet about the out-come of a scientific investigation. That seems at least imprudent. If I'm right, and Hornsby is wrong, would feminism *really* be in trouble? Here, I think, is an example of something that really "ought to seem ludicrous."

Let's consider the next argument, again unattributed.

> (1) A person who is the object of hate speech can always refute or verbally retaliate against the hateful speaker.
> Therefore,
> (2) "[I]nsofar as speech can cause hurt, the hurt can always be redressed."

Therefore,
(3) "[S]peech, though some of it may be hateful, is bound to be harmless overall." (pp. 98–99)

Once again, the most striking feature of the argument is its florid invalidity. Here are the problems. First, neither refutation nor retaliation necessarily constitutes "redress," so (2) does not follow from (1). Second, "redress" does not necessarily require full restoration; it might involve only compensation. (Cf. Gandhi: "an eye for an eye leaves everyone blind."[35]) Thus, even if "hurt can always be redressed," it would not follow that in a case of redressed harm, no harm had occurred: (3) does not follow from (2). Third, even if "redress" did imply full restoration, premise (1) asserts only that it is *possible* for every act of speech-assault to be redressed. That hardly is enough to support the conclusion that all instances—or even most instances—*will* be redressed. It is possible for, say, British Petroleum to redress (at least some of) the hurt it has recently caused; that is unfortunately not grounds for optimism.

Hornsby, however, ignores the *structural* problems in this argument and goes, once again, for the premise. Of course I agree with Hornsby that premise (1) is false. But it's false for a number of reasons, several of which have nothing to do with the sociolinguistic features of hate speech. A speaker may be unable to make any verbal response to a hateful remark because she doesn't know the language well enough to do so; she may be unable to say anything because it would be physically dangerous for her to antagonize her tormentor; she may already be too debilitated to respond. At the same time, the sociolinguistic point that Hornsby raises— the quite interesting observation that "hate words don't have obverses"— does *not* show that the premise is false. It would show this only if the only possible form of redress for a verbal insult involves a complementary verbal insult. But this is hardly so. If it were the case—and I'm not conceding that this would be a good thing—that hate speech was against the law, and the law was vigorously enforced by the powers that be, then individuals subjected to hateful speech *would* have redress despite the lexical gap noted by Hornsby.

Finally, there's the fact that Hornsby never shows why a Gricean could not acknowledge the power of specific words in exactly the way she does. Indeed, it might even be easier, on an intentionalist account of communication like Grice's, to explain why two perfectly co-extensive words, for example, "kike" and "Jew," can differ so completely in their expressive functions. A term like "kike" is insulting because it is a term with a history—because it came into being as a verbal means of expressing contempt for Jews. Since, on a Gricean account, anything about a speaker's precise choice of words may convey information that goes beyond the strict semantic content of the words, there's every reason to expect that particular words might have more fine-grained functions than the presentation of some particular referential content. For Grice, any violation of conversational norms raises a question about the intentions of a speaker. A speaker's choosing a term with a sordid history, especially when an innocuous term with the same extension is available, is clearly such a violation. The most likely explanation for the violation would be, in fact, malice—the speaker wants to convey contempt for Jews. But notice that this is not the only possible explanation—a hearer might conclude that the speaker is ignorant of the term's history, in which case the hearer might excuse the speaker and resolve not to take offense. (That doesn't mean that the term doesn't cause pain.) On Hornsby's nonintellectualist account, it is hard to see how a hearer could display this sort of nuanced understanding. If one's reactions to speech are "attuned directly and simultaneously to the significance of words," wouldn't the reactions to a particular set of words have to be the same on every occasion?

This is just one more way in which Hornsby's insistence that illocution involves "uptake" hinders, rather than helps us in characterizing the mechanisms of hate speech. Here is a further illustration of my point. Hornsby notes, in the course of her discussion of the first argument, that "a woman who is called 'a slag' may be directly hurt and insulted through no fault of her own" (p. 98). Yes! But I want to go further, and say that she may be hurt and insulted *without understanding what a "slag" is.* One can grasp *that* some word is a term of abuse, or know that it is, without knowing exactly what was meant by it. (This is the converse of the case where one understands the term of abuse, but does not take offense because of some excusing feature of the speaker's circumstances.) Take, for instance, me: I figured out from context (sometimes one *does* consciously and deliberately reflect on the meaning of what one has heard) that "slag" is insulting. But if I were to be called one, I wouldn't know which aspect of myself was being denigrated—is it my sexual mores? My personal hygiene? What? The point is that I take offense, not because I am "attuned" to the insulter's words, but rather because *I grasp her communicative intention.* I can tell what she's trying to do, even if I don't quite understand the verbal means by which she's trying to do it.

On Hornsby's view, as we've seen, this sort of situation must be impossible. On her view, grasp of the communicative intention of a speaker cannot be separated from an understanding of the speaker's words. It's not that she makes *insulting* into a *perlocutionary* act—she does not say that a victim must take offense in order for an insult to have been made—but she does make *something* about the victim's state of mind an essential part of the *illocutionary* act of insulting. If the victim does not instantiate "uptake," then, on Hornsby's view, no insult has been issued. Ironically, this rather puts her in league with the author of the first argument: Hornsby's notion of a communicative speech act makes it the case that the hearer *does* bear some responsibility for the occurrence of an act of hate speech—she does this by partly constituting it.[36]

There is a connection here with the first of the two abstractions present in Grice's theory. In his theory of implicature, Grice focused on cases where a speaker intends to communicate more than what the speaker's words literally meant. I think his general framework offers an excellent explanation of a variety of meaning/communication mismatches. He can explain, for example, how there can be cases where what I say means something different from what I intend to communicate. This can be perfectly innocuous, if embarrassing: when I was in high school, I wrote in an essay that the characters in Orwell's allegory *Animal Farm* were "phallic symbols." For some reason, I had picked up this term in a context that made me think it meant something like "symbol of something political." It does not. My teacher, however, understood what I intended, and informed me discreetly of my error.

But Grice's model equally well explains an important fact about the way hateful speech operates. The fact is that the power of derogatory terms and epithets can be independent of the intentions—and knowledge—of people who use them; that means that it is possible for me to give genuine offense without realizing I am doing so. When I lived with my family in North Carolina, my neighbor, a nice man with whom we had perfectly cordial relations, mentioned in a conversation with us that in recent business deal, he had managed to "jew down" a seller. As the words were leaving his mouth, he suddenly realized something he had never realized before—that that expression alluded to a pernicious stereotype about Jews. It was only when he was saying it while looking directly at my Jewish husband that he suddenly grasped the likely etymology of the expression.[37] What I want to say about this case is that my neighbor was not personally at fault for using the expression, but that he gave offense (at least initially) nonetheless. Having finally learned that the term was anti-Semitic, he *acquired* an obligation to cease using it, regardless of whether or not he ever intended to endorse, by its means, the pernicious stereotype it invokes in the minds of Jews (and other informed people).

There are other evils, outside the area of hate speech, in which language plays a role. For feminists interested in exposing the evil of acquaintance rape, there is a very serious point to preserving an analytical distinction between the literal meaning of an expression and the various messages that that an utterance of that expression can be used to convey. Consider an argument advanced by Douglas Husak and George C. Thomas III in connection with the question what sort of "mistake of fact" might serve as a defense in cases where rape has been charged.[38] They argue that, when prevailing local customs make it socially disadvantageous for a woman to admit to desiring sexual relations, she may well say "no" even if and when she actually does desire an intimate experience:

> How can it be possible for [a man] to make a reasonable mistake about [a woman's] consent when she says "no" or actively resists? The answer, of course, is that it is not impossible for the social convention [governing women's consent to have sex] to interpret no as yes when it comes on the heels of an incomplete rejection strategy.[39]

If, as Hornsby would have it, we are not permitted to abstract the linguistic meaning of the woman's words from the communicative speech act she performs in saying them, I do not see how we can avoid the conclusion that a woman acting in such a situation is not actually performing a speech act of refusing. A Gricean, on the other hand, may say that *even if* a woman says "no" while intending to convey the implicature that she consents to having sex in that instance, she has still *said no*. "No" still means no.[40]

This same case illustrates another of the difficulties, from the point of view of feminist analysis, in Hornsby's analysis, this time resulting from her making "uptake" necessary for the successful performance of an act of saying. We want to be able to say, it seems to me, that it is possible for a victim *to say no*, whether or not her assailant grasps her meaning.[41] Imagine a young woman who is, say, attending college in Texas, unaware of the complicated mores governing communication about sexual relations, and inclined, herself, to candor. A young man who is accustomed to women's deploying (in Husak and Thomas's terms) "incomplete rejection strategies," might very well fail to understand that the young woman means to refuse him if she simply says "no." In such a case,

Hornsby's account entails that the woman has not, in fact, performed the speech act of refusing. Perhaps it seems implausible that someone could really make such a mistake—if so, that would be relevant to the question whether or not the man in fact possessed *mens rea*. But it cannot be assumed that in all the cases we are concerned about, a hearer will always grasp what a speaker is saying. Indeed, Hornsby's own account of "silencing" depends on men's not understanding women in circumstances less unusual than those that allegedly prevail in Texas. If Hornsby is right, then dullness or idiocy on the part of a hearer can make it the case that the *woman did not actually say no*. This would be a whole new way of "silencing" women.[42]

I'll finish by just observing that Hornsby's view that saying something requires someone else's understanding what I say has some other pretty strange consequences. Hornsby is, of course, free to introduce "communicative speech-act" as a technical term, defined any way she likes. But the term so defined will fail to cover a lot of cases where people (of my acquaintance, anyway) would say that someone has said something. I can say to my class that the paper is due on the twentieth, even if no one is paying attention; no student may later complain that I never *said that* the paper was due on the twentieth. I may heartily thank a stranger for a kindness even if I do it in a language the speaker does not understand. (The stranger may understand that I'm *thanking* her, but not by understanding *what I have said*.) Indeed, it seems obvious to me that one can *say something* when one is all by oneself. I assert things when I write papers, even if no one ever reads the papers. (Sigh...)

It might be objected to this last example that when I write, I write with communication in mind. But this is irrelevant. *Expecting* there to be a listener does not bring the listener into existence. Either *actual* uptake is required for a communicative speech-act to have been performed, or it's not, and if the *prospect* of uptake is sufficient, then there's no conflict with individualism. And anyway, I don't have to have a reader in mind when I write something, nor a listener in mind when I say something. We do sometimes speak of "talking to ourselves," as if we are perched on the edge of consciousness, listening, raptly, to our own words. Yet even at the times this metaphor is apt, I find that I often don't listen. ("You don't need another glass of wine.") But, anyway, we also speak of "thinking out loud," which covers a lot of the cases, too. There are also cases in which I hope there will be no reader ("Read this only if I fail to return!") and cases where I intend there *not* to be a reader ("Private Diary!!! Do not open!!! This means *you*!"—Of course here I have a conditional intention that the *warnings* be read, but not the diary contents). Finally, it must be borne in mind that I can even perform some illocutionary acts by myself. I can vow to exercise more regularly; I can name my pet.

CONCLUSION—A PLEA FOR SPILLING INK PRACTICALLY

Here's what I have taken myself to have shown:

1. there is no incompatibility between believing that language is "social *au fond*," and seeing a place for a semantic theory in an overall account of human language use. One need not, in particular, accept any individualistic view of language or of language users.

2. Hornsby's theory of illocution, which takes a "communicative speech act" as an unanalyzed primitive, is problematic from both a philosophical and a political perspective.

Finally,

3. the etiological strategy is pointless.

I'll now go further: the etiological strategy is illegitimate. Not because it has some particular genealogy (I object to Wittgenstein because of his philosophy, not because of his gender), but because of its ill effects. To attempt to gain favor for one's own position in a substantive philosophical debate by alleging that the alternative is "malestream," and without consideration of objections registered against one's own position, or arguments offered for the alternative, is wrong for several reasons. Such a strategy is disrespectful to and exclusionary of feminists who support alternative views. It is philosophically unproductive, and probably coun-terproductive, since it short-circuits debate about the primary issue.

All of us who have chosen to make a career out of philosophy have been drawn to the subject because of some problem that bothered us, some dialectic that engaged us, or some thinker who moved us. To this extent, we felt ourselves at home in philosophy. But as women in a male-dominated field, we have also experienced isolation, alienation, rejection, or all of these, and many of us have looked to a community of feminist philosophers—partly actual, partly imagined—for relief. In such circumstances as these, many of us will of course try to unify our philosophical and political standpoints. My plea is that we do this constructively, by finding whatever matches we can between the theoretical questions generated by our politics, and the intellectual resources supplied by our philosophies. Let us not dishonor the appellation "feminist" by turning it into a bludgeon.

Notes

I'd like to thank Sharon Crasnow, Joseph Levine, Georges Rey, Jennifer Saul, and Anita Superson for comments on an earlier version of this paper. Errors of interpretation and intemperate phrasings that remain are entirely my fault and none of theirs.

1. I referred to this approach as "bare proceduralism" in an earlier essay, "Quine as Feminist: The Radical Implications of Naturalized Epistemology." There I rejected bare proceduralism as a model for feminist philosophical inquiry on the grounds that there were theoretical perspectives and philosophical projects that were inherently antithetical to feminist commitments, whether or not the philosophers who pursued them wanted to claim the label "feminist." I gave "feminist military science" as an example of a project that I thought didn't deserve this appellation. I now think that I was wrong to oppose bare proceduralism, and that my error lay in confusing two issues: (1) who gets to call their work "feminist"? And (2) what work ought I, as a feminist, to support? I can answer the second question—as can anyone else—without having to take a stand on any more general question, such as (1).

2. Sharon Crasnow reminds me that there might be yet another kind of project—what she calls a "transformative" project. Here the aim would be not to replace one philosophical framework with another, but rather to enrich an existing framework by taking gender into account in the questions one poses, the hypotheses one forms, or the considerations one adduces. Since one might undertake such a project in a largely theoretical spirit, with no particular practical issues in mind, a project could be transformative without fitting neatly into my rubric of "practical" feminist philosophy. Since a project of this sort seems not to depend on any prior demonstration that the framework it starts with is "masculinist," I can happily endorse it, too.

3. See, for example, Toril Moi's discussion of Freud's treatment of his patient Dora in her "Representation of Patriarchy: Sexuality and Epistemology in Freud's *Dora*".

4. See my "The Socialization of Epistemology."

5. Roger White, "You Just Believe That Because…" *Philosophical Perspectives* 24, no. 1 (December 2010): 573–615. White cites the late Gerald Cohen's observation that people who went to Oxford believe in the analytic/synthetic distinction, and people who went to Harvard don't; Cohen is happy to

concede that, had he gone to Harvard, he would have rejected the analytic/synthetic distinction, too. Fortunately, he says, he went to Oxford.

6. Hornsby, "Feminism in Philosophy of Language," p.87, fn. 1.

7. Austin, *How to Do Things With Words*; Searle, *Speech Acts: An Essay in the Philosophy of Language.*

8. Here is a partial list, in alphabetical order, and including only philosophers born before 1960: William Alston, Kent Bach, Stephen Barker, Robert Brandom, Michael Dummett, Carl Ginet, R. M. Hare, David Lewis, and Robert Stalnaker.

9. Mitchell Green, "Speech Acts," *Stanford Encyclopedia of Philosophy*, ed. Edward N. Zalta, http://plato.stanford.edu/entries/speech-acts/.

10. See her "Force and Meaning," "On Saying," and "Inscriptions and Indirect Discourse." In these papers, Frye pretty clearly endorses views of a kind Hornsby thinks arise from "decompositionalist thinking."

11. The full defense, to which I'm now alluding, is the basis of another essay, different from the one I'm focusing on in this paper. See Hornsby, "Illocution and Speech Act Theory."

12. Her tentative formulation is also sensible given how little evidence there is that there actually are any gendered "ways of thinking." For a review of relevant literature, with particular mention of the "separate vs. connected" cognitive styles, see Mary M. Brabeck and Ann G. Larned, "What We Do Not Know about Women's Ways of Knowing." Their conclusion: "Our literature review indicates that the studies that have tested the WWK claims are sparse and that explanations for variability in responses to the WWK interview questions are better attributable to factors other than gender" (p. 265). A great deal of the basis for claims about different ways of knowing came from Carol Gilligan's work alleging gender bias in Kohlberg's infamous test of moral development. What has not been widely acknowledged is that there is, in fact, no evidence of gender differences in performance on this scale, or on any other measure of moral reasoning or cognitive development. Apparently gender differences favoring men have been shown to be attributable to gender-correlated differences in educational level within the sample. The small (i.e., statistically insignificant) gender differences that remain when educational attainment is controlled for actually favor women. See Walker, "Sex Differences in the Development of Moral Reasoning: A Critical Review," Rest, *Development in Judging Moral Issues*, and Thoma, "Estimating Gender Differences in the Comprehension and Preference of Moral Issues."

13. See my "Sisters, Please, I'd Rather Do It Myself: A Defense of Individualism in Feminist Epistemology." Hornsby cites this article, takes note of our disagreement, but never discusses any of my arguments. I found that disappointing.

14. Footnote 35, p. 97.

15. Iris Young, *Justice and the Politics of Difference*, p. 99. See also Scheman, "Feminist Epistemology."

16. See Austin, *Sense and Sensibilia*.
17. See Hinton, "Visual Experiences" and "Experiences."
18. Dancy, "Arguments from Illusion."
19. References to works by these and other figures can be found in the bibliography of Byrne and Logue, eds., *Disjunctivism*.
20. Tarski showed how to define "truth-in-a-language" recursively, i.e., by building up semantic values compositionally from the semantic values of basic linguistic elements. For a given language, the result of this construction would be an axiomatized system that had, for every declarative sentence S, a theorem of the form: "S is true-in-L if and only if *p*" where *p* expressed the truth-conditions of S. Davidson argued, in "Truth & Meaning," that this recursive definition of "truth-in-L" could perform double-duty as a meaning-theory for L. See Davidson, "Truth and Meaning"
21. Quine, *Word and Object*.
22. See Davidson, "Rational Animals." Davidson took the same holistic view, incidentally about the characterization of *psychological* content. Useful as it might be to treat beliefs and desires *as if* they had determinate, individualistic contents, thought-content actually was holistic. See Davidson, "Mental Events." So anti-individualistic is Davidson's overall view that feminist philosopher Naomi Scheman commends it to feminist consideration in her early and influential article attacking psychological individualism. See "Individualism and the Objects of Psychology."
23. See *Ignorance of Language*. I argued that Devitt is wrong about this in my critical discussion of that book, "Meta-Linguistics: Methodology and Ontology in Devitt's *Ignorance of Language*."
24. I know that he would deny this, because he did, explicitly, in conversation with me, at a conference on the work of Donald Davidson at Rutgers in 1984. I had recently written a thesis on Dummett's work, in which I argued that the best way to understand his disagreement with Davidson was to take Dummett to be treating meaning-theories as characterizations of internalized representations. I was eager to know his reaction to my interpretation of his work. His reaction was: shock and dismay. Oops.
25. Antony, "Meaning and Semantic Knowledge."
26. Grice, "Meaning."
27. I have competing testimony about the extent of this convention from informants from the U.K. One informant (from the midlands) told me that it was local to London; another—an anonymous referee—insists that it is the informal law of the land. In my mind, this disagreement only underscores my cautions about resting very much on one's own impressions of "how things are."
28. As it happens, I am a roaring realist about mental representation, and I do think that intentionality is fundamentally a matter of the instantiation of mental symbols. But even people like me (there are about six of us—it's a niche religion) will insist on drawing a distinction between the *original* intentionality of mental states, and the *derived* intentionality of artifactual

symbols, like linguistic terms. Grice's story may be the correct one for the latter.

29. Again, even rabid realists about mental representation like me can allow that some attributions of intentionality have dispositional truth-conditions. We must just insist, as we do, that intentionality *fundamentally* involves explicit representation, and that it does whenever the *intensional* (i.e., non-extensional) features of a thought content are being exploited, as in practical reasoning.

30. There is (in my opinion) compelling evidence that children make attributions of intentionality and draw inferences from such attributions long before they are able to pass the standard "false belief" paradigm—indeed, before they have even acquired language. See Susan Johnson, "Reasoning about Intentionality in Preverbal Infants," and Renee Baillergeon et al., "False-belief Understanding in Infants."

31. Look—*dogs* can have Gricean intentions. My dear departed pet, Freya, once had one involving me, her leash, and a half-eaten doughnut outside on the sidewalk.

32. Grice, "Logic and Conversation."

33. See Uta Frith, *Autism: Explaining the Enigma*.

34. Here is a quotation from the introduction to a standard text in general linguistics: "In beginning the study of the structural properties of human language, it is useful to note a common theme that runs throughout part I: the structural analysis of human language can be stated in terms of (1) discrete units of various sorts and (2) rules and principles that characterize the way these discrete units can be combined, recombined, and ordered." See Akmajian et al., *Linguistics: An Introduction to Language and Communication.*

    John Trueswell and Michael Tanenhaus, in their important anthology *Approaches to Studying World-Situated Language Use* explain that despite some ingrained biases dividing members of the "product" school of linguistics (Chomskian) and the "action" school (Austin, Grice, and Searle), "it is clear that detailed complex linguistic knowledge is a central component of human-language comprehension and production." Trueswell and Tanenhaus, p. xv.

35. Hornsby allows for a weaker form of this argument, one that doesn't depend on the principle that two wrongs make a right: this one draws the "less implausible conclusion ... that there are no *particular* groups of people who need be at the losing end where there are no impediments to hate speech" (p. 99, n. 45). The conclusion may be less implausible, but that doesn't make the argument any closer to valid.

36. And here's another peculiar, and presumably unwanted consequence: as long as one is careful to speak in a language that one's intended victims cannot understand, one cannot be guilty of hate speech. (Thanks to Jennifer Saul for pointing this out.)

37. If you find it implausible that someone could use such a potent term without at least suspecting its disreputable origins, consider these

examples. I used the expression "paddy wagon," for years before an Irish-American friend explained its origins to me (and I'm Irish-American myself). I've found many people ignorant of the etymology of the term "gyp"—probably because it more commonly uttered than written. I don't know exactly what the term "Indian-giver" is alluding to, but I assume it involves some insult to Native Americans. I know that the *extension* of the terms "Dutch treat," and "Dutch courage," each of the first two—the first denotes a social arrangement whereby each member of a party pays for him- or herself, and the second refers to alcoholic drink—but I have no idea what the "Dutch" is doing in these expressions. But I don't even know what people are talking about when they use the term "Dutch uncle."

38. Husak and Thomas, "Date Rape, Social Convention, and Reasonable Mistakes."

39. Ibid., p. 122. Husak and Thomas contend that this is not merely a theoretical possibility, and cite a survey of Texas undergraduate women in which 60.8% of "sexually experienced" respondents said that they had said "no" when they wanted to have sex.

40. It might be objected that, since Grice's explication of linguistic meaning depends upon prevailing semantic *conventions*, Grice is in the same boat as Hornsby on this case. But he is not. Although it is conceivable that general conventions surrounding the use of the word "no" shift so drastically that there is no longer any contrast between "yes" and "no," the point is that if the shift in conventions involves only the use of the word "no" in a special set of circumstances, Grice can handle the phenomena through the construct of the implicature. Given the facts as Husak and Thomas report them, this seems much the more plausible analysis to me.

41. I am not saying that the woman's saying this would be sufficient for convicting the accused of rape. A situation in which, for example, the accused did not speak English at all would obviously raise issues not present in the usual case.

42. Ed Curley has written about an important case in England, in which a man, Morgan, convinced three male pals that his wife enjoyed "kinky" sex, and that she would enjoy "pretending" that she was being raped by them. On the strength of this report, the men returned with Morgan to his home, where the four of them forced Morgan's wife to have sex with them. Morgan's three friends were convicted of rape (Morgan could not be charged with rape because of the marital exclusion) and appealed. Although the conviction was upheld, the appeals ruling established a standard of *mens rea* for rape that allowed the defendant's *belief* in a woman's consent to count as a defense, *even if* such a belief was not reasonable. (The convictions were upheld because the appellate court found inconsistencies in the defendants' testimony about their own states of mind, and thus rejected the substance of the defense in their cases.) Curley argues

that the "Morgan rule" leaves women outrageously vulnerable, and argues for reform. Husak and Thomas are somewhat more sympathetic to the principle behind the rule (although they agree that acquittal in the Morgan case would have been wrong.)

References

Akmajian, Adrian, Richard A. Demers, Ann K. Farmer, and Robert M. Harnish. *Linguistics: An Introduction to Language and Communication.* 6th ed. Cambridge, Mass.: MIT Press, 2009.

Antony, Louise. "Quine as Feminist: The Radical Import of Naturalized Epistemology." In *A Mind of One's Own: Feminist Essays on Reason and Objectivity,* ed. Louise M. Antony and Charlotte E. Witt, pp. 110–53. 2nd ed. Boulder, Co: Westview Press, 1993/2002.

———. "Sisters, Please, I'd Rather Do it Myself: A Defense of Individualism in Feminist Epistemology." Special Issue: "Feminist Perspectives on Language, Knowledge, and Reality," ed. Sally Haslanger, *Philosophical Topics* 23, no. 2 (1995): 59–94.

———. "Meaning and Semantic Knowledge." *Proceedings of the Aristotelian Society,* supplementary vol. 71 (1997): 177–207.

———. "The Socialization of Epistemology." *Oxford Handbook of Contextual Political Studies,* ed. Robert Goodin and Charles Tilley. Oxford: Oxford University Press, 2006.

———. "Meta-Linguistics: Methodology and Ontology in Devitt's *Ignorance of Language.*" *Australasian Journal of Philosophy* 86, no. 4 (December 2008).

Austin, J. L. *How to Do Things With Words.* Oxford: Oxford University Press, 1962.

———. *Sense and Sensibilia.* Oxford: Oxford University Press, 1962.

Baillargeon, R., R. M. Scott, and Z. He. "False-belief Understanding in Infants." *Trends in Cognitive Sciences* 14 (2010): 110–118.

Brabeck, Mary M., and Ann G. Larned. "What We Do Not Know about Women's Ways of Knowing." In *Women, Men, and Gender: Ongoing Debates,* ed. Mary Roth Walsh, pp. 261–69. New Haven, Conn.: Yale University Press, 1997.

Byrne, Alex, and Heather Logue, eds. *Disjunctivism: Contemporary Readings.* Cambridge, Mass.: MIT Press, 2009.

Curley, E. M. "Excusing Rape." *Philosophy and Public Affairs* 5 (1976): 325–60.

Dancy, Jonathan. "Arguments from Illusion." *Philosophical Quarterly* 45, no. 181 (October 1995): 421–38.

Davidson, Donald. "Mental Events." In *Experience and Theory,* ed. Lawrence Foster and J. W. Swanson. London: Duckworth, 1970.

———. "Truth and Meaning." *Synthese* 17 (1967): 304–23.

———. "Rational Animals." *Dialectica* 36 (1982): 318–27.

Devitt, Michael. *Ignorance of Language.* Oxford: Oxford University Press, 2009.

Ferguson, Ann. "On Conceiving Motherhood and Sexuality: A Feminist Materialist Approach." In *Mothering: Essays in Feminist Theory*, ed. Joyce Trebilcot, pp. 153–82. Totowa, N.J.: Rowman and Allenheld, 1984.

Firth, Uta. *Autism: Explaining the Enigma*. Oxford: Blackwell Publishing, 2003.

Frye, Marilyn. "Force and Meaning." *Journal of Philosophy* 70, no. 10 (May 24, 1973): 281–94.

———. "On Saying." *American Philosophical Quarterly* 13, no. 2 (April 1976): 123–27.

———. "Inscriptions and Indirect Discourse." *Journal of Philosophy* 61, no. 24 (December 24, 1964): 767–72.

Grice, Paul. "Meaning." *Philosophical Review* 66 (1957): 377–88.

———. "Logic and Conversation." In *The Logic of Grammar*, ed. D. Davidson and G. Harman, pp. 64–75. Encino, Calif.: Dickenson, 1975.

Hinton, J. M. "Visual Experiences." *Mind* 76 (April 1967): 217–27.

———. "Experiences." *Philosophical Quarterly* 17 (1967): 1–13.

Hornsby, Jennifer. "Feminism in Philosophy of Language: Communicative Speech Acts." In *Cambridge Companion to Feminism in Philosophy*, ed. Miranda Fricker and Jennifer Hornsby, pp. 87–106. Cambridge: Cambridge University Press, 2000.

———. "Illocution and Speech Act Theory." In *Foundations of Speech Act Theory*, ed. Savas L. Tsohatzidis, pp. 187–207. London: Routledge, 1994.

Husak, Douglas, and George C. Thomas III. "Date Rape, Social Convention, and Reasonable Mistakes." *Law and Philosophy* 11, no. 1/2 Philosophical Issues in Rape Law (1992): 95–126.

Johnson, Susan C. "Reasoning About Intentionality in Preverbal Infants." In *The Innate Mind*, vol. 1: *Structure and Contents*, ed. Peter Carruthers, Stephen Laurence, and Stephen Stich, pp. 254–71. Oxford: Oxford University Press, 2005.

Moi, Toril. "Representation of Patriarchy: Sexuality and Epistemology in Freud's Dora." *Feminist Review* 9 (Autumn 1981): 60–74.

Quine, W. v. O. *Word and Object*. Cambridge, Mass.: Technology Press of MIT, 1960.

Rest, James. *Development in Judging Moral Issues*. Minneapolis: University of Minnesota Press, 1979.

Scheman, Naomi. "Individualism and the Objects of Psychology." In *Discovering Reality: Feminist Perspectives on Epistemology, Metaphysics, Methodology, and Philosophy of Science*, ed. Sandra Harding and Merrill B. Hintikka. Dordrecht: Reidel, 1983.

———. "Feminist Epistemology." *Metaphilosophy* 26, no. 3 (1995): 177–90.

Searle, John. *Speech Acts: An Essay in the Philosophy of Language*. Cambridge: Cambridge University Press, 1969.

Thoma, S. "Estimating Gender Differences in the Comprehension and Preference of Moral Issues." *Developmental Review* 6, no. 2: 162–80.

Thomson, Judith Jarvis. "A Defense of Abortion." *Philosophy & Public Affairs* 1, no. 1 (Fall 1971): 47–56.

Trueswell, John C., and Michael K. Tanenhaus. "Preface." *Bridging the Language-as-Product and Language-as-Action Traditions: Approaches to Studying World-Situated Language Use*, pp. xi–xxii. Cambridge, Mass.: MIT Press, 2004.

Walker, L. J. "Sex Differences in the Development of Moral Reasoning: A Critical Review." *Child Development* 55 (1984): 677–91.

White, Roger. "You Just Believe That Because…" *Philosophical Perspectives* 24 (forthcoming, 2010).

Young, Iris. *Justice and the Politics of Difference.* Princeton, N.J.: Princeton University Press, 1990.

11

MIRANDA FRICKER
Birkbeck, University of London

SILENCE AND INSTITUTIONAL

PREJUDICE

LET ME BEGIN WHERE I shall end: with the concept of *silence*. There are many kinds of silence; but at the most general level, we might say that silence has two aspects—a positive and a negative. In the negative aspect, there is the imposed silence of those who are in some way prevented from making their voices heard. This kind of silence is normally effected by way of an injustice. In the positive aspect, there is the active, attentive silence of those who are *listening*, perhaps trying to make out a voice that is seldom heard. This kind of silence belongs with a moral attitude of *attention* to others—an openness to who they are and what they have to say. Most of what I want to discuss in this paper can be brought under one or other of these aspects of silence.

There is a remark by Simone Weil that I find especially suggestive in this general connection, both politically and philosophically. Here is what she says:

> Human beings are so made that the ones who do the crushing feel nothing; it is the person crushed who feels what is happening. Unless one has placed oneself on the side of the oppressed, to feel with them, one cannot understand.[1]

The idea expressed here concerns a political dimension of knowledge and understanding—it expresses the thought that being in a position of social power tends to obscure or distort certain patches of reality. This broad idea is significant in two different connections that I would like to highlight and examine. The first connection concerns the contribution made by feminist work in philosophy of a certain, very general methodological insight about how to do philosophy. (This insight is perhaps beginning to take a genuine hold in the wider philosophical imagination.) Weil's remark anticipates this insight, which tells us that if we want to achieve a full understanding of a human practice, social phenomenon, or pattern of relationships, then we must take up the point of view of those on the losing end. If *you* are the one doing the crushing (to continue with Weil's formulation), then not only are you not in a position to know what it is like to be crushed, but also—and this is a separate point—your *general* picture of the social world in which such crushings take place will be in an unhelpfully partial perspective, the perspective of the powerful.

This is an idea at least as old as Marx, but feminism gave it a new and less theoretically burdened expression; and it is principally feminism that has made a recent gift of it to English-language philosophy. Most relevantly, we find in the feminist philosophy of the 1980s and onward an exploration of the notion of a "standpoint" from which the world is viewed, where a standpoint is a point of view afforded (though never guaranteed) by a given social identity positioning and the range of social experience that typically attends it—social positionings that we might begin to capture with categories such as "elderly," "woman," "gay," "straight," "disabled," "able-bodied," "man," and various complexes of such simple identity categories. In the macro-economic frame, the thought is that if you are at the top of the heap, you are not in a position to grasp fully the situation of those at the bottom. In the domestic frame, if you have always been used to having someone else take care of your everyday subsistence—feeding you and generally picking up after you—you are unlikely to have any realistic appreciation of just how much work goes into keeping you going. The *standpoints* of the economic underdog, or the unacknowledged provider of care, have been described as "epistemically privileged"—privileged, that is, both in terms of the greater expanse of social reality it brings into view, and in respect of the consequently less partial perspective in which the world more generally is understood.

Although these philosophical ideas were developing throughout the 1980s, I did not encounter them until 1990 when I took a Master's degree in Women's Studies. The B.A. in philosophy I had done previously did not expose me to any feminist philosophical literature—understandably: it was early days. But when I did get to read feminist philosophical literature, I was amazed. Manifestly this was philosophy; and yet, it seemed that this style of thinking was taking place somewhere in the silences of the English-speaking philosophical canon.

Philosophy after all is, among other things, a social-historical entity, a collective conversation extended over historical time and social space, and what I discovered as I read feminist philosophy for the first time was that to understand what philosophy is—that is, to gain a proper perspective on the historical formation of philosophy—one had to make an effort to listen to the silences. This illustrates, now at the level of philosophical canon, the methodological lesson already mentioned that is offered to us by feminist philosophy: If you want to understand a social phenomenon, you had better look at it from the perspective of those whose voices are hard to hear. One can see this as a milder application of the same idea to which Weil gives political expression when she says "unless one has placed oneself on the side of the oppressed, . . . one cannot understand."

This, then, is the first idea I want to bring out in relation to Weil's suggestive remark. To put the point quite generally: listening to silences tends to be instructive. But what is it to listen to silences when we are doing philosophy? It is one thing to take up an historical perspective on the canon in order to obtain an informed critical attitude to the business of what gets put in and what gets left out. It is quite another, someone might say, to suggest that *listening to silences* can be a useful methodological precept in philosophy, a guideline in how to proceed in the business of philosophical explanation. Let us suppose our methodological injunction to be as follows: Whatever you want to understand, try taking a look at it from the point of view of the powerless, those on the losing end of the practice you want to explain. Now it is perfectly true that for many questions or topics in philosophy this idea will find no application. If I am interested, for instance, in a metaphysical question such as, "Why is there anything rather than nothing?" I doubt I would know what to do with the methodological suggestion that I look at the question from the point of view of the powerless. Or again, if my interest is in some obstinately abstract question in epistemology—for instance, the question whether having a justified and true belief that the cat is on the mat is the same thing as *knowing* that the cat is on the mat—here once again, perhaps, I may draw a blank if I try to look at the question from the point of view of the powerless. But not all philosophical questions are like these. Indeed, not even all *epistemological* questions are like this epistemological question (or at least they are not any more). What if we are interested in the epistemology of testimony—that is, centrally, the question what justifies a hearer in believing something she is told by another person, thereby perhaps gaining knowledge from them. In the recent past, it did not occur to epistemologists interested in this question that it might be worth looking at the matter from the point of view of the powerless. But actually, it turns out that it is.

Getting into a position to see that this is so takes just two steps. First, we have to think of the epistemology of testimony as the epistemology of a *human social practice*, most basically, the practice of giving and receiving information, a practice in which hearers may accept what they are told with varying degrees of credence, or reject it, or perhaps reserve judgment. Coming to see testimony as a practice is actually a big step because of the historically prevalent self-conception of analytic philosophy, which casts it exclusively as inquiry into the nature of our concepts and the words we use to express them. (If the idea of practices got in at all, it was only in the form of our conceptual or linguistic practices). Fortunately, this idea that philosophy's subject matter is confined to the conceptual and linguistic has for some decades ceased to monopolize what philosophers do, and recently has come under explicit attack,[2] so that the linguistic turn can now be regarded as decisively superseded by alternative live conceptions of what philosophy can explain and illuminate. Now, having made this first step so that we have come to regard the subject matter of the epistemology of testimony to be *human practices of telling, and accepting (or not) what we are told*, we can begin to see how to take the second step. We can see what it might be to look at this practice from the point of view of the powerless, the point of view of the silenced. Practices of testimony involve attempts at conveying knowledge to others, but what if those others do not, cannot, or will not hear? At this point perhaps the speaker is silenced. A first formulation might be: When a speaker *should* be heard, but is not heard, he is silenced.

This would be too quick of course. There are other ways, after all, that speakers who should be heard might end up not being heard, where it would be a mistake to characterize them as "silenced." In particular, it would be quite wrong to accuse the hearer of having *silenced* them. A case of mistaken identity might do this, for example, as would simple ignorance of someone's expertise in a given area. Imagine a situation on an airplane where a passenger is taken seriously ill. The flight attendant is doing his best to cope, when another passenger starts barking instructions at him. Until the moment when the flight attendant realizes the bossy passenger is in fact a nurse (perhaps it's a few minutes before she says anything obviously medical), he might not take her suggestions all that seriously, giving her words little credence until her expertise manifests itself in some way. In examples like this, the speaker is not silenced, inasmuch as there is only innocent error on the part of the hearer.

But there are other kinds of examples. Imagine that a business executive—an attractive, blonde young woman—makes a good suggestion at a business meeting about how the company might improve one of its services, yet nobody around the table gives any serious credibility to her suggestion. Or imagine that a white police officer pulls over a black driver of an expensive car and asks him whether he is the owner, and the officer is skeptical of the driver's claim. In these kinds of examples, one person communicates an assertion of some kind (a suggestion, or a piece of testimony), and the hearer gives a deflated level of credibility to the speaker's word, but not this time through any innocent error. Rather, the deflation of credibility is owing to *prejudice*. The proper mechanism by which we receive the word of others, and gauge their credibility, is being corrupted by a prejudice in how the hearer *perceives* the speaker. The people at the meeting perceive the attractive blonde young woman in some way that is incompatible with her making useful informed business suggestions; the white police officer perceives the black male driver in a manner that makes him appear unlikely to be claiming truthfully that he is the rightful owner of the car.

Let me introduce a real example to focus our minds on the importance of the phenomenon. In the London Borough of Greenwich, on April 22, 1993, a teenager named Stephen Lawrence was fatally stabbed by a small gang of white teenagers. Stephen Lawrence and his friend Duwayne Brooks, with whom he was waiting at the bus stop, were black, and the murder was preceded by no provocation, indeed, no hostile *inter*action at all. This was an entirely one-sided, explicitly racially motivated attack—the only thing that preceded it was that one of the five or six assailants had called out racist abuse from across the road; the gang then engulfed Stephen Lawrence, one or possibly two of its members delivering two deep stab wounds, which minutes later ended his life. The now-notorious police handling of the murder investigation was so culpably botched that an independent inquiry was commissioned, headed by Sir William Macpherson, and the report on that inquiry is known as the Macpherson report. It is from that report that I gather my information, and the basis of the interpretation of its epistemic, ethical, and political aspects that I shall be offering.

Duwayne Brooks was the chief witness of the crime and, though physically uninjured, a fellow victim of the attack. There is clear protocol governing how any victim of a crime is to be treated: he must be comforted and treated according to his needs. One of the major shortcomings of the conduct of the police on that day was that Mr. Brooks was never cared for in the manner specified by the protocol. The report notes that no one tried to comfort him or calm him, even though he had manifestly experienced a horrifying trauma.[3] He had presumably narrowly missed being directly physically attacked himself, he had been terrorized, and had seen his friend bleed to death in front of his eyes while waiting for the ambulance to arrive—some time after the police had got to the scene. This order of arrival of the two emergency services was unfortunate, and did not help relations between Duwayne Brooks and the police officers present; but more importantly, the police apparently proceeded on the assumption that there had been some kind of fight that culminated in the stabbing, effectively treating Brooks, not to say his murdered friend, as party to the trouble. So he was a victim who was not cared for as a victim, and was instead spontaneously perceived as part of the trouble. But there is something else in all this—namely, the *epistemic* strand of the story, which is what I want to bring out. The police perception of Duwayne Brooks helps explain why, even though he was officially a witness—the primary source of information about the crime—he was not, at the scene, treated properly as a witness any more than he was treated properly as a victim. It is clear from the Macpherson report that the way the investigating officers perceived and heard the word of Duwayne Brooks was incompatible with their receiving his testimony about the attack as possessing any significant credibility for them. At paragraph 5.11 the report states:

> [T]he officers failed to concentrate upon Mr. Brooks and to follow up energetically the information which he gave them. Nobody suggested that he should be used in searches of the area, although he knew where the assailants had last been seen. Nobody appears properly to have tried to calm him, or to accept that what he said was true. To that must be added the failure of Inspector Steven Groves, the only senior officer present before the ambulance came, to try to find out from Mr. Brooks what had happened.

In this story of a racist murder of an eighteen-year-old man, and of a police investigation so mishandled and skewed by racial stereotyping that to this day no successful prosecution has been made (and probably never can be), we find a powerful example of the phenomenon I call testimonial injustice, whereby prejudice distorts a hearer's perception of a speaker so as to deflate the credibility given. In this case, it seems, what Duwayne Brooks had to say was barely heard at all by the police at the scene, and that prejudiced racial stereotyping was the cause. It is appropriate, therefore, to regard Duwayne Brooks as having been most unjustly silenced. Aside from the obvious ramifications of this silencing for the criminal investigation and subsequent legal procedures, there is the intrinsic epistemic injustice done to Duwayne Brooks, who was wronged in his capacity as knower—specifically, as a giver of knowledge. He was blocked by prejudice from passing on knowledge he had to give.

We might see him as blocked from passing on his knowledge in two ways worth distinguishing. First, he was *preemptively* silenced; that is, the police perception of him at the scene led them in large part simply not to bother soliciting much information from him. We have already seen in the Macpherson report that the only senior officer present before the ambulance arrived failed "to try to find out from Mr. Brooks what had happened." Second, insofar as Duwayne Brooks *was* given the opportunity to pass on his knowledge at the scene, it seems he was not properly heard. His agitation was perceived as hostility rather than traumatic stress, and his anxious, angry frustration at what he saw as a lack of police concern with saving the life of his friend who lay bleeding on the pavement until the ambulance arrived was taken as aggression toward the police; and so he was not properly recognized as the source of knowledge that he manifestly was.[4] Both of these forms of silencing are central forms of testimonial injustice.

The wrong of the testimonial injustice perpetrated here might strike someone as somewhat beside the point compared with the enormity of the legal injustice of the murderer or murderers evading prosecution. There is an obvious sense in which this is true: it is more important that a murder be properly investigated, and legal justice be done, than that someone avoid one instance of testimonial injustice. The silencing of Duwayne Brooks might seem just one in a catalogue of culpable police failures that culminated in the failed prosecution. But in fact I think the testimonial and the legal injustices at stake here are not separable, since the legal injustice of a police investigation so mishandled that no successful prosecution can be made was largely owing to the testimonial injustice perpetrated against Duwayne Brooks. That is to say, the silencing of Brooks was a proper part of the failed investigation and looks to have been a primary cause of its failure, since it was specifically this testimonial injustice which meant that the crucial opportunity for gathering evidence at the scene was missed. Insofar as legal justice directly depends on openness to what witnesses and other parties have to say, it directly depends on testimonial justice. Furthermore, if we think about the wrong involved in the testimonial injustice suffered by Duwayne Brooks, it is obvious that it is not isolated, fleeting, or singular in any way; it is part of a more general pattern of prejudiced perception and credibility judgment. Indeed, he was clearly not the only black person who suffered testimonial injustice at the hands of the police during the course of the investigation. The Macpherson report quotes Mrs. Doreen Lawrence, Stephen's mother, as she describes her encounters with the police during the time of the investigation when she and her husband, as the victim's parents, were supposedly receiving updates on progress. She states:

> Basically, we were seen as gullible simpletons. This is best shown by Detective Chief Superintendent Ilsley's comment that I had obviously been primed to ask questions. Presumably, there is no possibility of me being an intelligent, black woman with thoughts of her own who is able to ask questions for herself. We were patronised and were fobbed off....[5]

Consider the nature of the epistemic wrong involved here. The intrinsic wrong of testimonial injustice is the *epistemic insult*: the subject is undermined in their capacity as a knower, and so as a rational being. The insult goes deep. If we accept that our rationality is part of the essence of human beings' distinctive value, then to be perceived and treated as lesser in one's capacity as a knower is to be perceived and treated as a lesser human being. After the trauma of the murder, Duwayne Brooks sustained this extended epistemic insult from the police. That treatment of him is an ethical injustice. It is also a gross epistemic dysfunction, for the police lost out on knowledge they needed to build a case. Here we observe the curious hybridity of testimonial injustice, for it is at once ethical and epistemic: Duwayne Brooks was morally wronged, and the police (not to say the Lawrence family and society as a whole) lost out on knowledge that should have been taken from Mr. Brooks for the purposes of legal evidence.

I have written elsewhere about the nature of this kind of wrong and of the hope for how we, as individuals, might try to cultivate in ourselves a corrective virtue of *testimonial justice*, whereby we correct for any impact of prejudice in our judgments of credibility.[6] I cast it as a corrective virtue because there is no sensible general hope of plain freedom from prejudice in our judgments. This is because I take the (perhaps rather pessimistic) view that prejudicial stereotypes are in the social air we breath—that is to say, they persist in the collective social imagination—and so even if we do not have any sexist or racist *beliefs*, we are nonetheless susceptible to letting prejudicial stereotypes enter into our judgments of credibility so that we unwittingly allow a deflation of the credibility we give speakers of certain social types (depending to some degree, of course, on which social types *we* may belong to). Someone sitting on an appointments panel, for instance, may possess no ageist beliefs, and yet spontaneously perceive the younger applicant as therein more favorable, where the explanation may be nothing more than the surreptitious influence of a prejudicial stereotype of the slower, less flexible, less eager to please, older worker.

What individuals must aim to achieve is a certain *critical openness* to the word of others by way of an unprejudiced perception of those others as individuals. We might conceive this capacity to listen as a special kind of *attention* to others. Inspired by Simone Weil's notion of "attention," which Weil conceives ultimately as associated with the *unfocused* form of contemplation that she regards as distinctive of prayer, Iris Murdoch develops her own, more specifically ethical notion of "loving attention" as directed toward human persons and other individuals.[7] Despite the focused nature of Murdoch's loving attention, it shares with Weil's concept a kind of vision that is unobstructed, unprejudiced by any aspect of self—a kind of perception or, I want to say, *perceptiveness* that is fundamentally passive in nature, in the sense of being free from interference by the will.[8] In Murdoch's well-known, if now slightly dated, illustration of this sort of attention, she presents us with a mother-in-law at first perceiving her new daughter-in-law as "a silly vulgar girl,"[9] and lamenting that her son has married "beneath him." She manages to betray none of this in her behavior, so that no one aside from herself is aware of how she feels. And then over time she comes around to see her daughter-in-law differently. In particular, she achieves a new, non-snobbish perception of her through an admirable process of self-discipline. Murdoch imagines this woman saying to herself: "I am old-fashioned and conventional. I may be prejudiced and narrow-minded. I may be snobbish. I am certainly jealous. Let me look again." She then observes and reflects deliberately about her daughter-in-law, "until gradually her vision of [her] alters."[10]

What Murdoch describes here captures the essence of how we should think about the individual virtue of testimonial justice. First, it requires reflexive awareness that one might be prone to this or that prejudice; second, it exploits a stable motivation to overcome any such prejudice; and third, it ensures a reasonable degree of success in doing so. In the case of testimonial justice, the overcoming of the prejudice is a matter of readjusting one's perception of the speaker sufficiently to restore the proper level of credibility, or where it remains unclear what level that is, we may seek further evidence, or simply reserve judgment. This capacity for attention—the ability to see through prejudice to real human individuals—is indispensable in ethical life. It is indispensable in personal relations, as between Murdoch's mother- and daughter-in-law, and it is indispensable as part of social, institutional life too. If just one effective police officer present at the scene after Stephen Lawrence's murder had had any such capacity for this kind of attention, then Duwayne Brooks would have been *listened* to; he would not have suffered the epistemic injustice he did, and more evidence could have been gathered before opportunities were lost. But I shall not elaborate further on the business of individual virtue here, because virtuous individuals working within an institutional body are obviously only part of the story. Sometimes institutions have deeply entrenched vices, such as racism, even while the individuals working in them do not independently *as individuals* have the vice as such. Some of the most important instances of testimonial injustice concern the treatment of individuals by collectives, and in particular, institutional bodies such as appointments panels, corporations, juries, and, of course, police forces. And the fact is, there is more to such institutional bodies being racist (or whatever the vice might be) than the sum of racist individuals that work in it. What I would like to focus on, therefore, is the *collective* dimension of the racism that is at work in the story of racial prejudice on which we have been reflecting.

I am not in a position to address the question to what extent there were, or are still, racist individual officers in the London Metropolitan Police Service. But the most resounding and most publicly discussed conclusion of the Macpherson report was that London's Metropolitan Police Service was "*institutionally* racist,"[11] an idea which (at least in its pure form) is distinct from the claim that there were any number of individual officers who were racists. Indeed, the concept of institutional racism is as ethically important as it is hard to pin down, and the accusation against the Metropolitan Police Service inspired much confused and conflicted public discussion at the time. The confusion is anticipated in the publicly expressed advance fear on the part of the then-Commissioner of the Metropolitan Police Service that if the report were to label the police institutionally racist, then the average police officer and member of the public would understand the accusation to be that the majority of police officers "go about their daily lives with racism in their minds and in their endeavour."[12] The possibility of continued public misunderstanding of the role that police racism had played in the case, and the wise efforts made in the Macpherson report to improve that understanding, underline the social importance of the philosophical distinction between attitudes held at the level of the individual and attitudes held at the level of the group. More recently, there was renewed discussion of institutional racism in the U.K. media (occasioned by the tenth anniversary of the report's publication), and my impression is that our collective public understanding, at least in the United Kingdom, is still underdeveloped. I will attempt to say something useful about this kind of institutional vice, so that we may gain a firmer philosophical grip on it, and therefore on the causes of the kind of testimonial injustice that Duwayne Brooks suffered.

Many forms of institutional racism surely involve some significant number of racist individuals. But in order to isolate the institutional aspect, let us imagine an example where a group of coworkers in a given institution are not racist as private individuals, but still there is institutional racism. How can this be? One explanation relates only to procedures: certainly it is possible for an institution to have bad procedures that result in discriminatory outcomes, even while no individual workers have supporting discriminatory attitudes. Sometimes this is called indirect discrimination. An example is the existence of a height requirement for a certain profession, which indirectly discriminates against members of ethnic groups whose average height is lower than the national average. Procedures can be well-designed or poorly designed in relation to their outcomes. But it is not procedures themselves that I want to focus on. Rather, I want to focus on the tension there can be between individuals' private attitudes and attitudes held at the level of the group of which they are members.

The primary source of such a disconnect between group-level attitudes and individual-level attitudes is that human agents are social agents, with multiple social roles that generate distinct "practical identities."[13] Practical identities can generate role-specific reasons for action, so a single person can be in a situation of tension—even contradiction—between commitments and reasons generated by two different practical identities. I may have reasons to do something *as* a mother, *as* a teacher, *as* a university employee, *as* a daughter, *as* a friend, and all these would be practical identities of mine. Obviously, the reasons generated by my role as a teacher can come into conflict with reasons I have as a mother, as when a troubled student needs some last-minute help to prepare their dissertation in time, but the children are ill. Or, to take a quite different example, imagine a long-serving administrator of a local music society. As the administrator, he may be genuinely committed to the furtherance of the society, while as a local resident who is repeatedly inconvenienced by the fact that all the parking spaces get filled up early on the society's rehearsal nights, he may equally hold that it would be no disaster if the society folded. The mechanism here turns on our various commitments being *relative* to one or another practical identity we may have. The administrator's personal misgivings about the continuation of the music society are real, but even while he has these misgivings, he may still put on his hat as a music society member, and ingenuously join in with the collective commitment to the furtherance of the society. This is because he is committed, jointly with the other members, to going along with the enterprise of working for the future of the society.[14]

I think professional and semiprofessional commitments to goals, values, and even beliefs often take this practical-identity-relative form. And this is a good thing, too, for otherwise the only such commitments of which we would be capable would be those we had already taken on personally, independently from practical identities that go with our membership of professional or recreational groups. It must be said that very often the role-specific commitments may spill over into personal commitments, which can be helpful in shoring up our responsiveness to role-related obligations. Furthermore, if these roles are ethically significant ones, this can be part of a process of personal moral development—a process of expanding one's moral horizons in some way. For instance, a teacher may take care of his students' interests first out of sheer role-responsibility under the idea of professional duty; but soon this commitment may grow on him, so that it takes new root in the ground of more personal commitment. This might bring him to a more compassionate, more humanly informed outlook on, for instance, the significance that studying for a higher degree can have for students from non-standard university backgrounds. Given that such developments in moral consciousness are gained not instantly but over time, it is a good thing that such a teacher might be able to take on the attitudes of a conscientious giver of student pastoral care before he comes (if he does) to care in a more personally integrated capacity.

This general model of how people incur commitments as part of their different practical identities is applicable to our institutional racism case. Let us ask how there can be bad collective attitudes—for example, racism at the level of the group—without this stemming from racist attitudes possessed by officers as private individuals. My suggestion is that it works like the case of our music society administrator, as a matter of different practical identities bringing with them certain attitudes and commitments, whose character is irreducibly collective. Such commitments are instances of we-thinking, and the attitudes are irreducibly "we-attitudes."[15] As a private individual, an officer may personally have no active racial prejudices, and yet with his uniform on, he joins in with or goes along with a workplace culture of racism. Such a culture might be characterized by superficially friendly racist jokes and nicknames, a tendency to trade in racial stereotypes that affect how officers perceive black people at the scene of a crime or in the interview room. In the Macpherson report, members of the Black Police Association talked of just such a racist "occupational culture" in the Metropolitan Police. Let me cite two crucial points made about the particular nature of police work, and about the power of the workplace occupational culture to draw racially prejudiced attitudinal commitments from just about everyone, white or black. The officer is quoted as follows:

> Given the fact that these predominantly white officers only meet members of the black community in confrontational situations, they tend to stereotype black people in general. This can lead to all sorts of negative views and assumptions about black people, so we should not underestimate the occupational culture within the police service as being a primary source of institutional racism in the way that we differentially treat black people. Interestingly I say we because there is no marked difference between black and white in the force essentially. We are all consumed by this occupational culture. Some of us may think we rise above it on some occasions, but, generally speaking, we tend to conform to the norms of this occupational culture, which we say is all powerful in shaping our views and perceptions of a particular community.[16]

This comment alludes to the particular mechanism of institutional racism that I am trying to highlight (I do not doubt there are others). The institutional vice stems from group members effectively committing to a practice of racial stereotyping by going along with that practice as a matter of workplace culture. The collective commitment to the practice thereby becomes part of the very practical identity of a police officer in that force. And once that commitment is made, the group identification it helps define can make it costly to withdraw. Dis-identification with the racist attitudes comes to be tantamount to dis-identifying as a member of the force, given how that practical identity has been locally constructed. It is almost to say "I am not *one of us*" any more, not part of "we" anymore. This, at any rate, seems to be one way that a vice like racism can take hold in an institution, even without its necessarily being the case that any of the officers *as private individuals* could reasonably be described as racists. Needless to say, my aim is not to exonerate, but only to explain. Passively going along with a set of racist attitudes as a matter of professional identity *is* a way of being racist; but it is different from having preexisting racist attitudes that one brings to the collective from an independent practical identity. The passive phenomenon is consistent with personally having non-racist attitudes, and even anti-racist attitudes, but lacking the courage to stand up to the peer pressure from one's colleagues. It can take great courage to refuse to go along with an up-and-running workplace culture, however repellent it may be. And the difficulty can only be exacerbated by the fact that in going along with the values, goals, or beliefs of the group, one has actually made a *commitment* to the other group-members so to do. So dis-identification with the bad attitudes involves reneging on a real commitment—the commitment a person becomes party to by going along with those jokes, that way of talking, that set of attitudes. Of course, it is a commitment that should not have been made, and given that it has been made, should now be reneged on; but the fact remains that the commitment has some psychological force. Therein lies the internally coercive power that this sort of "we-attitude" can have.[17] It may well be that the best an ordinarily decent person can be expected to do in such a situation is to achieve an unspoken non-participation in that culture, still risking paying the price, no doubt, in terms of isolation.

If this is indeed how institutional vice can take hold, then we have also learned something about institutional virtue. For each can gain sway courtesy of the same mechanism. If the members of an appointments committee, a jury, or a police force jointly commit to a virtuous goal such as non-racist professional conduct, then that commitment can become associated with the practical identity that goes with membership of the group. This is one way of thinking about how an *ethos* establishes itself in an institution: value-related commitments that are worn on one's sleeve as part of one's identity as an officer of that institution.

The ethical importance of the institutional virtue of testimonial justice has been manifest in the discussion so far (Duwayne Brooks was wronged in his capacity as a giver of knowledge). And I have also tried to bring out its epistemic importance in terms of knowledge missed (the police missed out on valuable evidence at the scene). But there is also a *political* dimension to it that I would like at last to draw attention to. On one mainstream conception of political freedom, namely the republican conception, freedom is a matter of non-domination.[18] If, for example, you are married to a man in a society where there is no criminal category for rape within marriage, then you are dominated even if you can take it entirely for granted that your husband would never dream of hurting or coercing you. Your status as unfree is established by the counter-factual: *if* he were to hurt you, he would do so with impunity. The truth of that counter-factual means you are dominated, and to that extent not free. Similarly, if you are employed by someone who could sack you without due reason, leaving you with no redress, then you are dominated, and to that extent not free. What is doing the work here is the question of your safety or non-safety from certain forms of arbitrary interference, where what makes a form of interference count as arbitrary is that it is not geared to collective interests. Taxation is interference, but it is not arbitrary; being arrested for a crime is interference, but done properly it is not arbitrary. Now of course, in any society, bad things happen: people get assaulted, mugged, sacked without due reason, and so on. But what is crucial to such interference not counting as arbitrary is the victim's ability to *contest* the wrongful treatment. One might contest a crime by reporting it to the police or a wrongful sacking by taking one's case to an industrial tribunal. So long as one can contest it, the treatment no longer counts as arbitrary. On this conception of political freedom as non-domination, then, we are free insofar as we are properly protected from arbitrary interference, and being properly protected is a matter of our being able to contest it if it were to happen.

Freedom as non-domination, then, depends crucially on the power to contest. But what does contestation require? We should pursue the question in order to shine a light on the epistemic dimension of political freedom. Besides the basic linguistic conditions of communicative success, contesting wrongful treatment crucially requires that one be properly heard, without prejudice.[19] It requires, therefore, that the industrial tribunal, the complaints committee, the investigating police force, or whatever the relevant institutional body may be, *possess the virtue of testimonial justice*. Duwayne Brooks was not properly heard; he was silenced. Needless to say, he would not have been so silenced had the police possessed the institutional virtue of testimonial justice, that is to say, had the investigating team at the scene been jointly committed to hearing without prejudice the testimony of witnesses. But in addition to the testimonial injustice Duwayne Brooks suffered, and because of it, he is revealed as significantly politically unfree. His susceptibility to testimonial injustice means that his ability to contest was radically impaired. Indeed, on the night of his friend's murder, he was, among other things, trying to contest the attack in which *he* was a fellow victim; but he could not contest it, because the police at the scene were not ready to hear him without prejudice. In addition to the ethical and epistemic significance of testimonial injustice, then, we can now see its political dimension. On the republican conception we are considering, the institutional virtue of testimonial justice (for those institutions to which citizens may need to contest) is revealed as a *constitutive condition of political freedom.*

I have made this point in relation to a conception of freedom as non-domination. But the point can be generalized to other conceptions of political freedom insofar as they involve the power to contest. If freedom is conceived as negative liberty, then you are free insofar as you are not blocked from doing things you want to do. On this sort of liberal conception, freedom is a matter of de facto non-interference. Here, if your boss has the power to sack you without due reason, you are not *thereby* unfree. You remain free, unless and until he or she actually sacks you without due reason. On this kind of view, the power to contest is not built into freedom as a constitutive condition, but still we can see a direct causal connection: if you are a member of a group that is susceptible to testimonial injustice at the hands of institutions such as employers or industrial tribunals, then your boss knows he or she is more likely to get away with sacking you without due reason than the next employee. That makes your risk of such violations of your liberty significantly greater. So, on any such liberal conception of political freedom, we can see that a susceptibility to testimonial injustice generates a special vulnerability to infringements of political freedom.

It is now time to come full circle. I began with the idea that silence has positive and negative aspects. I have explored a negative kind of silence that comes with a certain injustice, namely, testimonial injustice. And I have discussed a positive kind of silence that goes with the kind of loving attention to an individual that allows one to *listen through* the white noise of prejudice. So let me now end by returning to my first thought about philosophical method, and the value of looking at any social practice from the point of view of those on the losing side when things go wrong. The very theme of testimonial *in*justice already signals a certain attention to the underbelly of epistemic practices—attention, that is, to how our various practices by which we gain, retain, or indeed lose knowledge can go wrong and do wrong. This is in itself a departure from the norm.

Philosophy tends to be focused on what it takes for a given practice to go well—what it takes for there to be justice, for instance. And the assumption tends to be that once we have got a clear account of what it takes for there to be justice in society, then injustice will just fall out of that positive account as the failure of one or another of its conditions.

But this makes the implicit methodological assumption that all the phenomena we are looking to explain in our philosophy will be present in the situation of justice, so that attention to mechanisms of injustice could never throw any light on the positive constitution and maintenance of justice. While I have allowed that this may be a sound principle for some topics, in the case of testimonial practice I have tried to show that there are aspects of the fully functional practice—the ideal practice even—that become visible only when we look at what goes on when things go wrong. The traditional philosophical ideal of testimonial exchange says only that the hearer's credence in what he is told be proportionate to the likelihood of its being true. Let us reflect, by contrast, on what ideal of testimonial practice has emerged from the present discussion. The ideal that has emerged is one in which everyone with something relevant to say has the opportunity to communicate it and be heard without prejudice. Such a situation would be one in which speakers could be confident they would encounter no testimonial injustice. Not only would hearers be intellectually and emotionally open (critically open, as I have put it) to the *content* of what is said, but they would also be open ("lovingly attentive," to use Murdoch's phrase) to the *person* of the speaker. A shorter way of describing what this involves is that hearers exercise an ability to neutralize the impact of prejudice in their judgments of credibility. On any given occasion that we achieve this—*if* we can achieve it: remember I am describing an ideal—achieving it might take significant self-critical effort and acquaintance over time, in the way it does for Murdoch's character of the mother-in-law who deliberates and disciplines her perceptual efforts so that she gradually learns to perceive her daughter-in-law differently, more passively, more truthfully. Let me add that it might also take some proper effort from the daughter-in-law, since the achievement of listening properly and attentively to someone may reasonably require that the speaker try to make themselves heard, try in effect to disrupt the hearer's normal patterns of perception and credibility judgment so that she is *enabled* to hear what is being said.

This conception of the ideal testimonial practice is a far cry from the skeletal traditional conception which emphasizes only that one's credence must somehow be proportionate to the likelihood of the testimony being true. That is the thinnest possible epistemic ideal of testimonial exchange, and in some guise or other it should remain present as the essential goal of the more fulsome ideal I have presented. But on its own, it is hopelessly methodologically under-informed. It is like advising people that the ideal adventure holiday is one in which nothing goes wrong and no one gets hurt, never bothering to mention any of the things that actively threaten to go wrong on an adventure holiday. An intelligent ideal of a practice is one informed by risk and what it takes to guard against it. By contrast to the traditional ideal of testimony, our more informed ideal includes crucial information about a type of risk that is endemic to testimonial practice—namely, the risk that prejudice is allowed to depress the level of credibility given to certain speakers, with the result that an injustice is done and knowledge is missed. The ever-presence of this risk has emerged from our discussion only because of the richly socially situated conception of speakers and hearers that is imported by our methodological commitment to looking at testimony from the point of view of those who lose out when things go wrong. Without that conception, none of the above could have made itself philosophically visible.

Attention specifically to these sorts of *dysfunction* in testimonial practice, then, is the key to a fuller understanding even of the ideally functional case. We can come to see that there is such a thing as testimonial *justice*, come to appreciate its ethical significance, and its connection to political freedom, only by exploring the phenomenon of testimonial *injustice*. I have presented this project as rooted in the feminist methodological insight with which we started, and which was anticipated in the opening remark recalled from Simone Weil. Philosophy that takes that insight as a guide hopes to achieve a more socially informed and so more philosophically rich picture of whatever human practice it aims to understand, by listening to silence.

Notes

1. Simone Weil, *Lectures on Philosophy*, trans. Hugh Price (Cambridge: Cambridge University Press, 1978), 139. I thank Clark Elliston for assistance in sourcing this quotation. This paper was first given as the 2009 Simone Weil Lectures on Human Value in Melbourne and Sydney, and it benefited greatly from discussions on those occasions. I would particularly like to thank C. A. J. Coady, Karen Jones, Martin Krygier, Genevieve Lloyd and Michael Smith for helpful discussion, and most of all Raimond Gaita— for the invitation, for philosophical insight on tap, and for his endlessly kind hospitality.

2. See Tim Williamson, *The Philosophy of Philosophy* (Oxford: Blackwell, 2007), though unfortunately his impressive defence of "armchair philosophy" substitutes something no more diversified than the linguistic conception he supplants.

3. See chapter 5 of the Macpherson report, especially 5.10–12 and 5.3. The report was published in 1999 and can be found at http://www.archive .officialdocuments.co.uk/document/cm42/4262/4262.htm.

4. The report makes clear (at 5.14) that while police treatment of Mr. Brooks at the scene, and even later at the hospital, was thoroughly inappropriate and inadequate, the way he was treated later at Plumstead Police Station was better, with one officer seeing him, giving him the opportunity to see his mother and to go home (which he declined), and taking a long statement from him through the night.

5. Macpherson, 4.4.

6. Miranda Fricker, *Epistemic Injustice: Power and the Ethics of Knowing* (Oxford: Oxford University Press, 2007), see chapters 4 and 7.

7. Iris Murdoch, *The Sovereignty of Good* (London: Routledge & Kegan Paul, 1970), 34.

8. "Simone Weil says that will does not lead us to moral improvement, but should be connected only with the idea of strict obligations. Moral change comes from an *attention* to the world whose natural result is a decrease in egoism through an increased sense of the reality of, primarily of course other people, but also other things. Such a view accords with oriental wisdom (and with Schopenhauer) to the effect that ultimately we ought to have no will" (Iris Murdoch, *Metaphysics as a Guide to Morals* [London: Chatto & Windus, 1992], 52.)

9. Murdoch, *Sovereignty of Good*, 17.

10. Ibid.

11. The Macpherson report deals with racism principally in chapter 6, and places great emphasis on the distinction between individual racist attitudes and unintentional racism of outcomes in terms of how black and ethnic minorities are treated by the police. At 6.34, it defines for the purposes of the report the concept of institutional racism as follows: "The collective failure of an organisation to provide an appropriate and professional service to people because of their colour, culture, or ethnic origin. It can be seen or detected in processes, attitudes and behaviour which amount to discrimination through unwitting prejudice, ignorance, thoughtlessness and racist stereotyping which disadvantage minority ethnic people." The paragraph continues: "It persists because of the failure of the organisation openly and adequately to recognise and address its existence and causes by policy, example and leadership. Without recognition and action to eliminate such racism it can prevail as part of the ethos or culture of the organisation. It is a corrosive disease."

12. He is quoted in the Macpherson report at 6.46.

13.   I borrow this term from Christine Korsgaard, *The Sources of Normativity* (Cambridge University Press, 1996), chapter 3.
14.   I am making allusive use of the joint commitment model of group agency that Margaret Gilbert has developed, most particularly what she says in relation to collective belief. See, for instance, her "Remarks on Collective Belief," *Socializing Epistemology: The Social Dimensions of Knowledge*, ed. Frederick F. Schmitt (Lanham, Md.: Rowman & Littlefield, 1994), 251; or "Collective Epistemology," *Episteme* 1 (2) (October 2004), 95–97: 102.
15.   This evocative label is used by Raimo Tuomela in his work on collective intentionality. See, for instance, *The Philosophy of Social Practices: A Collective Acceptance View* (Cambridge: Cambridge University Press, 2002).
16.   Macpherson report, 6.28.
17.   This point about the internal coercive force of joint commitment is made by Margaret Gilbert, whose model of plural subjectivity I am implicitly using.
18.   See Philip Pettit, *Republicanism: A Theory of Freedom and Government* (Oxford: Clarendon Press, 1997).
19.   This is an explicit commitment of Pettit's account (ibid., 63).

Bibliography

Fricker, Miranda. *Epistemic Injustice: Power and the Ethics of Knowing*. Oxford: Oxford University Press, 2007.
Gilbert, Margaret. "Remarks on Collective Belief." In *Socializing Epistemology: The Social Dimensions of Knowledge*, ed. Frederick F. Schmitt. Lanham, Md.: Rowman & Littlefield, 1994.
———. "Collective Epistemology." *Episteme* 1 (2) (October 2004): 95–97.
Korsgaard, Christine. *The Sources of Normativity*. Cambridge: Cambridge University Press, 1996.
Macpherson, Sir William, advised by Tom Cook, the Right Reverend Dr. John Sentamu, and Dr. Richard Stone. *The Stephen Lawrence Inquiry: Report of an Inquiry by Sir William Macpherson of Cluny* (February 1999), available at http://www.archive.officialdocuments.co.uk/document/cm42/4262/4262.htm.
Murdoch, Iris. *The Sovereignty of Good*. London: Routledge & Kegan Paul, 1970.
———. *Metaphysics as a Guide to Morals*. London: Chatto & Windus, 1992.
Pettit, Philip. *Republicanism: A Theory of Freedom and Government*. Oxford: Clarendon Press, 1997.
Tuomela, Raimo. *The Philosophy of Social Practices: A Collective Acceptance View* Cambridge: Cambridge University Press, 2002.
Weil, Simone. *Lectures on Philosophy*, trans. Hugh Price. Cambridge: Cambridge University Press, 1978.
Williamson, Tim. *The Philosophy of Philosophy*. Oxford: Blackwell, 2007.

12

H E I D I E. G R A S S W I C K
Middlebury College

KNOWING MORAL AGENTS:

Epistemic Dependence and the Moral Realm

RECOGNITION OF THE EXTENT and variety of our epistemic dependencies has been a common theme of contemporary feminist epistemologies. Feminist epistemologists argue that we can develop our capacities to know only through our engagement with others,[1] that knowledge depends on communal standards that may change over time,[2] that knowledge is a matter of critical exchange within communities,[3] and that we are often at the mercy of others' testimony for important knowledge that we need.[4] With respect to our dependence on testimony, Lorraine Code writes, "In an elaborated sense of learning from other people, from cultural wisdom embedded in everyday language, from books, media, conversations, journals, standard academic and secular sources of information, testimony makes knowledgeable living possible."[5] When considering various forms of epistemic dependence, it is worth attending to the fact that there is a wide variety of kinds of knowledge, and particular epistemic dependencies may play out differently accordingly. For example, although I may be dependent on others for the language and conceptual skills that allow me to articulate and comprehend my personal experiences, the direct testimony of others may be less relevant, whereas for scientific knowledge, as a layperson I may be very dependent on others' testimony. In this chapter, I examine feminist analyses of *moral knowledge* and consider their implications for one form of epistemic dependence: the possibility of knowing through testimony. I focus on the perspective of epistemic responsibility, considering whether feminist analyses of moral knowledge indicate circumstances in which we should rely on others' moral testimony rather than depend solely on our own moral assessment. Interestingly, within the testimony literature at large, there has been relatively little attention paid to the moral realm. I look particularly at feminist conceptions of moral knowledge, and I argue that they suggest some concerns, specific to the moral realm, about knowing through the testimony of others, while they also suggest that testimony may be very important in the moral realm. In this paper I reconcile these two directions of feminist thought. Using an example from Karen Jones, I discuss how feminists should understand the challenge of moral testimony, clarifying what we should expect from responsible moral knowers who remain epistemically dependent. I conclude that if we are to make sense of obtaining moral knowledge through testimony, while avoiding certain undesired ramifications of the analysis, feminist considerations of moral testimony must be embedded in a broader understanding of various forms of our epistemic *inter*dependence. Deferrals to moral testimony must be assessed within the context of certain practices that either engage our critical agency even as we defer, or not. Though I focus on feminist analyses with respect to moral testimony, my conclusions also help identify the shortcomings of nonfeminist analyses of testimony that isolate testimony from other forms of our epistemic dependence, and abstract instances of testimony from the context of practices.

FEMINIST EPISTEMOLOGIES AND THEORIES OF TESTIMONY

Feminist epistemologists have overwhelmingly rejected the vision of the self-sufficient and atomistic knower who must acquire knowledge on *his* own and is undifferentiated from other knowers in his capacity to know. Instead, they have drawn attention to the epistemic relevance of differently located knowers.[6] As a result, feminists have correspondingly attended to the epistemic importance of our reliance on others' testimonies. Since others may be in different and/or better positions to know than the agent herself, relying on others' testimony could be a very important source of knowledge. Recognizing the testimony of others as an important source of knowledge has also been a crucial prerequisite for feminists to interrogate the epistemic relevance of the power dynamics between knowers, investigating, for example, the social processes by which various knowers attain credibility.[7] Only when feminists turn their attention to the importance of testimony in the production and circulation of knowledge can they begin to see the complex power relations that lead to certain kinds of people carrying more cognitive authority than is warranted, and others less. For example, in her work on testimonial injustice, Miranda Fricker analyzes the "credibility excess" the socially privileged enjoy, and the "credibility deficit" experienced by the socially underprivileged.[8] The ability to theorize these economies of credibility is premised on a recognition of the significant role that testimony plays in our epistemic lives.

Feminist epistemologists have not been alone in turning their attention to testimony. Since the early 1990s, there has been a significant increase in philosophical work on testimony, growing alongside an increasing interest in social epistemology generally.[9] However, the feminist work on testimony, with its emphasis on differently situated knowers and its attention to the power relations involved in economies of credibility, is markedly different from most of the testimony work that is not explicitly feminist. Nonfeminist testimony theorists have recognized that the tradition of individualistic epistemology from Descartes on has failed to account for the extensive degree to which we do (and must) rely on testimony as a source of knowing.[10] In an effort to remedy this lack of attention, they have considered in detail what classifies something as a case of testimony, and they have debated possible sources of justification for a reliance on testimony. The main debate has been between the non-reductionists, who argue that testimony is just as basic a source of justification as familiar sources such as sense perception, memory, and inference, and the reductionists, who argue that knowers require positive reasons, based in another epistemically acceptable source, for their reliance on testimony. Examples are almost always isolated cases of two people, a speaker and a hearer, with little attention to structural economies of credibility such as we see in feminist analyses. Additionally, in spite of their break with the tradition of individualism by recognizing that the testimony of others is an important source of knowledge that needs to be analyzed, most testimony theorists have proceeded with a tendency to maintain certain features of the individualistic model of the knower, particularly the potential interchangeability of knowers.[11] For example, in standard discussions of testimony, Person A may happen to be in a position to have direct evidence that p, whereas Person B is not, and thus must rely on A's testimony. But the examples are usually mundane enough to suppose that had circumstances been different, their roles might have been reversed. Person B "happened" to lack access to the direct evidence.[12] Feminist discussions, in contrast, often focus on ways in which various knowers *could* not have access to certain evidence, given the relevance of their social location. Various versions of feminist standpoint theory, for example, argue that those in socially marginalized positions may carry an epistemic advantage in understanding social relations. One of the criticisms of feminist standpoint theory has been that the emphasis it places on the limitations of social location and material position results in epistemological chasms between knowers.[13] If one can only access sound knowledge of social relations directly from a position of social marginality, then the socially privileged will be unable to understand social relations by knowing on their own. This brings with it the worrisome implication that the privileged would not have any corresponding responsibilities to understand the workings of oppression: if you cannot know, then you cannot have an obligation to know. The epistemological chasm criticism suggests that feminist epistemologists may have an interest in exploring an even greater range of the possibilities of knowing through testimony than nonfeminist epistemologists. If testimony offers a legitimate form of knowing, the privileged could gain access to knowledge of social relations through the testimony of the underprivileged, potentially eliminating the problem of epistemological chasms while maintaining the feminist claims concerning the importance of social location for knowing.

FRAMING QUESTIONS OF TESTIMONY

Many feminist epistemologists have argued that it is a shortcoming of traditional epistemology that it focuses so much attention on the conditions of knowledge, at the expense of understanding the *activities* of knowing. As such, feminist epistemologists have been interested in reframing some of the key problems of epistemology in ways that take account of agent-centered activities of knowing. Lorraine Code, for example, in much of her work, shifts our attention to epistemic responsibility—asking how we can responsibly know well—and gives this concept a central place in her epistemology.[14] Similarly, here, I use the concept of epistemic responsibility to frame the question of moral testimony.

There are at least two ways of investigating the epistemic status of testimony, and both can be framed in terms of the epistemic responsibilities of agents. The first stems from arguments for the cognitive division of labor: is it acceptable to have someone else do the knowing *for* me? In the case of many kinds of specialized knowledge, we accept a cognitive division of labor without question. I do not need to know the details of physics or medicine or the techniques of making batik clothing. I trust others to do this knowing for me, and I am none the worse off as an epistemically responsible human being for my dependence on others in these fields. In fact, our epistemic communities are far better off if we are able to avail ourselves of certain cognitive divisions of labor. This is not to say we always think it appropriate to employ a cognitive division of labor. It depends on what kind of knowledge is at stake. Each of us is expected to know certain things and not others. But in cases where we are comfortable employing a cognitive division of labor, I do not so much know through another as I *let another do the knowing* for me, without having a responsibility to do that knowing myself or try to inquire on my own.

Yet another issue, however, concerns whether or not *I* can actually know *through* testimony. When I accept someone's telling me *p*, can *I* know that *p*, and under what conditions? This question often leads into more technical issues of the conditions of knowing, considering whether what we might *call* knowing through testimony is missing some crucial element of knowing, whether it is at best considered second-rate knowing, or whether and under what conditions it should be accepted as good knowing on a par with other individual-based forms of knowing that rely on skills such as perception, reasoning, and individual-based evidence gathering. Such technical questions have formed the bulk of the current mainstream literature on testimony, as theorists strive to understand the epistemic status of testimony and how it functions.

But this line of questioning need not be restricted to the technical definitions of what constitutes "knowing" and what the specific conditions of knowledge are. It can also be framed in terms of the epistemic responsibility of agents. In particular, a key question of interest is whether one can be epistemically responsible by deferring to another's testimony, and if so, under what conditions? This question, when framed in terms of epistemic responsibility, remains importantly different from the cognitive division of labor questioning set out above. In the case of allowing someone to know for me, it is a question of whether I can be epistemically responsible by allowing someone to "fill in" knowledge I lack in a particular area of inquiry, without investigation myself. In the latter line of questioning, the issue is whether or not part of my epistemically responsible inquiry might *involve* or even demand deference to another's testimony. Importantly, in the second case, the question arises of whether one's own assessment of a situation could be responsibly overridden by a deferral to another's testimony. So, for example, suppose I went car shopping with a friend last weekend, and in later conversation I comment that I really liked the mid-range model that came with a moonroof. My friend corrects me, claiming that only the high-end models came with a moonroof. My friend is no more expert than I am on such issues. The question at stake is whether or not it might be responsible for me to defer to her recollection over mine—perhaps, let's say, I knew I was overwhelmed by the choices that day and had had a hard time keeping track of the various car options.

The question of whether I can know through testimony presses on whether it can be epistemically responsible for me to defer to those around me, relinquishing my own judgment of the situation. I shall discuss both the cognitive division of labor question and the question of knowing through testimony, but it is in this second line of questioning that the work of feminist epistemology has the most potential to contribute to discussions of moral testimony. There are two reasons for this. First, as I shall discuss, cognitive division of labor arguments generally have less applicability in the moral realm than in other areas of knowledge. Second, feminists' focus on socially differentiated knowers directly confronts many situations where knowers are not equally positioned to access certain kinds of knowledge. In such cases, those not occupying the requisite position may need to defer to others who do in order to access this knowledge, overriding their own assessment of the situation in the process. Feminists deal with cases where one not only is not in a position to know *x* on one's own, but *cannot* be in a position to know *x* on one's own because of social position. While many have recognized certain kinds of phenomenological knowledge as being directly accessible only to certain kinds of people—men cannot know the pain of childbirth, for example—feminist epistemologists focusing on the social situatedness of knowing and the differentiation of knowers consider such cases to be much more widespread. For feminists, then, testimony may take on a new importance as a way of bridging epistemological chasms, and in the process may contribute significantly to our understandings of epistemically responsible deferral to moral testimony.

TESTIMONY AND THE MORAL REALM: FEMINIST CONCERNS

If we look specifically at moral knowledge, we see that most analyses, including feminist analyses, are less willing to apply cognitive division of labor arguments in the moral realm than for other forms of knowledge. This may be part of the reason for the relative inattention to the moral realm within the testimony literature. While it probably seems obvious not only that we *do*, but also that we *should* rely on others to do some knowing for us, particularly in areas of specialized knowledge such as the sciences, it is not so obvious in the moral realm. As Karen Jones notes, in the moral realm, "we are responsible for avoiding errors...in a way that we are not responsible for avoiding them in other areas."[15] So, for example, as long as I do not enter a medical profession, and I do not purport to have such knowledge, my lack of medical knowledge, which might lead me into error occasionally, is perfectly acceptable. I am not held accountable for such errors stemming from my ignorance of this particular specialized field of knowledge. The normative force of epistemology has always been a hypothetical: if you want to know, then do *x*.[16] But the moral realm is supposed to have pull on all of us regardless: *everyone* (barring exceptions of the incapacitated) is expected to conduct themselves within the moral realm, being held accountable for errors that occur due to moral ignorance. Unlike the case of medical knowledge then, there are much higher standards for each person's acquisition of moral knowledge, and few would support the acceptability of letting others do our moral knowing for us. As Elizabeth Fricker makes the point, "for deference on moral judgements, there are important ties with the idea of individual autonomy and responsibility which may place limits."[17]

These concerns hold for both feminist and nonfeminist moral epistemologists; however, it is worth noting that as a social and political movement, feminism has a particular interest in moral knowledge. If one is a skeptic about moral knowledge, one will not be able to justify the demands for social change away from oppression that are core to the feminist project. One of the interesting lines of argument we see in feminist work is the consideration of whether individuals are responsible for knowing that the practices of sexism and racism (and other oppressive practices) in which they participate are morally wrong. To claim that such individuals "ought to have known" is the first step in holding such individuals accountable for their contributions to the moral wrongs of sexism and racism. Michele Moody-Adams, for example, has challenged the idea that "one's upbringing in a culture simply renders one unable to know that certain actions are wrong."[18] Moody-Adams argues that in many cases, the problem is not one's inability to engage critically the culture and its practices but rather is the manifestation of "affected ignorance—choosing not to know what one can and should know" which sometimes "simply involves refusing to consider whether some practice in which one participates might be wrong."[19] I draw attention to the arguments of Moody-Adams here in order to show some of the parallels between feminist arguments for the responsibilities individuals carry for knowledge of moral wrongs such as sexism and racism and arguments that cognitive divisions of labor are inappropriate in the moral realm. In the case of affected ignorance, when I refuse to consider critically the moral status of the social practices in which I engage, there is a sense in which I am deferring to the culture, allowing others (well-established members of the community perhaps) to do the knowing for me, thus refusing to consider critically or investigate the moral status of these cultural practices for myself, just as I might let a specialist do the knowing for me, employing a cognitive division of labor. But feminist arguments such as those of Moody-Adams reject the acceptability of such a deferral, arguing that cultures continue only through the agency of individual members and that although it must be acknowledged that it takes significant effort on behalf of individuals to engage critically and come to realize the moral problems with some of their cultural practices, it remains important to hold them responsible for such knowledge and critical inquiry. Similar to the arguments to the effect that within the moral realm, we must not let others do our knowing for us, arguments such as those of Moody-Adams suggest that everyone bears some responsibility for inquiry into the moral status of our practices, even as those practices are deeply culturally bound. Along these lines, it is not surprising that feminists have increasingly become interested in manifestations of ignorance, seeing ignorance not as a gap in knowledge but often as the result of failures to exercise epistemic responsibilities to know well, which in turn have moral implications.[20]

But if reliance on moral testimony is not likely to be justified on the basis of a cognitive division of labor in the moral realm, there remains the second line of questioning concerning whether one can know something *through* moral testimony. Focusing on feminist analyses of moral knowledge, here too we can find reasons to think that moral knowledge may not be attainable through testimony, or at the very least, that moral knowledge gained through testimony must be somehow "second-rate" or merely, as Karen Jones uses the phrase, "borrowed knowledge."[21] Feminist analyses of moral knowledge are by no means uniform; however, there are certain themes that commonly appear. For example, evolving from the large amount of work in feminist care ethics, many feminists have argued that seeing the moral value of women's caring labor requires a shift in how we view moral knowledge itself. Moral knowledge comes to be understood as less abstract and theoretical knowledge of moral principles, and more a practical form of knowledge, involving sensitivity to others and the particular context of their plight. As Virginia Held writes, "caring, empathy, feeling with others, being sensitive to each other's feelings, all may be better guides to what morality requires in actual contexts than may abstract rules of reason, or rational calculation, or at least they may be necessary components of an adequate morality."[22] Stressing how to engage ethically across differences, Lorraine Code notes that there must be a "sensitively empathic listening committed to understanding 'others' worlds' (to borrow Sonia Kruks's phrase), to seeking out what one has to know in order to enter those worlds imaginatively, respectfully, with an intellectual-moral humility."[23] As Margaret Urban Walker characterizes the reconstructive project found in feminist ethics, across many distinctive projects is "a lattice of similar themes— personal relations, nurturance and caring, maternal experience, emotional responsiveness, attunement to particular persons and contexts, sensitivity to open-ended responsibilities."[24]

Taking into account the contextual nature of moral knowledge that these feminists describe, the sensitivity to others that they demand, and the emotional dimensions of this sensitivity, it becomes apparent that these feminist analyses are conceptualizing moral knowledge as akin to, or at least dependent upon, capacities of *perception*. We need to be able to perceive how things are with other people, becoming aware of the relevant moral details of the situation so that we will be able to respond appropriately. Feminists have been drawn to perception as a model for moral knowledge in its ability to incorporate both the cognitive and emotional aspects of moral knowledge and moral responsiveness that have been central to many feminist analyses.[25] Feminists are not alone in thinking of moral knowledge in this way, though Lawrence Blum credits the work of feminist ethicists as a major force in "keeping alive concerns with the emotional and the perceptual."[26]

For some feminist analyses, their emphasis on the perceptual amounts to a claim about the skills necessary to attain moral knowledge. Others go further, arguing that the feminist insights concerning the contextual and perceptual nature of morality suggest that the very idea of moral knowledge itself needs to be reworked. For example, Margaret Urban Walker is highly critical of the tradition of moral epistemology that views moral knowledge as a theoretical body of systematized universalist principles. Instead, she construes moral understanding as "a collection of perceptive, imaginative, appreciative, and expressive skills and capacities which put and keep us in unimpeded contact with the realities of ourselves and specific others."[27] For Walker, then, moral knowledge is fully practical rather than theoretical. It is a kind of "moral-practical intelligence."[28] There are, of course, close connections between what skills are necessary to attain moral knowledge and what kind of knowledge moral knowledge is. The questions are not isolatable: the form moral knowledge takes will in large part determine the appropriate methods of attaining it. However, what I want to note here is that even for those feminists who maintain a commitment to the role of abstract moral principles in morality (viewing a grasp of those abstract moral principles as being a form of moral knowledge), most still emphasize the need for moral agents to be able to perceive the contextual details of a situation to understand how a given moral principle applies, and they often argue that traditional moral theorists have not adequately emphasized the importance of such perceptions for moral knowledge. I am interested in the ramifications of this feminist emphasis on the epistemic importance of moral perception, without making any particular commitment to all moral knowledge as *thoroughly* practical.

Conceptualizing moral knowledge either as akin to perception or as heavily involving capacities of perception creates some tension with the idea of transmitting moral knowledge through testimony. Testimony involves purportedly transmitting knowledge by telling it to a hearer. This model fits when the knowledge in question is propositional. I can tell you *that* "it is raining outside," and the communicable content of my telling is a propositional claim.[29] Yet in moral cases, someone telling me how it is so in a given situation does not do the same work as my own perception of the rich moral dimensions of the situation. For those who understand moral knowledge as fully practical, ultimately there will be nothing to "tell," only things to "do" in response to moral situations. For those who maintain that there is a theoretical body of moral knowledge that can be expressed in propositional form, yet also emphasize the importance of perception in gaining moral knowledge, there may be significant limitations on the role of testimony in acquiring moral knowledge. Without the appropriate perceptual capacities, I will be unable to transfer the moral knowledge from one situation to another, making moral testimony potentially a poor substitute for the skills of moral perception that would allow me to read the morally salient features of highly variant situations. Perhaps more importantly, simply considering the particular situation at hand, it is questionable whether I would be able to grasp enough of the contextual details through the testimony to appreciate fully the moral dimensions of the situation and act appropriately.[30] In such a situation, we might question whether I can fully understand the moral dimensions of the situation, even if I accept someone's testimony on the matter.[31] If an important part of moral knowledge takes the form of a perceptual capacity, there may at most be a minor role for testimony within the moral realm.

Another element of the feminist conception of moral knowledge as crucially involving skills of perception can be found in feminist arguments that individuals have a responsibility to improve their capacities of moral perception. For example, Susan Sherwin argues that moral perception involves a skill that can be trained, and that "because an agent's capacity at moral perception is a necessary component of her ability to act in a morally responsible fashion, we each have a moral responsibility to develop our skills in this area."[32] Rebecca Kukla also emphasizes the importance of moral perception and notes that "overcoming moral blindness is itself a moral responsibility."[33] Claims such as these suggest that for these feminists, a practice of relying on the testimony of others who have sharper moral perception than oneself will be insufficient. Knowing by relying on others' testimony will either fail to yield the appropriate moral knowledge required for us to act well (thus perhaps allowing someone to know for me, but not allowing me to know through them), or it will at most serve as a short-term poor substitute for the development and exercise of one's own capacities of moral perception. According to these theorists, it is not acceptable to become aware of one's lack of acuity in moral perception and simply rely on others either to do that moral knowing for me or to accept their saying so as my way of knowing. Because feminists have focused on differently situated knowers and the insights they can provide, they have been particularly concerned with the possible abdication of responsibility for active knowing and inquiry that might come with a reliance on the testimony of one better positioned than oneself for the kind of knowledge in question. A good example is described by Sandra Harding. Writing of the problems a European American might encounter when simply adopting the insights of African American thinkers through their testimony, Harding notes:

> I cannot just repeat, robotlike, what African American thinkers say and never take responsibility for my own analyses of the world that I, a European American, can see through the lens of their insights. If I did so, I would be thought of as stupid, or as insidiously devaluing their thought and under-

mining the legitimacy of its analyses....I must learn how to see the world differently for myself in an active and creative way through the theoretical and political lenses that African American thinkers originally constructed to produce distinctive insights. A functioning antiracist—one who can pass "competency tests" as an antiracist—must be an actively thinking antiracist, not just a white robot "programmed" to repeat what blacks say.[34]

Here, Harding captures a serious ramification for the responsibilities of active inquiry if we are to place moral knowledge acquired through testimony on a par with other forms of moral knowing. This concern will need to be reconciled with any feminist insights concerning the value of moral testimony, and I return to it later.

THE FEMINIST CASE FOR MORAL KNOWING THROUGH TESTIMONY

Despite the apparent mismatch between feminist analyses that stress the importance of moral perception and the possible role of moral knowing through testimony, there are also indications within several feminist analyses that knowing through testimony may be a very important source of moral knowledge and our corresponding ability to act well. As Elizabeth Fricker notes, "learning from testimony is possible only in domains where it makes sense to think that one person can be better placed than another to make judgements."[35] Taking that to be the case in the moral domain, more than one feminist theorist has used the example of the inability of certain individuals to perceive the details of sexism to argue precisely for the importance of moral knowing through testimony.

For example, Cheshire Calhoun, in her important 1989 paper, "Responsibility and Reproach," distinguishes between "normal" moral contexts, where moral knowledge is the norm, and "abnormal" moral contexts, where moral ignorance is the norm.[36] Because moral knowledge is widespread in normal moral contexts, we can hold people accountable for failing to act on moral knowledge—they should have known better. But such is not the case in abnormal moral contexts, where we cannot rely on common knowledge for what to do. In abnormal contexts, we must rely on moral experts who have a better grasp of the relevant moral knowledge. Calhoun argues that a sexist society constitutes such an abnormal moral context, where moral ignorance concerning the appropriate treatment of women is the norm. She appeals to feminists as the experts who must offer guidance as to how to lead us to their appropriate treatment and out of the conditions of sexism.

Calhoun's suggestion that we rely on feminists to take on the role of moral *experts* concerning the treatment of women in a sexist society is not without its critics. Not only is the question of whether or not there is such a thing as a moral expert hotly debated within circles of moral theorists generally,[37] but other feminist moral theorists have questioned whether deferring to feminists as the experts is an appropriate model. Tracy Isaacs, for example, has questioned the supposition that feminists would all agree on what is appropriate treatment of women and suggests instead a model where dialogue rather than deference to designated experts leads us to a moral solution.[38]

Isaacs captures the worry that assigning an institutionalized role of moral expert may not be the most conducive to generating moral solutions, and this point is related to Harding's concerns regarding a practice of deferral to moral testimony. However, it must be noted that whatever one's view on an institutionalized role of moral expert, one can still acknowledge that in certain circumstances, moral expertise for a particular range of issues will not necessarily be equally shared by all.[39] Furthermore, there is reason to think that at least on some moral matters, experience might result in some persons having more expertise than others.[40] This could be through either more training or familiarity with the specifics at hand (Calhoun uses the example of biomedical ethics), or through a particular social situation that fosters certain sensibilities. For example, Laurence Thomas has argued that people who are "downwardly constituted" by oppression are owed a certain "moral deference" by the privileged with respect to some of their morally significant experiences and the emotional pain of those experiences that cannot be shared or adequately imagined by the privileged.[41]

Given feminist work on situated knowers, there is reason to think that the moral realm might be a particularly rich field for differentiated sensibilities based on social location.[42] Versions of the situated-knowledge thesis prominent in feminist epistemology were originally set out to emphasize how one's capacity for knowledge of social relations might be shaped by one's social location, and of course, understanding social relations is an important component of moral knowledge. Although critics of the situated-knowledge thesis have often questioned whether it applies in all domains of knowledge, it is generally understood to carry the most plausibility within the domain of knowledge of social relations.[43] In keeping with the earlier discussion of perception as a form of moral knowledge,

Rebecca Kukla argues that "there are plenty of morally relevant features of particulars that are perceptually available only to agents with the right kind of contingent capacities, where these capacities are rooted in their personal history and can be actualized only from certain positions and perspectives."[44] Kukla offers as an example the ways in which subcultures—the homosexual community, the orthodox Jewish community, the Korean Canadian community—develop semiotics that are accessible only to those already versed in them to express socially nuanced dimensions of their identities and situations.[45] An awareness of these socially nuanced dimensions is an important component of one's ability to treat such persons well, and not everyone will be in a position to have such an awareness. Kukla notes how "people from very sheltered backgrounds will often have a particularly deep insensitivity to the semiotics of groups who were taken by those around them as best kept invisible."[46] She offers the example of suburban white people in the United States, many of whom routinely feel threatened by urban black people. According to Kukla, such situations occur not because of the perception of threatening gestures where there are none, but rather "because [white suburban people] have had such little interaction with urban black people, the latter's gestures, speech, and behavior, differently nuanced from their own, will appear utterly foreign and uninterpretable."[47] They lack the appropriate sensitivity and perceptual capacity to properly interpret the behavior and hence cannot respond appropriately.

Assuming a reasonable case can be made that some may be better positioned than others to perceive some morally relevant features of our situations, we must still confront, from the potential hearer's perspective, whether or when it could be epistemically responsible to defer to such a knower. Should we avail ourselves of someone else's moral expertise—or more accurately, their superior acuity of moral perception—when ours is not up to the task? If the answer is yes, then this conclusion needs to be reconciled with the concerns of moral testimony and its implications for those responsibilities to improve one's own moral perception discussed in the previous section.

THE CHALLENGE OF MORAL TESTIMONY AND EPISTEMIC RESPONSIBILITY

Karen Jones's paper, "Second-Hand Moral Knowledge,"[48] examines a case that takes us to the crux of the matter in terms of allowing others' testimony to override one's own moral assessment of a situation. Jones sketches out the case of Peter, who is supportive of the principles of anti-sexism and antiracism, but not great at perceiving subtle instances of sexism and racism. Peter belongs to a cooperative household, with a practice of interviewing potential members of the household before their acceptance into the co-op. As part of this process, each household member has the authority to veto any particular applicant, though usually discussions suffice and no veto is necessary. Peter is well-meaning, and he has good relationships with the other household members. But he is puzzled by the perception of some of the women in the household of the subtle sexism and racism of some of the male applicants that Peter consistently fails to pick up on. He "could not grasp the reasons why the women were calling someone sexist, when he either could not see, or could not see as evidence, the considerations that the women thought supported viewing the would-be members as sexist."[49] In the end, Peter comes to believe that the decisions against some of these male applicants are arbitrary, and he decides that in good conscience, he should leave the cooperative household. Although the women in the household tell him to "just trust us, we know about this," Peter views such trusting an abdication of moral responsibility, and from his point of view, he sees the decisions as arbitrary and discriminatory.[50]

Jones argues that we must be quite cautious in accepting morally relevant testimony of others, suggesting that moral knowledge of the sort for which we might appeal to moral testimony must be difficult to come by (or else we'd be able to acquire it ourselves), requiring good character and the right kind of experiences from the testifier.[51] As a result, Jones argues that distrust is the appropriate default stance toward testifiers on the moral front.[52] However, she also argues that in Peter's case, this default stance is overridden and Peter should have deferred to the testimony of his housemates. Peter had an established relationship with his housemates, and with that came the knowledge of his housemates' characters and experiences that Jones demands for responsible deferral in moral matters. Importantly, Jones also argues that Peter had reason to "distrust his own distrust," given that his own track record on such matters demonstrated his tendency to call for fewer occasions requiring an antiracist or antisexist response than others.[53] Peter suffered a kind of moral blindness, and according to Jones, this is a case where he would do *better* attaining moral knowledge by relying on his housemates' testimony rather than trying to know the morally salient features of the situation on his own. I agree with Jones in her conclusion about Peter. However,

I think further discussion is necessary to understand exactly how Peter could exercise his epistemic responsibilities through a reliance on morally salient testimony.

Jones does not frame her arguments in terms of any insights specific to feminist theorists, though the case of Peter is of obvious interest to feminists, since it concerns the perception of subtle manifestations of sexism.[54] In the remainder of this paper, I consider Peter's case in light of my earlier discussion of specifically feminist analyses. To recap, having identified feminist analyses as conceptualizing an important form of moral knowledge as being akin to or at least heavily involving a perceptual capacity, I looked at two different directions that insight was taking feminists. On the one hand, the perceptual analyses indicate the moral importance of deeply contextual and practical knowledge that cannot be transmitted by testimony, leading some feminists to argue for the importance of individuals fulfilling their epistemic responsibilities by working to overcome whatever perceptual blindspots they have in the moral realm, and suggesting that knowing based on moral testimony is either unacceptable or at least second rate. On the other hand, the idea of situated knowing coupled with perceptual analyses suggests that in order to know well, knowers with blindspots *should* defer to those better situated than themselves in the case of morally relevant perceptions, accepting the testimony of well-positioned others. In both cases, of course, knowers must somehow become aware of their blindspots. While this is not easy, one can, of course, accumulate indirect evidence of one's blindspots, for example, by realizing that one is regularly "out of step" with others as in Peter's case with his poor track record at recognizing subtle cases of sexism and racism. But rather than focus on the issue of recognizing our blindspots, in what follows I hope to use a discussion of Peter's case that goes beyond Jones's analysis to reconcile these two different directions suggested by feminists: recommending working to overcome one's blindspots versus deferring to others in such moral situations. At the same time, my discussion will reveal some of the limitations of the standard literature on testimony.

The moral knowledge in question in Peter's case is the claim that particular applicants demonstrate sexism and racism. This is the basis upon which the housemates recommend not accepting particular applicants into the co-op. We are told that Peter already accepts the moral principles of antisexism and antiracism (that is, the moral wrong of sexism and racism), and Jones is clear that the fact that he already accepts these basic moral principles makes the case simpler (and less controversial). The difference between Peter's perception of the situation and that of his housemates concerns whether these moral principles apply to the case. We can formulate the knowledge claim of the housemates in propositional form: "applicant X is sexist and racist." By expressing the claim in propositional form, we make clear that it is the kind of claim that could be transmitted via testimony. However, it is worth noting that this propositional claim represents a judgment of the applicant's character and is not a simple observable fact. The housemates have come to conclude its truth on the basis of their interactions with the applicant in the interview and the morally salient features of those interactions. Their moral perception offers them evidence of the applicant's sexism and racism, whereas Peter fails to perceive any sexism or racism in the applicant's behavior. Because of the subtlety of the applicant's behavior, the housemates are unable to articulate their morally salient perceptions in a way that Peter could come to see them as reasons for their character judgment. Jones offers a sampling of the conversations between the housemates and Peter, describing their interactions with the applicant in question:

> HOUSEMATE: "Well, it wasn't that he didn't look at me and he didn't stare at my breasts, it was just a way of looking—a way of not quite being present as he answered me."
>
> PETER: "What way? I do not understand what way you mean."
>
> HOUSEMATE: "Well, it was just a feeling I got. A feeling that he didn't think me important."[55]

It is the perceptual nature of the morally relevant knowledge of the housemates that makes it difficult to articulate. What Peter lacks is a combination of the housemates' sensitivity to the subtle behavior directed at them, as well as the perception of that behavior as morally laden—that is, as sexist and racist. If Peter is going to access this knowledge and the conclusions his housemates draw from it, he needs to take it on trust by accepting their testimony. He is not in a position from which he can "check-up" on the reliability of his housemates' claims, or even their methods of generating these claims.

An important point to note is that the situation of Peter brings into focus the most serious challenge involved in knowing through moral testimony. It is not a question of whether the testimony of Peter's housemates can simply *add* to his wealth of moral knowledge. Rather, in order to grant the housemates' testimony the epistemic import Jones suggests it deserves, Peter has to allow it to override his own moral perception of the situation.[56] This is not a case of Peter's housemates reporting to him on an applicant interview for which he was not present. Peter takes part in the interviews, and yet he *fails* to see any sexism or racism in the behavior of the applicants. Somehow he must reconcile this with the conflicting testimony of his housemates. The very same argument that suggests that his roommates might be better positioned than him to perceive such subtle sexism implies that his own perceptual skills are not serving him well in this instance, and to know well he somehow must "give up" on his own perception. This could be seen as threatening his epistemic autonomy (and Peter does seem to see it this way), but I argue that it need not when we understand all that is involved in being a good moral inquirer.

Importantly, we must recognize that *regardless* of whether or not Peter defers, as soon as he is confronted with a difference in perception between himself and his housemates, there will be some remainder that needs explanation. If he defers, he must explain what to make of his own perception (that there is no sexism or racism evident in the applicant's behavior). But similarly, if he holds to his own perception and rejects that of his housemates, he is left in need of an explanation as to why his housemates saw things so differently from him. To be a good critical inquirer, Peter will need to grapple with these differences, accepting the fallibility of his epistemic capacities in the process.

Now we are in a position to consider a few of the more puzzling features of the Peter example, some of which Jones does not emphasize. Grappling with the differences in perception seems to be precisely what Peter does not do, and herein lies his weakness as a moral knower. Peter ultimately rejects his housemates' perception of the applicants, yet his reasoning as Jones outlines it—that it would be irresponsible to accept and act on a moral judgment based on another's word—seems to suggest that he did not feel it necessary to account for their different perceptions at all. Pure and simple, Peter thought knowing on his own was the only responsible way to gain moral knowledge. Peter's position is that to accept his housemates' position on the applicants, he would need to be *persuaded* by the reasons they offered. Faced with the housemates' incapacity to explain their subtle and highly contextualized perceptions in ways that can convince him, Peter concludes that his housemates' judgment must be a result of prejudice.[57] But this only pushes the need for an account of their differences further insofar as Peter would need to reconcile this judgment of his housemates' prejudice with what he knows about their character, the good relations he has enjoyed with them, the fact that they have accepted him within the co-op and have not shown prejudice toward him as a male and so on. Given his history with them, he has good reason to think that they would not exercise prejudice in their judgments of applicants. He is actually in almost an optimal situation for responsible deferral. Peter and his housemates are committed to certain common values that form the core of their co-op, and their practices for accepting new members into their community suggest that they essentially are engaged in a joint epistemic and moral project, trying to create an antisexist and antiracist community within the household. They hold lengthy discussions and clearly respect each other and each others' contributions, and as housemates they interact in a variety of ways, allowing them to know each other well. A high level of trust in each others' good characters and sincerity in approaching the issues has evolved through these practices. The context of his practices of engagement with his housemates makes Peter's deferral in this case more reasonable than his rejection of their claims, which would still leave in place a demand for an explanation of such sudden prejudice on the part of his housemates.[58] By contrast, explanations for Peter's inability to perceive the sexism and racism (explanations that are needed should he defer) are somewhat easier to come by; it is a plausible thesis that those who are positioned as the targets of sexism and racism experience it in such a way as to be able to perceive its subtle manifestations better than those who can observe it only indirectly, and as Jones suggests, Peter should have been aware of his fallibility through his poor track record on such issues.

Responsible knowing requires that one try to account for and reconcile all the sources of evidence, searching for the best explanation overall. In cases where we are engaged with others and hearing their testimonies, what needs accounting for will include beliefs about the characters and actions of others (such as, in this case, their propensity toward prejudice) as well as the content of their particular testimony, even when it conflicts with one's own perception of the situation. Recognizing that responsible knowing demands taking account of others' testimonies some way or other, we can see that deferral to someone else's testimony of their moral perception need not imply an abdication of epistemic responsibility at all. For responsible knowing, Peter needs to exercise his critical agency, but this can be done through his deferral, as he works to reconcile as best he can a wide variety of evidence. Understanding deferral as compatible with the exercise of critical agency enables us to reconcile his reliance on moral testimony with the feminist concerns I have outlined about moral perception being markedly different from knowledge available through testimony, and the corresponding responsibility for individuals to develop such capacities of moral perception.

Let us suppose that Peter does not leave the household, but rather he defers to his housemates' judgment. And let us suppose that he does so not just to give in for the sake of keeping the peace, but that he actually accepts their word regarding the subtle manifestations of sexism and racism in the applicants, and he chooses to remain in the co-op, where future conversations will ensue regarding more potential candidates as well as many other topics.

Jones takes us only as far as offering reasons that Peter could cite for his deferral (knowledge of his housemates' characters and a distrust of his own perceptual capacities, based on a poor track record). Yet I think that whether or not his deferral counts as epistemically responsible also depends upon the attitude Peter takes toward his deferral, with his attitude being a reflection of the kind of epistemic practice in which his deferral is embedded. If he just gives up on trying to understand how subtle sexism could occur and simply decides always to defer to his housemates on matters of sexism and racism without further consideration, he would be failing to engage fully in moral inquiry. I think this would be so *even if* he were to defer because he reasons that his housemates are better positioned than he is reliably to perceive sexism and racism in such cases. My point then is that these reasons on their own are not enough to make for responsible moral inquiry. If Peter were simply to defer regularly to his housemates on these matters and think no further about it, he would be like Sandra Harding's European American feminist I described earlier who, in accepting the testimonies of African American thinkers without learning to see the world differently herself, ends up "devaluing their thought and undermining the legitimacy of its analyses."[59] Such a practice would, I think, fail as responsible moral epistemic inquiry. One cannot accept that another has access to morally salient features of the world that one cannot perceive for oneself and fully engage as a responsible moral inquirer without also trying to further understand those morally salient features that currently seem blocked from one's perceptions.[60]

Here, then, I side with the likes of Sherwin and Kukla, who argue for a responsibility to try to increase one's capacity for moral perception. But importantly, rather than deferrals to testimony necessarily countering such a responsibility, the testimony of others can actually play an important role in developing one's moral perception. In Peter's case, I have argued that as a responsible inquirer, he needs to grapple with the differences between his perception of the situation and that of his housemates. By adopting a critical attitude toward his own perceptual capacities, and integrating his understandings of his own capacities and those of his housemates, Peter would be taking the first steps toward sharpening his skills of moral perception. He would not just be accepting his current (limited) skills of moral perception as reliable indicators of a morally infused world. Additionally, the testimony of others differently situated from him may be crucially important in describing for Peter what the moral experience of these situations is like for those who are the targets of sexism and racism. By listening to his housemates and engaging with them, he will likely be able to improve his grasp of the types of situations and the clues his housemates notice which manifest subtle sexism and racism. Of course, this will not be the only way Peter can learn to improve his moral perception. For example, Peter could also read about the experiences of those who are the targets of sexism and racism. But engaging with those in his community who experience oppression and listening to their testimonies will likely form a very important way of sharpening his moral perception. Far from testimony playing only a limited role in moral knowledge because of the importance of perception, the moral testimony of those differently positioned from oneself can play a very important role in moral knowing, precisely because of the need to develop one's moral perception and the difficulties and limitations of doing so on one's own. Although within the household community there may be occasions when Peter may do just as well morally by relying on his housemates' testimony, an improvement in his individual moral perception will not only allow him to better apply his moral understandings to circumstances outside the context of the household, it will also simply enhance his moral understanding overall.

Importantly, then, the source of the feminist concerns that we must strive to improve our skills of moral perception lies not in any sense that we must acquire knowledge on our own, but rather in a recognition of our responsibilities as moral inquirers. As individual agents, part of our moral task involves *investigating* the moral dimensions of our lives, not just acting on our current moral understandings.[61] If the history of feminism and feminist theory have taught us anything, it is that our understandings of oppression and our understandings of the ensuing moral demands on us change. There is cause for a healthy fallibilism with respect to our moral knowledge. For example, few feminists today would argue that patriarchy stands apart from relations of race and class oppression, and the shift toward a recognition of multiply dimensioned social locations has had ramifications for how we understand and engage in antisexism and antiracism. Moral inquiry must be an ongoing enterprise.

What feminists do not want is for Peter to get off the hook by becoming a lazy moral knower and regularly deferring to others who may or may not be better positioned than him, without laboring to try to sort out what is morally appropriate in certain situations—that is, without exercising his responsibilities as a moral inquirer. But as the household is described, Peter is engaged in discussions with his housemates, and if he chooses to remain in the co-op, such discussions and active engagements are likely to continue. A deferral to his housemates' testimony is not incompatible with his continued engagement in moral inquiry with his housemates, and such engagement will likely also help develop his individual moral perception.

To see how deferral to moral testimony can be epistemically responsible, then, we need to integrate it with an understanding of many of the other forms of epistemic interdependence that I referred to at the start of this paper. Peter is in a favorable position for responsible deferral in part because he shares certain moral and epistemic goals with his housemates, and he is critically engaged with his housemates in moral inquiry. To make sense of the epistemic importance of moral testimony, we must see it as embedded within various practices that demonstrate our interdependence on each other for epistemic pursuits, including moral inquiry. What we must examine is not just the *instances* of testimonial deferral, but rather the *practices* in which Peter is engaged and how those instances fit into the practices. I have argued that being engaged in relations of trust with others differently situated from oneself sets up a context where moral knowing through testimony can be both resourceful and responsible, when coupled with the exercise of critical agency directed at reconciling different perceptions of the situation. Peter is in just such a situation.

Of course, the example of Peter and his housemates does not represent all, or even the majority, of our contexts of moral inquiry. Many times we do not know people well enough to trust their characters or their sincerity with respect to moral concerns. Particularly in contexts of oppression, building relations of trust and contexts of positive moral engagement and sincere moral inquiry between those differently positioned may well be extremely difficult. But the point of Peter's case is to demonstrate that when embedded in the context of certain practices, deferral to moral testimony can be an important form of responsible moral inquiry, and engagement with others' moral testimony can be important for the development of one's skills of moral perception. The case of Peter illustrates that individuals need to engage in moral inquiry, but this is not a task that they must either undertake or succeed in on their own. It also suggests that the creation of contexts such as Peter's household, where differently situated persons can come to develop relations of trust, might be an important avenue for the development of sound moral inquiry as well as the sharpening of the moral perception of individuals less well situated than others.

IMPLICATIONS FOR ANALYSES OF TESTIMONY

I have focused my attention on reconciling two different directions of thought within specifically feminist analyses of moral knowledge. But the solution proposed—that we assess instances of deference to moral testimony within the context of particular practices of moral inquiry that demonstrate many dimensions of our epistemic interdependence—can also help identify the limitations of existing nonfeminist analyses of testimony.

As I noted earlier, current nonfeminist testimony literature has focused on many technical issues concerning how testimony might satisfy the conditions of knowledge and has had little to say specifically about testimony in the moral realm. The dominance of the debate between the reductionists and the non-reductionists has had a significant impact on the shape of the literature, with the focus being to determine how instances of testimony function differently (or similarly) from other sources of knowing. The goal is to resolve the one-way relation of epistemic dependence of the hearer on the speaker, either by granting testimony basic status as a meritorious source of knowledge different from other sources of knowledge (the non-reductionists) or by locating its epistemic merit in other sources of knowledge (the reductionists). This focus on comparing and contrasting testimony with other accepted sources of knowledge has worked against any recognition of how testimony might actually work in *conjunction* with other sources of knowledge within certain epistemic practices (without necessarily being *reduced* to these other sources as reductionists might have it). The reductionist/ non-reductionist debate structures discussion in such a way as to isolate particular instances of testimony to analyze, abstracting them from the multiple ways in which we interact with others in our efforts to know well. In an effort to identify and mark off cases of testimony from other forms of knowing, there has also been an emphasis on the linguistic aspect of testimony—that testimony is a telling. Yet absent from the analysis is a recognition that in any case of testimony, there is much more going on than mere telling: there is a telling within the context of a particular relationship of *inter*action. This relationship of interaction has often been left out of standard testimony accounts, as has an analysis of how testimony functions as an epistemic tool within practices of inquiry. In the case of Peter, we must remember that he engages with his housemates on more than just the issue of interviews for potential co-op members. For example, his friendship with his housemates suggests that they have a good rapport with him, that they respect him, and that presumably he has earned their respect through their interactions together. Their friendship with him and the relations of trust that have developed give him reason to think that they are not likely to veto just any male potential housemate. Peter cannot easily explain the vetoes they employ as a result of mere "man-hating." After all, in their acceptance of Peter, they demonstrate that they take seriously the possibility that a male can be antisexist. This makes a difference to how Peter is able to understand and assess their testimony. Indeed, as I have argued, to reject their testimony would leave Peter with a puzzle, unable to explain why their perception of the potential housemates was so different from his own.

My point is not to criticize the standard testimony literature for what it has achieved in trying to clarify what constitutes instances of testimony and analyze the difficulties peculiar to it compared with other sources of knowledge. But when we reframe the question of knowing through testimony in terms of epistemically responsible inquiry, the limitations of these analyses begin to show. Particularly for areas of knowledge such as the moral realm, where each of us has a responsibility to engage in inquiry rather than rely on others to do our knowing for us, the challenges of reconciling responsible deferrals to testimony with our critical epistemic agency loom large. Feminist analyses face these challenges head-on by working with a view of situated knowing such that there will be cases where deferral might mean overriding one's own assessment of the situation. I have argued that deferrals to testimony and critical agency can be reconciled by understanding instances of testimony as embedded in practices of engagement that carry with them a variety of features to which we can appeal.

The grounds for trust in another's testimony can be quite rich, stemming from a history of engagement with others. Additionally, by looking at our practices, it becomes apparent that such deferrals can form part of one's critical attempts both to know and develop one's capacities of moral perception across social locations.

Feminist analyses have contributed much in the way of coming to understand the challenges and subtleties of moral knowledge and our responsibilities to acquire such knowledge. While they offer some reasons to think that moral knowledge is particularly difficult to access by way of testimony, understanding moral knowing through testimony as one piece in our complex practices of social and moral interaction shows it to be much less troublesome than when viewed as an isolated activity of one individual telling another. When understood as embedded in such practices, feminists are able to reconcile their insights of the value of moral testimony given situated knowing and the epistemic responsibility of individuals to work toward improving their moral perception. Although my focus in this paper has been on feminist work, there is every reason to think that this line of reasoning will prove productive for a broader range of testimony theorists than just feminists, particularly in the moral realm.

Notes

1. Annette Baier, *Postures of the Mind: Essays on Mind and Morals* (Minneapolis: University of Minnesota Press, 1985), Lorraine Code, *What Can She Know? Feminist Theory and Construction of Knowledge* (Ithaca, N.Y.: Cornell University Press, 1991).
2. Helen E. Longino, *Science as Social Knowledge: Values and Objectivity in Scientific Inquiry* (Princeton, N.J.: Princeton University Press, 1990); Lynn Hankinson Nelson, *Who Knows: From Quine to a Feminist Empiricism* (Philadelphia: Temple University Press, 1990).
3. Longino, *Science as Social Knowledge.*
4. Annette Baier, *Moral Prejudices: Essays on Ethics* (Cambridge, Mass.: Harvard University Press, 1994); Code, *What Can She Know?*; Naomi Scheman, "Epistemology Resuscitated," in *Engendering Rationalities,* ed. Nancy Tuana and Sandra Morgen (Albany: State University of New York Press, 2001).
5. Lorraine Code, *Ecological Thinking: The Politics of Epistemic Location* (Oxford: Oxford University Press, 2006), p. 173.
6. Code, *What Can She Know?* and *Ecological Thinking*; Sandra Harding, *Whose Science? Whose Knowledge? Thinking from Women's Lives* (Ithaca, N.Y.: Cornell University Press, 1991), Donna Haraway, *Simians, Cyborgs, and Women: The Reinvention of Nature* (New York: Routledge, 1991).

7. Lorraine Code, *Rhetorical Spaces: Essays on Gendered Locations* (New York: Routledge, 1995), Linda Alcoff, "On Judging Epistemic Credibility: Is Social Identity Relevant?" in *Engendering Rationalities*, ed. Nancy Tuana and Sandra Morgen (Albany: State University of New York Press, 2001).

8. According to Fricker, credibility deficits that result due to prejudice constitute cases of testimonial injustice, where one is "wronged specifically in [one's] capacity as a knower." Miranda Fricker, *Epistemic Injustice: Power and the Ethics of Knowing* (Oxford: Oxford University Press, 2007), 20. Credibility excesses that can accrue in the socially privileged are also important to analyze (since they too affect one's capacity to know), though Fricker argues that these are not quite parallel to credibility deficits and do not usually constitute cases of testimonial injustice as she sets out the term.

9. Significant in the revival of attention to testimony is C. A. J. Coady, *Testimony: A Philosophical Study* (Oxford: Clarendon Press, 1992).

10. Frederick F. Schmitt, "Socializing Epistemology: An Introduction," in *Socializing Epistemology: The Social Dimensions of Knowledge*, ed. Frederick F. Schmitt (Lanham, Md.: Rowman and Littlefield, 1994), Philip Kitcher, "Contrasting Conceptions of Social Epistemology," in *Socializing Epistemology: The Social Dimensions of Knowledge*, ed. Frederick F. Schmitt (Lanham, Md.: Rowman and Littlefield, 1994).

11. Code, *Rhetorical Spaces*, 66.

12. For examples of recent nonfeminist work on testimony see Coady, *Testimony: A Philosophical Study*.

13. For a discussion of the worry of epistemological chasms in feminist standpoint theory see Sylvia Walby, "Against Epistemological Chasms: The Science Question in Feminism Revisited," *Signs: Journal of Women in Culture and Society* 26, no. 2 (2001).

14. See both Code's early pre-feminist work, *Epistemic Responsibility* (Hanover, N.H.: University Press of New England, 1987) and her later feminist work, especially *What Can She Know? Feminist Theory and Construction of Knowledge*.

15. Karen Jones, "Second-Hand Moral Knowledge," *The Journal of Philosophy* 96, no. 2 (1999): 57.

16. Of course, other dimensions of our lives create obligations to know certain things. When I travel in the backcountry with others and we rely on each other, it may be reasonable for my colleagues to expect me to learn some first aid, though a medical degree is too much to demand. Similarly, many would argue that responsible parenthood brings some responsibilities to learn about basic child health.

17. Elizabeth Fricker, "Testimony and Epistemic Autonomy," in *The Epistemology of Testimony*, ed. Jennifer Lackey and Ernest Sosa (Oxford: Clarendon Press, 2006), 238.

18. Michelle M. Moody-Adams, "Culture, Responsibility, and Affected Ignorance," *Ethics* 104, no. 2 (1994): 293.

19. Ibid., 296.

20. See, for example, two projects edited by Shannon Sullivan and Nancy Tuana: their 2006 special issue of *Hypatia* dedicated to Feminist Epistemologies of Ignorance, *Hypatia* 21, no. 3 (2006), and their edited volume on race and epistemologies of ignorance, Shannon Sullivan and Nancy Tuana, eds., *Race and Epistemologies of Ignorance* (Albany: State University of New York Press, 2007). In their introduction to the *Hypatia* special issue they explain that "feminist epistemologies of ignorance were born out of the realization that we cannot fully understand the complex practices of knowledge production and the variety of features that account for why something is known, without also understanding the practices that account for *not* knowing." Nancy Tuana and Shannon Sullivan, "Introduction: Feminist Epistemologies of Ignorance," *Hypatia* 21, no. 3 (2006): 1.

21. Jones, "Second-Hand Moral Knowledge." As I discuss more below, Jones argues *for* cases of our reliance on testimony for moral knowledge yet she also refers to such reliance as "borrowing moral knowledge."

22. Virginia Held, "Feminist Transformations of Moral Theory," *Philosophy and Phenomenological Research* 50, supplement (1990): 332.

23. Code, *Ecological Thinking.* Code's use of Kruks comes from Sonia Kruks, *Retrieving Experience: Subjectivity and Recognition in Feminist Politics* (Ithaca, N.Y.: Cornell University Press, 2001).

24. Margaret Urban Walker, *Moral Contexts* (Lanham, Md.: Rowman and Littlefield, 2003).

25. Alison M. Jaggar, "Love and Knowledge: Emotion in Feminist Epistemology," *Inquiry* 32 (1989), Walker, *Moral Contexts.*

26. Lawrence Blum, *Moral Perception and Particularity* (Cambridge: Cambridge University Press, 1994), 5.

27. Walker, *Moral Contexts*, 72.

28. Ibid., 79. For a more thorough discussion of Walker's alternative moral epistemology, see Margaret Urban Walker, *Moral Understandings: A Feminist Study in Ethics* (Lanham, Md.: Rowman and Littlefield, 1998).

29. Jennifer Lackey specifies that testimony must convey information in part in virtue of communicable content. She contrasts this with the example of singing "La, la, la" in a soprano voice, which conveys the information that I have a soprano voice purely in terms of perceptual content. Jennifer Lackey, "Introduction," in *The Epistemology of Testimony*, ed. Jennifer Lackey (Oxford: Clarendon Press, 2006), 3.

30. There are, of course, others besides feminists who have argued for the need for certain sensibilities or moral perceptual capacities in order to grasp the complexities of moral situations and the appropriate response, with much of this discussion taking place within virtue ethics. For example, Annette Baier claims Hume as "the women's moral theorist" noting that Hume's ethics focuses on developing virtuous character traits and reflective sentiment. Annette C. Baier, "Hume, the Women's Moral Theorist?" in *Women and Moral Theory*, ed. Eva Feder Kittay and Diana T. Meyers (Totowa, N.J.:

Rowman and Littlefield, 1987). A more contemporary example of the focus on virtue can be found in John McDowell, who articulates the possession of a virtue in terms of "a reliable sensitivity to a certain sort of requirement which situations impose on behaviour.... The sensitivity is, we might say, a sort of perceptual capacity." John McDowell, "Virtue and Reason," *Monist* 62, no. 3 (1979): 331–32.

31. Philip Nickel argues that for a person's actions to be morally good, they must understand the relevant moral reasons, and they may fail to meet this requirement in the case of reliance on moral testimony. Philip Nickel, "Moral Testimony and Its Authority," *Ethical Theory and Moral Practice* 4 (2001).

32. Susan Sherwin, "Moral Perception and Global Visions," *Bioethics* 15, no. 3 (2001): 177–78.

33. Rebecca Kukla, "Attention and Blindness: Objectivity and Contingency in Moral Perception," in *Feminist Moral Philosophy*, ed. Samantha Brennan (Calgary: University of Calgary Press, 2002), 339.

34. Harding, *Whose Science? Whose Knowledge*, 290–91.

35. Fricker, "Testimony and Epistemic Autonomy," 297.

36. Cheshire Calhoun, "Responsibility and Reproach," *Ethics* 99 (1989).

37. While there is debate and concern about how to deal with scientific experts, almost no one questions the plausibility of there actually being such a thing as a scientific expert (that is, an expert in a particular field of science—someone who knows more and understands more deeply a particular field of physics, or psychology, or chemistry). Yet philosophers have often questioned whether or not there is such a thing as a *moral* expert. We are at least a good deal less comfortable with the idea of a moral expert than with that of a scientific expert. For discussions on the possibility of a moral expert, see Arthur Caplan, "Moral Experts and Moral Expertise: Does Either Exist?" in *If I Were a Rich Man Could I Buy a Pancreas?* ed. Arthur Caplan (Bloomington: Indiana University Press, 1992), Peter Singer, "Moral Experts," in *The Philosophy of Experts*, ed. Evan Selinger and Robert P. Crease (New York: Columbia University Press, 2006).

38. Tracy Isaacs, "Cultural Context and Moral Responsibility," *Ethics* 107, no. 4 (1997).

39. Caplan, "Moral Experts and Moral Expertise."

40. Fricker, "Testimony and Epistemic Autonomy," 238. Fricker finds the idea of expertise in moral matters not all that controversial, calling it "an everyday and apparently sensible" idea (239).

41. Laurence Thomas, "Moral Deference," *The Philosophical Forum* 24, no. 1–3 (1992). Thomas does not express his argument explicitly in terms of moral testimony and knowledge since his focus is on the appropriate moral *attitude* to adopt towards those who have suffered injustice. But the moral deference he describes involves deference to a kind of moral testimony— testimony of the moral and emotional pain of oppression that goes beyond

a description of the events and cannot be imagined by those who are not similarly situated.

42. Of course, claiming social situation as relevant to some morally salient knowledge does not imply that there is no moral knowledge accessible to all, even with respect to understanding oppression. Anita Superson, for example, has argued that everyone, regardless of social position, has access to morally relevant "facts about humanity" such as that all persons possess dignity and are deserving of respect. Anita Superson, "Privilege, Immorality, and Responsibility for Attending to the 'Facts About Humanity,'" *Journal of Social Philosophy* 35, no. 1 (2004).

43. Heidi Grasswick. "Feminist Social Epistemology." In *The Stanford Encyclopedia of Philosophy*, ed Edward N. Zalta, Fall 2008 edition, http://plato.stanford.edu/archives/fall2008/entries/feminist-social-epistemology/. The issue of which areas of knowledge are affected by social location comes out most prominently in discussions of standpoint theorists and the epistemic advantage they claim for certain social locations. Alison Wylie has argued that the question of which areas of knowledge a particular standpoint might offer an epistemic advantage to is a contingent matter. Alison Wylie, "Why Standpoint Matters," in *Science and Other Cultures: Issues in Philosophies of Science and Technology*, ed. Robert Figueroa and Sandra Harding (New York: Routledge, 2003).

44. Kukla, "Attention and Blindness," 323.

45. Ibid., 323–24.

46. Ibid., 325.

47. Ibid., 325.

48. Jones, "Second-Hand Moral Knowledge."

49. Ibid.

50. Ibid., 60.

51. Ibid. Jones also puts forth a somewhat weaker argument, suggesting that an initial attitude of distrust might be appropriate in the moral realm because "the best way to convince others to go along with your interests is to convince them that morality requires them to do so" (72).

52. Across domains, Jones argues that there is no answer as to the appropriate stance to be taken toward testimony in general, since climate, domain, consequences, and metastances of trust are all relevant variables in ascertaining appropriate trust in testimony.

53. Jones, "Second-Hand Moral Knowledge," 74.

54. In fact, one of the few times Jones mentions feminist theories is in attempt to distance herself from them. While acknowledging that political engagement in liberation movements can lead to greater insight and understanding, she is quick to point out that this does not commit her to standpoint theory or any kind of theory of epistemic privilege.

55. Jones, "Second-Hand Moral Knowledge," 60.

56. Elizabeth Fricker contrasts such cases of "strong deferential acceptance," where another's testimony is allowed to override one's belief on the matter,

with "weak deferential acceptance," where one does not have a firm pre-existing belief on the matter. Fricker, "Testimony and Epistemic Autonomy," 233.

57. Jones, "Second-Hand Moral Knowledge," 60.

58. Additionally, though Jones only goes so far as analyzing Peter's particular decision not to defer, we should also note some further consequences. By deciding to leave the household because he cannot identify with its decisions, Peter is also setting himself up for future epistemic losses by removing himself from the joint epistemic and moral project of the co-op. By disengaging from his housemates, he will not benefit from continued interaction, discussion, and insights from his housemates in his epistemic pursuits.

59. Harding, *Whose Science? Whose Knowledge*, 290.

60. An additional argument can also be made here concerning fallibility. If deferral to others is justified in part due to a recognition of one's own fallibility as an epistemic agent, there will be ramifications for the status of others' testimony as well. Such fallibility in the moral realm will hold for all agents, not just oneself. A practice of regular deferral to others in the moral realm without critical consideration of their testimony or any attempt to understand their position would fail in acknowledging the fallibility of such agents.

61. We can also phrase this in terms of a distinction Helen Longino makes between knowledge producers and knowers (those who can know after the fact, but are not involved in the production of knowledge). Helen E. Longino, *The Fate of Knowledge* (Princeton, N.J.: Princeton University Press, 2002). In the moral realm, everyone has responsibilities to be knowledge producers, not just knowers.

References

Alcoff, Linda. "On Judging Epistemic Credibility: Is Social Identity Relevant?" In *Engendering Rationalities*, edited by Nancy Tuana and Sandra Morgen, 53–80. Albany: State University of New York Press, 2001.

Baier, Annette. *Moral Prejudices: Essays on Ethics*. Cambridge, Mass.: Harvard University Press, 1994.

———. *Postures of the Mind: Essays on Mind and Morals*. Minneapolis: University of Minnesota Press, 1985.

———. "Hume, the Women's Moral Theorist?" In *Women and Moral Theory*, edited by Eva Feder Kittay and Diana T. Meyers, 37–55. Totowa, N.J.: Rowman and Littlefield, 1987.

Blum, Lawrence. *Moral Perception and Particularity*. Cambridge: Cambridge University Press, 1994.

Calhoun, Cheshire. "Responsibility and Reproach." *Ethics* 99 (1989): 389–406.

Caplan, Arthur. "Moral Experts and Moral Expertise: Does Either Exist?" In *If I Were a Rich Man Could I Buy a Pancreas?* edited by Arthur Caplan, 18–39. Bloomington: Indiana University Press, 1992.

Coady, C. A. J. *Testimony: A Philosophical Study*. Oxford: Clarendon Press, 1992.

Code, Lorraine. *Ecological Thinking: The Politics of Epistemic Location*. Oxford: Oxford University Press, 2006.

———. *Rhetorical Spaces: Essays on Gendered Locations*. New York: Routledge, 1995.

———. *What Can She Know? Feminist Theory and Construction of Knowledge*. Ithaca, N.Y.: Cornell University Press, 1991.

———. *Epistemic Responsibility*. Hanover, N.H.: University Press of New England, 1987.

Fricker, Elizabeth. "Testimony and Epistemic Autonomy." In *The Epistemology of Testimony*, edited by Jennifer Lackey and Ernest Sosa, 225–50. Oxford: Clarendon Press, 2006.

Fricker, Miranda. *Epistemic Injustice: Power and the Ethics of Knowing*. Oxford: Oxford University Press, 2007.

Grasswick, Heidi. "Feminist Social Epistemology." In *The Stanford Encyclopedia of Philosophy*, edited by Edward N. Zalta. Fall 2008 edition. http://plato.stanford.edu/archives/fall2008/entries/feminist-social-epistemology/.

Haraway, Donna. *Simians, Cyborgs, and Women: The Reinvention of Nature*. New York: Routledge, 1991.

Harding, Sandra. *Whose Science? Whose Knowledge? Thinking from Women's Lives*. Ithaca, N.Y.: Cornell University Press, 1991.

Held, Virginia. "Feminist Transformations of Moral Theory." *Philosophy and Phenomenological Research* 50, supplement (1990): 321–44.

Isaacs, Tracy. "Cultural Context and Moral Responsibility." *Ethics* 107, no. 4 (1997): 670–684.

Jaggar, Alison M. "Love and Knowledge: Emotion in Feminist Epistemology." *Inquiry* 32 (1989): 151–76.

Jones, Karen. "Second-Hand Moral Knowledge." *Journal of Philosophy* 96, no. 2 (1999): 55–78.

Kitcher, Philip. "Contrasting Conceptions of Social Epistemology." In *Socializing Epistemology: The Social Dimensions of Knowledge*, edited by Frederick F. Schmitt, 111–34. Lanham, Md.: Rowman and Littlefield, 1994.

Kruks, Sonia. *Retrieving Experience: Subjectivity and Recognition in Feminist Politics*. Ithaca, N.Y.: Cornell University Press, 2001.

Kukla, Rebecca. "Attention and Blindness: Objectivity and Contingency in Moral Perception." In *Feminist Moral Philosophy*, edited by Samantha Brennan, 319–46. Calgary: University of Calgary Press, 2002.

Lackey, Jennifer. "Introduction." In *The Epistemology of Testimony*, edited by Jennifer Lackey, 1–21. Oxford: Clarendon Press, 2006.

Longino, Helen E. *Science as Social Knowledge: Values and Objectivity in Scientific Inquiry*. Princeton, N.J.: Princeton University Press, 1990.

———. *The Fate of Knowledge*. Princeton, N.J.: Princeton University Press, 2002.

McDowell, John. "Virtue and Reason." *Monist* 62, no. 3 (1979): 331–50.

Moody-Adams, Michelle M. "Culture, Responsibility, and Affected Ignorance." *Ethics* 104, no. 2 (1994): 291–309.

Nelson, Lynn Hankinson. *Who Knows: From Quine to a Feminist Empiricism.* Philadelphia: Temple University Press, 1990.

Nickel, Philip. "Moral Testimony and Its Authority." *Ethical Theory and Moral Practice* 4 (2001): 253–66.

Scheman, Naomi. "Epistemology Resuscitated." In *Engendering Rationalities,* edited by Nancy Tuana and Sandra Morgen, 23–52. Albany: State University of New York Press, 2001.

Schmitt, Frederick F. "Socializing Epistemology: An Introduction." In *Socializing Epistemology: The Social Dimensions of Knowledge,* edited by Frederick F. Schmitt, 1–27. Lanham, Md.: Rowman and Littlefield, 1994.

Sherwin, Susan. "Moral Perception and Global Visions." *Bioethics* 15, no. 3 (2001): 175–88.

Singer, Peter. "Moral Experts." In *The Philosophy of Experts,* edited by Evan Selinger and Robert P. Crease, 187–89. New York: Columbia University Press, 2006.

Sullivan, Shannon, and Nancy Tuana, eds. *Race and Epistemologies of Ignorance.* Albany: State University of New York Press, 2007.

Superson, Anita. "Privilege, Immorality, and Responsibility for Attending to the 'Facts About Humanity.'" *Journal of Social Philosophy* 35, no. 1 (2004): 34–55.

Thomas, Laurence. "Moral Deference." *Philosophical Forum* 24, no. 1–3 (1992): 233–50.

Tuana, Nancy, and Shannon Sullivan. "Introduction: Feminist Epistemologies of Ignorance." *Hypatia* 21, no. 3 (2006): 1–3.

Walby, Sylvia. "Against Epistemological Chasms: The Science Question in Feminism Revisited." *Signs: Journal of Women in Culture and Society* 26, no. 2 (2001): 485–509.

Walker, Margaret Urban. *Moral Contexts.* Lanham, Md.: Rowman and Littlefield, 2003.

———. *Moral Understandings: A Feminist Study in Ethics.* Lanham, Md.: Rowman and Littlefield, 1998.

Wylie, Alison. "Why Standpoint Matters." In *Science and Other Cultures: Issues in Philosophies of Science and Technology,* edited by Robert Figueroa and Sandra Harding, 26–48. New York: Routledge, 2003.

13

PHYLLIS ROONEY
Oakland University

WHAT IS DISTINCTIVE ABOUT FEMINIST

EPISTEMOLOGY AT 25?

1. TROUBLING THE QUESTION

What is distinctive about feminist epistemology, given that many of the characterizations of it (certainly many by non-feminists) have been misleading, if not false? Among the most persistent of these is the view that feminist epistemology is the epistemology of "women's ways of knowing." The idea of "women's/feminine ways of knowing" has indeed surfaced in feminist epistemology, but the primary focus has been on how problematic the idea is. It involves generalizations about women (across different races, classes, and cultures) that have been the focus of significant critical scrutiny in the past three decades of feminist theorizing. In addition, the idea of gender-marked ways of knowing is sustained by the persistence of gender stereotypes as much as it is informed by specific feminist analyses of particular processes of reasoning and knowing.[1]

Or, taking my question in another direction, what is distinctive about feminist epistemology, given that it shares many of the same goals, topics, and claims found in mainstream epistemology? (For now I use the term "mainstream" to refer to non-feminist epistemology—more on this term later.) At the outset, both feminist and mainstream epistemologists are committed to the value of knowledge, and both seek to theorize its nature and promote its acquisition. Both examine a range of epistemic concepts related to knowledge, including evidence, justification, reason, and objectivity. The central epistemological contention that knowledge claims ought to be well-justified by good evidence and reasoning is as significant in feminist epistemology as it is in mainstream epistemology. In fact, it was feminists' insistence on this very point when it came to knowledge about women (in the biological and social sciences especially) that provided an important starting point in the development of feminist epistemology and feminist philosophy of science in the 1980s. By then, as a result of the "second wave" feminist movement of the 1960s and 1970s, women had begun to enter traditionally male-dominated academic disciplines in greater numbers. In the sciences, in particular, feminists drew attention to the fact that scientific claims about women's different (often "inferior") biological, psychological, and behavioral nature were rarely based on careful empirical studies of women; instead, such claims drew significant inspiration from sexist cultural assumptions. As a result, feminist epistemologists and philosophers of science argued that philosophical analyses of evidence, objectivity, and knowledge need to pay closer attention (than mainstream analyses typically had) to the ways in which social and cultural assumptions and values work their way into knowledge communities, projects, claims, and theories.[2]

Yet this philosophical focus on the social conditions and institutions of knowledge production is not exclusive to feminist work. Those who work in mainstream *social epistemology* (by now a reasonably well-established area or approach in epistemology) share similar interests in examining the ways in which social practices and communities influence the development of knowledge.[3] As a result, many characterize feminist epistemology as a form of social epistemology. For example, Elizabeth Anderson notes that, since feminist epistemology pays particular attention to the social location of knowers and how that affects what they know, it "can thus be seen as a branch of social epistemology." Similarly, Heidi Grasswick thinks that "by far the majority of work in feminist epistemology is best understood as a form of social epistemology."[4] Assessing feminist epistemology as a form or type of social epistemology can, however, be taken to mean that it is not especially distinctive, even while we grant that feminist epistemologists pay significantly more attention than mainstream social epistemologists do to the epistemic effects of social locations marked by power or status differentials, such as those linked to gender, race, or class.

Not all feminist epistemological projects are readily assessed as forms of social epistemology, however, and some theorists stress the significance of epistemological individualism for feminist purposes.[5] In addition, some have argued for strong connections between feminist epistemology and other approaches or directions in mainstream epistemology, including, for example, *pragmatist epistemology*. Pragmatists challenge the traditional separation between philosophical theorizing and practical, social, and political engagement in the world—as many feminist philosophers do. More particularly, pragmatist epistemological developments promote understandings of knowers as engaged inquiring actors in the world. In drawing connections between practices of inquiry and broader social and political practices and concerns, pragmatists support the incorporation of political awareness into epistemological reflections, in a way that is quite consonant with many feminist projects.[6] In sum, while it is important to stress connections between feminist and mainstream projects or directions in epistemology, we need to be wary about attempts to identify feminist epistemology too readily with any one such project or direction.

While it is difficult to characterize feminist epistemology as a whole in terms of a single distinctive topic, method, or approach in epistemology, specific topics or concerns can prove to be helpful entry points into feminist epistemology, particularly when they reflect historical starting points for feminist reflections in epistemology. As we saw, feminist examinations of sexist sciences provide one such entry point. (I will note others below.) Yet starting points by themselves give little indication of the range of developments and views resulting from them, and this points to more general problems with attempts to identify feminist epistemology by picking out particular topics or projects that supposedly all feminist epistemologists engage with or by focusing on a specific claim or theory about knowledge (justification, objectivity) to which all or most feminist epistemologists subscribe. Such summary characterizations fail to capture the broad range of topics, questions, methods, and debates that have comprised the field as it has developed over the past 25 years. In their pursuit of many different projects, feminist epistemologists are no different from their mainstream counterparts. In addition, as with mainstream developments, feminist discussions and debates about a particular topic (objectivity, for example) are advanced by *differences* in perspectives or claims as much as they are advanced by notable agreement. Consequently, the question, "What is the feminist position on objectivity?" (the type of question I have encountered more than once) is likely to be as misguided as the corresponding question about a "mainstream position on objectivity" is.

There is an additional reason why we need to be especially wary of attempts to characterize feminist epistemology too neatly, and this reason provides an important clue to what I will argue *is distinctive* about feminist epistemology at 25.

2. SHIFTING THE QUESTION: GOING META

The additional reason I want to examine is this: neat characterizations of feminist epistemology, along with hasty generalizations about feminist epistemologists, are precisely what those not sympathetic to this work espouse in order to circumscribe or contain it. Such containment (or the "corralling of feminists" as I have heard some feminists describe this common phenomenon) regularly underwrites mainstream attempts to diminish or dismiss feminist work. The clue I want to pursue requires shifting attention from the term "feminist" to the term "mainstream" and addressing the following questions: What exactly is it about feminist epistemology that makes thereby self-categorized "mainstream" epistemologists seek to diminish its significance, to dismiss it by deciding that it is not proper or real epistemology, or even to comfortably continue to ignore it—a notable achievement a quarter century into its development? What is it that makes mainstream epistemologists *distinguish* feminist epistemology in this peculiar and virtually unprecedented way, in a discipline that normatively recommends openness to new perspectives and arguments?

That feminist epistemology is significantly ignored in the mainstream is evidenced, among other things, by the fact that few of the current standard textbooks in epistemology make any mention of it.[7] One well-regarded introductory text by Michael Williams includes what is, at best, an indirect reference to feminist epistemology, and it does not exactly encourage readers to take it seriously. This reference appears in Williams's discussion of *cultural relativism*, which he understands as the view that beliefs cannot be justified or true *simpliciter*; they can only be justified or true for particular cultures. (This view is typically contrasted with the view that there is objective knowledge, in particular, knowledge as truths that are transcultural.) Williams notes in a remark that he does not expand, "Cultural relativism sometimes leads to an embrace of 'standpoint epistemology,' according to which ethnic, class, gender, or other 'cultural' differences are associated with distinct 'ways of knowing.'"[8] *Standpoint epistemology* emerged as a significant theoretical approach in feminist epistemology, quite notably in Sandra Harding's *Science Question in Feminism*. It includes debates about the epistemic significance of the social and cultural locations of knowers, and it examines, in particular, whether and how epistemic advantage may accrue to the standpoint of the oppressed or marginalized, that is, whether and how those who occupy subdominant social locations may be in a position to know better at least some aspects of physical or social reality.[9] Williams's mention of standpoint epistemology and of gender-inflected "ways of knowing" thus indicates that he has feminist epistemology in mind in his remark, perhaps along with some other epistemological perspectives.

It is worth noting four ways in which Williams significantly misrepresents or dismisses feminist epistemology, especially since these moves are quite common. First, he seems to attribute to feminist epistemology some kind of uncritical embrace of "women's ways of knowing" (as well as other culturally inflected "ways of knowing") which, as we have seen, is a notable, though familiar, mischaracterization of feminist epistemology (and also of standpoint epistemology). Second, he associates feminist epistemology with a form of relativism that most feminist epistemologists have quite explicitly disavowed. For example, in her influential discussion of the role of the objectivity-relativism dichotomy in feminist epistemological work, Donna Haraway maintained, "Relativism is a way of being nowhere while claiming to be everywhere equally. The 'equality' of positioning is a denial of responsibility and critical inquiry."[10] Third, insofar as he reduces feminist epistemology to a form of cultural relativism, Williams exhibits the kind of reductive move often adopted in efforts to contain feminist epistemology. Finally, in his liberal use of scare quotes, Williams does not exactly distance himself from the tone of dismissal, if not derision, that, again, is not uncommon when feminist work is discussed or alluded to in mainstream circles.

Feminist epistemology does not fare much better when it is addressed directly and at greater length in mainstream scholarly works. There has been a persistent refrain there that feminist epistemology is not epistemology "proper," and thus not something with which epistemologists need concern themselves. This can be clearly gleaned from paper titles such as, "Why Feminist Epistemology Isn't," "Feminist Epistemology: Stalking An Un-Dead Horse," "The Failure of Feminist Epistemology," and "Feminist Epistemology as Folk Psychology."[11] More generally, mainstream responses to feminist epistemology have ranged from hostile to dismissive to, at best, limited acknowledgement. On the more hostile and dismissive side, feminist epistemologists are dogmatic ideologues, driven by "political correctness" and "agendas" rather than by the traditional methods of apolitical, value-free, rational investigation that have long been the hallmarks of good inquiry—including in epistemology itself. Stressing the political dimension, Susan Haack, for instance, has remarked, "The rubric 'feminist epistemology' is incongruous on its face, in somewhat the way of, say, 'Republican epistemology.'"[12] According to these critiques, feminist epistemology can be dismissed, or, at best, recognized as part of political philosophy.

On the limited-acknowledgement side, feminist epistemology might be assessed as a form of, or subarea within, social, pragmatist, or other mainstream epistemological projects, but, as such, as not especially new or distinctive. While, as noted above, it is important to recognize connections between feminist projects and mainstream ones, we need to resist the reductive move that frames feminist epistemology as "just" a form of a more mainstream project.[13] Indeed, once we acknowledge connections with various mainstream projects we thereby reject the neat containment of feminist epistemology within any one of them.[14] In effect, these forms of limited acknowledgement of feminist work also exhibit some of the containment and dismissive moves that are quite evident in more hostile reactions to the work.

Recognizing the persisting mainstream marginalization and dismissal of feminist epistemology is, I maintain, the first step toward articulating its distinctiveness at 25. But it is only the first step—as we will see, much more can be said in following through from this step. Yet this starting point helps to clarify the overall structure of my argument. When we say that something is distinctive (or has distinctive qualities) we are typically foregrounding a relationship: we are saying that this thing has some quality (or qualities) that distinguish it from other things that do not have this quality (or qualities)—or not in any noticeable degree. I am arguing that what makes feminist epistemology distinctive is that it can still be distinguished from non-feminist or mainstream epistemology, and significantly by the latter's seeming inability to meaningfully appreciate and incorporate feminist epistemological insights and developments. Thus, my attention is drawn not just to what feminist epistemologists are doing (which is a great variety of things), but to what non-feminist epistemologists are not doing or cannot, it seems, even countenance doing, as evidenced by their recurring moves to contain, marginalize, ignore, or dismiss feminist work—often in ways that conflict with standard epistemic norms of careful reading and reasoning. Despite its own significant diversity in topics, approaches, methods, and theories, mainstream (as non-feminist) epistemology has a more stable meaning than it would have, or should have, had feminist work been more substantially incorporated into the discipline as a whole. In short, what makes feminist epistemology distinctive is significantly determined by what makes mainstream epistemology (still) so distinctively non-feminist.

To begin to answer this question about what makes mainstream epistemology so distinctively non-feminist, we might start by considering the two ideas readily evoked by the term "feminist": *women* and *politics*. The political dimension is often noted as the main stumbling block to mainstream recognition and integration of feminist work: in a word, feminist epistemologists seek to inject their political values (if not "ideology") into an area where they do not properly belong. I think it is important that we address this concern, but we must first situate and examine it more carefully in connection with feminist epistemology's association with women.

The fact that so many initially assume that it is centrally concerned with some kind of endorsement of "women's ways of knowing" indicates that the association with women is prominent when people first encounter the term "feminist epistemology." While, as we have seen, this particular assumption mischaracterizes the field, there is another association with women that does mark something of its distinctiveness, including, I would suggest, the distinctiveness of its dismissal. Feminist epistemology is an epistemological project developed primarily (though not exclusively) by women and, as such, it is unique among epistemological projects. This fact, however, seems to trigger unacknowledged but historically reinforced assumptions to the effect that the work is likely be of an inferior sort and, consequently, does not merit the careful research and reading accorded projects in epistemology developed primarily by men. The strawperson caricatures, hasty generalizations, and misrepresentations that animate many dismissals of feminist work are more indicative of the lingering effects of philosophy's history of sexism and misogyny than they are of anything resembling the careful reading, research, and argumentation that the discipline usually promotes.[15] They thus evince a particular association with women that feminist epistemology does indeed examine: women's *epistemic subordination or disempowerment*, that is, the traditional dismissal or denigration of women as reasoners, serious knowers, and credible authorities. The concern with women's epistemic subordination not only defines significant projects in feminist epistemology, but it also underscores the significance of feminist epistemology within feminism more generally. It draws attention to the fact that women's social and political subordination was regularly underwritten by their epistemic subordination; in particular, women were considered to lack the intellectual and rational muscle required for academic, legal, political, or economic positions of public influence and authority. Thus addressing women's epistemic subordination is an important part of addressing their social and political subordination.

In her examination of the "backlash" against feminist scholars and scholarship in philosophy, Cressida Heyes clarifies this link between traditional sexist attitudes toward women and the dismissal of feminist scholarship as not "real" philosophy:

> [Feminist scholars are] read as intellectually narrow and ill-equipped, self-interested and hopelessly "biased," and dogmatically ideological with no standards for quality work or education. Of course, . . . such claims mesh neatly with sexist beliefs that have long and dishonorable histories; this culture commonly understands women as excessively concerned with the parochial and personal, incapable of seeing the "big picture," and as overly self-interested and subjective, unable to exercise our rationality to attain intellectual objectivity.[16]

Similarly, in his examination of the backlash against feminist epistemology in particular, Mark Own Webb has remarked, "Feminist epistemology has become one of the whipping-girls of choice for overtly and covertly sexist elements in philosophy."[17] Thus, with its marginalization of feminist work, the mainstream not only reflects forms of *epistemic injustice* evident in the larger culture (the very thing that many feminist epistemologists are interested in uncovering and challenging), but it reproduces politically problematic moves that draw inspiration from, among other things, Western philosophy's own history.[18] As I will argue in more detail below, when we examine the role of politics in feminist epistemology, particularly as that is regularly understood to mark something of its distinctiveness, we must situate that examination within a critical reappraisal of traditional epistemology's own political history, a history that necessitated specific feminist political intervention.

An important second step in determining what is distinctive about feminist epistemology at 25 can now be articulated. The first step, we will recall, involves noting the persisting marginalization of feminist work and asking what makes mainstream epistemology so distinctively non-feminist. The second step involves recognizing that feminist epistemology, like feminism more generally, does not start with women, or even with "feminist values." Feminism starts with facts about sexism, facts about the systematic subordination or disempowerment of women in relation to men. (If sexism didn't exist, neither would feminism—the term "feminism" would not have any meaning.) More particularly, feminist epistemology starts with a recognition of the historical and continuing epistemic and epistemological subordination of women and other marginalized groups that is, with the various forms of exclusion or distancing of women and other "others" from domains, conceptions, and idealizations of knowledge and of epistemology. In addressing both the practical and theoretical fallout of this subordination, feminist epistemology encompasses a significant range of specific inquiries. Yet this project is *distinctive* to the extent that proponents of other projects or perspectives in epistemology remain hostile to, dismissive of, or notably ignorant of it. Feminist work sheds light on mainstream epistemology as a disciplinary focus seemingly lacking the critical resources to reflexively examine its own sexist and racist history as well as the lingering epistemological and political effects of that history. Thus, as I see it, feminist work brings out from the shadows aspects of a tradition that, it seems, would otherwise remain there quite comfortably. Unpacking the discipline's lack, that is, articulating the new critical resources that feminist reflections bring to epistemology, will take up the remainder of my essay.

3. ANSWERING THE META-QUESTION

In order to elucidate the new critical perspectives that feminist work brings to epistemological theorizing (both within and about epistemology), it is useful to start with some notions that mainstream epistemologists assume when they determine (even passively through lack of serious attention) that it is feminist epistemology that belongs in the shadows, on the margins of epistemology. Dismissals of feminist work typically include suppositions such as the following: feminist epistemology is too historically and politically identified and situated to count as epistemology proper, which aims for general, apolitical, and ahistorical accounts and theories of knowledge and related concepts; feminist epistemologists seek to inject their particular feminist-political values, interests, and biases into their work, and this clearly differentiates them from the neutral, apolitical, value-free knowers of knowledge of epistemology proper; feminist epistemology deals, at best, with peripheral or applied questions and topics, not with the central or core concepts and questions of epistemology; in bringing moral and political norms and values to their work, feminist epistemologists confuse the distinction between moral or political normativity and epistemic normativity, an important distinction in epistemology.

These marginalizing characterizations draw attention to specific factors or features of epistemological theorizing that can serve as markers of differentiation between mainstream and feminist projects. These features include the historical and political situatedness of epistemology, the identity (political or otherwise) of epistemologists, starting or core concepts and questions in epistemology, and epistemic normativity. I will argue that these features do distinguishing work, but not in the way mainstream epistemologists regularly assume. The work they do involves recognizing that feminist critiques motivate distinctively enhanced understandings of these features and their role in epistemological theorizing. For example, we will see that while feminist epistemology is, in important ways, historically and politically situated, it also illuminates specificities of the historical and political situatedness of epistemology projects commonly accepted as part of "the tradition." In compelling greater reflexive awareness of such situatedness, feminist epistemology motivates new insights about epistemology, about its past limitations and about its future possibilities without these limitations. More generally, as we will see, when particular features of epistemological theorizing are noted in order to characterize and dismiss feminist work, these features usually tell us less about feminist epistemology than they tell us about the limited understanding of epistemology bound up in suppositions about a (non-feminist) epistemology proper. I now examine these features in sections (i)–(iv) below. I do not claim that the features I examine exhaust those we might draw on to articulate feminist epistemology's distinctiveness. Yet they connect and overlap in ways that yield a consistent and coherent account of that distinctiveness.

(i) Situating Epistemology (Historically)

Feminist epistemology *is* historically and politically situated. As we noted above, significant projects within its purview grew out of feminist advances in the academy that gained momentum in the second half of the twentieth century. These advances resulted, among other things, in women in many disciplines asking critical questions about the theoretical effects of the traditional exclusion or discouragement of women from those areas of inquiry. In philosophy, feminists drew attention to the tradition's embedded sexism and racism, which played a key role in the centuries-long epistemic subordination of women. As Genevieve

Lloyd clearly documented in her ground-breaking 1984 work, *The Man of Reason*, philosophers in the Western tradition regularly associated women or the symbolic "feminine" with that which is the "other" of reason.[19] Women literally or metaphorically represented embodiment, emotion, passion, instinct, or nature, that which "the man of reason" must control or transcend in order to become the ideal reasoner and knower.[20] Feminist epistemology's distinctiveness is thus significantly defined by that history. More specifically, feminist epistemology includes a commitment to uncovering the epistemic and epistemological fallout of particular aspects of the tradition's history and politics, while mainstream epistemology actively or passively distances itself from that commitment. This does not make mainstream epistemology less historically and politically situated, and certainly not in a way that renders it less problematic as an epistemological orientation. Let us elaborate on this point by first examining what it means to say that epistemology is historically situated.

Many feminist epistemologists pay particular attention to the claim that *knowledge is situated*, that knowledge reflects the interests, questions, and goals of individual knowers or communities of knowers that have particular social and cultural identities, locations, and histories.[21] More particularly, they maintain that epistemological theories that fail to take account of the situatedness of knowers and knowledge are limited at best. They question claims to generality in accounts and theories of knowledge that not only fail to recognize the variety of locations and perspectives that ground specific knowledge projects, but also implicitly privilege (or generalize from) particular groups of knowers, particular forms of knowledge, understanding, and insight, or particular topics and questions about human knowledge. Taking these insights to the meta-level, we can also understand epistemology (or knowledge about knowledge) as historically and culturally situated. In other words, specific epistemological projects, claims, or theories also reflect the interests, values, and questions of particular epistemologists in specific historical and cultural contexts, even when those interests and questions sincerely aim for general ahistorical accounts of knowledge and related epistemic concepts such as reason and objectivity. Not only does the history of epistemology reveal this, but feminist examinations of that history bring particular aspects of the tradition's historical situatedness into sharper relief.

In their *Introduction to Historical Epistemology*, Mary Tiles and Jim Tiles note that "the tradition" of epistemology is really a compendium of traditions, each with its own framework of assumptions "which determines what counts as an issue, what counts as a decisive consideration,

and what counts as a relevant consideration."[22] Contemporary epistemology is not wholly unmindful of its history, they argue, but it selects a
view of that history that accords with its particular framework of assumptions: "There are as a consequence many aspects of the history of our tradition which are commonly overlooked: historical figures such as Bacon
and Vico as well as the Hellenistic philosophers...; familiar figures such
as Plato, Hume and Kant, whose concerns with the relation between
knowledge and practice are frequently overlooked."[23] More careful historical attention also encourages us to rethink the meaning and role of what
is regularly posited as the constitutive core question of epistemology going
back to Plato: *What is the nature of knowledge?* Tiles and Tiles argue that
the original meaning of the Greek term *epistêmé* is derived from a verb
epistasthai, which means "to know how to do something" or "to be capable
of doing something." They continue: "[t]he traditional translation of
'*epistêmé*' into English as 'knowledge' tends to obscure the links which the
Greek has to 'know-how'...Plato's theorizing about knowledge begins
with an interest in expertise."[24] Thus, when epistemologists maintain that
epistemology is primarily concerned with propositional knowledge, that
is, with *knowing that* (the sky is blue, for instance), rather than *knowing
how* (to do something), they cannot unequivocally appeal to Plato as the
historical authority who established that central concern—though they
often do. We will return to consideration of core concepts and questions
in epistemology in section (iv).

Tiles and Tiles speak of "contemporary epistemology" in this context
as if it exhibits a kind of unity, framed by a particular set of background
assumptions. However, significant developments in these past decades of
(mainstream) epistemological theorizing belie an easy unity. Social epistemology and renewed interest in pragmatist epistemology count among
the new directions or approaches now regularly recognized as part of the
mainstream. *Naturalized epistemology* also stands out as a notable new
development, one that is linked to contemporary developments in the
cognitive sciences—in cognitive psychology, linguistics, and neuroscience, for instance. In his ground-breaking 1969 paper, W. V. Quine argued
for replacing epistemology as a purely philosophical analysis of epistemic
concepts with "epistemology naturalized," that is, with the study of
knowers, knowing, and knowledge as natural processes or phenomena
that lend themselves to scientific investigation.[25] Naturalized epistemology is, therefore, significantly situated by specific historical advances
in the empirical study of mind and cognition. Not unlike recent developments in social epistemology and renewed interest in pragmatism, it

has also inspired new metaepistemological thinking about what epistemology is, what its topics, methods, and goals are or should be. In
particular, developments in naturalized epistemology complicate a traditional view of epistemology as primarily a normative discipline about
how we *ought* to reason and form beliefs. Feminism-inspired readings of
the history of epistemology contribute additional insights into its historical situatedness, and they also encourage new thinking about how the
discipline is defined. The long-neglected work of women philosophers is
uncovered to fill gaps in the history of philosophy and to foreground
questions about how the canon in epistemology (as in other areas of philosophy) is established.[26] Understandings of canonical male figures are
also augmented by this inclusion. For example, we get better insight into
some of Descartes' positions and arguments by taking his correspondence
with Princess Elisabeth of Bohemia as seriously as he seemingly did.[27]
Moreover, feminist re-readings of canonical texts help uncover assumptions (linked to gender or race stereotypes, for instance) that shed new
light on historical arguments and projects, and on the ways those arguments or projects shaped the tradition. In elucidating the ways in which
some understandings or conceptions of *reason, knowledge,* or *epistemology* have been limited by historically entrenched, heretofore-unex-
amined cultural assumptions, feminist epistemologists thereby set the
stage for new assessments of the tradition and its continuing and future
impact. Lloyd also draws attention to the broader significance of feminist
re-readings of the history of philosophy:

> The effort to better understand the processes through which the history of
> western philosophy has excluded or denigrated women has brought with it
> a wider rethinking of the practices of history of philosophy, which goes
> beyond any explicitly feminist agenda....Reading strategies which may
> originally have been motivated by feminism are passing into broader
> attempts to treat the intelligent reading of history of philosophy as a
> conceptual resource for rethinking our present.[28]

Feminist examinations of the political and theoretical effects of epistemic
subordination also draw attention to its race and class configurations, to
the racist and classist assumptions involved in distancing "savage," "primitive," or "feeble-minded" peoples from philosophical idealizations of
reasoning and knowing.[29] As a consequence, characterizing feminist
epistemology as solely concerned with women's epistemic subordination
runs the risk of overlooking important feminist work examining the

interaction between gender and other social-status divisions, an examination that, feminist epistemologists maintain, is necessary for the fuller elucidation of the epistemic and epistemological effects of social and cultural subordination.

This examination of epistemology as an historically situated area of inquiry helps underscore three important points relating to feminist epistemology. First, claims to the effect that feminist epistemology is not epistemology proper, at least according to some supposed consistent traditional notion of "epistemology," are quite dubious, given that the tradition is a compendium of different, sometimes conflicting, projects. Second, the fact that feminist epistemology is linked to specific historical developments (feminism and advances in feminist research and theory) is certainly not grounds for dismissing it, since many epistemology projects were or are historically situated in this way. Naturalized epistemology is one such contemporary example, but so are many of the epistemological developments of the seventeenth century (Descartes', for instance) which were inspired by important developments in knowledge during the birth of modern science. Third, and perhaps most significantly, feminist epistemology situates most of what constitutes "the tradition" as specifically non-feminist. To the extent that mainstream epistemology still resists critical examinations of parts of the tradition that theorized and reinforced the epistemic subordination of those not favored by sexist and racist cultural assumptions, it still bears the mark of a particular history requiring epistemological interventions that are specifically feminist. Debates about feminism, epistemology, and politics need to be grounded in these understandings of the historical situatedness of epistemology.

(ii) Epistemology and Politics

Feminist interjections in epistemology that are framed by its history are also *political* to the extent that they address and challenge political dimensions of that history. When feminist epistemologists foreground concerns with the representation and status of women in epistemology, or address concerns with the ways in which understandings of reason were informed by and, in turn, reinforced gender and race stereotypes and assumptions, or concerns with the ways in which epistemological understandings of ideal knowledge and ideal knowers implicitly, if not explicitly, denigrated the epistemic lives and work of those in subordinate social locations, they are often characterized as injecting "politics" into epistemology, an area where it does not properly belong. But what feminists are really doing is pointing out how "politics" in the form of assumptions derived from broader social, cultural, *and political* arenas regularly worked their (subtle or not-so-subtle) way into epistemological understandings, questions, and the theories resulting from those understandings and questions. Does this make feminists problematically "political" in their epistemological work, in contrast to a supposedly apolitical tradition in epistemology?

There are different senses of "politics" and "the political" that would need to be elucidated in advance of settling questions about which connections between epistemology and politics are problematic and which are not. Louise Antony understands feminist epistemology to be "epistemology put at the service of feminist politics…[it] is dedicated to answering the many questions about knowledge that arise in the course of feminist efforts to understand and transform patriarchal structures."[30] Yet, even with her explicit political focus, there are different senses of "politics" at issue in Antony's characterization, insofar as feminist activists and theorists have differing and evolving views about what precisely constitutes *feminist politics* and what are the most pressing questions about knowledge that arise out of such politics. Antony's definition may also draw more exclusive attention to gender than is now warranted, given that gender is regularly theorized—in feminist epistemology and elsewhere—as a power/status social division that intersects with other epistemically significant power/status divisions such as race and class.

In her paper, "How is Epistemology Political?" Linda Alcoff argues that epistemology cannot but be political in quite specific ways. It has particular conditions of production, its theorists have specific identities, and it has distinct discursive effects in philosophy and in broader social and political arenas—it can, for instance, "[influence] whose arguments are considered plausible enough to be given consideration…[it can] authorize or disauthorize certain kinds of voices, certain kinds of discourses."[31] These specificities are all involved in some way with "politics," she maintains, in that they all "[have something] to do with relationships of power and privilege between persons, and the way in which these relationships are maintained and reproduced or contested and transformed."[32] Alcoff's use of "politics" makes explicit reference to power, yet it too lends itself to further elucidation, given feminist debates about the meaning of power and its legitimate and illegitimate uses. The epistemic deployment of power through practices and institutions that confer or withhold epistemic credibility and authority is a significant development in feminist epistemology, one that also helps to illuminate the role of the epistemological tradition in legitimating those practices and institutions that now require specific feminist political interventions.

Feminist work in epistemology provides important starting questions in the quest to determine which political interventions in epistemology promote the epistemic goals of truth, understanding, and knowledge, and which do not. For example, we might start with the question: Which types of political awareness, commitment, or intervention enhance epistemology and which detract from it? Many feminists are indeed interested in developing conceptions and accounts of *knowledge* and *understanding* that promote better knowledge and understanding of unjust social and political structures. What is *epistemologically* problematic about this? Or we might ask: Given that, historically, many epistemologists developed views and theories that (unwittingly or not) reinforced unjust political hierarchies, what is it about feminist examinations of the epistemic and epistemological fallout of that history that is *epistemologically* problematic? Or, perhaps more to the point, what is it about mainstream projects that actively disparage or distance themselves from these feminist examinations that is *epistemologically unproblematic* (as well as politically unproblematic)? By failing to distinguish among, and examine different senses of, "politics" and, in turn, different possible relationships between politics and epistemology, detractors of feminist epistemology, as promoters of some "apolitical" epistemology proper, risk reinforcing the traditional political interventions in epistemology that many of us (feminist or not do or should find problematic, for both political and epistemological reasons.

(iii) Epistemological Reflexivity

Acknowledging the significance of the historical and political situatedness of epistemology, or of specific epistemology projects and programs, naturally leads to considerations of what I call *epistemological reflexivity*. Reflexivity is regularly listed among the distinguishing methodological norms of feminist research, particularly, though not exclusively, in the social sciences. In calling for greater reflexivity, feminist researchers argue that we are better researchers and knowers ("better" in both political and epistemic senses) when we are reflective about the ways in which the processes and products of our inquiries are shaped by the specific interests, questions, and social and political values that *we bring* to our research—or, as the case may be, *fail* to bring to our research.[33] We might think of epistemological reflexivity as a form of second-order or metaepistemological reflection. It draws attention back *to us* as epistemologists (as knowers of knowledge) and the choices we make in deciding which first-order epistemic practices we will examine, which epistemic concepts we will favor (knowledge or understanding, for instance), or which methods (naturalist or pragmatist, for instance) we will use in our epistemological endeavors. Feminist epistemological and metaepistemological reflections draw particular attention to the need for greater reflexivity in epistemology.

My discussion above about the problematic construction of feminist epistemology as "political" in contrast to a supposedly "apolitical" epistemology proper is really a discussion about a particular deficiency in metaepistemological awareness and reflection on the part of those who dismiss feminist epistemology along such political lines. The issue is not whether feminist epistemology is too politically situated, but whether mainstream epistemology is *insufficiently* politically informed, not least when it continues to sustain ignorance about particular dimensions of its own political history and the continuing impact of that history. In her examination of the political dimensions of epistemology, Alcoff maintains that such examinations challenge what she calls "the stubborn persistence of epistemology's political blind spot," and they promote the development of epistemology's "own self-consciousness, so to speak, or an awareness of its own political character."[34] Similarly, in his examination of the epistemic and epistemological effects of philosophy's racial history, Charles Mills argues that mainstream evasions of that history contributed to what he calls "an epistemology of ignorance," which, among other things, is "a cognitive model that precludes self-transparency and genuine understanding of social realities."[35] By such lights, mainstream assertions about "apolitical" epistemology, as that is contrasted with "political" feminist epistemology, do little besides reinforcing a type of inoculation against specific forms of political awareness and critique in epistemology.

Helen Longino's idea of "doing epistemology as a feminist" to my mind also advances understandings of epistemological reflexivity. Longino maintains that terms such as "a feminist science" or "a feminist epistemology" can be misleading if they suggest that feminists think there is a distinctive female way of knowing, or if they imply that there is a set of feminist first principles to which all feminist adhere. She prefers the idea of "doing epistemology as a feminist," which is "to engage the questions of epistemology *with an awareness of…*" the many ways in which women or "the feminine" have been excluded from recognized knowledge and epistemology production.[36] Alison Wylie has noted that, in this case at least, Longino seems to be extending to the meta-level the insights derived from feminist advances in scientific research: "Longino seems committed to the . . . thesis that principles governing first-order practice should also govern second-order, philosophical inquiry."[37] Wylie takes up this extension of "reflexive strategy" from first-order practice to the meta-level quite explicitly, examining what Longino's first-order principles (that Longino calls "theoretical virtues") look like when applied to epistemological theorizing. For example, Wylie articulates meta-standards governing epistemology that draw upon Longino's "preference for ontological heterogeneity and complexity of relationship" as follows: "If knowledge and knowledge-making is complicated, interrelationally complex and responsive to context . . . then the practices of context-stripping and analytic reduction typical of mainstream epistemology may serve us badly; they may result in systematically misleading (simplistic) conceptions of what can reasonably count as 'knowledge' and of the principles governing its production and assessment. Certainly such philosophical practices disappear precisely the contextual factors, the diversity, and the dimensions of partiality that feminists, among others, are most interested in understanding."[38]

On an individual level, we as epistemologists promote epistemological reflexivity when we bring to our endeavors better understandings of *ourselves* as politically and historically situated knowers of knowledge(s). Such understandings involve our owning up to the assumptions, interests, values, and situated questions that frame our epistemological inquiries, including those interests and values that seem to be dictated by an impersonal ahistorical "tradition." These understandings also caution care in making general claims about knowledge or epistemology that extend beyond these interests and questions. Feminist work in epistemology reminds us that we make value-informed choices in epistemology when we favor, as worthy of philosophical attention, particular epistemic practices, particular areas or forms of knowledge, particular knowers, or particular aspects of knowledge or cognitive activity over others. As this work continues to make clear, these choices have moral and political as well as epistemological import.

Overall, this discussion of epistemological reflexivity again recommends a shift of focus from feminist to mainstream epistemology, from the fact that feminists epistemologists bring social and political interests, values, and awareness to their work, to the fact that mainstream epistemologists seem to have little reflexive awareness of *their* social and political (though admittedly historically reinforced) interests and values when they actively, or at this stage even passively, distance themselves from readily available feminist work.

(iv) Starting Concepts and Questions and Epistemic Normativity

Many of the discussions above (about different approaches in epistemology, about different forms of political intervention and awareness in epistemology) involve feminist metaepistemological reflections that can also be examined in connection with more mainstream metaepistemological discussions. The development of new approaches or projects in epistemology in recent decades, along with claims about the "end" of epistemology as it has been understood since the seventeenth century, have motivated renewed interest in metaepistemological questions.[39] In a chapter titled "Epistemology's End," Catherine Elgin draws attention to the considerations that she thinks should attend basic disagreements in or about epistemology: "To view [epistemological theories] as supplying alternative answers to the same questions is an oversimplification. For they embody disagreements about what the real questions are and what counts as answering them.... To understand a philosophical position and evaluate it fairly requires understanding the network of commitments that constitute it; for these commitments organize its domain, frame its problems, and supply standards for the solution of those problems."[40] Some marginalizing characterizations of feminist epistemology involve claims to the effect that it deals, at best, with peripheral rather than core concepts and questions in epistemology. Given substantial debate about what the core concepts and questions of epistemology are, such claims stand on shaky ground. Feminist work does, however, provide additional insights into what is at stake in choices about basic concepts and starting points in epistemology.

The concept of *knowledge* is not universally accepted as the core concept in epistemology. Given the endless production of Gettier counterexamples to proposed definitions of *knowledge* as *justified true belief* (that is, JTB analyses), in addition to skeptical arguments about whether any claim to knowledge can summon the level of justification thought necessary for indubitable "knowledge," many question the central epistemological focus on knowledge.[41] Mark Kaplan, for example, has questioned the significance of JTB analyses, particularly when these analyses are proposed as engaging the "traditional" or "classical conception" of knowledge going back to Plato. He concludes his specific historical examination (of Plato in particular) with the note: "Not only does the attempt to solve the Gettier problem fail to be a response to any problem that would have bothered Plato or Descartes; it now looks to be a project that cannot possibly address any problem *we* have in understanding or prosecuting the enterprise of inquiry."[42] Elgin maintains that a fuller epistemological accounting of the cognitive contributions of the sciences warrants a shift to *understanding* as the significant or key epistemic concept, arguing that "epistemology's emphasis on knowledge constricts and distorts its purview."[43] Taking a somewhat different direction, proponents of *virtue epistemology* shift central epistemological attention to knowers and the intellectual or epistemic virtues they should acquire. In terms of historical lineage, many virtue epistemologists locate their central concepts and "traditional" questions in Aristotle's work on the intellectual virtues.[44]

How do feminist projects distinctively contribute to discussions about core or starting concepts and questions in epistemology? While many of the key concepts of traditional and contemporary epistemology (*reason, evidence, justification, objectivity,* and *knowledge*) are also significant in feminist work, their significance is often situated and examined in terms of broader epistemological and moral-political considerations than is typically the case in mainstream projects. For example, Sally Haslanger has argued that an analysis of *knowledge* (of what it means to say that *S knows that p*, in particular) is not precluded by feminist work.[45] She notes, however, that when such analyses are informed by "our everyday" epistemic intuitions and practices they can be quite problematic from a feminist perspective, since everyday practices of epistemic evaluation and knowledge attribution incorporate sexist and other politically problematic norms and attitudes—as feminist research in psychology, sociology, education, and elsewhere has amply shown. For example, this research has revealed that evaluations of women's work (in journal refereeing, for instance) are higher when evaluators do not know the sex of the author. Admitting such feminist concerns does not require abandoning the analysis of *knowledge,* Haslanger maintains. However, she continues, epistemological analyses of knowledge as a *normative* concept (as concerned fundamentally with questions about how we *ought* to reason and form beliefs) does necessitate examining why we need the concept at all, why the concept is valuable for creatures like us who value certain kinds of moral/autonomous agency. She argues that when such considerations are in place, "an adequate definition of knowledge will depend on an account of what is cognitively valuable for beings like us, which raises moral and political issues on which feminists have much to contribute."[46]

What we take to be the starting concepts and questions in episte-mology (as well as what we take to be the appropriate considerations or methods of analysis we bring to such concepts and questions) sets the stage for more or less epistemological engagement with knowers, lives, and worlds informed by moral, social, and political complexity. Unfortunately, we rarely encounter such lives and worlds in epistemology texts populated with generic knowers and propositional knowledge sim-ples such as "The cat is on the mat" and "Jones owns a Ford." Some key terms that appear regularly in feminist works, including *knowledge that matters*, *genuine knowledge*, *real knowledge*, or *know(ing) well*, already foreground these broader considerations. For example, the term *knowledge that matters* already acknowledges that (at least some) knowledge matters in a way that unqualified "knowledge" does not. It thus more readily facilitates epistemological consideration of when, why, and how knowledge matters. Similarly, the concept *knowing well* invites consideration of broader social and political concerns, yet without over-looking the significance of good epistemic practices of careful evidence gathering and reasoning emphasized in traditional epistemology, prac-tices that are significant as part of the overall goal of aiming towards true beliefs.[47] Knowing well, as I understand it, is necessary to *living well*. At a very basic level, it requires knowing how to grow food or where to buy it, as well as knowing which foods are nutritional. But it also requires know-ing which actions are likely to harm other people or the environment, as well as knowing where to get reliable information about political candi-dates. An emphasis on *knowing well* thus reconnects epistemology with other areas of philosophy where other dimensions of living well (aesthetic, moral, or political, for instance) are prominent.

When we draw attention to epistemology's critical role in the anal-ysis and promotion of epistemic goods, values, or goals (which might include understanding, insight, and wisdom, in addition to truth, knowledge, or knowing well) we thereby engage questions about epi-stemic normativity, about the proper conduct of our cognitive or epi-stemic lives. Such conduct includes practices of reasoning, of gaining understanding, of attending to evidence, and of seeking out and listening to perspectives and opinions different from our own. Yet even if we take truth or true belief to be the core epistemic good or value that grounds many of our epistemic practices, we can still ask questions about which kinds of true belief we should seek. Are all items or kinds of belief, truth, knowledge, or understanding equally good? Insofar as we can often choose to pursue what we will justifiably believe, or know, or understand well or better, how do we choose well or wisely? More generally, what we take to be the core or constitutive concepts of epistemology matters, since such determinations presume in favor of some epistemic goods or values (and related norms of epistemic practice and conduct) over others. These considerations also help clarify links between epistemic normativity and moral or political normativity. The contention that philosophical examinations of *knowledge* or *knowing well* need to take account of moral and political concerns (or, as Haslanger maintains, need to take account of what is cognitively valuable for moral and political beings like us) is not, of course, the contention that epistemic normativity somehow reduces to moral or political normativity. But the epistemological promotion of robust forms of epistemic value and epistemic normativity requires linking these notions with social and political values and norms that show why and how good reasoning, good evidence, good knowledge, or knowing well matter, and, in the end, why epistemology matters.

What feminist epistemology promotes is a specific "value turn in epistemology." Yet this very turn is also claimed now by some working in mainstream epistemology. In announcing this turn in the title of his recent paper, Wayne Riggs identifies it: "[A] small but growing tendency to approach questions in epistemology in a refreshingly different way—a way that brings new resources to bear on old questions…, [value-driven epistemology] brings with it a way of conceiving epistemology that is less confining and intellectually richer than the more traditional way that tends to define epistemology as merely the 'theory of knowledge'…the most significant contribution that value-driven epistemology has to make is that it keeps epistemological theorizing on the track of those things that really matter to us."[48] Similarly, Duncan Pritchard has recently remarked on the growing interest in *epistemic value*, claiming it is "one of the most interesting developments in recent work in epistemology."[49] He adds that this renewed focus on epistemic value "grew out of one of the last big developments in epistemology—that of virtue epistemology, which arose to prominence from the mid-1980s onward…the interest in epistemic virtues stimulated a rapprochement between epistemology and ethics."[50] Nowhere in their papers do Riggs or Pritchard mention feminist epistemology or cite any work in or about feminist epistemology. Nor do the works in virtue epistemology they cite make any reference to specific developments in feminist epistemology.[51] Although the new developments they discuss engage central concerns and debates in feminist epistemology, that particular development in epistemology seems to be quite invisible to them. This particular phenomenon, the relegation of feminist work to the margins along with the appropriation of feminist insights and innovations without recognition of feminist origins or influences, is, unfortunately, not uncommon in the academy. In their recent review of feminist work in sociology, Karen Rosenberg and Judith Howard remark on "sociology's tendency to relegate gender to studies of the family while continuing to conceptualize other major institutions (e.g., the economy) as ungendered."[52] The corresponding tendency in epistemology is to relegate feminist work to concerns with gender or "women's ways of knowing," while continuing to conceptualize other major concepts (reason or objectivity, for instance) as having nothing to do with gender. Rosenberg's and Howard's remark about "the assimilation of feminist innovations into [sociology's] mainstream disciplinary theory and practice, with a consistent untethering of these practices from their feminist roots," has, alas, a familiar ring with some mainstream developments in epistemology.[53]

There is an additional cognitive entity or concept that warrants epistemological examination and normative attention. Although it has immediate relevance for feminist epistemological projects, it clearly has broader significance for epistemology as a tradition and discipline. Significant work in psychology and social psychology reveals that gendered social divisions are kept in place by *gender schemas* as much as they are by overt sexist or gender-limiting beliefs. Virginia Valian has drawn effectively on this work to explain how, despite the removal of more overt barriers, the advancement of women in many professional and academic arenas is still so slow. Gender schemas, which function as "a set of implicit, or nonconscious, hypotheses about sex differences," play a significant role. Held by both women and men, gender schemas affect "our expectations of men and women, our evaluations of their work, and their performance as professionals."[54] Although Valian gives them less attention in this context, similar schemas inform race and class perceptions and evaluations. As cognitive entities, schemas also lend themselves to feminist and naturalist epistemological investigation and normative evaluation. Thus, while epistemological projects that draw attention solely or primarily to consciously available *beliefs* continue to be important from a feminist perspective (after all, lots of people still have poorly justified sexist, gender-limiting, or racist beliefs), such exclusivity of attention can also serve to render invisible the more subtle cognitive workings of sexism and racism.

Changing limiting and damaging schemas requires new forms of epistemic *and* epistemological attention, insight, and activism, over and above those long championed by normative epistemology. Epistemologists might begin this project by examining the operation of gender schemas right on our own doorstep, in our own discipline. As I have argued, the continued, notable marginalization of feminist epistemology is significantly sustained by the workings of gender schemas linked to forms of epistemic subordination that were developed and reinforced in the tradition of Western epistemology.[55] I hope that, as I conclude, these schemas are somewhat less implicit and more conscious. Not only do they continue to shape specific types of epistemic injustice that feminist epistemologists still experience within the discipline, these schemas also significantly constrain mainstream epistemology, keeping it in a distinctively more limited place than it might be.

4. CONCLUSION

My examination of what it is that make feminist epistemology distinctive, a quarter century into its development, involves a bad news/good news situation. The bad news, certainly for those of us who seek to develop the field, is that this work is still—too often—trivialized, mischaracterized, dismissed, or simply ignored in the wider discipline of epistemology. But good news also emerges from my analysis of this professional resistance. Feminist work helps to illuminate persisting limited ideas about what epistemology is, about what its history and its political impact have been, and about what we as morally and politically aware theorists of knowledge (and related concepts) might bring to the field. As I have argued, feminist work provides important insights and critical resources that help move us beyond these limitations and guide us toward an improved epistemology future. It will stand as a somewhat ironic mark of its significant success, if, a quarter century hence, feminist epistemology is no longer distinctive in the ways I have examined in this essay.

Notes

I presented earlier versions of this essay (or parts of it) at a BayFAP (Bay Area Feminism and Philosophy) workshop in 2006, the Society for Analytical Feminism conference at the University of Kentucky in 2008, the FEMMSS (Feminist Epistemology, Methodologies, Metaphysics, and Science Studies) conference at the University of South Carolina in 2009, the Hypatia 25th Anniversary conference at the University of Washington in 2009, the American Philosophical Association's Central Division Meeting in 2010, and at a philosophy colloquium at Michigan State University in 2011. I am grateful to these audiences for their comments and suggestions. I am also indebted to Sharon Crasnow and Anita Superson for their generous feedback and support with the development of this essay.

1. See, for example, Noretta Koertge, "Feminist Epistemology: Stalking an Un-Dead Horse," in *The Flight from Science and Reason*, ed. Paul R. Gross, Norman Levitt, and Martin W. Lewis (Baltimore, Md.: John Hopkins University Press, 1996), 413–19. Koertge begins her essay as follows: "Feminist epistemology consists of theories of knowledge created *by* women, *about* women's modes of knowing, *for* the purpose of liberating women. By any reasonable standard, it should have expired in 1994" (413). Lorraine Code examines the problematic epistemological references to "women's ways of knowing" in *What Can She Know? Feminist Theory and the Construction of Knowledge* (Ithaca, N.Y.: Cornell University Press, 1991), esp. 251–62. The problematic use of a female-inflected "care reasoning" as different from a male-inflected "justice reasoning" has also garnered significant attention in feminist moral epistemology. For an examination of this problem, see my "Gender and Moral Reasoning Revisited: Reengaging Feminist Psychology," in *Feminists Doing Ethics*, ed. Peggy DesAutels and Joanne Waugh (Lanham, Md.: Rowman & Littlefield, 2001), 153–66. In particular, I argue there that claims about different voices in moral deliberation and reasoning owe as much to gender associations and stereotypes as they do to clear empirical evidence.

2. Many feminist critiques of the biological and social sciences are examined in *Feminism and Methodology: Social Science Issues*, ed. Sandra Harding (Bloomington: Indiana University Press, 1987), in *Sex and Scientific Inquiry*, ed. Sandra Harding and Jean F. O'Barr (Chicago: University of Chicago Press, 1987), and in *Feminism and Science*, ed. Nancy Tuana (Bloomington: Indiana University Press, 1989). The methodological and epistemological questions raised by these feminist critiques are further explored in *Beyond Methodology: Feminist Scholarship as Lived Research*, ed. Mary Margaret Fonow and Judith A. Cook (Bloomington: Indiana University Press, 1991), and in *Feminism and Science*, ed. Evelyn Fox Keller and Helen E. Longino (New York: Oxford University Press, 1996). Sandra Harding's *The Science Question in Feminism* (Ithaca, N.Y.: Cornell University Press, 1986) was a ground-breaking work in the development of feminist epistemology and feminist philosophy of science. Further developments in these areas, including work drawing on multicultural and global feminist perspectives, appear in *Feminism, Science, and the Philosophy of Science*, ed. Lynn Hankinson Nelson and Jack Nelson (Boston: Kluwer Academic Publishers, 1997).

3. An important volume examining central questions in social epistemology is *Socializing Epistemology: The Social Dimensions of Knowledge*, ed. Frederick F. Schmitt (Lanham, Md.: Rowman & Littlefield, 1994). Schmitt notes that

feminist philosophy of science was a significant inspiration in the development of social epistemology since 1980 (p. 3).

4. Elizabeth Anderson, "Feminist Epistemology and Philosophy of Science," in *The Stanford Encyclopedia of Philosophy* (Fall 2009 Edition), ed. Edward N. Zalta, http://plato.stanford.edu/archives/fall2009/entries/feminism-epistemology/. Heidi Grasswick, "Feminist Social Epistemology," in *The Stanford Encyclopedia of Philosophy* (Fall 2009 Edition), ed. Edward N. Zalta, http://plato.stanford.edu/archives/fall2009/entries/feminist-social-epistemology/.

5. Grasswick, in "Feminist Social Epistemology," notes, for example, that Louise Antony's defense of epistemological individualism (where the primary or sole focus of analysis is individual believers and knowers) resists at least certain elements of a social epistemology. See Antony, "Sisters, Please, I'd Rather Do It Myself: A Defense of Individualism in Feminist Epistemology," *Philosophical Topics*, 23, no. 2 (1995): 59–94.

6. See Charlene Haddock Seigfried, *Feminism and Pragmatism: Reweaving the Social Fabric* (Chicago: University of Chicago Press, 1996). Among other things, Seigfried pays particular attention to feminist influences in the development of American pragmatism in the late nineteenth and early twentieth centuries. For further exploration of connections between feminist epistemology and pragmatist epistemology, see my "Feminist-Pragmatist Revisionings of Reason, Knowledge, and Philosophy," *Hypatia* 8, no. 2 (1993): 15–37.

7. Of the fifteen or so standard single-authored epistemology textbooks on my shelf that I have recently examined, only two make any mention of feminist epistemology. In *Contemporary Epistemology* (Fort Worth, Tx: Harcourt Brace College Publishers, 1995), Ralph Baergen devotes his last, though relatively short, chapter to feminist epistemology. In his recent new edition of *An Introduction to Epistemology*, 2nd ed. (Peterborough, Ontario: Broadview Press, 2009), Jack S. Crumley also devotes a chapter to feminist epistemology. In what we hope is a harbinger of more constructive mainstream recognition and integration of feminist work, Crumley avoids reductionist moves in that he examines a range of topics in feminist epistemology, and acknowledges that it comprises a "family of views" (234).

8. Michael Williams, *Problems of Knowledge: A Critical Introduction to Epistemology* (New York: Oxford University Press, 2001), 220.

9. The view that social subordination automatically grants epistemic advantage or privilege—a view often associated with feminist standpoint epistemology—has been at best a controversial view there. See *The Feminist Standpoint Reader: Intellectual and Political Controversies*, ed. Sandra Harding (New York: Routledge, 2004). This volume contains many important papers in the development of standpoint epistemology.

10. See Donna Haraway, "Situated Knowledges: The Science Question in Feminism and the Privilege of Partial Perspective," *Feminist Studies* 14, no. 3 (1988): 575–99, quotation on 584. The objectivity-relativism dichotomy is

also examined by Lorraine Code in *What Can She Know?* Code also explicitly disavows the kind of cultural relativism that Williams seems to associate
with feminist epistemology. She argues for a "mitigated relativism, constrained by objectivity and a commitment to realism…" (251). Many feminist epistemologists have, like Code, argued that some forms of epistemological
relativism are politically regressive, and that a substantial notion of *objective
truth* is required for feminism—not least in the recognition of objective
truths about women's inequality. Indeed, the project of redefining or reconceptualizing *objectivity* has been a predominant one in feminist epistemology
and philosophy of science. See Sharon Crasnow, "Can Science Be Objective:
Feminism, Relativism, and Objectivity," in *Scrutinizing Feminist Epistemology:
An Examination of Gender in Science*, ed. Cassandra Pinnick, Noretta
Koertge, and Robert Almeder (New Brunswick, N.J.: Rutgers University
Press, 2003), 130–141, for a discussion of objectivity in feminist philosophy
of science, particularly in the work of Helen Longino.

11. See Janet Radcliffe Richards, "Why Feminist Epistemology Isn't," in *Flight
from Science and Reason*, ed. Gross, Levitt, and Lewis; Koertge, "Feminist
Epistemology"; Jim Shelton, "The Failure of Feminist Epistemology,"
Academic Questions 19, no. 2 (2006): 82–92; and Robert Klee, "Feminist
Epistemology as Folk Psychology," in *Scrutinizing Feminist Epistemology*,
ed. Pinnick, Koertge, and Almeder, 31–44.

12. Susan Haack, "Knowledge and Propaganda: Reflections of an Old Feminist,"
in *Scrutinizing Feminist Epistemology*, ed. Pinnick, Koertge, and Almeder,
7–30, quotation on 8. A significant number of the essays in Pinnick,
Koertge, and Almeder, eds., *Scrutinizing Feminist Epistemology*, adopt a
disparaging attitude toward the field. In their reviews of this volume, both
Elizabeth Potter and Elizabeth Anderson draw attention to these critical
assessments of the field as a whole. Most of the authors are animated not
by the impulse "to make it better [but] to make it go away," notes Potter,
"The Science War Front," *The Women's Review of Books* 22, no. 1 (2004):
7–8, quotation on 7. They aim "to show that the entire enterprise [of feminist epistemology] is a failure," remarks Anderson in "How Not to Criticize
Feminist Epistemology: A Review of *Scrutinizing Feminist Epistemology*,"
Elizabeth Anderson's Philosophy Home Page, http://www-personal.umich.
edu/~eandersn/hownotreview.html (accessed January 2008). Anderson
notes, in particular, the recurring accusation of "political correctness" that
is leveled against feminist epistemology, where feminist epistemologists
are characterized as seeking to inject "feminist values" into scientific and
other forms of "honest inquiry." (She adds, however, that unlike most of the
other essays, those by Sharon Crasnow and Janet Kourany "are models of
respectful, intellectually serious critical scholarship.") The idea that feminist epistemology can be accepted or rejected as a whole is also evident in
a special issue of *The Monist* devoted to the topic: "Feminist Epistemology—
For and Against" (*The Monist* 77, no. 4 [1994]). This "astonishing topic,"
Lynn Hankinson Nelson has remarked, "suggested that whether one is 'for'

or 'against' 'feminist epistemology' is a matter of subscribing to one of two clearly delineated, complete, and mutually exclusive sets of tenets . . . [which] badly mischaracterized much of the work at the intersections of feminism, epistemology, and philosophy of science." See Nelson, "The Very Idea of Feminist Epistemology," *Hypatia* 10, no. 3 (1995): 31–49, quotation on 32. I have examined in more detail the marginalization of feminist epistemology in Rooney, "The Marginalization of Feminist Epistemology and What That Reveals about Epistemology 'Proper'" in *Feminist Epistemology and Philosophy of Science: Power in Knowledge,* ed. Heidi Grasswick (Dordrecht, Holland: Springer, 2011), 3–24.

13. I have developed this point in more detail in Rooney, "Marginalization of Feminist Epistemology." I also examine there the relationship between feminist epistemology and two additional areas or directions in contemporary mainstream epistemology, naturalized epistemology and virtue epistemology.

14. Also on the limited acknowledgement side, feminist epistemology might be characterized as a type of practical or applied epistemology, something that has practical applications in knowledge contexts where gender or other social divisions are epistemically salient. Feminist work certainly does have practical applications in, for example, helping to uncover sexist or racist assumptions in what had been considered "neutral" concepts, methods, or theories. However, such applications also help to refine understandings and theoretical accounts of key epistemological concepts such as knowledge, evidence, objectivity, and reason. Thus, assessing feminist epistemology as "just" applied epistemology, particularly in an effort to distance it from theoretical epistemology "proper," overlooks the significant interaction between theory and practice that has been a notable achievement in feminist epistemological work. The works listed in note 2 above include many examples of the interaction between feminist theorizing and feminist practice in research across many disciplines. For helpful overviews of connections between feminist theory and practice, see Fonow and Cook, eds., *Beyond Methodology,* and more recently, Fonow and Cook, "Feminist Methodology: New Applications in the Academy and Public Policy," *Signs: Journal of Women in Culture and Society* 30, no. 4 (2005): 2211–36.

15. Again, I argue this point in more detail in Rooney, "Marginalization of Feminist Epistemology." Both Anderson, in "How Not to Criticize Feminist Epistemology," and Potter, in "Science War Front," note the recurring lapses in reasoning and argumentation that arise in critiques of feminist epistemology, including "gross misrepresentations of feminist epistemology" (Anderson) and "unrecognizable caricatures of feminist scholars" and their work (Potter). In her recent paper examining feminist work in philosophy of science, Sarah Richardson also addresses the problem of the "continuing marginalization" of feminist scholarship. She notes, "Feminist philosophical critiques of gender bias in science are frequently simplified,

distorted, or truncated when translated by scientists, non-feminist philosophers, and general readers...A well-documented translation problem is the persistent reception of feminist critiques of sciences as 'anti-science.'" See Richardson, "Feminist Philosophy of Science: History, Contributions, and Challenges," *Synthese* 177, no. 3 (2010): 337–62, quotation on 352–53.

16. Cressida J. Heyes, "The Backlash against Feminist Scholars and Scholarship: Introduction," *American Philosophical Association Newsletter on Feminism and Philosophy* 99, no. 1 (Fall 1999): 36–40, quotation on 37.

17. Mark Owen Webb, "Feminist Epistemology as Whipping-Girl," in *Theorizing Backlash: Philosophical Reflections on the Resistance to Feminism*, ed. Anita M. Superson and Ann E. Cudd (Lanham, Md.: Rowman & Littlefield, 2002), 49–65, quotation on 49.

18. For an analysis of *epistemic injustice* (including its connection with women's epistemic subordination), see Miranda Fricker, *Epistemic Injustice: Power and the Ethics of Knowing*. (New York: Oxford University Press, 2007), and Karen Jones, "The Politics of Credibility" in *A Mind of One's Own: Feminist Essays on Reason and Objectivity*, 2nd ed., eds. Louise M. Antony and Charlotte E. Witt (Boulder, Colo.: Westview Press, 2002), 154–176.

19. See Genevieve Lloyd, *The Man of Reason: "Male" and "Female" in Western Philosophy* (Minneapolis: University of Minnesota Press, 1993 [1984]).

20. For further analysis of the metaphorical construction of reason as masculine, see Rooney, "Gendered Reason: Sex Metaphor and Conceptions of Reason," *Hypatia* 6, no. 2 (1991): 77–103, and Genevieve Lloyd, "Maleness, Metaphor, and the 'Crisis' of Reason," in *Mind of One's Own*, ed. Antony and Witt. I have also examined the more literal distancing of women from reason and rationality in Rooney, "Rationality and the Politics of Gender Difference," *Metaphilosophy* 26, no. 1/2 (1995): 22–45.

21. Specifically feminist examinations of the epistemic significance of the social and cultural location of knowers underscore claims about the situatedness of knowledge. Haraway's "Situated Knowledges" is regularly cited as a significant work in these feminist discussions. Haraway maintains that "feminist objectivity is about limited location and situated knowledge, not about transcendence and splitting of subject and object. It allows us to become answerable for what we learn how to see" (583).

22. Mary Tiles and Jim Tiles, *An Introduction to Historical Epistemology* (Oxford: Blackwell, 1993), 2.

23. Tiles and Tiles, *Introduction to Historical Epistemology*, 5.

24. Tiles and Tiles, *Introduction to Historical Epistemology*, 11–12.

25. Quine, "Epistemology Naturalized," in *Ontological Relativity and Other Essays* (New York: Columbia University Press, 1969). Also see Hilary Kornblith, *Naturalizing Epistemology*, 2nd ed. (Cambridge, Mass.: MIT Press, 1994) for further developments in naturalized epistemology. Not all naturalist-inclined epistemologists argue for the replacement of epistemology by empirical studies of cognition and knowledge production, but

they maintain that such studies should inform some nontrivial part of (philosophical) epistemology. Important papers examining links between naturalized epistemology and feminist epistemology are included in *Feminist Interpretations of W. V. Quine*, ed. Lynn Hankinson Nelson and Jack Nelson (University Park: Penn State Press, 2003). I have examined an "uneasy alliance" between these two areas of epistemology in Rooney, "Feminist Epistemology and Naturalized Epistemology: An Uneasy Alliance," in *Feminist Interpretations of W. V. Quine*, ed. Nelson and Nelson, 205–239.

26. See Mary Ellen Waithe, ed., *A History of Women Philosophers*, vols. 1–4 (Dordrecht, Holland: Springer, 1987–94). The many volumes in the *Re-reading the Canon* Series published by Penn State Press (under the general editorship of Nancy Tuana) are an important resource for examining the history of Western philosophy from a feminist perspective.

27. See Margaret Atherton, ed., *Women Philosophers of the Early Modern Period* (Indianapolis, Ind.: Hackett Publishing Company, 1994), especially 9–21.

28. Genevieve Lloyd, *Feminism and History of Philosophy* (New York: Oxford University Press, 2002), quotation on 3.

29. Historically, philosophers regularly claimed that, like women, people of "inferior races" lacked the kinds of intellectual capacity needed for admittance to realms of social and political influence. See Charles Mills, *The Racial Contract* (Ithaca, N.Y.: Cornell University Press, 1997) and Shannon Sullivan and Nancy Tuana, eds., *Race and Epistemologies of Ignorance* (Albany: State University of New York Press, 2007) for further examinations at the intersection of philosophy of race and epistemology.

30. Louise Antony, "Situating Feminist Epistemology." *Proceedings of the Twentieth World Congress of Philosophy* 8, ed. Jaakko Hintikka, Robert Neville, Ernest Sosa, and Alan Olson, 31–40. (Bowling Green, Ohio: Philosophy Documentation Center, 2000), quotation on 31.

31. Linda Alcoff, "How Is Epistemology Political?" in *Radical Philosophy: Tradition, Counter-tradition, Politics*, ed. Roger S. Gottlieb (Philadelphia: Temple University Press, 1993), 65–85, quotations on 69, 73.

32. Alcoff, "How is Epistemology Political?" 72.

33. In the introduction to their influential volume of essays on feminist methods and feminist methodology, Mary Margaret Fonow and Judith Cook define "reflexivity" as follows: "By reflexivity we mean the tendency of feminists to reflect upon, examine critically, and explore analytically the nature of the research process." See Fonow and Cook, eds., *Beyond Methodology*, 2. In their examination of feminist scholarship in the field of communication, Bonnie Dow and Celeste Condit note that "[f]eminist research ... is generally more self-reflective about operating from an orientation that links its specific data or theoretical or methodological concerns to a perspective that seeks to ameliorate the systems of domination that

operative through the axis of gender (although never exclusively so)." See
Bonnie J. Dow and Celeste M. Condit, "The State of the Art in Feminist
Scholarship in Communication," *Journal of Communication* 55, no. 3
(2005): 448–78, quotation on 449.

34. Alcoff, "How is Epistemology Political?" 79, 80.
35. Mills, *Racial Contract*, 18.
36. Helen Longino, "In Search of Feminist Epistemology," *The Monist* 77, no. 4
(1994): 472–85, quotation on 475, my emphasis.
37. Alison Wylie, "Doing Philosophy As a Feminist: Longino on the Search for
a Feminist Epistemology," *Philosophical Topics* 23, no. 2 (1995): 345–58,
quotation on 350.
38. Wylie, "Doing Philosophy As a Feminist," 352.
39. Claims about the "end" or "death" of epistemology (particularly as the discipline has been constituted since the seventeenth century) are attributed to
Richard Rorty in *Philosophy and the Mirror of Nature* (Princeton, N.J.:
Princeton University Press, 1979). Sharyn Clough in *Beyond Epistemology:
A Pragmatist Approach to Feminist Science Studies* (Lanham, Md: Rowman
& Littlefield, 2003) draws on Rorty's skepticism about epistemology (as a
meaningful project) in her argument for "a pragmatist approach to feminist
science studies." Quine's argument for the replacement of epistemology (as
a purely philosophical discipline) by "naturalized epistemology" might also
be interpreted as a type of "end" claim. The essays in Stephen Hetherington's
edited volume, *Epistemology Futures* (New York: Oxford University Press,
2006) provide a good examples of this metaepistemological discussion. In
his introduction, Hetherington lists some key metaepistemological questions that frame these essays. These include back-to-the-drawing-board
questions about what the purpose or goal of epistemology is, what cognitive
or epistemic phenomena it should study, what core concepts it should
examine ("maybe other epistemic concepts…[besides] knowledge, evidence, warrant…would be more penetrating and apt"), what methods it
should use, and what should count as epistemological progress or achievement. See *Epistemology Futures*, especially pp. 1–9. In connection with this
essay, it is instructive to note that in none of the thirteen essays in
Hetherington's volume is feminist epistemology mentioned or referenced,
though, taken together, the essays engage a range of directions or approaches
in epistemology—in standard analytical, naturalist, pragmatist, and virtue
epistemology. According to this text, not only is feminist epistemology
nonexistent in the present, but it does not figure into any epistemology
future either.
40. Catherine Elgin, *Considered Judgment* (Princeton, N.J.: Princeton
University Press, 1996), 3.
41. Gettier counter-examples are examples involving situations or cases in
which someone's belief is true and well justified but is not considered
knowledge, at least not according to epistemologists' intuitions about what

knowledge is. These counter-examples get their name from Edmund Gettier's much-discussed paper, "Is Justified True Belief Knowledge?" *Analysis* 23 (1963): 121–23.

42. Mark Kaplan, "It's Not What You Know that Counts," *Journal of Philosophy* 82, no. 7 (1985): 350–63, quotation on 359.

43. Catherine Elgin, "From Knowledge to Understanding," in *Epistemology Futures*, ed. Hetherington, 199.

44. A significant work in the development of virtue epistemology is Linda Zagzebski's, *Virtues of the Mind* (Cambridge: Cambridge University Press, 1996). She argues that "intellectual virtue is the primary normative component of both justified belief and knowledge" (p. xv).

45. Sally Haslanger, "What Knowledge Is and What It Ought to Be: Feminist Values and Normative Epistemology," in *Philosophical Perspectives 13*, ed. James Tomberlin (Cambridge, Mass: Blackwell, 1999).

46. Haslanger, "What Knowledge Is and What It Ought to Be," 473.

47. I have noticed that many works in or closely related to feminist epistemology place particular emphasis on *knowing*, for example, Linda Alcoff, *Real Knowing* (Ithaca, N.Y.: Cornell University Press, 1996); Lorraine Code, *What Can She Know?*; Michele Le Doeuff, *The Sex of Knowing* (New York: Routledge, 2003); and Lynn Hankinson Nelson, *Who Knows* (Philadelphia, Pa: Temple University Press, 1990).

48. Wayne Riggs, "The Value Turn in Epistemology," in *New Waves in Epistemology*, ed. Vincent F. Hendricks and Duncan Pritchard (New York: Palgrave Macmillan, 2008), 300–23, quotations on 300, 319.

49. Duncan Pritchard, "Recent Work on Epistemic Value," *American Philosophical Quarterly* 44, no. 2 (2007): 85–110, quotation on 85.

50. Pritchard, "Recent Work on Epistemic Value," 85.

51. Some work in (or substantially informed by) feminist epistemology is, however, included in Adrian Haddock, Alan Millar, and Duncan Pritchard's recent co-edited volume, *Social Epistemology* (Oxford: Oxford University Press, 2010)—a welcome advance, even if it presents feminist work as significantly contained within social epistemology. See Haddock, Millar, and Pritchard, *Social Epistemology*.

52. Karen Esther Rosenberg and Judith A. Howard, "Finding Feminist Sociology: A Review Essay," *Signs* 33, no. 3 (2008): 675–96, quotation on 675.

53. Rosenberg and Howard, "Finding Feminist Sociology," 689.

54. Virginia Valian, *Why So Slow? The Advancement of Women* (Cambridge, Mass.: MIT Press, 1998), 2.

55. See Sally Haslanger, "Changing the Ideology and Culture of Philosophy: Not By Reason Alone," *Hypatia* 23, no. 2 (2008): 210–23. Haslanger draws specific attention to gender schemas in her analysis of "the ideology and culture of philosophy," a culture that still sustains a chilly climate for women and minorities and, she maintains, contributes the hostile reception that feminist philosophy and feminist philosophers have often received.

References

Alcoff, Linda. "How Is Epistemology Political?" In *Radical Philosophy: Tradition, Counter-tradition, Politics*, ed. Roger S. Gottlieb, 65–85. Philadelphia: Temple University Press, 1993.

———. *Real Knowing: New Versions of the Coherence Theory*. Ithaca, N.Y.: Cornell University Press, 1996.

Anderson, Elizabeth. "How Not to Criticize Feminist Epistemology: A Review of *Scrutinizing Feminist Epistemology*." Elizabeth Anderson's Philosophy Home Page. http://www-personal.umich.edu/~eandersn/hownotreview.html (accessed January 2008). A shorter version of this review appeared in *Metascience* 13 (2004): 395–99.

———. "Feminist Epistemology and Philosophy of Science." In *The Stanford Encyclopedia of Philosophy* (Fall 2009 Edition), ed. Edward N. Zalta. http://plato.stanford.edu/archives/fall2009/entries/feminism-epistemology/.

Antony, Louise. "Sisters, Please, I'd Rather Do It Myself: A Defense of Individualism in Feminist Epistemology." *Philosophical Topics* 23, no 2 (1995): 59–94.

———. "Situating Feminist Epistemology." *Proceedings of the Twentieth World Congress of Philosophy* 8, ed. Jaakko Hintikka, Robert Neville, Ernest Sosa, and Alan Olson, 31–40. Bowling Green, Ohio: Philosophy Documentation Center, 2000.

Atherton, Margaret, ed. *Women Philosophers of the Early Modern Period*. Indianapolis, Ind.: Hackett Publishing Company, 1994.

Baergen, Ralph. *Contemporary Epistemology*. Fort Worth, Tx: Harcourt Brace College Publishers, 1995.

Burgess-Jackson, Keith. "The Backlash against Feminist Philosophy." In *Theorizing Backlash: Philosophical Reflections on the Resistance to Feminism*, ed. Anita M. Superson and Ann E. Cudd, 19–47, Lanham, Md.: Rowman & Littlefield, 2002.

Clough, Sharyn. *Beyond Epistemology: A Pragmatist Approach to Feminist Science Studies*. Lanham, Md: Rowman & Littlefield, 2003.

Code, Lorraine. *Epistemic Responsibility*. Hanover, N.H.: University Press of New England, 1987.

———. *What Can She Know? Feminist Theory and the Construction of Knowledge*. Ithaca, N.Y.: Cornell University Press, 1991.

Crasnow, Sharon L. "Can Science Be Objective: Feminism, Relativism, and Objectivity." In *Scrutinizing Feminist Epistemology: An Examination of Gender in Science*, ed. Cassandra Pinnick, Noretta Koertge, and Robert Almeder, 130–141. New Brunswick, N.J.: Rutgers University Press, 2003.

Crumley, Jack S., II. *An Introduction to Epistemology*. 2nd ed. Peterborough, Ontario: Broadview Press, 2009.

Dow, Bonnie J., and Celeste M. Condit. "The State of the Art in Feminist Scholarship in Communication." *Journal of Communication* 55, no. 3 (2005): 448–78.

Elgin, Catherine Z. *Considered Judgment.* Princeton, N.J.: Princeton University Press, 1996.

——— . "From Knowledge to Understanding." In *Epistemology Futures,* ed. Stephen Hetherington, 199–215. New York: Oxford University Press, 2006.

Fonow, Mary Margaret, and Judith A. Cook, eds. *Beyond Methodology: Feminist Scholarship as Lived Research.* Bloomington: Indiana University Press, 1991.

——— . "Feminist Methodology: New Applications in the Academy and Public Policy." *Signs: Journal of Women in Culture and Society* 30, no. 4 (2005): 2211–36.

Fricker, Miranda. *Epistemic Injustice: Power and the Ethics of Knowing.* New York: Oxford University Press, 2007.

Gettier, Edmund. "Is Justified True Belief Knowledge?" *Analysis* 23 (1963): 121–23.

Grasswick, Heidi. "Feminist Social Epistemology." In *The Stanford Encyclopedia of Philosophy* (Fall 2009 Edition), ed. Edward N. Zalta. http://plato.stanford.edu/archives/fall2009/entries/feminist-social-epistemology/.

Gross Paul R., Norman Levitt, and Martin W. Lewis, eds. *The Flight from Science and Reason.* Baltimore, Md.: Johns Hopkins University Press, 1996.

Haack, Susan. "Knowledge and Propaganda: Reflections of an Old Feminist." In *Scrutinizing Feminist Epistemology: An Examination of Gender in Science,* ed. Cassandra Pinnick, Noretta Koertge, and Robert Almeder, 7–30. New Brunswick, N.J.: Rutgers University Press, 2003.

Haddock, Adrian, Alan Millar, and Duncan Pritchard, eds. *Social Epistemology.* Oxford: Oxford University Press, 2010.

Haraway, Donna. "Situated Knowledges: The Science Question in Feminism and the Privilege of Partial Perspective." *Feminist Studies* 14, no. 3 (1988): 575–99.

Harding, Sandra. *The Science Question in Feminism.* Ithaca, N.Y.: Cornell University Press, 1986.

——— , ed. *Feminism and Methodology: Social Science Issues.* Bloomington: Indiana University Press, 1987.

——— , ed. *The Feminist Standpoint Reader: Intellectual and Political Controversies.* New York: Routledge, 2004.

——— , and Merrill B. Hintikka, eds. *Discovering Reality: Feminist Perspectives on Epistemology, Metaphysics, Methodology, and Philosophy of Science.* Dordrecht, Holland: D. Reidel Publishing Company, 1983.

——— , and Jean F. O'Barr, eds. *Sex and Scientific Inquiry.* Chicago: University of Chicago Press, 1987.

Haslanger, Sally. "What Knowledge Is and What It Ought to Be: Feminist Values and Normative Epistemology." In *Philosophical Perspectives 13,* ed. James Tomberlin, 459–480. Cambridge, Mass.: Blackwell, 1999.

——— . "Changing the Ideology and Culture of Philosophy: Not By Reason Alone." *Hypatia* 23, no. 2 (2008): 210–23.

Hendricks, Vincent F., and Duncan Pritchard, eds. *New Waves in Epistemology*. New York: Palgrave Macmillan, 2008.

Hetherington, Stephen, ed. *Epistemology Futures*. New York: Oxford University Press, 2006.

Heyes, Cressida J. "The Backlash against Feminist Scholars and Scholarship: Introduction." *American Philosophical Association Newsletter on Feminism and Philosophy* 99, no. 1 (Fall 1999): 36–40.

Jones, Karen. "The Politics of Credibility." In *A Mind of One's Own: Feminist Essays on Reason and Objectivity*. 2nd ed. Eds. Louise M. Antony and Charlotte E. Witt, 154–176. Boulder, Colo.: Westview Press, 2002.

Kaplan, Mark. "It's Not What You Know that Counts." *Journal of Philosophy* 82, no. 7 (1985): 350–63.

Keller, Evelyn Fox, and Helen E. Longino, eds. *Feminism and Science*. New York: Oxford University Press, 1996.

Klee, Robert. "Feminist Epistemology as Folk Psychology." In *Scrutinizing Feminist Epistemology: An Examination of Gender in Science*, ed. Cassandra Pinnick, Noretta Koertge, and Robert Almeder, 31–44. New Brunswick, N.J.: Rutgers University Press, 2003.

Koertge, Noretta. "Feminist Epistemology: Stalking an Un-Dead Horse." In *The Flight from Science and Reason*, ed. Paul R. Gross, Norman Levitt, and Martin W. Lewis, 413–19. Baltimore, Md.: John Hopkins University Press, 1996.

Kornblith, Hilary. *Naturalizing Epistemology*. 2nd ed. Cambridge, Mass.: MIT Press, 1994.

Le Doeuff, Michèle. *The Sex of Knowing*, translated by Kathryn Hamer and Lorraine Code. New York: Routledge, 2003.

Longino, Helen. "In Search of Feminist Epistemology." *The Monist* 77, no. 4 (1994): 472–85.

Lloyd, Genevieve. *Feminism and History of Philosophy*. New York: Oxford University Press, 2002.

———. *The Man of Reason: "Male" and "Female" in Western Philosophy*. Minneapolis: University of Minnesota Press, 1993 [1984].

———. "Maleness, Metaphor, and the 'Crisis' of Reason." In *A Mind of One's Own: Feminist Essays on Reason and Objectivity*, ed. Louise M. Antony and Charlotte E. Witt. 2nd ed. Boulder, Colo.: Westview Press, 2002.

Mills, Charles. *The Racial Contract*. Ithaca, N.Y.: Cornell University Press, 1997.

Nelson, Lynn Hankinson. *Who Knows: From Quine to a Feminist Empiricism*. Philadelphia, Pa: Temple University Press, 1990.

———. "The Very Idea of Feminist Epistemology." *Hypatia* 10, no. 3 (1995): 31–49.

———, and Jack Nelson, eds. *Feminism, Science, and the Philosophy of Science*. Boston: Kluwer Academic Publishers, 1997.

———, eds. *Feminist Interpretations of W. V. Quine*. University Park: Penn State Press, 2003.

Pinnick, Cassandra, Noretta Koertge, and Robert Almeder, eds. *Scrutinizing Feminist Epistemology: An Examination of Gender in Science*. New Brunswick, N.J.: Rutgers University Press, 2003.

Potter, Elizabeth. "The Science War Front." *The Women's Review of Books* 22, no.1 (2004): 7–8.

Pritchard, Duncan. "Recent Work on Epistemic Value." *American Philosophical Quarterly* 44, no. 2 (2007): 85–110.

Quine, W. V. "Epistemology Naturalized." In *Ontological Relativity and Other Essays*. New York: Columbia University Press, 1969.

Richards, Janet Radcliffe. "Why Feminist Epistemology Isn't." In *The Flight from Science and Reason*, ed. Paul R. Gross, Norman Levitt, and Martin W. Lewis, 385–412. Baltimore, Md.: John Hopkins University Press, 1996.

Richardson, Sarah S. "Feminist Philosophy of Science: History, Contributions, and Challenges." *Synthese* 177, no. 3 (2010): 337–62.

Riggs, Wayne. "The Value Turn in Epistemology." In *New Waves in Epistemology*, ed. Vincent F. Hendricks and Duncan Pritchard, 300–23. New York: Palgrave Macmillan, 2008.

Rooney, Phyllis. "Gendered Reason: Sex Metaphor and Conceptions of Reason." *Hypatia* 6, no. 2 (1991): 77–103.

———. "Feminist-Pragmatist Revisionings of Reason, Knowledge, and Philosophy." *Hypatia* 8, no. 2 (1993): 15–37.

———. "Rationality and the Politics of Gender Difference." *Metaphilosophy* 26, no. 1/2 (1995): 22–45.

———. "Gender and Moral Reasoning Revisited: Reengaging Feminist Psychology." In *Feminists Doing Ethics*, ed. Peggy DesAutels and Joanne Waugh, 153–166. Lanham, Md.: Rowman & Littlefield, 2001.

———. "Feminist Epistemology and Naturalized Epistemology: An Uneasy Alliance," In *Feminist Interpretations of W. V. Quine*, ed. Lynn Hankinson Nelson and Jack Nelson, 205–239. University Park: Penn State Press, 2003.

———. "The Marginalization of Feminist Epistemology and What That Reveals about Epistemology 'Proper.'" In *Feminist Epistemology and Philosophy of Science: Power in Knowledge*, ed. Heidi Grasswick, 3–24. Dordrecht, Holland: Springer, 2011.

Rorty, Richard. *Philosophy and the Mirror of Nature*. Princeton, N.J.: Princeton University Press, 1979.

Rosenberg, Karen Esther, and Judith A. Howard. "Finding Feminist Sociology: A Review Essay." *Signs* 33, no 3 (2008): 675–96.

Schmitt, Frederick F., ed. *Socializing Epistemology: The Social Dimensions of Knowledge*. Lanham, Md.: Rowman & Littlefield, 1994.

Seigfried, Charlene Haddock. *Pragmatism and Feminism: Reweaving the Social Fabric*. Chicago: University of Chicago Press, 1996.

Shelton, Jim D. "The Failure of Feminist Epistemology." *Academic Questions* 19, no. 2 (2006): 82–92.

Sullivan, Shannon, and Nancy Tuana, eds. *Race and Epistemologies of Ignorance*. Albany: State University of New York Press, 2007.

Superson, Anita M., and Ann E. Cudd, eds. *Theorizing Backlash: Philosophical Reflections on the Resistance to Feminism.* Lanham, Md.: Rowman & Littlefield, 2002.

Tiles, Mary, and Jim Tiles. *An Introduction to Historical Epistemology: The Authority of Knowledge.* Oxford: Blackwell, 1993.

Tuana, Nancy, ed. *Feminism and Science.* Bloomington: Indiana University Press, 1989.

Valian, Virginia. *Why So Slow? The Advancement of Women.* Cambridge, Mass.: MIT Press, 1998.

Waithe, Mary Ellen, ed. *A History of Women Philosophers.* Vols. 1–4. Dordrecht, Holland: Springer Academic Publishing, 1987–1994.

Webb, Mark Owen. "Feminist Epistemology as Whipping-Girl." In *Theorizing Backlash: Philosophical Reflections on the Resistance to Feminism*, ed. Anita M. Superson and Ann E. Cudd, 49–65. Lanham, Md.: Rowman & Littlefield, 2002.

Williams, Michael. *Problems of Knowledge: A Critical Introduction to Epistemology.* New York: Oxford University Press, 2001.

Wylie, Alison. "Doing Philosophy as a Feminist: Longino on the Search for a Feminist Epistemology." *Philosophical Topics* 23, no. 2 (1995): 345–58.

Zagzebski, Linda Trinkaus. *Virtues of the Mind.* Cambridge: Cambridge University Press, 1996.

14

ELIZABETH ANDERSON
University of Michigan–Ann Arbor

USES OF VALUE JUDGMENTS IN SCIENCE:

A General Argument, with Lessons from a Case Study of Feminist Research on Divorce

THE UNDERDETERMINATION ARGUMENT ESTABLISHES that scientists may use political values to guide inquiry, without providing criteria for distinguishing legitimate from illegitimate guidance. This paper supplies such criteria. Analysis of the confused arguments against value-laden science reveals the fundamental criterion of illegitimate guidance: when value judgments operate to drive inquiry to a predetermined conclusion. A case study of feminist research on divorce reveals numerous legitimate ways that values can guide science without violating this standard.

I. RETHINKING THE UNDERDETERMINATION ARGUMENT FOR VALUE-LADEN SCIENCE

Feminist science is science guided by feminist values. To its critics, the very idea of feminist science—or any science guided by moral or political values—is paradoxical and dangerous (Susan Haack 1993; Clifford Geertz 1990; Paul Gross and Norman Levitt 1994; Janet Richards 1995). Advocates of feminist science have offered able defenses of value-laden science (Helen Longino 1990; Lynn Hankinson Nelson 1990). Their core argument begins with the observation that the link between evidence and hypothesis is mediated by background assumptions. Scientists must therefore select their background assumptions before they can determine which hypotheses are supported by the evidence. According to Quine's underdetermination thesis, theories are, in principle, underdetermined even by all the empirical evidence that could ever be gathered. So there is always room for choice in the selection of background assumptions. Since various background assumptions could be legitimately selected for any reason, no logical or methodological principles prevent scientists from choosing some on account of their congruence with their moral or political values. A fortiori, feminists are permitted to choose their background assumptions on account of their congruence with feminist values.

The underdetermination argument has served feminist scientists well. But the time has come to rethink the way it models the relations between values and hypotheses. As the argument stands, it does not help us evaluate the different ways that values might be deployed in inquiry. Yet surely some uses of values to select background assumptions are illegitimate. Feminists object to the deployment of sexist values to select background assumptions that insulate the theoretical underpinnings of patriarchy from refutation. Critics of feminist science similarly worry that feminists will use their values in ways that insulate feminist theories from refutation. We need criteria to distinguish legitimate from illegitimate ways of deploying values in science.

The underdetermination argument also assumes that all moral and political values are on a par with respect to their epistemic value. It's just a lucky break if some values are more congruent than others with what turn out to be the most epistemically fruitful background assumptions. To the extent that feminists are simply interested in making room for the legitimacy of feminist science, we should not demand more than this. No one should be persuaded by an argument that *immediately* infers, from the claimed normative superiority of particular moral and political values, their superiority as tools for generating scientific knowledge. Yet we might wonder whether some values are systematically more epistemically fruitful than others.

Finally, as stated, the underdetermination argument represents values as an exogenous influence on theory choice. Yet it would seem reasonable that if values can legitimately influence empirical theories, then empirical theories can legitimately influence our value judgments. Some feminist philosophers, notably Lynn Hankinson Nelson (1990, 248–54, 300–317), have stressed this possibility. On her model, factual and evaluative judgments are integrated into a unified web of belief. However, her commitment to Quinean holism, in which our factual and evaluative theories confront, as a body, the totality of the evidence, prevents her from modeling the specific ways that particular empirical observations can be used to support or undermine particular value judgments. This lack of specificity lends an air of hand waving to the underdetermination argument.

These deficiencies of the underdetemination argument can be traced to a common cause. Feminist philosophers of science have focused on analyzing science, while mostly taking value judgments for granted.[1] This undertheorization of value judgments has made it hard to identify precisely the concerns of advocates of value-free science. It has impeded the development of criteria to distinguish legitimate from illegitimate uses of values in science. It has also made it difficult to model the knowledge-enhancing roles of value judgments in science. To make progress on these problems, we need to integrate moral philosophy and the philosophy of science.

I shall address these problems by focusing attention on value judgments and their epistemic character: on what facts count as evidence *for* value judgments, and what facts value judgments help us see. In the next section of this paper, I review the orthodox case for the claim that good science is value-free or neutral among moral and political values. I show that the orthodox case depends on the claim that value judgments are science-free—that is, that no empirical observations can count as evidence for a claim that something is good. In section three, I show that the real worry advocates of neutrality have about value judgments in science is what they take to be the *dogmatic* character of value judgments, which is derived from the supposition that value judgments are science-free. The worry is that if we allow value judgments to guide scientific practice, they will infect it with dogmatism, thereby rendering it blind to the evidence. I address this worry by arguing that we have evidence about the value of different states of affairs. One important source of evidence consists in the representations that ground our emotional responses to these states. If we condition our acceptance of value judgments on evidence, we will not hold our values dogmatically, and they can be integrated into scientific theorizing without making it dogmatic. In part four, I explore the bidirectional influences of factual and value judgments, identifying specific paths of legitimate and productive interaction, in an exemplary case of feminist research. Part five draws conclusions from this case study for the questions with which we began.

II. THE ORTHODOX CASE FOR VALUE-NEUTRAL SCIENCE

Let us distinguish two senses to the claim that science is value-free (Hugh Lacey 1999, 2–6):

1. *Neutrality*: Scientific theories do not a) presuppose or b) support any non-cognitive (moral and political) intrinsic value judgments.
2. *Impartiality*: The only grounds for accepting a theory are its relations to the evidence and its manifestation of cognitive values. These grounds are impartial among rival noncognitive values.

According to impartiality, theories are to be assessed on the basis of their realization of cognitive values, such as empirical adequacy, consistency, scope, simplicity, and consonance with established theories (Thomas Kuhn 1977). How well a theory realizes these cognitive values can be assessed independently of one's moral and political values. It is a delicate matter to arrive at a sound formulation of the claim of impartiality. I shall assume for the purposes of this paper the existence of a sound formulation of this claim, suitably qualified (Hugh Lacey 1999, 224–31).

Impartiality is logically independent of neutrality. It poses no logical barriers to the possibility that a scientific theory, impartially supported by the evidence and manifesting cognitive values to a high degree, provides greater support for some noncognitive intrinsic value judgments (value judgments, for short) than for others. If this were true, then some value judgments would be impartially justified, or at least better justified than rival value judgments. And this would be a fact that adherents of rival value judgments would have to admit. Similarly, a scientific theory might presuppose certain noncognitive value judgments—for instance, in classifying data according to a preferred normative theory. Such a theory might manifest cognitive values to a higher degree than rival theories that refuse to classify the data in the same value-laden way. If this were true, then some value judgments would be epistemically fruitful, as judged by impartial standards, and their deployment in science would be epistemically justified on impartial grounds.[2]

In this paper, I focus on the arguments for neutrality—the idea that sound empirical theories neither a) presuppose nor b) support any non-cognitive value judgments. Call these claims presupposition neutrality and implication neutrality, respectively. The two claims of neutrality entail one another. If a hypothesis is confirmed by independent evidence, it may legitimately be used as a tool for uncovering and interpreting observations bearing on some other hypothesis. For example, if the evidence supports the theory of carbon dating, then one may legitimately presuppose the validity of carbon dating in choosing among rival archaeological theories about the origin of agriculture. By parallel reasoning, if scientific evidence existed that supported a particular value judgment, then it could legitimately be used to interpret data relevant to some *other* scientific theory. And if a sound scientific theory were entitled to presuppose certain value judgments, it could provide support for further value judgments. For example, if a scientific theory were entitled to presuppose that x is valuable, and it discovered that y causes x, then it would support the judgment that y is instrumentally valuable.

Let us turn to the standard case for neutrality. It rests on two arguments, one psychological, the other ostensibly logical but really dependent on a claim about practical reason. The psychological argument addresses presupposition neutrality. It claims that scientists who bring to inquiry value judgments concerning the subject of investigation—for instance, the judgment that the subordination of women is unjust—will be unable to impartially assess empirical theories concerning that subject—in this case, phenomena of women's subordination. "Whenever the person of science introduces his personal value judgment, a full understanding of the facts *ceases*" (Max Weber 1946, 146). Good scientists should bracket their value judgments and adopt a neutral, "objective" attitude toward their subject matter.

What is the psychological mechanism by which value presuppositions interfere with impartiality? Several candidates have been suggested. Geertz worries that investigators doing science as feminists will be compromised by wishful thinking (1990, 19). Gross and Levitt believe that such investigators will dishonestly reject an impartially justified scientific theory "if and when it inconveniences [their] political program" (1994, 162). Haack argues that they will be close-minded, rejecting any reasoning or evidence that did not reach a foregone conclusion supported by their political preferences (1993, 37–38).

The logical argument is addressed to implication neutrality. Supporters cite "Hume's law," that there is no deductively valid inference from "is" to "ought," from factual to value judgments (Haack 1993, 35). This facile claim does not get to the heart of the matter. Even if we grant that no substantive value judgment *logically* follows from any conjunction of factual statements, this merely puts value judgments on a logical par with scientific hypotheses. For it is equally true that there is no deductively valid inference from statements of evidence alone to theoretical statements. Theories always logically go beyond the evidence adduced in support of them. The question of neutrality is not whether factual judgments logically entail value judgments, but whether they can stand in evidentiary relations to them.

Behind the logical argument lie two lines of thought, one existentialist, the other instrumentalist. Max Weber (1946) articulated the existentialist route in the *locus classicus* of the doctrine of scientific neutrality, "Science as a Vocation." He argued that rationalization, the fundamental feature of modernity, results in the "disenchantment of the world": a representation of the world as value-free, neither governed by teleological laws nor containing objectively normative properties. It also leaves us without prophets or gods—those who could speak authoritatively for one ultimate value over others. Modern times therefore force us to confront the necessity of choosing our ultimate values—our "gods"—for ourselves, without authoritative guidance from the world or others. "Life...interpreted in its own terms...[is] an unceasing struggle of these gods with one another...The ultimately possible attitudes toward life are irreconcilable, and hence their struggle can never be brought to a final conclusion. Thus it is necessary to make a decisive choice" (Weber 1946, 152).

Weber holds that there is no way to adjudicate between conflicting world-views, because each rejects the value of what the other presupposes. For example, science shows that there is no basis in fact for beliefs in God or miracles. But this does not pose an unanswerable challenge to the religious believer. To be sure, the religious person *must* acknowledge that if science can explain supposedly supernatural phenomena in naturalistic terms, then the scientific explanation is epistemically superior. But "the believer can do this without being disloyal to his faith" (Weber 1946, 147). For the genuinely religious can, indeed must, make the "intellectual sacrifice" of rejecting reason (Weber 1946, 155). Science cannot refute this choice, since it can only presuppose and not prove the value of guiding belief in light of evidence and reasoning.

Weber's heroic existentialism does not prove the neutrality of science, but rather the opposite. By his own account, science supplies evidence against the truth of religious world-views. And religion itself presupposes that the authority of its values depends on the truth of its factual claims—divine creation, revelation, and so forth. So, science supplies evidence against the authority of religious values. Christian fundamentalists are under no illusions about this, which is why they vigorously assault the epistemic credentials of evolutionary theory. They want to have their religion *and* reason, too. Weber's argument gives them only a Hobson's choice.

Weber represents the choice of values as a matter of arbitrarily joining forces in the titanic clash of competing gods, where the intellectually honest courageously recognize both that the battle must be joined and that there are no grounds for choosing one side or the other. The need to reconcile two competing thoughts—that the choice must be regarded as of momentous importance, even though nothing objectively matters—leaves one wondering whether the feeling of profundity generated from viewing life from Weber's elevated perspective is merely a symptom of hypoxia. Strip out Weber's hyperbolic rhetoric, and what remains is the instrumentalist theory of practical reason. According to instrumentalism, reason can only inform us about means to our ends. It cannot guide the choice of final ends. For our ends are given to us by our motives, which are beyond rational criticism. Thus, there can be no considerations favoring the choice of one final end over another. *A fortiori*, there can be no empirical evidence in favor of one end over another. If we take a final end to be what the agent judges to be intrinsically valuable, it follows that no evidence can exist for intrinsic value judgments. So values are science-free.

Let us defer until the next section an evaluation of these arguments. Assuming that science is neutral and impartial, what are its proper relations to noncognitive values? Even the most orthodox advocates of value-free science accept the following:

1. In the "context of discovery," noncognitive values may play a role in selecting the phenomena to be investigated and suggesting hypotheses to be tested. (They must be excluded, however, from the "context of justification" in which hypotheses are evaluated in light of how well they manifest the cognitive values.)
2. In the context of scientific investigation (designing a study, collecting data) noncognitive values may justify the imposition of practical or informational constraints on scientific procedures—for example, requiring that experimental subjects be treated humanely, and that human subjects give informed consent. But these constraints are in the service of noncognitive values only. Any positive impact they may have on cognition is accidental.
3. In the context of application, noncognitive values may play a role in determining what level of certainty in a scientific theory is demanded before it is accepted as a guide for action.
4. Science may guide action by informing people of the means to their ends and the possibility of attaining their ends.
5. Science may make "assessments"—informing people how far certain values are realized (Ernest Nagel 1979, 492–93). For

example, if one counts as a standard of justice that no woman shall be subject to domestic violence, science can assess how just the world is by this criterion. But it cannot tell us whether this standard is normatively authoritative.

The question of neutrality is the question of whether scientific and value judgments may be more intimately related than in these ways. In particular, we want to know whether, when investigators allow their non-cognitive evaluative presuppositions to structure the context of investigation, this can have *systematically* favorable effects on the cognitive values manifested in the results of the investigation, precisely in virtue of the normative validity of those presuppositions (contrary to 2 and presupposition neutrality). We also want to know whether scientific findings can provide evidential support for the normative authority of some value judgments over others (contrary to 5 and implication neutrality).

III. THE ORTHODOX CASE EVALUATED: CAN THERE BE EVIDENCE FOR VALUE JUDGMENTS?

I have argued that science is value-free if and only if values are science-free. The thesis of scientific neutrality therefore depends more on the character of ethical thought than is usually supposed. I shall argue in this section that the arguments for neutrality depend on contradictory and crude models of how value judgments work.

Observe that the psychological argument for presupposition neutrality contradicts the "logical" argument for implication neutrality. The psychological argument postulates that value judgments give people motives to believe or assert certain factual claims, even when the evidence does not support those claims. *Which* claims do they have an interest in believing? Let us not be deceived by the suggestion that non-neutral investigators will be tempted to illegitimately infer "P is true" from "P ought to be true," where P is whatever state they judge to be good (Haack 1993, 42, n. 19). This is a red herring. Feminists believe that women ought to be free from rape, forced reproduction, and material deprivation. This does not give us the slightest interest in believing that we *already* live in a feminist utopia, where women enjoy these freedoms! To the contrary, it heightens our awareness of when these feminist values are *not* realized.

The judgments non-neutral inquirers are thought to have an interest in believing, regardless of the evidence, are rather *the factual claims that provide evidential support for their noncognitive value judgments.* When feminist scientists are suspected of "wishful thinking," they are suspected of thinking, for example, that the paucity of women among political leaders is not due to any innate inferiority of women in leadership ability, and wishing away evidence to the contrary. This accusation would make no sense unless one thought that feminists staked the normative claim for expanding women's political leadership on a factual claim that women's natures do not disable them from performing in leadership roles. The same point applies to Gross and Levitt's charge that feminist inquirers will be tempted to dismiss any facts "inconvenient" to their political program (1994, 162). There could be no such "inconvenient" facts, if facts could not provide evidence for or against value judgments. Gross and Levitt here merely echo Weber's view that science teaches us to recognize "facts that are inconvenient" for people's "party opinions" (1946, 147).

People who are disposed to believe a judgment regardless of the evidence are called dogmatists. Value judgments are not inherently dogmatic. "Disillusionment" is another name for learning from experience that one's deepest value judgments were mistaken. Millions of people in Eastern Europe, once dedicated communists, were disillusioned of it when they found out what living under communism was like. "Growing up" is another name for learning from experience that one's childish and adolescent values weren't what one had chalked them up to be, an experience that most people undergo. Thus, the psychological argument against scientists who bring value judgments to their investigations is another red herring. The argument is properly framed against dogmatism, not value judgments.

Now consider the instrumentalist model of value judgments that underlies the "logical" argument for implication neutrality. On this model, we cannot reason about whether our ultimate values are right are wrong; we can only reason about what means would realize what we value. This supposes that nothing could ever count as *evidence* that some things are good or bad. This is why value judgments are thought to be held dogmatically. If no considerations can support value judgments, then none can defeat them. So we can go on holding our value judgments regardless of the state of the world.

It is possible to construct world-views in which certain value judgments are held dogmatically, insulated from the give-and-take of the rest of the web of belief. More typically, as in religious worldviews, ultimate value judgments are taken to rest on factual claims about God or the divine that are themselves held dogmatically. But value judgments *needn't* be held in these ways. I would suggest that for most people—those who are not fanatically in the grip of some ideology—they *can't* be held in these ways. The mark of a nonfanatical valuer is that she treats her intrinsic value judgments as open to revision in light of experience. These are the people who are capable of learning, growth, even wisdom.

Among the experiences that provide evidence for value judgments are emotional experiences. By "emotional experiences" I refer to affectively colored experiences of persons, things, events, or states of the world. Examples include joy in seeing someone, satisfaction and pride in the fulfillment of one's objectives, misery over some process, and relief at its end. Emotional experiences have the following features. First they have objects: they are *about* persons, things, events, or states. Second, they have a positive or negative aspect: they present their objects in a favorable or unfavorable light. Emotional experiences are *appearances* of objects as *important*. Third, they reflect the perspective or point of view of subjects who care about themselves or others. Emotions appear to signal the importance of things *for* what their subject cares about—the self, loved ones, or others with whom the subject identifies. Standing attitudes of concern (that is, dispositions to feel emotions, which may be negative, as in hatred) serve the epistemic function of making salient to subjects the features of the world that appear to have import for what they care about. They seem to reveal the world insofar as it is related, positively or negatively, to the subject's concerns. But emotions can also lead subjects to question their attitudes of concern. (Zina may love John. But daily contact with his petty scheming could arouse her contempt, in the light of which he appears unworthy of her love.)

Do emotional experiences *really* provide evidence for value judgments? This is to ask whether we should take seriously the appearances they present to us as bearing on our value judgments and hence on the choice of our final ends and objects of concern. In fact, we do take such experiences seriously. We tend to judge what arouses our favorable emotions as good, and what arouses our unfavorable emotions as bad. If we experience a hobby as boring, we seem to take this as evidence that it isn't worthwhile, at least for those of us who find it boring. If we view the giant California redwoods with awe, we seem to take this as evidence that they are splendid. To vindicate these thoughts, we must show, first, that emotional experiences have a form and relation to value judgments that makes them *capable* of standing in an evidentiary relation to them; and second, that they can be *reliable* or *trustworthy* sources of evidence.

Consider first the question of capability. To count as presenting evidence, a mental state must a) have cognitive content, b) be independent of what it is supposed to be evidence for, and c) be defeasible—accountable and hence responsive to the way the world is. Emotional experiences satisfy all three conditions: a) It is now widely acknowledged that emotions have cognitive content, that they represent the world as having certain features.[3] b) They can exist independently of the value judgments for which they purport to provide evidence, and of the desires or final ends supported by those value judgments. In other words, they are not merely reflections of judgments and desires the agent had prior to the experience. Diane might take up a career in politics, eager to attain elected office, anticipating with relish its challenges and prospects for achievement and power. Despite these desires and value judgments, she might find her life as a politician intolerable—she is dispirited by the backbiting; she feels compromised by what she needs to do to raise campaign funds; legislative victories feel hollow. These experiences come as an unwelcome surprise to Diane, undermining both her conviction that politics is a worthwhile career for her and her desire to pursue it. They are the basis of her disillusionment with politics, a process that would be impossible if her emotional experiences were merely the creatures of her preexisting value judgments and desires.

Finally, c) we hold our emotional experiences accountable to the way the world is. If we find that the representational content of an emotional experience is defective—erroneous, blinkered, confused—we rationally discount its import. Imagine Sharon, a political ally of Diane's, trying to persuade Diane that her disappointment with what seems to be a merely symbolic victory reflects an unduly narrow perspective. Granted, it achieves little when considered in isolation. But in the long view it can be seen as fundamentally shifting the terms of debate. What seems like a hollow victory is a watershed event. This judgment could be tested over a longer stretch of experience. Sharon is trying to persuade Diane that if she viewed the significance of the victory in its wider context, she should feel triumphant, not disappointed. Such persuasion would make no sense unless our emotions were of a kind to be systematically responsive to the way the world is.[4]

It is clear, then, that emotional experiences are *capable* of functioning as evidence for value judgments. But are we wise to treat them as evidence? Should we trust our emotions? Once they have passed the tests of representational adequacy applied to their cognitive contents, it is hard to see, apart from special cases (for example, when our emotional reactions are dulled by drugs or depression), why we shouldn't. Indeed, we would be *crazy* not to.[5] This would be to tell Diane that she should stick to her original judgments about the value of her pursuing a career in politics, and the ambitions it underwrites, even though the pursuit makes her miserable and she is just going through the motions while gritting her teeth. It would be to counsel Diane to hold her value judgments *dogmatically*.

Let us retrace our steps. The psychological argument for presupposition neutrality assumes that there can be empirical evidence for value judgments, since it worries that people will dogmatically insist on the factual claims that support their values. The "logical" (instrumentalist) argument for implication neutrality denies that evidence can exist for value judgments (that is, rational grounds for our final ends), and so implies that they can only be held dogmatically. I have argued that there is a body of evidence to which value judgments can and ought to be held accountable. Values are therefore not "science-free." From an epistemological point of view, value judgments function like empirical hypotheses.[6]

IV. THE BIDIRECTIONAL INFLUENCE OF FACTS AND VALUES: A CASE STUDY OF FEMINIST SCIENCE

The argument so far clears the way for feminist science by relocating the objections to value-laden science. Deep down, what the objectors find worrisome about allowing value judgments to guide scientific inquiry is not that they have evaluative content, but that these judgments might be held dogmatically, so as to preclude the recognition of evidence that might undermine them. We need to ensure that value judgments do not operate to drive inquiry to a predetermined conclusion. This is our fundamental criterion for distinguishing legitimate from illegitimate uses of values in science.

This criterion may leave us wondering whether any value-laden research could satisfy it, while still giving values some epistemic function. Consider that much empirical research in the social sciences is devoted to answering evaluative questions, especially about the relations of various phenomena to well-being. We need a model of the bidirectional influence of facts and values in which the evaluative presuppositions brought to inquiry do not determine the answer to the evaluative question in advance, but leave this open to determination by the evidence. At the same time, these presuppositions must help us uncover the evidence that bears on our question.

To construct such a model, we need to focus on a case study. Abigail Stewart, Anne Copeland, Nia Lane Chester, Janet Malley and Nicole Barenbaum's *Separating Together: How Divorce Transforms Families* (1997) offers an exemplary case study of feminist research on divorce. Such research is controversial, because the evidence it uncovers bears on the value of divorce, which is contested. Yet discovery of such evidence, with the purpose of informing value judgments, and consequently, practical recommendations concerning divorce, is the primary reason for such research. Let us consider the interaction of evaluative presuppositions, evidence, and evaluative conclusions at each stage of the Stewart team's research. To clarify these interactions, I offer the following stylized division of the stages of research: a) Researchers begin with an orientation to the background interests animating the field, b) frame a question informed by those interests, c) articulate a conception of the object of inquiry, d) decide what types of data to collect, e) establish and carry out data sampling or generation procedures, f) analyze their data in accordance with chosen techniques, g) decide when to stop analyzing their data, and h) draw conclusions from their analyses.

a) *Orientation to background interests.* All sides in the empirical controversies surrounding divorce are interested in understanding phenomena concerning divorce in relation to the well-being of the affected parties. This shared interest enables us to see researchers on different sides as addressing one another, even when they are answering different questions. Feminist research in this area most perspicuously challenges those oriented toward what we may call "traditional family values." Proponents of traditional family values idealize a model of the family in which the husband and wife are married for life, live in same household, and raise their biological children. The key feature of this model is the inseparability of the role duties of spouses and parents. The wife's role is to be mother to her husband's children; the father's role is to be the husband of his children's mother. According to its proponents, this arrangement is in the best interest of the children, and probably also the parents. Alternative family arrangements are judged progressively worse the further they depart from this ideal. Divorce, because it separates parental from spousal roles, is conceived as "breaking up" the family, thereby harming the children. Traditionalists blame the divorcing adults for failing to identify sufficiently with their role duties, for selfishly seeking personal fulfillment (Barbara Whitehead 1983). They also blame feminists for drawing women away from the homemaker role that unified the duties of wife and mother (George Gilder 1986; James Wilson 2002).

Feminists approach divorce with greater ambivalence. Although feminists are critical of the patriarchal family, Stewart's team was initially unsure how to assess divorce from the standpoint of opposition to sexism (author's interview with Stewart, March 14, 2002). Does divorce reinforce women's disadvantages, enabling men to leave their wives while undermining wives' interests? Or is it a way for women to liberate themselves from oppressive marriages? While keeping an open mind on this point, the Stewart team's feminist values did lead them to question whether post-divorce family forms should be evaluated in terms of how well they approximated the relationships of "traditional" families.

b) *Framing the research questions.* The different value orientations of traditionalists and feminists suggest different research questions. Traditionalists, viewing married parents as the ideal, are apt to ask: does divorce have negative effects on children and their parents? A natural way to answer this question would be to compare the members of families with and without divorce on measures of well-being, especially negative outcomes (for example, sickness, poverty, behavior problems). Stewart's team was skeptical of this approach, on both methodological and normative grounds. Methodologically, it is virtually impossible to distinguish the effects of divorce from the effects of the problems in the marriage that led to divorce (Stewart et al. 1997, 26–28). Trying to measure the value of divorce by comparing the well-being of members of families with and without divorce is like trying to measure the value of hospitalization by comparing the health of people in and out of the hospital. In both cases, we need to control for pre-existing sickness—in the marriage or the body. But whereas objective controls can be devised for hospitalization studies, the same is not true for divorce studies. Even when families with divorce are compared with families without divorce, but experiencing similar problems (for example, high spousal conflict), the two types of families always differ in other respects (Stewart et al. 1997, 26)—perhaps most importantly with respect to whether the spouses judge that their problems are so bad that divorce is warranted.

Aside from these methodological problems, Stewart also had normative objections to the traditional research question. Focusing on negative outcomes reduces the possibility of finding positive outcomes from divorce. Focusing on aggregate differences between the married and the divorced implicitly supposes that each group is internally homogeneous, that the evaluations supported by the group comparisons apply to each member of the group. Distinguishing groups simply by the presence of a particular life event is to assume that the importance of this event does not change over time. These choices of focus make normative sense from a traditional point of view, which assumes that the key to human flourishing is everyone's performance of traditional role duties. One system for living fits all. Disruptions of traditional roles have a fixed, enduring meaning. But feminists reject these assumptions, holding instead that different people may find different life plans fulfilling. Moreover, they regard people as agents, actively interpreting and shaping the meanings of events in their lives, rather than as simply defined by their status ("married" or "divorced"). An event such as divorce, initially experienced as disruptive, may recede in significance as individuals cope with it and engage the new experiences that it makes possible (Stewart et al. 1997, 30). Given this value orientation, Stewart's team thought it made more sense to ask how individuals vary among themselves and over time in the meanings they ascribe to divorce, its effects, and their coping strategies.

c) *Conceiving of the object of inquiry.* Longino (1990, 98–102) argues that value presuppositions play an important role in determining how some research conceives of the object of inquiry. This depends on the point of view one takes on the object of inquiry, which may be a function of one's professional and moral relations to it. Research on divorce confirms her argument. Judith Wallerstein, a clinical psychologist who studies divorce, argues that it scars the affected children for life (Judith Wallerstein and Joan Kelly 1980; Judith Wallerstein, Julia Lewis, and Sandra Blakeslee 2000). She constructed her conception of divorce from her involvement with individuals in a clinical setting. The conception of divorce drawn from a clinical perspective focuses on the *individual's* problems with an event in the *past*, stressing its *negative* aspects. Divorce is conceived in terms of "trauma" and "loss"; it is seen as a "life stress" that puts children "at risk" for problems later in life.

The phrases in quotations use what is known as "thick evaluative concepts"—concepts that simultaneously express factual and value judgments. For example, the thick concept "trauma" applies only to sudden injurious events. The factual components of thick concepts are selected to track their underlying evaluative point. Extending their application to new factual contexts—for example, extending the concept "trauma" from cases of physical to psychological injury (Ian Hacking 1995, 183–89)—involves normative and not just factual reasoning (Bernard Williams 1985, 141–42). Conceiving of the object of inquiry in thick evaluative terms is thus not a value-neutral activity, not the neutral matter of "assessment" as understood by Ernest Nagel (1979).

Yet, the evaluative content of thickly described conceptions of the object of inquiry does not prevent such conceptions from fruitfully and legitimately guiding empirical research. A conception of divorce as trauma and loss leads researchers to *look* for certain kinds of evidence, guiding their selection of research tools—for example, measures of psychological disturbance. Since such evidence would be relevant to answering research questions about the value of divorce, such a conception is potentially fruitful. Since the conception does not guarantee that such evidence will be *found*, it is legitimate.

Stewart's team, likewise, adopted a thickly described conception of divorce. But their conception included both negative and positive dimensions. Stewart's team, like our hypothetical Sharon in the section above, also questioned the *temporal* frame through which the trauma-loss-stress school views divorce. The conception of divorce as a "trauma" represents it as a sudden *event* "occurring in an otherwise benign stream of events" (Stewart et al. 1997, 9). On this view, divorce brings about or constitutes the failure of a marriage. Yet, from the point of view of at least one spouse, the marriage has typically been failing for years before divorce. To them, divorce is not an event, but a long *process* of coming to grips with that failure. The conception of divorce as a "loss" represents the post-divorce condition as lacking some good that was present prior to the divorce. It fixes attention on the significance of divorce in relation to the past. This conception may make sense in clinical settings, for patients who can't get over their past. But it is at odds with the perspective of those seeking divorce, who are through that very act trying to put some of their problems in the past so as to construct a better future. Stewart's team therefore decided to conceive of divorce not only as loss but also as an "opportunity for personal growth" (Stewart et al. 1997, 19) and as an extended process of adjustment to a new set of life circumstances that could go better or worse over time (1997, 23–24). This longer temporal perspective of evaluation guided research by dictating a longitudinal study design. It permitted Stewart's team to test whether divorce receded in significance as the affected individuals learned to cope with its consequences. This is legitimate: to look for evidence of change over time is not to ensure that one will find it.

Stewart's team also questioned the individualistic orientation of traditional research that focuses on factors involving the individual, considered in isolation. This orientation meshes with the traditional conception of divorce as "breaking up" the family, as if it threatens to reduce its members to free-floating atoms. As feminists, the members of Stewart's team were open to seeing alternative family forms as *families*. They therefore conceived of divorce not as breaking up the family, but as transforming it by separating parental from spousal roles (Stewart et al. 1997, 20–21). The members of the divorcing couple remain related to one another as co-parents living in separate households. They saw this alternative family system as having needs of its own, which could not necessarily be determined by taking the traditional family as a model. Their systems perspective on individuals as participants in social relationships, as well as their pluralistic conception of families, enabled them to explore whether post-divorce families that more closely approximate the traditional family model—for example, in the regularity of the noncustodial parent's contact with children, and authority relations between the custodial parent and children—are better for children.

d) *Deciding what types of data to collect.* Divorce researchers agree that the central focus of study is the well-being of the persons and relationships involved in divorce. Value judgments are inherent in this line of research. This does not leave the content of research up to the whims of the investigator. There is little dispute over the evaluative implications of many standard measures of well- (or ill-) being—for example, physical illness, stress symptoms such as sleep disturbance, financial security, and children's behavior problems. However, measures of such objective phenomena don't capture all aspects of well-being. I argued above that individuals' emotional responses to and emotionally colored interpretations of their situations constitute vital evidence of value. Congruent with this argument, Stewart's team gathered data on subjects' post-divorce feelings and interpretations of changes they underwent, in addition to reports of more objective phenomena. This provided crucial data confirming the conception of divorce as an opportunity for personal growth. Women especially found this to be so, with 70 percent judging that their personalities had improved since divorce (Stewart et al. 1997, 66).

The decision to gather qualitative data on subjects' feelings and self-interpretations reflects a background value presupposition of according normative authority to the subjects of study, to judge values for themselves. The results of taking subjects' self-assessments seriously put objective data on divorce in a revealing light. For example, other researchers have found that divorce leaves women in worse objective financial condition than when they were married (Lenore Weitzman 1985). However, Stewart's team found that many divorced women, although acknowledging their lower incomes, were pleased by the change divorce brought to their financial condition because it let them enjoy greater financial autonomy over the income they had (Stewart et al. 1997, 102).

e) *Data sampling.* Conceptions of the object of inquiry function as tools of inquiry, shaping study questions and design. Conceptions of divorce as loss or as opportunity for personal growth, as family breakup or as family transformation, facilitate the exposure of different aspects of the object of inquiry. How do we prevent such value-laden conceptions from simply confirming their own presuppositions? Consider sampling procedures. It is a standard methodological rule that causal inquiries should not select cases on the dependent variable. Doing so introduces biases that cannot be corrected through the introduction of controls.[7] In the case of divorce studies, this means that a clinically obtained sample is *not* a sound basis for comparing conceptions of divorce as loss against conceptions of divorce as an opportunity for growth. A sample drawn from psychological clinics will be biased toward those experiencing great difficulties coping with divorce, or mis-attributing their difficulties to divorce, and against those who find divorce liberating. Wallerstein's work on divorce has been criticized on this ground (Wallerstein and Kelly 1980; Wallerstein, Lewis, and Blakeslee 2000). Her error lies not in adopting a value-laden conception of divorce, but in failing to draw a random sample of cases. Stewart's team, by contrast, drew a less biased sample of cases from the divorce dockets. It still contained some biases. For example, more mothers were willing to participate than fathers (Stewart et al. 1997, 34). But precautions were taken to prevent the gender bias in the sample from affecting the conclusions, by analyzing mothers and fathers separately.

f) *Data analysis.* Quantitative studies typically contain numerous variables. Not every logically possible combination of and relationship among these variables is significant, either statistically, clinically, or normatively. Researchers must therefore choose which ones to analyze. With respect to any outcome variable, they also must decide whether to focus on *main effects* of independent variables on the outcome or to look for *interaction effects*. Suppose, for example, we are interested in measuring children's psychological adjustment after divorce. We could regress adjustment on measures of the children's maturity—for example, how skilled they are at grasping other people's perspectives. A significant, positive coefficient on mature perspective taking would indicate that children who are more mature in this respect have better post-divorce adjustment. Stewart's team found no main effect of mature perspective taking on post-divorce psychological adjustment (Stewart et al. 1997, 255, table 6.5). It does not follow that mature perspective taking is irrelevant to children's adjustment, however. Perspective taking may affect children's adjustment through its interaction with other variables. Indeed, Stewart's team found that it was associated with better adjustment among children whose parents were high in conflict (Stewart et al. 1997, 127). But it was associated with *worse* adjustment among children whose parents were low in conflict. On reflection, this makes sense. Mature perspective taking enables children to come to terms with their parents' fighting. But when they don't see their parents fighting, it leads to confusion, as the perceptive children try to make sense of their parents' divorce with inadequate information (Stewart et al. 1997, 128).

The decision to focus on main effects, or to look for interaction effects, reflects background values. A main effects analysis accepts the average outcome as representative of the group, discounting individual variation. This makes sense if one believes that a single way of life is best for everyone. But for researchers who doubt this, attention to within-group heterogeneity is imperative (Longino 1994, 477). Ways of life should be tailored to individual differences. Knowing that perceptive children of low-conflict divorces have greater difficulties in adjustment, what should parents of such children do? Maybe they should avoid situations that stimulate perceptive children's needs to make sense of them. Concretely, this suggests that custodial mothers should obtain employment out of the home, so their perceptive children aren't constantly confronted with their mothers' own psychological issues. Indeed, contrary to the traditionalists' view that children are better off with the mother at home, Stewart's team found that perceptive children were better adjusted when their mothers went to work (Stewart et al. 1997, 130–33).

g) *Deciding when to end an analysis.* Given that scientists cannot explore every possibility contained in their data, how should they decide when to stop their analysis and publish their conclusions? The great temptation is to stop an analysis as soon as it reaches findings pleasing to the researchers, but to continue analyzing displeasing findings in the hope of explaining them away. To be sure, it is almost impossible to accept unwelcome findings at face value. Stewart's team found that some children appeared to suffer from regular visitation by their noncustodial fathers. Unhappy with this result, the team engaged in further analysis and discovered that high levels of post-divorce parental conflict inter-acted with regular father visitation to produce their finding. For parents still fighting after the divorce, regular visits were the occasion for regular arguments, which the children presumably anticipated with anxiety (Stewart et al. 1997, 238). This account enabled Stewart's team to offer happier recommendations to fathers in high-conflict divorces: not to stay away, but to visit on a more spontaneous basis—a pattern they observed to work better for children whose divorced parents were still fighting.

Perhaps any divorce researchers would have insisted on further ana-lyzing the disturbing result. Stewart's team considered this point in criti-cally reflecting on its own practice. Team members argued that if they insisted on digging deeper into unwelcome findings, they should apply the same rigorous analysis to the controversial findings that they wel-comed (author's interview with Stewart, March 14, 2002). This led them to reopen their analysis of their finding, congenial to feminists, that divorced mothers were better adjusted if they worked full-time. Might this main effect mask a negative interaction between work and some other variable? Further analysis found that it did. Mothers who were working prior to the divorce did much better if they continued working after the divorce. But mothers who had previously stayed at home did worse if they went to work after the divorce (Stewart et al. 1997, 100–101).

h) *Drawing conclusions.* The main point of divorce research, as of much other research in the social sciences, is to answer evaluative ques-tions on the basis of empirical evidence. Are children better off if parents who want a divorce stay together? What coping strategies make divorce go better or worse for the affected parties? The enterprise of answering these questions on the basis of evidence would make no sense if science were value-neutral in implication—that is, if ethics were science-free. It is not. We can learn from experience what modes of life are better and worse, and correct our prior value judgments in light of experience. Stewart's team was bolder than most social scientists in drawing normative conclusions in explicitly moral vocabulary. They even ventured to describe some of their subjects as "wise" in their willingness to learn from their experiences, even when the conclusions they drew bucked conventional wisdom (Stewart et al. 1997, 232). For example, some mothers rejected the traditional assumption that families do best when parents maintain firmly authoritative relations with their children. They found that after divorce, they needed to consult their children about family decisions more than they used to. As evidence of the wisdom of this, Stewart's team found that children did no worse, and custodial mothers did better with more flexible parent-child role boundaries (1997, 239). Freed "from a constraining family ideology," such families were more creative in solving their problems (1997, 219).

V. HOW TO USE VALUE JUDGMENTS TO GUIDE SCIENCE IN LEGITIMATE AND FRUITFUL WAYS

This paper has raised several questions for value-laden research: 1) Can we distinguish legitimate from illegitimate uses of noncognitive value judgments in research? 2) Can we distinguish more from less epistemically fruitful non-cognitive value judgments? 3) Is the epistemic value of a noncognitive value judgment ever due to its normative authority? 4) Can science ever reach beyond instrumental value judgments and "assessments," providing evidence that bears on noncognitive intrinsic value judgments? 5) How should we model the bidirectional influence of factual and value judgments? Let us sketch some answers to these questions, drawing on the evidence about value-laden research found in our case study.

Legitimacy. Value-laden research is often accused of being "biased." Whether this is illegitimate depends on what is meant by bias. Let us distinguish three kinds of bias: in relation to the object of inquiry, in relation to the hypotheses to be tested, and in relation to a question or controversy. A research design is biased in relation to the object of inquiry if it (truthfully) reveals only some of its aspects, leaving us ignorant of others. It is biased in relation to its hypotheses if it is rigged in advance (whether wittingly or not) to confirm them. It is biased in relation to a question or controversy if it is more likely to (truthfully) uncover evidence that tends to support one side rather than the other sides of the controversy.

Bias in relation to the object of inquiry is inevitable. *All* research designs open up some lines of research into their objects, while closing off others. Scientific research programs necessarily adopt an abstract—that is, selective—conception of their objects of inquiry. For example, a conception of cancer as a genetic disease can guide research into genetic causes of cancer, but the tools it recommends (genetic tests, twin studies, family histories) won't tell us much about dietary causes of cancer. This is innocuous, as long as we do not confuse our abstract conception of the object of inquiry with the object itself.

Bias in relation to hypotheses is illegitimate. If a hypothesis is to be tested, the research design must leave open a fair possibility that evidence will disconfirm it. Failure to do this is the flaw I have labeled "dogmatism." Critics of feminist science claim it is inherent to value-laden research that it will only confirm the researchers' evaluative presuppositions. Our case study shows that this claim is false. Stewart's team discovered and reported results (on fathers' visitation, mothers' employment, and children's maturity) that they found unwelcome or surprising, as well as many null results. They left it open to determination by the evidence whether the coefficients of the variables in their regression models were significant or insignificant, positive or negative, large or small. They took precautions against sampling biases, and analyzed their data so as to circumvent known biases.

The larger lesson to be drawn from this study is that when bias in relation to hypotheses does exist, it has nothing intrinsically to do with the evaluative content of the presuppositions guiding inquiry. Wallerstein's research is biased toward confirming her conception of divorce as loss, not because this conception is described in thick evaluative terms, but because she failed to draw a fair sample of evidence. A fairly drawn sample would have left open to empirical determination whether divorce entails any losses, and how large they might be. Illegitimate biases that may exist in value-laden research can be corrected using the same sorts of methodological precautions that are available to value-neutral research. From an epistemological and methodological point of view, research guided by evaluative presuppositions functions just like research guided by any other presuppositions.

This does not mean that value-laden research cannot drive methodological innovation. Recall the temptation to stop analysis when one makes controversial findings one welcomes, but to continue analysis when one makes unwelcome findings. This demonstrates the value of symmetrical treatment of controversial results, whether they are welcome or unwelcome from the researchers' perspective. Stewart's team demonstrates that feminist researchers can live up to this standard. The dangers of asymmetrical treatment are more salient in value-laden research, making it easier for us to arrive at this rule in this context. But even scientists engaged in value-neutral research would prefer that their research programs be vindicated, since they have an interest in career success. A symmetry rule is equally applicable to them.

Fruitfulness. Turn now to bias in relation to questions and controversies. All inquiry begins with a question, the answer to which is sometimes sought to settle a controversy. This means that the findings of any inquiry can be evaluated along two dimensions. They can be evaluated according to whether they are true or warranted, and they can be evaluated with respect to whether they are relevant to answering a particular question or controversy. Call a true or warranted finding *significant*, relative to a controversy, if it bears on the answer to that controversy. A research design is *biased* in relation to that controversy if it is more likely to discover evidence that supports one side than the others. One research design is more *fruitful* than another, with respect to a controversy, if it is more likely to uncover evidence supporting (or undermining) all, or a wider range of sides of the controversy.

Thus, a noncognitive value judgment is more epistemically fruitful than another, relative to a controversy, if it guides a research program toward discovering a wider range of evidence that could potentially support any (or more) sides of a controversy. For example, the conception of divorce as loss, presupposing a negative evaluation of divorce, will be able to guide research toward discovering the negative but not the positive features of divorce. By comparison, the Stewart team's value-laden conception of divorce as involving both loss and opportunities for growth is more epistemically fruitful, relative to controversies about the *overall* value of divorce, in that it allows us to uncover evidence bearing on both the pros and the cons of divorce.

Our case study shows that some moral and social values have *asymmetric* epistemic value—that is, unequal fruitfulness, or powers to uncover significant phenomena. A "one size fits all" value orientation favors a main effects analysis, which *precludes* discovering that certain variables that are good for some people in the group, or "on average," are bad for others. By contrast, the Stewart team's feminist value orientation, because it accepts individuality and difference, is *open* to such discoveries, *but does not rule out the possibility of discovering otherwise.* The latter possibility would be realized if the coefficients on the interaction variables in a regression were insignificant—a common finding in the Stewart team's regressions.

Different noncognitive value judgments can be more or less fruitful, relative to specific questions, without calling into question the legitimacy of research programs guided by them. Although a conception of divorce exclusively oriented around loss is less fruitful, relative to the divorce controversies, than one open to seeing positive features, it does not follow that such a conception is useless for uncovering important evidence. It may be legitimately used, provided we keep in mind its limitations for answering particular questions.

Normative authority. Suppose we analytically divide a thick evaluative judgment into its factual and normative components—that is, into the empirical features of the world it picks out, and its claim to normative authority. Then we may ask whether the epistemic fruitfulness of such a judgment can be attributed to its normative authority. According to presupposition neutrality, the answer is no. Whatever epistemic value it has is solely due to its factual elements. Our case study shows that this is false. The normative validity of the Stewart team's evaluative presuppositions directly explains their epistemic value in guiding research. It is precisely because individuals have a privileged (not infallible) normative authority to make judgments about their own well-being that research programs that draw on individuals' self-assessments are more fruitful than research programs that don't, relative to questions about the relations of phenomena to well-being. It is precisely because subjective emotional responses and emotion-laden interpretations are normatively relevant to judgments of well-being that the Stewart team's inclusion of such measures makes their research more fruitful than research programs that focus only on objective measures. Matters could hardly be otherwise, when the questions a research program is designed to answer—such as the relations of divorce to well-being—are essentially evaluative. One simply cannot answer an evaluative question adequately without letting normatively adequate evaluative presuppositions guide one's inquiry.

Noncognitive intrinsic value judgments. According to implication neutrality, science can question whether something is *instrumentally* valuable for a given end by showing that it does not cause the end. It can determine, *given* an empirical criterion of value, how far something meets that criterion. But it can never supply evidence that bears on a judgment of intrinsic value.

This dogma depends on a confusion of intrinsic value—value as an end—with unconditional value—the idea that something could have value in all possible worlds (regardless of any contingent states of our world).[8] When people accept something as a final end, that does not commit them to thinking that its status as an end would remain fixed regardless of their experiences. Once we grant the bearing of emotion-laden interpretations of experience on value judgments, it is hard to imagine any empirically defined ends having such a status.

Consider, in light of this, the traditional family values position that parents should maintain firmly authoritative relations to their children. This practical judgment does not simply reflect a judgment that firm role boundaries are instrumentally valuable for promoting well-being. It reflects an ideal of family order, based on a conception of proper parent-child relations assumed to have intrinsic value. So its claim to value cannot be undermined *simply* by a demonstration that life in such relations fails to cause this or that good—for example, the Stewart team's finding that it does not promote the well-being of divorced mothers. Such a demonstration would show that attempts to realize this traditional family value come at some cost, but not that authoritative parent-child relations do not have some value as final ends.

Stewart's team did not stop their analysis with an external causal claim, however. It explored mothers' interpretations of their relations to their children. One of their "wise" subjects, reflecting on her own experiments in redefining parent-child role boundaries, explained why her former firmly authoritative stance *no longer made sense* after divorce. Family life requires an "interaction partner" with which to "meet the adventure [of life] together." No longer having a husband to fill that role, she found that it made more sense to draw her children more into it, while taking care "that you don't use your children in an adult capacity" (Stewart et al. 1997, 239). To find that a certain mode of life no longer makes sense in one's own experience, that it no longer presents a lived experience of family orderliness, is to grasp *evidence* that something once valued as a final end is not intrinsically valuable in the current context. So, Stewart's team did uncover evidence against the intrinsic value of a certain way of life for certain people.

Models. Let us conclude with some reflections on how to model the relations of factual to value judgments in science and ethics. We have seen that the argument for the value-neutrality of science depends on the assumption that values are science-free. This, in turn, depends on a model of the structure of beliefs as occupying sharply demarcated spheres, with factual judgments on one side, value judgments (and perhaps a set of dogmatically held factual judgments, as of supernatural phenomena) on the other, each isolated from logical or evidentiary connections with the other. This model identifies the epistemically problematic feature of value judgments with their supposed *dogmatism*, their stubbornness in the face of any conceivable evidence. But what is the status of that very supposition? Is it supposed to be a fact, or a value? It cannot be a fact, because we are confronted with daily evidence that people do take their experiences as evidence for and against value judgments. It must, then, be a value: thou shalt hold one's value judgments dogmatically. But this is absurd.

We often ask evaluative questions, such as, does divorce help or hurt people? What should parents do to help their children cope with divorce? The best way to answer such questions is not to defer to dogmatically held value judgments. It is to look at people's experiences with divorce and try to sort out the factors that make things go better or worse for them. This requires empirical inquiry. Done properly, this opens us up to the possibility of finding out that our value judgments were mistaken. The fact that we can do this shows that factual and value judgments do not occupy separate spheres. They are integrated in the same web of belief. Evaluative inquiry is empirical inquiry devoted to answering evaluative questions.

Thus, ethical inquiry and scientific inquiry are of a piece. This does not mean that factual and value judgments play the same roles in inquiry. Value judgments guide inquiry toward the concepts, tools, and procedures it needs to answer our value-laden questions. But facts—evidence— tell us which answers are more likely to be true. These two roles must be kept distinct, so that inquiry does not end up being rigged simply to reinforce our evaluative preconceptions. So long as they are distinct, the active direction of scientific inquiry by value judgments is not only legitimate, but indispensable.

Notes

I thank Abigail Stewart and the referees of *Hypatia* for helpful thoughts on this paper.
1. A notable exception is Richmond Campbell (1998).
2. An anonymous referee of this paper has questioned my distinction between impartiality and presupposition neutrality. If a noncognitive value

judgment is presupposed by a theory, then must it not be part of the basis for accepting a theory? To be sure, those who already accept the value judgment may find the theory more acceptable for presupposing it. But the key question is whether we can identify grounds for *anyone* to accept the theory, whatever their noncognitive values. Such grounds would be impartial grounds. The thesis of impartiality is that such grounds exist, and consist in the theory's manifestation of *cognitive* values (empirical adequacy, scope, consistency, and so forth). Impartiality and presupposition neutrality are distinguishable, so long as we can identify cognitive values independently of noncognitive values.

3. John Deigh (1994) disputes this, on the ground that we share some emotions, such as fear, with animals who lack propositional attitudes. However, he acknowledges that some emotions have cognitive content, when they are modified by reflection. I therefore confine my claims about the evidentiary value of emotional experiences to those with cognitive content.

4. To be sure, emotions are not as responsive as beliefs to the way the world is. They are more akin to perceptions than beliefs. Like perceptual illusions, emotions can sometimes persist even when we know they are misleading.

5. For an allied argument that this would be crazy, in that it would threaten the unity of the self, see Elijah Millgram (1997).

6. This has similar implications as Peter Geach's (1965) argument that from a logical point of view, value judgments function like any factual claim. My argument does not presuppose any particular metaethical view about the meaning of value judgments. Any acceptable metaethical account of value judgments must take their epistemological functioning as a constraint, just as it takes their logical functioning as a constraint.

7. Douglas Dion (1998) offers a sophisticated discussion of this point, noting qualifications that should be made for small n case studies.

8. Christine Korsgaard (1983) discusses this distinction at length, although she reserves the term "intrinsic value" for unconditional values.

References

Campbell, Richmond. 1998. *Illusions of paradox: A feminist epistemology naturalized.* Lanham, Md.: Rowman & Littlefield.

Deigh, John. 1994. Cognitivism in the theory of emotions. *Ethics* 104 (4): 824–54.

Dion, Douglas. 1998. Evidence and inference in the comparative case study. *Comparative Politics* 30 (2): 127–45.

Geach, Peter. 1965. Assertion. *Philosophical Review* 74 (4): 449–65.

Geertz, Clifford. 1990. A lab of one's own. *New York Review of Books* 37 (8 November): 19–24.

Gilder, George. 1986. *Men and marriage.* Gretna, La.: Pelican Publishing.

Gross, Paul, and Norman Levitt. 1994. *Higher superstition: The academic left and its quarrels with science.* Baltimore: Johns Hopkins.

Haack, Susan. 1993. Epistemological reflections of an old feminist. *Reason Papers* 18 (fall): 31–43.

Hacking, Ian. 1995. *Rewriting the soul: Multiple personality and the sciences of memory*. Princeton: Princeton University Press.

Korsgaard, Christine. 1983. Two distinctions in goodness. *Philosophical Review* 92 (2): 169–95.

Kuhn, Thomas. 1977. Objectivity, value judgment, and theory choice. In *The essential tension*. Chicago: University of Chicago Press.

Lacey, Hugh. 1999. *Is science value free? Values and scientific understanding*. New York: Routledge.

Longino, Helen. 1990. *Science as social knowledge*. Princeton: Princeton University Press.

———. 1994. In search of feminist epistemology. *Monist* 77 (4): 472–85.

Millgram, Elijah. 1997. *Practical induction*. Cambridge: Harvard University Press.

Nagel, Ernest. 1979. *The structure of science*. Indianapolis: Hackett.

Nelson, Lynn Hankinson. 1990. *Who knows? From Quine to a feminist empiricism*. Philadelphia: Temple University Press.

Richards, Janet Radcliffe. 1995. Why feminist epistemology isn't (and the implications for feminist jurisprudence). *Legal Theory* 1 (2): 365–400.

Stewart, Abigail, Anne Copeland, Nia Chester, Janet Malley, and Nicole Barenbaum. 1997. *Separating together: How divorce transforms families*. New York: Guilford Press.

Wallerstein, Judith, and Joan Kelly. 1980. *Surviving the breakup*. New York: Basic.

Wallerstein, Judith, Julia Lewis, and Sandra Blakeslee. 2000. *The unexpected legacy of divorce*. New York: Hyperion.

Weber, Max. 1946. Science as a vocation. In *From Max Weber: Essays in sociology*, ed. H. H. Gerth and C. Wright Mills. New York: Oxford University Press.

Weitzman, Lenore. 1985. *The divorce revolution*. New York: Free Press.

Whitehead, Barbara. 1983. Dan Quayle was right. *Atlantic Monthly* 271 (4): 47–50.

Williams, Bernard. 1985. *Ethics and the limits of philosophy*. Cambridge: Harvard University Press.

Wilson, James Q. 2002. *The marriage problem: How our culture has weakened families*. New York: Harper Collins.

15

SHARYN CLOUGH
Oregon State University

THE ANALYTIC TRADITION, RADICAL

(FEMINIST) INTERPRETATION, AND THE

HYGIENE HYPOTHESIS

INTRODUCTION

Within philosophy of science in the analytic tradition, and in the public understanding of science more generally, there has been a tendency to view any political influence as a source of bias and error in scientific research.[1] As feminist studies of science throughout the 1980s and 1990s have documented, there have indeed been many cases where political influences, such as sexism and racism, have negatively affected the empirical adequacy of scientific studies.[2]

However, as feminist and other progressive scientists and philosophers of science have worked to address sexism and racism in science, they have found themselves in the awkward epistemic position of criticizing these political influences, while simultaneously offering prescriptions for better scientific research—prescriptions that are themselves explicitly aligned with yet another (e.g., feminist) set of political interests. What has become clear, though, is that in a number of well-documented cases, feminist-informed prescriptions for science have made improvements over sexist research.[3] Can it be, then, that while some political interests simply bias scientific research, some other political interests (such as feminist interests) can be used as effective resources for increasing the empirical adequacy of research? And if so, how? Much work in feminist science studies is aimed at answering precisely these questions.[4]

My own research as an analytic feminist philosopher focuses on three elements of these questions. The first identifies the particular political interests at play in feminist science projects; the second addresses the empirical improvements to scientific research that these feminist interventions allow; and the third concerns how it is that we can evaluate the empirical adequacy of political interests at all. Each of these features is best addressed in the context of specific cases and I focus here on a compelling set of epidemiological and immunological studies that inform the "hygiene hypothesis"—a hypothesis made more empirically robust, I argue, by augmenting it with a particular set of feminist political interests.

As will be discussed in more depth, below, the hygiene hypothesis was developed to explain the correlation between increased sanitation, and increased prevalence and incidence of allergies, asthma, auto-immune diseases, and even certain kinds of depression. Especially in the industrialized nations of the North and West, it is hypothesized, our lower rates of exposure to certain kinds of bacteria and other micro-organisms have had unintended negative consequences for our immune health. In the words of neuroscientists Rook and Lowry, as "a consequence of diminished exposure," especially in childhood, to a variety of micro-organisms once prevalent in the human evolutionary past, populations in developed countries have a "lack of appropriate levels of immunoregulatory pathways."[5]

Over the last few years, support for the hypothesis has increased with the discovery that populations in those less industrialized areas of the rural South and East that are still regularly exposed to certain parasitic worms (helminthes), also have a lower incidence and prevalence of chronic inflammatory diseases such as Crohn's, than do populations in the industrialized North and West that are not regularly exposed.[6] In India, the incidence of Crohn's, while lower than in nations of the North and West, is on the increase, reliably tracking rates of industrialization and sanitation.[7] Most recently, a study of children in the Philippines found that increased exposure to microbes in childhood predicted increased immune health in adulthood.[8]

The hygiene hypothesis has also been suggested as a further piece of the causal story in some cases of depression,[9] although, as I discuss below, the documentation for this link is less robust than that between the hygiene hypothesis and the other pathologies mentioned. Briefly, the current literature shows that some kinds of depression can be linked to failures of immune regulation and higher levels of pro-inflammatory cytokines (signaling molecules produced by the immune system).[10]

To foreshadow my argument that feminist political interests can empir-ically strengthen the hygiene hypothesis, it is worth noting that in the industrialized North and West, women are over-represented in all the relevant clinical populations, *and this pattern has received no critical attention by hygiene hypothesis researchers.* Women have higher rates than men of asthma, allergies, auto-immune disorders,[11] as well as depression.[12] The "feminization" of these diagnostic categories has been well-acknowledged by clinicians who treat and study these illnesses, but not by the immunologists and epidemiologists involved in studying the hygiene hypothesis.

Despite the fact that the clinicians who treat and study these illnesses have noticed sex differences in the populations they treat, their own explanatory weakness comes from a tendency to focus exclusively on reductionistic biomedical explanations for these differences, relying on physiological, hormonal, and genetic accounts, with little to no attention paid to the ways these biological processes are affected by complex environmental factors, such as patterns of hygiene and sanitation, or social factors, such as the interweaving of the effects of gender, race, and economic hierarchies.[13]

For example, sex hormones, such as the family of estrogens, have been hypothesized to account for the differential rates of auto-immune disorders in women compared to men, as have a variety of genetic phenomena, such as X-chromosome mosaicism.[14] Similarly, sex hormones have featured in explanations for the higher rates of depression in women.[15] To be fair, compared to the literature on asthma, allergies, and auto-immune disorders, the literature on sex differences in depression includes far more attempts, especially by feminist clinicians and researchers, to examine the role of more complex social factors such as the social and cognitive effects of sexism.[16] The fact remains, however, that in each attempt, biomedical or otherwise, to account for the differences in the relevant morbidity rates between women and men, a significant amount of variation is left unexplained.

This is precisely the explanatory gap that the hygiene hypothesis is suited to address, especially, I argue, when a feminist understanding of the gendered socialization of children is added to the epidemiological and immunological picture. As I discuss in more detail below, feminist social scientists have shown that standards of cleanliness are generally higher for girls than boys, especially under the age of five, when children are more likely to be under close adult supervision.[17] These gendered patterns form a robust phenomenon in industrialized nations, and some studies point to a cross-cultural pattern.[18]

Note that, while I attend to differentiations in nationality and socio-economic status, I continue to use the gender categories "girls" and "boys" as if they were unproblematic *within* categories of nation and SES. These coarse-grained gender categories will probably capture the relevant variation of interest, epidemiologically speaking. However, it is important to acknowledge that a broader discussion of gender identity and gender expression, including (data from) populations of people who are transgender/transexual, though beyond the scope of this paper, has the potential to enrich the explanatory account.

In what follows, I review the case for the hygiene hypothesis.

I argue that *insofar as the hygiene hypothesis successfully identifies standards of hygiene and sanitation as mediators of immune health*, then, properly augmented by feminist analyses of the gendered standards of cleanliness in children, the hypothesis can account for the unexplained variation in the relevant morbidity rates between men and women. The augmented hygiene hypothesis also responds to a number of outstanding puzzles in current epidemiological and immunological research on allergens and parasites. I then present new sources of evidence for the hygiene hypothesis in the form of cross-cultural and other natural experiments involving gender differences.

The hygiene hypothesis as it stands already enriches, and indeed moves beyond, reductionistic biomedical approaches to immunological problems by attending to complex environmental factors such as sanitation and hygiene standards. Adding a feminist analysis of child-rearing practices, and the gendered standards of cleanliness—standards that are generally higher for girls than boys—imports important empirical resources to the explanatory picture.

The feminist-informed sociological and anthropological research makes clear that feminine gender-role socialization includes higher standards of cleanliness than does masculine gender-role socialization, and I argue that this difference in standards might play an important explanatory role in the sex differences between women and men reported in asthma, allergies, auto-immune disorders, generally, and depression.

I incorporate in the discussion of feminine gender-role socialization a presentation of the feminist political commitments (that is, my own feminist commitments and those of the feminist sociologists and anthropologists I cite) and show how these commitments make the link between gender and the hygiene hypothesis salient. I argue that, by making the link visible, these political commitments do not bias the immunological and epidemiological research. Instead, the political commitments I discuss, and indeed prescribe, have the effect of *increasing* the empirical adequacy of that research, specifically by reconceiving relevant sources of evidence and opening up further avenues for study.

Traditional analytic philosophy of science has little to say about politically fueled scientific research like that modeled in the current study beyond discouraging it *tout court* as biased and subjective. Despite the paucity of traditional philosophical accounts regarding the potential benefits of political interests in science, however, there are some analytic philosophical tools available that feminists can use to provide such an account. I conclude by reviewing the case for a feminist use of Davidson's method of radical interpretation (hence radical [feminist] interpretation). I offer a feminist approach to Davidson's philosophy of language that shows how we can differentiate between those political interests that are beneficial in a particular scientific context and those that are not. This requires showing that political interests can be evaluated using the same sorts of empirical analyses that are deployed in other aspects of scientific decision-making.[19] I then show how this sort of evaluative process explains the improvements to the immunological and epidemiological research on the hygiene hypothesis that are made available by attending to a feminist political view of gendered child-rearing practices.

THE HYGIENE HYPOTHESIS[20]

Germs, Allergies, and Asthma

Industrialized nations of the North and West have experienced increasing rates of asthma and allergies. In a recent study, Maziak and his colleagues note that "There is a wide consensus that asthma and allergies are witnessing a rising trend among children in Western societies. In some Western countries asthma and allergies have reached alarming proportions, affecting up to one-third of children within the general population."[21] This increase has been explained by increased standards and practices of cleanliness and sanitation—the so-called "hygiene hypothesis."

Recent experimental support with mice has shown that a variety of allergic responses can be decreased via exposure to particular bacteria.[22] Support for the hypothesis also comes from studies of human populations which document the protective effects of farm environments for children.[23] Compared to children raised in urban settings, children raised on farms have lower rates of allergic rhinitis and/or conjunctivitis.

Kilpeläinen's research team concludes that "environmental exposure to immune modulating agents, such as environmental mycobacteria . . . could explain the finding."[24] A more recent study argues that exposure to two or more domestic pets has a similar protective effect: "exposure to 2 or more dogs or cats in the first year of life was associated with a lower prevalence of allergic sensitization at age 6–7 years."[25]

Parasites and Inflammatory Diseases

Elliott, Summers, and Weinstock have theorized that the increase in other immune-system malfunctions such as inflammatory-bowel disease (IBD) and Crohn's disease may also be related to the hygiene hypothesis.[26] They observed that in contemporary urban environments where humans are largely free of contamination by parasitic worms, rates of these sorts of diseases have increased dramatically. In Israel, for example, Zvidi and colleagues report that "the prevalence rate rose from 25.53/100,000 in 1987 to 65.11/100,000 in 1997, and then to 112.99 in 2007."[27] Since some parasitic worms seem to have a "calming" effect on the immune system, it seems likely that the trends are related. Indeed, clinical trials have shown that exposure to the eggs of the *Trichuris suis* whip worm can reduce the severity of symptoms in patients with Crohn's.[28]

Bacteria and Depression

That certain sorts of depression might be explained by the hygiene hypo-thesis[29] is the most recent and surprising finding in this collection of studies. As I have noted, the documentation for this link is less robust than that between the hygiene hypothesis and the other pathologies mentioned. Neuroscientists Rook and Lowry argue that "depression and anxiety are associated with markers of ongoing inflammation, even without any accompanying inflammatory disorder"[30] and that one effect of SSRIs (the most-commonly-prescribed form of antidepressant) is to lower the inflammatory response.[31] Whether the association between depression and clinically significant inflammatory response is a causal association is currently supported by clinical evidence that "proinflammatory cytokines can induce depression"[32] and that in an example of the inverse pattern, cancer patients who were treated with a harmless version of the bacterium *M. vaccae* reported "higher quality of life," even though the bacterium had no effect on their survival rates from cancer.[33] The relation between "quality of life" and depression is not well-examined in these studies.

Insofar as lower levels of bacterial loads generally can be linked to the standards and practices of cleanliness and sanitation found in industrialized nations, and insofar as the currently weak link between depression and immune health proves to be accurate, Rook and Lowry expect that depression rates too would differ between industrialized and non-industrialized nations. There is some data to support their expectation. They write:

> Estimates of the incidence of depression in rich industrialized nations are consistently higher than in poor rural nations. Indeed, in young adults (15–29 year olds), the incidence of depression in men in the United States and Canada is estimated to be twice, while that in women is estimated to be three times, that seen in Africa, and within Europe depression tends to be more prevalent in urban than in rural communities.[34]

Rook and Lowry admit that the data from these latter studies is "fraught with problems in interpretation."[35] An examination of the studies they cite[36] reveals that while there has been some success at unifying diagnostic criteria across populations, problems in estimating prevalence and incidence across cultures remain and are well-acknowledged.[37] However, despite the problems in cross-cultural comparisons of this sort, what remains robust is the finding that no matter what population is being sampled, within that population, more women than men satisfy criteria for depression, and this is particularly the case in countries of the industrialized North and West. Additionally, as Bird and Rieker note, "it is now well-established that women's higher rates of depression reflect a real [sex] difference in health, rather than an artifact of help-seeking behavior or willingness to report symptoms."[38]

Rook and Lowry do not comment on this difference between women and men, a pattern that is well-documented within nations of the North and West. They focus instead on the less reliably documented differences in depression rates across societies, that is, for women and men from industrialized nations of the North and West, when compared to women and men of the more rural nations of the South and East. As supporters of the hygiene hypothesis, which predicts the latter pattern *across* societies, it makes sense that they would have nothing to say about the differences *within* societies—in contrast, my augmented hypothesis offers a cogent explanation for these latter differences within any society that has higher hygiene standards for girls than boys.

FEMINIST POLITICAL INTERESTS AND THE HYGIENE HYPOTHESIS

What is required to make this gender link more salient is some level of feminist political commitment to the project of documenting, deconstructing, and ameliorating the varying social pressures that inform what it means to be a gendered body. Within this feminist political project is embedded a cluster of views that are at once both descriptive and prescriptive, for instance, the view that the content of the social roles assigned to boys and girls, men and women, is significantly driven by deeply held cultural commitments that are in some important sense: (a) arbitrarily assigned relative to features such as secondary sex characteristics; and (b) vigorously, though often unconsciously, enforced and rewarded from a very young age.

While this latter feature means that our current assignment of social roles is not easily modified, most feminists believe that the historical evidence regarding human flourishing shows us that there are more relevant criteria for assigning social roles, such as individual interest and/or skill. Indeed, when girls are given the same chances, training, and encouragement as boys, they seem to be just as capable as boys in a variety of tasks not often associated with femininity; the pattern holds similarly for boys and tasks not often associated with masculinity.

Social scientists with feminist commitments have amassed a great deal of empirical data supporting this cluster of political views, and, indeed, these political views might seem to many readers of this volume to be uncontroversial, straightforward matters of fact. However, the relationship between empirical evidence and feminist political theory often needs to be carefully explained, rather than assumed, since the view that gender-role assignments are less than arbitrary, perhaps "natural" or mandated by theological design is still widespread and often uncritically presupposed. Because of this, showing the relationship between empirical evidence and feminist political interests is an important project to undertake. In the penultimate section of this essay, I make use of Davidson's philosophical theory of meaning in order to argue for and further clarify the empirical nature of feminist political interests.

The feminist political claim of particular relevance to my analysis of the hygiene hypothesis is that the masculine gender-role assignment, broadly construed, involves a social acceptance of playing in dirt and mud for those (typically boys) so assigned, an acceptance that does not extend to the feminine gender role, broadly construed (and typically assigned to girls). These differential social expectations regarding clean-liness are reflected in and reinforced by gender differences in children's clothing, participation in sports, and adult supervision of children's play.

Gendered Norms of Cleanliness

Feminist-informed sociologists in the industrialized North and West have documented that girls are dressed more often than boys in clothing that is not supposed to get dirty and that restricts the sorts of movements that would get one dirty in the first place.[39] Young girls do not participate in sports with the same frequency as young boys, and girls more often than boys play indoors.[40] Insofar as many sports, and outdoor play gen-erally, increase the chances for exposure to the micro-organisms found in dirt—and there is abundant evidence to support this[41]—then boys will have greater rates of exposure to these micro-organisms than girls. Finally, parents structure and supervise the play of girls more than that of boys,[42] which is likely to result in girls being kept cleaner than boys.

Not surprisingly, given that girls receive more parental supervision and direction regarding cleanliness than do boys, girls more than boys are taught to police themselves—to be vigilant about their appearance and cleanliness. In a 1938 Boston study of the content of preschool chil-dren's speech, psychologist Shirley found marked gender differences with respect to the concepts of cleanliness and clothes. Shirley noted that these two concepts are mentioned in conversations "about twice as often by girls as by boys."[43] Even by preschool, traditional strictures about cleanli-ness have been differentially absorbed by girls.

While these gender differences in hygiene standards might seem a relic of a distant sexist past, research suggests otherwise. As recently as 1991, research showed that a significant number of students training to be preschool teachers in the United Kingdom expected the children in their classes to conform to fairly standard gender roles, including gendered norms of cleanliness. In one study, over 25% of preschool student teachers "expected boys, but not girls to be reckless, untidy, cheeky, brave, noisy and naughty; and expected girls, but not boys to be tidy, lean, quiet, sen-sible, obedient, passive and well-behaved."[44]

Many parents continue to reinforce traditional gendered norms of hygiene in their preschool children, as expressed, for example, in how children are dressed. In a 1998 study of American children in a preschool setting,[45] one-third of the five-year-old girls came to school in dresses *each day*. Of relevance to the question of cleanliness, Martin, the study's author, noted that being in a dress limited the girls' "physicality." She added, "it is not only the dress itself, but knowledge about how to behave in a dress that is restrictive. Many girls already knew that some behaviors were not allowed in a dress. This knowledge probably comes from the families who dress their girls in dresses."[46] One particular observation of five-year-old girls in Martin's study is worth quoting at length:

> Vicki, wearing leggings and a dress-like shirt, is leaning over the desk to look into a "tunnel" that some other kids have built. As she leans, her dress/shirt rides up exposing her back. Jennifer (another child) walks by Vicki and as she does she pulls Vicki's shirt back over her bare skin and gives it a pat to keep it in place. It looks very much like something one's mother might do.[47]

These young children have already internalized the rule that when wearing a dress, even a dress-like tunic with leggings, they must constantly monitor their decorum—who knows what immodesty might otherwise result, what dirt (metaphorically and literally) might cling.

The linking of dirt and immorality is a robust phenomenon historically in the industrialized North and West. In the schools and playgrounds of nineteenth-century Britain and the United States, education about physical cleaning was meant to introduce moral cleanliness as well, especially for the immigrant and working classes.[48] For girls in general, though, education about keeping clean and tidy was not just important for physical hygiene, it also helped them to "adopt particular [feminine] ways of carrying and presenting their bodies."[49]

Returning to the present day, sociologist Thorne documents gender norms in children's play at the elementary school level in her book, *Gender Play*.[50] Of particular relevance is her discussion of "cooties" and other "pollution rituals"—concerns that are especially prevalent, she notes, in children ages six to nine. The term "cooties" here refers to invisible "germs" that children play at passing on to others through touch, or more pointedly, that children play at *avoiding* by ostracization of those assigned as carriers. Thorne's observations, taken from field work in the late 1970s and early 1980s at schools in Michigan and California, show that girls are far more likely than boys to be associated with cooties and to be ostracized as carriers of cooties.[51] The clear message is that, unlike boys, girls need to guard against these and other forms of pollution: "Girls as a group are treated as an ultimate source of contamination."[52] While individual boys are sometimes also so marked, she notes that in these cases, it is the boy's ethnicity or physical ability that is used to set him up as a source of pollution rather than his gender per se. She also notes a common pattern in this research, namely, that boys, more often than girls, played outdoors.[53]

As a final note regarding research about girls policing their own hygiene, it seems unlikely to be a coincidence that among sufferers of Obsessive Compulsive Disorder, hand washing and cleaning compulsions are far more common in women than men.[54]

Women and Immunological Disorders

As noted earlier, there are a number of immunological health outcomes in adults that attention to gender and hygiene in children might help explain: the fact that women far more than men suffer from asthma, allergies, as well as many auto-immune disorders, including rheumatoid arthritis, multiple-sclerosis, Grave's disease, Lupus, as well as IBDs and Crohn's disease. In the case of Crohn's disease, the sex difference is less marked; at the other extreme—Lupus—women patients outnumber men as much as 9:1.[55] Insofar as depression too can be tied to hygiene, then the alarming fact of women's high rates of depression might also fall, at least partially, under the explanatory umbrella of the augmented hygiene hypothesis.

Beginning with the case of asthma, age complicates the issue in a way that is consistent with my augmented hygiene hypothesis regarding the gender socialization of children. Before puberty, boys have higher rates of asthma than girls.[56] After puberty, the gender difference reverses, with women having higher rates than men. Osman reports that the reasons for the age link remain unclear.[57] As mentioned, there are certainly a number of competing biomedical explanations for the "over-active" immune systems of women relative to men;[58] however, there are no accepted explanations available (biomedical or otherwise) for the over-active immune systems of boys relative to girls. The augmentation to the hygiene hypothesis that I have offered suggests an explanation. It might be that there is a critical period involved, a developmental period during which the immune system, properly exposed to potential allergens, responds with asthmatic symptoms, and after which shows a "settling effect." Those children, typically boys, who are properly exposed during the critical period, respond with asthmatic symptoms early on, but then their symptoms abate. Those children, typically girls, who are not exposed during the critical period, respond with asthmatic symptoms later, and for the rest of their lives.

In fact, a critical period of just this sort was found in the study mentioned earlier that showed that two or more pets in the home at infancy protected children against allergies at six years of age.[59] The positive effect was not found if the pets were introduced later than infancy. And, in what the authors note as a "puzzling" aside, the protective effect of pets in the home was significantly more marked for boys than girls.[60]

That women are over-represented among the clinically depressed across numerous cultures is, as reported above, another well-supported finding.[61] Debates continue about the causal explanation of this gender difference. Altemus believes that the robust cross-cultural effect requires a biomedical explanation appealing to, for example, estrogen or genetics, though she admits that such an explanation has proven elusive.[62] Completing a meta-analysis of the literature, Kuehner argues for the importance of linking biological arguments with appeals to well-documented social "risk factors": "Consistently, intrapsychic and psychosocial gender role related risk factors have been identified which may contribute to the higher depression risk in women. Gender role aspects are also reflected in endocrine stress reactions and possibly influence associated neuropsychological processes."[63] A hygiene hypothesis that takes into account the differential gender-role socialization of boys and girls might be able to provide the missing link between the biological and social risk factors called for by Kuehner. But, of course, the link has to be made salient before it can be evaluated by epidemiologists and immunologists.

INCREASING THE EMPIRICAL ADEQUACY OF THE HYGIENE HYPOTHESIS

Recall that I began with the general question regarding whether and how it is that while some political interests can bias scientific research, other political interests (such as some feminist interests) can empirically strengthen research. Particular interests and particular case studies are needed to defend this claim, and as promised, I began by identifying a particular case study, the hygiene hypothesis, and the particular feminist political interests that strengthen that hypothesis. The next feature of my project is to address in more detail the improvements to scientific research that attention to feminist interests allow, and it is to this second feature that I now turn.

The hygiene hypothesis is currently well-supported, but, as I noted, there remains a "puzzle" concerning the interaction of age and sex differences in rates of some auto-immune disorders. I have argued that feminist-informed research regarding the differential socialization patterns of girls and boys and their relationship to dirt and germs suggests a solution to the puzzle.

Thinking in terms of gender differences in hygiene also helps identify new relevant sources of evidence for the hygiene hypothesis and opens up further avenues for study. While epidemiologists and immunologists have not yet linked gendered norms of cleanliness to morbidity rates for allergies, asthma, immune disorders more generally, and/or depression, there are some epidemiological studies of children that mention gender differences in exposure to dust, dirt, and germs, and these studies, not previously believed to be relevant, could be used to provide support for and point toward the further development of the hygiene hypothesis.

Eating dirt—geophagia—is a very reliable way to ingest micro-organisms, and in a study from rural Guinea that examined the ingestion of parasites via geophagia, boys under the age of ten are significantly more likely than girls to be infected by these parasites.[64] Studies of children with bloodstream infection (BSI) from Acinobacter species show similar results.[65] For adults in the industrialized North and West, exposure to Acinobacteria is generally associated with a hospital stay. New research has shown that in children, the pattern is different—for children, infection is significantly more likely to be developed in the home and by patients who are male. That is, consistent with my augmented hypothesis, under the gendered supervision of parents in home settings, more boys than girls are exposed to this bacteria.[66]

Consider also studies of the transmission of *Ascaris lumbricoides* (a harmful intestinal roundworm) among rural populations in Southern Ethiopia.[67] The transmission route typically involves "ingestion of infective eggs from soil contaminated with human feces or uncooked vegetables contaminated with soil containing infective eggs."[68] In Southern Ethiopia, homes typically have dirt floors, infants are often accompanied by domestic dogs throughout the day, and livestock are brought into homes at night. The dogs and livestock as well as the dirt floors are all sources of the eggs. Children are the primary victims of roundworm infection.[69] At one clinic, "70% of all outpatients treated for helminthiases [intestinal parasites] were children under fourteen years of age,"[70] with infection rates highest among one- to four-year-olds. Of note here is the sex difference: 20.5% of males in this age group, as opposed to only 13.5% of females, had Ascariasis infection. The researchers remarked that this gap closes in later ages, that is, five- to fourteen-year-olds, where rates lower—in males to 8.9% and females to 11.3%—"making it difficult to establish statistically significant sex-differences in worm infection."[71]

However, the change across age groups might be explained by differential hygiene expectations for boys and girls (more on the cross-cultural strength of these expectations below). Both male and female infants are likely to be under greater parental supervision than are older children, and for females more than males, greater supervision is likely to come with increased restrictions on how and where they play. Perhaps these gendered facets of parental supervision explain the fact that in the one to four age group, significantly fewer girls than boys were found to have parasites. In addition, the reported decrease in parasitic load with age might be similar to the decrease in asthma rates with age that is reported in boys and girls in countries in the industrialized North and West. Again, a critical period for exposure to the relevant parasites might be at work, disadvantaging those children, typically girls, who have fewer opportunities for exposure.

If the modalities of exposure to harmful micro-organisms such as Acinetobacter species and the *Ascaris lumbricoides* parasite are similar to those for the more helpful micro-organisms that calm over-active immune systems (such as *M. vaccae*, and the *Trichuris suis* whip worm), then epidemiological studies like these, attending to gendered norms of cleanliness, could serve as further sources of evidence in support of the hygiene hypothesis. If the augmented hygiene hypothesis is correct, that is, if increased hygiene negatively affects immune health, and immune health differs by sex (as research shows it does), then we should see sex differences in the morbidity rates for these illnesses. And here we do.

The epidemiological research in rural Guinea and Southern Ethiopia, cited above, introduces another avenue of study that could provide evidence for the hygiene hypothesis. Such research, outside the industrialized North and West, provides the opportunity for a number of cross-cultural natural experiments.

The first sort of experiment would evaluate whether the gender norms that place higher standards of cleanliness on girls than boys hold across different cultures. Some of the sociological and anthropological research on gendered norms of cleanliness in the nonindustrialized settings of the South and East suggests that this is the case.

In her field work in Bengal, India, anthropologist Lamb found that women and girls are expected to bathe more often than men and boys— expectations that are related to views of women and girls as naturally dirtier than men and boys.[72] For these women and girls, the practice of bathing, often two or more times daily, consists mostly in a ritual rinsing with water, rather than wringing one's hands with anti-bacterial soap or guarding against cooties, but the gender differences in cleanliness here clearly run parallel to the purity notions associated with femininity in the North and West. A similar trend was found in the Caribbean country of Guyana where sociological research on parental socialization preferences showed that parents rated neatness and cleanliness as "more desirable for girls [than boys] in all age groups."[73]

One difference between the activities of children in nations of the industrialized North and West and children in the more rural settings of the South and East is that in the latter societies, children are typically given far greater freedom from parental supervision through their assigned chores, such as minding cattle and sheep.[74] It remains to be examined whether and how this freedom affects standards of hygiene for boys and girls. One might expect that in this case, girls are under less parental supervision and have more freedom to play in the dirt. Are they also more healthy, immunologically speaking, as adults? Research on this question would be helpful.

A second kind of natural experiment involves examining whether those studies of the rural South and East that reported higher levels of ingestion of micro-organisms in boys also reveals this to be correlated with those boys having a lower incidence of allergies, asthma, IBD, and depression. We already know that the incidence and prevalence of these diseases is lower in the more rural nations of South and East, relative to the industrialized North and West, but we do not know whether morbidity patterns in the South and East feature the same sex differences that are found in the North and West. Insofar as the gendered socialization patterns that have been well-identified in the industrialized North and West continue in the nonindustrialized, primarily rural settings of the South and East, we can expect that there will be sex differences in the relevant morbidity rates.

One study comes close to confirming this expectation. Researching allergies among the Hiwi settlements of Venezuela, an anthropology team led by Hurtado noted that, consistent with the hygiene hypothesis, these populations had lower rates of allergies than are typically found in populations of the industrialized North and West.[75] They also noted that Hiwi girls spend significantly more time than do boys engaging in "grooming behaviors," and that these behaviors "serve to eliminate ecto-parasites."[76] What they did not note in their study was whether there were any sex differences in parasite exposure between Hiwi boys and girls, though the grooming behavior suggests there is. They also did not note whether there were any sex differences in incidence and prevalence of allergies in either children or adults. However, the presentation of their data suggests that they have this information available (they present data comparing Hiwi girls and women to girls and women from Western populations, for example). In the absence of attention to the socialization processes that differentially affect hygiene expectations for boys and girls, it is likely that the researchers did not think that sex differences within the Hiwi populations were relevant for analysis and presentation. Paying attention to gender differences in hygiene provides a means of recognizing potential evidence for the hygiene hypothesis that might be otherwise ignored.

Of course, in the industrialized North and West it is not just sanitation policies and practices that have decreased children's exposure to micro-organisms. Sociologists who study play behaviors have noticed a marked decrease in the rates at which both boys and girls play outdoors in the dirt. This change in play pattern is yet another evidential link that could be used to support the hygiene hypothesis, a link that becomes relevant when gender roles are taken into consideration.

In a study of American playgrounds in the United States, Frost notes that, increasingly, children in the United States find "their places for play dominated by manufactured equipment, regimented games, and paved surfaces," and he ties this trend directly to support for the hygiene hypothesis.[77] He also notes that public schools are increasingly deleting recess, and that even public playgrounds are being visited less often as parents fear injury and violence.[78]

The hygiene hypothesis is used to explain the increased rates of immune-related morbidity in populations of the industrialized North and West as a whole. The morbidity rates at issue have increased for both women *and* men, girls *and* boys. Given the relatively recent decrease in access to outdoor play, a number of natural experiments suggest themselves once gender roles are made salient. Especially in the suburbs of cities in the industrialized North and West, boys are more likely to have been affected by these restrictions in the type and place of play than are girls. In these populations, have the relevant morbidity rates increased more markedly among boys than girls? One would expect so if my augmented hygiene hypothesis is correct. These are just a few of the natural experiments on the hygiene hypothesis that become obvious once gender socialization is made salient.

FEMINIST POLITICAL INTERESTS AND THE PHILOSOPHY OF LANGUAGE

I conclude now with the third aspect of my project, a review of the case for "radical (feminist) interpretation"—a feminist approach to Davidson's philosophy of language that shows how political interests, like the feminist political interests I have identified as important to the hygiene hypothesis, are related to empirical evidence and can themselves be empirically evaluated. It is this sort of evaluative process that can be used to differentiate between those political interests that have a negative, biasing effect on research and those that can empirically strengthen research.[79]

One of the ways that feminist and other progressive philosophers of science have tackled the problem of bias in science has been to document the frequency with which a variety of political interests present in early stages of the discovery of a scientific hypothesis can, and do, go on to bias hypothesis testing and results.[80] It seems clear from this careful documentation that political interests are ubiquitous in all aspects of scientific activity. But it should also be clear by now that not all political interests are of a piece. As I have argued, some political interests can actually increase the empirical adequacy of scientific research in a variety of ways.

For many readers of this volume, the relationship between empirical evidence and the feminist political interests of relevance to the hygiene hypothesis might seem obvious, and the inclusion of such political interests in a scientific study, uncontroversial. However, accepting that (some) political interests can play a positive role in science runs contrary to the value-free ideal prescribed by analytic philosophy of science, and, as I noted at the outset, contrary to the public idealization of science more generally.

One of the reasons for this ideal is the long-standing and widely held belief that it is only straightforwardly factual claims that stand in relation to empirical evidence and that while we have well-known methods for empirically adjudicating between competing factual claims, these methods cannot be used when adjudicating between competing value claims, including those claims informed by feminist political interests. If claims informed by political interests are not themselves capable of empirical adjudication, then it seems difficult to imagine that those claims could be used to build the empirical adequacy of a particular descriptive hypothesis within a scientific setting.

Anderson is one of the few analytical feminist philosophers who has argued that in particular cases, political interests, in particular feminist interests, can increase the empirical adequacy of scientific research.[81] In her discussion of social science research on divorce, Anderson argues that feminist approaches to this research make for empirically stronger results.[82] The feminist political interests at play in this research are represented in the claim that women, like men, cannot be adequately defined by exclusive attention to their relationships to their spouses and children. Both women and men have needs, desires, and concerns that focus on aspects of their lives other than their families and homes.

Again, the truth of this latter sort of claim might seem obvious because it is a statement of empirical fact rather than value, but alas, it is not an uncontroversial claim and there are many in the contemporary United States, for example, who would see it as being shot through with feminist values, and reject it on those grounds. So it is important that Anderson shows that, by including feminist claims of this sort, the feminist researchers she discusses were encouraged to frame questions for the participants in their study that allow for a wider range of responses and hence arrived at a more *empirically accurate description* of the phenomenon of divorce. As a result of starting from empirically informed feminist political interests, they were able to see what traditional researchers did not, namely, that divorce might not always be seen as a negative life event.[83]

My only concern with Anderson's account is that she maintains that value judgments, such as those reflected in feminist and other political interests, *have no empirical content*, but they can be used to help shape and support those factual judgments that do. The problem is that while she believes that value judgments can be evaluated, without viewing them as bearers of empirical content, it is difficult to see how the evaluation might proceed.

At this point my account diverges from hers: I make the Davidsonian argument that, like factual judgments, value judgments have empirical content, and this content can be evaluated using the same sorts of empirical analyses that are deployed in other more straightforwardly factual aspects of scientific decision-making.[84] Insofar as we can make distinctions between those factual judgments that are better supported by the empirical evidence and those that are not, so too we can make such distinctions in the case of value judgments.[85] Where relevant, political interests that are empirically supported can play a positive role in science.

On Davidson's view, the evaluative symmetry between judgments of fact and value is possible because value judgments are, first and foremost, beliefs, the semantic content of which is formed no differently from the content of factual beliefs. Together, all of our beliefs form a holistic web of meaning, to use the Quinean metaphor. Factual and value judgments might be used for different rhetorical purposes in our explanations and research, but that is different from saying that one kind of judgment has empirical content and the other does not.

While a complete review of Davidson's philosophy of language does not fall under the scope of this essay, some of the basics can be teased out by focusing on the question, "How are our beliefs, political or otherwise, formed in the first place?" Davidson's model of belief formation is based on the holistic epistemology of Quine. and concerns the interpretational strategies of a "radical interpreter"—an adult who finds herself in the midst of speakers of a language completely foreign to her.[86] In the absence of a translation manual or any collateral information about the new language, Davidson asks how this idealized interpreter should proceed to cope with her radically unfamiliar world. Davidson notes that initially all she has to go on, and, indeed, all she needs, is the development of a triangular relationship between (i) the beliefs of native speakers expressed as sentences, (ii) the features of the world to which the sentences refer, and (iii) her attention to (i) and (ii).[87] As I have argued elsewhere,[88] there are two important implications of this model of belief formation for analytic feminists studying the effects of political interests on scientific knowledge. These two implications are discussed below and then applied to the feminist political interests of relevance to the hygiene hypothesis.

The first is Davidson's argument that whatever there is to the meaning of any of our beliefs, must, in principle, be available from the radical interpreter's external, third-person perspective. We can all imagine and/ or have experienced successful immersion experiences in completely unfamiliar language communities. On what can this success depend? Surely not on some internal private stock of beliefs about, or expressed in, the new language that are then tested, since initially in these situations, we, as radical interpreters, have no such semantic content available to us in the new language. Yet eventually we can learn the new language, or at least we know people who have done so. The reason is that in at least the simplest cases, the content of the beliefs of the native speakers can be publicly accessed through radical interpretation.

Although beliefs are held by individuals and are in some sense idiosyncratic and/or a product of particular social forces such as gender or nationality, still, the content of any belief must in principle be publicly accessible and communicable, for it is the public process of communication that gives rise to those beliefs in the first place. And if the content of a belief can be publicly communicated, then through triangulation, the relationship between the content of the belief and the empirical features of the world to which it refers, more or less directly, can be evaluated by anyone who cares enough to take the time to do so.

The second important implication for analytical feminist work in science is that Davidson's holistic model shows there is no principled, substantive difference in the triangulation process by which we form beliefs concerning basic descriptive features of the world and beliefs concerning evaluative features of the world, such as those that inform our political interests.[89] That is, just as with descriptive beliefs, feminist and other political interests get their semantic content from their relationship to the world—a relationship that can, in principle, be empirically adjudicated.

While it is certainly possible that some of the more complex feminist political beliefs that make up our belief webs might be more geographically remote from the simpler perceptual beliefs at the edge of our belief webs, the holism of Davidson's model indicates that, insofar as they have any meaning at all, the complex beliefs are still connected by some semantic threads to those simpler beliefs. The case is similar for the more geographically remote beliefs that make up the theories of, say, high energy physics. The links to the empirical content of any complex set of feminist interests are as available for empirical evaluation as are the complex descriptive beliefs of physics (which is to say, not immediately available to any given undergraduate student, for example, but still empirically accessible—indeed, that's why the students attend class).

Returning to the feminist political interests of relevance to the hygiene hypothesis, recall that these include the beliefs that (a) the social roles assigned to boys and girls, and men and women, are significantly driven by deeply held cultural commitments that are arbitrarily assigned relative to features such as secondary sex characteristics, rather than being assigned relative to the interests or skills of the individuals involved; and (b) that these social roles are vigorously, though often unconsciously, enforced and rewarded from a very young age. The features of gender-role socialization affecting the hygiene hypothesis most directly include the further belief that masculine gender-role assignment, broadly construed, involves a social acceptance of playing in dirt and mud for those (typically boys) so assigned, an acceptance that does not extend to the feminine gender role, broadly construed (and typically assigned to girls).

This set of feminist political interests is layered and complex. However, if we take Davidson's semantic holism seriously, then even these more complex political beliefs are importantly linked in publicly accessible ways to our more simple perceptual beliefs and, more generally, to our everyday shared experiences about and in the world. We appeal to our students' experience of sexism, and other social constraints and prejudices, to draw out inferences to the more complicated aspects of feminist theory that have been developed in response to these experiences. It is these complicated but, in principle, publicly accessible set of inferential links that give our more complex feminist political beliefs their meaning. Conversely, by tracing the inferential relationship between our political interests and our everyday shared experiences, we can begin to adjudicate the empirical adequacy of our more complex political interests. Such evaluation is possible, though often, of course, difficult.[90] Again, compare these beliefs with the theories of high energy physics that are similarly layered and complex, and similarly removed from more immediate empirical experience. There is little doubt that the beliefs contained in the theories of physics can be connected to empirical experiences and then evaluated for the viability of those connections. Our current working theories of both high energy physics and feminist politics require careful examination and training to be properly evaluated.

CONCLUSION

While feminist researchers have amassed a great deal of empirical data supporting the cluster of political interests that I have shown to be relevant to the hygiene hypothesis, we should not assume that this empirical support is obvious, nor that the connections between more or less straightforwardly empirical claims and feminist political interests is clear, easy to follow, and in no need of further argument. In this essay, I have gone some way to providing such an argument.

I have argued that hygiene hypothesis researchers have not sufficiently attended to, or accounted for, the "feminization" of the morbidity rates they seek to explain, a lapse that is especially problematic as these sex differences are very well-documented in nations of the industrialized North and West. While clinicians who treat and study these illnesses have noticed sex differences in the populations they treat, they have tended toward reductionistic biomedical explanations for these differences that put the focus on physiological, hormonal, and genetic accounts. This is a second kind of lapse that has resulted in little to no attention being paid to the ways these same physiological, hormonal, and genetic phenomena are affected by complex environmental factors, such as patterns of hygiene and sanitation, or social factors, such as the interweaving of the effects of gender, race, and class hierarchies.

The problem with the first lapse is that important sources of evidence for the hygiene hypothesis have been ignored, a number of natural experiments remain unpursued, and a number of interaction effects, such as age by sex, remain unaccounted for. The problem with the second lapse is that the reductionistic focus on biomedical processes continues to leave large amounts of variation unexplained.

Having conducted an interdisciplinary review of feminist research on the gender socialization of children, I have argued for an augmented hygiene hypothesis informed by feminist political interests. In particular, I have argued that insofar as social preferences for cleanliness are enforced more aggressively for girls than boys, this gender difference leaves girls with lower rates of exposure than boys to an array of micro-organisms. The feminist political interests that inform the augmented hypothesis help fill in some of the explanatory gaps in our current understanding of why it is that, in industrialized nations of the North and West, at least, women are more likely than men to suffer from allergies, asthma, auto-immune diseases, and depression. These political interests also respond to a number of outstanding puzzles in the hygiene hypothesis research, make available new sources of evidence, and suggest designs for a number of cross-cultural and other natural experiments.

Insofar as adding a gender analysis increases the empirical adequacy of the hygiene hypothesis, and insofar as this analysis requires a particular set of feminist political interests to be in play, then we have a case where the addition of political interests to a scientific project proves empirically beneficial. While traditional philosophy of science is unable to explain this type of case, a feminist application of Davidson's philosophy of language provides us with the analytic resources we need to show how the inclusion of particular feminist political interests can play a legitimate role in scientific research.

Notes

Many thanks to Kristin Barker, Sharon Crasnow, Jonathan Kaplan, Kristen Intemann, and the anonymous referees who provided helpful comments on earlier drafts of this paper. Thanks also to Meghan Kahnle for her research assistance.
1.   See, for example, the public views surveyed in Steel et al. (2004).

2. Many of these cases are reviewed by Fausto-Sterling in *Myths of Gender: Biological Theories about Women and Men* (1992 [1985]); Schiebinger in *The Mind Has No Sex? Women and the Origin of Modern Science* (1989); Tavris in *The Mismeasure of Woman* (1992); Harding in *The "Racial" Economy of Science* (1993); and Spanier in *Im/partial Science: Gender Ideology in Molecular Biology* (1995).
3. Fausto-Sterling (2000); Anderson (2004).
4. Beginning, of course, with Harding (1986); see also Antony (1993), Intemann (2001), Clough (2003), Wylie and Nelson (2007), and de Melo-Martin and Intemann (2007) for more recent reviews of this work.
5. Rook and Lowry (2008, 150).
6. Elliot, Summers, and Weinstock (2007).
7. Desai and Gupta (2005).
8. McDade et al. (2009).
9. Rook and Lowry (2008).
10. Ibid.
11. Bird and Rieker (2008).
12. Hankin and Abramson (2001).
13. See Bird and Rieker (2008); Epstein (2007); and Barker (2005, esp. ch. 2) for a critical discussion of the trend toward the reductionistic biomedicalization of these diagnoses.
14. For a critical discussion of these biomedical approaches to immune health in women, see Beeson (1994) and Richardson (2008).
15. E.g., Altemus (2006).
16. E.g., Kuehner (2003); Nolen-Hoeksema (2001).
17. E.g., Pomerleau et al. (1990).
18. Lamb (2005).
19. A case I have made in a number of places, e.g., Clough (2006a; 2006b; 2008).
20. My presentation of the hygiene hypothesis case study was published originally in *Social Science and Medicine* (Clough 2011a).
21. Maziak et al. (2003).
22. Zuany-Amorim et al. (2002) and Ricklin-Gutzwiller et al. (2007).
23. Kilpeläinen et al. (2000).
24. Ibid., p. 201.
25. Ownby, Johnson, and Peterson (2002, p. 969).
26. Elliot et al. (2007).
27. Zvidi et al. (2008).
28. E.g., Summers et al. (2005); Elliott, Summers, and Weinstock (2007); Erb (2009).
29. Rook and Lowry (2008); Lowry et al. (2007); Spiga et al. (2006).
30. Rook and Lowry (2008, p. 150).
31. Ibid., p. 153.
32. Ibid., p.150, 152.
33. O'Brien et al. (2004).

34. Rook and Lowry (2008, p. 153).
35. Ibid.
36. Chisholm et al. (2004); and Ayuso-Mateos et al. (2001).
37. See Horwitz and Wakefield (2007) on problems comparing, for example, the diagnostic criteria of the DSM and the ICD—the International Statistical Classification of Diseases and Related Health Problems, published by the World Health Organization.
38. Bird and Rieker (2008, p. 32).
39. Martin (1998). Certainly equity policies such as Title IX in the United States have increased the participation of girls in sports, but this is a fairly recent change, and has had the greatest effect on girls' participation in sports in high school and college, well beyond the early childhood period when exposure to pathogens seems to be key.
40. Pomerleau et al. (1990).
41. E.g., Lanphear and Roghmann (1997).
42. Caldera, Huston, and O'Brien (1989).
43. Shirley (1938, p. 336).
44. Sikes (1991).
45. Martin (1998).
46. Ibid., p. 498.
47. Ibid.
48. Gagen (2000, p. 225); Tomes (1998).
49. Gagen (2000, p. 225).
50. Thorne (1993).
51. Ibid., pp. 73–75.
52. Ibid., p. 74.
53. Ibid., p. 91.
54. Castle and Groves (2000); Bogetto et al. (1999); Lensi et al. (1996); Minichiello et al. (1990); Rachman and Hodgson (1980).
55. See, for example, U.S. Department of Health and Human Services, Office on Women's Health (2009); Jacobson et al. (1997); Walsh and Rau (2000).
56. Osman (2003); Johnson, Peterson, and Ownby (1998).
57. Osman (2003).
58. For a critical discussion of these explanations, see Howes (2007); Bird and Rieker (2008).
59. Ownby, Johnson, and Peterson (2002).
60. Ibid., p. 970.
61. See Kuehner (2003) for a review of this literature.
62. Altemus (2006, p. 364).
63. Kuehner (2003, p. 169).
64. Glickman et al. (1999).
65. Segal et al. (2007).
66. Ibid.
67. Vechiatto (1997).
68. Ibid., p. 241.

69. Ibid., p. 245.
70. Ibid.
71. Ibid., p. 246.
72. Lamb (2005, p. 213).
73. Wilson, Wilson, and Berkeley-Caines (2003, 217).
74. Punch (2000).
75. Hurtado et al. (1997).
76. Ibid., p. 63.
77. Frost (2007, p. 24).
78. Ibid., pp. 17–18.
79. E.g., Clough (2006a; 2006b; 2008).
80. E.g., Okruhlik (1984); Longino (1987).
81. E.g., Anderson (2004).
82. Ibid., pp. 12–18.
83. Ibid., p. 13.
84. For more detail on my differences with Anderson, see Clough (2006b).
85. I acknowledge that my argument here hinges on an undefended assumption that empirical adjudication is efficacious for factual judgments.
86. E.g., Davidson (1990; 1991a; 1991b).
87. This characterization of radical interpretation comes from Clough (2001, p. 82).
88. Clough (2011b).
89. Davidson ([1995a] 2004); Clough (2006a, 2006b, 2008); Clough and Loges (2008).
90. See Davidson ([1995b] 2004); see also Clough (2010), for a discussion of the practical problems involved in this sort of evaluation.

Bibliography

Altemus, Margaret. 2006. Sex differences in depression and anxiety disorders: Potential biological determinants. *Hormones and Behavior* 50: 534–38.

Anderson, Elizabeth. 2004. Uses of value judgments in science. *Hypatia* 19 (1): 1–24. [Reprinted as Chapter 14 of this volume.]

Antony, Louise. 1993. Quine as feminist: The radical import of naturalized epistemology. In *A mind of one's own: Feminist essays on reason and objectivity*, ed. Louise Antony and Charlotte Witt. Boulder: Westview Press, 185–226.

Ayuso-Mateos, J. L., et al. 2001. Depressive disorders in Europe: Prevalence figures from the ODIN study. *British Journal of Psychiatry* 179: 308–16.

Barker, Kristin. 2005. *The Fibromyalgia story: Medical authority and women's worlds of pain*. Philadelphia: Temple University Press.

Beeson, Paul B. 1994. Age and sex associations of 40 autoimmune diseases. *American Journal of Medicine* 96 (5): 457–62.

Bird, Chloe E., and Patricia P. Rieker. 1999. Gender matters: An integrated model for understanding men's and women's health. *Social Science and Medicine* 48: 745–55.

————. 2008. *Gender and health: The effects of constrained choices and social policies*. Cambridge: Cambridge University Press.

Bogetto, F., S. Venturello, U. Albert, G. Maina, & L. Ravizza. 1999. Gender-related clinical differences in obsessive-compulsive disorder. *European Psychiatry* 14: 434–41.

Caldera, Y. M., A. C. Huston, and M. O'Brien. 1989. Social interactions and play patterns of parents and toddlers with feminine, masculine, and neutral toys. *Child Development* 60: 70–76.

Castle, David J., and Aaron Groves. 2000. Heart of the matter: The internal and external boundaries of obsessive-compulsive disorder. *Australian and New Zealand Journal of Psychiatry* 34: 249–55.

Chisholm, D., et al. 2004. Reducing the global burden of depression: population-level analysis of intervention cost-effectiveness in 14 world regions. *British Journal of Psychiatry* 184: 393–403.

Clough, Sharyn. 2001. Donald Davidson. In *The Routledge encyclopedia of postmodernism*, ed. Charles E. Winquist and Victor Taylor. London: Routledge, p. 82.

————. 2003. *Beyond epistemology: A pragmatist approach to feminist science studies*. Lanham, Md.: Rowman and Littlefield.

————. 2006a. On the very idea of a feminist epistemology of science: Response to commentators on *Beyond epistemology: A pragmatist approach to feminist science studies*. *Metascience* 15: 27–37.

————. 2006b. Commentary on Elizabeth Anderson's "Uses of value judgments in science." *MIT symposium on gender, race and philosophy*, Symposium I: 1–6. http://web.mac.com/shaslang/SGRP/Archive.html.

————. 2008. Solomon's empirical/non-empirical distinction and the proper place of values in science. *Perspectives in Science* 16 (2): 265–79.

————. 2010. Drawing battle lines and choosing bedfellows: Rorty, relativism, and feminist strategy. In *Feminist interpretations of Richard Rorty*, ed. Marianne Janack. University Park: Penn State Press, 155–172.

————. 2011a. Gender and the hygiene hypothesis. *Social Science & Medicine* 72 (4): 486–93.

————. 2011b. Radical interpretation, feminism, and science. In *Dialogues with Davidson*, ed. Jeffrey Malpas. Cambridge, Mass.: MIT Press, 405–426.

————, and Bill Loges. 2008. Racist value judgments as objectively false beliefs: A philosophical and social-psychological analysis. *Journal of Social Philosophy* 39 (1): 77–95.

Davidson, Donald. 1990. Meaning, truth and evidence. In *Perspectives on Quine*, ed. Robert Barrett and Roger Gibson, Jr. Oxford: Basil Blackwell.

————.1991a. Epistemology externalized. *Dialectica* 45 (2–3): 191–202.

————.1991b. Three varieties of knowledge. In *A. J. Ayer memorial essays*, ed. A. Phillips Griffiths. Cambridge: Cambridge University Press, 153–166.

————. [1995a] 2004. The problem of objectivity. Reprinted in *Problems of rationality*. Oxford: Clarendon Press, 3–18.

————. [1995b] 2004. The objectivity of values. Reprinted in *Problems of rationality*. Oxford: Clarendon Press, 39–51.

Desai, H., and P. Gupta. 2005. Increasing incidence of Crohn's disease in India: Is it related to improved sanitation? *Indian Journal of Gastroenterology* 24: 23–24.

Elliott, D. E., R. W. Summers, and J. V. Weinstock. 2007. Helminths as governors of immune-mediated inflammation. *International Journal of Parasitology* 37 (5): 457–64.

Epstein, S. 2007. *Inclusion: The politics of difference in medical research*. Chicago: University of Chicago Press.

Erb, K. 2009. Can helminths or helminth-derived products be used in humans to prevent or treat allergic diseases? *Trends in Immunology* 30 (2): 75–82.

Fausto-Sterling, Anne. 1992. Myths of gender: Biological theories about women and men, 2nd ed. New York: Basic Books.

———. 2000. *Sexing the body: Gender politics and the construction of sexuality*. New York: Basic Books.

Frost, Joe L. 2007. Genesis and evolution of American play and playgrounds. In *Investigating play in the 21st century* (*Play and Culture Studies*, vol. 7). Dorothy Justus Sluss and Olga S. Jarrett, eds. New York: University Press of America, 3–31.

Gagen, E. A. 2000. An example to us all: Child development and identity construction in early 20th-century playgrounds. *Environment and Planning A* 32 (4): 599–616.

Glickman, L.T., A. O. Camara, N. W. Glickman, and G. P. McCabe. 1999. Nematode intestinal parasites of children in rural Guinea, Africa: Prevalence and relationship to geophagia. *International Journal of Epidemiology* 28: 169–74.

Harding, Sandra. 1986. *The science question in feminism*. Ithaca, N.Y.: Cornell University Press.

——— (ed). 1993. *The "racial" economy of science*. Bloomington: Indiana University Press.

Hankin, Benjamin L., and Lyn Y. Abramson. 2001. Development of gender differences in depression: An elaborated cognitive vulnerability-transactional stress theory. *Psychological Bulletin* 127 (6): 773–96.

Horwitz, Allan V., and Jerome C. Wakefield. 2007. *The loss of sadness: How psychiatry transformed normal sorrow into depressive disorder*. New York: Oxford University Press.

Howes, Moira. 2007. Maternal agency and the immunological paradox of pregnancy. In *Establishing medical reality: Essays in the metaphysics and epistemology of biomedical science*, ed. Harold Kincaid and Jennifer McKitrick. Netherlands: Springer, 179–98.

Hurtado, A., K. Hill, I. Arenas de Hurtado, and Selva Rodriguez. 1997. The evolutionary context of chronic allergic conditions: The Hiwi of Venezuela. *Human Nature* 8 (1): 51–75.

Intemann, Kristen. 2001. Science and values: Are value judgments always irrelevant to the justification of scientific claims? *Philosophy of Science* 68 (Proceedings): S506–18.

Jacobson, D. L., S. J. Gange, N. R. Rose, and N. M. Graham. 1997. Epidemiology and estimated population burden of selected autoimmune diseases in the United States. *Clinical Immunology Immunopathology* 84 (3): 223–43.

Johnson, C., E. Peterson, and Dennis R. Ownby. 1998. Gender differences in total and allergen-specific Immunoglobulin E (IgE) concentrations in a population-based cohort from birth to age four years. *American Journal of Epidemiology* 147: 1145–52.

Kilpeläinen, M., E. O. Terho, H. Helenius, and M. Koskenvuo. 2000. Farm environment in childhood prevents the development of allergies. *Clinical and Experimental Allergy* 30 (2): 201–208.

Kuehner, C. 2003. Gender differences in unipolar depression: An update of epidemiological findings and possible explanations. *Acta Psychiatrica Scandinavica* 108: 163–74.

Lamb, Sarah. 2005. The politics of dirt and gender: Body techniques in Bengal, India. In *Dirt, undress and difference: Critical perspectives on the body's surface*, ed. Adeline Masquelier. Bloomington: Indiana University Press, 213–32.

Lanphear, B., and K. Roghmann. 1997. Pathways of lead exposure in urban children. *Environmental Research* 74: 67–73.

Lensi, P., G. B. Cassano, G. Correddu, S. Ravagli, J. L. Kunovac, and H. S. Akiskal. 1996. Obsessive-compulsive disorder: Familial developmental history, symptomatology, comorbidity and course with special reference to gender-related differences. *British Journal of Psychiatry* 169: 101–7.

Longino, Helen. 1987. Can there be a feminist science? *Hypatia* 2 (3): 51–64.

Lowry, C. A., J. H. Hollis, A. de Vries, B. Pan, L. R. Brunet, J. R. F. Hunt, et al. 2007. Identification of an immune-responsive mesolimbocortical serotonergic system: Potential role in regulation of emotional behavior. *Neuroscience* 146: 756–72.

De Melo-Martin, Inmaculada, and Kristin Intemann. 2007. Can ethical reasoning contribute to better epidemiology? A case study in research on racial-health disparities. *European Journal of Epidemiology* 22: 215–21.

Martin, Karin A. 1998. Becoming a gendered body: Practices of preschools. *American Sociological Review* 63 (4): 494–511.

Maziak, W., T. Behrens, T. M. Brasky, H. Duhme, P. Rzehak, S. K. Weiland, and U. Keil. 2003. Are asthma and allergies in children and adolescents increasing? Results from ISAAC phase I and phase III surveys in Munster, Germany. *Allergy* 58: 572–79.

McDade, Thomas W., Julienne Rutherford, Linda Adair, and Christopher W. Kuzawa. 2009. Early origins of inflammation: Microbial exposures in infancy predict lower levels of C-reactive protein in adulthood. *Proceedings of the Royal Society of Britain, Biological Sciences*. Published online 9 December 2009.

Minichiello, W. E., L. Baer, M. A. Jenike, and A. Holland. 1990. Age of onset of major subtypes of obsessive-compulsive disorder. *Journal of Anxiety Disorder* 4: 147–50.

Nolen-Hoeksema, Susan. 2001. Gender differences in depression. *Current Directions in Psychological Science* 10 (3): 173–76.

O'Brien, M. E., et al. 2004. SRL172 (killed *Mycobacterium vaccae*) in addition to standard chemotherapy improves quality of life without affecting survival, in patients with advanced non-small-cell lung cancer: Phase III results. *Annals of Oncology* 15: 906–14.

Okruhlik, Kathleen. 1994. Gender and the biological sciences. *Biology and Society Canadian Journal of Philosophy* Supplementary Vol. 20: 21–42.

Osman, M. 2003. Therapeutic implications of sex differences in asthma and atopy: Community child health, public health, and epidemiology. *Archives of Disease in Childhood* 88 (7): 587–90.

Ownby, D., C. Johnson, and Edward L. Peterson. 2002. Exposure to dogs and cats in the first year of life and risk of allergic sensitization at 6 to 7 years of age. *JAMA* 288 (8): 963–72.

Pomerleau, A., D. Bolduc, G. Malcuit, and Louise Cossette. 1990. Pink or blue: Environmental gender stereotypes in the first two years of life. *Sex Roles* 22 (5–6): 359–67.

Punch, Samantha. 2000. Children's strategies for creating playspaces: Negotiating independence in rural Bolivia. In *Children's geographies: Playing, living, learning*, ed. Sarah Holloway and Gill Valentine. London: Routledge, 48–62.

Rachman, S., and R. Hodgson. 1980. *Obsessions and compulsions*. Englewood Cliff, N.J.: Prentice Hall.

Richardson, Sarah S. 2008. When gender criticism becomes standard scientific practice: The case of sex determination genetics. *Gendered innovations in science and engineering*, ed. L. Schiebinger. Palo Alto: Stanford University Press, pp. 22–42.

Ricklin-Gutzwiller, M. E., et al. 2007. Intradermal injection of heat-killed *Mycobacterium vaccae* in dogs with atopic dermatitis: A multicentre pilot study. *Veterinary Dermatology* 18: 87–93.

Rook, G. A. W., and C. A. Lowry. 2008. The hygiene hypothesis and psychiatric disorders. *Trends in Immunology* 29 (4): 150–58.

Segal, S., T. Zaoutis, S. J. Kagen, and S. Samir. 2007. Epidemiology of and risk factors for Acinetobacter species bloodstream infection in children. *Pediatric Infectious Disease Journal* 26 (10): 920–26.

Shirley, Mary. 1938. Common content in the speech of preschool children. *Child Development* 9 (4): 333–46.

Sikes, Patricia. 1991. "Nature took its course"? Student teachers and gender awareness. *Gender and Education* 3 (2): 145–62.

Schiebinger, Londa. 1989. *The mind has no sex? Women in the origins of modern science*. Cambridge, Mass.: Harvard University Press.

Spanier, Bonnie. 1995. *Im/partial science: Gender ideology in molecular biology*. Bloomington: Indiana University Press.

Spiga, F., S. L. Lightman, A. Shekar, and C. A. Lowry. 2006. Injections of Urocortin 1 into the basolateral amygdala induce anxiety-like behavior and c-Fos expression in brainstem serotonergic neurons. *Neuroscience* 138: 1265–76.

Summers, R. W., D. E. Elliott, J. F. Urban Jr., R. Thompson, and J. V. Weinstock. 2005. *Trichuris suis* therapy in Crohn's disease. *Gut* 54 (1): 87–90.

Steel, B., P. List, D. Lach, and B. Shindler. 2004. The role of scientists in the environmental policy process: A case study from the American west. *Environmental Science & Policy* 7: 1–13.

Tavris, Carol. 1992. *The mismeasure of woman*. New York: Simon and Schuster.

Thorne, Barrie. 1993. *Gender play: Girls and boys in school*. New Brunswick, N.J.: Rutgers University Press.

Tomes, N. 1998. *The gospel of germs: Men, women, and the microbe in American life*. Cambridge, Mass.: Harvard University Press.

U.S. Department of Health and Human Services, Office on Women's Health. 2009. Lupus: Frequently asked questions. http://www.womenshealth.gov/faq/lupus.pdf. Accessed February 21, 2011.

Vechiatto, Norbert. 1997. "Digestive worms": Ethnomedical approaches to intestinal parasitism in Southern Ethiopia. In *The anthropology of infectious disease: International health perspectives*, ed. Marcia Inhorn and Peter Brown. Amsterdam: Gordon and Breach Publishers, 241–66.

Walsh, S. J., and L. M. Rau. 2000. Autoimmune diseases: A leading cause of death among young and middle-aged women in the United States. *American Journal of Public Health* 90 (9): 1463–66.

Wilson, Leon C., Colwick M. Wilson, and Lystra Berkeley-Caines. 2003. Age, gender and socioeconomic differences in parental socialization preferences in Guyana. *Journal of Comparative Family Studies* 34: 213–27.

Wylie, Alison, and Lynn Hankinson Nelson. 2007. Coming to terms with the values of science: Insights from feminist science studies scholarship. In Harold Kincaid, John Dupré, and Alison Wylie (eds.), *Value-Free Science? Ideals and Illusions*. Oxford: Oxford University Press, 58–86.

Zuany-Amorim, C., et al. 2002. Suppression of airway eosinophilia by killed *Mycobacterium vaccae*–induced allergen-specific regulatory T-cells. *Nature Medicine* 8: 625–29.

Zvidi, I., R. Hazazi, S. Birkenfeld, and Yaron Niv. 2008. The prevalence of Crohn's disease in Israel: A 20-year survey. *Digestive Diseases and Sciences* 54 (4): 848–52.

16

MIRIAM SOLOMON
Temple University

THE WEB OF VALIEF:

An Assessment of Feminist Radical Empiricism

1. INTRODUCTION

Willard Van Orman Quine has had an amazing influence on feminist analytic philosophers. Several wrote their doctoral dissertations on his work: Sharyn Clough, Sandra Harding, Catherine Hundleby, Alison Jagger, Lynn Hankinson Nelson, Alessandra Tanesini, Nancy Tuana, and I.[1] Others, such as Elizabeth Anderson, Louise Antony, and Richmond Campbell, explicitly adopt much of the Quinean epistemic framework of a holistic network of beliefs with occasional tethering in experience. Most if not all of these feminist philosophers are happy to identify themselves as "feminist empiricists" in one way or another.[2] The purpose of this chapter is to display the appeal and evaluate the plausibility of its most Quine-inspired and most empiricist version, which I call "feminist radical empiricism." I appropriate Quine's metaphor of "the web of belief" to characterize this feminist view as "the web of valief." "Valief," as will be explained in this paper, is not a typo, but my term for the all-encompassing network of beliefs and values that is described by feminist empiricists in the Quinean tradition.[3] My assessment is that "the web of valief" characterizes a few epistemic situations, but is not plausible or appropriate for many others. The underlying reason for this is that "the web of valief" is too simple a model to give an account of the ways in which values work. I think that it is also too simple a model to give an account of the ways in which beliefs work across domains of inquiry, but that is a topic to be addressed elsewhere.

2. FOUR TYPES OF FEMINIST EMPIRICISM

In this section, I will give an explication of the range of positions that are regularly called "feminist empiricism" in the analytic tradition and specifically in the Quinean analytic tradition.[4] The term "feminist" is generally understood as modifying the term "empiricist," signifying the use of some special feminist empirical tools. I discern *four* distinct types of feminist empiricism: *spontaneous feminist empiricism* (the term is due to Sandra Harding [1993]); *reliabilist feminist empiricism* (a term I shall use for the position taken by Louise Antony [1993]); *gap feminist empiricism* (the term is from Kristen Intemann's [2005] discussion of "the gap argument"); and what I shall call *feminist radical empiricism* (so termed because what is radical is the empiricism, not the feminism).

First, a word about terminology. The terms "spontaneous" and "gap" are not the greatest labels, but they are familiar and are used as placeholders for more accurate and aesthetic terminology that I hope someone will coin. "Reliabilist feminist empiricism" is a simple term for a position that is attractive to feminist *naturalistic* analytic philosophers (rather than more traditional feminist *aprioristic* analytic philosophers, who might belong in the "spontaneous feminist empiricist" category).[5] "Feminist radical empiricism" is a dull-sounding phrase, but so precise and so reasonably concise that I cannot bring myself to give it up for something with more zing! At least it is explicated with a memorable metaphor, "the web of valief" (to be explained below).

Let me also include a word about the practice of classifying feminist empiricisms (and feminist epistemologies and epistemologies in general). I have learned from feminist philosophers to be wary of such general classifications, suspecting that they may reflect unconscious cognitive hierarchies or that they may crudely prune ideas and leave out the interesting complexities and tensions. Nevertheless, some classification is helpful in this context, for the issues discussed in this chapter.

Spontaneous feminist empiricism is the view that a traditional logical empiricist framework (say, the framework of Hempel [1966]), supplemented by the experiential knowledge that gender bias is a pervasive cause of error in science, is sufficient for a feminist critique of science. If I was coining a term for this position, it would be "traditional feminist empiricism," but I prefer to keep "spontaneous feminist empiricism" to honor Sandra Harding. The traditional empiricist framework characterizes scientific objectivity as, among other things, freedom from bias. By "spontaneous," Harding means "unreflective" or "business as usual" in science: this feminist critique is continuous with widely accepted critical practices among scientists for identifying and correcting for erroneous thinking. This is not surprising, if we bear in mind that scientists are typically trained in, at best, Baconian and logical empiricist methodology. They are trained to try to keep scientific reasoning free of all bias, and to test hypotheses rigorously against the evidence, keeping those that are predictively and explanatorily successful and also preferring those that have "cognitive virtues" such as simplicity. According to spontaneous feminist empiricism, gender bias—in common with all biases—produces inferior science, sometimes called "bad science." Examples of work in spontaneous feminist empiricism are works by Bleier (1986), Fausto-Sterling (1992), Hubbard (1990), Lloyd (2005), and the Biology and Gender Study Group (1988).[6]

Reliabilist feminist empiricists have given up the traditional normative goal of bias-free science. They acknowledge that it is both impossible and unnecessary for scientists to reason without some heuristics, interests, or values. Instead, they advocate distinguishing the good "biases" from the bad "biases," on grounds of conduciveness to epistemic goals. Then, the recommendation is to use the good biases and avoid the bad ones. Louise Antony's widely reprinted paper, "Quine as Feminist" (1993), is written in this spirit and gives an interpretation of the history of modern philosophy, including the rationalist/empiricist debate, in a reliabilist framework, which takes truth to be the ultimate epistemic goal.[7] Antony is primarily thinking of innate heuristics, such as those for language learning and visual perception, which predispose infants toward learning languages and perceiving objects correctly, even though the heuristics are not justified by experience. Antony generalizes from such cases to cognitive mechanisms in general, assessing them instrumentally (in terms of conduciveness to truth) rather than procedurally (in terms of conformity to traditional ideas about good reasoning). Reliabilism is an occasional theme in Quine's work that is developed more thoroughly by Alvin Goldman (1986) and other analytic epistemologists. Reliabilism gives a more generous epistemological account of "bias" than Quine would do most of the time; Quine always espoused traditional cognitive virtues, even though his overall views permit a less pristine epistemology.[8]

Feminist reliabilist empiricism includes gender bias along with all other kinds of bias, to be assessed instrumentally, in terms of the quality of the knowledge that each bias produces. Reliabilist feminist empiricism makes two empirical claims: that gender bias is a "bad" bias because it often leads scientists to incorrect conclusions, and that scientists can learn to reason without this epistemically "bad" bias. Any epistemically good biases (those leading to true beliefs) should be kept. Biases are not inherently epistemically good or epistemically bad.

Both spontaneous and reliabilist feminist empiricisms treat gender bias like any other bias, to be countered by clear bias-free thinking (spontaneous feminist empiricism) or instrumental assessment followed by elimination or acceptance (reliabilist feminist empiricism). These critical frameworks have sufficed for the occasional dip into gender critique. However, the more examples of gender bias that are discovered, and the more difficult it turns out to be to root out the undesirable biases, the more tempting it becomes to give a richer epistemological account of bias, perhaps also giving gender bias special treatment through discussion of concepts such as "standpoint." Ruth Bleier, Anne Fausto-Sterling, and Ruth Hubbard, who began as spontaneous feminist empiricists, have moved beyond spontaneous feminist empiricism in this way. Standpoint theories, which privilege the epistemic perspective of politically engaged feminists, have been especially fruitful in feminist philosophy of science, beginning with the pioneering work of Sandra Harding (1986) and continuing to the present.[9] In my view, standpoint theories should not be viewed as an alternative to "feminist empiricism" (despite Sandra Harding's [1993] widely adopted classification of feminist epistemology into feminist empiricism, feminist standpoint theories, and feminist postmodernism) but as a crucial methodological tool for feminist empiricists of all kinds. I am in agreement with Alison Wylie (2004) that successful feminist standpoints are not general all-purpose epistemic tools, but specific interventions for specific domains. Their usefulness is a contingent matter rather than an armchair privilege. Standpoint is particularly useful for understanding the social power relationships that subjugate those with standpoint; it is less helpful for understanding other social power relationships (for example, those who have feminist standpoint may not have knowledge of race and class relationships) and it may be unhelpful in natural (rather than social) sciences.[10] Gap feminist empiricism is a more philosophical view about "bias" (and/or "values") than spontaneous feminist empiricism, unlikely to be taken by practicing scientists who do not have the time or the motivation to reflect more deeply on scientific method. According to gap feminist empiricism, empiricist constraints (such as predictive power and explanatory success) are vital but insufficient for theory choice. Scientific theories are underdetermined by the available evidence. Sometimes this is called the "underdetermination argument" for feminist empiricism. This is a better description but uses a clumsy word that is always flagged by spell checkers. Underdetermination is, of course, a regular theme in the work of Quine, who was credited with the term "Duhem-Quine thesis" first proposed by Pierre Duhem (1954).[11]

An overall pluralism—with different scientists pursuing different theories—is recommended by Helen Longino, who articulated gap feminist empiricism in her *Science as Social Knowledge* (1990).[12] Scientists are free to choose among the available competing, equally (but, Longino allows, differently) empirically successful theories. Their choices may be based on their values when different theories express or assume different ideologies. The "gap" between the constraints of empiricism and theory choice is bridged with values. The language of "gap" is misleading because you can't see, or mind, or fill, or even bridge the gap; values pervade theory. For Longino, there are no constraints on the *content* of the values, but all values should be *made explicit* through a process of mutual criticism of theories, which is the foundation of scientific objectivity. Some of these values are the traditional cognitive values of science such as simplicity and fruitfulness; they have the same epistemic status as more feminist values such as novelty and mutuality of interaction (Longino, 1995). Longino is not an empiricist about the values themselves; in personal correspondence she has said that her "naturalism is curbed" when discussing the justification of values.[13]

Why is gap feminist empiricism thought of as a *feminist* view, especially when Longino herself rarely uses this adjective to characterize her "critical contextual empiricism"? To be sure, it allows feminist values to be used in theory choice. But equally, it allows—indeed encourages—other values, including morally objectionable values, to determine choice. It does not privilege feminist values. Pluralism, of a critical variety, is the scientifically desirable state of affairs. One answer that I expect Longino would give is that feminist values have been especially productive as critical and creative stances in recent science. So the feminism in gap feminist empiricism is a contingent feature of recent successful science criticism. It is not that feminist values produce better science, but rather good criticism produces better science, and feminist values create a fruitful stance for criticism of contemporary science, which is, for historical reasons, mostly steered by non-feminist values.

Another reason that Longino's view is feminist is that good criticism, as Longino understands it, is itself constituted by democratic discursive practices, and democratic discursive practices in turn are grounded in feminist commitments that do not "disappear" gender or other kinds of diversity. Longino's four criteria for objectivity—tempered equality of intellectual authority, public forums for criticism, responsiveness to criticism, and overlapping values—supplement her "gap feminism" and are not empiricist commitments themselves. In fact, the four criteria are applicable to all knowledge domains, constituting objectivity whether or not one of the shared values is empirical adequacy (Longino, 1990; Longino, 2002). This is a special feature of Longino's view, not present in other gap feminist views such as those of Nelson (1993) and Lacey (1999).

Does it follow for gap feminist empiricists that if contemporary science were largely guided by feminist values, sexist values would be productive of criticism? I think that this *is* a consequence of Longino's view, and that gap feminist empiricists should just bite the bullet and allow that morally bad values might be scientifically useful in this situation, which is after all hypothetical. If the only theories of human behavior we had were complex and interactionist, it would be helpful to introduce some linear hierarchical alternatives, even though linear hierachical theories can fuel inflexible and reductionist views of human nature. Thinking about such hypothetical situations produces concern only because they are so alien to our usual experience.

Another option, at this point—which Longino does not take, but others (Anderson, 2004; Campbell, 1998; Clough, 2004; Nelson, 1990) take—is to argue that values (as well as scientific theories) should be empirically criticized, and that only those which survive criticism be kept. In this kind of account, there may be no gap to be filled since both values and theories are part of the complex network of beliefs.[14] In this more radical empiricism, values, including feminist values, are put to the test and not taken as given. But what kind of evidence is appropriate for criticizing the values that are used in science? Moral and political objections to particular values, such as the undemocratic values expressed in linear hierarchical accounts of biological processes, are irrelevant in that biological context, even if they could be construed as evidentiary. For example, it would be inappropriate to criticize Francis Crick's "central dogma" that information flow is one way only from the DNA to the cytoplasm on the grounds that this theory is not sufficiently egalitarian. Crick would laugh off the criticism with a remark that natural processes are not designed to reflect democratic values, or any values. They are not designed at all. The only appropriate question to ask of linear hierarchical values is whether or not, and to what extent, linear hierarchical accounts of biological processes are generally *scientifically* successful. This is a question about the reliability of the use of a heuristic ("look for linear hierarchical accounts") in biological contexts. And the only way to judge that is to look at the empirical successes of linear hierarchical accounts, comparing their success with the empirical successes of other kinds of accounts. This amounts, in Quinean holistic terms, to looking at the empirical success of the values (in addition to the empirical success of the particular theories themselves). And this is the basis of feminist radical empiricism. Helen Longino resists going this far; as I reported above, she is not an empiricist about values.

Lynn Hankinson Nelson (1990) was the first feminist empiricist to suggest that values be considered along with scientific theories for the empirical success of the aggregate.[15] Using the metaphor of Quine's "web of belief" (Quine and Ullian, 1970) she suggests that moral and political values "face the tribunal of sense experience" (Quine, 1963; 1961) along with the theoretical claims for which they function as background assumptions. So there can be evidence for some values and against other values. Keeping the Quinean language, I suggest that this radicalization of Quine's views, feminist radical empiricism, be thought of as the "web of valief," where "valief" includes both beliefs and values.[16]

Nelson (1996) has a peculiarly broad understanding of "evidence" as including cognitive values such as coherence. This is a departure from the usual terminology and I have not found a convincing justification for it. So I will present feminist radical empiricism with the usual understanding of what is meant by "evidence." "Evidence," in most accounts, includes predictive, retrodictive, experimental, explanatory, and technological success, but does not include "cognitive" values—traditional or feminist—such as simplicity, coherence, conservativeness, novelty, or mutuality of interaction.[17]

Nelson's general view—that values are tested empirically, together with the theories that they underwrite—is also put forward by Liz Anderson (2004), Sharyn Clough (2004) and Richmond Campbell (1998). These philosophers argue that the facts and values are both part of the Quinean holistic framework of belief. And they suggest that feminist values do *better* than sexist values at getting good scientific theories and are thereby better confirmed. They put feminist values to the test of experience and come out singing. They concur that science is not value-free and that values are not science free.

3. FEMINIST RADICAL EMPIRICISM

Let's explore how feminist radical empiricism applies to a classical feminist case, Evelyn Fox Keller's story of Barbara McClintock (1983). Barbara McClintock used the feminist value of "respecting difference" to develop her classical genetics inquiries, yielding a successful account of genetic transposition, in which the movement of one gene to another part of the chromosome affects the expression of another gene. Instead of ignoring the few facts that did not fit, she cherished and explored the few exceptions to Mendelian inheritance in the genetics of maize. So it looks like this feminist value is confirmed in her work. But before drawing any conclusions, let's reflect that Francis Crick's sexist values of "expecting hierarchy" yielded a good deal of success in the early years of molecular genetics. For example, extensive genetic maps were produced for *Drosophila*, taking for granted that the location of genes on the genome does not affect their functioning (what we would call their expression). These maps made successful predictions for genetic experiments. The "master molecule" theory was scientifically successful, although it was not responsible for all the scientific successes in genetics.

Values are applied in many domains; any particular value may fare well in some domains (or for some occasions) and less well in others (or for other occasions). Making the claim that feminist values are well-confirmed in a manner that justifies their wider application requires showing their fruitful applicability to a range of domains (and occasions), as well as showing that they do better than sexist values in this range of domains (and occasions). However, no one has even begun to think about how to individuate and aggregate the successes and failures of values in different domains (or occasions). Perhaps feminist values can be confirmed and shown to be more empirically successful than sexist values, but we are nowhere on the way to doing that.

Values, like mathematics and logic, can operate in many domains and thus pervade the "web of valief." Unlike mathematics and logic, however, they may not be entrenched, and it may not take that much in the way of counter-evidence to drop them. The feminist radical empiricist must be willing to revise values—including any favored feminist values—when they are not working. For example, suppose Longino's (1995) proposed feminist value "prefer novelty" (which contrasts with the sexist value of conservatism) is used to evaluate and select a new theory of high temperature superconductivity over the traditional Bardeen, Cooper, and Schrieffer (BCS) theory. And suppose that new theory turns out not to work. Feminist radical empiricists should take that as evidence not only that the new theory is wrong, but also that there is a strike against the feminist value of "prefer novelty." This result is perplexing because, frankly, the worth of the feminist value of novelty should not depend on the outcome of theoretical debates in high temperature superconductivity. Likewise, the plausibility of the feminist value of mutuality of interaction should not rest, even partially, on how interactive the nucleus is with the cytoplasm. After all, what theoretical physics and intercellular biology have to say about their respective microprocesses is *irrelevant* to the question of human values. Humans are neither superconductors nor cells. We may *use* human values, at least metaphorically, when reasoning in scientific domains, and some of these uses may turn out to be better than others at answering some of our questions, but we do not typically *test them for their moral correctness* there.

There is more to say here about testing and using values. In particular, I would like to unpack the idea of "relevance," which may not be understandable through the usual Quinean metaphor of a web of belief, which treats all connections between beliefs as the same in kind and bidirectional (Quine writes of a "field of force," and conceives of it on analogy with a web constructed of elastic threads where tensions are equal and opposite) and which rejects over-semantic tools. I will explore the concept of "relevance" in the next section of this chapter. But first I want to take a look at Elizabeth Anderson's essay, "Uses of Value Judgments in Science: A General Argument with Lessons from a Case Study of Feminist Research on Divorce" (2004; reprinted as chapter 14 of this volume). Anderson argues that value judgments are empirically testable, and that, in her case study, feminist values are supported by the evidence.[18] It is a refreshing article, avoiding the hand-waving generality and abstractness that characterizes the earlier (Campbell, Nelson) statements of feminist radical empiricism.

Anderson's strategy is to present the work of Abigail Stewart and her team on the psychological consequences of divorce, contrasting it with the work of more traditional researchers such as Barbara Whitehead, Judith Wallerstein, George Gilder, and James Wilson. Stewart's team, guided by feminist values, framed the research questions differently from the traditionalists. They looked for positive as well as negative consequences of divorce. And they investigated more complex interaction effects of marital conflict, maturity of children, maternal employment, and so on. They expected to find, and found, individual differences. The traditional researchers worked with the assumption that divorce is always a loss and a trauma and used simpler models, expecting fewer individual differences. Stewart's team obtained more comprehensive results, including some surprising results about divorce and well-being. Anderson concludes, plausibly, that the research done by Stewart and her team is much better than the traditional research, and thus that feminist values are conducive to scientific success. In this way, she claims, feminist values are *confirmed* by empirical work.

Anderson thinks we are familiar with using evidence to assess values; she claims that we should be open to finding out that our values do not work and to changing our values. As an example—one that I will examine more closely in a little while—she says that communist values are disconfirmed by the several failures of communist governments.

Anderson's argument is different in an important respect from the feminist radical empiricist arguments of Nelson and Campbell just discussed. The domain in which feminist values are said to be tested is a *relevant* domain. The domain is human well-being before and after divorce, not, for example, epigenetics, quantum mechanics, or geological change. Anderson's argument does not work in the irrelevant domains in which feminist values are sometimes used, because feminist values are independent of disputes in quantum mechanics.

Another feature of Anderson's argument is that the feminist values under investigation could be stated as facts (or assumptions) rather than values, that is, it could be stated that "a variety of family styles are associated with human flourishing." In my view and that of many others, not all values can be stated as facts. Those that contain irreducible, evaluative terms, for example, "democracy is the right form of government," are not factual (although facts may enter into their assessment). Those values that cannot be stated as facts may not be disconfirmable by evidence. They may, instead, rest on preferences or goals. This alerts us to the possibility that Anderson's example may not be representative.[19]

As an example of her claim that values can be challenged by data, Anderson claims that communism is disconfirmed by the recent experience with communist governments in Eastern Europe. But this is too quick. To be sure, the former Soviet Union was oppressive, inefficient, punitive, and so on. But committed communists, quite reasonably, argue that the totalitarian aspects of the Soviet Union ruined the potential benefits of communism, just as, we might admit, the capitalist structure of the United States is ruining the benefits of democracy. We do not assess the value of democracy by looking at the United States. In fact, the idea of democracy is supported by more general values such as the desire for fairness and equality. Is there any evidence that could count for or against equality? Or is this a value that is irreducible to fact, a statement of preference for how we wish to live our lives?

Anderson's case study works extremely well within its own domain and particular range of values. My reservation is that it does not generalize to all values used in science, or to values used in irrelevant domains. This means that we are not justified in using cases such as this one to argue for the general conclusion of feminist radical empiricism.

4. MORE ABOUT "RELEVANCE"

Quine rejects the a priori intuition that any parts of the web of belief are *logically* immune from revision at times when the web is empirically unsatisfactory. He allows that we may prefer as a matter of convenience to tinker with localized and less established claims than with general and entrenched claims. He terms this "pragmatism," and sometimes even thinks of it as a "rational" constraint on belief revision which he conceptualizes as a mixture of simplicity and conservatism (Quine, 1963; 1961).

Confronted with my example of high temperature superconductivity above, a feminist radical empiricist (that is, someone who is a Quinean holist about both facts and values) would say that there is, indeed, a strike against Longino's feminist cognitive value of "prefer novelty." And confronted with the example of theories of intracellular processes, a feminist radical empiricist would say that the feminist value of "mutuality of interaction" is confirmed to the degree that nucleus-cytoplasm interactions are non-hierarchical. A feminist radical empiricist would say that our intuitions about the oddness of such judgments are explained (away) by the fact that our commitment to (or against) particular values is so entrenched and so dependent on an entire network of applications in different domains (i.e., not only in high temperature physics and cellular biology).

I think that Lynn Hankinson Nelson might endorse this feminist radical empiricist position about "relevance." Many of us would not, because our confidence in our intuitions about relevance is currently stronger than our confidence in the metaphor of a web of valief in which valiefs stand in such general and pervasive relation to the world. Many of us—since the contributions of Ludwig Wittgenstein, John Dewey, Arthur Fine, Ian Hacking, and Nancy Cartwright in philosophy, and the general mood of post-structuralism, post-modernism, and anti-essentialism outside of philosophy—reject the traditional epistemological and ontological view that our beliefs and practices function (or should function) as universals.

Of course, feminist empiricists are well aware that scientists *use* values outside the domains of their relevance. The question is whether the results of this use should reflect back on the use of the values in their intended domains of application. A feminist radical empiricist (of the Quinean variety, that is, someone who endorses the web of valief) would say yes. Those who have rejected the presumption of a very general web of valief, myself included, would say no.

5. CONCLUSIONS

Values are heterogeneous. Some (such as "family values" in sociology) are relative to particular domains, others (such as simplicity) are quite general and often abstract, needing precise and variable tailoring to apply to specific situations. Sometimes values are used relevantly (e.g., assumptions about hierarchy in social processes), sometimes they are used irrelevantly (e.g., assumptions about hierarchy in biological processes). Some (e.g., the use of "family values" in sociological research) can be supported or disconfirmed, and others (e.g., the value of empirical success in scientific research) are more fixed and constitutive of practice. Feminist radical empiricism overlooks this heterogeneity of values in favor of a Quinean simplicity that treats all values as nodes in the all-encompassing network of valief. As I have argued, this does not correspond to the way in which values are handled in practice.

I suggest a more nuanced understanding of value, as follows. Where values are relevant to the domain of inquiry and can be put to the test, they should be put to the test, as feminist radical empiricists urge. Where values are irrelevant in their domain of application, "gap" feminist empiricism is the best understanding of the epistemic role of those values. Such use of values is epistemically appropriate—indeed necessary for creativity—but domain irrelevant. Where values are constitutive of a practice, such as the value of empirical success in scientific research, we may choose whether or not to engage in that practice on the basis of our broader personal or societal goals, but the values themselves can only be slightly negotiated.[20]

Notes

Sharyn Clough's (2008) response to my book, *Social Empiricism* (Solomon, 2001) raised questions about the epistemic status of values that deserved a fuller response than I could make at the time; this chapter is the beginning of that fuller response. I am grateful to Liz Anderson, Louise Antony, Sharyn Clough, Sharon Crasnow, Sandra Harding, Kristen Intemann, Anita Superson, Kenny Walden and two anonymous reviewers for Oxford University Press for their generous and thoughtful comments on an earlier draft of this paper.

1. I may not have a complete list here. I compiled it from personal knowledge as well as queries to the SWIP and the FEMMSS e-lists, and an examination of the list of Quine dissertations on Douglas Quine's website, www.wvquine. org. I would be interested to hear about any omissions. My dissertation was written at Harvard University (Quine's academic home from 1930–2000) in 1986, under the direction of Burton Dreben, Warren Goldfarb, and Hilary Putnam. I was fortunate to have several occasions to speak with (then-retired) Quine about his work as I was working on my dissertation.

2. Louise Antony prefers not to be called an "empiricist" since she associates the term with the claim in philosophy of mind that there are no innate structures. However, methodologically speaking, she is an empiricist, in requiring empirical support for all scientific claims.

3. I was inspired to coin this neologism by Tamar Szabo Gendler's recent work on an unrelated concept, that of "alief"; it showed me the advantages of judicious creation of new terms ("Alief and Belief" *Journal of Philosophy* 105(10), 634–63, 2008).

4. Burton Dreben said that "Quine *is* analytic philosophy." This extreme claim may have unduly influenced me and others who also learned their Quine through Burton Dreben (rather than, for example, through Donald Davidson's different interpretation).

5. "Naturalistic" approaches claim that contingent facts are relevant to philosophical conclusions; a prioristic approaches typically deny this.

6. Some of these authors have gone on to produce more methodologically nuanced work, usually espousing some version of standpoint theories.

7. Antony prefers not to call her views "empiricist" because she sides, on the whole, with the rationalist tradition in the history of philosophy. However, she is a naturalist about the rationalism, talking about innate mechanisms rather than a priori mechanisms. And these innate mechanisms are discovered by experimental psychology, an empirical science. For the epistemic purposes of this paper, it is fair to call her a reliabilist empiricist.

8. In contrast with Antony, Elizabeth Anderson keeps to a more classically Quinean framework, taking the epistemic goal to be achievement of the "cognitive virtues" of science such as predictive success, simplicity, and conservatism.

9. Sandra Harding reminds me that she developed her own version of standpoint theory in conversation with the sociologist Dorothy Smith and the political scientist Nancy Hartsock. An important recent anthology on standpoint theories is S. G. Harding's (2004). A special issue of *Hypatia* on the continuing relevance of standpoint theories to feminist philosophy of science recently appeared in volume 24(4) in 2009.

10. (a) Perhaps a standpoint theorist would say that standpoint is still useful in all these domains because, having learned the lesson once that social power relations affect knowledge, one is more willing to apply it more widely. But, as intersectionalist accounts have shown us more recently, each instance of social power requires separate detailed analysis and particular expertise.

 (b) The content of natural sciences may benefit from political critique if social power is playing a metaphorical role in theory construction, for example, the "master molecule" theory.

11. The Duhem-Quine thesis states that hypotheses cannot be tested in isolation; they must always be tested together with other hypotheses and assumptions. This result is extrapolated to the likely result that there will be a choice of how to respond to the results of any particular test, yielding underdetermination. Duhem argued this thesis only for physics; Quine for all of knowledge, including logic and mathematics.

12. Longino does not call her own views "gap feminism"; I use Kristin Intemann's (2005) language to describe the view.

13. The personal correspondence was in late 1992 or early 1993; I am happy to show it to anyone who is interested. I have Helen Longino's permission to quote this portion of the correspondence. So far as we can remember, she has not addressed the matter in print.

14. There may, however, still be underdetermination. Whether or not theories-plus-values are underdetermined by experience is an empirical matter. So there may still be a "gap" although not one that is bridged by values alone.

15. Of course, other thinkers (Marx, postcolonial studies, etc.) have paid attention in one way or another to values in scientific inquiry. The issue here is, rather, a specific kind of attention: treating values in the same way as theoretical claims in the theory.

16. Values can often be stated in the form of factual beliefs (e.g., "The nuclear family is the best family organization"). Nevertheless, (I would argue, along with many others) values are not ultimately reducible to facts. In this case, the term "best" marks values that are not facts (although they may be goals).

17. I explore this issue in much greater depth in Solomon (2001), chapter 2.

18. Sharyn Clough describes her own approach, focusing on particular case studies rather than general epistemic considerations, in the same way.

19. It is also likely that the term "human flourishing" includes an irreducible value component, and is thus not straightforwardly testable by the data about life after divorce.

20. A good analogy is that we can choose whether or not to play Scrabble based on our other interests and our general views about the value of playing Scrabble, but we can't do much about the overall value/goal of making as many high scoring words as possible without giving up playing Scrabble altogether (and maybe playing some other game with Scrabble pieces). So empirical success may be slightly negotiated (emphasizing, say, predictive success or deemphasizing technological success) but not radically changed

(say, requiring psychic tools for perception), without creating something other than science.

References

Anderson, E. (2004). Uses of value judgments in science: A general argument, with lessons from a case study of feminist research on divorce. *Hypatia* 19(1): 1–24.

Antony, L. M. (1993). Quine as feminist: The radical import of naturalied epistemology. In L. M. Antony, & C. Witt (Eds.), *A mind of one's own: Feminist essays on reason and objectivity* (pp. 185–225). Boulder, Colo.: Westview Press.

The Biology and Gender Study Group [A. Beldecos, S. Bailey, S. Gilbert, K. Hicks, L. Kenschaft, et al.]. (1988). The importance of feminist critique for contemporary cell biology. *Hypatia* 3(1, Feminism and Science 2): 61–76.

Bleier, R. (1986). *Feminist approaches to science.* New York: Pergamon Press.

Campbell, R. (1998). *Illusions of paradox: A feminist epistemology naturalized.* Lanham, Md.: Rowman & Littlefield.

Clough, S. (2004). Having it all: Naturalized normativity in feminist science studies. *Hypatia* 19(1): 102–18.

———. (2008). Solomon's empirical/non-empirical distinction and the proper place of values in science. *Perspectives on Science* 16(3): 265–79.

Duhem, P. M. M. (1954). *The aim and structure of physical theory* [Théorie physique: son objet et sa structure.] Princeton, N.J.: Princeton University Press.

Fausto-Sterling, A. (1992). *Myths of gender: Biological theories about women and men* (2nd ed.). New York: Basic Books.

Goldman, A. I. (1986). *Epistemology and cognition.* Cambridge, Mass.: Harvard University Press.

Harding, S. (1993). Rethinking standpoint epistemology: What is "strong objectivity"? In L. Alcoff and E. Potter (Eds.), *Feminist epistemologies* (pp. 49–82). New York: Routledge.

———. (1986). *The science question in feminism.* Ithaca, N.Y.: Cornell University Press.

———. (2004). *The feminist standpoint theory reader: Intellectual and political controversies.* New York: Routledge.

Hempel, C. G. (1966). *Philosophy of natural science.* Englewood Cliffs, N.J.: Prentice-Hall.

Hubbard, R. (1990). *The politics of women's biology.* New Brunswick, N.J.: Rutgers University Press.

Intemann, K. (2005). Feminism, underdetermination, and values in science. *Philosophy of Science* 72(5): 1001–12.

Keller, E. F. (1983). *A feeling for the organism: The life and work of Barbara McClintock.* San Francisco: W. H. Freeman.

Lacey, H. (1999). *Is science value free? Values and scientific understanding.* London: Routledge.

Lloyd, E. A. (2005). *The case of the female orgasm: Bias in the science of evolution.* Cambridge, Mass.: Harvard University Press.

Longino, H. E. (1990). *Science as social knowledge: Values and objectivity in scientific inquiry.* Princeton, N.J.: Princeton University Press.

———. (1995). Gender, politics, and the theoretical virtues. *Synthese* 104(3, Feminism and Science): 383–97.

———. (2002). *The fate of knowledge.* Princeton, N.J.: Princeton University Press.

Nelson, L. H. (1990). *Who knows: From Quine to a feminist empiricism.* Philadelphia: Temple University Press.

———. (1993). Epistemological communities. In L. Alcoff and E. Potter (Eds.), *Feminist epistemologies* (pp. 121–59). New York: Routledge.

———. (1996). Empiricism without dogmas. In L. H. Nelson and J Nelson (Eds.), *Feminism, science and the philosophy of science* (pp. 95–119). Dordrecht: Kluwer Academic Publishers.

Quine, W. V. (1963; 1961). *From a logical point of view; 9 logico-philosophical essays* (2nd rev. ed.). New York: Harper & Row.

———, and J. S. Ullian. (1970). *The web of belief.* New York: Random House.

Solomon, M. (2001). *Social empiricism.* Cambridge, Mass.: MIT Press.

Wylie, A. (2004). Why standpoint matters. In S. Harding (Ed.), *The feminist standpoint reader: Intellectual and political controversies* (pp. 339–51). New York: Routledge.

17

MARIAM THALOS
Philosophy Department, University of Utah

SELF-CONSTRUCTIONS:

An Existentialist Approach to Self and Social Identity

SUMMARY

This essay proposes a naturalistic account of social identity (both individual Self-identity and group/collective identity) that is inspired by Simone de Beauvoir's conception of existentialist social struggle. Identities, on this still-preliminary account, are constituted by an interlocking network of ascriptions, with self-ascriptions being the most weighty elements in the net. But identities—both individual and collective—are no less real, for all that. Ascriptions, and especially self-ascriptions, are profoundly important features of any agent because they are constitutive of an individual's social identity, both as an individual Self and as a member of a range of social entities and institutions. Through ascription, and especially self-ascription, an individual manages to align herself with, and so comes to behave from that time forward as a part of a larger *agentic entity* (singular or plural in subject, as the case may be) that takes action on the ground. In human beings, identity mediates agency through a nexus of ascriptions.

This *nexus* account of identity carves a space for treating the important role that groups of various kinds play in human life. The human experience is throughout marked by a collectivist dimension: humans are bonding entities.[1] This collectivist thread in the human experience— and in particular the fact that individuals suffer or enjoy consequences in virtue of group membership—has been at the heart of numerous insights contributed by analytical feminism, and has shaped much of race theory as well.[2]

Illumination of the functions of group-membership ascription illuminates also, as will be illustrated here, the identity symbolism implicit in many historical episodes, both real and legendary—how to construe, for instance, the giant headline on September 12, 2001, in the French newspaper *Le Monde*: "WE ARE ALL AMERICANS NOW." And it will provide theoretical resources for explaining the fundamental role played by institutions and other social groups in history, thereby de-centering the individual as the focal historical player, while at the same time affirming radical (indeed, existential-grade) human freedom for individuals. The present essay will (somewhat ironically) show that this freedom—whose chief manifestations are precisely in exercises of the power of self-creation—is the very fundament of power exercised by those larger players on the stage of history, whose reality destabilizes triumphalist individualistic narratives. The message here is that groups play fundamentally important roles in the human experience, and their power comes from the radical freedom individuals sometimes exercise in shaping their identities in relation to these groups. But of course this reality must not be allowed to overshadow the fact that much human misery derives from highly visible and involuntary group membership.

Thus, as will become clear, groups come in many varieties, especially as to the nature of their membership. And the roles they play in human life depend crucially on the structure of entry and exit pathways into and out of these groups. While there is no space here to discuss most of the subtleties of this topic, we will nevertheless discuss the importance of it. For the collective use we as free individuals make of groups in our social dealings is precisely what makes these groups powerful, both as agents and as patients.

This account, like many other feminist theories (see for instance Mackenzie and Stoljar 2000, and Koggel 1998) is one that places emphasis on relations among individuals, as well as the totality of these relations that constitutes the web of human social interactions, even as it seeks to account for Selfhood, actively deemphasizing intrinsic or biological characteristics of individuals. Social relations, according to this account, are at the heart of what it is to be a human Self. And the network enlivens them all.

INTRODUCTION

Jean-Paul Sartre famously remarked that human beings are "condemned to be free." Coiled tightly within this observation is the distinctive principle of existential philosophy—at once a hyperbole and a paradox. The observation articulates, first of all, the idea that the inescapable essence of human experience is the profound *freedom-to-be* encountered in it. At the same time, it makes clear there is no avoiding this fact—that indeed it rests upon thoroughly commonplace human capacities for social engagement with others, especially in face-to-face contexts. And while it was Sartre who framed this paradox, it was Simone Beauvoir who confronted it most viscerally, in both her fictional work and her nonfiction—especially her first philosophical opus *Pyrrhus and Cinéas*, where she wrestled with the disturbing reality of freedom in the context of Others' radical freedom, and the barriers to intimacy and authenticity that ensue thereupon, and of course in *The Second Sex*. Freedom, for Beauvoir, was also a source of constriction for the Other. This pair of ideas, in rough outline, is at the heart of my proposal concerning the nature of social identity. I will be advancing the idea that the freedom-to-be lies in *both* embracing membership in some groups (via adoption of the corresponding group labels) *and* in resisting it vis-à-vis other groups (via rejecting certain group label).

Feminism, or at any rate Beauvoir's existential brand of it, is a guiding beacon for the present project which, as will become clear, is situated within analytical philosophy and assembled with the aim of providing foundations for the human sciences. We begin by observing that Beauvoir's feminism is existential in a certain raw way: its ultimate target is the transformation of social arrangements, especially with respect to gender differentials, and the exercise of freedom in the struggle for transformation to a more equitable society. This feminist endeavor presupposes constructionism in two important ways: (1) it is committed to the notion that at least some social structures are fundamentally human constructions; and consequently (2) that these structures are susceptible to *modification* or *overhaul* through exercises of radical freedom.

At the core of all existential thought lies a feminist thought which, in turn, is fundamentally a liberationist thought (and so subject to articulation by other oppressed social groups too) to the effect that the truth about the human "life-world"—the world of human experience and of entities-as-experienced—is not at odds with human freedom to remake it in line with a liberationist vision, rather than in line with limitations and immutables. And that this truth *too* is part of the truth about being human—about human *being*. This is a more prosaic statement of Sartre's paradox about humans being condemned to freedom.

At certain points in its development, feminism has regarded its wisdom as an anti-science sentiment—involving as it does a resistance to limiting human universals, particularly as regards gender. My thesis, countering the anti-science conception of the feminist wisdom, is that the existential wisdom at the core of feminism will lead to a *better* science of human nature—and in particular to a better social science of *individuals, as such,* in society. In this way, feminist insights, entwined throughout with existential wisdoms, will be responding to traditional concerns of analytic philosophy regarding sound foundations for the human sciences, and in particular foundations for the sciences that treat of the Self. It will turn out that feminist instincts are much more finely attuned to the needs of such sciences than philosophical approaches to that topic that focus exclusively upon general cognitive capacities or other biological features. For, while these latter approaches have maintained that True Science is to be found in the Universal rather than in the Particular, a science of Selves and self-conceptions—a science of social identities—must finesse this trope, because of the very nature of human freedom. And in the process, such a science must reconceptualize the subject matters of sciences that treat of human Selves.

I will be defending here the existential feminist notion that social identities and root self-conceptions (in other words, Selves) are socially constructed in an interconnected fashion—that, in other words, there is nothing "given" about them. And that they can be reinvented, literally at-will. I will not be insisting that *all* of social reality is a human construction; I do not need to do so. (Indeed it has already been attempted,[3] and it is not my intention here to suggest moderations, amplifications, or qualifications.) It is simply enough for my purposes that *some* of social reality be so constructed. So I am content to leave space for the potentially immutable; but this space must not encroach upon the space that must be left clear for the exercise of individual self-construction out of genuinely plastic elements, substitutions on given ones, or recombinations and reaggregations of preformed elements. My efforts here will be devoted to articulating how Selves are constructed, and the phenomenology that both occasions and enables self-construction. We will find that there are obstacles to self-construction. And herein lies moral courage.

I shall be using the term "Self" here, in line with its usage in social psychology, to mean "self-concept," and not "agent" or "person." There is now, and there has always been, philosophical controversy over just how to conceptualize the agent and (perhaps alternatively) the person, as an entity interacting with others of its kind. Fortunately, I do not need to settle this question. My focus is upon the steps individuals take to construct self-conceptions, and not upon the object (agent or person) to which that construction subsequently adheres as a label or description. Of course, if what I say is correct, there will no doubt be consequences for our theories of agency and personhood—and I will be discussing some of the consequences here. But everything I will be contending can be made compatible with a wide range of philosophical views regarding agents and persons.

The psychological literature on self-concept is permissive, allowing all descriptors into the self-concept. For instance, one recent experimental paradigm, designed to take the collectivistic/individualistic pulse of a culture, asks subjects to fill twenty blanks with self-descriptors.[4] Statistical analysis of the answers ensues, focusing upon the extent to which subjects self-ascribe categorical or relational attributes ("smart" is an example of the former, "brother" of the latter). I will be focusing primarily on category labels that are readily construed as labels for (nonlatent) groups. Thus I am strictly speaking focusing upon partial self-conceptions, if indeed self-ascription of other labels is important to the self-concept. But this fact will in no way affect the argument to be presented.

There is indeed something paradoxical in the idea of a *self*-construction, just as there is something apparently paradoxical in the juxtaposition of universality and individuality, genus and differentiae. The paradoxicality in the notion of self-construction lies in the idea that something that does not yet exist is bringing something (namely, itself) into existence. (It is, in slightly different terms, the same sort of paradoxicality as we find in the slogan "Existence precedes essence.") The paradoxicality in the idea of self-construction in this case is dispelled immediately once the distinction is made between the Self as self-concept and the agent or person as such. The Self as self-concept is *not* an agency per se, nor is it a center of consciousness. It is instead a *conception* of one's identity in the terms (self-ascribable language) found in and made salient by one's culture or community, which indeed *must* be constructed because it cannot be innate; but once constructed, it becomes the ground of further constructions and other actions. It becomes the basis of further self-development. Indeed, I believe this is the best reading of Sartre's phrase to the effect that existence precedes essence. Mine is thus a commitment to focus on the particular-in-society in preference to the biological universal; it is a commitment to a discipline that puts the individual—the Particular—first, and so must take its existence for granted. I understand Sartre as laying the foundations for inquiry into the social, as fundamental to human life and not purely derivative in relation to biology. And so it is quite easy, in this context, to attribute consciousness to an organism (a snake, for instance, if you like) without attributing to it also a Self. Selves, according to this conception, are easily subject to construction; and who better to construct them but the organisms that will ultimately bear them? And so we should no longer feel suspicious of a natural science that (at this admittedly late date) seeks to harvest the insights of an existentialist movement whose very force is "a gesture of protest against academic philosophy, [with] its anti-system sensibility, [and] its flight from the 'iron cage' of reason" (Crowell 2006). As will become clear, I do not view existential insights as demanding a flight from those exercises of reason characteristic of scientific inquiry.

What I hope to make clear here is that the human sciences stand to benefit from employing some of the methodologies and intellectual insights of existentialism, particularly its commitment to the phenomenology of agency, self, and power—that the human sciences will benefit from taking seriously that circle of interlocking concepts that include *freedom, commitment, alienation,* and *authenticity,* all of which come with a characteristic regulative cast and with an emphasis upon the activities of individuals as such. This profound circle of concepts is, as I hope to show, bound up with practical norms that universally govern human thought about membership in human social groups. The norms so embodied govern the ways in which agents practice commitment and self-limitation, and thereby agents self-create their Selves. By the same token, commitment to groups, practiced universally by humans, can form the subject matter of a scientific discipline.

The pervasive influence existential concepts have exercised all the world over, expressed in courageous efforts at self-determination—and not only (albeit also) in the context of social and political resistance—is substantial testimony to the fact that this circle of concepts is at the core of understanding human experience. It should then come as no surprise that these concepts illuminate important features of the social and political landscape, and as such are conspicuously ripe for co-optation by the empirical disciplines, even if the timing is so piteously belated. True: existentialism in its original historical setting drew on a distinction, made widely in phenomenology, between objects of the so-called *life-world,* on the one hand, and the various objects of scientific inquiry, on the other. The life-world is the world as immediately or directly experienced in the subjectivity of everyday life, and this world was to be sharply distinguished from the "objective worlds" of the sciences. Although empirical inquiry originates in the life-world, its targets, according to some phenomenological doctrines, are not those in view in everyday life. The objectivism of science, according to many practitioners of phenomenology, obscures both its origin in the subjective perceptions of the life-world and the life-world itself. But the life-world also includes individual, social, perceptual, and practical experiences. What I will be insisting here is that (at least) one dimension of the subjectively apprehended materials in the life-world—specifically, various acts of self-ascription utilizing social entity/group labeling—is important for empirical inquiry, indeed fundamental for the human sciences (as psychologists have known for many years), and that by following the contours of things on this dimension we shall be able to make sense of at least some features of individual identity and make them fit for the scrutiny of science. This dimension illuminates the individual as against the category under which she falls—the specimen as against the taxon—in terms that are also appropriate for an empirical science.

This essay will thus embed the existential axiom of freedom, as Beauvoir might have articulated it, in a decidedly naturalistic conception of self and identity, both individual and plural. And it will seek to do this in a way that helps make better sense of the role of personal narratives and their liberatory promise. It will illuminate how the narrative of an individual life can be a narrative of liberatory power and freedom.

The fundamental proposition I will be defending here is that, while individual humans cannot always exercise choice in their associations, or even in the bulk of their group memberships, they often nonetheless enjoy choice in their *affiliations* as well as in how they construe those affiliations. Affiliation, as I will be using the term here, is the alignment of one's *will* (and by that I will mean *agentic resources*) with that of another entity (group or individual).[5] It is therefore the source of new social group alignments, but also of self-construals in group-membership terms. And these alignments are performed predominantly via self-ascriptions or avowals, which may be either private or public.

This fundamental proposition is the basis for an account of identity—both individual and group/collective. And the account of identity will at once qualify as constructionist at the same time as it makes clear that self-constructed Selves belong to a special natural kind category—one that can help provide more illuminating historical analyses.

RECENT ANATOMIES OF THE SELF: FREUD REDISCOVERED?

Existential philosophy developed alongside the fledgling discipline of psychology. Sigmund Freud had only rather recently speculated that the modern human being living in civilized society is obliged to repress, via a battery of subconscious processes, a host of urges and instincts, largely to do with sex, in response to social pressures and expectations. Dividing the human agent into three parts (three, as it happens, reminiscent of Plato), Freud set in motion questions about how these parts interact in the repression process, and what to do about it, by way of therapy. The postulated repressions and their fallout subsequently become players in a kind of subterranean drama that becomes the subject, according to one (psychological) school of Analysis, of psychological science. According to Freud's conception of the human psyche, Nature and Society are in conflict within the individual, with representatives of each locked in moral combat therein. Freud's project indeed aims at a science of the individual, and in that way it is kin to existentialism—as much as existentialists sought to distance themselves from Freudian ideas. Whereas Freudians concentrate on repression, existentialists concentrate on *expression*. But expression has not been the focus of the preponderance of recent scientific investigations of individuality.

The human individual in prevailing approaches in cognitive psychology and anthropology fares no better than it does in Freud's hands, and in some regards much worse. The human individual is now studied in these disciplines as a specimen of something larger—the Human Being, or Human Nature. And ever since the later 1970s, when Edward O. Wilson, a zoologist specializing in the social insects, launched a program to study behaviors—human and nonhuman—as adaptations to ecological conditions encountered in evolutionary history, and to discern similarities to and precursors of human ethology in the behaviors of nonhuman species, the academy has been plunged in "human nature wars" over the following question: are human traits (for example, the characteristically human emotions) or human divisions (ethnic or other social categories, including gender and class, whose members share traits or clusters of traits, including and especially, dispositions to think and behave in similar ways) produced by culture or instead strictly by biology? It seems that however we answer the question, whether we affirm or deny the role of biology narrowly construed in realization of human traits, we will vindicate the existence of something deserving of the label "human universals." In 1991, anthropologist Donald Brown, then at the University of California, Santa Barbara, published *Human Universals*, a survey of hundreds of candidate "human universals," from domains as diverse as language, kinship, and status systems, to concepts of time, number, and incest taboos. Today the University of California, Santa Barbara, leads in evolutionary psychological research—part empirical psychology and part voodoo evolutionary anthropology. This discipline is premised, with scant argument, on three dogmas: that (a) human nature is the same wherever there are humans; (b) the elements of human behavior are "psychological mechanisms" that are themselves adaptations to ecological challenges faced in the "environment of evolutionary adaptedness" (which, according to practitioners of this tradition, is the Pleistocene period); and (3) the "psychological mechanisms" are evoked by cues in the environment, rather than developmental or other "plastic" processes that might include socialization. Thus, they maintain that human behavior is orchestrated by a massively modular mind, consisting of independent modules for handling a range of adaptive problems. "Human nature," as that view now goes, "can finally be defined precisely as the set of universal, species-typical, information-processing programs that operate beneath the surface of expressed cultural variability."[6] On this picture, it's as if the human mind-brain were a Swiss Army Knife comprised of a small set of tools, each running an algorithm suited to a restricted domain of inputs and outputs, paradigm among these the processing of optical information, mate selection, and predator avoidance. There is no space for individuals in the discipline of evolutionary psychology.

In the 1970s, in reaction to E. O. Wilson's magnificent *Sociobiology*, resistance to the study of human beings through a biological lens was mounted. The critics were concerned that study of humans through this lens was an invitation to rationalize and perhaps even deepen oppression of persons and groups already unjustly oppressed (women, the lower classes, aboriginals, and non-Europeans generally), but whose prospects were improving under increasingly favorable social arrangements—developments imperiled by a dangerous innatist orientation. Critics of early sociobiology demonstrated that studying behavior as an evolved phenomenon is more difficult than Wilson and comrades were prepared to make it seem, not least because if one is to have anything at all to say, one is bound to speculate—to make under-substantiated, potentially tainted assumptions—about certain unknown features of the Darwinian natural histories of those behaviors. And so for a time, anthropologists in particular maintained a diversity of views on universals, resisting the "biologization" of human nature. Clifford Geertz, for instance, was a champion of traditional anthropology who wrote,

> The notion that the essence of what it means to be human is most clearly revealed in those features of human culture that are universal rather than in those that are distinctive to this people or that is a prejudice that we are

> not obliged to share....It may be in the cultural particulars of people—in their oddities—that some of the most instructive revelations of what it is to be generically human are to be found. (Geertz 1968)

Feminists too were once upon a time enemies of the biologization of human nature. But today numerous feminists are at the forefront of a high-paced Darwinian movement to study behavior within the context of the evolutionary history of life on the planet: Mary Jane West-Eberhard, Sarah Blaffer-Hrdy, Barbara Smuts, and many others.[7] They are now themselves spearheading a movement to eradicate deplorable prejudice, proceeding with eyes deliberately critical of all that threatens, in unscientific and unsubstantiated fashion, to divide humans—and other species too—into ranked castes. And there are, to be sure, differences of emphasis, of methodology, and of reliance upon bodies of empirical findings in comparative phylogeny, primatology, developmental psychology, and human and animal cognition, that go along with the choice of label among "evolutionary psychology," "behavioral ecology," and "evolutionary anthropology." And exchanges among those who adhere to different labels (or who have the labels adhered to them) have been positively acrimonious.[8]

Thus biological ideas have decidedly earned their keep and deserve representation at the human-nature table. But now it seems they are occupying the lion's share of seats. From a scientist's perspective, we are now all uniformly the same, and there seems to be no room for scientific scrutiny of the personal space—where the Self is manifested and expressed. No methodology for a discipline of the individual seems to exist, except among personality psychologists, who study universal dimensions along which individuals differ from one another. Even they have adopted a methodology that admits nothing but vast kinds, whether the kinds are biological or environmentally or culturally mediated.

And philosophy too has been affected by this dogma. In the last several decades, philosophical assaults have been launched against the very existence of character differentials—clusters of properties that vary in the population. The very notion of individual character differences has been challenged. Building on recent social psychology, certain philosophers have been arguing that the better predictors of human behavior are situational or contextual factors—features of the landscape (both natural and social), rather than stable cross-situational personal/individual traits. Indeed, sometimes very trivial situational factors are better predictors of human behavior than so-called character.[9] Humans, as this argument goes, do not exhibit cross-situational consistencies: apparent behavioral consistencies are explained entirely by situational consistencies. This idea resonates with the near-ideological research program pursued by many evolutionary psychologists.

Thus today the preponderant view favors the proposition that Nature's universals are expressed within the individual, and within Society, too. The vast majority of experts in our time looks upon human nature—conceived as a legacy of *tendencies* to certain behaviors—as indeed universal. And not only are human beings cut from the same cloth, but the individual articles of clothing made from this cloth are all cut to the same size and style, with modest variations by way of concessions to local climate. The differences between us are, as David Stamos puts it, "statistical" (Stamos 2008). The chorus of massive universality has become the common currency, a political mantra with undertones of fatalistic inevitability. Against the backdrop of this common ideology, Kwame Anthony Appiah can declare, without mustering authorities of any kind, in the opening lines of his manifesto, *Cosmopolitanism*: "Our ancestors have been human for a very long time. If a normal baby girl born forty thousand years ago were kidnapped by a time traveler and raised in a normal family in New York, she would be ready for college in eighteen years" (Appiah 2006, xi). All the insights of existentialism have thus been evacuated, their challenge to remake the world according to unscripted visions forgotten. In this process of universalization, we have lost such space as one might like for the very notion of a recognizably individual reality, a uniquely personal space, distinct from the purely physiological and cultural features shared with one's kind—distinct from the universal. And of course we have lost the capacity to examine the role of freedom in creating that space. True: existentialists did not even seek a place at the human nature table. But their sentiments on this matter were misguided. At any rate, this is my contention. Theirs was a failure of imagination, a failure of ambition.

And so I am, first of all, insisting that the case for massive universality has been greatly exaggerated.[10] The contemporary evolutionary universalist vision of the human being is hardly different from Freud's. True: evolutionary psychologists offer no psychodynamical story—no mythos—to help us understand and subsequently navigate the irrepressible dynamics of the various semi-autonomous mental algorithms. Indeed, they take it for granted we are better off without such a mythos. But this, to my mind, is really to their disadvantage. Evolutionary psychology has nothing of substance to offer the clinician.[11] What should be quite striking to a neutral observer is that both Freud and the evolutionary psychologists, in invoking a subterranean dynamics, are substantially in agreement that there is no one locus of analysis that ultimately can be thought of as the referent of "I," "he," or "she"—for on each account, there is nowhere near enough in the way of unity to be found in the human organism to halt the reduction from proceeding downward into such depths as there might still be, unbeknownst even now to science.

What I will be offering here is defense of the thesis that, while the great span and sweep of evolution might be the right place to look for a natural history of the human mind-brain and its many capacities, an evolutionary timetable is not the right place to look for Selves and social identities. Natural history all by itself cannot give a complete picture of being human in a social setting—and certainly not of the nature of being human at a decidedly local scale. This is because human life is decidedly socially and culturally conditioned. To complete the picture, we must look to history as told by traditional historians, cultural and social anthropologists, sociologists, social psychologists, and many others. And the turn to such disciplines must be justified—as I'll justify it here—partly by reference to existentialist conceptions within the circle we discussed above. The approach I will describe is an "historical" approach too, but not one whose aim is to illuminate kinds or universals. It is *not* meant to illuminate a history in which the primary figures in the drama are *kinds* in competition with one another. And so, before we can get to the argument for the central thesis of the chapter, we will make one last stop—this time to examine the case against historical approaches quite globally. There are indeed good reasons for opposing a "great man" approach to history so well-illustrated in the work of historian Thomas Carlyle, who famously remarked that "the history of the world is but the biography of great men," thereby approving the thesis that heroes shape history through personal attributes that might just as well be divinely gifted.

The "great man" approach is best countered by that approach implicit in the formal literature of the social and economic sciences. Not seeking to take a stand on the human nature issue explicitly, economists generally adopt a certain *generalist* position (as I will call it) on the subject of human behavior.[12] The generalist position seeks to explain behavior by directing attention purely to advantages conferred by the behavior on individuals who engage in it, without making any attempt to identify the relevant psychological machinery for achieving that behavior. Thus, what the generalist proposal lacks in detail, it makes up for with a kind of robustness. The generalist proposal is simply to identify behavior that can outperform a range of competing behaviors (in evolutionary terms, during a certain period in evolutionary history), and subsequently to claim that this advantage makes the behavior inevitable even for those of us who come so much later. Advocates of the generalist position argue that a less generalist account, one that trades in strictly biological, psychological, or historical details, might obscure this fact. It might suggest that details matter, when they don't. For if the behavior weren't achieved through the particular ways it was actually achieved (the persons and their proprietary characteristics), it would have been achieved some other way (different persons with different proprietary characteristics). And this is the generalist's point. We can quite profitably—at least for purposes of scientific explanation—simply conceive of the human being as an entity that aims at advantage, without in any way dispensing with what science cares about. We can adopt, for example, as a certain brand of economist does, a rationally self-interested model of the human being.

The single-minded self-loving hero of so many economic theories (elevated by such epithets as "economic man" and "rational agent") has come in for some criticism. (Even Adam Smith, to whom the rational man is often attributed, had profound doubts about him [Brennan and Pettit 2004]). But up until very recently, "modern economic theory has proceeded as if these doubts were of marginal concern and easily brushed off."[13] Not any more. For the generalist's economic man has proved too elusive. He is not the entity we meet on the streets. And because this is the case, the generalist position is spoiled. Will the "great man" rise again to fill the void? No. Economists are identifying a new hero, which I will be championing as well.

Most recently the criticisms of economic man—*Homo e.*, as I will call him—have been to the effect that this so-called rational man fails to do as real-life people are observed to do, even in laboratory-based controlled studies.[14] *Homo e.*, as a model, does not predict the behavior of *Homo sapiens.* And now even economists are undertaking reevaluation of their construal of rationality as self-service by looking also at "loyalty as an aspect of rationality, or at any rate as a 'filter.'"[15] I propose we refer to the model of loyal entity as *Homo filiatus;* I will call him *Homo f.*

Within the discipline of economics, Amartya Sen has been at the forefront of taking account of the perception of identity and measuring its impact upon preferences and economic behavior (Sen 2002). Individuals belong to many groups, some more visible than others (for example, the group of people who wear size 8 shoes is not, as Sen observes, one that enjoys notable solidarity, under present circumstances, although it might have done, had circumstances been different). Individuals have to judge which of their identities are relevant to their decisions, and then rank the relevant identities in importance on any given occasion of choice. And these tasks exercise *both* rationality *and* freedom.

Now this *Homo f.*, unlike the *Homo e.* that is the brainchild of the generalist modeling strategy, contrasts strongly with the evolutionary psychologist's model, concerned as it is with a concept of identity that the evolutionary psychologist, in the name of science, declined from the beginning. I will be defending the scientific credentials of *Homo f.* as a scientific model, in such a way as deserves calling existentialist: *Homo f.* will be the first Self (with a capital S) in his lineage. With a Self comes a sense of "I," an identity. My defense is by no means a decisive ouster of the Swiss Army Knife model, but rather a demonstration of the robustness of *Homo f.*, especially as contrasted to *Homo e.* The main point, roughly, will be that identity is constructed in a (social) process of ascriptions, and in particular self-ascriptions. Identity is a personal historical matter, and done primarily through a process of self-construction.

To be sure, the human-nature debate has been playing out in one theatre of an even more global and comprehensive debate: the realist/ constructionist debate. Realists, on a target subject, contend that a target classificatory term refers to a natural—or at least to an objec-tive—kind, while their constructionist (or even anti-realist) opponents contend that there is either a failure of reference, because no such entity exists as a kind, or else that the kind is "constructed." And while a great deal of heat has been generated over the nature of construction, the salient feature of *being constructed* seems to be that there is nothing inevitable or unavoidable about falling into the target category (Hacking 1999, 6), and that there is in fact an element of human choice—either in the labeling process and in the acquisition of such features as make one eligible of the label, or both.[16] In this essay, I shall be less concerned with the formal meaning of construction and more concerned with specific proposals for the construction of one kind: the kind *Self* (cf. Mallon 2007, 2006b). I propose that we give a social-scientific rationale for the proposition that the most fundamental political act is the act of self-construction, because it is the kind of act that brings social agents, both individual and collective, into existence. In acceding to this pro-posal, an academic investigator will be injecting academic life into the feminist activists' slogan: "The personal is political." For in acceding to this proposal, one affirms that identify politics is politics at its most fundamental.

THE ONE FROM THE MANY: THE SELF-CONSTRUCTION OF THE SELF

According to Freud's model of the human being, there are three parts, running in parallel but independently of one another, with nothing unifying them. The same holds of the massively modular mind of the evolutionary psychologist, but the parts are now indefinitely many. In both models, we are simply invited to regard the three and the many as in some way held together. But how precisely? Is the union of three into one wrought through simple proximity or through simple cohabitation of the same organism? If that is the case, it is a unity that obtains only as a vacancy obtains: as a simple space- and place-holder, as an availability for occupation, whether by dramatis per- sonae or computational algorithms or what-have-you, more or less of them according to space or other resource limitations. The Self—indeed the very agent—is nothing over and above these occupying (or, more correctly, frag- menting) parts or dimensions, on either model. So nothing is required to account for its doings, as the doings of a unified entity. There is no further, transcendent I. No further self-determining being.

And so it is fitting that the psychologist Bernard Baars should pro- nounce a "gathering consensus" in the scientific disciplines of mind: the whole affair is orchestrated by a "distributed society" of specialists operating upon a shared space consisting of working memory—what he refers to as a "global workspace" (Baars 1988). This consensus, as he sees it, has been forged by the work of many neuroscientists and psycholo- gists, many of them studying subjects with brain damage or cognitive deficits, or who have been the subjects of surgical procedures such as a cutting of the *corpus collosum*. As Michael Gazzaniga puts it, "the human brain is more of a sociological entity than a psychological entity" (Gazzaniga 1985, 28). This sort of account (which has a more modest precursor in Fodor 1983) has been taken up and propounded in a radical form by Daniel Dennett (esp. 1991), and Thomas Metzinger (2003, 1: "No such things as selves exist in the world: Nobody ever was or had a self"). Similar themes can be found in the literature on computational theories of mind, especially the embodied and distributed cognition literature. Andy Clark, for example, asks us to focus attention on our species' dependence upon technological tools, how technologies of every kind alter the way human brains utilize and process information, and how they change the organism's very sense of itself—its capacities, its possibil- ities, its very extension in space and time. As we do so, we are made more and more aware of how "plastic" or "soft" our Selves are. As Clark puts it, "we just *are*...shifting coalitions of tools" (Clark 2003, 137). The resulting skepticism about Selves is profound. And, if correct, positively demoralizing—morally numbing. For if there are no true Selves, who or what is to respond to moral imperatives? Who is to be held accountable?

But there is another way with these questions, even within a naturalistic paradigm. A way that turns back from skepticism about the Self, by explicitly making room for it. And this way is to distinguish the Self per se from the *source* of behavior—to separate the Self from both the cognizer and/or the agent, however distributed or divided each of these latter entities might be. The Self is instead construed as the self-conception *constructed* by an agent.[17] I am thus positing that Self and agent can and should come apart, if we are to make sense of what transpires on the ground. Agents are born, at least in embryonic form; they also develop, and their development is at least partly an organic matter.[18] But Selves are made. And indeed largely self-made. And (or at any rate so I shall argue) can be made in a liberationist way. Of course an account of this sort requires a metaphysics of self-construction. And the balance of this essay is devoted to producing at least the beginnings of one. The account begins with acknowledgement of some important features of the larger evolutionary landscape, as well as some important features specific to the human species. They concern the forging of alliances.

Before I begin that account, I wish to distinguish it from another account of identity that resists skepticism about self to a lesser extent. I have in mind the so-called *narrative theories of identity* or theories of Self as *center of narrative gravity*. According to this cluster of theories, Selves are narratives cooperatively articulated in social contexts (see Hutto 2007 for discussions of the proposal). This account of identity is compatible with Selves as fictions (explicitly so identified in Dennett 1991). But it is also compatible with realism about the Self—or at any rate, realism about narratives as products of natural selection. For instance, Don Ross (2005, 2007, forthcoming) insists on narrative selves as "a crucial evolved basis for guiding socialized individuality":

> People insist that others with whom they enter into coordination exercises tell dramatically structured, publicly ratifiable stories about themselves and conform their behavior to these stories. This enables not only public predictability, but, for organisms with enormous information-processing devices that are largely opaque to their direct inspection, *self*-predictability....Thus people become and remain distinct while simultaneously remaining comprehensible and predictable. (Ross, forthcoming)

I have sympathies with this account, while recognizing it stops altogether too short: certainly, it has the space we require to articulate a story about individuality, but stops short of an account of any construction process whereby Selves come into being and go on to impact the social drama. The account I will propose makes no bones about the sociological basis of the construction of Selves. Neither does it balk at pronouncing their reality and fundamental importance for social and political processes in which they vigorously participate. Finally, it is unafraid to speak of the space of freedom that is sometimes encountered as these processes unfold.

THE BONDING SPECIES *HOMO FILIATUS*

Microscopic cells form an alliance we refer to as an organism (a biological individual), which itself amounts to an interlocking set of alliances among organs that perform different functions. This so-called "biological hierarchy" in which subcellular entities come together to form cells, cells come together to form organs, and organs hang together in organisms, has itself come into existence over evolutionary time. But this hierachical-ization did not stop with individual organisms. For individuals in their turn form dyads or mating groups. And mating groups form as packs, herds, flocks, troops, prides, tribes, and so on, all the way to ecosystems. The mechanisms by which this variety flourishes are themselves varied. We will focus here only on inter-organism processes, acknowledging that they have their origins—as they must—in the same sorts of processes as transformed the single-cellular into the multi-cellular.

Now, because inter-organism cohesion itself is not one single process or achievement, but a genus that comprises at least three different processes, we require a taxonomy, or at any rate an itemization or index, of these things.[19]

The first and simplest form of inter-organism bonding is found in many species that invest care and nurture in their young: it is called *imprinting*, and it is as common among fowl as it is among mammals such as sheep. The second and less common form involves *feeling* (especially sympathy) and emotional *attachment*, and this prevails among mammals, particularly higher mammals. The third and most complex form is *identificational* bonding, and it is arguably unique to the human species. (And it might well be the defining feature of E. O. Wilson's "fourth pinnacle" of social evolution: human society, the company of strangers.)

This third form of bonding will be the focal point of our account of identity—it is at once the basis for I as well as We. Here is how identificational bonding works.

Human cognitive capacities are so configured as to allow for adjustment of motivation by means of purely conceptual acts, many of which lead to group formation. This phenomenon is hugely robust and is responsible for mob phenomena.[20] Humans will group themselves according to numerous labels—*Star Trek* fans, sports team boosters, professional groups, bus passengers—and accordingly seek to promote the fortunes of the groups to which they belong, as groups. For instance, even subjects grouped arbitrarily in laboratory settings will readily accept their arbitrarily chosen mates as a "we." Social researchers agree that groups are formed via a dazzlingly wide range of different routes. These include (but are not limited to): common interests that can only be achieved by working together ("interdependence" [Sherif et al. 1961]), shared experience, face-to-face interaction (Dawes et al., 1997), the perception of a common fate (Rabbie and Horwitz 1969), membership in merely ad hoc categories (Tajfel 1970), and perhaps most surprisingly, exposure to the pronouns "we," "our," and so on (Perdue et al., 1990).

So, for example, each member of a family or clan or interest group (or even just a group of strangers exposed to plural pronouns) can conceive of their ensemble as a "we." And this conception acts upon the configuration of motivations of each of them individually, via changing or creating collective motivation: each is now not only someone with personal interests, but also someone with *collective* or *communal* interests, with consequences for individual interests. This is *social identifying* and is "the cognitive mechanism that makes group behavior possible."[21] This restructuring of motivation can be the basis of action that accords with this conception of things.[22] Similarly, the recognition, among the members of an arbitrarily assembled group of human beings, of commonalities in taste, fate, or interest may be enough to sustain among them the existence of a "we," and concomitantly motivations favoring a (collective) good, as has repeatedly been shown even in the laboratory (Kramer and Brewer, 1986). Essential to identificational bonding of this latter variety is characteristic development—*not of emotion* or *feeling*—but rather of a certain *conception* of how the world now divides. (Atoms bond to form molecules, but their bonding, while not founded upon emotions, is not founded upon conceptions either.)

The social human being is, essentially, an entity that draws distinctions, groups conspecifics according to those distinctions, and locates itself within some cell created in the space of these cross-cutting distinctions. Each individual human's space of distinctions functions, for her, as a map to the alliances in the world—a map to the way that agencies fall together on the ground. And this map is also a source of her own motivations, as well as her expectations of conspecifics. And of the self-concept.

It is this conceptual capacity, which allows for identificatory bonding, that serves to unify both groups and individuals. Indeed, development of the first-personal "I" is perhaps the first appearance of bonding of the identificational variety. And it is quite rare in the animal kingdom. At least typically, when an entity takes into account how its current actions will affect its future self, the entity in question does it by means of identification with its future self. Although one sometimes reasons from the point of view of oneself-now, one usually proceeds from the point of view of oneself-as-a-temporally-extended-being or from the point of view of some "we" of which one is part. Such reasoning involves identification, but need not involve emotion; in particular, it need not involve any feeling of sympathy. And it results in a *concept*, as contrasted with a mere *perception*, of a self. In that role, it has the power to change behavior.

This fact of a network of identificatory bondings is what makes human folk tribal. And it helps to explain not only how alliances actually form and spread on the ground, but also how human folk conceive of those allegiances. It is important to note, however, that a given individual's map of the alliances, even if it should accord with any number of other such maps, may not reflect the true reality of alliances on the ground.

The individual, as a unified concern-bearing entity, is as much a creature whose existence depends upon capacities for bonding as does that of a collectivity. But the self depends upon the higher capacity for conceptualization—unlike, for example, alliances forged through emotional bonding.

It is well-documented that sense of self is something that very few species possess, as well as a developmental matter among those that do.[23] Ironically, then, helping behavior is quite common (bees and ants do it), but Selves are relatively rare. Rarer still is that helping behavior which *rests upon a conception* of Self, Other, or community.

But how are identificational bonds actually forged? They are formed through ascription—both self-ascription and other-ascription. Let's begin with how they are forged between individuals.

PRELIMINARY REMARKS ON ASCRIPTION

Membership in social organizations is not a straightforward matter, and there is a spectrum of transparency for membership conditions. There are on the one end of the spectrum, the straightforward cases: when someone claims membership in, say, the Book-of-the-Month Club, the truth of this claim is determined entirely by the rules of membership inscribed above the "dotted line." Entry and exit rules are both simple and transparent. But things become cloudy very quickly, even when the groups in question have explicit rules of membership, and the performances these call for are all apparently voluntary. Suppose, for example, that someone claims membership in Hamas; this is a much trickier sort of case than Book-of-the-Month. There may be rules of membership, inscribed in a constitution (written or unwritten) of the organization, perhaps involving a ritual of initiation. Perhaps there is no constitution, and no ritual of membership. And even in the instance where a constitution and rules of initiation are explicit and have been applied, a member in the process of reevaluating her membership (that is, considering exit) might nonetheless begin to cross an unwritten line—a zone of ambiguity—on the way out. So there are zones of ambiguity on the way out, as well as on the way in. What seems clear from these initial remarks is that in cases where performance of entry is in fact transparently voluntary, membership must be earned—it's not a matter of simple self-ascription.

But the converse is not true: there are cases where there seem to be clear performance criteria (and so entry must be wrought through performance), but performance of entry requirements under such criteria does not settle the question of whether the performance was itself voluntary. Consider, for example, membership in the prototypical religious societies. Being a Baptist or a Catholic is at least partly a matter of—among other things—acculturation to familial expectations and conformity with familial obligations. So that when one performs such initiation rituals as are called for by Baptist or Catholic tradition, it is not altogether beyond disputation whether that performance was voluntary. Still, it seems that performance of such initiation rituals counts as having earned the ascription, whether voluntarily or not. And so from here on I will use the term "performance" to include both non-voluntary and involuntary, as well as voluntary fulfillment of conditions of entry. (So, for example, it will count as performance to have white hair, or blue eyes, or stand in a particular line of ancestry, even if none of the relevant properties can be said to have been wrought voluntarily by the entity who bears them. They nonetheless "earn" her or him entry into some types of groups.) So in many such cases, ascriptions can be earned through performance of entry requirements.

While I've been claiming that membership that must be earned can be tricky, these are for my purpose the simple cases. They present the true foil to those social entities I now wish to introduce, by way of analysis of self-construction. My goal from here on will be to demarcate earned membership from the other kind, and to show the latter as a fundamental analytical tool for analysis of Selves. It would be misleading to call membership in what I've just referred to as the "other kind" of group "unearned," as this sort of membership might be hugely demanding in ways that matter a great deal—and even in ways that are not open to third-personal checking up by ordinary citizens in the press of life.

My contention is that self-ascription of membership in this "other kind" of social entity can be *itself* the ticket of entry, or the primary ticket of entry (if there are further demands).[24] And as we all know from personal experience, self-ascriptions can be costly to the ascriber. (Second-personal ascription might also be enough, but it is not my purpose here to settle this matter, so I will just leave it open.)

So, now to the cases of social entities for which performance of entry requirements are not defining of membership. What is conspicuously troubling about such social entities, from a purely empirical standpoint, is the ambiguity or strange open-endedness about membership in them. But this is what suits them so remarkably well for self-construction: they are the fertile ground for Selves, because in relation to the question of membership in them, we enjoy—or at any rate can enjoy, in numerous cases—freedom.

The class of these important but empirically ambiguous social entities includes, remarkably enough, many among the following: ethnic groups, social cliques, political parties, sewing circles, book groups, benevolent societies, community and youth organizations, and possibly even some secret organizations for espionage or political action. Where membership in such collectivities or organizations involves (among other things) payment of an entrance fee, payment might function as a kind of proxy or badge of performance—just as badges themselves work as proxies. But many groups falling in the categories I named at the head of this paragraph defy attempts to delineate their composition, and routinely any attempts to nail down their membership, at any given time on the ground, are fraught with peril under the best of circumstances: it is one thing for history to proclaim the existence of such groups, but another thing entirely to give an exhaustive list of members or membership qualifications. And a self-ascription of membership in one of these entities has to be understood within this context.

What does ascription of membership in such an organization or collective amount to? An ascription of membership is a speech act like any other. And, as with every speech act, self-ascription is performed in a specific context. An ascription of membership in the Book-of-the-Month club is performed in the context of the familiar reality that the composition of the Book-of-the-Month Club is determined definitively by the rules of membership inscribed in the club's membership literature. But an ascription of membership in the Democratic Party of the United States will be performed within the context we have just described—a context familiar to those in the audience of the ascription, aware that the composition of the Democratic Party is not definitively determined by performance criteria of the transparent sort. And so ascriptions will fill a certain vacancy—a vacancy of material evidence for the truth value of such an ascription.

THE OTHER KIND OF SOCIAL GROUP

Let's now work with the following case: a certain voter is registered as a Democrat, but self-ascribes membership in the Republican Party. Is there a truth of the matter as to this voter's political membership, and so political loyalties? It would, I think, be a mistake to deny a truth of the matter. Just as equally it would be mistaken to ask for conditions that qualify the self-ascriber as having earned the ascription. Here is why.

To deny a truth of the matter is to assert that there is no basis in fact for ascriptions of membership in such groups as the Democratic Party, in the face of there being a certain abundance of materials that ordinarily functions as evidence. (And make no mistake: it is a relevant fact that the noted self-ascription will be particularly salient for ascriber and audience alike, in the moment of the self-ascription.) Of course, the contention that there is no basis in fact for ascription of "Democrat" is not exactly tantamount to asserting that there is no point to ascriptions of membership in such groups. Still, I think it would be a mistake to deny a basis in fact for such ascriptions.

My point is this: once such a function of such self-ascriptions (or indeed second- or third-personal ascriptions of membership in these groups) is identified, the denial of truth to the ascription of membership will be more difficult to maintain. My contention is that the point of a speech act consisting of such an ascription *itself* forms the basis for ascriptions of this type. And so denying truth to such ascriptions will be untenable, once we have identified this function of making them. And the reason is that, once it becomes clear that membership ascriptions serve a particular function in the social context—the function of self-admission into a group whose membership is open to that kind of entry—it is crucial to ask whether that function can be well-served if the subject of ascription must also earn the ascription through satisfaction of some condition. My contention is that the function of self-admission to a group of this sort is not consonant with performance criteria having been fulfilled. And so we have to abandon the notion that performance criteria are required for correct ascription of membership in such groups. Certain groups simply leave their doors open to self-admission. This creates space for a certain kind of social freedom—a freedom of entry.

The same goes for conditions of exit. The same groups that leave the door open to self-admission often also leave the door open to self-exit via the same doorway. Other groups may leave the door open to self-exit that do *not* countenance self-admission: one can with a word withdraw membership from the Catholic Church, despite having to have performed all the rites of entry to get in on the other end.

Now, when I say "leave the door open to entry," I do not mean this to be construed as an action on the part of the relevant agents individually or the relevant groups collectively. Indeed, I do not believe that entry and exit conditions can be up to groups and their members in any straightforward way. Obviously there is a great deal to be said on this topic—vast territories to explore. Here, unfortunately, is not the place.

Finally, it is important to keep in mind the contrast to this special class of groups: the contrast is that class of groups that countenance neither self-admission nor self-exit, by ordinary measures. For example, the group "women" does not permit of self-admissions or self-exit, except by extraordinary medical measures. The same goes for groups structured by race or ethnicity. No performances can get someone into these groups who is not already admitted via satisfaction of a condition, often nonvoluntarily. And, more importantly, self-ascription cannot succeed where performances fail. But in such cases, there may be something else one can do to express solidarity with such groups, if one is of a mind to do so. One can make a symbolic self-ascriptive gesture which, although it does not succeed in gaining the gesturer entry, nonetheless does something equally important: it creates the category of sympathizer or supporter. This is a very important category in its own right, as some examples below will show. Such "satellite" groups play important roles in history and society, in spite of their merely penumbral nature.

THE MANY FINE POINTS OF IDENTITY ASCRIPTION

Identity ascriptions obviously play an important role in the conduct of personal life. When someone declares: "I am a Hatfield!" that someone is taking a particular kind of stance. And no less so when the person pronounces instead, "I am no Hatfield!" Arguably, identity ascriptions play an even more important role in public life, and so must command the attention of historians and other students of the social.

But identity ascriptions play a wide variety of roles in public life. And we turn attention now to some examples of such ways, so as to begin the task of taxonomy. These examples are decidedly not exhaustive, but rather suggestive of how advancing this taxonomy will be most productive.

Arturo Toscanini was one of the very few non-Jewish musicians who took a strong public stand against Hitler's regime, refusing invitations to take part in the 1933 Wagner Festival, but accepting engagements in Palestine to conduct groups consisting of Jewish émigrés who had fled Hitler's Germany. The Italian media consequently branded him an "honorary Jew who should be shot." And so, having aligned him with a certain socially problematic group, the Italian media summarily passed judgment and pronounced sentence in the very same breath. Toscanini's identity, constructed for him, left a certain mark upon his legacy, if not upon his person.

To take another instance, Leon Uris (*Exodus*, 1958) recounts the legend of the King of Denmark and the yellow star of David:

> From the German occupation headquarters at the Hotel D'Angleterre came the decree: ALL JEWS MUST WEAR A YELLOW ARMBAND WITH A STAR OF DAVID. That night the underground transmitted a message to all Danes. "From Amalienborg Palace, King Christian has given the following answer to the German command that Jews must wear a Star of David. The King has said that one Dane is exactly the same as the next Dane. He himself will wear the first Star of David and he expects that every loyal Dane will do the same." The next day in Copenhagen, almost the

entire population wore armbands showing a Star of David. The following day the Germans rescinded the order.

While some readings of the legend have King Christian and his subjects demonstrating solidarity with fellow Jews through voluntary adoption of identity markers imposed upon their fellows by a tyrant, Uris's account has the king displaying the badge in a courageous effort at effacing an ethnic identity as the ground of public political discriminations. Which is the right way to construe the king's display of the yellow badge?

What is the point of ascribing to oneself membership in the Democratic Party, or in the Hatfield tribe, or in ascribing to oneself (or for that matter expunging from the public record) a national, tribal, or ethnic identity? My answer is that ascription plays many roles, from positive alignment (which makes a center of gravity more prominent) to effacements or cancellations (which seek to deemphasize the center of gravity as a force to be reckoned with). But each and every such role serves either to identify or erase some one or more features of the ascriber's allegiances as an agent on the ground. The *function* of identity self-ascriptions is primarily to align the subject of ascription with a certain set of goals, ideals, or movements, by way of a kind of announcement of where one's efforts must perforce be directed from that point forward, whether voluntarily or not. Self-ascriptions might serve other functions as well, but I am contending that this is their primary or characteristic function—the function that will be associated with them by someone who hears a speech with an identity-ascriptive content. And this is due entirely to the fact that identity ascription locates the subject of ascription within a network of agents and agencies—a network of allegiances. Location of agency is the very function of identity ascriptions.

What, now, is the point of ascribing to someone *else* membership in the Democratic Party, or in Hamas, or in the Jewish people? Ascriptions of identity to others serve the same function as self-ascriptions: such ascriptions serve to identify some one or more features of the ascriptive subject's allegiances as an agent on the ground, by way of announcing where that subject's efforts must perforce be directed, whether voluntarily or not. Because—once again—identity ascriptions locate the subject of ascription in a network of agents and agencies.

This is a constructionist position, as I will now explain. According to the present view, identity is a matter of ascriptions, performed in the context of a culture of ascription practices. The practices of identity ascription are governed by local rules, but these rules might very well share universal features—at any rate, the question is open to empirical enquiry. What makes certain identities *constructed* is that the rules that govern their ascription do not demand that the ascriptions in question be earned in the way that membership in the Book-of-the-Month Club must be earned. Consequently the construction of ethnic identities involves a strategic element. (Toscanini's and King Christian's Jewish markers are especially strategic, but for all of that, other ethnic markers are not lacking in strategy.) Ascriptions of identity are thus moves in a social and political game—moves that have social and political consequences.

This insight will allow us to comprehend the function of the headline in *Le Monde*, "WE ARE ALL AMERICANS NOW," as an effort—a "move"—of re-alignment through membership ascription. In *Le Monde*'s case, it must reckoned a purely symbolic gesture, as a self-ascription all by itself does not make one an American. But in spite of this, the audience can be satisfied that the statement is asserting the important point behind self-ascription, the point that self-ascription itself is good for: it expresses solidarity. And so it creates the category of American sympathizer, into which self-admission is indeed possible. The existential framework we have adopted makes this construal of the statement possible. And the analytical framework for construal of identity ascriptions, in the context of a distinction between "earned" ascriptions and the "other kind," makes the function intelligible.

Now: can the function of alignment efforts, illuminated here as moves in a social and political game governed by local membership rules, be served by self-ascription *if these ascriptions have to be earned in the way that membership in the Book-of-the-Month is earned*? Decidedly No. For if ascriptions require being earned, then ascriptions cannot be doing the job of alignment, but rather they must be reporting on the fulfillment of membership conditions. Declaring oneself to be a Democrat, if all self-ascription required being earned, could (contrary to fact) be proven false, and the Italian media's branding of Toscanini as an honorary Jew would (contrary to fact) be nothing but a dishonest mistake. Toscanini could not take pleasure in accepting such a label, as an act of solidarity. And in no way could the heroes of the Danish legend be correctly viewed as performing an act of solidarity—theirs can only be an act of brave perjury or mendacity. And so if an identity self-attribution can ever be a formative act, it cannot also be a report on a condition already earned.

One thing we must not fail to notice is that it must be possible for someone to say this: "In order to discharge my membership obligations to X (of which I am a member), I need to maintain or initiate affiliational bonds with Y." This feature of identities suggests strongly interlocking, mutually dependent affiliational structures. I propose a model according to which individuals are not exactly static nodes or vertices in an otherwise dynamic network of ties—a model that is more consonant with an anti-constructionist notion of identity—but instead a model more like a system of interlocking rubber bands, the stability of which depends upon the strength of the bonds, their relative directionality and the extent to which they are stretched by any given tie. According to such a model, there will be enormous numbers of shifting "centers of gravity," and these will be the "institutions" (families, clubs, religious institutions, community organizations, activist societies, nations and so on). The individuals will be the (highly dynamic and shifting) points at which the rubber bands cross. Discerning the centers of gravity will not always be easy on the ground. And what they share in common is that they are centers, but nothing about them says they are especially clubbish, or family-ish, or ethnic. By looking at what the individual "rubber bands" that constitute them have in common, we might be able to identity some "thread"—some color, or texture, or thickness, or what-have-you. And in fact these are the features that allow for their coalescing. But the features are, from the point of the view of the model in its current developmental state, unpredictable.

INSTITUTIONS AND THEIR MEMBERS

Problematizing their membership as sometimes-open-ended makes social institutions and groups, as such, stand out—finally—as the enormously important players they are on the social and political landscape. At last, they can take their places as centers of gravity, with capacities for attraction and repulsion. And this view of things underscores the dynamism of institutions as players on the stage of history. Individuals are prominent on this stage, make no mistake. But their prominence, or lack of it, is enhanced or diminished (as the case might be) in accordance with the alliances they have made or have been obliged to make. (The power of alliance is no less important in nonhuman societies, and chimpanzee society in particular; see de Waal 1989.) The prominence of individuals masks the fact that this prominence is often due to the identities they have constructed through the alliances they have forged. And once we see how this construction occurs, we can see the importance of alliance, as such, on the stage of history.

So as individual actors recede in importance on the stage of history, another sort of player emerges as vital: the alliance. An alliance is a variant of one sort or another on the theme of socially organized collectivity. Alliances range from family groups up through ethnic groups, and they are the basis of the phenomenon of solidarity, and have been variously organized by different scholars in different time periods. Focus on the variations and demographics of alliances is hugely important for: (1) understanding the ways that actors (both individuals and groups) organize themselves, both interacting and intersecting, and thereby forming centers of gravity, in that network of agencies whose history just is the history of human life on the planet; and (2) crafting social and political policies that foster or curb the actions of alliances.[25] Alliance is the stuff of politics.

This being so, a certain conclusion is necessitated by our considerations up to this point: the construction of a Self is a fundamentally political act, because it is the basis of the construction of alliances, and alliances are the stuff of politics. However personal or private an alliance might be, it is the basis of actions on the larger stage of human history—the stage of human politics. Thus the personal—as feminists have famously proclaimed—is political. This is not to say that there is no room whatever for the simple interpersonal, or the private, as such. Rather, it is to say that what one sometimes does in private, by way of forging bonds, is elemental to political life.

EXITENTIALIST CREDENTIALS: A RUDIMENTARY PHENOMENOLOGY OF SOCIAL IDENTITY POLITICS

A conception of Selves as natural entities in a natural world is nowadays not very sexy. We have thoroughly imbibed the doctrine that a construal of identity purely in social-group-membership terms is sociology, not philosophy. In particular, it is not obviously compatible with conceptions of freedom and the normative, so central to philosophy since Kant. Much more philosophically respectable are naturalistic conceptions of self in cognitive terms. But better still—indeed, most modern—are those conceptions that invoke updated or enlightened versions of Descartes or Kant, in which Selves are articulated in terms of self-regarding cognitions/judgments, on the one hand, and practices of evaluation, on the other (à la Strawson 1974, Korsgaard 1996, even Bilgrami 2006). These accounts are apparently much more attractive to contemporary philosophical scholars. To philosophical minds trained in the contemporary era, no social science is to be trusted to prize what is important in a human self, what the analytical tradition prizes in a self—namely the capacity for conceptualization, for thought and for evaluation, all from a first-personal perspective.[26] And it's no good insisting that classical philosophy—neither Plato nor Aristotle—made not even the slightest fuss about first-personality and were more concerned simply with rehabilitating ill-behaved individuals or citizens with bad habits. In this section, I will argue that Plato and Aristotle had their priorities straight. The importance of first-personality in moral terms can and must be "gotten over," and when once it has been, we will see that first-personality as such is morally neutral—as it is as much a platform for reprehensible exercises of power as much as for liberation. There is nothing in first-personality to ensure good will or even reasonability. Furthermore, first-personality is only a small piece of the larger puzzle of social identity. My account will draw on Sartre for support of this thesis. This will fill out the existentialist credentials of my proposal, as well as further stress the feminist nature of it.

Sartre taught us how to conceive of the first-personal perspective as an object in the world—and, even more profoundly, as a target of social engagements. Sartre was the first philosopher since Aristotle to take seriously the elementality of social contact in human life. He maintained that our natural appreciation of social nuances formed the backbone of our social "intelligence"—of our appreciation of the minds of others. He illuminated this via analysis of the experience of perceiving the gaze of another—via a phenomenology of being looked upon. When I observe a stranger at a distance, I am free to speculate wildly about his relationship to the entities in his environment. For instance, when I see a man sitting on a park bench in the distance, I might speculate as to how he manages to avoid being swayed with the breeze, as nearby objects of similar size and heft are. But this would be the case *only* if I have never interacted face-to-face with objects of his kind. If—strictly hypothetically, of course—I have been until the present moment entirely innocent of social interactions with other human beings, able to boast of experience of them only as distant objects in my world, I should certainly speculate a great deal about the sources of that stranger's behavior now. In that (strictly hypothetical) condition, I might experience the whole world—indeed, spatiality itself—as emanating from my point of view (my Self) as its center, a Cartesian point without extension that "transcends" the world centered about it, just as it is said that divine entities do. I am a Subject—an entity with a view—upon a universe of Objects themselves without "windows," without *orientation* toward entities in their local universe, without Selves. I might indeed experience the inhabitants hereabouts as populating space at my pleasure, collateral upon my having actively perceived and categorized them according to such lights as I have established from the very beginning of my self-centered universe. I can arrogate as much power as I please to myself, in the style made so famous by Descartes in his armchair by the fire—if I have never once gazed close-up upon another live human face.

But just once let me be looked upon—for example, by that man as I approach his park bench and he catches my gaze—and I am locked into an unprecedented experience of vertigo. I am displaced from center of the universe, even as I experience that very center fleeing from me and toward him (NOT me!!) as Subject. And suddenly I become, no longer Subject, but now one of many objects—Others—in that universe I once transcended absolutely. An "Other" is an object distinct from myself, bearing a spatial location relative to me, and with an immanence—a boundedness in space and time. To be an Other is to be an object or body, bounded in time and space, within some Subject's universe, not mine; it is, as Sartre puts it, "to be-for-another" rather than "to be-for-oneself." The experience of "objectification" is absolutely transforming, as Sartre was at pains to explain. Because it is at once an experience of another's subjectivity and an experience of one's own boundedness. (The question of how, in organic terms, an organism can experience this "disorientation"—of having the very orientation of the universe "reversed" upon it—is of course vexed. No doubt it is bound up with facets of proprioception. But nowise will an explanation of the process detract from the evidence that the experience itself provides of other Selves.)

Ordinary human folk, embedded in workaday social contexts, have been experiencing objectification—an experience that amounts to a transcending of their self-centered universe—from the very moment of birth. They have repeatedly experienced objectification within the ameliorating orbit of nurturing adults, and in that way overcome the illusion of being at the very center of the universe. For persons having repeatedly imbibed the experience of displacement from center, the experience is considerably less disorienting than it could be. To the social human being, the experience of being trapped in another's gaze is so familiar, in fact, so bound up with everyday life, an inalienable dimension of our experience, that we hardly notice it as a displacement. Some of us in fact thrive upon the experience. And each of us appreciates the experience as simply the fact of the subjectivity of others with whom we have made eye contact.

The kernel of this profound argument in Sartre's magnum opus illuminates the fact that so much of what we can conceptualize about other people (for example, that they have minds and are capable of judgments just like we are) lies in our natural endowment as social beings who, through encountering each other face-to-face, appreciate each other's points of view. Thus Sartre was first to grasp the fundamental idea that the capacity for seeing another's gaze is elementally conditioning, not only of developmental pathways into adulthood, but also conditioning of adulthood itself—indeed of full-throated social life. Appreciation of gaze, and the judgments that are sometimes bound up in it, whether liberating or confining, conditions all our cognitions as social beings. What's more, it is becoming more and more clear that the ability to navigate the world as entities locked in permanent possibilities of mutual gaze (and collaterally, of joint attention upon some third object of mutual interest) is an achievement that not all humans can attain: some autistic individuals have profound deficits in this area (Moore and Dunham 1995). Nowadays, the topic of joint attention is very lively, as psychologists have discovered how hard it is to overestimate the importance, in human social development, of being able visually to perceive another person's gaze (see the articles in Eilan et al. 2005, as well as Moore and Dunham 1995). But Sartre was onto this idea first and much more fully (as we will discuss further in the next section).

As social beings, we appreciate gaze as action; gaze is only rarely passive reception of sensory information. Gaze, in addition to mediating so much of our social lives in the facilitative role of helping us identify what others are referring to, also involves exercises of power overwhelming. For the gaze socializes, invites, and reproduces social distinctions that mark social prejudice, for example regarding gender. Thus gaze can also be enormously aversive. In exchanges of social gaze one individual can lose their liberty, via (for instance) becoming marked as a "second." Simone de Beauvoir deserves credit for an acute and penetrating articulation of this point. With the aim of illuminating power relations via the phenomenological categories articulated by Sartre, Beauvoir used the language of Self and Other to capture, not only conditions of subjectivity, but also conditions of subjugation. In her phenomenologies of power relations, she describes power relations as working through categories of gender. She describes, for instance, the phenomenology of woman-and-not-man as one of being *pen-*

umbral and *antithetical* to man: the negative, the "abnormal," the deficient, and therefore the "marked" case within an overarching class of which "man" is the central and normal. "Humanity is male," she writes, "and man defines woman not in herself but as relative to him... She is defined and differentiated with reference to man and not he with reference to her; she is the incidental, the inessential as opposed to the essential. He is the Subject, he is the Absolute—she is the Other" (Beauvoir 1984 [1949], Introduction).

These observations allow Beauvoir to raise the poignant question of the meaning of freedom in a context in which neither rejecting nor accepting the label "woman"—given its conceptual positioning—is an especially powerful mode of social resistance. Damned if you do (since it is tantamount to accepting the subordinate position), damned if you don't (since the act affirms the label as negative). For what could resistance amount to, under such conditions? And where nothing can be done by way of meaningful resistance, in the medium of social transactions, how can there be freedom? So for Beauvoir, there is a genuine question of freedom.

Since Beauvoir, many persons on "the margins" have answered that sometimes embracing a derogating label (for example, "gay") is itself a way of upturning and restructuring the conceptualization associated with categories that enjoy a dominant/inferior or healthy/diseased conceptual structuring; at any rate, embracing—not merely accepting passively—is a way of resisting, a way of *re*-valuing the penumbral, even of casting it adrift of its orbit around the "normal," so as ultimately to render it an independent term of approval, or at any rate as simple matter-of-fact, no longer one of abuse. It takes many such acts of embrace to achieve true re-valuation; therein lies the hard work of resistance. But sometimes a reorientation takes place, and the resistance can indeed triumph.

So consider a certain gaze of a superior male upon a young and inexperienced female. It says "You are a woman; you exist only for domestic work or mothering; you have no genius, and you are therefore my subordinate." (How it says this is of course a matter of expressions, postures, perhaps even through exercises of physical force.) There is perhaps contempt in this look, a bloodless smugness, or simply a matter-of-fact condescension. Sometimes this same message comes from another woman, whose attitude of course is one of being a co-slave—someone who, as a slave, judges me as no better than she herself. I experience each gaze, the judgment, the devaluation in it commanding an assent in an acknowledging return-gaze. In some cases, I acquiesce in the judgment and feel the shame of being looked upon in these terms, so I break the gaze in response to the pain of the feeling. Or NOT! I can resist the judgment while accepting the label itself. These are thus acts of free affiliation, in the terms we have already discussed. In such cases I continue to return the gaze, label accepted, judgment unshared. Or I can refuse the gaze entirely, not even notice the judgment, or at any rate pay it no mind—refusing the very experience of seeing being "looked down" upon. (I might for instance refuse the judgment that as a girl one must be poor at math, in view of ample evidence to the contrary.) Or I can simply refuse from that time forward any circumstances that make gazes like it possible: I remove myself from the reach of the gaze and its kin wherever possible.

Each of these strategies has it champions, as well as its many performances. These performances are ultimately second-hand evidence of freedom—freedom to choose one's labels, one's identity, to some extent. It is not decisive evidence. For there is no undiluted freedom. Our freedom is bounded on all sides, but perhaps bounded most significantly by the interests and motivations that structure our goal-directed lives. But limited freedom there sometimes is—for instance, when our motivations support acts of affiliative resistance. And it is the right kind and of the right grade: the kind that allows for self-construction.

But you might ask: where is the freedom? Where is the exercise of will? This is harder to see, why Sartre simply took it as an axiom. We are looking for an absence—an absence of constraint. And even Sartre, who was skilled in the perception of elemental absences, did not report a direct experience of it. We are allowed indirect glimpses of it, for instance, when Sartre discusses the experience of being an object in someone's universe: "I am a slave to the degree that my being is dependent at the center of a freedom which is not mine and which is the very condition of my being. In so far as I am the object of values which come to qualify me without my being able to act on this qualification or even to know it, I am enslaved" (1969, 267). The freedom to choose one's or at least some of one's qualifiers is precisely the freedom this essay has sought to illuminate.

Just as with self-admissions, the range of possible strategies, vis-à-vis a gaze, varies by label. For category labels for race and gender ("black," "negro," "nigger," "woman," "girl," and the like), the range is somewhat fixed by the possibilities for credibly refusing the label. It is implausible to refuse the label "woman" or "black."[27] However, explicitly derogatory labels for the same category are more credibly refused: "I'm no girl, I'm a woman!" Or "Nigger!" "Take that back!" and so on.

For categories in which conditions of entry are subject to some choice, either in the form of entry conditions or simply self-ascription, the phenomenology is somewhat different. Sports fans rarely cringe at being caught in a gaze that labels them as such. And to the extent that one's profession or line of work leaves one located within an acceptable social stratum, one is rarely unwilling to refuse identification in the relevant category. Still, one may squirm in the gaze of someone who jeers or satirizes contemptuously one's occupation or recreational preferences. Squirm phenomenology suggests discomfort with joint attention upon a feature of oneself, however comfortable one may actually be with the associated label itself. It suggests a discomfort with the phenomenology of self-presentation to that contemptuous Other.

You might think I'm saying that accepting a label, especially a label fraught with moral peril, is constitutive of falling under the category labeled by it. (This is language prevalent in Kantian scholarship and its contemporary extensions.) I am resisting the sterility of this thesis as a general characterization of my proposal. I think it is true in some cases—in the cases involving labels for groups of the "other kind." When the thesis is true, it makes good sense to speak of behavior rationalized by reference to the relevant group membership, as explainable in terms of the act of accepting the label.[28] Indeed, in such cases, it can make sense to criticize someone for accepting or rejecting labels of that sort, on the grounds that they render it possible to "make certain statements." For example, someone who rejects the label of "Democrat" might view that rejection as making a statement about the condition of the Democratic Party. And someone who accepts the label "American" in the wake of 9/11 might well view that acceptance as making a statement about the status of American-style democracy in a freedom-hostile world.

But there is scant philosophical mileage to be gained from formulations in the language of "constitution." For one thing, such language is inapt vis-à-vis the phenomenology discussed above in rejection of labels, both false and true. For another thing, it fails to grapple with the phenomenology of freedom and slavery in acts of ascription. It is sterile because it bleaches out the colors in which labels come, and also the "colored" experience of freedom one has in either accepting or rejecting them; for these experiences are tinted by feeling and emotion, as too are the acts that flow out of them. The language of constitution, as the sole analytical category for describing what people do with labels, bleaches out the experience of "dis-orientation" that comes with recognizing the Selfhood of another, in the context of an ascription; correspondingly, it makes invisible the power relations that attend the various interactions in the political arena. To make sense of all the phenomenology within the sweep of one theoretical framework, an existentialist phenomenology is exceptionally well-placed.

CONCLUSION: TOWARD A NATURAL SCIENCE OF IDENTITY

Cognitive science is still insufficiently attuned to the significance of gaze. The highly influential work of Baron-Cohen (1995a, 1995b), for instance, treats the appreciation of gaze in an organism as appreciation only of *direction* of gaze, something shared by a very wide range of organisms on the planet. By no means, however, does appreciation of direction of gaze exhaust the significance of gaze as Sartre understood it (or as I've sought to do in the discussion above). Gaze in the restricted eye-direction sense cannot be that instrument exploited by persons in positions of conceptual privilege to "put others down," and thereby to exercise enormous power in human social contexts. Indeed, we cannot even be seeing eyes if we are perceiving gaze. As Sartre tells us: "The Other's look hides his eyes; he seems to go *in front of them*." To perceive gaze fully is to perceive, *not* eye directionality, but to see the Other as a first-personal entity in whose first-personal world the Self is caught like a fly in amber.

Without appreciation of gaze as the mark of subjectivity, out of which might flow power overwhelming, social scientists will not appreciate the importance of gaze in its deepest political workings. But perhaps this too will come, in time, to natural science. Tomasello (1995) is some evidence that there are developments afoot in this direction—movement in the direction of a gaze-as-revealing-goal psychology. But there is a long way to go from goal-appreciation cognitions to a full-throated naturalistic analysis of gaze-as-subjectivity-in-which-the-gaze-is-caught-as-Object, and the power that can flow in such transactions in social contexts. Still, I have hope that conception will soon be an ordinary one in the toolkit of social scientists. And, when once she has arrived at the more existentially nuanced analysis of gaze, the natural scientist will be in possession of a wider range of tools of such analysis as is required to treat the experiences and facts of identity. Feminist insights already abound as to the power of the put-down; perhaps they can help light the scientist's way forward.

Flat-footed and graceless as my articulation has been throughout this essay, I hope that it is nonetheless suggestive of the direction in which these ideas might take us. My essay is a mere gesture at a naturalistic conception of human Selfhood and social identity, and a naturalistic conception as well of their construction. Still, unsubtle as this essay has been, the ideas coiled within it are palpably liberating. Folk psychology is comparatively lame, focusing upon propositions spoken or thought as the contents of beliefs and desires, but clueless as to the power of dynamic states of "attention capture" such as ebb and flow in real-time phenomenology in the appreciation of gaze. The next step will be to put flesh on two ideas we have sought to develop in the last several pages: (1) the power of gaze can be power overwhelming; but (2) the potential liberatory power that resides in self-ascription, and that might flow out in a return gaze, should not be underestimated, least of all by social scientists. First and primarily, this latter is power over self. But secondarily, it is power over shared concepts of group membership. And the latter has far-reaching consequences.

Notes

It is a pleasure to be able to thank Anita Superson and Sharon Crasnow for their single-minded commitment to this anthology project. Their advice has been invaluable and their energy limitless. Their vision of a collection of essays that showcases feminist insights blazing trails and building castles on the frontiers of philosophical innovation will be a positive force for de-ghettoizing feminist philosophy. Thanks also to those in attendance at the energizing 2008 meeting of the Society for Analytical Feminism in Lexington, Kentucky, organized by Sharon and Anita. I am indebted too to fellow travelers: to Ann Cudd, Lije Millgram, Chrisoula Andreou, and Meg Bowman for friendship and challenging conversations; and to my partner Robert Richardson and my sons, Oliver and Eli, for intimate glimpses into lives striving mightily for freedom-to-be.

1. Thalos and Andreou (2009) elaborates on this point.
2. In regard to the former, see especially Friedman and May (1985); and in regards to the latter, see Omi and Winant (1986).
3. I refer here to John Searle (1997).
4. This is the twenty-question test described by Heine (2007, chapter 5), designed to measure a society's temperature on the individualism-collectivism scale.
5. For more on agentic resources, see Thalos (2008a).
6. Taken from the book jacket of Barkow et al. (1995).
7. For instance: Sarah Blaffer-Hrdy (1981) and (1999); West-Eberhard (1996) and (1998); Smuts (1996); see also Margo Wilson and Martin Daly (1995), David Buss (1994) and Peter Singer (2000), for philosophical discussion of Darwin's uneasy relationship with the political Left.

8. See Downes (2001).

9. For instance, Doris (2002).

10. I have argued (Thalos 2003) that these contentions are not borne out either in their theory or in their practice. There is nothing "universal" about human nature as conceived by the contemporary sciences of behavior. Universality is not substantiated—and indeed is contradicted—by those very evolution studies, no less than by findings in developmental and cognitive psychology. In line with my contention is a substantial review of languages by Evans and Levinson (2009).

11. I have taken the clinician's side on human nature in Thalos (2003).

12. This is Robert Batterman's term (Batterman 1998), to refer to the work of Robert Axelrod (1984) and Brian Skyrms (1994) and (1996).

13. Sen (2006, 22). Sen's own criticisms have been sustained for decades: Sen (1977) and (1987).

14. The literature on these studies is massive. A few key pieces: Dawes, van de Kragt, and Orbell (1997), Kramer and Brewer (1986).

15. Akerlof (1984).

16. Mallon (2006a) engages this question succinctly.

17. Social psychologists have been making this distinction for some time. See the many excellent essays in Baumeister (1999).

18. My position on agency is articulated in Thalos (2008a) and (2007).

19. This taxonomy derives from ideas set forth in Thalos and Andreou (2009).

20. More on this phenomenon in Thalos (2008b).

21. The term "social identity" is due to Turner (1982, 1984); the quotation is from Turner (1984, 527).

22. This description of things is not uncontroversial, but there is a broad spectrum of evidence for it, as well as a great deal of argumentation. Some of this literature is listed in the References.

23. Leary (2004) provides a window onto the topic of self-awareness, and Markus and Kitayama (1991), Markus and Kunda (1986), Markus and Nurius (1986) provide a developmental and cross-cultural perspective.

24. There are some echoes of this idea in Bilgrami (1992).

25. Hannan and Carroll (1992) present an attractive theoretical framework, using ecological modeling tools, for handling the lives of organizational entities.

26. Obviously this point needs fleshing out. I have sought to do this in Thalos (2007).

27. Still, it is not impossible. In my own case, for example, I did not know I was "not white" until the age of eleven, more than two years after first arrival as an immigrant in the United States. My instruction occurred on the playground. Before that time, I had been apprised only of certain more specific facts: for instance, that I evinced strange habits of dress, strange manners, and of course strange speech. It took 5th-graders to put it all together into a racial profile. Later on, I would be surprised by the strength

of anger and resentment aroused in persons poorly qualified or not qualified at all for coveted vacancies, when it turned out that members of protected classes into which I fell received special consideration—but only if especially well qualified. And then there were the administrators who wanted it both ways—for reporting purposes to count me among the nonwhite, but for salary purposes not to do so. Damned if you do, damned if you don't.

28. Indeed, one may take Bilgrami (2006) as describing such cases.

References

Akerlof, George. 1984. *An Economic Theorist's Book of Tales.* New York: Cambridge University Press.

Appiah, Kwame Anthony. 2006. *Cosmopolitanism.* New York: Norton.

Axelrod, Robert. 1984. *Evolution of Cooperation.* New York: Basic Books.

Baars, Bernard. 1988. *A Cognitive Theory of Consciousness.* Cambridge: Cambridge University Press.

Barkow, J., L. Cosmides, and J. Tooby, eds. 1995. *The Adapted Mind: Evolutionary Psychology and the Generation of Culture.* New York: Oxford University Press.

Baron-Cohen, S. 1995a. The Eye Direction Detector (EDD) and the Shared Attention Mechanism (SAM): Two Cases for Evolutionary Psychology. In Moore and Dunham (1995), 41–59.

———. 1995b. *Mindblindness.* Cambridge, Mass.: MIT/Bradford Books.

Batterman, Robert. 1998. Game Theoretic Explanations and Justice. *Philosophy of Science* 65: 76–102.

Baumeister, Roy, ed. 1999. *The Self in Social Psychology.* Philadelphia: Psychology Press.

Beauvoir, Simone de. 1984 [1949]. *The Second Sex.* Translated by H. M. Parshely. Harmondsworth: Penguin.

Bilgrami, A. 2006. *Self-Knowledge and Resentment.* Cambridge, Mass.: Harvard University Press.

———. 1992. What Is a Muslim? Fundamental Commitment and Cultural Identity. *Critical Inquiry* 18 (4): 821–42.

Blaffer-Hrdy, Sarah. 1999. *Mother Nature.* New York: Ballantine Books.

———. 1981. *The Woman that Never Evolved.* Cambridge, Mass.: Harvard University Press.

Brennan, Geoff, and Philip Pettit. 2004. *The Economy of Esteem: An Essay on Civil and Political Society.* New York: Oxford University Press.

Buss, David. 1994. *The Evolution of Desire: Strategies of Human Mating.* New York: Basic Books.

Clark, Andy. 2003. *Natural-Born Cyborgs.* New York: Oxford University Press.

Crowell, Steven. Existentialism. *The Stanford Encyclopedia of Philosophy* (Spring 2006 Edition), ed. Edward N. Zalta, http://plato.stanford.edu/archives/spr2006/entries/existentialism/.

Dawes, Robin M., A. J. C. van de Kragt, and J. M. Orbell. 1997. Not Me or Thee but We: The Importance of Group Identity in Eliciting Cooperation in Dilemma Situations: Experimental Manipulations. In *Research on Judgment and Decision Making*, ed. W. M. Goldstein and R. M. Hogarth. Cambridge: Cambridge University Press.

Dennett, Daniel. 1991. *Consciousness Explained*. Boston: Little, Brown and Company.

De Waal, Frans. 1989. *Chimpanzee Politics: Power and Sex among Apes*. Baltimore: Johns Hopkins Press.

Downes, Stephen. 2001. Some Recent Developments in Evolutionary Approaches to the Study of Human Cognition and Behavior. *Biology and Philosophy* 16: 575–95.

Doris, John. 2002. *Lack of Character*. Cambridge: Cambridge University Press.

Eilan, N., C. Hoerl, T. McCormack, and J. Roessler. 2005. *Joint Attention: Communication and Other Minds*. New York: Oxford University Press.

Evans, N., and S. Levinson. 2009. The Myth of Language Universals: Language Diversity and its Importance for Cognitive Science. *Behavioral and Brain Science* 32: 429–492.

Fodor, Jerry. 1983. *The Modularity of Mind*. Cambridge, Mass.: MIT Press/ Bradford Books.

Friedman, Marilyn A., and Larry May. 1985. Harming Women as a Group. *Social Theory and Practice* 11: 207–34.

Gazzaniga, Michael. 1985. *The Social Brain: Discovering the Networks of the Mind*. New York: Basic Books.

Geertz, Clifford. 1968. The Impact of the Concept of Culture on the Concept of Man. In *Man in Adaptation*, ed. Y. A. Cohen. Aldine Publishing.

Hacking, Ian. 1999. *The Social Construction of What?* Cambridge, Mass.: Harvard University Press.

Hannan, Michael T., and Glenn R. Carroll. 1992. *Dynamics of Organizational Populations: Density, Legitimation and Competition*. New York: Oxford University Press.

Heine, S. 2007. *Cultural Psychology*. W. W. Norton.

Hutto, D., ed. 2007. *Narrative and Understanding Persons*. Cambridge: Cambridge University Press 2007.

Koggel, Christine M. 1998. *Perspectives on Equality: Constructing a Relational Theory*. Lanham, Md.: Rowman and Littlefield.

Korsgaard, C. 1996. *Sources of Normativity*. New York: Cambridge University Press.

Kramer, R. M., and M. B. Brewer. 1986. Social Group Identity and the Emergence of Cooperation in Resource Conservation Dilemmas. In *Experimental Social Dilemmas*, ed. H. Wilke, D. Messick, and C. Rutte. Frankfurt am Main: Verlag Peter Lang.

Leary, M. 2004. *The Curse of the Self: Self-Awareness, Egotism, and the Quality of Human Life*. Oxford University Press.

Mackenzie, Catriona, and Natalie Stoljar, eds. 2000. *Relational Autonomy: Feminist Perspectives on Autonomy, Agency, and the Social Self.* Oxford: Oxford University.

Mallon, Ron. 2007. Human Categories Beyond Non-Essentialism. *Journal of Political Philosophy* 15 (2): 146–68.

———. 2006a. A Field Guide to Social Construction. *Philosophy Compass Online* 2 (1): 93–108.

———. 2006b. Race: Normative, not Metaphysical or Semantic. *Ethics* 116 (3): 525–51.

Markus, H., and S. Kitayama. 1991. Culture and the Self: Implications for Cognition, Emotion, and Motivation. *Psychological Review* 98: 224–53.

Markus, H., and Z. Kunda. 1986. Stability and Malleability in the Self-Concept in the Perception of Others. *Journal of Personality and Social Psychology* 51 (4): 858–66.

Markus, H., and P. Nurius. 1986. Possible Selves. *American Psychologist* 41 (9): 954–69.

Metzinger, T. 2003. *Being No One: The Self-Model Theory of Subjectivity.* Cambridge, Mass.: MIT Press.

Moore, C., and P. J. Dunham. 1995. *Joint Attention: Its Origins and Role in Development.* New Jersey: Lawrence Erlbaum Associates.

Omi, Michael, and Howard Winant. 1986. *Racial Formation in the United States: From the 1960s to the 1980s.* New York: Routledge.

Perdue, C., J. Dividio, M. Gurtman, and R. Tyler. 1990. Us and Them: Social Categorization and the Process of Intergroup Bias. *Journal of Personality and Social Psychology* 59: 475–86.

Rabbie, J., and M. Horwitz. 1969. Arousal of Ingroup-Outgroup Bias by a Chance Win or Loss. *Journal of Personality and Social Psychology* 13: 269–77.

Ross, D. [forthcoming]. Coordination and the Foundations of Social Intelligence. *Interaction Studies.*

———. 2007. H sapiens as Ecologically Special: What Does Language Contribute? *Language Sciences* 29: 710–31.

———. 2005. *Economic Theory and Cognitive Science: Microexplanation.* Cambridge, Mass.: MIT Press.

Sartre, Jean-Paul. 1969. *Being and Nothingness: An Essay on Phenomenological Ontology.* Routledge.

Searle, John. 1997. *The Construction of Social Reality.* Free Press.

Sen, Amartya. 2006. *Identity and Violence.* New York: Norton.

———. 2002. *Rationality and Freedom.* Cambridge, Mass.: Harvard University Press.

———. 1987. *On Ethics and Economics.* Oxford: Blackwell.

———. 1977. Rational Fools: A Critique of the Behavioral Foundations of Economic Theory. *Philosophy & Public Affairs* 6 (4): 317–344.

Sherif, M., O. J. Harvey, B. J. White, W. Hood, and C. Sherif. 1961. *Intergroup Conflict and Cooperation.* Norman: University of Oklahoma.

Singer, Peter. 2000. *A Darwinian Left.* New Haven, Conn.: Yale University Press.

Skyrms, Brian. 1996. *Evolution of the Social Contract*. New York: Cambridge University Press.

———. 1994. Sex and Justice. *Journal of Philosophy* 91: 305–20.

Smuts, Barbara. 1996. Male Aggression against Women: An Evolutionary Perspective. In *Sex, Power, Conflict: Evolutionary and Feminist Perspectives*, ed. D. Buss and N. Malamuth. New York: Oxford University Press.

Stamos, David. 2008. *Evolution and the Big Questions*. Wiley.

Strawson, P. F. 1974. *Freedom and Resentment and Other Essays*. London: Methuen and Co.

Tajfel, Henri. 1970. Experiments in Intergroup Discrimination. *Scientific American* 223: 96–102.

Thalos, Mariam. 2008a. On Planning: Towards a Natural History of the Will. *Philosophical Papers* 37: 289–317.

———. 2008b. Two Conceptions of Collectivity. *Journal of the Philosophy of History* 2: 83–104.

———. 2007. Sources of Behavior: Towards a Control Account of Agency. *Distributed Cognition and the Will*, ed. Don Ross and David Spurrett, 123–67. Cambridge, Mass.: MIT Press.

———. 2003. From Human Nature to Moral Philosophy. *Canadian Journal of Philosophy*, supplementary vol. 28: 85–128.

Thalos, Mariam, and Andreou, Chrisoula. 2009. Of Human Bonding. *Public Reason* 1 (2): 46–73.

Tomasello, M. 1995. Joint Attention as Social Cognition. In Moore and Dunham (1995), 103–30.

Turner, J. C. 1984. Social Identification and Psychological Group Formation. In *The Social Dimension: European Developments in Social Psychology*, ed. H. Tajfel, vol. 2, 518–38. Cambridge: Cambridge University Press.

———. 1982. Towards a Cognitive Redefinition of the Social Group. In *Social Identity and Intergroup Relations*, ed. H. Tajfel, 15–40. Cambridge: Cambridge University Press.

West-Eberhard, Mary Jane. 1998. Evolution in the Light of Developmental and Cell Biology, and Vice Versa. *Proceedings National Academy of Sciences* USA 95 (15): 8417–19.

———. 1996. Wasp Societies as Microcosms for the Study of Development and Evolution. In *Natural History and Evolution of Paper Wasps*, ed. S. Turillazzi and M. J. West-Eberhard. Oxford: Oxford University Press.

Wilson, E. O. 1975. *Sociobiology: The New Synthesis*. Cambridge, Mass.: Harvard University Press.

Wilson, Margo, and Martin Daly. 1995. The Man Who Mistook his Wife for a Chattel. In *The Adapted Mind: Evolutionary Psychology and the Generation of Culture*, ed. J. Barkow, L. Cosmides, and J. Tooby. New York: Oxford University Press.

18

ANN GARRY
California State University, Los Angeles

WHO IS INCLUDED?

Intersectionality, Metaphors, and the Multiplicity of Gender

INTERSECTIONALITY, THE SUBJECT OF this essay, is intertwined with my hopes for both traditional philosophy and feminist philosophy. I want to encourage traditional philosophers to do philosophy that is "part of the solution" rather than "part of the problem." To continue to be part of the problem, all philosophy has to do is to leave unquestioned the ways in which its concepts, theories, frameworks, and methods have contributed directly or indirectly to perpetuating oppression and other forms of injustice. I want to encourage feminist philosophers to be more genuinely pluralistic, especially to de-center white, middle-class women in our theories and practices. Intersectionality, which I characterize in more detail later, includes the idea that various forms of oppression and privilege interact with each other in multiple complex ways. I focus on intersectionality here in order to encourage philosophers to appreciate the multifaceted relationships among kinds of oppression and privilege, and to value the roles that complex social identities play in the construction of their own theories, specifically the complicated ways in which gender, race/ethnicity, class, sexual orientation (and the "embarrassed, 'etc.'"[1]) are interwoven. If philosophers, both traditional and feminist, more fully appreciate these complexities, then the possibilities increase that many theories will be richer, better, and, dare I say, true. In addition, I hope that philosophers of whatever theoretical, moral, and political bent want their theories not only to be plausible but also, where relevant, to exhibit respect for all human beings.[2] Understanding the complex nature of human social identities and systems of oppression moves us toward this goal.

Of course, feminist philosophers think of ourselves as already "part of the solution" or surely at least moving toward it. Unlike many traditional philosophers, we intend for our work to be applicable to daily life and have a bearing on social justice. We contribute to the dialogues and practices that will lessen oppressions of various kinds and improve the lives of women everywhere. To do this seriously and realistically, we must ensure that feminist philosophy is inclusive and pluralistic. Offering lip service to these goals is much easier than doing the hard work to accomplish them. Unfortunately, most feminist philosophers are still drawn from dominant races/ethnicities/classes/nationalities in our societies, so we must work more diligently to overcome layers of denial and resistance. In North America and Europe, this means that in order to create inclusive and pluralistic feminist philosophy that moves white women far from center stage, white women must (i) learn a great deal about the lives and thinking of women of color and women from the global south, (ii) understand more deeply the ways in which various oppressions/privileges are intermeshed, and (iii) acknowledge and remedy the ways in which our practices have marginalized women from non-dominant groups. This is old news, but it is old news that white feminist philosophers must take seriously and integrate more fully into our work.

I maintain that intersectionality offers the best framework at present in which to do the work that I want feminist and traditional philosophers to do (although I would be pleased with any framework that could do at least as much of the same kind of work without its limitations). This might seem an uncontroversial claim, since intersectionality is a concept that has been part of feminist discourse since Kimberlé Crenshaw introduced the term in 1989, and grew from an already existing discourse of women of color.[3] Until fairly recently, feminist theorists and activists welcomed the concept for the most part uncritically, both for theoretical and everyday political purposes. We were relieved to have a way to discuss the interactions among race, ethnicity, gender, sexual orientation, social class, and so forth, that (i) rejected ranking them, and (ii) enabled both our activism and our theories to move forward with at least a minimal understanding of the ways in which the major axes of oppression interacted with each other and affected human lives, and helped us start to grasp the complexities of our similarities, differences, and the networks of hierarchical relationships among us.

For well over a decade, even the most conceptually nitpicky feminist theorists, among whom we would have to number feminist philosophers, were not inclined to tinker with the concept of intersectionality.

This might have been in part because so many feminist philosophers are white women who did not want to tinker with a fruitful concept introduced by feminists of color, but it might also be attributed to a phenomenon observed by Kathy Davis, namely, "that, paradoxically, precisely the vagueness and open-endedness of 'intersectionality' may be the very secret to its success" (2008, 69). Using the work of sociologist of science Murray S. Davis (1971, 1986), Kathy Davis argues that "successful theories appeal to a concern regarded as fundamental by a broad audience of scholars, but they do so in a way which is not only unexpected, but inherently hazy and mystifyingly open-ended" (K. Davis 2008, 70). This explanation seems apt and squares with the apparent lack of interest in refining the details of the concept of intersectionality for quite a long time after its introduction. We did not want to mess with a good thing that addressed a number of strongly felt needs!

Today intersectionality has its critics, some of whom I have argued against elsewhere and discuss briefly here (Garry 2007, 2008a, 2008b). However, in spite of (or perhaps because of) my advocacy of intersectionality, I find it very important to understand the limitations and scope of intersectionality. It has many practical, political, and theoretical virtues, but it is only a framework—some would even say a tool.[4] It does not do the hardest work of investigating the "intersections" in the lives of real people or analyzing the ways that structural oppressions interact in social contexts. What it needs to do is to provide a basis for a good strategy and conceptual structure that we can use for practical feminist politics as well as for at least two theoretical purposes: the first is to enable feminist theorists, critical race theorists, queer and trans theorists, and others creating emancipatory theories to understand human social complexity, oppression, and privilege in ways that improve both their theories and the conditions of our lives; the second is to help traditional philosophers (and other traditional academics) both to understand and to care about what it takes to become "part of the solution."[5] The traditional group is, of course, the tougher nut to crack. It is especially difficult to persuade some traditional academics to care enough about the lives, experiences, and oppressions of people sufficiently unlike them that they see the need to modify their previous theories. However, we should try to crack the toughest nuts with the best strategy and conceptual structure possible. This does not imply that the most precise concept of intersectionality is best, for precision might fly in the face of the complex variety of expressed needs of members of oppressed groups. Instead, a concept of intersectionality that is modest, broadly conceived, and "good enough" is the best approach we have at this point.

In order to support intersectionality, I pull several threads together. My overall aim is to clear the way for the use of intersectionality, that is, to make it "safe" for feminist and traditional philosophers to use it. This requires explaining its scope and limitations and addressing some of the objections to it. In section 1, I briefly lay out some benefits and limitations of intersectionality; in section 2, I discuss limitations of the images used to explain it; section 3 considers María Lugones's position on intersectionality and gender(s); section 4 sets out an intersectional family resemblance position that supports Lugones's aims, but differs with her view of the number of genders that women have.

1. THE BASICS, THE BENEFITS, AND THE LIMITATIONS

I propose to use a broad, inclusive concept of intersectionality in order to see whether it gives us a structure in which to start addressing traditional philosophers and to meet the theoretical and practical needs of feminists:

> Oppression and privilege by race, ethnicity, gender, sexual orientation, class, nationality, and so on, do not act independently of each other in our individual lives or in our social structures; instead, each kind of oppression or privilege is shaped by and works through the others. These compounded, intermeshed systems of oppression and privilege in our social structures help to produce (a) our social relations, (b) our experiences of our own identity, and (c) the limitations of shared interests even among members of "the same" oppressed or privileged group.

I use the term "intersectionality" for the concept in order to affirm continuity with the tradition from which it springs, not because it is identical with everyone else's usage.[6] I also want to emphasize that my support is for this *kind* of concept, rather than with the particularities of my expression of it.

In this section, I retrace some familiar steps to explain why we need such a concept. I start with the most fundamental needs—ones that apply only to traditional philosophers who have yet to see the relevance of feminism or critical race theory, queer theory, or other liberatory theories.

From "square one," I move in increments to considerations that realistically will apply only to those with a commitment to social change.

Many traditional philosophers still fail to grasp that human beings cannot be treated generically in their theories, let alone that philosophers should consider the various complexities of our identities and our structures of oppressions and privileges. Assuming that they want their theories to be more applicable to real human beings (or perhaps they have a naturalized bent and are willing to reflect a more complex world in their naturalizations[7]), what can intersectionality do for them?

First, it can help them understand not only that gender matters to philosophy but also that people are not simply men and women. By noting this, I do not mean to begin a discussion about people who are intersex or transgender, interesting though it would be, but to make the "intersectional point": we all have other important facets to our identities and are differently impacted by multiple interacting systems of oppression and privilege depending on what those other facets are. Perhaps intersectional analyses can help traditional philosophers fast-forward through earlier decades of feminist and critical race theory that did not adequately address the impact of multiple intertwined systems of oppression and privilege.[8] There will be no need to be sidetracked by attempts to rank competing oppressions or to make facile false generalizations about social groups. For example, intersectionality gives philosophers working on personal identity a framework in which to understand the relevance of work by Gloria Anzaldúa (1987), María Lugones (2003, 2006, 2007), and Cherríe Moraga (1983), just to cite a few. They have all detailed many ways in which dominant theories render their lives invisible. They explain how and why their identities contain multiplicity, but are unified, not fragmented (although others' labels try to split them) and the ways in which they construct identities by resistance to oppressions. Philosophers who take these views seriously might well need to rethink the way they frame issues of personal identity and assess differently which theories succeed.[9]

Second, if we assume, as I do, that self-understanding and awareness of one's social location can help improve one's philosophical views, then it's important to note that intersectionality can aid those willing to examine their own social identities and especially their unacknowledged privileges, including the privilege of remaining ignorant of marginalized people. Many white people do not consciously see themselves or their conceptual frameworks as raced. Similarly, heterosexuals of any race/ethnicity or class often render gay men and lesbians conceptually invisible. Patricia Hill Collins finds intersectional analysis helpful in our ability to identify "the oppressor within us" (acknowledging Audre Lorde); she applies this not simply to those in privileged groups, but to all people (1993/2008, 98). The value of self-knowledge is not simply for moral self-improvement, but also to enable us to undertake the very hard work of understanding the implications of philosophy's Eurocentrism. It is difficult for philosophers to look at the colonial legacies and deep biases based on race, class, and gender that permeate Western philosophy in its methods, formulation of issues, and substantive positions.[10]

Recent work on "epistemologies of ignorance" have called attention to the ways in which dominant groups' ignorance is constructed and maintained, explorations of whose power is served by such ignorance, and the ways that our current interests, beliefs, and theories block why we sometimes do not even know that we do not know, or if we do know it, why we do not care (see Mills 1997, Tuana and Sullivan 2006, Sullivan and Tuana 2007).

Alison Bailey's discussion, directed toward white analytic feminist philosophers, but applicable to all analytic philosophers, illustrates the difficulties of dealing with deep biases and shows that philosophers need to rethink the reasons that we value certain methods and styles of philosophy over others. Analytic philosophers can be averse to the idea of tinkering with their methods of argument or with the high levels of abstraction and generality in which they discuss issues. Intersectional approaches can feel threatening to philosophers who believe that such approaches put the "purity" of philosophical methods at risk. They then try to label the work of philosophers who value intersectionality and want to reflect upon the thinking and actual diverse conditions of the lives of women of color as "not philosophy" (Bailey 2010).

Third, intersectionality can point all of us to the locations where we need to begin identifying issues and constructing our theories. Here again, I am making a very basic point. Feminist standpoint theorists have explained to us for decades the importance of starting our thinking or our research from the lives of marginalized people (for example, Harding 1991). Intersectionality helps to point us to fruitful, complex marginalized locations. It does not do the work for us, but tells us where to start and suggests kinds of questions to ask. It sets the stage to counteract the deep Eurocentrism referred to above by trying to formulate issues from the lives of those not part of the Western philosophical canon. Starting with the African-American woman's life experience and structures of authority might well lead a naturalized epistemologist to shape his/her questions and strategies differently about the ways in which epistemic authority is constructed, how we choose "experts," and whose views carry weight and whose are not even acknowledged when a working-class African-American woman has a disagreement over medical symptoms or a factual dispute with a middle-class white man.[11]

Although feminist philosophers certainly need to be reminded about the points above, our focus *should* have incorporated these ideas and moved along. Let us review quickly some of the other benefits of intersectionality for feminists as well as for any traditional scholars who are motivated to become part of the solution.

Fourth, the focus on systemic interaction, compounding, and intermeshing avoids several misunderstandings of the ways oppression and privilege work as structural forces. These arguments are well known in feminist theory. For example, race, gender, and sexual orientation, whether used to oppress or to privilege human beings, are not simply added together in Black lesbians or added/subtracted in white gay men. Additive or "pop-bead" models of identity or oppression do not work.[12] Although intersectionality builds on a rich literature by feminists of color about multiple oppressions and double consciousness, it does not merely repeat that women of color or lesbians of any ethnicity are multiply oppressed. Instead it points to the ways in which oppressions intermesh with each other or are used to construct each other. This can be seen both in the ways they act as structural forces and are applied to individuals. Consider, for example, the ways in which racist stereotypes of African-American, Asian-American, and Latina women are used to objectify these women sexually as well as to assign them to "appropriate" jobs. Or consider Anna Stubblefield's analysis of the ways advocates of eugenic sterilization in the first half of the twentieth century intertwined classism with racialized theories of intelligence and sexist views of moral depravity in the concept of feeblemindedness (Stubblefield 2007).

Fifth, as noted above, the inclusion of both privilege and oppression in intersectionality implies that members of dominant groups must consider the factors of privilege in their own identity and positionality. Intersectionality applies to everyone, not simply to members of subordinated or marginalized groups. This is important to me not only because I think it is correct, but also because it overcomes the objection raised by Naomi Zack to some analyses of intersectionality, namely, that intersectional analyses keep white women central to feminism and exclude women of color and women from the global south from the feminist conversation table. Zack believes that intersectionality helps to maintain the distinction between "feminism" on the one hand and "multi-cultural feminism" and "global feminism" on the other (2005). Given that all people, not just the oppressed, have race/ethnicity, then intersectionality as I conceive it undermines Zack's conceptual basis for dividing feminists. In fact, it can facilitate moving white feminists from center stage, make them less likely to overgeneralize about "women," and decrease the extent to which they are "arrogant perceivers" of other women.[13] It can also increase the awareness of "relationality" and hierarchical power relations among women, for example, the extent to which privileged women's lives are dependent on the work of other women who care for their children and their homes.[14]

Sixth, intersectionality has many other practical advantages for feminists as well. It can enable us to face squarely and understand the reasons why we might have different interests at stake in a particular issue, for example, lesbian interest in marriage. It can support alliances and solidarity even when there are salient differences; for example, East Asian women have formed alliances across historically conflicting nationalities to work on behalf of "comfort women" pressed into sexual service by the Japanese military in World War II.

We need to consider also the *limitations* of intersectionality: what it is not capable of doing or does not imply. I do not consider these "objections" to intersectionality, but a realistic assessment of the scope of the concept. Of course, not everyone agrees with me.

First, although I hesitate to use the word "methodology" because its meaning varies widely across and within disciplines, I doubt that intersectionality is one.[15] The term I used earlier, "framework," is loose, but apt. One can develop methods and methodologies that support an intersectional framework (or even an intersectional picture). Intersectionality's positive value can be seen in its function as a "method checker" (or even a "framework checker") that provides standards that a method or methodology should meet.

Second, by itself, intersectionality provides neither any structural analyses of oppressions and privileges nor any particular analysis of anyone's complex identity or experiences. Instead it points out what kinds of analyses might be useful, namely, ones that consider mutually constructed or intermeshed axes of oppression or facets of identities.

Third, it is not a theory of power, of oppression, or of any other central concept of social and political theory.[16]

Fourth, it provides neither a theory of identity formation nor a theory of agency.[17]

Fifth, it does not abolish identity categories; instead they become more complex, messy, and fluid. A number of critics have argued that the treatment of identity categories in intersectional analyses is problematic. These would include (i) poststructuralist critiques that seek to undermine identity categories deeply, (ii) critiques that pushing identity categories to a higher level remains problematic, and (iii) Lugones's critique that identity categories embody a "logic of purity."[18]

Sixth, it does not imply that all situations are intersectional to the same extent. The degrees and kinds of intersectional intermeshing need empirical investigation. For example, the degree to which a gay couple is subject to economic oppression will need a thoroughgoing intersectional analysis. We need to consider whether they are gay men or lesbians, what their races/ethnicities and social classes are, whether they speak the dominant language of the country, how these all fit together, and so forth. In contrast, if we want to know whether this gay couple is discriminated against by the legal prohibition of same-sex marriage, we need to know far less about them. The laws under which they live determine whether they can marry (whether rich or poor, white, Asian, Latino, or Black, gay man or lesbian). I am not saying that marriage laws are completely devoid of relevant intersections, just that there are differences in the degree of intersectional analyses needed in different situations.[19]

Having noted some of the benefits of intersectionality as well as a few limitations on what it can do or provide, let us turn to the limitations of the images in which intersectionality has been explained.

2. METAPHORS AND IMAGES

Explaining a concept, especially a concept that goes against the grain of dominant institutional structures and thought, often requires metaphors, images, or analogies. Intersectionality is no exception, although it itself is a metaphor. I want to look at some of the ways in which intersectionality has been visualized in order to understand some of the critiques of it, and consider whether the problem is the concept of intersectionality itself or the metaphors and images used to discuss it.

Crenshaw originally used a traffic intersection to explain the ways in which Black women were harmed by existing U.S. legal categories that allowed African-American women to be disadvantaged by only one axis of discrimination at a time.

Consider an analogy to traffic in an intersection, coming and going in all four directions. Discrimination, like traffic through an intersection, may flow in one direction, and it may flow in another. If an accident happens in an intersection, it can be caused by cars traveling from any number of directions and, sometimes, from all of them. Similarly if a Black woman is harmed because she is in the intersection, her injury could result from sex discrimination or race discrimination [or both]. (1989, 149)[20]

This image of intersectionality caught on in a way that a more sterile intersection of sets in mathematics or a Venn diagram would not have. Even if streets are more linear and horizontal than axes of oppression, the vivacity of the images of multi-car collisions and of Black women being battered by multiple vehicles representing oppressions helped people to expand their thinking beyond legal frameworks that were based on analyses of equality that relied on the "single-axis" model of discrimination: "but for" this one oppression, they'd be treated equally.

As I have visualized intersectionality over two decades, I have added many more streets to the intersection and placed a roundabout in its center. We need these changes in order to distinguish intersectionality from more simplified cases of multiple oppressions. Being hit by two different cars does not show the ways that oppressions can interact. A roundabout works better if we want to point out that one axis of oppression uses another to oppress a single person, or that axes can sometimes blend together to produce a distinct mixture (consider, for example, Carla Trujillo's treatment of Chicano Catholic homophobia [1991] or Lugones's position on the colonial/modern fusion of race and gender [2007]). In a roundabout, different axes can intermesh in various ways after they enter the central space. The central space is up for grabs! There might not even be an "island" in the middle, just an open space. A person standing anywhere in the central space could be hit by any number of axes either in combination or singly. Cars, trains, buses, and motorcycles all could be vehicles carrying different axes of oppression into the central space. Vehicles could even crash or fuse together first before hitting the person. No need to keep it simple. Imagine here the life of a U.S. Muslim lesbian with family members in Afghanistan trying to enlist in the U.S. military between 2001 and 2011.

This more fluid roundabout allows us to visualize more facets of intersectionality. It is now easier to expand the axes of oppression beyond race and gender to include sexual orientation, class, and other factors; in addition, the central area is suitable for incorporating several types of intersectionality. By "types" I include the interactions among axes in institutions or social issues as well as intersectional effects on an individual. For example, Patricia Hill Collins explains the ways in which Black slavery exemplified patriarchy and class hierarchy as well as racism (consider the many reasons for controlling slave women's sexuality and fertility) (1993/2008, 100–1). Crenshaw, in addition to discussing the importance of intersectionality in dealing with domestic violence, details the interaction of axes of oppression on each other in a more structural way and distinguishes among structural intersectionality, political intersectionality, and representational intersectionality (1991, 1993).

However, a horizontal roundabout presents a problem, particularly if we adopt a concept of intersectionality that includes privilege as well as oppression.[21] If a person is subject to axes of privilege/oppression rather than just oppression, how or where do we locate her on the axes and in the intersection? Suppose our U.S. Muslim lesbian above is white with family in Europe, not Afghanistan. Is she standing on a "white curb" protected from racism while being hit by a combination of heterosexualism and anti-Muslim bigotry? Or perhaps an axis in terms of which she is privileged simply bypasses her as she stands in the roundabout. Or imagine that no cars are allowed to enter the intersection from the privileged end of the axis, so battering an oppressed pedestrian is done by cars, trucks, and buses on one-way streets from the oppressive end.

Something is still wrong: a person with privilege can sometimes choose to mitigate a few of the damaging effects of oppression, not just bypass that axis. A wealthy Chicana lesbian can choose to use her wealth to mitigate some of the damage done by her ethnic/religious community's homophobia. For example, she could donate funds to organizations that resist homophobia in her community or move away from the neighborhood in which her daily social interactions are oppressive, even if such a move has emotional costs in other respects. The possibility of mitigation makes it look as if a multi-dimensional matrix of axes of oppression and privilege would be needed. In addition, we must also keep in mind that social forces do not merely "strike one differently" depending on one's location in this complex matrix, but that agents choose to act differently within their locations. They can resist oppressions even without other privileges; those with some privilege can use their privilege in a variety of ways (or not). It might be worthwhile to explore Collins's image of the matrix of domination to assist us here, but that will have to wait for another occasion.[22]

In order to address the horizontality of the model and its lack of ability to incorporate the ways in which privilege in one respect can mitigate or modify oppression in another, let us introduce mountains to add verticality. Intersections can be found on various places on the side of a mountain. A heterosexual's intersections are found higher up on the "heterosexualism mountain," or if the heterosexual is also middle class, higher up on the mountain of combined heterosexualism and classism.

Once we have mountains, we can replace vehicles with liquids to show the ways in which some oppressions or privileges seem to blend or fuse with others. Different liquids—milk, coffee, olive oil, nail polish, beet borscht, paint in several colors—run down from different places at different altitudes into a roundabout. Some of the liquids run together, some are marbled with others, and some stay more separate unless whipped together. To me, this image captures intersectionality better than many others, but it still cannot capture agency well.

Although I yearn for a rich concept of intersectionality that can be visually captured, it is, in fact, difficult to find visual images that both capture all the features of intersectionality and are simple enough to help explain the concept. This fact has always made me somewhat uncomfortable. However, this difficulty does not imply that the fault is with the concept of intersectionality. Perhaps we simply need to realize that intersectionality itself is a metaphor that, as it has evolved, encompasses too many facets for any image to capture completely: the interaction of the axes of oppression and privilege across a variety of social structures and situations; the agency of people within these structures; the conflicting interests of members of an oppressed group; individuals' social identities—how people see and represent themselves and each other; and so on. I mean here to allude not simply to Crenshaw's categories of structural, political, and representational intersectionality, but also to the sheer array of cases and uses at hand. We might recall Kathy Davis's claim that it is precisely the somewhat amorphous character of intersectionality—coupled with the needs it satisfies—that gives it such a wide appeal.

3. LUGONES: INTERSECTIONALITY, COLONIAL/MODERN POWER, AND GENDERS

Although we now turn to María Lugones's work, we continue our discussion of metaphors, visual images, and the need for messiness in them. Not only is Lugones's writing full of rich imagery, but she is also especially concerned that intersectionality and related concepts not leave our key concepts pure, tidy, and separate from each other. I consider her work in some detail not only because of her valuable contributions, but also because it challenges the position I develop in section 4.

I concentrate on two of her essays, "Purity, Impurity, and Separation" (in Lugones 2003) and "Heterosexualism and the Colonial/Modern Gender System" (2007), focusing on her treatment of the role of inter-sectionality and her position that women differently situated by oppres-sions have different genders. Although I argue against Lugones on the latter issue, her work has influenced my thinking for decades. I strongly support her overall aims to make feminist theory pluralistic, to make women of color visible, and to push white feminists and men of color (I would add white men) to appreciate more fully the importance of work done by and the interests of women of color. I explain later the ways in which my work supports Lugones's aims.

In "Purity, Impurity, and Separation," Lugones develops a frame-work built on the contrast between the logics of "purity/splitting" and "impurity/curdling." The logic of purity/splitting encompasses domi-nance, control, hierarchy, categorizing, and selves that are either unified, fragmented, or both. In this view, "unification and homogeneity are related principles of ordering the social world" (2003, 127). This logic fragments the identities of women of color. The contrasting logic of impurity/curdling resists intersected oppressions, sees that the social world is "complex and heterogeneous and each person is multiple, non-fragmented, embodied" (2003, 127), and has "potential to germinate a nonoppressive pattern, a mestiza consciousness" (2003, 133).

The image that is most vivid is that of "curdle-separation" in contrast with "split-separation." Lugones draws on our knowledge of emulsions: if mayonnaise is curdled, the egg yolk, oil, and water are not separated cleanly and completely; instead "they coalesce toward oil or toward water...[there are] matter[s] of different degrees of coalescence....you are left with yolky oil and oily yolk." (2003, 122). If curdled mayonnaise is beyond a reader's grasp, Lugones offers another image of "impurity": our frequent inability to separate the two parts of an egg completely. We leave some yolk in the egg white. Curdle-separation is the act of a subject resisting the logic of purity. It gives a way to characterize the identity of *la mestiza* and the nature of mestiza consciousness. Lugones, of course, acknowledges that she is writing within the mestiza tradition of Gloria Anzaldúa and others (see Moraga 1983, Anzaldúa 1987). For our discussion here, it is important to note that curdled identities are intersectional identities, but not split or fragmented identities. A passage from Anzaldúa is illustrative of curdled identities that are misperceived by others as fragmented or split:

> I am a wind-swayed bridge, a crossroads inhabited by whirlwinds.... What am I? *A third world lesbian feminist with Marxist and mystic leanings.* They would chop me up into little fragments and tag each piece with a label.... One foot on brown soil, one on white, one in straight society, one in the gay world, the man's world, the women's, one limb in the literary world, another in the working class.... Who, me confused? Ambivalent? Not so. Only your labels split me. (1983, 205)

We need to be explicit about the relation between intersectionality and Lugones's concepts. That oppressions intersect is a necessary condition for (or an assumption of) Lugones's analysis. Nevertheless, she usually speaks in more specific terms. Oppressions that are *interlocking* are part of the logic of purity that fragments people; they require that fragments are "unified, fixed, atomistic, bounded...."(2003, 231, n. 1).[23] They do not change the nature of what is interlocked. In contrast, *intermeshed* or *enmeshed* oppressions more closely approach the logic of impurity/curdling she uses—although a "mesh is still too much separability." (2003, 231, n. 1). Although I cannot discuss her theory of resistance here, resisting multiple oppressions is central to Lugones's long-term work. It is important to note that curdle-separation resists both interlocking and intermeshed oppressions.

In "Heterosexualism and the Colonial/Modern Gender System," Lugones weaves together two frameworks: the coloniality of power, as exemplified in the work of Anibal Quijano (1991, 2000a, 2000b, 2001–2002), and theories emphasizing intersectionality that detail the exclusion of women of color and Third World women from "liberatory struggles in the name of women," work done primarily by Third World feminists and women of color feminists or critical race theorists (Lugones, 2007, 189). This essay and Lugones's larger project of decolonial feminism pose complications for my view of intersectionality.

Lugones offers an historicized analysis that includes gender oppression, heterosexualism, racial classification/oppression, colonialism, and capitalism as "impossible to understand apart from each other" (Lugones, 2007, 187). I focus here on her view that colonial/modern power and the colonial/modern gender system mutually constitute each other. Lugones states: "Colonialism did not impose precolonial, European gender arrangements on the colonized. It imposed a new gender system that created very different arrangements for colonized males and females than for white bourgeois colonizers. Thus it introduced many genders and gender itself as a colonial concept and mode of organization of relations of production, property relations, of cosmologies and ways of knowing" (2007, 186).

Lugones explains the "light" and "dark" sides of gender in the colonial/modern gender system, drawing on work by Quijano, Oyerónké Oyéwumi (1997), and Paula Gunn Allen (1986/1992) among others. The "light side" includes "biological dimorphism, heterosexualism, and patriarchy" (Lugones 2007, 190) and applies only to the gender of the colonizers. Women on the "light side" are thought to be fragile and sexually passive (2007, 203). The gender characteristics on the "dark side" result from white colonists' need for many kinds of labor coupled with their fears of the sexuality of the native people. Indigenous people were thought to be intersexed or hermaphrodites with both penises and breasts (2007, 195), with their sexuality characterized in animalistic terms (2007, 203). Colonized women were thought to be sexually aggressive, sometimes perverse, and capable of doing any kind of labor (2007, 203).

On these bases, Lugones maintains that the colonized women and colonizers' women have different genders. They are parts of different systems of distinctions. All are different from precolonial Yoruban society as explained by Oyéwumi (1997). Oyéwumi says that the Yoruba categories of *obinrin* and *okunrin* are mischaracterized by using "female/woman" and "male/man." Instead the terms "*obinrin*" and "*okunrin*" refer to only anatomical features: she uses the terms "anafemale" and "anamale" (1997, 32–34). She maintains that gender was not an organizing principle for the Yoruba until colonial powers imposed it. The distinction between *obinrin* and *okunrin* is "one of reproduction, not one of sexuality or gender" (1997, 37). Her claim that gender is absent rests on her identification of gender with social categories containing hierarchy or binary opposition (1997, 34), neither of which she finds in the relation of anamales and anafemales. She offers detailed explanations of the mistaken attribution of gender in various social contexts in Yoruban life by other scholars—usually anthropologists, both feminist and nonfeminist. She finds hierarchy among the Yoruba, but it is based on seniority and is context relative.

Although there are no doubt many controversial issues in Oyéwumi's account, it is at least inspiring to think about a culture in which physical

reproductive differences played a minor role in social organization—
whether or not Oyéwumi's denial of gender is precisely correct (or relies
too heavily on her definition of gender). But even if Oyéwumi is wrong
and there were precolonial genders among the Yoruba, Lugones can still
make a point about the existence of multiple gender systems. She will
need to clarify the sense in which "gender itself as a colonial concept"
(2007, 186), the ways that gender and colonial/modern power constitute
each other or fuse, and the ways that the imposed systems relate to the
Yoruban precolonial gender system. Assuming she can do this successfully, then she can increase the number of genders from four to at least
six: at least two precolonial genders and two others imposed by the colonizers, all of which are different from the Europeans' own two genders.
However, what is more important here than the precise number of genders, four or six, is that colonial/modern force imposed a different and
very vicious set of rules and norms on indigenous men and women than
on themselves, that the Yoruban anafemales became inferior in all spheres
of life (cognitive, economic, political, as well as control over reproduction),
and that the process was accomplished with the cooperation of the
Yoruban anamales (Lugones, 2007, 198). It is these truths that require
continued feminist focus.

   Because I focus on the roles that intersectionality plays in Lugones's
position, I cannot do justice here to her very rich project. Her exploration
of mutually constructed colonial/modern intersections promises to
expand feminist thinking.[24] Her position relies on intersectionality, as did
her position in "Purity, Impurity, and Separation"; not surprisingly,
Lugones again advocates the need to avoid separability in the intersection
(2007, 193). Avoiding separability here is not expressed in terms of "cur-
dling"; instead it means that systems of oppression, namely, colonial/
modern power and the colonial/modern gender system (along with heterosexualism, racial classification/oppression, and capitalism), literally
constitute each other and cannot be understood apart from each other.
This is a strong position.

   Lugones explicitly addresses the relation of intersectionality (as conceived by Crenshaw) to Quijano's structural axes such as colonial/modern
power:

   I think the logic of "structural axes" does more and less than intersectionality. Intersectionality reveals what is not seen when categories such as
   gender and race are conceptualized as separate from each other. The move
   to intersect the categories has been motivated by the difficulties in making

visible those who are dominated and victimized in terms of both categories. . . . It becomes logically clear then that the logic of categorical separation [the logic that identifies women with white bourgeois women, blacks with black heterosexual men, etc.] distorts what exists at the intersection, such as violence against women of color. Given the construction of the categories, the intersection misconstrues women of color. So, once intersectionality shows us what is missing, we have ahead of us the task of reconceptualizing the logic of the intersection so as to avoid separability. It is only when we perceive gender and race as intermeshed or fused that we actually see women of color. (2007, 192–93)

Using Lugones's own terminology, I want to sort out four positions to help us determine whether there is any leeway in the kinds of analysis that make women of color visible, and whether intersectionality remains part of the logic of purity. These positions include those that Lugones rejects as well as the one that she holds.

A.   The most "pure" position within the *logic of purity* conceptualizes categories of oppression in ways that do not allow for differences within categories such as gender or race. It cannot distinguish "transparent" interests (those of the dominant group within a category, for example, straight Black men among Blacks) and "thick" interests of those who are marginalized within that group, for example, Black women, gay Black people of either gender (Lugones 2003, 140–41). This position is often identified with essentialism of some kind and with "pop-bead" metaphysics. It is difficulties in positions of this kind that lead to the need for intersectional analyses.

B.   Views that focus on *multiple oppressions* and *multiple jeopardies* of women of color are precursors to intersectional analyses; however, these analyses do not explore the inseparability of the intersections in a way that moves nearly far enough toward Lugones's goal. In fact, they might not even speak in terms of interactions or intersections. Lugones's other views imply that this kind of position is still part of the logic of purity.

C.   *Intersectionality of interlocked oppressions* does not change the nature of what is interlocked: for example, in this view racism is not mutually constructed by patriarchy or heterosexualism, nor are identities curdled. Lugones sees this kind of position as part of the logic of purity.

However, although the natures of the interlocked oppressions have not changed, even this kind of intersectionality takes extremely important steps toward making the "thick" interests of Black women or Latina lesbians visible. The point of Crenshaw's original intersectional analysis and examples were to do precisely this (1989, 1991). Something similar could be said about Collins's analyses (1990). And as we have seen from the uptake on early intersectional analyses over two decades, they were effective theoretically by helping to break down essentialism, and effective practically by encouraging complex institutional changes to benefit the lives of women of color, for example, in programs of domestic violence. My own sense is that there is a very big difference between "pre-intersectionality" purity of categories (pop-beads, essentialism, and so on) and "post-Crenshaw-intersectionality" categories of oppression and identity. The latter categories do not continue to imply essentialism, even if they are not themselves as "impure" as Lugones desires. They also encourage, as Lugones repeatedly recognizes, continued explorations in the right locations. So even if intersectionality of interlocking oppressions does not go as far as Lugones wants toward her view that women of color can be seen only by perceiving "gender and race as intermeshed or fused" (2007, 193), it is important to acknowledge how extensively it moved feminists both in theory and in practice.[25]

D. *Mutually constituted and fused oppressions:* This is Lugones's considered view that I explained above—joining together the tradition of intersectional analyses with Quijano's analysis of the modern coloniality of power. The conceptual content at the intersections explains the inseparability of oppressions. The logic of impurity reigns.

4. MY VIEW: FAMILY RESEMBLANCE INTERSECTIONALITY

Where does my view of intersectionality fit into these four positions? The short answer is between (C) and (D): intersecting oppressions change each other, but are not necessarily fused. My framework pairs intersectionality with a Wittgenstinian family resemblance analysis of the "identity categories"—the approach I find most appropriate for thinking about women, men, Latinos, Anglos, gay men, or transwomen. Take women as an example. A family resemblance view acknowledges that although there is nothing—neither a property, an experience, nor an interest—that all women have in common, we know what a woman is and who women are because of crisscrossing, overlapping characteristics that are clear within social contexts.[26] In this way, we can say that women share a gender (or that woman is a gender). Of course, the contexts as well as the properties, characteristics, and gendered roles are all intersectional. Race, sexual orientation, class, and so on are part of the family resemblance analysis of woman. Similarly, gender, sexual orientation, and class are part of the family resemblance analysis of African-American. We should not take "resemblance" too literally or narrowly; our terms are not merely "descriptive" here. For example, suppose a feminist wants to argue that subordination in a hierarchy or other prescriptive features are important to a characterization of women; these would be fine in my analysis.[27] Family resemblances can, I believe, be much messier and more politically laden than any of Wittgenstein's own examples of games or numbers.

I have argued elsewhere that a position that pairs a family resemblance analysis with intersectionality can accommodate a wide variety of feminist positions, is anti-essentialist without the need to argue against the existence of categories in a thoroughly postmodern manner, gives us a strategy to answer the most problematic objections to intersectionality, and provides plausible accounts of women for everyday politics (Garry 2008a, 2008b). It is also very useful in my argument here against Lugones's position that women have many genders. In terms of political metaphysics, it falls between a view such as Naomi Zack's, which requires that women have a disjunctive nominal essence to ground inclusive feminism, and views that thoroughly critique identity categories or advocate a "solidarity" view of feminism not based on identities at all.[28]

I discuss only two issues here: I first argue that my position is not part of the logic of purity and so, although more open-ended than Lugones's position, is compatible with some facets of it.[29] Then I turn to the question, "How many genders do women have?" in order to see whether an intersectional family resemblance account or a multiple genders account better serves Lugones's (and feminism's) overall aims.

My commitment is to a framework in which intersecting oppressions are mutually shaped and changed rather than to any particular substantive analysis in the intersections. Lugones's project shapes the substantive analysis in more detail. My terms are weaker than Lugones's; for example, I say that gender oppression works through and is shaped by racism, classism, or heterosexualism. Mutual construction seems to be a good way to state their relations in many circumstances (although Lugones might not agree with my usage). In any case, she uses a variety of expressions including "co-construction," "mutual constitution," and "fusion" apparently inter-changeably (2007). I do not interchange the terms because fusion seems the most restrictive and, although it is harder to argue for it, I hear a nuanced difference between co-constructing and mutually constituting race and gender as well. As fruitful as I find Lugones's discussion of fused categories, I want to leave open the possibility of a wider range of relations among oppressions.

I worry about how many kinds of oppression must mutually construct each other at once (not to mention fuse), how these will vary from case to case, and the multiple, precise ways they apply in our lives. Recall an example I used earlier: economic discrimination against gay couples is much more thoroughly intersectional than is legal discrimination against their marry-ing. In general, I want to be able to (i) claim that most of the time oppres-sions are inseparable in individual people's lives (though not necessarily to the same degree in every single instance), and (ii) state the conceptual rela-tions among oppressions in such a way that we leave open to be explored the details of lives and experiences in the intersections. Although oppres-sions *might be* conceptually fused from the start, the fact that they are enmeshed in people's lives does not necessitate their antecedent conceptual fusion.[30]

Let me explain briefly why my view of intersectionality is not linked to Lugones's logic of purity. In addition to my explicit statements that the categories are in fact changed by intersecting, there is a simple logical point. The fact that a logic of purity *can* use intersectional analyses of certain kinds (interlocking oppressions) does not imply that intersec-tionality *must* be part of the logic of purity. Intersectionality is useful within both curdled and pure logics.[31]

Although Lugones says that "the intersection misconstrues women of color" (2007, 193), she also realizes that intersectional analyses move at least part way out of the logic of purity to set the stage—give necessary conditions—for intermeshed oppressions that are resisted in impure/curdled logic as well as for the fusion of the colonial/modern gender/power system. Granted that intersectionality (with or without family resemblances) does not entail either of Lugones's analyses, it can still be consistent with the direction she wants to go. What's important for Lugones's position on intersectionality is that oppressions not be thought of as unchanged or separated. My account and hers do not differ in this regard.

We must also not be misled into thinking that an intersectional anal-ysis, whether mine or anyone else's, is part of the logic of purity because of the way it retains the terminology of race, gender, class, and so forth. We do not imply that categories are static or have internal homogeneity simply by using the term "gender" or "class." Given that we must have some way to speak of the factors that intersect, mutually construct each other, or even fuse, we simply speak in the everyday terms available to us.

Let us turn to the final issue of the number of genders that women have. I address it here because critics of intersectionality such as Zack appeal to theoretical and political fragmentation resulting from women's allegedly multiple genders as a reason to repudiate intersectional analyses (Zack 2005). As an advocate of intersectionality, I aim to clear away this avenue of critique so that a broad range of people can feel comfortable developing intersectional analyses.

Zack argues that intersectional theories are harmful because they fragment feminist theory and solidarity. Specifically, she maintains (i) that intersectionality entails that each ethnic group of women has a different gender, and (ii) that this proliferation of genders promotes both *theoretical fragmentation* (because each "virtually incommensurable" group can produce theories applicable only to itself) and *political fragmentation* that can easily preclude "common goals as well as basic empathy" (2005, 7–8). She visualizes segregated groups of feminists engaging in "parallel play" unable to find common ground (2005, 7).

I disagree with all of these claims, but because my principal dialogue here is with Lugones rather than Zack, I must be brief. Against claim (i) I offer my family resemblance approach. In addition, if each new intersection of ethnicity and gender constitutes a different gender, it obscures intersectionality's conceptual logic and makes it harder to explain how ethnicity affects one's gendered experience. Nevertheless, Lugones (unlike many other advocates of intersectionality) would agree with claim (i).

Both clauses in claim (ii) are highly controversial. However, we can construct weaker, more plausible claims: that multiplying genders *can encourage* theoretical and political fragmentation or that there is *a risk* that postulating multiple genders for women can lead to fragmentation. If one believes that ontological, conceptual, or linguistic framing influences theory construction and politics at all, one could not deny that there is at least *a risk* of theoretical fragmentation here.[32] If we have an alternative position that avoids this risk, it makes sense to use it. Why take a chance with a more risky position?

Lugones's position is exactly the kind that Zack believes promotes fragmentation: colonized women have a different gender from European women; women from different ethnic groups have different genders.

I aim to avoid a Zack–Lugones dispute by changing the terms of the discussion to family resemblances.

One advantage of coupling intersectionality with a family resemblance analysis is precisely to have a framework that can block the implication that differences among women mean that we cannot share the gender woman. Theory fragmentation does not get off the ground because we are women in virtue of the crisscrossing resemblances, similarities, reasons for places in the hierarchies of power, possible relations to reproduction, and so on. This precludes neither "opting out" nor borderline or ambiguous cases; indeed, we should have troublesome cases because binary gender systems are problematic on many grounds.[33] Family resemblances can easily accommodate Lugones's analyses of curdle-separation and curdled identities, for nothing precludes curdled family resemblances or curdled identities among women. No purity is needed in family resemblances. Lugones wants to give visibility to women of color—to their resistance to the logic of purity and to their previously "thick" interests. A family resemblance analysis can support her aims.

However, Lugones's discussion of the fused colonial/modern/ gender/power analysis moves in a different direction from a family resemblance analysis. Of course, we could stretch a family resemblance analysis to the point that a precolonial Yoruban anafemale (regardless of everything else about her life and experience) will be in the same gender as a European woman colonizer by noting that they have in common one of the many characteristics of the gender woman—they are both the kind of human being who typically can give birth. However, since Lugones takes there to be no precolonial Yoruban gender at all, there is no conceptual space for woman in this picture. Unless I am prepared to mount both a conceptual and empirical argument against Oyéwùmi's account of the absence of gender (including the way it was based on making hierarchy part of the definition of gender), I cannot simply insert a family resemblance gender concept into it. If the reader will allow a bit more Wittgenstein, we can say that gender makes sense within certain forms of life (common as they are). In Oyéwùmi's account, the precolonial Yoruba did not have such a form of life.

When the concept of gender clearly enters the picture, mutually constructed with race and modern colonial power, Lugones can speak of different genders for the colonizers and the colonized, but does not necessarily need to do so. I understand her motivation for postulating four genders, but since a move that proliferates genders is open to Zack's fragmentation objection, let us try to accommodate Lugones's central points without proliferation. If we speak in terms of family resemblances among the colonized women and the European women, it could actually illuminate rather than disguise both the hierarchies of power and the mutual construction of modern colonial power, race, and gender by pointing to the extreme differences among the characteristics of European women and colonized women (for example, in the norms for their sexual behavior and their labor). There is no need for these women to occupy different genders in order to explain the male colonizers' motivation or implementation of different norms and expectations for different groups of women within the hierarchies they imposed. Nor do multiple genders for women help to explain the relations of dependency that the European women have on the colonized women.

Of course, I cannot talk Lugones out of multiple genders. They are integral to her decolonial feminist project (see Lugones 2010). Lugones is likely to reject Zack's critique as part of the logic of purity because Zack uses nominal essences to overcome fragmentation among women. Both Zack and Lugones want to overcome fragmentation, but focus on different kinds. Zack does not want women as a group fragmented—severed from each other theoretically or politically. Lugones opposes fragmenting or splitting the elements in identities of women of color. She maintains that white women are already split from women of color and tend not see them. So Lugones tries to make visible women of color (with coherent, nonfragmented, but multiple identities as well as agency that resists oppression) and to make intelligible the reasons for their current invisibility. I interpret Lugones as taking a step toward solidarity, toward improving empathy among women. Zack is unlikely to agree; she would reject it as a wrong-headed way to go about it. One might think that Zack would find my approach more amenable because I place women in one gender, a move that should promote empathy as well as theoretical cohesion. However, Zack also rejects family resemblances, although I do not know whether she would consider them a lesser evil than multiple genders.[34]

It is clear, I hope, that my family resemblance approach supports Lugones's overall aims despite my disagreement with her on the number of genders women have. If we speak as if women have one gender (*not* defined in terms of a single kind of hierarchy) and use intersectional family resemblances, we can discuss the intermeshed, mutually constructed systems of oppression and encompass the enormous variations in their characteristics, roles, and experiences. I believe that it is an asset, not a liability, that this view is almost as wide-ranging as Lugones's is. Yet because it stops with family resemblances, and does not take Lugones's step to multiple genders, we can stop theory fragmentation and proliferation and have an anti-essentialist flexible framework from which to think about women's lives. Lugones and I will still disagree about how widely we can apply "woman" because she means literally that gender is a colonial concept (2007, 186). In any case, the historical and contemporary varieties of intersectional gender systems offer plenty to keep feminist theorists busy.[35]

My view also has a communicative advantage over Lugones's because I use everyday terminology in both theoretical and practical contexts. Even if ordinary language is rightly considered conservative, being able to explain "the diverse and sometimes contradictory interests of women" (or even "curdled identities of women") in everyday speech has a better chance of success than a theoretical approach that eschews our standard uses of "woman" or "gender."[36] In fact, without everyday concepts it is more difficult to explain the ways in which oppressions intersect and to express or even locate our intersecting identities. As noted earlier, we are not necessarily using the logic of purity if we say that a bit of stability in terminology, especially terminology that people already understand, can be valuable in explaining how differing by race, class, or sexual orientation changes women's lives. Consider the example of an Ecuadorian woman of European ancestry who moves to Chicago. In Ecuador she was a member of the dominant group; in Chicago she might well be thought of by feminist theorists as a woman of color (she might or might not also think of herself that way). I find it neither plausible nor useful to think that she changes genders by moving to Chicago. Instead, understanding her situation requires attention to the intersecting changes that her gender and her move from dominant group to immigrant group have on each other. Creating a new gender for each new intersection does nothing in itself to help us explore the intersection. Instead, intersectional analysis becomes more difficult without this bit of conceptual stability to express the Ecuadorian woman's intersectional life changes.[37]

Nevertheless, there is a serious downside to my strategy. If women from many different groups share a gender, we must constantly be vigilant to keep dominant (for our purposes, white or Western) women de-centered, off center stage—historically, now, and in the future. Otherwise we cannot construct pluralist, inclusive feminist theory. I know this will be difficult; we are battling not only history, but also the perceived self-interest of certain white women. However, it is very powerful for women of color to refuse to let white women "own" a gender that is not white women's to own. My account recognizes that exploring the many specific historical and contemporary intersections requires hard, fascinating work of exploration and analysis. White women's lives are likely to be irrelevant to these explorations and analyses.

I understand the appeal of Lugones's multiple genders: we can de-center white women by excluding them from the analyses of other women's genders; we make women of color visible; and we can attend to the details of intermeshed (fused) oppressions in their lives in specific historical contexts. This approach speaks to the worry that a family resemblance framework could dilute the experience of colonized women and women of color.[38] Although it makes sense to worry, being alert to this possibility is not the same as prejudging the results of intersectional analyses. I think the best plan is to remember that exploring intersections in their specificity is an empirical activity. Of course, we will have some theoretical framework or strategy within which we do it, but both Lugones's and mine allow specificity to flourish. And both of us need to speak about the relations among women—in whatever terms we choose to do it.

I also understand the pull of saying that different gender systems imply different genders. However, I do not think we are required to say it without considering the costs, namely, the likely promotion of theory fragmentation, and the conceptual problem concerning how multiple and shifting genders will intermesh with other axes of oppression. Because both Lugones's account and mine encourage exploration of the intersections that result from mutually constructed categories, and because an intersectional family resemblance concept of women is designed to increase, not decrease, the visibility of women of color, I do not think we have to choose between prioritizing the experiences and lives of women of color and having coherent, flexible concepts that end theoretical fragmentation and simplify communication.

5. FINAL REMARKS

I have advised caution lest we overextend or expect too much of the concept of intersectionality. It is neither a methodology nor a theory of power or oppression. It provides a framework or strategy for thinking about issues, a set of reminders to look at a wider range of oppressions and privileges to consider their mutual construction or at least their intermeshing (if these are different). The hard work is in digging into the details of the ways that the full range of oppressions and privileges interact in our societies, lives, and theories. In order to encourage this hard work and the use of an intersectional framework, I have undertaken the tasks below in this essay:

- To convince philosophers that intersectional thinking is important for many reasons, both philosophical and political.
- To convince feminist philosophers that intersectional analyses are the best strategy we have at the moment for developing truly pluralistic and inclusive feminist philosophy.
- To assure all readers that intersectionality, especially when paired with family resemblances, is a safe and useful strategy or tool without dangerous implications of gender proliferation or theory fragmentation.
- To support Lugones's aims to increase the visibility of women of color and to create pluralist feminist theory at the same time that I disagree with her position on multiple genders.

Notes

My thanks go especially to Alison Bailey and Talia Bettcher for comments on this paper and for several years of very enlightening conversations and sharing their work, and more recently to Anna Carastathis, Sharon Crasnow, Sally Markowitz, Diana Meyers, Anita Superson, and reviewers for *Hypatia*. Sections of this paper or its forbearers were presented at conferences of the Society for Analytic Philosophy (2008), Feminist Ethics and Social Theory (FEAST) (2009), National Women's Studies Association (NWSA) (2009), and the Critical Race Studies Symposium at UCLA Law School (2010). An abbreviated version appeared in *Hypatia* 26:4 (2011).

1. This is Judith Butler's expression (1999, 182), but my point in this footnote is not related to her. In the original intersectional analyses given by African-American women and other women of color, the central kinds of oppression were race and gender (see note 3 below). Then, over time, the kinds of oppressions/privileges that are mentioned and become salient on the list change with the context of consideration. For example, colonialism, nationalism, disability, immigration status, age, or religion might be at least as important in some contexts as the ones mentioned in the text. We should also remember that oppression due to gender (gender identity and expression) encompasses transgender oppression as well as sexism. The general move is to "ask the other question" (Matsuda 1996, 64) in order to understand what oppressions are interwoven.
2. My hope for philosophy is consistent with what Anna Stubblefield calls "postsupremacist philosophy" (2005).

3. Some trace intersectional thinking to Anna Julia Cooper (1892). Nevertheless, two early essays of Kimberlé Crenshaw (1989, 1991) strongly influenced thinking about intersectionality in contemporary feminist theory and critical race theory. "Demarginalizing the Intersection of Race and Sex: A Black Feminist Critique of Antidiscrimination Doctrine, Feminist Theory and Antiracist Politics" (1989) concerned compounded discrimination in seniority-based layoffs, promotions, and awards of back pay. In her 1991 essay, "Mapping the Margins: Intersectionality, Identity Politics, and Violence against Women of Color," Crenshaw explains the ways in which intersectionality helps us to understand and better address violence against women of color. The women of color discourse that immediately preceded and surrounded intersectionality includes, for example, "The Combahee River Collective Statement" (1978), reprinted in Barbara Smith (1983) (now widely available on the internet); bell hooks (1981, 1984); Gloria Hull et al. (1982); Cherríe Moraga and Gloria Anzaldúa (1983); Anzaldúa (1987); Deborah King (1988); Elizabeth Spelman (1988); Patricia Hill Collins (1990); Mari Matsuda (1996).

4. Alison Bailey, also an advocate of intersectionality, analogizes its status as a tool to a spell checker (2009). I would say a "framework checker"—if only our software had such a thing! More on this point later.

5. From this point on, I speak in terms of traditional and feminist philosophers rather than broader disciplinary groups. Most of the points I make are relevant to wider groups, including activists as well as scholars, but brevity beckons.

6. Initially, intersectionality and related concepts concerned only oppressions, not privileges (and only gender and race, but it's usually not controversial to include other oppressions). Still today the major focus of intersectional analysis is, quite rightly, on oppressions and multiply oppressed people. María Lugones puts it nicely: "Though everyone in capitalist Eurocentered modernity is both raced and gendered, not everyone is dominated or victimized in terms of their race or gender" (2007, 192). Jennifer Nash addresses as an open question whether intersectionality "is a theory of marginalized subjectivity or a general theory of identity" (2008, 10). Ange-Marie Hancock advocates mainstreaming intersectional methods to include dominant groups (2007a); Rita Dhamoon has worries about this strategy, including that to do so might weaken intersectionality's central focus of critique (2008). One reason that I believe it is important to include privilege is that if the analysis overlooks the fact that men are gendered, white people have a race, and straight people have a sexual orientation, those in dominant groups are more likely to remain in denial (or ignorance) of their privileged statuses and to continue to marginalize "the others" in thinking about the categories. I will say more later about why the move to include privilege helps to overcome certain objections to intersectionality.

7. My use of "naturalized" is both broad and weak. Philosophers who engage in naturalized forms of epistemology, metaphysics, ethics, etc., believe that empirical evidence/facts about human beings and the world are relevant to doing normative philosophy. So, for example, understanding how people can and do act, acquire beliefs and moral emotions, and develop a sense of self would all be relevant to philosophy.

8. I sincerely hope that they do not need to work through all of this step by step, but I cannot help thinking of Wittgenstein's remark in *Zettel*: "In philosophizing we may not terminate a disease of thought. It must run its natural course, and slow cure is all important. (That is why mathematicians are such bad philosophers.)" (1967, #382). I am hoping that the "natural course" of this disease has already run long enough.

9. I know of no traditional philosopher, and very few feminist philosophers, who have attempted this. One related example in feminist philosophy is Diana Meyers's "Intersectional Identity and the Authentic Self" (2000), which considers the impact that intersectional identities make on philosophical treatments of autonomy. In the course of it she reexamines notions of self-knowledge, self-definition, authenticity, and so on. It is a big, complex job! Charles Mills, who has written widely on race, has a chapter, "Intersecting Contracts" (2007).

10. Helpful suggestions on race can be found, for example, in Mills (1997, 1998), Yancy (2004), Stubblefield (2005), and Bailey (2010).

11. In *Epistemic Injustice*, Miranda Fricker introduces the terms "testimonial injustice" for the ways credibility is deflated by prejudice and "hermeneutical injustice" for disadvantages experienced by not having "collective interpretive resources... [to make sense] of their social experiences" (2007, 1). Kristie Dotson (2011) lays out practices of silencing testimony.

12. "Pop-bead" metaphysics is Spelman's expression (1988). Authors in the tradition being referred to in this paragraph are cited in note 4 above.

13. On arrogant perception, see Lugones (2003, 77–100) and Frye (1983, 66–72).

14. In note 23 below, I mention a position that identifies relationality among women with "interlocking oppressions" rather than with intersectionality (Razack 1998). However, I do not use Razack's distinction in this essay. Bailey (2009) and others agree with my use here.

15. Social scientists are particularly interesting on this topic, for example, McCall (2005) and Nash (2008). Political scientist Hancock argues that it should be thought of as a normative and empirical research paradigm (2007a, 2007b). I noticed in conversation with feminist political scientists at NWSA (November 2009) that they call "intersectional methods" what I term "strategies or methods that support an intersectional framework." For example, we need to note who is left out at the policy table or not called to testify in front of Congress or the FDA about women's reproductive health, and then attend to the positions of those who have been excluded. Social scientists at NWSA also spoke of intersectionality's being

a "paradigm shift." I believe that this is not a technical Kuhnian use of the term, but a way to claim emphatically that we must start thinking very differently to do intersectional work.

16. In fairness, one might want to explore whether it *should* be such a theory. For example, see Anna Carastathis (2008) and Wendy Brown (1997) on the problems with intersectionality's not being or having a theory of power or oppression. I should acknowledge that there are a number of critiques of intersectionality that I have not engaged at all here or elsewhere. They deserve to be considered carefully. For example, see Carastathis (2008 and n.d.), Brown (1997).

17. Nash believes that intersectionality will need to provide both of these (2008).

18. On (i) see Butler (1999) and Brown (1997), on (ii) Carastathis (2008), and on (iii) Lugones (2003 and 2007). Because I return to Lugones later, but not to the others, let me note here that even those who believe that subjects are constituted through regulatory power still often note the mixtures of various kinds of power in terms of race, gender, etc., so proceed on a path in some ways analogous to intersectional analyses.

19. For example, gay transpeople who want to marry are affected by heterosexualism/oppression. In addition, heterosexualism mixed with sexism probably motivates much opposition to same-sex marriage.

    S. Laurel Weldon is among the other theorists who support great flexibility in thinking about the empirical details of intersectionality and other relationships of structural oppressions, e.g., multiplicative, additive, or autonomous (Weldon 2006).

20. "Or both" was not in the original essay, but was added as clarification at some point in the many reprintings of the 1989 essay, for example, in David Kairys (1998, 361). Crenshaw uses other variations on intersections and crossroads, including a crossroads image cited by Bailey (2009, 16) and Yuval-Davis (2006, 196): "The main highway is 'racism road'. One cross street can be Colonialism, then Patriarchy Street.... She has to deal not only with one form of oppression but with all forms, those named as road signs, which link together to make a double, a triple, multiple, a many layered blanket of oppression." [The original website with this passage is no longer available.] In a talk at U.C. Santa Barbara, Crenshaw spoke of the great depth of the multiple roads in the intersection—racism, sexism, heterosexualism, classism; she pictured contemporary issues and effects of these oppressions as the traffic that flows on the roads (2008). I am not totally satisfied that any of these images captures the ways the oppressions intermesh or mutually construct each other.

21. It is not that Crenshaw lacks vertical imagery; it is just that it doesn't transfer well to an explanation of intersectionality. Her other image in her 1989 essay is vertical—the narrow door in the floor through which those with the fewest disadvantages (standing on the shoulders of others) can climb through into the non-oppressive space, for example by affirmative

action. Carastathis (n.d.) has an excellent critique of horizontal imagery and discussion of Crenshaw. My concerns are somewhat different from hers.

22. Collins uses the language of intersectionality as well as the matrix of domination; the images do not seem to compete in her eyes (1993/2008). Although it is tempting to run through possible permutations of Collins's matrix image, I will instead make only a few points about it. If the matrix is at least three-dimensional rather than flat, this is already an advantage. But it would be a mistake to visualize this matrix with straight lines at right angles because this doesn't capture the ways in which oppressions and privileges intersect. If I were to rely on a matrix image, I would move quickly to a tangled ball of many strands of yarn, some of which are themselves woven together. In addition, the issue of the kinds of agency that are possible within different points on the matrix complicates the problem further.

23. Two points here about "interlocking oppressions." First, Lugones says in this same endnote that "interlocking does not alter the monadic nature of the things interlocked. In Elizabeth Spelman's words, it does not trouble the 'pop bead' metaphysics (Spelman 1988:15)" (Lugones 2003, 231, n.1). I appreciate Lugones's point here, but I think that even a *minimal* intersectional analysis such as interlocking oppressions takes decisive steps to undermine "pop bead" metaphysics simply by questioning essentialism. ("Essentialism" can mean many things. I use it here to refer to positions of the following kinds: (i) that there is a set of necessary and sufficient conditions for the application of a concept such as woman, or (ii) that there is a set of experiences that women universally share.)

    Second, although Lugones refers briefly in this same endnote (2003, 231, n.1) to transnational or postcolonial contexts, she does not make explicit the extent to which she means to engage transnational feminist/anti-racist discussions of interlocking oppressions *in their own terms*. There is more work to be done here for many reasons, not the least of which is that terms are given different meanings by different writers. For example, Sherene Razack's use of "interlocking" is different from Lugones's. Razack states, "I use the word interlocking rather than intersecting to describe how the systems of oppression are connected. Intersecting remains a word that describes discrete systems whose paths cross. I suggest that the systems *are* each other and that they give content to each other" (Razack 2007, 343). And: "Analytical tools that consist of looking at how systems of oppression interlock differ in emphasis from those that stress intersectionality. Interlocking systems need one another, and in tracing the complex ways in which they help to secure one another, we learn how women are produced into positions that exist symbiotically but hierarchically [e.g., domestic workers and professional women]" (Razack 1998, 13).

24. Lugones understands her 2007 essay as the beginning of a larger decolonial feminist project that requires detailed work with historically specific

concepts, immersion in nonwestern ontologies/frameworks, collaboration among researchers, and so on (2007, 207 and conversation at NWSA 2009). In this way, women as historical subjects become visible. Lugones further develops her view in "Toward a Decolonial Feminism," published after I wrote this essay (Lugones 2010). Her 2010 essay helps us understand more fully the meaning of her 2007 statement that gender is a colonial concept (2007, 186).

25. Two points. First, I take Lugones to be critical of Crenshaw from her claim in the passage quoted, "Given the construction of the categories, the intersection misconstrues women of color" (2007, 193). However, nothing in my essay hangs on whether Lugones intends to place Crenshaw explicitly in "the logic of purity." Second, see note 23 above concerning differing uses of "interlocking."

26. Wittgenstein uses the term "family resemblance" to evoke the wide variety of kinds of resemblances among family members: those who share coloring might not have similar chins or noses; others share only a chin; still others share temperament but no physical features (1958, § 67). In the preceding section, Wittgenstein illustrates his position about family resemblances by using the example of games (1958, § 66). We cannot give a set of properties that are necessary and sufficient for something's being a game, but game is still an important and useful concept with clear applications.

   If space permitted, it would be fruitful to analyze further the family resemblance metaphor. Both José Medina (2003) and Marilyn Frye (2011) provide useful work here (Frye includes as well Wittgenstein's image in PI § 67 of a spun thread of twisted fiber on fiber). Shelley Park pointed out in discussion (FEAST 2009) that since families are formed in a variety of ways, we need not focus only on "resemblances." I agree, and believe that Wittgenstein's talk of families of cases or of meanings is consistent with this strategy. Remember, too, that family resemblance concepts are sometimes called "cluster concepts" by others.

27. Other feminists have used a Wittgenstinian analysis of woman or gender, for example, Jacob Hale (1996), Cressida Heyes (2000), Hilde Lindemann Nelson (2002), and Natalie Stoljar (1995) in addition to Frye and Medina (see note 26). Unfortunately, I cannot take time to differentiate the ways in which my view differs from each of theirs. Linda Zerilli uses Wittgenstein's views in *On Certainty* to argue that feminists (and others) are held captive by a misleading picture of woman (1998). A "prescriptive" analysis is given by Alessandra Tanesini (1996). Concerning hierarchy, I am thinking of Sally Haslanger's definition of woman (2000) that includes systematic subordination. (However, I differ from Haslanger in that I would make systematic subordination merely one factor in a family resemblance analysis; Haslanger incorporates it into necessary and sufficient conditions.)

28. Zack's position is that "[a]ll women share the nonsubstantive, relational essence of being assigned to or identifying with the historical, socially constructed, disjunctive category of female birth designees, biological mothers,

or heterosexual choices of men—category FMP" (2005, 162). F=designated female at birth; M=biological mother; P=primary sexual choice of [heterosexual] men (2005, 8). Butler(1999) is among those offering a thoroughgoing critique of identity categories. An early "solidarity" approach is found in hooks (1984), and a recent one is in Carastathis (2008). An alternative strategy is Mikkola's: feminist politics can avoid definitions of "woman" and rely on our intuitions about the extension of "woman" (not the content of the concept) in order to explain on whose behalf feminists struggle (Mikkola 2009). Space does not permit engagement with the decades-long "essentialism" debate.

29. I was motivated to give this argument by comments of Alison Bailey.

30. Again, see Weldon 2006.

   One other difference between Lugones's view and mine is that I do not specifically focus on capitalism or the modern/coloniality of power in my characterization of intersectionality. They are obviously extremely important factors in oppression, ones to which we should all attend. Nevertheless, they are more central to Lugones's ongoing decolonial feminist project than to my much smaller project here—to make intersectionality plausible and useful.

31. Alison Bailey points out that because intersectionality is very useful in everyday politics to advance the interests of women of color, they would not reject it as a tool simply because it sometimes falls into a logic of purity (email correspondence, August 28, 2009). Bailey suggests that a "curdled approach" can see intersectionality as both curdled and pure. Lugones does, after all, see think that the two logics co-exist (Lugones 2003, 126).

32. I cannot enter into a full discussion of any of the following: the extent to which metaphysics can influence politics, factors that increase or undermine empathy, or thorough explanation or critique of Zack's argument (see Garry 2007, 2008a, 2008b for reasons to prefer my view to Zack's). If I could pursue Zack's claim (ii) here, I would start by noting the ways in which groups of women are, in fact, commensurable and that theorists can indeed go (and have gone) beyond their own group in constructing theories. I would also note that what promotes or undermines empathy is a complex empirical question. Metaphysics might well be relevant to it, but it is not likely to do all the heavy lifting! See Bailey's critique of Zack on empathy (Bailey 2009). I particularly like Bailey's statement, "It is not women's relations to the FMP category that are important; it is women's relationships to each other" (2009, 31). Note 28 above explains "FMP."

33. Although the binary gender system needs critique, I am not undertaking it here. It is important to note that a family resemblance analysis can be used with more than two genders. Some transpeople reject an identity within the binary gender system at all. So do some lesbians, for example, Wittig (1992) and Calhoun (1994). However, family resemblance analyses that give no special place to women's heterosexuality take away a principal

reason that lesbians advocate opting out of the category woman. Intersexuals have often been forced to adopt one of the binary gender identities.

34. Zack explicitly rejected my family resemblance analysis as a replacement for her own disjunctive nominal essences in remarks on a SWIP-sponsored panel on her book, *Inclusive Feminism* (2005), at the American Philosophical Association, Pacific Division meeting in March 2005.

35. One might wonder about an issue that is beyond the scope of this essay. Do I want to extend a family resemblance analysis (or a family resemblance analysis within forms of life) to gender systems or class systems, or systems of race-class-gender-sexual orientation? Yes. I do not know a better way to think about their relation to each other than this. Sally Markowitz is currently considering an approach along these lines (n.d.).

36. Mikkola makes a similar point (2009). In general, I think one needs a very good reason to use language in a revisionary (non-ordinary) way when doing feminist theory. In addition, it is extremely difficult not to rely on ordinary usage (that is, to smuggle it in) to support one's arguments. Although Lugones's 2010 essay is beyond the scope of this chapter, it presents a stark challenge to ordinary usage. She states, "The semantic consequence of the coloniality of gender is that 'colonized woman' is an empty category: no women are colonized; no colonized females are women" (Lugones 2010, 745). She advocates care in using "woman" and "man," wanting to "bracket them" when needed (2010, 749).

37. This point is somewhat modified from what I wrote in 2008: "Intersectionality need not multiply genders for each different ethnicity/race or social class; indeed, an intersectional analysis does not make sense if it does so. After all, gender, class, and race/ethnicity must intersect. The individual axes must have a least a minimal degree of stable meaning for the analysis to work. If every intersection produced a new gender or a new race (or both!), there would be no way to make sense of the ways in which ethnicity affects one's gendered experiences" (2008a, 616). This passage sounds misleadingly like "the logic of purity," which I did not intend.

38. Lugones expressed this worry to me in conversation at NWSA 2009.

References

Allen, Paula Gunn (1986/1992). *The Sacred Hoop: Recovering the Feminine in American Indian Tradition.* Boston: Beacon Press.

Anzaldúa, Gloria (1983). "La Prieta." In *This Bridge Called My Back*, 2nd ed. Ed. Cherríe Moraga and Gloria Anzaldúa. Watertown, Mass.: Persephone Press, 198–209.

——— (1987). *Borderlands/La Frontera: The New Mestiza.* San Francisco: Spinsters/Aunt Lute.

Bailey, Alison (2009). "On Intersectionality, Empathy, and Feminist Solidarity: A Reply to Naomi Zack." *Journal for Peace and Justice Studies* 19(1): 14–26.

————— (2010). "On Intersectionality and the Whiteness of Feminist Philosophy." In *The Center Must Not Hold: White Women on the Whiteness of Philosophy*. Ed. George Yancy. Totowa, N.J.: Rowman and Littlefield.

Brown, Wendy (1997). "The Impossibility of Women's Studies." *differences: A Journal of Feminist Cultural Studies* 9(3): 79–101.

Butler, Judith (1999). *Gender Trouble: Feminism and the Subversion of Identity*. New York: Routledge.

Calhoun, Cheshire (1994). "Separating Lesbian Theory from Feminist Theory." *Ethics* 104(3): 558–81.

Carastathis, Anna (2008). "The Invisibility of Privilege: A Critique of Intersectional Models of Identity." *Ateliers de l'éthique* 3(2): 23–28.

————— (n. d.). "Spatial Metaphors for Oppression: Intersectional and Hierarchy in Law, Feminist Theory and Practice." Typescript.

Collins, Patricia Hill (1990). *Black Feminist Thought: Knowledge, Consciousness, and the Politics of Empowerment*. New York: Routledge.

————— (1993). "Toward a New Vision: Race, Class, and Gender as Categories of Analysis and Connection." *Race, Sex, and Class* 1(1): 25–46. Reprinted in Ferber et al. 2008: 97–108. Page references are to Ferber et al. 2008.

————— (2003). "Some Group Matters: Intersectionality, Situated Standpoints, and Black Feminist Thought." In *A Companion to African-American Philosophy*. Ed. Tommy L. Lott and John P. Pittman. Malden, Mass.: Blackwell, 205–29.

Cooper, Anna Julia (1892). *A Voice from the South*. Xenia, Ohio: The Aldine Printing House.

Crenshaw, Kimberlé (1989). "Demarginalizing the Intersection of Race and Sex: A Black Feminist Critique of Antidiscrimination Doctrine, Feminist Theory and Antiracist Politics." *University of Chicago Legal Forum* 1989: 139–67.

————— (1991). "Mapping the Margins: Intersectionality, Identity Politics, and Violence against Women of Color." *Stanford Law Review* 43(6): 1241–99.

————— (1993). "Beyond Racism and Misogyny: Black Feminism and 2 Live Crew." In *Words That Wound*. Ed. Mari J. Matsuda, Charles R. Lawrence III, Richard Delgado, and Kimberlé Crenshaw. Boulder, Colo.: Westview Press, 120–31.

————— (2008). "On Gendered Violence and Racializing Prisons: A Tale of Two Movements." Given at U.C. Santa Barbara, February 15, 2008. http://www.youtube.com/watch?v=d1v9E83yTNA (accessed November 18, 2009).

Davis, Kathy (2008). "Intersectionality as Buzzword: A Sociology of Science Perspective on What Makes a Feminist Theory Successful." *Feminist Theory* 9: 67–86.

Davis, Murray S. (1971). "That's Interesting! Towards a Phenomenology of Sociology and a Sociology of Phenomenology." *Philosophy of the Social Sciences* 1: 309–44.

————— (1986). " 'That's Classic!' The Phenomenology and Rhetoric of Successful Social Theories." *Philosophy of the Social Sciences* 16: 285–301.

Dhamoon, Rita (2008). "Considerations in Mainstreaming Intersectionality as an Analytic Approach." Presented at the Western Political Science Association meeting, March 2008. http://www.allacademic.com//meta/p_mla_apa_research_citation/2/3/7/9/9/pages237996/p237996-1.php (accessed January 9, 2011).

Dotson, Kristie (2011). "Tracking Epistemic Violence, Tracking Practices of Silencing." *Hypatia* 26(2): 236–57.

Ferber, Abby L., Christina M. Jiménez, Andrea O. Herrera, Dena R. Samuels, eds. (2008). *The Matrix Reader: Examining the Dynamics of Oppression and Privilege*. New York: McGraw-Hill.

Fricker, Miranda (2009). *Epistemic Injustice: Power and the Ethics of Knowing*. New York: Oxford University Press.

Frye, Marilyn (1983). *The Politics of Reality: Essays in Feminist Theory*. Trumansburg, N.Y.: Crossing Press.

——— (2011). "Metaphors of Being a Φ." In *Feminist Metaphysics: Explorations in the Ontology of Sex, Gender and the Self*. Ed. Charlotte Witt. New York: Springer, 85–95.

Garry, Ann (2007). "Should Feminist Philosophers Care about Essences?" Published as "Feministo tetsugakusha ha honshitsu o ki ni kakeru beki ka." *Tetsugaku-Zasshi [Philosophical Studies]* 122: 113–39.

——— (2008a). "Essences, Intersections, and American Feminism." In *The Oxford Handbook of American Philosophy*. Ed. Cheryl Misak. New York: Oxford University Press, 595–625.

——— (2008b). "Intersections, Social Change, and 'Engaged' Theories: Implications of North American Feminism." *Pacific and American Studies* 8 (March): 99–111.

Hale, C. Jacob (1996). "Are Lesbians Women?" *Hypatia* 11(2): 94–121.

Hancock, Ange-Marie (2007a). "Intersectionality as a Normative and Empirical Paradigm." *Politics and Gender* 3(2): 248–54.

——— (2007b). "When Multiplication Doesn't Equal Quick Addition: Examining Intersectionality as a Research Paradigm." *Perspectives on Politics* 5(1): 63–79.

Harding, Sandra (1991). *Whose Science? Whose Knowledge? Thinking from Women's Lives*. Ithaca, N.Y.: Cornell University Press.

Haslanger, Sally (2000). "Gender and Race: (What) Are They? (What) Do We Want Them to Be?" *Nous* 34(1): 31–55.

Heyes, Cressida J. (2000). *Line Drawings: Defining Women through Feminist Practice*. Ithaca, N.Y.: Cornell University Press.

hooks, bell (1981). *Ain't I a Woman: Black Women and Feminism*. Boston, Mass.: South End Press.

——— (1984). "Sisterhood: Political Solidarity among Women." In *Feminist Theory: From Margin to Center*. Cambridge, Mass.: South End Press, 43–67.

Hull, Gloria T., Patricia Bell-Scott, and Barbara Smith, eds. (1982). *All the Women Are White, All the Blacks Are Men, but Some of Us Are Brave: Black Women's Studies*. Old Westbury, N.Y.: Feminist Press.

Kairys, David, ed. (1998). *The Politics of Law*. New York: Basic Books.

King, Deborah (1988). "Multiple Jeopardy, Multiple Consciousness: The Context of a Black Feminist Ideology." *Signs* 14(1): 42–72.

Lugones, María (2003). *Pilgrimages/Peregrinajes: Theorizing Coalition against Multiple Oppressions*. Lanham, Md.: Rowman and Littlefield.

——— (2007). "Heterosexualism and the Colonial/Modern Gender System." *Hypatia* 22(1): 186–209.

——— (2010). "Toward a Decolonial Feminism." *Hypatia* 25(4): 742–59.

Mackenzie, Catriona and Natalie Stoljar, eds. (2000). *Relational Autonomy: Feminist Perspectives on Autonomy, Agency, and the Social Self*. New York: Oxford University Press.

Markowitz, Sally (n.d.). "Thinking About Intersectionality: What Intersects with What?" Presented at the Society for Women in Philosophy, Pacific Division meeting, October 2009.

Matsuda, Mari J. (1996). *Where Is Your Body? And Other Essays on Race, Gender and the Law*. Boston: Beacon Press.

McCall, Leslie (2005). "The Complexity of Intersectionality." *Signs* 30(3): 1771–800.

Medina, José (2003). "Identity Trouble: Disidentification and the Problem of Difference." *Philosophy and Social Criticism* 29(6): 655–80.

Meyers, Diana T. (2000). "Intersectional Identity and the Authentic Self: Opposites Attract." In *Relational Autonomy: Feminist Perspectives on Autonomy, Agency, and the Social Self*. Ed. Catriona Mackenzie and Natalie Stoljar. New York: Oxford University Press, 151–80.

Mikkola, Mari (2009). "Gender Concepts and Intuitions." *Canadian Journal of Philosophy* 39(4): 559–84.

Mills, Charles W. (1997). *The Racial Contract*. Ithaca, N.Y.: Cornell University Press.

——— (1998). *Blackness Visible: Essays on Philosophy and Race*. Ithaca, N.Y.: Cornell University Press.

——— (2007). "Intersecting Contracts." In *Contract and Domination*. By Carole Pateman and Charles Mills. Malden, Mass.: Polity Press, 165–99.

Moraga, Cherríe (1983). *Loving in the War Years: Lo Que Nunca Pasó por Sus Labios*. Boston: South End Press.

———, and Gloria Anzaldúa, eds. (1983). *This Bridge Called My Back: Writings by Radical Women of Color*, 2nd ed. Watertown, Mass.: Persephone Press.

Nash, Jennifer, C. (2008). "Re-Thinking Intersectionality." *Feminist Review* 89: 1–15.

Nelson, Hilde Lindemann (2002). "Wittgenstein Meets 'Woman' in the Language-Game of Theorizing Feminism." In *Feminist Interpretations of Ludwig Wittgenstein*. Ed. Naomi Scheman and Peg O'Connor. University Park: Penn State University Press, 213–34.

Ortega, Mariana (2006). "Being Loving, Knowingly Ignorant: White Feminism and Women of Color." *Hypatia* 21(3): 56–74.

Oyéwumi, Oyerónké (1997). *The Invention of Women: Making an African Sense of Western Gender Discourses*. Minneapolis: University of Minnesota Press.

Quijano, Anibal (1991). "Colonialidad, Modernidad/Racionalidad." *Peru Indigena* 13(29): 11–29.

———(2000a). "Colonialidad del Poder y Clasificacion Social." *Journal of World Systems Research* 5(2): 342–86.

———(2000b). "Colonialidad del Poder, Eurocentrismo y America Latina." Colonialidad del Saber, Eurocentrismo y Ciencias Sicales. Buenos Aires: CLACSO-UNESCO. Reprinted: Michael Ennis, trans. (2000). "Coloniality of Power, Eurocentrism, and Latin America." *Nepantla: Views from South* 1(3): 533–580.

———(2001–2002). "Colonialidad del Poder, Globalización y Democracia." *Revista de Ciencias Sociales de la Universidad Autónoma de Nuevo León* 4(7–8): 1–23.

Razack, Sherene H. (1998). *Looking White People in the Eye: Gender, Race, and Culture in Courtrooms and Classrooms.* Toronto: University of Toronto Press.

———(2007). "How Is White Supremacy Embodied? Sexualized Racial Violence at Abu Ghraib." *Canadian Journal of Women and the Law* 17(2): 341–63.

Smith, Barbara (1983). *Home Girls: A Black Feminist Anthology.* New York: Kitchen Table–Women of Color Press.

Spelman, Elizabeth V. (1988). *Inessential Woman: Problems of Exclusion in Feminist Thought.* Boston: Beacon Press.

Stoljar, Natalie (1995). "Essence, Identity and the Concept of Woman." *Philosophical Topics* 23(2): 261–93.

Stubblefield, Anna (2005). "Meditations on Postsupremacist Philosophy." In *White on White, Black on Black.* Ed. George Yancy. Lanham, Md.: Rowman and Littlefield, 71–81.

———(2007). "Beyond the Pale: Tainted Whiteness, Cognitive Disability, and Eugenic Sterilization." *Hypatia* 22(2): 162–81.

Sullivan, Shannon, and Nancy Tuana, eds. (2007). *Race and Epistemologies of Ignorance.* Albany: State University of New York Press.

Tanesini, Alessandra (1996). "Whose Language?" In *Women, Knowledge, and Reality*, 2nd ed. Ed. Ann Garry and Marilyn Pearsall. New York: Routledge, 353–65.

Trujillo, Carla M. (1991). *Chicana Lesbians: The Girls Our Mothers Warned Us about.* Berkeley, Calif.: Third Woman Press.

Tuana, Nancy, and Shannon Sullivan, eds. (2006). *Hypatia Special Issue: Feminist Epistemologies of Ignorance* 21(3).

Weldon, S. Laurel (2006). "The Structure of Intersectionality: A Comparative Politics of Gender. *Politics and Gender* 2(2): 235–48.

Wittgenstein, Ludwig (1958). *Philosophical Investigations.* Trans. G. E. M. Anscombe. New York: Macmillan.

———(1967). *Zettel.* Trans. G. E. M. Anscombe. Oxford: Blackwell.

Wittig, Monique (1992). *The Straight Mind and Other Essays.* Boston: Beacon Press.

Yancy, George, ed. (2004). *What White Looks Like: African-American Philosophers on the Whiteness Question*. New York: Routledge.

—— (2010). *The Center Must Not Hold: White Women on the Whiteness of Philosophy* Totowa, N.J.: Rowman and Littlefield.

Yuval-Davis, Nira (2006). "Intersectionality and Feminist Politics." *European Journal of Women's Studies* 13: 193–209.

Zack, Naomi (2005). *Inclusive Feminism: A Third Wave Theory of Women's Commonality*. Lanham, Md.: Rowman and Littlefield Publishers.

Zerilli, Linda (1998). "Doing without Knowing: Feminism's Politics of the Ordinary." *Political Theory* 26(4): 435–58.

INDEX